GLOBAL ISSUES
2022 Edition

Sara Miller McCune founded SAGE Publishing in 1965 to support the dissemination of usable knowledge and educate a global community. SAGE publishes more than 1000 journals and over 800 new books each year, spanning a wide range of subject areas. Our growing selection of library products includes archives, data, case studies and video. SAGE remains majority owned by our founder and after her lifetime will become owned by a charitable trust that secures the company's continued independence.

Los Angeles | London | New Delhi | Singapore | Washington DC | Melbourne

GLOBAL ISSUES

SELECTIONS FROM *CQ RESEARCHER*

2022 EDITION

$SAGE | CQPRESS

FOR INFORMATION:

CQ Press

An Imprint of SAGE Publications, Inc.

2455 Teller Road

Thousand Oaks, California 91320

E-mail: order@sagepub.com

SAGE Publications Ltd.

1 Oliver's Yard

55 City Road

London EC1Y 1SP

United Kingdom

SAGE Publications India Pvt. Ltd.

B 1/I 1 Mohan Cooperative Industrial Area

Mathura Road, New Delhi 110 044

India

SAGE Publications Asia-Pacific Pte. Ltd.

18 Cross Street #10-10/11/12

China Square Central

Singapore 048423

Sponsoring Editor: Anna Villarruel

Product Associate: Lauren Younker

Production Editor: Astha Jaiswal

Typesetter: Hurix Digital

Proofreader: Lawrence W. Baker

Cover Designer: Candice Harman

Marketing Manager: Jennifer Jones

Copyright © 2022 by CQ Press, an Imprint of SAGE Publications, Inc. CQ Press is a registered trademark of Congressional Quarterly Inc.

All rights reserved. Except as permitted by U.S. copyright law, no part of this work may be reproduced or distributed in any form or by any means, or stored in a database or retrieval system, without permission in writing from the publisher.

All third-party trademarks referenced or depicted herein are included solely for the purpose of illustration and are the property of their respective owners. Reference to these trademarks in no way indicates any relationship with, or endorsement by, the trademark owner.

Printed in the United States of America

ISBN: 978-1-0718-3528-9

This book is printed on acid-free paper.

21 22 23 24 25 10 9 8 7 6 5 4 3 2 1

Contents

ANNOTATED CONTENTS vii
PREFACE xiii
CONTRIBUTORS xv

CONFLICT, SECURITY, AND TERRORISM

1. **The New Arms Race** **1**
   The Issues 1
   Background 9
   Current Situation 17
   Outlook 21
   Notes 21
   Bibliography 24
   The Next Step 25

2. **Medical Tourism** **29**
   The Issues 29
   Background 37
   Current Situation 44
   Outlook 47
   Notes 48
   Bibliography 51
   The Next Step 52

3. **Pandemic Preparedness** **55**
   The Issues 55
   Background 59
   Current Situation 64
   Outlook 67
   Notes 68
   Bibliography 71
   The Next Step 72

4. **U.S. Foreign Aid** **75**
   The Issues 75
   Background 80
   Current Situation 83
   Outlook 86
   Notes 88
   Bibliography 91
   The Next Step 93

INTERNATIONAL POLITICAL ECONOMY

5. **Supply Chains at Risk** **95**
   The Issues 95
   Background 102
   Current Situation 111
   Outlook 113
   Notes 114
   Bibliography 119
   The Next Step 121

6. **China Rising** **123**
   The Issues 123
   Background 131
   Current Situation 140
   Outlook 144
   Notes 145

	Bibliography	148
	The Next Step	149
7.	**The Natural Gas Industry**	**153**
	The Issues	153
	Background	157
	Current Situation	160
	Outlook	163
	Notes	164
	Bibliography	166
	The Next Step	167
8.	**K-pop**	**169**
	The Issues	169
	Background	173
	Current Situation	176
	Outlook	180
	Notes	180
	Bibliography	183
	The Next Step	184

RELIGIOUS AND HUMAN RIGHTS

9.	**Global Protests Movements**	**187**
	The Issues	187
	Background	194
	Current Situation	203
	Outlook	207
	Notes	207
	Bibliography	211
	The Next Step	212
10.	**The Abraham Accords**	**215**
	The Issues	215
	Background	224
	Current Situation	234
	Outlook	236
	Notes	237
	Bibliography	240
	The Next Step	242
11.	**Immigration Overhaul**	**245**
	The Issues	245
	Background	250
	Current Situation	256
	Outlook	260
	Notes	260
	Bibliography	265
	The Next Step	266

12.	**Targeted Killings**	**269**
	The Issues	269
	Background	276
	Current Situation	284
	Outlook	287
	Notes	288
	Bibliography	291
	The Next Step	292
13.	**Child Trafficking**	**295**
	The Issues	295
	Background	303
	Current Situation	312
	Outlook	316
	Notes	317
	Bibliography	320
	The Next Step	321

ENVIRONMENTAL ISSUES

14.	**Fuel Efficiency Standards**	**325**
	The Issues	325
	Background	332
	Current Situation	340
	Outlook	343
	Notes	344
	Bibliography	348
	The Next Step	349
15.	**Zoonotic Diseases**	**353**
	The Issues	353
	Background	361
	Current Situation	368
	Outlook	371
	Notes	372
	Bibliography	376
	The Next Step	377
16.	**The Future of Meat**	**379**
	The Issues	379
	Background	387
	Current Situation	395
	Outlook	398
	Notes	399
	Bibliography	405
	The Next Step	406

Annotated Contents

CONFLICT, SECURITY, AND TERRORISM
The New Arms Race
In recent years, the United States and Russia have withdrawn from several major agreements developed over 40 years to control the spread of nuclear weapons, citing violations by the other side. Those treaties created a climate of strategic stability, minimizing the chances of nuclear war. Without them, a new arms race, reminiscent of the Cold War years, has begun, as both sides develop ultramodern, super-fast weapon systems capable of delivering a nuclear device anywhere on the globe within 15 minutes. U.S. and Russian military leaders also have embraced doctrines that maintain that a limited nuclear war using small, tactical nuclear weapons can be won. The last remaining treaty limiting U.S. and Russian nuclear arsenals will expire next February unless both countries agree to extend it. President Trump says he prefers to negotiate a broader pact that includes China, but Beijing has said it is not interested, and critics say a year is not enough time to negotiate such an ambitious accord. Meanwhile, a stalemate in talks over North Korea's denuclearization has added uncertainty to the future of arms control, as has the U.S. withdrawal from an international agreement halting Iran's development of nuclear weapons.

Medical Tourism
The steady growth in U.S. health care costs may lead to a renewal of interest in medical tourism, once international travel becomes feasible again. Before the coronavirus outbreak, one group had projected that as many as 2.2 million people would leave the United

States this year for medical treatments. Yet even that would have been far short of the 16 million once expected, as enactment of the Affordable Care Act in 2010 initially caused interest to wane. But despite the act's protections, many Americans are finding medical care unaffordable. More Americans may be willing to look abroad for bargains, as is already seen in cases of retirees going to Mexico for dental care, experts say. And cheaper costs are not the only reason Americans and others have left home for medical care. They have also gone abroad for experimental treatments they cannot obtain in their own countries. Many physicians and ethicists have warned about the risks of treatments abroad, saying some are unproven and the danger of costly complications is substantial.

Pandemic Preparedness

With a vast public health infrastructure, a wealth of drugs, hospitals, health care providers and scientists, the United States seemed well positioned to be one of the best prepared countries to contain a pandemic. Yet the nation's response to COVID-19 has revealed otherwise. The virus has now infected over 6 million Americans, more than any other country, and killed over 184,000. The nation's leaders have struggled to implement basic infectious disease control management measures, such as data gathering, testing, contact tracing and distribution of critical medical supplies to health care providers. Some experts say President Trump failed to follow the pandemic-response plan established during the Obama administration, while others complain that Congress has never fully and reliably funded existing pandemic plans. Meanwhile, other new pathogens, perhaps more deadly than the coronavirus, likely will jump from animals to humans, according to experts. This reality is spurring lawmakers to examine what went wrong with the U.S. pandemic response and to create a more workable plan for future outbreaks. But such federal reform is unlikely to occur until after November's election.

U.S. Foreign Aid

President Biden's inauguration speech promised to "repair our alliances and engage with the world once again." As he pursues these goals, international development aid will be a key tool. Biden's promise, however, comes in the context of the shock waves created by the COVID-19 pandemic and an American public with divergent views about the country's role in the world. Support for international development assistance has typically been bipartisan and advocates are optimistic about its future, but there are escalating needs that could compete with foreign aid for attention and dollars. In addition, development progress achieved prior to the pandemic may be set back decades by the effects of COVID-19. And critics complain about corruption and self-interest in aid programs. As Biden's team settles into the many agencies administering foreign assistance, the key questions to be answered are whether there will be a strategic alignment of aid priorities—and whether aid will get to those needing it most.

INTERNATIONAL POLITICAL ECONOMY
Supply Chains at Risk

President Trump's approach to trade policy—using import tariffs and other punitive measures as leverage when negotiating international agreements—is forcing many companies to restructure their global supply chains, which often took decades to develop. International trade rules established after World War II, combined with technological breakthroughs such as robotics, cloud computing and software, have resulted in intricately connected worldwide supply chains that have cut costs and boosted profits. The shifts also have cost thousands of U.S. manufacturing jobs. Trump says his strategy will change that, but many companies and economists say imposing tariffs at levels unseen since the 1930s will not rein in rivals such as China, the world's second-biggest economy and America's biggest trading partner in 2018. As U.S. companies scramble to find non-Chinese suppliers and brace for lower profits, they warn that the cost of the tariffs eventually will mean higher consumer prices. And China has retaliated by imposing its own tariffs on U.S. goods or halting purchases of American farm products, triggering fears of a prolonged "cold" trade war between the two countries.

China Rising

Over the past year, China has been moving aggressively to secure a leading role on the global stage. Its assertiveness was on display most recently in Hong Kong, where a new law tightened Beijing's control over the semiautonomous city. China's influence has grown at the United Nations, part of an effort to overturn the norms of the U.S.-led world order. China also has strengthened its grip on the South China Sea, ramped up efforts to intimidate Taiwan, bloodied Indian troops along the disputed Himalayan border and waged a public relations offensive during the coronavirus pandemic that portrays itself as a model to emulate. An alarmed United States and other advanced democracies are challenging Beijing's territorial claims and trying to prevent China from dominating new technologies that will determine economic and military power for years to come. Through tariffs, President Trump is attempting to decouple the U.S. and Chinese economies—an effort that many economists say would cause massive dislocation in both nations if successful.

The Natural Gas Industry

Liquefied natural gas (LNG) production has jumped over the past decade, helping make the United States a net exporter of energy for the first time in more than 70 years. The growth of LNG—gas cooled to at least minus 260 degrees Fahrenheit, which reduces its volume and allows it to be transported long distances—has elevated the role of natural gas in politics and national security. Natural gas was the fastest-growing fossil fuel in 2019, but the coronavirus pandemic has cut sharply into demand and prices have tumbled, creating a volatile marketplace. In addition, the gas sector faces numerous long-term challenges, including environmental questions and competition from renewable energy. Opponents of fracking—the process that extracts gas by drilling deep underground and injecting chemicals into rock—say it is damaging the environment. President-elect Joe Biden, meanwhile, has vowed to strengthen the limits on methane, a greenhouse gas that is emitted during the production and transportation of natural gas.

K-pop

Korean pop music, aka K-pop, fuses musical genres to create a distinctive, dance-oriented sound that has become popular in the United States and worldwide, boosting the South Korean economy. BTS, the leading K-pop band, reportedly generates about $4.6 billion annually for the economy, based on music sales, product promotion and increased tourism. The genre is so popular that it has helped make South Korea the world's fastest-growing music market. K-pop groups have sought to extend their influence beyond music by supporting Black Lives Matter, speaking out against child poverty and warning about climate change. But critics accuse K-pop of cultural insensitivity in its use of symbols from Black, Indian and other cultures. One band's video drew condemnation for featuring the statue of a Hindu god, another for performers appearing in blackface. Critics also voice concern about K-pop's grueling training system, known for long hours and low pay. The genre's growing use of digital—that is, fake—musicians is proving controversial as well.

RELIGIOUS AND HUMAN RIGHTS
Global Protest Movements

Protest movements swept the globe last year—so widely that some experts said there were more protests, and more protesters, in 2019 than at any other time in history. Millions of citizens in dozens of countries took to the streets to protest a host of grievances, ranging from higher consumer prices to government corruption and social inequality. Thousands died; national leaders were forced from office. Experts differ on whether the wave of protests is a sign of failing democracy or of healthy citizen empowerment. But the deadly global spread of the coronavirus this year halted most street protests, at least temporarily, as governments enforced social distancing restrictions in hopes of preventing further infections—and perhaps in some cases in hopes of breaking the protests' momentum. Many movements took their campaigns online, but how successfully remains to be seen. Social media enables protesters to organize effectively and promote their causes widely. Yet some observers argue that a social media campaign dissipates quickly if organizers cannot meet their followers' expectations.

The Abraham Accords

Israel's normalization of ties with the United Arab Emirates, Bahrain and Sudan shatters the status quo in which Arab states withheld recognition of Israel until it allowed creation of an independent Palestinian state in the West Bank and Gaza. The U.S.-brokered agreement is excellent news for the signatories. Security cooperation and coordination regarding Iran—a country that all the parties to the agreements view as a threat—will increase. And officials anticipate around $500 million in deals and investments annually through the marriage of Gulf Arab petrodollars and Israel's scientific and technological expertise. But the deals leave the Palestinians in the cold, with few options. They are hoping for more sympathetic treatment from the incoming Biden administration. But President-elect Joe Biden first must tackle America's COVID-19 and economic crises before investing the time and political capital needed to revive the Middle East peace process. Meanwhile, Saudi Arabia and other Arab countries are waiting to see how the normalization agreements function before signing on.

Immigration Overhaul

On his first day in office, President Biden began advancing measures that would reverse his predecessor's hardline immigration policies, eventually legalize millions of undocumented immigrants and ensure that the United States meets what he called "its responsibilities as both a nation of laws and a nation of immigrants." But advocates of a fresh approach to immigration face major challenges. New waves of asylum-seekers, including record numbers of unaccompanied minors, are reaching Southern border checkpoints, straining facilities and fueling opposition to a less restrictive immigration policy. Congressional Republicans have panned Biden's legislative proposal as "blanket amnesty," and a federal judge quickly blocked his early bid to suspend deportations. Immigrants' advocates and progressive lawmakers want Biden to dismantle former President Donald Trump's restrictive asylum policies more quickly, even as a massive backlog of immigration court cases threatens to undermine Biden's plans. In addition, experts say, many of Trump's hundreds of immigration policy changes are so deeply woven into the federal bureaucracy, it could take years to undo them.

Targeted Killings

The targeted killing of suspected terrorists and other nonstate actors, pioneered by Israel, is being utilized with growing frequency by the United States and other nations as a warfare and anti-terrorism tactic. The rise of targeted killings, often with armed drones and other precision weapons, has changed the nature of military operations, allowing states to intervene remotely in long-running conflicts. The United States killed up to 16,900 people in drone strikes between 2010 and 2020, including as many as 2,200 civilians, mainly in Yemen, Pakistan, Somalia and Afghanistan, according to the Bureau of Investigative Journalism, a British media organization. Often occurring outside defined battlefields with little accountability, the practice is raising ethical and legal issues. Critics also question the effectiveness of targeted killings, saying the strikes can create sympathy for terrorist groups and momentum for their causes. But its defenders say assassinating key individuals can stop imminent terrorist attacks, weaken terrorist organizations and, in the case of Iran, slow its development of nuclear weapons.

Child Trafficking

The worldwide trafficking of children for commercial sex and forced labor is rising rapidly, despite more than a century of laws, treaties and protocols banning the practice. Some 10 million children are trafficked each year, the majority of them girls forced into the underground sex trade. Poverty, natural disasters and now the COVID-19 pandemic have left destitute families and their children vulnerable to traffickers. The use of the internet to sell images of child sex abuse to pedophiles around the world has exploded. Law enforcement officials say they do not have the resources to stop the traffickers, who net some $150 billion a year—second in profit only to the drug trade. A new U.S. law enables states to prosecute internet platforms that knowingly facilitate such trafficking, but critics have challenged the law in court, arguing it restricts free speech. Some experts say the best way to defeat trafficking is to align government policy with a sweeping United Nations sustainable development agenda that will add untapped resources to the battle.

ENVIRONMENTAL ISSUES

Fuel Efficiency Standards

President Trump is significantly reducing federal fuel efficiency and emissions standards for vehicles to below those set by the Obama administration. The Obama regulations required automakers to build vehicle fleets that would average about 54 mpg by 2025. The Trump rule cuts the requirement to about 40 mpg by 2026. Trump has also revoked a waiver that allowed California to set stricter standards, which are followed by several other states. The Trump administration contends its rule will save consumers billions of dollars in vehicle costs and will spur a move to new, cleaner and safer vehicles. Opponents say the rule will endanger public health and accelerate climate change by putting into the air more pollutants and greenhouse gases that cause global warming, especially carbon dioxide. The battle over the standards has divided automobile manufacturers and led a coalition of states headed by California, along with a dozen environmental groups, to sue to block the Trump administration's fuel efficiency and emissions rollback.

Zoonotic Diseases

The pandemic circling the globe is only the latest instance of a disease that jumped from animals to humans, known as a zoonotic disease. COVID-19 likely came from a bat; AIDS, severe acute respiratory syndrome (SARS), Ebola, West Nile virus and Lyme disease also originated in animals. Zoonotic disease outbreaks have been occurring more often since the 1940s as an expanding human population pushes deeper into forests for hunting, agriculture, mining and housing. Demand for exotic meat also brings live wildlife to food markets, where they can transmit viruses to other animals and humans. How to prevent the next pandemic is a matter of vigorous debate: Some scientists are pushing for more research into animal viruses, while others stress stopping human activities, such as deforestation, that can spur contagion. Conservation groups urge a ban on the wildlife trade, but critics say that will only encourage a black market. Some researchers and environmentalists say preserving wilderness and biological diversity is key to preventing more outbreaks.

The Future of Meat

Nearly all sectors of the global meat industry face unprecedented challenges. In the United States, a handful of companies control much of the $218 billion industry, making it difficult for smaller players to compete. And the COVID-19 pandemic has taken a high toll, killing more than 200 workers and infecting 42,000 others in U.S. beef, poultry and pork processing plants and forcing dozens of those facilities to temporarily shut down. Globally, meat conglomerates increasingly are interconnected—animal feed, livestock and meat being shipped across the planet. Growing worldwide demand for meat is raising environmental concerns, with many experts saying the industry exacerbates climate change, threatening global food supplies. Other experts disagree, saying animal agriculture is a relatively small source of planet-warming greenhouse gases. The industry's critics say factory farms pose human health risks due to their routine use of antibiotics, their storage of large concentrations of manure and by serving as ideal incubators for pathogens that can jump from animals to humans. Meanwhile, plant-based meat substitutes are challenging the industry, but they face obstacles of their own.

Preface

In this pivotal era of international policymaking, scholars, students, practitioners and journalists seek answers to such critical questions as: Do U.S.-China tensions over the coronavirus increase the chances for a military clash between the two world powers? Does the new Israel-Gulf Arab coalition threaten Iran? Does industrial meat production threaten human health? Students must first understand the facts and contexts of these and other global issues if they are to analyze and articulate well-reasoned positions.

The 2022 edition of *Global Issues* provides comprehensive and unbiased coverage of today's most pressing global problems. This edition is a compilation of 16 recent reports from *CQ Researcher*, a weekly policy brief that unpacks difficult concepts and provides balanced coverage of competing perspectives. Each article analyzes past, present and possible political maneuvering, is designed to promote in-depth discussion and further research and helps readers formulate their own positions on crucial international issues.

This collection is organized into four subject areas that span a range of important international policy concerns: conflict, security, and terrorism; international political economy; religious and human rights; and environmental issues. *Global Issues* is a valuable supplement for courses on world affairs in political science, geography, economics and sociology. Citizens, journalists and business and government leaders also turn to it to become better informed on key issues, actors and policy positions.

CQ RESEARCHER

CQ Researcher was founded in 1923 as *Editorial Research Reports* and was sold primarily to newspapers as a research tool. The magazine was renamed and redesigned in 1991 as *CQ Researcher*. Today, students are its primary audience. While still used by hundreds of journalists and newspapers, many of which reprint portions of the reports, *Researcher*'s main subscribers are now high school, college and public libraries. In 2002, *Researcher* won the American Bar Association's coveted Silver Gavel Award for magazine excellence for a series of nine reports on civil liberties and other legal issues.

Researcher writers—all highly experienced journalists—sometimes compare the experience of writing a *Researcher* report to drafting a college term paper. Indeed, there are many similarities. Each report is as long as many term papers—about 10,000 words—and is written by one person without any significant outside help. One of the key differences is that the writers interview leading experts, scholars and government officials for each issue.

Like students, writers begin the creative process by choosing a topic. Working with *Researcher*'s editors, the writer identifies a controversial subject that has important public policy implications. After a topic is selected, the writer embarks on one to two weeks of intense research. Newspaper and magazine articles are clipped or downloaded, books are ordered and information is gathered from a wide variety of sources, including interest groups, universities and the government. Once the writers are well informed, they develop a detailed outline and begin the interview process. Each report requires a minimum of ten to fifteen interviews with academics, officials, lobbyists and people working in the field. Only after all interviews are completed does the writing begin.

CHAPTER FORMAT

Each issue of *CQ Researcher*, and therefore each selection in this book, is structured in the same way. A selection begins with an introductory overview, which is briefly explored in greater detail in the rest of the report.

The second section chronicles the most important and current debates in the field. It is structured around a number of key issues questions, such as "Should federal health insurance programs cover medicines and therapies obtained abroad?" and "Has a U.S. law blocking websites that facilitate child sex trafficking inadvertently endangered its victims?" This section is the core of each selection. The questions raised are often highly controversial and usually the object of much argument among scholars and practitioners. Hence, the answers provided are never conclusive but rather detail the range of opinion within the field.

Following those issue questions is the "Background" section, which provides a history of the issue being examined. This retrospective includes important legislative and executive actions and court decisions to inform readers on how current policy evolved.

Next, the "Current Situation" section examines important contemporary policy issues, legislation under consideration and action being taken. Each selection ends with an "Outlook" section that gives a sense of what new regulations, court rulings and possible policy initiatives might be put into place in the next five to ten years.

Each report contains features that augment the main text: sidebars that examine issues related to the topic, a pro/con debate by two outside experts, a chronology of key dates and events and an annotated bibliography that details the major sources used by the writer.

ACKNOWLEDGMENTS

We wish to thank many people for helping to make this collection a reality. For many years, Thomas J. Billitteri, managing editor of *CQ Researcher*, gave us his enthusiastic support and cooperation as we developed this edition. Now, Kenneth Fireman, managing editor of *CQ Researcher*, is carrying on the tradition of help with our new edition texts. He and his talented editors and writers have amassed a first-class collection of *Researcher* articles, and we are fortunate to have access to this rich cache. We also thankfully acknowledge the advice and feedback from current readers and are gratified by their satisfaction with the book.

Some readers may be learning about *CQ Researcher* for the first time. We expect that many readers will want regular access to this excellent weekly research tool. For subscription information or a no-obligation free trial of *Researcher*, please contact CQ Press at www.cqpress.com or toll-free at 1-866-4CQ-PRESS (1-866-427-7737).

We hope that you will be pleased by the 2022 edition of *Global Issues*. We welcome your feedback and suggestions for future editions. Please direct comments to Anna Villarruel, Sponsoring Editor for International Relations, Comparative Politics, and Public Administration, CQ Press, an imprint of SAGE, 2600 Virginia Avenue, NW, Suite 600, Washington, DC 20037; or send e-mail to *Anna.Villarruel@sagepub.com*.

—*The Editors of CQ Press*

Contributors

Jonathan Broder is a Washington-based reporter and editor. He was a senior writer for *Newsweek*, a senior editor at *Congressional Quarterly* and served as a foreign correspondent in the Middle East, South Asia and the Far East for the *Chicago Tribune*. Broder's writing also has appeared in *The New York Times Magazine, The Washington Post, Smithsonian* and the *World Policy Journal*, among other publications. He previously reported for *CQ Researcher* on financial services deregulation and on India.

Zarrín Caldwell is an Arizona-based freelance writer. She has written for print and online publications on U.S. foreign policy, global issues and international development. She has also worked as a contractor for the U.S. Department of State and holds a master's degree in public and international affairs from the University of Pittsburgh.

Lorna Collier has written about business, technology and other topics for *AARP Bulletin, U.S. News & World Report, Chicago Tribune, Discover* and others. She has reported about universal basic income, college debt and COVID-19's impact on mental health for *CQ Researcher*.

Val Ellicott is a Washington-based writer and editor and a former editor at *CQ Researcher*. Before that, he worked for 14 years as an editor at Gannett and *USA Today* in Washington, and spent 12 years covering investigative stories, court news and the medical beat at *The Palm Beach Post* in Florida. He received a master's degree in journalism in 1986 from Columbia University.

Sarah Glazer is a New York-based freelancer who contributes regularly to *CQ Researcher*. Her articles on health, education and social-policy issues also have appeared in *The New York Times* and *The*

Washington Post. Her recent *CQ Researcher* reports include "Manipulating Human Genes" and "Global Migration." She graduated from the University of Chicago with a B.A. in American history.

Reed Karaim, a freelance writer in Tucson, Ariz., has written for *The Washington Post, U.S. News & World Report, Smithsonian, American Scholar* and other publications. He is the winner of the Robin Goldstein Award for Outstanding Regional Reporting and other journalism honors. He is also the author of two novels, the most recent of which, *The Winter in Anna*, published by W. W. Norton & Co., is set at a small-town weekly newspaper. He is a graduate of North Dakota State University in Fargo.

Rachel Layne is a Boston-based freelance journalist whose work has appeared in outlets including CBS, *USA Today, HBS Working Knowledge* and *MIT Technology Review*. She also spent 20 years at *Bloomberg News*, where she covered multinational corporations, among other roles.

Sara Toth Stub is a Jerusalem-based U.S. journalist who has written for *The Wall Street Journal, The Atlantic, U.S. News & World Report* and other publications. She usually covers business, culture and travel.

Bara Vaida is a Washington-based freelancer with more than 25 years' experience as a journalist, primarily covering health care policy issues. She has worked for Agence France-Presse, Bloomberg News, *National Journal* and *Kaiser Health News*. She also has published articles in, among others, *Cancer Today, Stateline*, WebMD and *Washingtonian* magazines.

Bill Wanlund, a former Foreign Service officer, is a freelance writer in the Washington, D.C., area. He has written for *CQ Researcher* on abortion, intelligence reform, the marijuana industry and climate change as a national security concern.

Kerry Dooley Young is a freelance writer based in Washington, D.C. She specializes in health care, writing often for publications owned by WebMD. She earlier covered Medicare for *CQ Roll Call* and the pharmaceutical industry and the Food and Drug Administration for *Bloomberg News*.

The New Arms Race

Are new treaties needed to control modern nuclear weapons?

By Jonathan Broder

Intercontinental nuclear missiles are displayed during a military parade in Beijing in October 2019 to celebrate the founding of the People's Republic of China. Nonproliferation advocates say China is racing to catch up to Russia and the United States in a global arms race.

THE ISSUES

Russia recently announced the deployment of its Avangard boost-glide vehicle, which rides a powerful rocket into orbit just above Earth's atmosphere. From there, the vehicle, armed with a nuclear warhead, can strike anywhere on the planet within 15 minutes, moving toward its target at more than 20 times the speed of sound, according to Russian military officials.[1]

With its ability to steer around air and missile defenses at hypersonic speeds, the Avangard is "practically invulnerable," Russian President Vladimir Putin has said.[2] And it is just one of half a dozen new nuclear weapons delivery systems being developed by Moscow. Meanwhile, China has deployed its own hypersonic delivery vehicle.

The United States is years behind Moscow and Beijing in developing nuclear-capable hypersonic missiles but is working hard to modernize its nuclear arsenal, including the missiles, bombers and submarines that deliver the weapons, senior defense officials say. The modernization could cost up to $1.2 trillion over the next three decades, according to a Congressional Budget Office study.[3]

"We have lost our technical advantage in hypersonics," said Gen. Paul Selva, then-vice chairman of the Joint Chiefs of Staff. But, he added: "We haven't lost the hypersonics fight."[4]

Arms control advocates say the competition to develop more advanced nuclear weapons and faster delivery systems signals a

From *CQ Researcher*, February 14, 2020

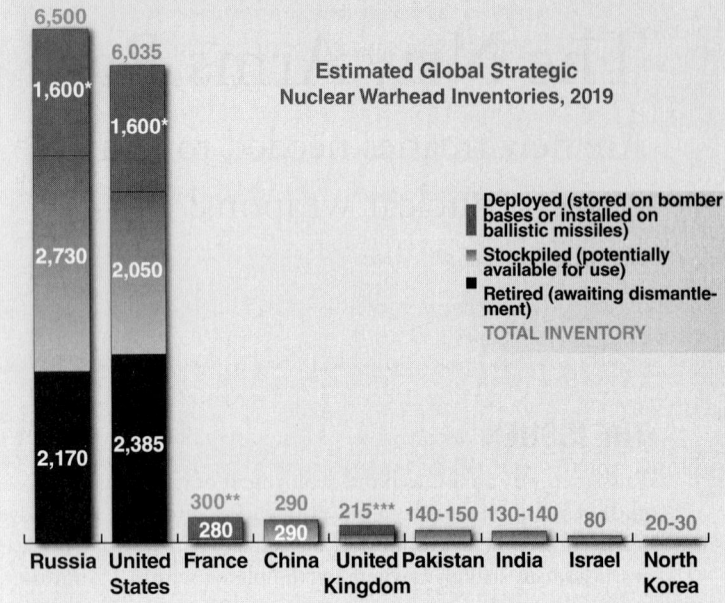

U.S., Russia Have Most of the World's Nuclear Weapons

Although the world's nuclear arsenals have declined significantly since the 1980s, about 90 percent of the nearly 14,000 strategic nuclear weapons that still exist are controlled by Russia and the United States. The two countries have 6,500 and 6,035 weapons, respectively, far more than any of the other seven nuclear-armed nations. About a third of the U.S. and Russian weapons are retired and awaiting dismantlement; the rest are either deployed or available for use.

* These figures exceed the 1,550 allowed in New START because they include bombs stored on bomber bases, which the START cap does not cover.
** France has 280 warheads deployed and 20 stockpiled.
*** The U.K. has 120 warheads deployed and 95 stockpiled.

Source: Hans M. Kristensen and Matt Korda, "Status of World Nuclear Forces," Federation of American Scientists, May 2019, https://tinyurl.com/junbna7

The crumbling of the international arms control architecture also comes as two new strategic competitors—Iran and North Korea—are asserting themselves in ways that further heighten nuclear risks, experts say. With denuclearization talks between the Trump administration and North Korea stalled, the North's leader, Kim Jong Un, recently declared he no longer feels bound by his self-imposed moratorium on nuclear and long-range missile testing. Analysts say that while his message has left the door open for diplomacy, it also could set the stage for another angry confrontation with President Trump, who threatened North Korea with "fire and fury" in previous face-offs.[5]

In addition, after a U.S. drone in January killed Iran's top military commander, Tehran announced it was resuming its enriched uranium production, signaling what many analysts regard as the death knell of a landmark 2015 international agreement to curb Iran's nuclear weapons program.[6]

"The risk that the world will stumble its way into nuclear war is higher today than it's been since the end of the Cold War," says Thomas Countryman, a former assistant secretary of State for international security and nonproliferation.

dangerous, new three-way arms race among the United States, Russia and China, sparked after Washington and Moscow withdrew from several key arms control treaties in recent years. (*See Box.*) In this new age of hypersonic nuclear weapons, cyber warfare and the growing militarization of space, U.S. defense hawks argue such accords are outdated and no longer serve the nation's interest. And amid the new, great-power contest, they insist the best way to deter an apocalyptic nuclear war is to be fully ready and willing to fight one, unconstrained by obsolete treaties. Some now even contend that a limited nuclear war can be won.

Such nuclear alarm bells represent a sharp turnabout from a few years ago, when the threat of nuclear war was successfully managed through a matrix of arms control agreements between the United States and Russia, which together hold more than 90 percent of the world's nearly 14,000 nuclear weapons, according to the Arms Control Association, a Washington-based advocacy organization.[7] (*See Graphic.*)

By imposing transparency, predictability and limits on each side's nuclear forces, those agreements created what officials have called a state of "strategic stability"

The Pentagon's top two experts on China's military say the Asian giant is on track to double its roughly 300 strategic warheads in the next 10 years, fueled by a stockpile of enriched uranium and plutonium that exceeds the country's civilian nuclear power needs.

In addition, say these officials, China is also developing its own hypersonic missiles as well as new intermediate- and long-range missiles with higher accuracy than older versions, stealthy long-range bombers and advanced missile-firing submarines. As a result, they estimate, China could attain nuclear parity with the United States and Russia within one or two decades.

But with China unwilling to consider a three-way treaty with Washington and Moscow, Trump administration aides are struggling to attract Beijing to a treaty that Moscow and domestic critics would approve, says Countryman, the former State Department arms control chief. So far, Trump's aides have suggested three possible approaches, none of which is acceptable to all parties, says Countryman, who is currently board chair of the Washington-based Arms Control Association advocacy group.

In one, China would increase its deployed nuclear arsenal fivefold to 1,550 warheads—the same as the United States and Russia—but this is a nonstarter for Washington and Moscow, Countryman says. Another approach would require the United States and Russia to reduce their nuclear arsenals fivefold to the size of China's, which neither the Pentagon nor the Kremlin is prepared to do. Under a third option, the United States and Russia would agree to freeze their nuclear arsenals at the New START ceiling of 1,550 warheads while China would agree to keep its arsenal at 300 warheads, a proposal China rejects.

Glossary of Nuclear Weapons Terminology

Nuclear weapon—A bomb that releases enormous amounts of explosive energy as a result of either nuclear fission, a reaction that occurs when the nucleus of an atom is split into two or more fragments, or nuclear fusion, which occurs when two or more atomic nuclei fuse to form a heavier nucleus.

Atomic bomb—A type of nuclear weapon that draws its explosive power from the sudden release of large amounts of atomic energy through fission. The United States is the only country to have detonated atomic bombs in wartime, in Hiroshima and Nagasaki, Japan, in 1945.

Hydrogen (thermonuclear) bomb—About 1,000 times more powerful than an atomic bomb; draws its explosive force from a fusion reaction.

Strategic nuclear weapon or warhead—Large, high-yield weapons that can destroy entire cities.

Tactical nuclear weapons—Low-yield devices with about a third of the explosive power of the atomic bomb used in Hiroshima; designed for battlefield use; can take the form of artillery shells, bombs or short-range missiles.

Deployed—Mounted on a missile or ready to be loaded onto a long-range bomber.

Ballistic missiles—Rocket-powered delivery vehicles that travel in a ballistic (free fall) trajectory.

Intercontinental ballistic missile (ICBM)—A ballistic missile that can travel more than 3,400 miles.

Delivery vehicle—A land-based or submarine-launched ballistic or cruise missile or long-range bomber that can deliver one or more warheads to a target.

Hypersonic—Many times faster than the speed of sound.

Sources: "Glossary," Nuclear Threat Initiative, https://tinyurl.com/ukzwvml; "Glossary of Terms," Nuclear Reduction/Disarmament Initiative, https://tinyurl.com/vu6oe9s; "How does stealth technology work?" HowStuffWorks, April 1, 2000, https://tinyurl.com/ybnglspb; and "NATO/Russia Unclassified," North Atlantic Treaty Organization, 2007, https://tinyurl.com/tuvoj72

"If there's a more creative idea, it has escaped me," Countryman says. "And it has escaped the administration officials who have been discussing how to realize the president's strategy for nine months now, when in fact, no such strategy is possible."

Some critics suspect Trump's tripartite treaty strategy is a ploy, designed to distract arms control advocates while New START expires, which would appease defense hawks who never liked the treaty in the first place.

"Trump and the hawks don't want to have limits on the United States' ability to increase its nuclear force," says Joseph Cirincione, president of the Ploughshares Fund, a foundation dedicated to nuclear nonproliferation, arms control and disarmament. "It's mostly about their belief that China could rapidly expand its arsenal, so they feel we have to be in a position to match it. Their view is that they protect American national security through American military might, not by pieces of paper like the New START treaty. They see that treaty as an arms control trap and its expiration next year as an opportunity to get out of it. And if that means an arms race, fine."

Defense hawks say China's rise as a military power with advanced hypersonic nuclear weapons has rendered New START obsolete. "Technology has moved," said Secretary of State Mike Pompeo.[14]

"If you want to pursue arms control, you can't do it an in old-fashioned, outmoded, Cold War-era style," said then-National Security Adviser John Bolton in June 2019. "So to extend [New START] for five years and not take these new delivery system threats into account would be malpractice," he said, referring to hypersonic missile systems. He also cited the absence of limits on tactical nuclear weapons as another flaw in New START.[15]

Although Bolton left the administration last September, the president still agrees with Bolton's criticism of New START, White House officials say.

Arms control experts argue that the need to address the threats from Chinese and Russian tactical nuclear weapons should not blind Trump to the benefits that an extended New START would bring to U.S. national security.

Rose Gottemoeller, the chief U.S. negotiator for New START, told lawmakers in December that since the treaty entered into force in 2011, it has established strategic weapons parity between the United States and Russia, providing Americans with a stable and predictable security environment. Extending the treaty for another five years, she argued, would preserve that predictability while the Pentagon modernizes its nuclear forces. It would also give the United States time to negotiate a new treaty that includes China, she said.

"Without the treaty, things could change drastically and quickly," Gottemoeller told the House Foreign Affairs Committee in December, 2019. "There is no faster way for the Russians to outrun us than to deploy more nuclear warheads on their missiles."[16]

Is a limited nuclear war a viable option?

In a striking illustration of the return to Cold War thinking, Russian and U.S. military planners now believe it is possible to wage limited nuclear war without it escalating into a nuclear apocalypse.

In such a war, each side would use low-yield, or tactical, weapons on the battlefield. Depending on its size and radiation yield, a single tactical nuclear weapon could kill thousands of troops and contaminate its blast radius for decades.

Since the start of the Cold War in the 1940s, U.S. and Soviet military leaders envisioned using smaller nuclear weapons to halt a major armored thrust by the other side in Europe, or to block the enemy's advance through a strategic mountain pass. Nowadays, they are regarded as effective weapons against military or nuclear installations buried deep underground, or to save one's forces from a conventional defeat while discouraging the enemy from waging further hostilities.

Moreover, say U.S. military experts, Russia has adopted an "escalate-to-de-escalate" strategy, believing that using such tactical nuclear weapons on the battlefield would quickly de-escalate a military confrontation with U.S. and NATO forces, because Washington would balk at a full-scale nuclear response that would lead to global annihilation.

In response, the United States has begun producing more tactical nuclear warheads for its cruise missiles and submarine-launched ballistic missiles so it can deter the threat of any tactical nuclear strike and retaliate proportionally should one be used against U.S. or allied forces. The Pentagon refers to such deterrence as "escalation dominance."

The National Nuclear Security Administration, the federal agency responsible for the effectiveness of the U.S. nuclear weapons stockpile, said new tactical warheads have been rolling off a production line in Texas since this past January. And in February, the Pentagon announced it has equipped the Navy's Trident ballistic missiles with a new tactical warhead, the W76-2, which has less than a third of the destructive power of other U.S. nuclear weapons.[17]

The Pentagon's 100-page "2018 Nuclear Posture Review" outlined the buildup of tactical nuclear weapons as a key element of the Trump administration's nuclear policy: "Expanding flexible U.S. nuclear options now, to include low-yield options, is important for the preservation of credible deterrence against regional aggression. It will . . . help ensure that potential adversaries perceive no possible advantage in limited nuclear escalation, making nuclear employment less likely."[18]

But the Trump nuclear doctrine is controversial. The Ploughshares Fund's Cirincione warns that it would blur the line between the use of conventional and nuclear weapons and expand the circumstances in which the U.S. military would go nuclear. For example, the administration's nuclear review says the United States could use nuclear weapons in response to "significant non-nuclear strategic attacks," such as a crippling cyberstrike on the nation's power grid or other essential infrastructure.[19]

Another Pentagon document, titled simply "Nuclear Operations," outlined a broad range of additional scenarios in which the U.S. military might use nuclear weapons.

The document said integrating nuclear weapons with conventional and special operations "is essential to the success of any mission or operation." Furthermore, it said, "The spectrum of nuclear warfare may range from tactical application, to limited regional use, to global employment by friendly forces and/or enemies. . . . Employment of nuclear weapons can radically alter or accelerate the course of a campaign. A nuclear weapon could be brought into the campaign as a result of perceived failure in a conventional campaign, potential loss of control or regime, or to escalate the conflict to sue for peace on more favorable terms."[20]

Further expanding the potential use of nuclear weapons in conventional combat, the Pentagon document said field commanders "can nominate potential targets to consider for nuclear options that would support [the commander's] objectives in ongoing operations."[21]

Arms control advocates, including former senior Defense officials, said the U.S. and Russian embrace of a limited nuclear war doctrine represents a highly dangerous throwback to the Cold War years.

"Anybody that thinks you can use a tactical weapon and not have a profound risk of escalation all the way to an all-out nuclear war is risking the world on a pretty naive assumption," says Sam Nunn, a former chairman of the Senate Armed Services Committee and co-founder of the Nuclear Threat Initiative, a research organization that educates policymakers on the dangers of nuclear weapons. "It's very high risk," he says.

But Elbridge Colby, a former senior Defense Department official, cautioned that with the return of great-power competition, Russia and China have developed strategies to defeat the United States in a military confrontation and that tactical nuclear weapons are a key part of their strategies.[22] He supports the U.S. production of tactical nuclear weapons, which could help defeat a Russian or Chinese attack "without provoking a nuclear apocalypse," he said, adding that demonstrating such a capability to U.S. adversaries "is the best way to avoid ever having to put it into practice."[23]

Another proponent of the limited nuclear war doctrine, Keir Lieber, a nuclear arms expert at Georgetown University, says if deterrence fails and the use of a nuclear weapon is required, a tactical weapon diminishes the chances of a full-scale nuclear exchange in certain cases. He paints a possible scenario in which Russia overruns the former Soviet republic of Estonia and explodes a low-yield nuclear weapon to get NATO forces to sue for peace. That would prompt the Western alliance to retaliate with its own tactical nuclear weapon, he says.

"Is it going to stop there?" he asks. "I don't know why one would assume that it will continue to escalate from there."

In response to the emerging doctrine of limited nuclear war, researchers at The Lab—part of Princeton University's Program on Science and Global Security, which studies nuclear arms control, nonproliferation and disarmament—recently used extensive data on U.S. and Russian nuclear forces, war plans and targets to produce a four-minute video showing how the limited use of nuclear weapons could quickly escalate into a full-scale nuclear war, killing or wounding more than 90 million people in a few hours.[24]

Underscoring the difficulty of limiting a nuclear exchange to tactical weapons, Nunn and other skeptics note that U.S. and Russian leaders would not know whether an incoming missile is carrying a tactical nuclear warhead or a city-destroying strategic weapon, raising the chances of a full-blown nuclear exchange.

"Hey all you nuclear powers out there. We're just going to trust that you recognize this is just a little nuclear weapon and won't retaliate with all you've got," tweeted Melissa Hanham, an expert on nuclear weapons at One Earth Future, a Washington-based foundation that advocates arms control. "Remember! The U.S. only intends to nuke you 'a little bit.'"[25]

Is a denuclearization agreement with North Korea possible?

In June 2017, Trump upended decades of American policy and diplomatic norms by meeting with North

Japanese schoolchildren take cover under their desks during a drill in 2017 to prepare for a possible North Korean missile attack. Even though President Trump became the first sitting U.S. president to meet with a North Korean leader in 2017, progress between the United States and North Korea on a denuclearization agreement has stalled.

Korean dictator Kim Jong Un in Singapore to discuss the denuclearization of the communist country in return for sanctions relief and U.S. economic aid.

Until then, successive administrations had held low-level negotiations with North Korean officials, offering food and other forms of assistance in a bid to get Pyongyang to curtail its fledgling nuclear program. Several times the talks produced agreements, but eventually they all collapsed amid mutual misunderstandings, charges of cheating and deep distrust left over from the 1950-53 Korean War.

To his credit, many arms control advocates say, Trump shattered that diplomatic model. In Singapore, he became the first sitting U.S. president to meet with a North Korean leader, convinced that their personal rapport could pave the way for an historic denuclearization agreement. "We fell in love," Trump said of his new relationship with Kim.[26]

At the end of that summit, the two leaders pledged to "work toward the complete denuclearization of the Korean Peninsula."[27] As a confidence-building measure, Trump scaled back joint military exercises with South Korea, and Kim reciprocated by declaring a moratorium on North Korea's nuclear and ballistic missile tests. Commentators noted that after a year in which the two leaders had publicly hurled insults and threats at each other, the simple act of talking had changed perceptions on both sides and made conflict less likely.

But the Singapore talks, and subsequent summits in 2018—in Hanoi in February and in the Demilitarized Zone (DMZ) between North and South Korea in June 2019—failed to translate their personal rapport into any meaningful progress. The biggest hurdle, arms control experts say, has been the inability of U.S. and North Korean officials to agree on how the denuclearization process should proceed.

The Trump administration says North Korea must first abandon its nuclear weapons program before Washington provides any sanctions relief, while Pyongyang insists on a gradual process, in which Washington lifts some sanctions in return for each concrete step Pyongyang takes toward denuclearization.

John D. Maurer, an expert in nuclear weapons and geopolitics at the conservative American Enterprise Institute think tank, says the failure of the Hanoi and DMZ meetings publicly embarrassed Kim, who had raised hopes at home that his diplomacy with Trump would result in economic relief. Meanwhile, Trump continued to tout his summit diplomacy with Kim as one of his signature foreign policy achievements.

Kim's loss of face prompted North Korea's warning on Dec. 1, 2019, that unless Washington made further concessions by year's end, Pyongyang would adopt a more confrontational posture.

Trump ignored the deadline. And on New Year's Day, Kim told his ruling Workers Party Central Committee that he no longer felt constrained by the testing moratorium, he would not surrender North Korea's nuclear weapons and North Korea would achieve economic prosperity on its own.

Despite Kim's tough tone, analysts say his speech left the door open for further negotiations by not declaring an end to diplomacy or the resumption of nuclear and long-range missile tests. Going forward, several experts said, Pyongyang's next moves would be based on Trump's ability to win a second presidential term in the November election.

"Donald Trump happens to be the first sitting U.S. president to view North Korea as a source of political victory, for domestic purposes," said Go Myong-Hyun, a research fellow and expert on North Korea at the Seoul-based Asan Institute for Policy Studies think tank. As the election approaches, Go said, North Korea likely will view Trump's habit of boasting to his base about his accomplishments as a source of leverage in future negotiations.[28]

But "if they calculate that President Trump won't be re-elected next year, then their approach is going to fundamentally change," Go said. North Korea could test another nuclear bomb, he said, resume missile tests or take other provocative steps that would effectively end the diplomatic dialogue that Trump and Kim began.²⁹

Some Democrats say a deal with Pyongyang is still possible, but only if Trump agrees to embrace a step-by-step approach to North Korea's denuclearization. In a letter to Trump in late December, eight senior Democrats on the Senate Foreign Relations Committee urged him to consider an interim agreement under which North Korea would freeze and roll back some of its nuclear weapons programs in return for some sanctions relief as a first step in executing a "serious diplomatic plan before it is too late."³⁰

"While such an interim agreement would of course only be a first step in a longer process, it would nonetheless be an important effort to create the sort of real and durable diplomatic process that is necessary to achieve the complete denuclearization of North Korea," the senators wrote.³¹

Some analysts believe the prospects are dim for a North Korean denuclearization agreement with any U.S. administration, in part because of Pyongyang's deep ideological antipathy toward, and distrust of, the United States. But perhaps the biggest obstacle to North Korea's denuclearization, says Maurer, is Washington's record of eliminating troublesome foreign leaders, such as Iraq's Saddam Hussein and Libyan leader Moammar Gadhafi.

"The North Korean leadership has to look at anything the U.S. government says about cooperation with extreme skepticism," Maurer says. "From their perspective, the United States goes around the world, killing off all the people on its naughty list. And who's at the top of that list today? Kim Jong Un."

Thus, he argues, Kim's nuclear weapons are not just a tool to win sanctions relief from the United States, they are his insurance that he will not end up like Saddam or Gadhafi.

BACKGROUND
Nuclear Age Dawns

The nuclear age dawned with a blinding flash on Aug. 6, 1945, when an American B-29 Superfortress dropped an atomic bomb on the Japanese port city of Hiroshima.

The explosion leveled the entire city, instantly killing 80,000 people. Three days later, the United States dropped a second nuclear bomb on Nagasaki, another port city, killing another 40,000 people. Tens of thousands of wounded would die later from severe burns and radiation poisoning. On Aug. 15, Japanese Emperor Hirohito, citing the immense power of "a new and most cruel bomb," surrendered unconditionally, ending World War II.³²

The atomic bomb dropped by the United States on Hiroshima in 1945 leveled the Japanese port city. Today's hydrogen weapons are about 1,000 times more powerful than the atomic bomb.

After years of bloody fighting in Europe and the Pacific, the war's end unleashed scenes of jubilation across the United States. But the bomb's enormous destructive power also forced a moral reckoning among some of the physicists who created it. One of them, J. Robert Oppenheimer, said that as he watched the fiery mushroom cloud rise over the New Mexico desert during the bomb's first test, he remembered a sentence from the Hindu scripture, the Bhagavad-Gita: "I am become death, the destroyer of worlds."³³

Such moral qualms drove the earliest debates in Washington over controlling the spread of nuclear weapons know-how. One group in the Truman administration worried that America's monopoly over nuclear weapons would spark a dangerous arms race with the Soviet Union, which was competing with the United States in a budding Cold War for global influence. This group proposed sharing the nation's nuclear secrets with Moscow to establish a parity that would stabilize relations. Another group opposed giving up America's strategic advantage over the Soviets.³⁴

In 1946, the United States proposed that the newly formed United Nations establish an international agency to control the proliferation of nuclear weapons, but preserve Washington's status as the world's only nuclear power. The Soviets, already on their way to developing

CHRONOLOGY

1939-1949 *The nuclear age dawns, and the U.S.-Soviet arms race ensues.*

1939 With Nazi Germany's discovery of nuclear fission, physicist Albert Einstein warns President Franklin D. Roosevelt of the potential for a new type of "extremely powerful bombs"; Roosevelt institutes the Manhattan Project to explore the feasibility of atomic weapons.

1945 The United States drops atomic bombs on the Japanese cities of Hiroshima and Nagasaki, ending World War II.

1949 The Soviet Union explodes an atomic bomb, marking the beginning of the U.S.-Soviet nuclear arms race.

1950-1963 *Cold War competition eventually leads to arms control efforts.*

1952-53 The United States detonates the world's first hydrogen bomb, far more powerful than the atomic bomb used at Hiroshima. . . . Britain becomes a nuclear power.

1957 The arms race moves into space after the Soviets launch the satellite *Sputnik*.

1960 France tests an atomic bomb.

1962 The Cuban missile crisis brings the U.S. and the Soviet Union to the brink of nuclear war.

1963 Washington and Moscow establish a hotline and sign the Limited Test Ban Treaty, banning nuclear weapons testing in the atmosphere, underwater and outer space but allowing underground tests.

1964-1979 *Major arms control agreements advance despite Cold War tensions.*

1964 China becomes the fifth nuclear-armed nation.

1968 The United Nations adopts the Treaty on the Non-Proliferation of Nuclear Weapons, which recognizes the five nuclear-armed countries; all other signatories commit to use nuclear power only for peaceful purposes.

1972 The United States and the Soviet Union sign SALT I agreement, freezing the number of long-range ballistic missiles at 1972 levels, and the Anti-Ballistic Missile (ABM) Treaty, which limits each side to a single anti-missile battery with 100 missiles and launchers.

1979 U.S. and Soviet leaders sign SALT II, limiting each country to 1,320 long-range missiles with multiple nuclear warheads, but the Senate fails to ratify it after the Soviets invade Afghanistan; both countries honor the treaty's limits anyway.

1980-1993 *Arms control progresses; the Soviet Union collapses.*

1987 President Ronald Reagan and Soviet leader Mikhail Gorbachev sign the Intermediate-Range Nuclear Forces (INF) Treaty, eliminating all ballistic missiles with a range of 300 to 3,400 miles.

1991 Gorbachev and President George H.W. Bush sign START I, capping each country's arsenal at 6,000 deployed nuclear warheads and 1,600 deployed long-range delivery systems. . . . After the Soviet Union collapses, the Cooperative Threat Reduction Program secures Soviet nuclear weapons and fissile material held in former satellite states.

1993 U.S. and Russia sign START II, limiting each side to 3,500 deployed strategic nuclear warheads.

2000-2015 *Cracks appear in arms control, but other agreements follow.*

2002 President George W. Bush withdraws from ABM Treaty, citing alleged threats from rogue nations such as Iraq; in response, Russia withdraws from START II. . . . Iraq is later found not to be building nuclear weapons.

2010 Obama and Russian President Dmitry Medvedev sign New START, further reducing their respective deployed nuclear arsenals to 1,550 warheads and 700 delivery systems.

2015 Iran signs agreement with six world powers, promising to curtail its nuclear program in exchange for relief from U.N. economic sanctions.

2016-Present *Trump administration begins abandoning arms control agreements.*

2016 Donald Trump wins the presidency, calls Iran nuclear agreement and New START "bad deals."

2018 Russian President Vladimir Putin unveils nuclear weapons delivery systems that can travel more than 20 times the speed of sound; Trump withdraws from Iran nuclear deal, imposes unilateral sanctions on Tehran. . . . Trump says he prefers a new arms reduction treaty that includes China instead of a five-year extension of New START. . . . Trump meets North Korean President Kim Jong Un in Singapore; they agree to work toward denuclearization of the Korean Peninsula; Kim voluntarily freezes nuclear and missile testing.

2019 Trump and Kim fail to agree on how negotiations should proceed. . . . Trump withdraws from INF Treaty, citing alleged Russian violations. . . . Iran restarts part of its nuclear program.

2020 In a New Year's Day speech, Kim declares he is no longer bound by his freeze on nuclear and missile testing. . . . After U.S. drone kills Iran's top military commander, Tehran announces it will fully resume uranium enrichment, signaling the de facto collapse of the Iran nuclear deal (January).

---

their own atomic bomb, rejected the proposal, and the United States spurned a Soviet counterproposal to ban all nuclear weapons.[35]

The Soviets successfully tested a nuclear bomb in September 1949, sparking the arms race some had feared. Oppenheimer spoke out publicly against U.S. efforts to develop a hydrogen bomb, which would be far more destructive than the atomic bombs used in Japan, angering many in the administration.

Coming at the height of the so-called Red Scare stirred up by Sen. Joseph McCarthy, R-Wisc., Oppenheimer's objections led to an FBI investigation that revealed the physicist had sympathized with communism when he was a young professor at the University of California, Berkeley. At a hearing to rule on the revocation of Oppenheimer's security clearance, Edward Teller, another prominent nuclear physicist, portrayed him as a security risk. Stripped of his clearance, Oppenheimer continued to lecture widely on the dangers of nuclear weapons, but he had no impact on the burgeoning arms race.[36]

Over the next two decades, the Americans and Soviets developed immensely destructive hydrogen bombs, along with neutron bombs, which leave structures standing but kill people with high levels of radiation; intercontinental ballistic missiles capable of carrying multiple nuclear warheads; and a vast arsenal of small, tactical nuclear weapons for battlefield use, such as nuclear landmines, artillery shells and torpedoes. With the Soviet's successful 1957 launch of *Sputnik*, the first artificial Earth satellite, the two countries extended their rivalry into outer space. During that period, Britain, France and China also became nuclear weapons states.

In 1962, the Cold War rivalry between the superpowers reached a crisis when U.S. intelligence discovered the Soviets had deployed nuclear-armed missiles in Cuba, 90 miles from the U.S. mainland. In response, President John F. Kennedy deployed a naval blockade around Cuba to prevent additional Soviet missiles from reaching the island. He also demanded that Moscow remove the existing missiles, warning he was prepared to use military force to neutralize the Soviet threat.[37]

Over the next 13 days, a tense standoff ensued that brought the two countries to the brink of nuclear war. "I thought it was the last Saturday I would ever see," Robert McNamara, Kennedy's Defense secretary, later told Cold War historian Martin Walker.[38]

Eventually, Kennedy and Soviet leader Nikita Khrushchev resolved the crisis peacefully. Kennedy agreed to Khrushchev's proposal to remove the missiles in return for a U.S. pledge not to invade Cuba. Privately, Kennedy also agreed to remove U.S. missiles from Turkey, which the Soviets saw as a threat.[39]

Experts Say Nuclear Terrorism Threat Is Overstated

"Countries won't give nuclear weapons to terrorists."

Ever since the 9/11 terrorist attacks in the United States in 2001, Western leaders, lawmakers and national security officials have feared that terrorists would obtain a nuclear weapon, or the fissile material to make one, and use it to attack Western capitals or regional rivals.

After 9/11, President George W. Bush explained the need to invade Iraq by lumping it with Iran and North Korea in his 2002 State of the Union speech, calling them "an axis of evil" that threatened world peace. "By seeking weapons of mass destruction, these regimes pose a grave and growing danger," he said. "They could provide these arms to terrorists, giving them the means to match their hatred."[1]

President Barack Obama echoed Bush's concerns when he told a 2016 White House summit on nuclear security: "There is no doubt that if these madmen ever got their hands on a nuclear bomb or nuclear material, they most certainly would use it to kill as many innocent people as possible."[2]

And former CIA Director R. James Woolsey (1993-95) famously said in 1994, "Terrorists don't want a seat at the table, they want to destroy the table and everyone sitting at it."[3]

But some terrorism experts say those assumptions are based on cartoonish perceptions of anti-American regimes and terrorists as single-minded, suicidal fanatics. Counterterrorism officials could better avoid catastrophe by approaching such threats with an eye toward terrorists' strategic priorities, they say, and not simplistic assumptions that detonation is their primary goal.

Moreover, they note, citing detailed studies and empirical data, the likelihood of a government providing a nuclear bomb or fissile material to a terrorist group is vastly overstated.

"Countries won't give nuclear weapons to terrorists," says Keir Lieber, an expert on nuclear weapons and geopolitics at Georgetown University. And "it is implausible that terrorists could develop a nuclear weapon on their own."

Even a state sponsor of terrorism would avoid giving a nuclear weapon to a proxy terrorist group, according to Lieber and Daryl G. Press, an associate professor of government at Dartmouth College and an expert on nuclear deterrence. "Nuclear weapons are the most powerful weapons a state can acquire," the two wrote in a 2013 article in the journal *International Security*. "Handing that power to an actor over which the state has less than complete control would be an enormous, epochal decision—one unlikely to be taken by regimes that are typically obsessed with power and their own survival."[4]

In addition, they argued, forensic examination of the radioactive isotopes that remain after a nuclear blast would reveal the uranium mines, reactors and enrichment facilities where the bomb originated, exposing the state sponsor to

Decades later, former advisers to Khrushchev disclosed that 43,000 Soviet soldiers had secretly amassed on the island to defend the missiles against a U.S. invasion, according to a new history of nuclear warfare by *Slate* defense reporter Fred Kaplan. In his review of the book for *The Washington Post*, author Evan Thomas noted that those troops were armed with tactical nuclear weapons.[40]

Arms Control Treaties

Shaken by the missile crisis, Washington and Moscow agreed the following year to establish a communications hotline between their leaders to mitigate the risk of accidental nuclear warfare. The two countries also signed the Limited Test Ban Treaty, which forbade most nuclear test explosions.[41]

Another major arms control effort occurred in 1968 with the signing of the U.N.-sponsored Nuclear Non-Proliferation Treaty. It recognized the five existing nuclear-weapons states—the United States, the Soviet Union, Britain, France and China—and required their pledge to work toward nuclear disarmament. The treaty also obligated non-nuclear states not to acquire nuclear

retaliation. Plus, they added, a state sponsor would worry that terrorists might use such a weapon in an unexpected way or provoke a response that would end the sponsor's regime.[5]

However, there is still some cause for concern, experts say. If a terrorist group obtained a nuclear weapon, its leaders would more likely be guided by strategic considerations, such as potential rewards, rather than sheer rage. Knowing the impact a nuclear blast and the ensuing retaliation would have on public opinion, the group's leaders would seriously consider other options than detonation, they say. But that could still create some painful dilemmas for the terrorists' targets.

For instance, a group could engage in nuclear blackmail, declaring that it has a nuclear weapon and threatening to use it unless the group's conditions were met.

Joseph Cirincione, president of the Ploughshares Fund, a foundation that advocates for nuclear disarmament, paints a frightening nuclear blackmail scenario in which a terrorist group somehow obtains two nuclear bombs, places one in Washington and one in New York City and threatens to destroy the nation's capital unless the United States withdraws its forces from the Middle East. Then, to prove the group's capability, it could detonate the bomb in New York or off the coast.

"What does a U.S. president do" in such a situation? Cirincione asks. "There is no good response."

Christopher McIntosh and Ian Storey, terrorism experts at Bard College, say a nuclear-armed terrorist group also could announce that it has a nuclear weapon but present no demands, instilling fear among its enemies, "without committing the organization to a definite strategic path," they wrote.[6]

Or a terrorist group could simply suggest—but not confirm—that it has a nuclear weapon, a strategic posture used by Israel for 50 years, according to Avner Cohen, author of the 1999 book *Israel and the Bomb*.

McIntosh and Storey say a terrorist group also could keep its nuclear capability a secret until it decides conditions are right to unveil it and issue demands.

But numerous studies have shown that terrorist groups try to avoid stepping over a line that will draw catastrophic damage to their organizations and communities. For example, after a border attack in 2006 by the Iranian-backed military group Hezbollah that killed several Israeli soldiers, Israel launched a full-scale war that killed or wounded some 5,600 people, displaced another million and destroyed much of Lebanon's civilian infrastructure.

Many Lebanese blamed Hezbollah for their suffering, causing Hassan Nasrallah, the group's leader, to declare that, had he known Israel's response would be so devastating, he would never have ordered the attack.

—*Jonathan Broder*

---

[1] "Text of President Bush's 2002 State of the Union Address," *The Washington Post*, Jan. 29, 2002, https://tinyurl.com/rq8zyq4.

[2] David Smith, "Barack Obama at nuclear summit: 'madmen' threaten global security," *The Guardian*, April 1, 2016, https://tinyurl.com/t4o9r3e.

[3] Nicholas Lemann, "What Terrorists Want," *The New Yorker*, Oct. 22, 2001, https://tinyurl.com/qmgejrz.

[4] Keir A. Lieber and Daryl G. Press, "Why States Won't Give Nuclear Weapons to Terrorists," *International Security*, Vol. 38, No. 1, Summer 2013, https://tinyurl.com/uwua7p8.

[5] *Ibid.*

[6] Christopher McIntosh and Ian Storey, "Would terrorists set off a nuclear weapon if they had one? We shouldn't assume so," *Bulletin of the Atomic Scientists*, Nov. 20, 2019, https://tinyurl.com/s3h69no.

---

weapons but guaranteed them the right to civilian nuclear power, subject to certain safeguards. Eventually, 187 countries signed on, making the treaty one of the pillars of a global arms control architecture. (Israel, India and Pakistan refused to sign and later became nuclear weapons states. Cuba and South Sudan have refused to join the treaty but do not have nuclear weapons.)[42]

In 1972, President Richard M. Nixon, long an anticommunist hawk, traveled to China, fostering a rapprochement that upended the balance of power between Washington and Moscow. Worried about a new Sino-American alliance, Moscow quickly reached two major arms control agreements with Washington that same year.

The first, the Strategic Arms Limitation Treaty, or SALT I, froze the number of each country's long-range ballistic missile launchers and submarine-launched ballistic missiles at existing levels. The second accord, the Anti-Ballistic Missile (ABM) Treaty restricted the number of anti-missile batteries each side could deploy.[43]

The Erosion of Arms Control Will Extend to Outer Space

China and Russia are developing missiles that can destroy satellites.

If the United States and Russia allow the New START arms control pact to expire next year, the subsequent end of all remaining limits on their nuclear arsenals will affect not only strategic stability on Earth but also in outer space, experts say.

The expiration will eliminate prohibitions on interfering with each other's intelligence satellites and other methods for verifying treaty compliance, warns a new study by Aerospace Corp.'s Center for Space Policy and Strategy, a research center that analyzes space programs for the U.S. military.[1]

"This will mark a significant change in the strategic context within which U.S. national security space forces operate," the study said. "U.S. space forces' resources will be taxed, and the stability of the space domain will face new risks."[2]

The study came out weeks after President Trump, authorized by Congress, announced creation of the U.S. Space Force, the military's sixth branch, which aims to defend the United States and its satellites and spacecraft from hostile forces. With New START due to expire in February 2021 and no sign from Trump that he will activate the treaty's five-year extension provision, the study details some of the challenges the Space Force and intelligence agencies will face in a post-New START world.

Michael Gleason, a senior strategic space analyst and co-author of the study, told reporters at a Jan. 15 news conference that on-site inspections conducted by U.S. and Russian officials as part of the treaty's verification provisions will end. Thus, he said, there will be greater demand—and costs—for U.S. satellite surveillance of Russia's nuclear forces.

Gleason also warned that after decades during which the United States and Russia left each other's reconnaissance and military satellites alone, the Pentagon should be prepared for the possibility that Russia may try to challenge U.S. satellite overflights of its territory by interfering with them.

According to a U.S. intelligence analysis of open-source documents, Russia is developing a satellite system called Burevestnik, believed to be designed to disrupt and destroy other countries' satellites. The documents suggest the Burevestnik will be a co-orbital satellite, or one that is deployed in an orbit similar to its target, capable of assessing the functions of Russian satellites as well as inspecting or killing an adversary's satellites.[3]

U.S. intelligence officials also have cited Russia's extensive testing of its PL-19 Nudol anti-satellite missile, which is fired from a mobile launcher and targets enemy satellites in low-Earth orbit, 250 miles above the planet.[4] The Pentagon's "2019 Missile Defense Review" cited such anti-satellite missiles as one of several Russian threats, including laser weapons.

Russia is developing a diverse suite of anti-satellite capabilities, including ground-launched missiles and laser weapons, "and continues to launch 'experimental' satellites that conduct sophisticated on-orbit activities to advance counterspace capabilities," the report said.[5]

U.S. officials acknowledge the Pentagon is developing anti-satellite capabilities, but details remain classified.

Meanwhile, studies published last April focus on counterspace activities by China, which in 2007 stunned the U.S. defense community by firing a missile that destroyed one of its own defunct weather satellites, creating a large field of space debris that continues to pose risks to the International Space Station and other satellites.[6] China demonstrated further technological advances in space last

But the budding detente quickly dissipated after Washington and Moscow lined up on opposing sides of the 1973 Arab-Israeli War. After two weeks of fierce fighting, Israeli forces had blunted a Syrian attack on the Golan Heights and advanced to within artillery range of Damascus while Israeli tanks had crossed the Suez Canal and surrounded Egypt's Third Army. With Moscow threatening to intervene with nuclear weapons to save its beleaguered Arab clients, Nixon placed U.S. nuclear forces on a midlevel alert, once again bringing the two superpowers to the precipice of nuclear war. Eventually, a battlefield ceasefire defused the crisis.

year when it became the first country to land a probe on the dark side of the moon.[7]

The April studies—one conducted by the Center for Strategic and International Studies (CSIS), an independent Washington think tank, and the other by the Secure World Foundation, a research organization that promotes the peaceful uses of space—noted that China continues to test the ability of its SJ-17 satellite to maneuver close to another to inspect, repair or monitor its functions. China also appears to have deployed mobile jammers on Mischief Reef in the South China Sea's Spratly Islands that can disrupt other countries' ground-to-space communications, according to the CSIS study.[8]

Both studies say China is developing at least three types of missiles capable of hitting satellites orbiting between 250 miles and 22,236 miles above Earth. The Secure World Foundation study says one of the three anti-satellite missiles is probably operational and may already have been deployed on mobile Chinese launchers.[9]

"China is clearly investing in its counter-space capabilities," the CSIS study says. "Evidence confirms that in 2018 alone, China tested technologies in three of the four counter-space weapon categories."[10]

The four categories include kinetic weapons, such as missiles and killer satellites, designed to smash into or explode next to a satellite; nonkinetic weapons, such as lasers, high-powered microwaves or electromagnetic pulses that can blind or disable satellites; electronic weapons that can jam satellite communications or trick them with fake signals; and cyber-weapons that target the data from satellites.[11]

"The big changes to Chinese doctrine and space organization happened a few years ago when they created their Strategic Support Force," said Brian Weeden, director of program planning at the Secure World Foundation and co-editor of its study. "This is a new military organization that combines space, electronic warfare and cyber capabilities."[12]

Military technology experts say China probably began building up its counterspace capabilities when the U.S. military started relying heavily on its constellation of communications, surveillance and intelligence-gathering satellites at the outset of its wars in Afghanistan and Iraq.

But with New START's expiration looming, Russia is the most immediate concern, the Aerospace study stressed. Urging the Trump administration to begin planning for the day after the treaty expires, the study suggested either a negotiated understanding or a formal agreement with Moscow not to interfere with one another's satellites.

"No alternative future foresees the existing status quo surviving after New START expires," the study said.

—*Jonathan Broder*

---

[1] Michael P. Gleason and Luc H. Riesbeck, "Noninterference With National Technical Means: The Status Quo Will Not Survive," Center for Space Policy and Strategy, Aerospace Corp., January 2020, https://tinyurl.com/uqgs2v9.

[2] *Ibid.*

[3] "Russia develops co-orbital anti-satellite capability," *Jane's Intelligence Review*, 2018, https://tinyurl.com/uycd8mo.

[4] "Russian Space Wars: U.S. Intelligence Claims Kremlin Made Seventh Test of Nudol ASAT Missile," Spacewatch.global, 2019, https://tinyurl.com/s7pwx7b.

[5] "2019 Missile Defense Review," Office of the Secretary of Defense, Department of Defense, January 2019, https://tinyurl.com/y9hkqfnj.

[6] Michael Safi and Hannah Devlin, "'A terrible thing': India's destruction of satellite threatens ISS, says NASA," *The Guardian*, April 2, 2019, https://tinyurl.com/yyuezl8l.

[7] Trefor Moss, "China Lands Probe on the 'Dark Side' of the Moon," *The Wall Street Journal*, Jan. 3, 2019, https://tinyurl.com/yborl7kj.

[8] Todd Harrison *et al.*, "Space Threat Assessment 2019," Center for Strategic and International Studies, April 2019, https://tinyurl.com/vwo77oh.

[9] Brian Weeden and Victoria Samson, "Global Counterspace Capabilities: An Open Source Assessment," Secure World Foundation, April 2019, https://tinyurl.com/qmnndgj.

[10] Harrison *et al.*, *op. cit.*

[11] *Ibid.*

[12] Kelsey D. Atherton, "The chicken-and-egg debate about new threats in space," C4ISRNET, April 8, 2019, https://tinyurl.com/t9m5wjq.

A year later, Nixon resigned over the Watergate scandal. U.S.-Soviet Arms control talks resumed, and in June 1979, President Jimmy Carter and Soviet General Secretary Leonid Brezhnev signed the SALT II accords, further limiting the number of each side's nuclear warheads and ICBMs. But six months later, the Soviets invaded Afghanistan, prompting Carter to ask the Senate to delay consideration of the treaty. Although the Senate never ratified SALT II, both sides honored it, underscoring the value each placed on its controls.[44]

President Ronald Reagan made arms control a priority with his bold 1981 "zero-option" proposal, which called for the removal of all U.S. and Soviet intermediate-range nuclear missiles from Europe. He followed up the following year with a proposal to reduce the number of each side's strategic nuclear warheads.[45]

In 1983, Reagan introduced a plan for a space-based missile shield against Soviet nuclear attack. Some experts questioned the effectiveness of the initiative, which they nicknamed "Star Wars." But the program alarmed the Soviets, who feared they were falling behind the Americans in both defense technology and spending.[46]

That same year, Mikhail Gorbachev became the Soviet Communist Party's general secretary and introduced greater openness along with economic and political reforms, transformative policies that set the stage for more cooperation on arms control.

In 1986, Reagan and Gorbachev met in Reykjavík, Iceland, for what arms control experts have called one of the most extraordinary U.S.-Soviet summits ever held. The two leaders nearly agreed to complete nuclear disarmament within 10 years. Gorbachev's demand to limit tests for Reagan's space missiles killed the deal, but experts say their talks paved the way for later arms control agreements.[47]

One was the Intermediate-Range Nuclear Forces, or INF, Treaty, which Reagan and Gorbachev signed in December 1987. It banned all intermediate-range nuclear missiles, an arms control milestone, experts say, because it was the first agreement to abolish an entire class of nuclear arms, as opposed to limiting their number.[48]

On Nov. 9, 1989, the Berlin Wall fell, marking the beginning of the end of the Cold War and greater progress on arms control. In July 1991, Gorbachev and President George H.W. Bush signed the Strategic Arms Reduction Treaty (START I), which limited the United States and the Soviet Union each to deploy 6,000 warheads and 1,600 delivery vehicles.[49]

After the Soviet Union collapsed in late 1991, Bush signed bipartisan legislation creating the Cooperative Threat Reduction Program. The brainchild of Democratic Sen. Nunn of Georgia and Republican Sen. Richard Lugar of Indiana, the legislation provided financial and technical assistance to former Soviet republics to dismantle thousands of nuclear weapons, remove their stockpiles of plutonium and highly enriched uranium needed to make such weapons, and provide their nuclear scientists with civilian jobs.[50]

In 1993, Russia and the United States signed START II, banning the use of multiple nuclear warheads deployed on ICBMs. Although the U.S. Senate and the Russian Duma, or parliament, ratified the agreement, it never went into effect because of unresolved differences in other areas of arms control.[51]

Cracks Appear

Those differences opened the first cracks in the arms control edifice. In June 2002, President George W. Bush, the son of the former president, withdrew from the Anti-Ballistic Missile Treaty Nixon had signed 30 years earlier, arguing that it limited U.S. ability to deploy missile defenses against rogue states. Russia's new president, Vladimir Putin, strongly opposed the move, and in response, he also pulled out of the treaty, preventing it from taking effect.[52]

Tensions between Washington and Moscow escalated in 2007 when Bush announced plans to base antimissile batteries in Poland and the Czech Republic, former Soviet-controlled Warsaw Pact countries that joined NATO after the Soviet Union's demise. Bush maintained the missiles were needed to defend NATO allies against Iran's missiles. But Putin saw them as antimissile systems that could potentially be turned against Russia, blunting its nuclear arsenal.

U.S.-Russia relations improved after President Barack Obama took office in 2009. Eager to enhance cooperation, Obama announced he would scrap Bush's plan for the Eastern European anti-missile sites and rely instead on the anti-missile systems aboard U.S. Navy warships.

The following year, Obama and Russian President Dmitry Medvedev signed New START, capping each country's deployed nuclear warheads at 1,550 and its long-range delivery systems at 700. Like the previous U.S.-Russia treaties, New START included extensive verification procedures, providing transparency for both sides.[53]

In 2012, in another major nonproliferation effort, the United States and five other world powers began negotiating with Iran to halt its nuclear program, which many experts suspected was close to developing a nuclear bomb. In 2015, Tehran agreed to curtail its nuclear program in return for relief from international sanctions that had hobbled Iran's economy.

Israel and its supporters in Congress condemned the deal, arguing that once key provisions expired after 10 years, Iran would be free to resume its weapons development. In his 2016 campaign for the presidency, Republican nominee Trump echoed those allegations, vowing if elected to withdraw from the Iran deal and negotiate a tougher accord permanently halting Iran's nuclear and ballistic missile programs and ending its support for proxy military forces across the Middle East.

After winning the 2016 election, Trump turned his attention to North Korea, which was testing its nuclear weapons and long-range ballistic missiles capable of reaching the United States. Trump and North Korean leader Kim taunted each other with personal insults and threats.

In early 2018, the Pentagon released its updated "Nuclear Posture Review," detailing the administration's plans to modernize the nation's nuclear arsenal and presenting limited tactical nuclear war as a viable battlefield strategy.[54]

On May 8, that year, Trump made good on his promise to withdraw from the Iran deal. Six months later, he reimposed crippling sanctions on the Islamic Republic and gave its leaders a stark choice: sign a tougher accord or watch Iran's economy collapse. A defiant Iran refused and slowly reactivated its nuclear program.

In June of that year, Trump stunned arms control advocates and defense hawks by becoming the first sitting U.S. president to meet with a North Korean leader. Gambling that their personal diplomacy could sweep away decades of hostility and distrust, Trump and Kim held talks in Singapore and agreed to begin negotiations toward denuclearization of the Korean Peninsula.[55]

Meeting Kim for a second time in Hanoi in February 2019, Trump abruptly walked out of their summit after rejecting what U.S. officials said was the North Korean leader's demand for relief from all U.S. sanctions in return for dismantling his main nuclear facility at Yongbyon. North Korea said it had asked for a partial lifting of sanctions.[56]

Last August, the two leaders met a third time, in the Demilitarized Zone between the two Koreas, and Trump even stepped briefly into North Korean territory—another first for a U.S. president. But their differences remained over how negotiations should proceed. North Korea experts say Kim wanted a step-by-step process in which the United States would reward North Korea's gradual denuclearization with gradual sanctions relief and the removal of U.S. nuclear forces from the region. On the advice of his hawkish advisers, Trump insisted North Korea first surrender all of its nuclear and ballistic missile programs before the United States would provide any sanctions relief.

Arms control withered further last August when Trump withdrew from the Intermediate-Range Nuclear Forces Treaty with Russia. Like Obama before him, he accused Russia of covertly developing and deploying a banned intermediate-range cruise missile that could threaten both Europe and Asia, a charge Russia denied. Congress later authorized $10 million for tactical nuclear warheads to be mounted on intermediate-range ballistic missiles capable of reaching Russia after being launched from submarines in the region.[57]

The Defense and Energy appropriations bills signed into law in December provided the Trump administration with $30.8 billion to maintain and modernize the military's nuclear arsenal and to pay for new nuclear-armed missiles, missile-launching submarines and long-range bombers.[58]

In what arms control advocates considered a hopeful sign, Putin announced late last year that he was ready to extend New START until 2026. Trump, however, refused to commit to its extension, citing his preference for a treaty that would include China.

In the end, 2019 came to a close with the future of New START, North Korea's denuclearization and Iran's nuclear program under clouds of uncertainty.

CURRENT SITUATION
Korean Diplomacy Fizzles

Many analysts believe North Korean leader Kim is embarking upon a defiant path for 2020 with his year-end policy speech announcing he no longer feels bound by his self-imposed moratorium on missile tests. Kim cited

President Trump's failure to reciprocate with any relief from sanctions that have hobbled North Korea's economy.

"If the U.S. persists in its hostile policy toward the DPRK, there will never be the denuclearization on the Korean Peninsula, and the DPRK will steadily develop necessary and prerequisite strategic weapons for the security of the state until the U.S. rolls back its hostile policy," Kim said, using the initials of his country's official name, the Democratic People's Republic of Korea.[59]

Nevertheless, Trump continues to believe his personal rapport with Kim holds the promise for an historic agreement that would see the communist nation give up its nuclear weapons.

"Look, he likes me, I like him, we get along," Trump said about his relationship with Kim while speaking to reporters on New Year's Eve at his Mar-a-Lago resort. "But he did sign a contract, he did sign an agreement talking about denuclearization.... I think he's a man of his word, so we're going to find out."[60]

In his speech, Kim appeared to leave the door open to further diplomacy by saying the nuclear tests would resume if Washington refused to drop its demands that North Korea first fully denuclearize. Further complicating any future negotiations is North Korea's definition of denuclearization, which includes the removal of all U.S. nuclear forces from South Korea.

Since then, there has been no sign that Trump has softened his position. But Trump sent Kim birthday greetings in early January in a gesture that analysts said was aimed at defusing tensions and preparing the ground for another summit. In a response, carried by the official Korean Central News Agency, North Korean Foreign Ministry adviser Kim Kye Gwan said it would be "stupid" to expect that Kim's personal relationship with Trump would be enough to restart negotiations.[61]

Talks will resume, he said, when Washington agrees to the proposal Kim put forward at his Hanoi summit with Trump last June: That North Korea would dismantle its principal nuclear facility at Yongbyon in exchange for the partial lifting of U.N. sanctions on North Korea. "There is no need for us to be present in such talks, in which there is only unilateral pressure," Kim Kye Gwan said, "and we have no desire to barter something for other things at the talks, like traders."[62]

On Capitol Hill, the eight Democratic senators who wrote to Trump in December urged him to come up with a comprehensive strategy to advance denuclearization talks, including a "phased process to verifiably dismantle the Yongbyon nuclear complex and other nuclear facilities."[63]

But Kori Schake, who has served in senior policy positions at the Pentagon, State Department and National Security Council in both Democratic and Republican administrations, says the prospects for any progress toward North Korea's denuclearization appear slim. "The Trump administration doesn't appear to think that agreements require any compromise from them," says Schake. "Most negotiations work better when your position isn't 'Give me everything first, and then I'll give you something.' They're not invested in a process that builds confidence as it builds momentum."

According to several independent experts who closely follow North Korean issues, the administration's position has thwarted Stephen Biegun, Trump's top North Korea negotiator, who has been unable to persuade Trump and Secretary of State Mike Pompeo to adopt a step-by-step negotiating process.

In an appearance on ABC's *This Week* just before the new year, Robert O'Brien, Trump's fourth national security adviser, echoed the president's hard line, warning the United States will respond if North Korea resumes nuclear weapons and long-range ballistic missile tests.

U.S. President Barack Obama and Russian President Dmitry Medvedev shake hands after signing the New Strategic Arms Reduction Treaty (New START) in 2010 in Prague. The pact committed the two nations to major nuclear arms cuts.

AT ISSUE

Is limited nuclear war a viable battlefield option?

YES
John D. Maurer
Jeane Kirkpatrick Fellow, American Enterprise Institute

Written for *CQ Researcher*, February 2020

The most viable way to prevent a limited nuclear war is to be ready to fight one. As such, the United States must modernize its arsenal of tactical or so-called low-yield nuclear weapons, whose explosive power can range from the equivalent of 20 tons of TNT to as high as a Hiroshima-sized bomb, which was 16,000 tons. Fielding such weapons will ensure that U.S. leaders have options short of all-out war to respond to nuclear provocation and will signal to adversaries that they cannot hope to escalate their way out of a losing conventional battle. By closing off options for escalation, low-yield U.S. weapons will help deter adversaries from embarking on militarized crises in the first place. Furthermore, improving and expanding U.S. low-yield capabilities will create an incentive for rivals to take seriously proposals to eliminate such weapons.

Those who oppose the United States developing tactical nuclear weapons argue that they are destabilizing because the collateral damage they cause is small enough that decision-makers might be tempted to use them in a crisis. But nuclear war is only likely to occur against the backdrop of a major conventional war between the great powers. If one of those powers fears defeat on the conventional battlefield, it will face strong pressures to use nuclear weapons to stave off that loss.

The escalatory pressure emerges not from the character of the nuclear weapons themselves but from the looming threat of conventional military humiliation. If the losing great power has low-yield weapons that it can use without fear of reprisal, nuclear war is all but assured. Only the threat of a proportional nuclear response would deter adversaries from using such weapons to stave off defeat.

Modernizing the U.S. low-yield nuclear arsenal also provides the clearest path to eliminating tactical nuclear weapons entirely. Rivals such as Russia and China already maintain large numbers of these weapons and have no incentive to dismantle them if the United States does not have a similar capability to trade away in negotiations. Critics of low-yield nuclear weapons who are serious about eliminating their escalatory potential should support U.S. nuclear modernization as a first step toward bringing adversaries to the bargaining table.

The United States cannot abide a world in which adversaries such as Russia and China have low-yield weapons, while the United States does not. As our adversaries engage in increasingly threatening behavior toward U.S. allies, the United States needs a nuclear arsenal that will ensure deterrence—not just on good days, but also on the worst days.

NO
Joseph Cirincione
President, Ploughshares Fund

Written for *CQ Researcher*, February 2020

We refuse to learn from history. Almost 40 years ago, Defense Secretary Robert McNamara wrote: "It is inconceivable to me, as it has been to others who have studied the matter, that 'limited' nuclear wars would remain limited—any decision to use nuclear weapons would imply a high probability of the same cataclysmic consequences as a total nuclear exchange." McNamara concluded, along with his British colleagues, that "under no circumstances" would they have recommended "that NATO initiate the use of nuclear weapons."

But that is precisely what a new generation of Dr. Strangeloves recommends today. They have embraced the Cold War theory of "escalation dominance" and favor new, more usable nuclear weapons to fight even conventional conflicts. They argue that if the United States has greater military force on every rung of the "escalatory ladder," it can convince an enemy to surrender early in a conflict.

But that attractive theoretical concept has little relationship to any conceivable conflict scenario, in which even a militarily inferior adversary has multiple ways of escalating a conflict. For example, the United States is militarily superior to Iran, but with a few mines and speedy patrol boats, Tehran could close the Strait of Hormuz, crippling oil flows and plunging the world economy into recession.

Yet, Iran is precisely where some in Washington favor using nuclear weapons. A 2017 Pentagon war game used U.S.-based bombers to drop a low-yield nuclear weapon on Iran. But because it would take a 10-hour flight to deliver this weapon, the Trump administration has just deployed—with congressional approval—a low-yield nuclear warhead that can be launched from submarines off Iran's coast. This Hiroshima-sized bomb could explode within 15 minutes of launch.

Supporters justify this scenario by arguing it offers "multiple options" and "maximum flexibility," providing military solutions to even the most difficult political problems. Most serious analysts recognized long ago that this strategy leads to disaster.

"A nuclear weapon is a nuclear weapon," warned former Secretary of State George Shultz. "You use a small one, then you go to a bigger one."

Iran does not have nuclear weapons, but Russia and China do. The first use of nuclear weapons against those countries would not be the last. Commanders can have no confidence that they can control or contain a limited nuclear war. Rather than being a strategy for victory, it guarantees defeat for all sides.

"We will take action, as we do in these situations," O'Brien said. "If Kim Jong Un takes that approach, we will be extraordinarily disappointed, and we will demonstrate that disappointment." He declined to provide any specifics but said the administration has many "tools in its tool kit" to respond to any such tests.[64]

Other White House officials say Trump is not looking for another confrontation with Kim in an election year. If the tests resume, they say, Trump is likely to press the United Nations to tighten sanctions against North Korea—a strategy that previous administrations have used to little effect.

Nuclear weapons experts say in the year and a half since the Singapore summit, Kim has built up his missile stores and produced enough bomb-grade nuclear fuel for about 38 warheads—double an earlier estimate issued by U.S. intelligence analysts.

Pressure for New START

Meanwhile, lawmakers are stepping up pressure on the Trump administration to extend New START, introducing bipartisan legislation in both chambers that would strengthen a requirement to assess the costs and implications of allowing the treaty to expire next February.

With Trump still unwilling to commit to the pact's extension in order to explore including China, the House and Senate bills would require the administration to provide intelligence estimates on how much Russian and Chinese nuclear forces could expand if New START expires. Lawmakers also want to know how much it would cost for U.S. intelligence to ascertain such developments without an extension of New START's verification provisions.

The bills echo a provision in the new fiscal 2020 National Defense Authorization Act, which requires the administration to estimate how large Russia's tactical nuclear arsenal and China's nuclear modernization program will grow if New START is allowed to lapse.[65]

Congressional aides say the legislation reflects serious concerns on Capitol Hill that the administration has not sufficiently analyzed the strategic implications of allowing New START to expire. Moreover, lawmakers from both parties and arms control experts say they are unaware of any concerted administration effort to formulate a negotiating strategy for China.

Countryman, the former assistant secretary of State for international security and nonproliferation, notes that while Trump announced his plan for a tripartite arms control treaty last May, the State Department only invited China to begin what it called a bilateral "strategic security dialogue" in December. "After saying they wanted to negotiate with China, it took them nine months to officially communicate that," he says.

State Department officials will not say whether China has responded to its invitation, but Beijing repeatedly has said it has no interest in three-way nuclear arms reduction talks, because the Russian and U.S. arsenals are already 20 times the size of China's.

In February 2020, national security adviser Robert O'Brien said the Trump administration would soon open nuclear arms control negotiations with Russia. His remarks came 10 months after Secretary of State Mike Pompeo told lawmakers the administration was at the "very beginning of conversations about renewing" New START, indicating it had made no serious diplomatic efforts in the interim.[66]

With the administration struggling to deal with North Korea and Iran, some arms control experts suggest it may not have the bandwidth to focus on Trump's trilateral treaty proposal. The State Department's Office of Strategic Stability and Deterrence Affairs, responsible for negotiating arms control treaties, reportedly has gone from having 14 staffers when Trump took office in 2017 to four. The State Department's top two arms control officials were among those who left, says Bell, the former State Department arms control adviser, and neither has been replaced. The State Department has not commented on the report.

"We simply don't have enough people doing this," says Bell, now the senior policy director at the Council for a Livable World, a Washington-based organization that advocates for nuclear disarmament. "To create these kinds of agreements, you need patience and high-level, disciplined attention paid to those goals. It's hard to see that forthcoming from this administration."

And without the robust verification procedures allowed by New START, it would cost billions of dollars to create new intelligence programs to determine the disposition of Russia's nuclear arsenal, with no guarantees that such programs would succeed, say former arms control officials. The treaty's expiration also would remove any restrictions on the numbers of new hypersonic nuclear weapons Russia could deploy, experts say.

"It is hard to overstate, from my perspective as a senior military leader, how much we benefit from the knowledge and predictability the treaty provides about Russia's nuclear forces and operational practices," Mullen, the former Joint Chiefs chairman, told the House Foreign Affairs Committee in December 2019. "Without the treaty and its verification provisions, we'd be flying blind."[67]

OUTLOOK
Grim Future

The Ploughshares Fund's Cirincione says the future of arms control looks grim. "It's on life support," he says, citing the steady erosion of treaties that once formed the pillars of the arms control architecture.

The United Nations will conduct its five-year review of the nuclear Non-Proliferation Treaty in April and May of 2020, providing a comprehensive assessment of arms control, nonproliferation efforts and progress toward disarmament. Arms control experts expect poor report cards for the United States, Russia and China regarding their commitments to nuclear disarmament.

Arms control experts predict that the review will cite the development of new hypersonic nuclear weapons, cyberwarfare capabilities and the militarization of space as troubling technological advances that will only make nuclear disarmament more difficult. The review is also expected to raise concerns over the collapse of the Intermediate Nuclear Forces Treaty, the stalemate in U.S.-North Korean negotiations, President Trump's withdrawal from the Iran nuclear deal and the possible lapse of the New START and Open Skies treaties.

Meanwhile, the Council for a Livable World's Bell says U.S. investments in both new missiles and missile defenses and the Pentagon's buildup of tactical nuclear weapons are foreboding signs. "This looks like a recommitment to the concept of nuclear war fighting," she says.

Nunn, of the Nuclear Threat Initiative, says a key factor for the future of arms control is sustained communication between the United States and Russia over maintaining strategic stability. Although Putin and Trump have agreed to hold such talks, few meetings between their military representatives have taken place. "When we're not having a military-to-military dialogue, arms control is eroded," Nunn says.

The American Enterprise Institute's Maurer believes arms control will probably remain dormant for the next 10 to 30 years—the time it will take for the United States to fully modernize its nuclear weapons and delivery systems. At that point, he predicts, Russia and China will make arms control a priority because the technical superiority of America's arsenal will leave them vulnerable.

"Once our capabilities mature, that's when we'll see the Russians and the Chinese become interested in arms control negotiations," Maurer said. "We saw this during the Cold War. The Russians were always the most eager for arms control talks when we had a big military program coming down the pipeline, whether it was our missile defense system in the 1970s that resulted in the ABM Treaty, or our Pershing II and Trident missiles in the 1980s that led to the INF and START treaties."

But Nunn fears that kind of thinking is an enormous gamble.

"We've gone 75 years without a nuclear explosion," he says. "To think we're going to go another 50 years without an awful lot of cooperation between the nuclear powers is pretty naive. We've become accustomed to thinking that because it hasn't happened, it won't happen. But that defies both the odds and history."

NOTES

1. "Russia deploys new hypersonic nuclear-capable missiles that can travel 27 times the speed of sound," *The Associated Press*, *The Straits Times*, Dec. 28, 2019, https://tinyurl.com/wb7k59q; R. Jeffrey Smith, "Hypersonic Missiles Are Unstoppable. And They're Starting a New Global Arms Race," *The New York Times*, June 19, 2019, https://tinyurl.com/y2nberq2.

2. Brad Lendon, "Russia's 'invulnerable' nuclear missile ready to deploy, Putin says," *CNN*, Dec. 27, 2018, https://tinyurl.com/y7b674l9.

3. David E. Sanger and William J. Broad, "To Counter Russia, U.S. Signals Nuclear Arms Are Back in a Big Way," *The New York Times*, Feb. 4, 2018, https://tinyurl.com/ybufvz59.

4. Aaron Mehta, "Hypersonics 'highest technical priority' for Pentagon R&D head," *Defense News*, March 6, 2018, https://tinyurl.com/y8ckzk27.

5. Choe Sang-Hun, "North Korea Is No Longer Bound by Nuclear Test Moratorium, Kim Says," *The New York Times*, Dec. 31, 2019, https://tinyurl.com/uefzf3f.

6. Max Burman and The Associated Press, "Iran pulling out of nuclear deal commitment following U.S. strike that killed Soleimani," *NBC News*, Jan. 5, 2020, https://tinyurl.com/r42hksc.

7. "Nuclear Weapons: Who Has What at a Glance," Arms Control Association, July 2019, https://tinyurl.com/6ovpr2v.

8. Ibid.

9. Vladimir Isachenkov, "Putin offers US an immediate extension to key nuclear pact," *The Associated Press*, Dec. 5, 2019, https://tinyurl.com/vgxb884.

10. Nicole Gaouette, "US to start negotiating with Russia on nuclear arms control soon," *CNN*, Feb. 5, 2020, https://tinyurl.com/rlf6kwl.

11. Ed Pilkington and Martin Pengelly, "'Let it be an arms race': Donald Trump appears to double down on nuclear expansion," *The Guardian*, Dec. 24, 2016, https://tinyurl.com/zyz4elr.

12. Gaouette, *op. cit.*

13. David Hale, testimony before the Committee on Foreign Relations, U.S. Senate, Dec. 3, 2019, https://tinyurl.com/tdkxcbp.

14. Rebecca Kheel, "Pompeo: Russia complying with nuclear treaty that's up for renewal," *The Hill*, April 10, 2019, https://tinyurl.com/y2gjqe5v.

15. Bill Gertz, "Bolton: China Continuing Cyberattacks on Government, Private Networks," *The Washington Free Beacon*, June 18, 2019, https://tinyurl.com/y674ua97.

16. Rose Gottemoeller, testimony before the Committee on Foreign Affairs, U.S. House of Representatives, Dec. 4, 2019, https://tinyurl.com/vv6drv3.

17. Gordon Lubold, "U.S. Deploys New, Less Destructive Nuclear Warhead," *The Wall Street Journal*, Feb. 5, 2020, https://tinyurl.com/ufqrg9j.

18. "2018 Nuclear Posture Review," Office of the Secretary of Defense, February 2018, https://tinyurl.com/yc7lu944.

19. Ibid.

20. "Nuclear Operations," Joint Chiefs of Staff, June 11, 2019, https://tinyurl.com/y4khdm2r.

21. Ibid.

22. Elbridge Colby, "If You Want Peace, Prepare for Nuclear War," *Foreign Affairs*, November/December 2018, https://tinyurl.com/vkruuy3.

23. Ibid.

24. Matthew Gault, "Even 'Limited' Nuclear War Could Cause 90 Million Casualties in a Few Hours," *Vice News*, Sept. 16, 2019, https://tinyurl.com/y3egjc4y.

25. Melissa Hanham, Twitter post, Jan. 27, 2019, https://tinyurl.com/rglk8g2.

26. Roberta Rampton, "'We fell in love:' Trump swoons over letters from North Korea's Kim," *Reuters*, Sept. 30, 2018, https://tinyurl.com/ybpomjgc.

27. Simon Denyer, "Confusion over North Korea's definition of denuclearization clouds talks," *The Washington Post*, Jan, 16, 2019, https://tinyurl.com/y7jfz33w.

28. Anthony Kuhn, "Why North Korea's Kim Jong Un May Be Leaving The Door Open To Nuclear Talks," *NPR*, Jan. 1, 2020, https://tinyurl.com/yxxghmsq.

29. Ibid.

30. "Letter from Senior Democratic senators to President Donald Trump on the administration's North Korea policy," Senate Foreign Relations Committee, Dec. 18, 2019, https://tinyurl.com/vngdnv5.

31. Ibid.

32. "Truman's Legacy: Breakout Box Activity," Harry S. Truman Library and Museum, https://tinyurl.com/s6vqelg; Emperor Hirohito, "Accepting the Potsdam

Declaration, Radio Broadcast," Federal Communications Commission, Aug. 14, 1945, https://tinyurl.com/ycvld9t8.

33. James A. Hijiya, "The Gita of J. Robert Oppenheimer," *Proceedings of the American Philosophical Society*, Vol. 144, No. 2, June 2000, https://tinyurl.com/yx7m5nkx.

34. "The United States presents the Baruch Plan," History.com, July 17, 2019, https://tinyurl.com/up34tul.

35. *Ibid.*

36. "J. Robert Oppenheimer Biography," Biography.com, July 26, 2019, https://tinyurl.com/st34k9h.

37. "Cuban Missile Crisis," *Encyclopaedia Britannica*, Feb. 4, 2020, https://tinyurl.com/ybyumlfj.

38. "Cuban Missile Crisis," History.com, June 10, 2019, https://tinyurl.com/yb83yomu.

39. *Ibid.*

40. Evan Thomas, "America's history of preparing for, and trying to avoid, nuclear war," *The Washington Post*, Jan. 30, 2020, https://tinyurl.com/wc6vqcn.

41. "Hot Line Agreement (1963)," Atomicarchive.com, https://tinyurl.com/ru9yt95; "Limited Test Ban Treaty (1963)" Atomicarchive.com, https://tinyurl.com/tymckbf.

42. "Nuclear Non-Proliferation Treaty (1968)," Atomicarchive.com, https://tinyurl.com/wm2azag.

43. "Strategic Arms Limitation Treaty I," Atomicarchive.com, https://tinyurl.com/vngomxq; "Anti-Ballistic Missile Treaty (1972)," Atomicarchive.com, https://tinyurl.com/yx6u676m.

44. "Strategic Arms Limitation Treaty II (1979)," Atomicarchive.com, https://tinyurl.com/smqmmly.

45. "The zero option," *The Christian Science Monitor*, Nov. 19, 1981, https://tinyurl.com/wldt6ho; Daryl G. Kimball, "Looking Back: The Nuclear Arms Control Legacy of Ronald Reagan," Arms Control Association, https://tinyurl.com/7gskwlm.

46. *Ibid.*

47. *Ibid.*

48. *Ibid.*

49. "Strategic Arms Reduction Treaty (1991)," Atomicarchive.com, https://tinyurl.com/2dd9sc.

50. Justin Bresolin and Brenna Gautam, "Fact Sheet: The Nunn-Lugar Cooperative Threat Reduction Program," Center for Arms Control and Non-Proliferation, June 1, 2014, https://tinyurl.com/wfbk47l.

51. "Strategic Arms Reduction Treaty (START II)," Federation of American Scientists, https://tinyurl.com/vd39j3x.

52. *Ibid.*

53. "New Strategic Arms Reduction Treaty (New START) (2010)," Atomicarchive.com, https://tinyurl.com/rsn3m34.

54. Sanger and Broad, *op. cit.*

55. Mark Landler, "Trump and Kim See New Chapter for Nations After Summit," *The New York Times*, June 11, 2018, https://tinyurl.com/y8d3ptod.

56. Kevin Liptak and Jeremy Diamond, "'Sometimes you have to walk': Trump leaves Hanoi with no deal," *CNN*, Feb. 28, 2019, https://tinyurl.com/yxr5oulm.

57. David E. Sanger and William J. Broad, "U.S. Suspends Nuclear Arms Control Treaty With Russia," *The New York Times*, Feb. 1, 2019, https://tinyurl.com/y8oakt5y; "Summary: House-Senate Conference Agreement on FY2020 National Defense Authorization Bill (S.1790)," Center for Arms Control and Non-Proliferation, Dec. 11, 2019, https://tinyurl.com/tl7qpek.

58. Kingston Reif, "Congress OKs Trump Nuclear Priorities," Arms Control Association, January/February 2020, https://tinyurl.com/uuasmf7.

59. Kim Tong-Hyung, "North Korea's Kim touts strategic weapon amid stall in talks," *The Christian Science Monitor*, Jan. 1, 2020, https://tinyurl.com/qnx35wl.

60. Adam Forrest, "Trump insists Kim is a 'man of his word' despite North Korea ramping up nuclear programme," *The Independent*, Jan. 1, 2020, https://tinyurl.com/yx7ozrcl.

61. Kanga Kong, "North Korea Says Won't Trade Nuclear Weapons for Sanctions Lift," *Bloomberg*, Jan. 11, 2020, https://tinyurl.com/v6y6t6v.

62. *Ibid.*
63. "Democratic senators' letter to Trump regarding North Korea talks," *op. cit.*
64. "'This Week' Transcript 12-29-19: Amb. Robert O'Brien, Sen. Chris Van Hollen, Andrew Yang," *ABC News*, Dec. 29, 2019, https://tinyurl.com/s9fbyew.
65. "Summary: House-Senate Conference Agreement on FY2020 National Defense Authorization Bill (S.1790)," *op. cit.*
66. Gaouette, *op. cit.*
67. Michael G. Mullen, testimony before the Committee on Foreign Affairs, U.S. House of Representatives, Dec. 5, 2019, https://tinyurl.com/vw6r7of.

BIBLIOGRAPHY
Books

Hersey, John, *Hiroshima*, Vintage Press, 1989.
In the 49th printing of a 1946 book, a journalist interviews six survivors shortly after the atomic bomb fell on Hiroshima.

Kaplan, Fred, *The Bomb: Presidents, Generals and the Secret History of Nuclear War*, Simon & Schuster, 2020.
A veteran defense reporter uses recently declassified documents and interviews with former presidents and generals to recount how they considered using nuclear weapons in war.

Perry, William J., *My Journey at the Nuclear Brink*, Stanford University Press, 2015.
The former U.S. Secretary of Defense (1994-97) recounts how he changed from a nuclear weapons hawk to an advocate for disarmament.

Roberts, Brad, *The Case for Nuclear Weapons in the 21st Century*, Stanford University Press, 2015.
A senior Pentagon official in the Obama administration argues the United States needs a strong nuclear arsenal to deter other nuclear powers.

Sherman, Wendy R., *Not For The Faint At Heart: Lessons in Courage, Power and Persistence*, Public Affairs, 2018.
A former senior U.S. diplomat recounts her experiences negotiating the Iran nuclear agreement and past accords with North Korea.

Articles

Borger, Julian, "US nuclear weapons: first low-yield warheads roll off production line," *The Guardian*, Jan. 28, 2019, https://tinyurl.com/y7x3mzjs.
A veteran British national security journalist reports on the U.S. buildup of smaller tactical nuclear weapons.

Choe, Sang-Hun, "North Korea Is No Longer Bound by Nuclear Test Moratorium, Kim Says," *The New York Times*, Dec. 31, 2019, https://tinyurl.com/uefzf3f.
The North Korean leader says U.S. concessions will determine whether he resumes nuclear and missile testing.

Gault, Matthew, "Even 'Limited' Nuclear War Could Cause 90 Million Casualties in a Few Hours," *Vice News*, Sept. 16, 2019, https://tinyurl.com/y3egjc4y.
A journalist details a Princeton University study showing a limited nuclear war would quickly become unlimited, with catastrophic results.

Gould, Joe, "Trump upbeat on nuclear talks with Russia and China, but lawmakers warn of 'blow up,'" *Defense News*, Dec. 4, 2019, https://tinyurl.com/qsqk6lf.
The president is optimistic China and Russia will join in three-way negotiations for a new arms reduction treaty despite Beijing's stated refusal to take part.

Kong, Kanga, "North Korea Says Won't Trade Nuclear Weapons for Sanctions Lift," *Bloomberg*, Jan. 11, 2020, https://tinyurl.com/v6y6t6v.
Pyongyang hardens its negotiating position on denuclearization in response to Trump's tough line.

Kristensen, Hans, "The New START Treaty Keeps Nuclear Arsenals In Check and President Trump Must Act To Preserve It," *Forbes*, Dec. 10, 2019, https://tinyurl.com/vwd86rp.
A nuclear weapons expert discusses why the New START Treaty should be extended for another five years.

Mohammed, Arshad, and Jonathan Landay, "U.S. Congress pressures Trump to renew arms control pact," *Reuters*, Dec. 17, 2019, https://tinyurl.com/wen3v52.

Two reporters detail lawmakers' concerns that President Trump may let the New START Treaty expire next year.

Moniz, Ernest J., and Sam Nunn, "The Return of Doomsday," *Foreign Affairs*, September/October 2019, https://tinyurl.com/yyxqquhl.

Former Energy secretary and a former Democratic senator who is a nuclear nonproliferation advocate detail how the arms control regime constructed over 50 years has unraveled.

Sanger, David E., and William J. Broad, "To Counter Russia, U.S. Signals Nuclear Arms Are Back in a Big Way," *The New York Times*, Feb. 4, 2018, https://tinyurl.com/ybufvz59.

Two reporters detail the Trump administration's nuclear weapons policies.

Tannenwald, Nina, "The Vanishing Nuclear Taboo? How Disarmament Fell Apart," *Foreign Affairs*, Oct. 15, 2018, https://tinyurl.com/wj679gl.

A Brown University expert on nuclear policy examines how arms control has withered during the Trump administration.

Reports

Gleason, Michael P., and Luc H. Riesbeck, "Noninterference with National Technical Means: The Status Quo Will Not Survive," Center for Space Policy and Strategy, Aerospace Corporation, April 2019, https://tinyurl.com/uqgs2v9.

Two experts in the military uses of space explain the challenges facing U.S. satellite surveillance of Russia's nuclear arsenal if the New START treaty expires in 2021.

Harrison, Todd, *et al.*, "Space Threat Assessment 2019," Center for Strategic and International Studies, April 2019, https://tinyurl.com/qulgrwm.

Space war experts detail the weapons other countries have or are developing to counter U.S. military dominance in space.

Hruby, Jill, "Russia's New Nuclear Weapon Delivery Systems," Nuclear Threat Initiative, November 2019, https://tinyurl.com/rn7ux3k.

A nuclear weapons expert describes Russia's new lines of hypersonic boost-glide vehicles, nuclear-powered torpedoes and other systems to deliver nuclear warheads.

"2018 Nuclear Posture Review," Office of the Secretary of Defense, 2018, https://tinyurl.com/yc7lu944.

The Trump administration lays out its nuclear weapons policy, which includes waging limited nuclear war with tactical nuclear weapons.

THE NEXT STEP

China's Weapons

Chan, Minnie, "China nuclear missile development steps up a gear with test of weapon capable of hitting US mainland," *South China Morning Post*, Jan. 4, 2020, https://tinyurl.com/t93cf64.

China tested a new submarine-launched nuclear missile capable of hitting the continental United States.

"China displays new hypersonic nuclear missile on 70th anniversary," *Al Jazeera*, Oct. 1, 2019, https://tinyurl.com/y5s958ew.

China unveiled a new weapon believed to be capable of breaching all existing U.S. anti-missile shields.

Wainer, David, "Chinese nuclear plans cloud prospects for new U.S.-Russia missile deal," *Bloomberg*, Oct. 18, 2019, https://tinyurl.com/svlbdfn.

China plans on rapidly expanding its nuclear arsenal and seems unlikely to join Russia and the United States in an extension of New START, the arms control accord that is due to expire in early 2021.

New START

Arkhipov, Ilya, "Russia Says U.S. Silence on Last Nuclear Treaty May Be 'Fatal,'" *Bloomberg*, Aug. 26, 2019, https://tinyurl.com/y3pxf9hx.

A Kremlin spokesman raised concerns about the lack of controls on nuclear weapons if New START, the arms reduction treaty signed by the United States and Russia in 2010, is allowed to expire.

Brennan, David, "America is Risking a Nuclear 'Free-For-All' By Delaying New START Extension With Russia: Former National Security Official," *Newsweek*, Jan. 16, 2020, https://tinyurl.com/uy6wpzu.
A White House National Security Council staffer during the Obama administration is concerned that delaying, even for a short time, the extension of New START will create long-term security risks for the United States.

Zengerle, Patricia, "Senior U.S. official: Russia in compliance with New START weapons treaty," *Reuters*, Dec. 3, 2019, https://tinyurl.com/vc3tmgt.
A top U.S. State Department official said Russia remains in compliance with New START, even as it fails to comply with most other arms control obligations.

Space

Erwin, Sandra, "Pentagon report: DoD needs to test how satellites would perform under attack," *Space News*, Feb. 1, 2020, https://tinyurl.com/svf8zaw.
In a new report the Pentagon warns that the U.S. military currently cannot assess the durability of its satellites if they came under attack.

Kiang, Charlotte, "What Exactly Is The Space Force?" *Forbes*, Jan. 27, 2020, https://tinyurl.com/wf69cw4.
The recently established U.S. Space Force's work includes procuring and operating space vehicles and satellites and rockets to launch them into orbit.

Strout, Nathan, "What we know about Iran's counterspace weapons," *C4ISRNET*, Jan. 8, 2020, https://tinyurl.com/rfxlvc4.
While it is unlikely that Iran has strong anti-satellite weaponry, defense experts believe the Islamic Republic can jam U.S. satellite communications and GPS.

Tactical Weapons

Brumfiel, Geoff, "U.S. Has Deployed New, Small Nukes on Submarine, According to Group," *NPR*, Jan. 29, 2020, https://tinyurl.com/vb4xctn.
A U.S. submarine has begun carrying one or two low-yield nuclear warheads, according to the Federation of American Scientists.

Ioanes, Ellen, and Dave Mosher, "A terrifying new animation shows how 1 'tactical' nuclear weapon could trigger a US-Russia war that kills 34 million people in 5 hours," *Business Insider*, Jan. 23, 2020, https://tinyurl.com/yyrqpfta.
A simulation from Princeton University shows how the use of one tactical nuclear weapon could lead to a worldwide nuclear conflict.

Meier, Lauren, "Putin to develop new 'tactical' nuclear missiles after Trump spikes weapons treaty," *The Washington Times*, Sept. 5, 2019, https://tinyurl.com/vwxhy7m.
After the United States abandoned the Intermediate-Range Nuclear Forces (INF) Treaty in August 2019, Russia said it planned to develop short-range tactical nuclear weapons.

For More Information

American Enterprise Institute, 1789 Massachusetts Ave., N.W., Washington, DC 20036; 202-862-7177; aei.org. Conservative think tank that analyzes U.S. nuclear policy and takes generally hawkish positions.

Arms Control Association, 1200 18th St., N.W., Suite 1175, Washington, DC 20036; 202-463-8270; armscontrol.org. Nonpartisan organization that advocates for arms control through briefings, seminars and its magazine, *Arms Control Today.*

Carnegie Endowment for International Peace, 1779 Massachusetts Ave., N.W., Washington, DC 20036; 202-483-7600; ceip.org. Centrist think tank with experts on strategic nuclear weapons and nonproliferation.

Council for a Livable World, 820 First St., N.E., Suite LL-180, Washington, DC 20002; 202-543-4100; Livableworld.org. Advocacy organization that promotes peace through arms control, nonproliferation and disarmament.

European Council on Foreign Relations, 4th Floor, Tennyson House, 159-165 Great Portland St., Marylebone, London W1W 5PA, UK; +44 20 7227 6860; ecfr.eu. Centrist think tank that provides the European perspective on U.S. and Russian nuclear arms policy, arms control and national security issues.

International Institute for Strategic Studies, 2121 K St., N.W., Suite 801, Washington, DC 20037; 202-659-1490; iiss.org. Nonpartisan think tank that produces papers and briefings and holds conferences on nonproliferation and nuclear policy.

Nuclear Threat Initiative, 1776 I St., N.W., Suite 600, Washington, DC 20006; 202-296-4810; nti.org. Nonpartisan research organization whose staff includes former senior government officials and nuclear weapons experts who provide studies and other materials aimed at reducing the threat of nuclear, chemical and biological weapons.

Ploughshares Fund, 1100 Vermont Ave., N.W., Suite 300, Washington, DC 20005; 202-783-4401; ploughshares.org. A public grantmaking foundation that supports initiatives aimed at preventing the spread and use of nuclear weapons.

2

Medical Tourism

Will rising health costs trigger a post-coronavirus revival?

By Kerry Dooley Young

People crowd the street outside a dental clinic in Los Algodones, Mexico, in 2017. Americans travel to the town, located on the U.S.-Mexican border, in search of cheaper dental care.

THE ISSUES

Howard Staab remains a big fan of medical tourism.

Sixteen years ago, the self-employed carpenter, lacking health insurance, traveled to India to replace a failing heart valve. The cost: about $6,700—far less than the $200,000 typically charged at a U.S. hospital.[1]

Staab, now 68, is still leading an active life and is restoring a home in Spain. While he had a second valve replacement at a U.S. hospital in 2018—Medicare paid for this operation—Staab says he would not have hesitated to return to India for the procedure. And he recommends that others in need of cardiac care consider treatment at the facility in New Delhi where he had his first valve replacement.

"I had such a great experience in India," he says.

Although the coronavirus outbreak has largely frozen medical tourism because of the international travel restrictions, many experts expect it to resume once the pandemic subsides. And the key driver will continue to be the high cost of medical care at home, says Josef Woodman, CEO of Patients Beyond Borders, a group that advises government agencies and hospitals about medical tourism.

"No one wants to travel for medical care," says Woodman, who also publishes guides for consumers. "That's not on the top of the list for a vacation agenda. It's about saving money."

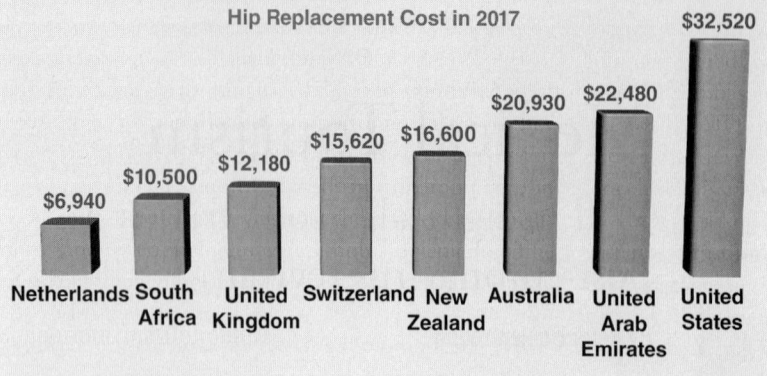

Hip Replacement Costs in the U.S. Top Other Countries

A hip replacement in the United States cost $32,520 on average in 2017, more than $10,000 higher than in the United Arab Emirates and nearly five times higher than in the Netherlands. The procedure also cost less in South Africa, the United Kingdom, Switzerland, New Zealand and Australia.

Hip Replacement Cost in 2017

- Netherlands: $6,940
- South Africa: $10,500
- United Kingdom: $12,180
- Switzerland: $15,620
- New Zealand: $16,600
- Australia: $20,930
- United Arab Emirates: $22,480
- United States: $32,520

Source: John Hargraves and Aaron Bloschichak, "International comparisons of health care prices from the 2017 iFHP survey," Health Care Cost Institute, Dec. 17, 2019, https://tinyurl.com/rz2ceqr

Wealthier Americans have long gone abroad in search of treatments unavailable to them at home, including unproven therapies. Staab's journey to India made him perhaps the most famous American medical tourist to seek care abroad due to cost. There was a splash of news coverage and even a 2006 Senate hearing about his Indian heart surgery. But his far-flung experience is far from the norm for the majority of Americans seeking medical care abroad, says Valorie Crooks, a researcher at British Columbia's Simon Fraser University.

"There's an idea of the mythical American patient. It's sort of like a unicorn," Crooks says. "A lot of the coverage tends to exoticize the practice of medical tourism. It suggests that people are traveling all the time from Missouri, for example, to India or that people are crossing into different hemispheres."

Instead, Crooks cites as more typical the dense cluster of dentists in Los Algodones, Mexico, catering to Americans and Canadians. It is a two-and-a-half-hour drive from San Diego and three hours from Phoenix.

I. Glenn Cohen, a professor at Harvard Law School and the author of *Patients with Passports: Medical Tourism, Law, and Ethics,* agrees with Crooks. He says the most common form of medical tourism in recent years has been "driving to our southern border with Mexico."

Familiarity remains the key predictor of where an American might seek care abroad, says Cohen. Immigrants might return to their country of origin for medical care, and their children and even grandchildren may be likely to do so if families have maintained cultural ties, Cohen says. People with connections to Thailand or South Korea, for example, may return to these nations for care, he notes.

David Boucher, the chief business transformation officer at Thailand's Bumrungrad International Hospital, is also anticipating a rebound in business. People who were considering traveling abroad for orthopedic procedures before the pandemic hit will still need hip and knee replacements and rotator cuff treatments when coronavirus infections subside, says Boucher, whose hospital is a major hub for medical tourism.

"Once this clears and the airlines open up the flights, they will be back in the air and they will be coming here," he says.

Boucher says he is confident about the future of Bumrungrad, a giant hospital in Bangkok, which cares for more than 1.1 million patients from more than 190 countries each year.[2] But a shakeout is likely among smaller participants in medical tourism. Some agencies that connect patients with hospitals and clinics abroad probably will close due to the pandemic, said Ian Youngman, an author who specializes in writing about the business of medical tourism.

"The restrictions and virus fears have hit tourism hard, and medical tourism is expected to be hit the hardest," Youngman said.[3]

While U.S. insurers and employers have not rushed to embrace medical tourism, there have been some notable pioneers. Privately owned HSM Solutions, a North Carolina manufacturer, for example, has let its employees share in the savings if they get elective procedures in places such as Costa Rica and the Cayman Islands.

It is easy to understand why some Americans look for medical bargains abroad. But these patients may be underestimating the high costs of treating potential complications, says Dr. Usamah Mossallam, medical director for international initiatives at Detroit's Henry Ford Health System.

Patients seen abroad sometimes return home with infections or find their knee and hip replacements must be redone, Mossallam says. These patients then may need to find specialists in the United States.

"It's a whole host of things that are scary to see and deal with. They can't go back to the place" that treated them, Mossallam says. "They don't trust them anymore."

He contrasts this with the experience of overseas patients who travel to America for medical care. The United States is a leader among nations drawing medical tourists, with many wealthy people seeking care at medical centers. Those undergoing a joint replacement at Henry Ford would commit to spending about a month living near the hospital, allowing physicians to monitor their condition, according to Mossallam.

"We feel like we own that person's health. We own that person's process as well as whatever it takes to get them healthy, instead of it being a case of 'send us a large sum of money and we'll do the procedure and then you are on your own,'" Mossallam says.

But Cohen, the Harvard law professor, says Americans can be "very parochial" in their attitudes about the quality of care.

"We assume we have the best health care in the world, but in fact there are many hospitals across the world that do particular things as well as the Mayo Clinic does," he says. "So the average hospital you go to in the United States may actually be worse than the very best hospitals in Thailand or India."

The exact number of Americans traveling abroad for health care is unknown, say Crooks, Cohen and other medical tourism experts. But they agree that certain estimates have been too bullish. A widely cited 2008 report from the Deloitte Center for Health Solutions predicted that the number of American medical tourists would rise to 16 million by 2017.[4]

That was far above Patients Beyond Borders' estimate—made before the coronavirus outbreak—that about 2.2 million Americans were likely to travel outside the United States for medical care this year.

The group estimated recent spending by medical tourists as averaging $3,550 per visit. That includes medical-related costs, cross-border and local transport, inpatient stay and outside accommodations.[5] Costa Rica, India and Thailand are among the most popular destinations.

One reason why the higher projections for U.S. medical tourism failed to materialize may have been the passage in 2010 of the Affordable Care Act (ACA), which dropped the number of Americans lacking health insurance from almost 47 million in 2010 to about 28 million in 2018.[6]

But some consumers still have difficulty finding affordable plans. And the costs imposed by the coronavirus pandemic could produce a spike in the price of medical insurance next year, causing employers and consumers to drop medical coverage, said Covered California, the state health insurance exchange created by the ACA. Covered California's researchers in March predicted health insurance premium increases next year ranging from a low of 4 percent to more than 40 percent.[7]

Cohen says the study of medical tourism relies in part on "anec-data," with the numbers available used to illustrate points promoters of certain procedures and locales want to make. Crooks of Simon Fraser University uses the phrase "triple U's" to describe medical tourism. "It's untracked, untraced and unregulated," she says.

Countries do not collect information about whether citizens have had care abroad. "We do things like ask if somebody has been on a farm because we're concerned about zoonotic disease," Crooks says, referring to maladies spread between animals and humans. "But we don't ask if somebody has accessed care abroad."

The coronavirus pandemic might prompt governments around the world to reconsider their laissez-faire approach to citizens seeking health care abroad, says Heather Wipfli, an associate professor at the University of Southern California's Keck School of Medicine.

Even before the new virus emerged as a major threat, scientific bodies, including the U.S. Centers for Disease

Control and Prevention, raised alarms about the spread of drug-resistant bacteria through medical tourism. With the coronavirus carried into many nations by travelers returning home, governments and scientific leaders are newly reminded just how intertwined nations should be in fighting diseases, says Wipfli, who has published research on international efforts to coordinate health initiatives.

"We might want to have some rules in place to be able to conduct surveillance and monitoring of procedures and patients in order to track whether these kinds of microbes are crossing borders," she says.

As patients, medical professionals and scientists consider the future of medical tourism, here are some of the issues they are discussing:

Should federal health insurance programs cover medicines and therapies obtained abroad?

A Utah experiment with pharmacy tourism should be copied by federal agencies and programs such as the Department of Veterans Affairs, Medicare and Medicaid, says state Rep. Norm Thurston, a Republican.

Utah's Public Employees Health Program lets employees share in savings if they travel to pharmacies in Mexico or Canada to purchase certain costly drugs. Utah so far says it has saved about $225,000 on drugs bought in Mexico by patients who required certain expensive medications, mostly treatments for multiple sclerosis and other autoimmune disorders.[8]

"Why can't we do this, for example, for the Medicaid program?" says Thurston, who earlier served as Utah's health reform coordinator. "We could do it safely, and it would save taxpayers a ton of money, both state and federal."

Combined annual spending for Medicaid and Medicare tops $1 trillion, with more than 100 million covered between the two programs.[9] Medicare offers health insurance to those age 65 and older, while Medicaid provides coverage for lower-income adults.

Many states already are interested in tapping into Canadian pharmacies for the same medicines sold in the United States. In response, the Trump administration in December released a proposal for creating a safe pathway for certain cross-border sales.[10] This represents a major shift in attitude by the U.S. Food and Drug Administration, which long has said it could not guarantee the safety of these imported medicines.[11] The American Medical Association in 2018 endorsed the practice of people buying their medicines in person from licensed Canadian pharmacies.[12]

Why not have Medicare follow a strategy popular with many corporations and seek the aid of offshore partners to lower costs for surgical procedures, asks Dean Baker, senior economist with the Center for Economic and Policy Research, a liberal Washington think tank. Medicare could cover the cost of some elective procedures at foreign hospitals with good track records in these fields, Baker says.

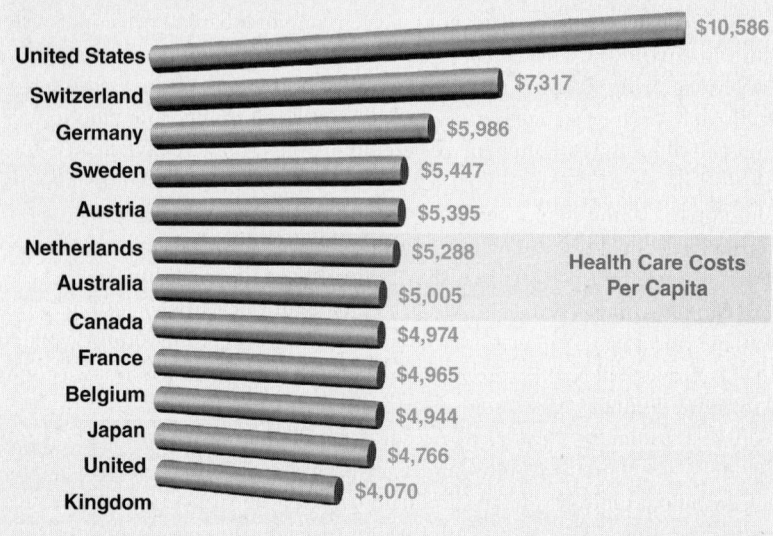

U.S. Health Care Cost Tops Other Developed Nations

The per capita U.S. health care cost in 2018 was $10,586, far more than for other developed nations. Of 12 countries studied, the United Kingdom had the lowest per capita cost.

Health Care Costs Per Capita

United States	$10,586
Switzerland	$7,317
Germany	$5,986
Sweden	$5,447
Austria	$5,395
Netherlands	$5,288
Australia	$5,005
Canada	$4,974
France	$4,965
Belgium	$4,944
Japan	$4,766
United Kingdom	$4,070

Source: "How Does the U.S. Healthcare System Compare to Other Countries?" Peter G. Peterson Foundation, July 22, 2019, https://tinyurl.com/tmc47sg

"The savings could be quite large," he says.

Marc Joffe, a senior policy analyst at the Reason Foundation, a libertarian Los Angeles think tank, also has raised the idea. "Given the very large savings available, it may even be appropriate for Medicare to provide cash incentives to patients choosing medical tourism," Joffe wrote.[13] "Further, a medical tourism benefit could be added to Medicaid and to federal employee benefit systems."

Federal officials could test this approach in a limited way through an experiment involving Medicare Part D pharmacy plans, says Joffe. "That might get traction because there have been a lot of issues with prescription drug costs and people complaining about them," he says.

In a 2009 op-ed in *The New York Times*, Dr. Arnold Milstein, now a professor of medicine at Stanford University, and Jerome Kassirer, a former editor of *The New England Journal of Medicine*, suggested a path testing whether other countries could offer the same level of care for American senior citizens that U.S. medical providers do.

"Medicare should invite accredited offshore hospitals and their affiliated doctors to participate in all of its comparative performance reporting systems," they wrote. "Beyond informing Americans contemplating treatment abroad, such comparisons would allow us to learn if our care is the world's best and to accelerate our improvement efforts if it is not."[14]

To date, no federal agency has taken up that challenge. There are only a few cases where the federal government now pays for medical care delivered abroad.

The Department of Veterans Affairs pays for health services provided for eligible veterans living or traveling abroad through its foreign medical program, accounting for a sliver—about $59 million—of a $90 billion annual budget for medical care.[15] Medicare covers foreign health care only in very limited circumstances. These include cases where a foreign hospital is closer to a senior citizen's home in the United States than the nearest American hospital.[16]

U.S. hospitals likely would strongly object to a plan to use federal health care funding to pay for nonemergency surgeries performed abroad even if performance on surgical quality measures was equivalent to U.S. hospitals, according to Milstein. That would make it difficult for lawmakers to support legislation to test federal payments for medical tourism, he says.

"It would be politically improbable . . . and courageous," says Milstein, medical director for the Pacific Business Group on Health, which advises large corporations and public agencies.

Even before the coronavirus pandemic hit, insurers who worked with Medicare showed little appetite to test medical tourism, says Matthew Downs, a lawyer based in Washington.

Downs, a former Senate staffer, created a nonprofit organization, the Center for Medicare Portability, in 2011 to gauge interest in extending Medicare coverage for Medicare-eligible Americans living abroad. Downs says he intended to see if the program would cover treatments in Mexico, where a sizable community of U.S. expatriates lives.

Congress often allows Medicare Advantage plans—Medicare coverage delivered through private insurers—more flexibility in testing approaches to health care, such as offering dental plans or hearing aids.[17]

But Downs says he dropped his project in 2015 after finding there was little active interest among insurers with Medicare Advantage plans for this kind of expansion.

Mossallam, of the Henry Ford Health System, says he opposes expanding Medicare payment for overseas medical treatments—or even testing the idea.

"That's actually a scary idea," Mossallam says. "If we are even suggesting to send people out of this country, what kind of message does that send? It's saying, 'We're the highest quality care, but we're so expensive we're going to look at options outside of our own country.' That's just insane to me."

Should developing countries promote medical tourism?

While the coronavirus outbreak has halted the arrival of foreign patients in Thailand for now, the beneficial impact of medical tourism will be felt in Boucher's Bumrungrad International Hospital, he says. It will have a greater capacity to respond to local people suffering from the infection.

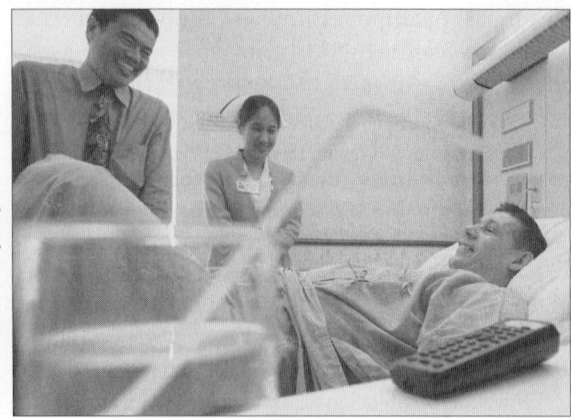

British patient Richard Newman talks with a doctor and nurse following surgery at Yanhee International Hospital in Bangkok to remove fat in 2005. After the 1997 Asian financial crisis, Thai hospitals began promoting their medical care as a less expensive alternative.

This is one example of the benefits of medical tourism for a host nation, Boucher says. "There is no doubt at all," he says. "It's a definite asset."

In 2018, Bumrungrad treated patients from more than 190 countries. In that year, international patients accounted for two-thirds of its revenue, with the nations of Myanmar, Oman and the United Arab Emirates contributing the largest shares of revenue.[18]

Bumrungrad's foray into medical tourism has its roots in the 1997 Asian financial crisis. The private hospital opened in January of that year. By July, demand for care at private hospitals had all but evaporated, Mack Banner, then the hospital's CEO, said in a 2009 interview. The hospital could have slipped into insolvency—but for a plunge in the Thai currency, the baht, as a result of the financial crisis.[19]

Bumrungrad "became half price almost overnight for those paying for their care in U.S. dollars," Banner said, prompting the hospital to start marketing to patients in nearby countries. "That really began our foray into caring for international patients," he said.[20]

Medical tourism need not be viewed as an either-or proposition for developing countries, said David A. Reisman, an economics professor at Nanyang Technological University in Singapore. Investments needed to attract wealthy foreigners may serve local communities as well, he argued.

"Health tourism can deliver the goods. Foreigners get quality care at an acceptable price and without a wait. Professionals are retained who might otherwise have gone abroad," Reisman said. "The unskilled and the semiskilled obtain jobs and on-the-job training. Economies of scale become possible even if the domestic market lacks critical mass."[21]

Vijay Govindarajan, a professor at Dartmouth College's Tuck School of Business, and Ravi Ramamurti, a business professor at Northeastern University, have depicted medical tourism as a potential driver of improved medical care. They cited India's Narayana Health, a hospital system developed by cardiologist Devi Shetty, as an example of how richer medical tourists may subsidize care of the poor.[22]

"The poor increase volume, which improves the quality of outcomes for all, including the rich. It is a perfect matchup: Rich and poor create value for each other, and the hospitals become high-quality, ultra-low-cost players," Govindarajan and Ramamurti wrote.[23]

The Medical Tourism Association, a Florida-based trade group, posts on its website information intended to attract clients interested in drawing patients as medical tourists. The group also hosts conferences and sells other services to aid organizations and countries interested in expanding in this market. The association has a medical tourism calculator, which it describes as "an adaptable tool used by all industry stakeholders to demonstrate the total economic impact of creating a medical travel program."

"Important factors such as job creation and tax revenues as well as the impact to hospitality and tourism have been less emphasized in medical tourism forecasts," the association said.[24]

Some developing nations, particularly in Asia, are vying to attract foreign patients to their hospitals. They see these patients both as sources of revenue and a way to foster improved medical care.

There is a potential for a trickle-down effect on the health systems of poor and developing nations by bringing in medical tourists from wealthier ones, says Swati Gola, a lecturer at the University of Exeter in Britain, who has published research on the ethics of medical tourism.

"I'm not against medical tourism, but what's important is regulation," she says.

But often, corruption within national governments can make them ineffective in keeping private medical interests in check, Gola says.

Ronald Labonté, a professor of public health at the University of Ottawa, said nations sometimes subsidize the care of foreigners at the expense of their own citizens. Legal action was required to get Indian hospitals that had given tax breaks for care of the wealthy to deliver on promised care for the poor, according to Labonté.[25]

In Colombia, hospitals constructed for medical tourists were "tax-free zones" with lower tax rates on commercial activities. In many cases, nations are using medical staff trained at public expense to attract foreign patients.[26]

"Meanwhile, the money governments spend promoting or subsidizing this economic sector comes with opportunity costs in the areas it doesn't invest in, like constructing much needed comprehensive primary health facilities," Labonté said.[27]

Harvard's Cohen also questions how well profits from medical tourism have served the poor of the host nations. "Although one cannot reach a conclusive judgment on the subject, there is thus far no good evidence that there have been major trickle-down benefits from medical tourism," Cohen said.[28]

Could global standards be established for medical tourism?

Wipfli of the University of Southern California says global regulation of medical tourism is needed. She suggests the Framework Convention on Tobacco Control as a model.

Overseen by the World Health Organization (WHO), the convention came into force in 2005 when more than 160 nations signed on. Public health experts credit this voluntary agreement with helping many nations adopt policies, such as raising taxes and stepping up warnings about the risks of smoking, to curb tobacco use.[29]

The WHO would have the organizational experience to aid with an effort to create a more unified global approach to monitoring or regulating medical tourism, says Wipfli, the author of the 2015 book *The Global War on Tobacco: Mapping the World's First Public Health Treaty.*

"If WHO wanted to take the lead again on a treaty on medical tourism, they would have a lot of in-house capacity that they wouldn't have had at the beginning of the tobacco treaty," Wipfli says.

There is a natural ebb and flow to international attitudes toward global agreements, Wipfli says. While there has been a tendency away from such cooperation in recent years, the coronavirus pandemic could lead to renewed interest.

"Coming out of this current outbreak, there might be more heightened desire to formulate more binding rules, given the appreciation at the moment for the interdependence" of nations in health care, Wipfli says.

Y.Y. Brandon Chen, a researcher at the University of Ottawa who teaches health and immigration law, has published work on the profound effects of medical tourism on low- and middle-income countries. In a 2013 paper, he argued for regulating medical tourism.[30] People who travel abroad for medical services may be unaware of the toll that medical tourism can take on national health systems, Chen says.

"I don't think people are thinking about that question, and our argument is that they should when they are making the decision to travel abroad," Chen says. "Most often they are thinking, 'I have a medical condition that requires attention and if I cannot get it in my home country, for whatever reason, and there are other options available, I'm going to try them.'"

At a minimum, there should be a shift toward educating people about the risks not only to their own health, but to the impact their visits have on receiving countries, Chen says.

Chen says he does not oppose medical tourism, and having standards could prevent "a free-for-all" developing: "When medical tourism is solely driven by the private sector, which I think to a . . . large extent it is, the for-profit motive comes to the forefront." In addition, he asks, when allegations of malpractice arise, "which countries' law do we use . . . and where do we litigate?"

Creating a global standard for medical tourism, however, would be difficult, says Dr. Lloyd I. Sederer, a physician and former chief medical officer for the New York State Office of Mental Health. "There are so many different procedures and so many different countries," he says. "There's so much variance."

Sederer, who also is an adjunct professor at Columbia University's School of Public Health, was a medical

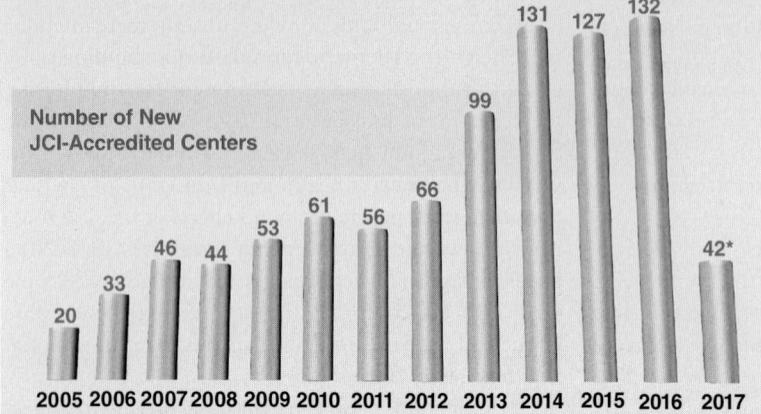

Global Accreditation of Hospitals and Clinics Rises

The Joint Commission International (JCI) annually accredited more than 100 medical facilities around the world from 2014 to 2016, continuing a decade-long upward trend. The group provides information for traveling patients to find facilities with safe and ethical care abroad. The increasing frequency of accreditations reflects the recent growth of the medical tourism industry.

Number of New JCI-Accredited Centers

2005	2006	2007	2008	2009	2010	2011	2012	2013	2014	2015	2016	2017
20	33	46	44	53	61	56	66	99	131	127	132	42*

* Through June 2017

Source: Amber Mehta, Seth Goldstein and Martin A. Makary, "Global trends in center accreditation by the Joint Commission International growing patient implications for international medical and surgical care," *Journal of Travel Medicine*, Vol. 24, Issue 5, Aug. 21, 2017, https://tinyurl.com/r9d67p7

tourist, disclosing in 2012 that he was among the patients—who included basketball star Kobe Bryant and Pope John Paul II—seeking "a novel form of anti-inflammatory arthritis/tendinitis treatment" that then was only available in Germany.[31]

Sederer says he was unaware when he had his overseas treatment of a group called the Joint Commission International (JCI) that performs voluntary assessments of foreign hospitals and clinics. As of March, 1,013 hospitals, clinics and other medical facilities outside the United States held the international group's accreditation, meaning they had passed the group's inspections, the JCI says.

The JCI, founded in 1994, is an affiliate of the U.S. Joint Commission, a nonprofit group that has considerable clout over the operations of U.S. hospitals and clinics. About 22,000 U.S. hospitals and other medical clinics and centers have Joint Commission approval.

The federal government accepts the Joint Commission's accreditation as a qualification for Medicare and Medicaid payments, the financial lifeblood of many American hospitals. But the work of its international branch may not carry the same clout.

"Losing Joint Commission accreditation is very meaningful in this country. I don't know about other countries," Sederer says.

The JCI's parent organization, the Joint Commission on Accreditation of Healthcare Organizations, is dependent on the fees paid by hospitals and other medical organizations in the United States and abroad for its services. The organization's 2018 financial statement shows it had $238.6 million in revenue that year, including $95.5 million in on-site survey fees and $85.1 million in annual accreditation subscription fees.[32] The clients for these surveys, services and publications are the hospitals that the Joint Commission and JCI rate. "We pay them, so there is a sort of inherent lack of independence," Sederer says.

Sederer says the Joint Commission has made improvements over the years in its evaluations of medical care. It now focuses more on the procedures in place than on how well paperwork is done. Still, the group's work is for the most part no more than a basic benchmark for acceptable quality. "I wouldn't go to a hospital that isn't Joint Commission accredited, but beyond that, some are a lot better than others," Sederer says of his experience with U.S. hospitals.

There has been rapid growth in the number of JCI accreditations, said Marty Makary, a surgeon and the author of the 2012 book, *Unaccountable: What Hospitals Won't Tell You and How Transparency Can Revolutionize Health Care*. In a 2017 paper in the *Journal of Travel Medicine*, Makary and two colleagues said the annual number of newly JCI-accredited medical centers rose from one center in 1999 to 132 in 2016. By that year, there were 939 accredited by JCI.[33]

These international facilities do not report outcomes to any kind of a central database, making it impossible to compare hospitals in the United States and elsewhere. Makary and his colleagues suggested adding a new accreditation requirement for reporting outcomes, such as the number of infections, lengths of stay and cases where subsequent operations were needed.

But Paula Wilson, the CEO of the JCI, says her organization's mission is not about promoting transnational health care.

"We're neutral when it comes to medical tourism," she says. "We're not against it or for it."

The JCI's growth in accreditation stems in part from doctors from other nations seeking to replicate in their home countries the standards they experienced in the U.S. hospitals where they trained, Wilson says. Nations such as the United Arab Emirates use the program to bolster their domestic health systems, she says.

Neither the U.S. Joint Commission nor its international branch delves into data on how well patients fare in a specific hospital. Instead, they examine how well institutions carry out procedures that are known to improve safety. With global medical officials immersed in the fight against coronavirus in early 2020, Wilson cited as an example preventing the spread of disease among hospital patients and staff. JCI looks at whether organizations employ infection-control officers and what strategies and procedures are in place to prevent the spread of viruses and bacteria.

"We ask, 'Do you have an infection control plan?'" Wilson says. "And is it a good plan? And did you follow it?"

BACKGROUND
Ancient Pilgrims to Jet Set

The impulse to seek medical care in foreign lands dates from the earliest days of recorded human history. Ancient Greeks and Romans traveled in search of better health to temples of the god Aesculapius, whose symbol of a serpent coiled around a staff remains associated with medicine to this day.[34]

These temples were often built on hills outside towns and near wells that people believed to have healing powers. They thus attracted many people experiencing ill health and have been compared to modern hospitals.[35] By the 16th century, wealthy Europeans traveled to towns such as Bath, England, and St. Moritz, Switzerland, in search of healing waters.[36]

In the early 20th century, the popularity of psychoanalyst Sigmund Freud and his followers drew many wealthy foreigners to seek mental health care abroad.

"Analysts in Austria and Germany usually spoke several languages," wrote historian Eric Shiraev. "They saw an influx of cash-paying foreign patients, especially from France, Great Britain, and even the United States." [37]

In 1963, Brazilian plastic surgeon Ivo Pitanguy opened a private clinic. His work and that of the surgeons he trained created a cottage industry for face-lifts and other cosmetic procedures.[38] By the 1970s, so many wealthy people and celebrities traveled to South America for such procedures that the phrase "vacation in Brazil" became a synonym for a restorative visit to a plastic surgery clinic.[39] In 1980, *The New York Times* profiled Pitanguy in an article titled "Doctor Vanity: The Jet Set's Man in Rio."[40] Writer Warren Hoge described what happened when foreigners sought Pitanguy's care:

"After arriving in Rio, patients receive a precautionary examination from an internist and pose for the crucial photographs," Hoge wrote. "'Pictures are to a plastic surgeon what X-rays are to a general practitioner,' says a Venezuelan surgeon studying with Pitanguy."

Brazilian plastic surgeon Ivo Pitanguy reviews a patient's photographs in 2000. After he opened a private clinic in 1963, Brazil became a destination for wealthy foreigners seeking face-lifts and other cosmetic surgeries.

Actor Steve McQueen also drew attention to medical tourism during his battle against an aggressive cancer, mesothelioma. He traveled to Mexico for treatments not approved in the United States that included laetrile, a controversial alternative therapy made from apricot pits. Even though McQueen succumbed to his cancer in 1980, his fight sparked interest in medical tourism.

"In so doing, he put Mexico on the map, popularized unapproved treatments, and touched off a trend toward seeking medical care beyond America's borders," wrote authors Kathy Merlock Jackson, Lisa Lyon Payne and Kathy Shepherd Stolley.[41]

Ethical Quandaries

Other celebrities have followed McQueen's path and sought out treatments that are not approved at home.

Reports of sports stars traveling abroad for stem cell treatments have triggered increased public interest. In 2018, actor Mel Gibson told sports commentator Joe Rogan that he thought a course of stem cells had helped rejuvenate his aging father. Rogan's interview of Gibson and the doctor who administered the treatment in Panama has been watched more than 3 million times on YouTube.[42]

These kinds of reports frustrated scientists, who saw media accounts overselling the potential of stem cells. These cells can develop into many different cell types, from muscle to brain cells, and thus are seen as having the potential to repair damaged tissues.[43] Stem cell transplants have been found to aid in treatment of leukemia. Scientists are studying whether they might have use as well in treating conditions such as Alzheimer's disease, but the results have been mixed at best.

In 2008, the International Society for Stem Cell Research issued guidelines on the use of these treatments, highlighting in particular the risks for people undergoing care outside of their home countries.

"The marketing of unproven stem cell interventions is especially worrisome in cases where patients with severe diseases or injuries travel across borders to seek treatments purported to be stem cell-based 'therapies' or 'cures' that fall outside the realm of standard medical practice," the society said.[44] In 2016 it issued new guidelines urging scientists and clinicians not to participate in stem cell treatments that lack clear scientific evidence.[45]

But for-profit stem cell clinics continued to flourish, due to a mix of lack of regulation and patients' desperate searches for cures. When celebrities undergo and then endorse unproven treatments, they may get better without knowing if there is any connection between their improvement and the procedure, researchers said.[46]

Physicians who sell these treatments have a responsibility to put their theories through rigorous scientific testing, said Dr. George Q. Daley, the dean of Harvard Medical School, who has been a leader in developing the society's guidelines.[47] In medicine, physicians seek to show new medicines and treatments work by comparing results of patients given these drugs and procedures against similar patients who do not get them in clinical trials.

"If you apply these criteria, most of the clinics that are involved in stem cell tourism will fall quite short," Daley said.[48]

In the same vein, transplant surgeons and kidney specialists in 2008 called for an end to abuses seen in trafficking of donated organs and associated medical tourism.

In what came to be known as the Declaration of Istanbul, the group sought to curb abuses in transplant organs, particularly cases where people living in poor nations were coerced into selling their kidneys. It is unclear how many Americans travel abroad to obtain new kidneys, but clearly some do, Harvard's Cohen says. The federal government has not moved strongly to end or address this practice, he says. Medicare, for example, covers the cost of drugs needed to prevent organ transplant rejection even in cases where a patient had the operation abroad.

"They could disallow them," Cohen says. "But they don't ask too many questions about the provenance of organs."

Reproductive assistance has long been an important niche for medical tourism, due in part to poor insurance coverage for procedures intended to help people conceive and carry children, Cohen says. This field includes in vitro fertilization (IVF), where an egg is combined with sperm outside the body and then implanted in the body. But it also extends to cases of surrogacy where women who live in poor nations carry children for peo-

CHRONOLOGY

1960s-1980s *A Brazilian doctor sparks a trend.*

1963 Brazilian plastic surgeon Ivo Pitanguy opens a private clinic, spurring wealthy Americans in the 1970s to travel to South America for cosmetic surgery.

1980 Actor Steve McQueen sparks interest in medical tourism when he travels to a Mexican clinic for controversial treatments to fight cancer. The treatments do not prevent his death from mesothelioma later in the year.

1990s-2000 *Accreditations are instituted for international facilities.*

1990 British medical journal *The Lancet* publishes articles on complications suffered by men who traveled to India for kidney transplants.

1994 The Joint Commission, a well-known accreditor of U.S. hospitals, forms the Joint Commission International (JCI) to evaluate foreign hospitals.

1997 After Thailand's currency collapses, the government hopes to boost revenues by directing tourism officials to market the country as a destination for plastic surgery. Thailand goes on to become a leading medical destination.

1999 Brazil's Einstein Hospital in São Paulo becomes the first health institution outside the United States to be certified by the Joint Commission International.

2002 The JCI awards its first accreditation in Asia, to Thailand's Bumrungrad International Hospital in Bangkok.

2005 *CBS*'s "60 Minutes" airs a profile of Bumrungrad International Hospital.

2006 U.S. Senate Special Committee on Aging holds a hearing on medical tourism, drawing more attention to the practice.

2007 HSM Solutions, a North Carolina manufacturing company, institutes a program to send some employees abroad for medical care, sharing part of the resulting savings with the workers.

2008 An international team of experts creates the Declaration of Istanbul in an effort to combat organ trafficking and curb transplant tourism. . . . The International Society for Stem Cell Research releases guidelines for patients who are seeking stem-cell treatments.

2010-Present *Medical tourism spreads, and controversy grows.*

2010 President Barack Obama signs the Affordable Care Act, which aims to reduce the number of the uninsured and help make medical care more affordable for Americans.

2016 The International Society for Stem Cell Research urges physicians to refrain from giving unproven stem cell treatments.

2017 The U.S. Centers for Disease Control and Prevention (CDC) issues an alert about risks for serious infections seen in people who returned to the United States after having cosmetic surgery in the Dominican Republic.

2018 The state of Utah begins its pharmacy tourism program, paying people to travel abroad to get certain costly medicines.

2019 The CDC issues an alert for travelers about the risk of infection in connection with weight loss surgery in Mexico.

2020 The coronavirus pandemic puts global travel and medical tourism on hold.

---

ple from wealthier ones. This form of medical tourism raised questions about exploitation of women and the role of medical go-betweens.

India in 2002 legalized commercial surrogacy as part of its broader efforts to boost medical tourism. One Indian industry group estimated that within a decade the surrogacy industry could generate $2.3 billion a year. While a surrogate pregnancy in a Western nation could cost more than $90,000, the cost in India was about a third of that price, with the surrogate receiving about $6,500 to $7,500.[49]

Black Market in Organs Persists Despite Anti-Trafficking Efforts

"We should not have foreigners coming here to buy kidneys."

People considering traveling abroad to black-market clinics for organ transplants should understand the risks involved, including the likelihood that donors have been coerced or exploited, researchers say.

In a paper published in November, five Canadian researchers emphasized the need to boost domestic organ donation rates across nations, while also making the public more aware of how organs can sometimes be obtained unethically.[1]

"I wanted to bring this issue back to the forefront," says one of the authors, Dr. Zaid Hindi, a gastroenterology fellow at Ontario's London Health Sciences Centre.

In addition, a 2008 study by UCLA researchers suggested that patients may be at higher risk of complications, such as acquiring serious infections, through medical tourism.[2]

Global efforts to end organ trafficking have curbed, but not ended, this illegal trade. Perhaps as many as 5 to 10 percent of all kidney and liver transplants involve illegally or improperly obtained organs, the United Nations Office on Drugs and Crime said in a 2018 report. Brokers in nations such as India have found ways around medical and legal restrictions, which are intended to allow altruistic donations of organs, but not sales, the report said.[3]

"A lot of patients would rather purchase a kidney from a stranger than ask a family member," says Seán Columb, a lecturer at the University of Liverpool's School of Law and Social Justice, who has interviewed participants in illegal transplants. "They weren't convinced you could live a healthy life with just one kidney."

These purchasers of black-market organs intend to spare their relatives and loved ones the risks associated with donating kidneys, says Columb, who this year will publish a book on these illicit sales. These buyers may even see their purchase as a benefit for the organ donor, with their payments helping to lift people out of poverty, Columb says.

But the donors may not benefit from these sales. Columb last year wrote in *The Guardian* newspaper about an Eritrean immigrant in Egypt who donated a kidney in return for passage to Europe. But the immigrant said he was tricked out of his payment, Columb wrote.[4]

There have been several high-profile prosecutions of organ brokers in the past decade, including a U.S. case. Levy Izhak Rosenbaum, of Brooklyn, N.Y., was sentenced in 2012 to 30 months in prison for brokering illegal kidney transplants.[5] According to federal prosecutors, Rosenbaum found people in Israel willing to sell their kidneys and then charged New Jersey residents between $120,000 and $150,000 for his services. He said the high price was due in part to payments that would be made to people in Israel for their assistance in locating donors.[6]

Rosenbaum admitted to helping kidney donors and recipients fabricate cover stories to fool hospital employees into believing that the transplant in question was the product of a genuine donation, the prosecutors said.[7]

In 2016, arrests of 14 people, including four physicians and a hospital executive, dubbed the "Great Indian Kidney Racket" by local news media, stemmed from the persistence of 23-year-old Sundar Singh Jatav. He was cheated by an organ broker after serving as a donor, Jatav told the *Los Angeles Times*.[8]

Instead of paying Jatav, a broker put him to work as an assistant, Jatav said. That is how Jatav discovered falsified paperwork to show relationships between donors and

---

Many women saw these payments as opportunities to escape poverty. Ranju Rajubhai told *The Guardian* newspaper that her roughly $6,225 payment for a surrogate pregnancy would pay for surgery her husband needed for his burns and perhaps contribute toward the purchase of a house. "One pregnancy won't be enough, so I am thinking of coming back," Rajubhai said.[50]

But concerns emerged about the treatment of the Indian women carrying children for foreigners. "His surrogate mother dead, baby boy 'all right,'"

recipients that did not exist. Jatav, for example, was listed as the sibling of the recipient of his kidney, a woman to whom he is not related.[9]

The transplantation community has made efforts over the years to increase use of living donors, but the demand for kidneys still greatly exceeds the supply. About 95,000 people were on the U.S. waiting list for kidneys as of April.[10] The average U.S. wait time for a kidney from a deceased donor is five years.[11]

To date, the leading effort to curb black-market kidney sales has come from the transplantation community itself. In 2008, a global group of physicians and researchers created the Declaration of Istanbul, an agreement intended to curb abusive practices in connection with organ donations.[12]

The group's work, carried out through the Declaration of Istanbul Custodian Group, helped pressure surgeons in China to lobby internally to end the use of prisoners as a source for donor organs, says Alexander Capron, former director of ethics for the World Health Organization. The group also has offered advice and encouragement to nations such as Qatar and Israel as they have worked on policies to increase kidney donation rates, says Capron, now a professor at the University of Southern California's Gould School of Law.

The key to the Custodian Group has been its ability to build peer pressure among physicians for more ethical practices, says Capron, who was among the leaders in the creation of the Declaration of Istanbul.

"It provided a clear statement to the transplant community from the transplant community" about what should be considered acceptable, he says of the declaration.

That helped advocates for changes in places such as Pakistan and the Philippines where large commercial organ transplant operations were running, Capron says. These physicians could count on participants in the Custodian Group for advice and support as they lobbied their governments for stronger efforts to prevent black-market sales. The Custodian Group also helped physicians seeking to persuade their fellow transplant specialists to stop participating in organ sales.

"Local champions had the benefit of support and advice as they turned to their colleagues who were on the fence and saying to them, 'You should be on the side of building up our voluntary related programs. We should build up our deceased donation, and we should not have foreigners coming here to buy kidneys,' " Capron says.

—*Kerry Dooley Young*

---

[1] Zaid Hindi *et al.*, "Liver Transplant Tourism," Liver Transplantation, Nov. 25, 2019, https://tinyurl.com/w9ujllq.

[2] Jagbir Gill *et al.*, "Transplant Tourism in the United States: A Single-Center Experience," *Clinical Journal of the American Society of Nephrology*, Nov. 3, 2008, pp. 1820-1828, https://tinyurl.com/s57bwya.

[3] "Global Report on Trafficking in Persons 2018," United Nations Office on Drugs and Crime, 2018, p. 30, https://tinyurl.com/yxhmzbun.

[4] Seán Columb, "Organ trafficking in Egypt: 'They locked me in and took my kidney,' " *The Guardian*, Feb. 9, 2019, https://tinyurl.com/y4mdwd58.

[5] "First Federal Defendant Convicted For Profiting From Illegal Kidney Transplants Sentenced To Prison," press release, Department of Justice, July 11, 2012, https://tinyurl.com/vckj4nh.

[6] *Ibid*.

[7] *Ibid*.

[8] Shashank Bengali and Parth M.N., "Duped into selling his kidney, this 23-year-old exposed an illegal organ racket in India," *Los Angeles Times*, Sep. 15, 2016, https://tinyurl.com/samx53q; V Narayan & Malathy Iyer, "Kidney racket: Hiranandani CEO, medical director, 3 docs held," *Times of India*, Aug. 10, 2016, https://tinyurl.com/ue2ykz9.

[9] Bengali and Parth, *ibid*.

[10] "Organ Procurement and Transplantation Network: National Data," U.S. Department of Health and Human Services, https://tinyurl.com/yckqcv2c.

[11] "Transplant Waiting List," American Kidney Fund, https://tinyurl.com/sz87j2c.

[12] "The Declaration of Istanbul on Organ Trafficking and Transplant Tourism," *Clinical Journal of the American Society of Nephrology*, pp. 1227-1231, Aug. 13, 2008, https://tinyurl.com/v58xug4.

The *Indian Express* newspaper headlined a story about the 2012 death of Premila Vaghela. The child was born at eight months.[51]

"Premila was like many other economically marginalized surrogates, who may suffer or even lose their lives while carrying a child, and are quickly forgotten," wrote Kishwar Desai, an author who had researched medical tourism for a novel. "The highly secretive and largely unregulated baby factories (many of which are dressed up as legitimate IVF clinics) now mushrooming all over

India are usually only concerned with the end product: the child."[52]

India barred surrogacy for foreigners in 2015. Thailand that year also barred foreigners from paying for surrogacy, while Nepal banned it even when unpaid.[53] The laws were intended to protect women from exploitation and harm, with operators of clinics sometimes neglecting postpartum care and failing to explain medical risks to the surrogates. In the wake of these bans, though, the surrogacy business merely shifted to Greece, Laos, Kenya and other nations, according to experts.

Ethical questions also arise when people seek medical procedures that are approved in their home countries,

Medical Tourists Can Bring Home Drug-Resistant Infections

"Even the most obscure pathogens can leap over continents and oceans."

A 61-year-old man living in the United States bet on beating the long wait for a domestic kidney transplant by buying an organ through a black-market clinic in Pakistan. Instead, he brought home a potentially deadly pathogen, New Delhi metallo-beta-lactamase 1 (NDM-1), which nearly cost him his life, University of Washington researchers reported in a 2019 paper.[1]

The man, who was not identified in the paper, lost the new kidney and survived only due to multiple operations and anti-microbial treatments, the researchers wrote.[2]

Medical travel has fostered the spread of dangerous pathogens such as NDM-1, which is a fragment of DNA that helps many strains of bacteria withstand antibiotics, wrote Sonia Shah, a journalist who has conducted in-depth research on infectious diseases. "Thanks to the power, speed and relative comfort of air travel, even the most obscure pathogens can leap over continents and oceans," Shah wrote.[3]

The coronavirus pandemic has served as a reminder of how easily travelers can bring infections back home with them. Coronavirus emerged in Wuhan, China, in late 2019.[4] By early April, more than 1 million cases had been confirmed globally, with almost all of the world's nations having reported instances of this infection, known as COVID-19.[5] In March, the U.S. Centers for Disease Control and Prevention (CDC) warned Americans to avoid international travel due to the pandemic.[6]

The CDC has also in recent years issued warnings specific to medical tourism, made in connection with weight loss and cosmetic procedures. In January 2019, the agency issued a public alert for travelers about the risk of infection in connection with weight loss surgery in Mexico, although it later removed the alert.[7] Two years earlier, it had issued a similar alert about risks for another infection, nontuberculous mycobacteria, seen in people who returned to the United States after having cosmetic surgery in the Dominican Republic.[8]

In some cases, patients may not volunteer information to their doctors about their medical tourism, complicating efforts to track pathogens acquired abroad, according to Mary E. Wilson, an adjunct professor at Harvard University's T.H. Chan School of Public Health. At the same time, there has been aggressive promotion of "beach vacations" combined with cheaper elective procedures, such as face-lifts, Wilson says. The high cost of medical care in the United States remains a driving force in medical tourism, and the attendant risk for contracting serious infections, she says.

The high cost "leads people to look for other options and makes them vulnerable to hearing about places where they're told everything is safe and easy," Wilson says.

The American Society for Aesthetic Plastic Surgery has sought to gain a better understanding of how often people seek its members' help to address complications of surgeries done abroad. More than half of its members who participated in a 2018 survey said they had seen two to five

but for which they do not qualify, says Crooks of Simon Fraser University.

People may travel to Mexico for bariatric surgery, for example, if they do not qualify for this weight loss procedure at home, Crooks says. In these procedures, physicians may shrink the size of the stomach, restricting how much people can eat and how many calories their bodies can absorb.[54] Some people may want to lose only 20 or 30 pounds and thus not qualify for insurance coverage for bariatric surgery or easily find a surgeon willing to operate on them. In other cases, people may seek more repeat knee replacements than their physicians at home would allow or ask for orthopedic procedures for which they are considered too old or too young, she says.

---

patients in the previous 12 months with complications from cosmetic tourism.[9]

"Why do patients pursue cosmetic tourism if there are known increased risks?" wrote plastic surgeon Ali A. Qureshi and his co-authors in a paper discussing the survey. "Without question, cost is a key factor, with several studies describing the average cost of a breast augmentation in the United States at $6,000 vs. $2,200 in India," they found.[10]

But treating complications can erase the savings. The society's paper pegged the estimated costs for U.S. management of complications connected to medical tourism at between $1,001 and $5,000 for almost one-third of patients, with bills topping $10,000 in about 15 percent of cases.[11]

An Arkansas woman, Tamika Capone, told *The Washington Post* she incurred about $30,000 in follow-up bills due to a rare infection acquired as a medical tourist.

With her weight nearing 300 pounds, Capone wanted to improve her health through bariatric surgery. But her family's medical insurance would not cover the $17,500 cost of the procedure, which shrinks the size of the stomach, restricting how much people can eat and how many calories their bodies can absorb. So in 2018 she followed the example of a friend who had it done for about $4,000 in Tijuana, Mexico.[12]

The Post last year reported that Capone, then 40, acquired a bacteria, *Pseudomonas aeruginosa*, that resists almost all antibiotics. Arkansas health officials told Capone that hers was the first case in which they had seen this organism. News of Capone's case helped a CDC investigator identify a cluster of these infections seen in people who had weight loss surgery in Tijuana.[13]

"We pounce when we see them [extremely antibiotic-resistant infections] because we know they can smolder and spread," said Maroya Spalding Walters, an epidemiologist leading the CDC team investigating the outbreak. "And no one may recognize it until this becomes an out-of-control wildfire."[14]

— *Kerry Dooley Young*

---

[1] Jenell Stewart *et al.*, "Transplant tourism complicated by life-threatening New Delhi metallo-ß-lactamase-1 infection," *American Journal of Transplantation*, Oct. 3, 2018, https://tinyurl.com/vjseqmz.

[2] *Ibid.*

[3] Sonia Shah, *Pandemic: Tracking Contagions, From Cholera to Ebola and Beyond* (2016), p. 54.

[4] Derrick Bryson Taylor, "A Timeline of the Coronavirus Pandemic," *The New York Times*, April 7, 2020, https://tinyurl.com/wb48cut.

[5] "Coronavirus COVID-19 Global Cases by the Center for Systems Science and Engineering at Johns Hopkins University," Johns Hopkins University Medicine, accessed April 3, 2020, https://tinyurl.com/rnjqnnh.

[6] "Global COVID-19 Pandemic Notice," Centers for Disease Control and Prevention, March 27, 2020, https://tinyurl.com/szkv2vs.

[7] "Drug-Resistant Infections in Patients Who Had Weight-Loss Surgery in Mexico," Centers for Disease Control and Prevention, last reviewed May 3, 2019, https://tinyurl.com/weyf24q.

[8] Joanna Gaines *et al.*, "Notes from the Field: Nontuberculous Mycobacteria Infections in U.S. Medical Tourists Associated with Plastic Surgery—Dominican Republic, 2017," Centers for Disease Control and Prevention, March 30, 2018, https://tinyurl.com/stw578h.

[9] Ali A. Qureshi *et al.*, "Report on Current Experience of ASAPS Membership and Management of Cosmetic Tourism Complications," *Aesthetic Surgery Journal Open Forum*, April 9, 2019, https://tinyurl.com/r552ns4.

[10] *Ibid.*

[11] *Ibid.*

[12] Lena H. Sun, "They went to Mexico for surgery. They came back with a deadly superbug," *The Washington Post*, Jan. 23, 2019, https://tinyurl.com/yd6eve2h.

[13] *Ibid.*

[14] *Ibid.*

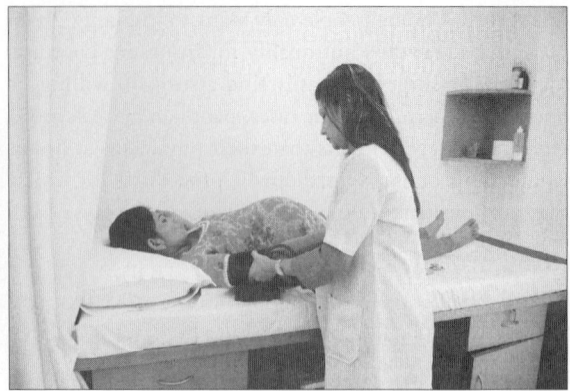

A surrogate mother gets her blood pressure checked at a clinic in New Delhi in 2013. Two years later, India banned surrogacy for foreigners, amid concerns about the treatment of Indian women carrying children for foreigners.

"They are looking for a place where they can circumvent the guidelines, where their money can pay for access to something they would not be a candidate for," Crooks says. "This practice creates a lot of ethical concerns for physicians."

Thailand Emerges

The Thai government in 2003 began a campaign to promote the country as the "medical hub of Asia."[55] The previous year, the JCI awarded its first accreditation in Asia to Bumrungrad International Hospital.

The image of medical tourism was boosted with the airing in 2005 of a segment on *CBS'* "60 Minutes" about Bumrungrad. The hospital received more than 3,000 emails from prospective patients within days of the show.

"Former naysayers, including many in the American medical community, could no longer dismiss international medical tourism in general nor Bumrungrad in particular," wrote Jackson, Payne and Stolley.[56]

In 2006, the Senate Special Committee on Aging held a hearing featuring Staab's decision to have heart surgery in India.[57] Among the witnesses was Rajesh Rao, chief executive and co-founder of North Carolina-based IndusHealth, a firm that coordinates medical care abroad as a benefit employers can offer their workers. Rao described medical tourism as an option that could help curb rising U.S. health care costs, even if most Americans never would leave home for medical treatments.

"I don't believe we will ever run into a situation where everyone just chooses to go," Rao said. "It will be a healthy form of competition that gets introduced into the system and not one that basically goes out of control."[58]

IndusHealth has worked with the American firm perhaps best known for its participation in medical tourism, HSM Solutions of Hickory, N.C. HSM makes a variety of products, including components for bedding and seats for school buses. Since 2007, it has offered its workers the option to share in the savings and receive cash payments if they travel abroad for elective surgeries.

HSM shares 20 percent of the savings up to $10,000, says Tim Isenhower, director of benefits for HSM Solutions.

"We did that to get people interested in the program," Isenhower says. "They are taking time away from home, they have to hire babysitters and things such as that."

HSM's program has been the subject of several news stories over the years, including one in *Kiplinger's Personal Finance* and an *ABC News* broadcast.[59] In February, a Denver television station broadcast a story about HMS employee Tony Martin traveling to Costa Rica's CIMA Hospital for a knee replacement. The average cost of a total knee replacement is almost $50,000 in the United States. The same procedure might cost just over $20,000 in Costa Rica.[60]

Isenhower says he gets calls from other companies about medical tourism. Fellow adopters include Ashley Furniture of Arcadia, Wis. Kaiser Health News last year reported on an Ashley Furniture employee's trip to Cancún, Mexico, for knee surgery. *The New York Times* ran the article with the headline, "A Mexican Hospital, an American Surgeon, and a $5,000 Check (Yes, a Check)."[61]

Still, to date, employers have not embraced this approach as quickly as Isenhower had expected.

"It's been slow. A lot of people aren't grasping it like I thought they would, but I am not concerned about selling it," Isenhower says. "It works for us."

CURRENT SITUATION
'Sticker Shock'

Changes in U.S. health insurance likely will keep Americans shopping abroad for elective procedures, once they are able to travel again, says Woodman, of Patients Beyond Borders.

The spotty coverage of health insurance plans is leaving many Americans directly responsible for more of their health costs. Some 28 percent of workers who get insurance from their employer face deductibles of at least $2,000. One in eight—13 percent—have deductibles topping $3,000.[62]

There is also the prospect of so-called surprise billing, the unexpected and sometimes devastatingly high cost for the services of physicians who are not part of patients' insurance networks. In the past two years, about one in five insured adults had an unexpected medical bill, according to the Kaiser Family Foundation. And two-thirds of adults are worried about facing these kinds of high costs for themselves and their family, Kaiser found.[63]

Woodman said about 80 million people are now underinsured due in part to inadvertent changes in health coverage resulting from the Affordable Care Act. Employers and insurance companies have looked to shift more medical costs onto consumers through increased premiums, higher co-pays and policies that exempt the insurers from paying for care.

"An acquaintance of mine with a decent enough health plan was surprised to hear that a single hip replacement was going to set her back $12,000," Woodman said. "In brief, the false sense of security offered by employer 'skinny' plans often result in extreme sticker shock—and patients shopping cross-border for care."[64]

Woodman wrote that $6,000 was the dividing line for whether traveling abroad was worth it. A procedure costing less than that amount in the United States was best performed domestically; for those costing more than this amount, patients would probably save money going abroad, he wrote.[65]

Woodman also cautioned against promotions that emphasize the fun activities people could potentially combine with medical travel, such as beach time and shopping sprees. He said people instead should think of medical travel more as a business trip than a leisure junket.

"Websites and health travel brochures peppered with zealous recreational promotion tend to ignore the realities of health travel," Woodman said. "Long flights, post-treatment recovery, and just plain being alone in a faraway place can be overwhelming, even for the most optimistic health traveler."[66]

HSM's Experience

Isenhower of HSM says his company started its medical tourism arrangement with an Indian hospital, but has shifted over the years to use centers closer to home, including facilities in Cancún and Costa Rica.

The trips to India proved to be too taxing, he says, describing calls from workers who awoke after 20-plus-hours of travel yearning for familiar sights like a Taco Bell. HSM employees in need of orthopedic care in Costa Rica stay at resorts, which are more suited to their needs, he says.

"We're manufacturing people. A lot of these people have never been out of the state of North Carolina, much less flying to India," Isenhower says. "I've not had anybody call homesick from" Costa Rica, he adds.

With pharmacy tourism, lawmakers are eyeing ways to get savings from certain state workers making only short trips from home.

Washington state Sen. Karen Keiser, a Democrat, this year introduced a pharmacy tourism bill based on the Utah model. It seeks to create a pharmacy tourism program that would let people covered by Washington's Public Employees' Benefits Board and the School Employees' Benefits Board use a pharmacy in nearby Canada to buy certain costly drugs, as well as insulin.[67]

Cost is not the only factor driving Americans to consider health care abroad. People who have had treatments in other nations cite a straightforward approach to billing and the friendly attitude of medical professionals as an advantage over domestic care. In a posting for the *Medium* website titled "Oh My God, You're Going To MEXICO For Medical Care?" journalist Shelly Fagan gave a glowing review to both the cost of her care and the approach of her dentist and his staff.[68]

Fagan said she decided to look across the border after her dentist retired and she struggled to find a replacement. One dental office said she would need to start her treatment there with a $150 consultation fee.

That "experience aptly demonstrates one of the more subtle issues I have with American health care," Fagan wrote. "They treat you like you are a problem—not a customer—and taking your money is doing you some sort of favor."

AT ISSUE

Can people be treated as safely abroad as at home?

YES — Karen Timmons
CEO, Global Healthcare Accreditation
Written for *CQ Researcher*, April 2020

Before the coronavirus pandemic, one group estimated that between 21 million and 26 million patients globally crossed borders to receive care, with a market size of between $74 billion and $92 billion.

While people have traveled for treatment for thousands of year, most commonly the rich traveling to more-developed countries, medical tourism has undergone fundamental change in recent decades, especially in the last one. Disparate motivations are fueling the growth in medical tourism: more affordability, better and quicker access to care, higher quality, specialty treatments (e.g., clinical trials, robotic surgery) unavailable in their home country and anonymity.

These trends will only grow in a world of increasing costs of care, rising numbers of noninsured or underinsured, growing middle classes in developing countries such as China and India, and long wait times in countries with single-payer systems such as Canada and the United Kingdom. Self-insured U.S. employers have begun to contract with providers overseas in narrow networks for treating employees for specific conditions, using quality and safety metrics that providers must meet. Employers share the savings with employees, providing cash payouts as incentives, with employees exempt from deductibles and travel costs for the patient and a companion.

A key factor in enabling trust and confidence is accreditation. With the introduction of internationally recognized standards of quality and patient safety in 1998, the Joint Commission International facilitated global standardization of hospital care by applying consensus standards based on quality improvements and evidence-based practices. Since then, numerous other international and national accreditation schemes have also applied standards to hospitals and clinics. The Global Healthcare Accreditation (GHA) Program for Medical Travel Services was established in recognition that medical travel encompasses much more complexity along the entire continuum, and has established standards and norms for organizations treating medical travel patients.

It is likely in the next decade that patients, insurers and employers will be the main drivers for more transparency from hospitals, health care organizations and physicians. There is a need for more data on clinical and patient experience outcomes, and to have more comparable information to make sound

NO — Dr. Gregory A. Greco, DO, FACS
Chief, Division of Plastic Surgery,
Monmouth Medical Center, Long Branch, N.J.
Written for *CQ Researcher*, April 2020

The American Society of Plastic Surgeons (ASPS) represents greater than 8,000 board-certified plastic surgeons in the United States. Our society advocates for excellence in plastic surgery training and certification and holds its members to the highest standards.

Cosmetic surgery tourism can seem attractive to U.S. citizens. Cosmetic surgery at a reduced price in a foreign, sometimes exotic country may seem enticing. However, the consumer must ask the ultimate question: "Where am I comfortable having my complications?" Plastic surgery is still surgery and poses inherent risks.

Surgical complications can occur with any surgery. These include blood loss, blood clots (deep vein thrombosis, or DVT) in the legs that can travel to the heart (pulmonary embolism), infections and wound complications. Complications can range from minor to life-threatening and may occur hours to weeks after surgery. Experiencing a complication in a foreign country can potentially jeopardize your life. Often, patients may not allow ample time at their surgical destination for appropriate preoperative assessment and postoperative care.

Patients should consider the following factors when contemplating foreign travel for surgery:

- Is your surgeon qualified? What resources are available to check and verify your surgeon's credentials? Are they certified to perform the intended surgery? In the United States, a physician's credentials can be verified with multiple regulatory agencies.
- Are you having your procedure in a licensed facility? ASPS requires all members to operate in nationally accredited operating rooms. They are held to the highest standards for delivering safe surgical services, focusing on infection control, patient safety and medical emergency preparedness of the facility and the staff.
- Communication barriers: Depending on the destination country, a patient may not be able to effectively communicate with their surgeon and care team. Effective communication is essential for successful outcomes.
- Limited legal recourse: Patients may have signed waivers to file a lawsuit, either with the physician or the medical tourism company. It remains difficult to establish jurisdiction in U.S. courts for foreign defendants.
- Air travel and surgery: Flying and surgery may increase your risk of developing blood clots in the legs, a sometimes fatal complication.
- The hidden costs: The initial reduced fee for surgery may seem enticing; however, if there are complications resulting from your

> choices regarding cross-border medical travel: infection rates, complications, mortality and morbidity rates as well as by procedure and cost, much like Trip Advisor does for the hospitality industry. With this information, a patient can receive safe and highly satisfactory care abroad.
>
> procedure, you may be faced with several realities. Extended stays in the destination country, airline reservation change fees, complications back in the United States that are treated by a new physician and possibly your personal health insurance denying any resulting hospitalizations. Caveat emptor!

Fagan said some dentists in the United States often will try to upsell patients with dire warnings about the state of their teeth. But in Mexico, there were "no hysterical warnings of imminent structural failure." She had a filling done for $45, less than a third of the $150 cost in the United States.

As more people test cross-border health care, there could be increased medical travel due in part to the greater emphasis on patient satisfaction, Isenhower of HSM says.

He relates his own experience when he ruptured his knee's posterior cruciate ligament (PCL) while skiing in Colorado. Isenhower says he first sought care from his physician at home in North Carolina, who told Isenhower he likely would need a knee replacement and might not ski again. The doctor ordered an MRI and said he would call Isenhower back. While waiting weeks to hear back from the physician, Isenhower contacted a physician in Costa Rica. The medical staff there often deals with PCL injuries in soccer players. They replaced two tendons, and Isenhower says he was skiing again within about six months.

"It's just a totally different experience" getting care in Costa Rica, Isenhower says. "If people in the U.S. saw that, they would realize how behind things are in the U.S. The service is not what it should be for the cost we pay."

Coronavirus Impact

Travel bans and restrictions due to the threat of coronavirus infection have put a quick dent in businesses dependent on medical tourism.

The U.S. State Department in March warned Americans to avoid all international travel due to the global impact of the outbreak.[69]

IndusHealth, which has worked with HSM and Ashley, announced on its website in March that it had temporarily suspended all planned international medical travel.[70]

In the Mexican border town of Juárez, across from El Paso, Texas, the travel ban dried up sales for businesses that cater to visiting Americans.[71] Lucio Cano, a pharmacist in Juárez, has sold medicines to Americans for 23 years, knowing repeat customers by name.

"Sales are down . . . I estimate by 60 percent," said the pharmacy owner. "I've only seen this happen once before, during the drug violence of 2009-10. Back then, nobody came. Now, business is just as bad."[72]

OUTLOOK
Disruption Ahead?

For the next six to 18 months, medical tourism will be at a standstill, says Labonté of the University of Ottawa. Even an easing of travel restrictions might not be enough to immediately revive the industry, he says.

Until the coronavirus outbreak is brought under control, the private hospitals set up for medical tourism would risk censure if they were to resume care of foreign patients.

"Border closures, self-isolation requirements, bed and medical supply shortages, will lead to triaging of remaining health care capacities," Labonté says.

This will be the case even in the low- and middle-income countries that have promoted medical tourism for economic purposes, he says. Many of these countries will soon face a rise in coronavirus cases. Their public health systems could face substantial consequences if they were to allow foreign patients to occupy hospital beds for elective procedures. And fewer people from rich nations may be willing to go abroad in search of care, due to concerns about emerging infections, Labonté says.

"Given the extent to which tourism of any form is presently in a downwards tailspin, one can only imagine medical tourism to fare even worse," Labonté says. "Even over the longer term, the fear of novel pathogens like [coronavirus] may particularly impact transborder health care, in both supply and demand."

The coronavirus presents an unprecedented challenge to medical tourism, but this industry has overcome other disruptions so far in this century, says Woodman of Patients Beyond Borders. These include terrorist attacks and bombings in India, a 2014 coup in Thailand and the SARS virus outbreak of 2002-03, as well as major disruptions in airline traffic following the 9/11 attacks in the United States and a 2010 volcanic eruption in Iceland.

"It always bounces back, and it's always for the same reason," Woodman says.

Once international travel resumes, many people likely will seek abroad the medical treatments they cannot afford at home, he says. Americans likely will shoulder more of their health costs in the years ahead, according to the Centers for Medicare & Medicaid Services (CMS), the federal agency that administers those programs. It said consumers' out-of-pocket spending on health care likely rose 4.8 percent in 2019. For the 2020-27 period, it predicts an average annual growth rate of 5.0 percent.[73]

The average annual growth in total U.S. medical spending is projected to be 5.7 percent from 2020 to 2027, CMS said.[74] The calculations do not factor in a potential increase due to spending this year on the response to the coronavirus.

"To ask if there is a future for medical tourism is to ask if there is going to be a structural change in the U.S. health care system, and I would say probably not," Woodman says. "Nothing kills medical tourism as long as prices remain as high as they are in the United States."

NOTES

1. Howard Staab and Maggi Ann Grace, testimony before the Senate Special Committee on Aging, June 27, 2006, https://tinyurl.com/wfeugwj.

2. "About Bumrungrad," Bumrungrad International Hospital, https://tinyurl.com/tzb7kds.

3. Ian Youngman, "Now a Pandemic, Coronavirus Will Hit Medical Tourism Hard," *International Medical Travel Journal*, March 12, 2020, https://tinyurl.com/tpvb78f.

4. Ronald Labonté and Arne Ruckert, *Health Equity in a Globalizing Era* (2019), p. 207.

5. "Quick Facts About Medical Tourism," Patients Beyond Borders, https://tinyurl.com/w3wcfdj.

6. Jennifer Tolbert *et al.*, "Key Facts about the Uninsured Population," Kaiser Family Foundation, Dec. 13, 2019, https://tinyurl.com/uyjvvo6.

7. "The Potential National Health Cost Impacts to Consumers, Employers and Insurers Due to the Coronavirus (COVID-19)," Covered California, March 22, 2020, https://tinyurl.com/vzcoqtz.

8. Erin Alberty, "Prescriptions from Mexico? Utah is paying public employees to make the trip," *Salt Lake Tribune*, Jan. 5, 2020, https://tinyurl.com/tcp-nan4.

9. "Total Medicaid spending," Kaiser Family Foundation, https://tinyurl.com/y7q958lf; "2019 Annual Report of the Boards of Trustees of the Federal Hospital Insurance and Federal Supplementary Medical Insurance Trust Funds," Centers for Medicare & Medicaid Services, April 22, 2019, p. 6, https://tinyurl.com/y5llkja9; "December 2019 Medicaid & CHIP Enrollment Data Highlights," Medicaid, https://tinyurl.com/gl2bqha; and "People Dually Eligible for Medicare and Medicaid," Centers for Medicare & Medicaid Services, March 2020, https://tinyurl.com/rpsee99.

10. "Trump Administration Takes Historic Steps to Lower U.S. Prescription Drug Prices," press release, Department of Health and Human Services, Dec. 18, 2019, https://tinyurl.com/wt7m2bn.

11. "Personal Importation," U.S. Food and Drug Administration, Aug. 3, 2018, https://tinyurl.com/rhwyf6s.

12. "AMA policy on in-person importation of prescription drugs from Canada," American Medical Association, Nov. 12, 2018, https://tinyurl.com/vec28p2.

13. Marc D. Joffe, "Medical Cost Containment: A Microeconomic Approach," Mercatus Center, April 2014, https://tinyurl.com/rda6f4j.

14. Arnold Milstein, Mark D. Smith and Jerome P. Kassirer, "Overseas, Under the Knife," *The New York Times*, June 9, 2009, https://tinyurl.com/tlb6opa.

15. "Foreign Medical Program (FMP)," Department of Veterans Affairs, https://tinyurl.com/y5lgsrv9; "FY 2021 Budget Submission: Medical Programs and

Information Technology Programs," Department of Veterans Affairs, February 2020, https://tinyurl.com/qpzrl27.

16. "Medicare Coverage Outside of the United States," Centers for Medicare & Medicaid Services, revised April 2018, https://tinyurl.com/yyy94tl4.
17. "Dental services," Medicare, https://tinyurl.com/w4v54nr.
18. "Company profile," Bumrungrad International Hospital, https://tinyurl.com/qkfrpuf.
19. "Bangkok's Bumrungrad Hospital: Expanding the Footprint of Offshore Health Care," Wharton School of Business, Sept. 2, 2009, https://tinyurl.com/vf5jmw2.
20. *Ibid.*
21. David Reisman, "The economics of health and medical tourism," *Handbook on Medical Tourism and Patient Mobility*, 2015, p. 90, https://tinyurl.com/qlhzxvd.
22. Vijay Govindarajan and Ravi Ramamurti, *Reverse Innovation in Health Care: How to Make Value-Based Delivery Work* (2018), Kindle edition, location 742.
23. *Ibid.*
24. "Calculator," Medical Tourism Association, https://tinyurl.com/v43to5u.
25. Labonté and Ruckert, *op. cit.*, p. 210.
26. Ronald Labonté, "Medical tourism isn't always a fair deal for developing countries," *The Conversation*, Feb. 25, 2015, https://tinyurl.com/s5ugfn9.
27. *Ibid.*
28. I. Glenn Cohen, *Patients with Passports: Medical Tourism, Law, And Ethics* (2014), p. 226.
29. Lorraine Craig *et al.*, "Impact of the WHO FCTC on tobacco control: perspectives from stakeholders in 12 countries," *Tobacco Control*, May 30, 2019, https://tinyurl.com/wpalxqc.
30. Y.Y. Brandon Chen and Colleen M. Flood, "Medical Tourism's Impact on Health Care Equity and Access in Low- and Middle-Income Countries: Making the Case for Regulation," *Journal of Law, Medicine and Ethics*, April 1, 2013, https://tinyurl.com/rasatac.
31. Lloyd Sederer, "An Arthritis Treatment Worthy of the Pope and Kobe," *The Atlantic*, Oct. 15, 2012, https://tinyurl.com/u3udr6h.
32. "Consolidated Financial Statements and Supplemental Schedules: December 31, 2018 and 2017," prepared by KPMG, April 25, 2019, https://tinyurl.com/r7yelae.
33. Amber Mehta, Seth Goldstein and Martin A. Makary, "Global trends in center accreditation by the Joint Commission International growing patient implications for international medical and surgical care," *Journal of Travel Medicine*, Vol. 24, Issue 5, Aug. 21, 2017, https://tinyurl.com/r9d67p7.
34. Rade Nicholas Pejic, "The Symbol of Medicine: Aesculapius or Caduceus?" *Journal of the American Medical Association*, April 24, 1996, https://tinyurl.com/u36annv.
35. William Smith, ed., *Dictionary of Greek and Roman Biography and Mythology*, vol. 1 (1844), p. 45, https://tinyurl.com/tozjcuq.
36. Stephen T. Green, "Medical Tourism," in *Hunter's Tropical Medicine and Emerging Infectious Disease* (2012).
37. Eric Shiraev, *A History of Psychology: A Global Perspective* (2014), pp. 260-261.
38. Natasha Singer, "Ivo Pitanguy, Plastic Surgeon to the Stars and a Celebrity Himself, Dies at 93," *The New York Times*, Aug. 7, 2016, https://tinyurl.com/tw8bhdg.
39. *Ibid.*
40. Warren Hoge, "Doctor Vanity: The Jet Set's Man in Rio," *The New York Times*, June 8, 1980, https://tinyurl.com/qvdslkj.
41. Kathy Merlock Jackson, Lisa Lyon Payne and Kathy Shepherd Stolley, *The Intersection of Star Culture in America and International Medical Tourism: Celebrity Treatment* (2015), p. 26.
42. "Joe Rogan Experience #1066—Mel Gibson & Dr. Neil Riordan," YouTube, Jan. 17, 2018, https://tinyurl.com/s9nsp76.
43. "Guidelines for the Clinical Translation of Stem Cells," International Society for Stem Cell Research, 2008, p. 4, https://tinyurl.com/yx4a2vom.

44. *Ibid.*

45. "Guidelines for Stem Cell Research and Clinical Translation," International Society for Stem Cell Research, 2016, p. 25, https://tinyurl.com/vsxrqzs.

46. Liz Szabo, "Superstar Athletes Popularize Unproven Stem Cell Procedures," *Kaiser Health News*, Aug. 5, 2019, https://tinyurl.com/y58xr2vg.

47. Jessica Lau, "The path to responsible stem cell therapies," Harvard Stem Cell Institute, Sept. 19, 2019, https://tinyurl.com/srsfcpn.

48. *Ibid.*

49. Divya Gupta, "Inside India's surrogacy industry," *The Guardian*, Dec. 6, 2011, https://tinyurl.com/sslwo5k.

50. *Ibid.*

51. "His surrogate mother dead, baby boy 'all right,'" *Indian Express*, May 18, 2012, https://tinyurl.com/sbkwbow.

52. Kishwar Desai, "India's surrogate mothers are risking their lives. They urgently need protection," *The Guardian*, June 5, 2012, https://tinyurl.com/vv22tyu.

53. "Help wanted: As demand for surrogacy soars, more countries are trying to ban it," *The Economist*, May 13, 2017, https://tinyurl.com/t6su4vu.

54. "Bariatric surgery," Mayo Clinic, https://tinyurl.com/us65a4b.

55. Cohen, *op. cit.*, p. 16.

56. Jackson, Payne and Stolley, *op. cit.*, p. 177.

57. "The Globalization of Health Care: Can Medical Tourism Reduce Health Care Costs?" Senate Special Committee on Aging, June 27, 2006, https://tinyurl.com/wfeugwj.

58. *Ibid.*

59. Miriam Cross, "Travel Abroad for Low-Cost Care," *Kiplinger's Personal Finance*, January 2017, https://tinyurl.com/shlfs89; Byron Pitts and Nikki Battiste, "As More Americans Have Surgeries Overseas, US Companies Consider 'Medical Tourism' a Health Care Option," *ABC News*, Sept. 30, 2013, https://tinyurl.com/spkvvda.

60. "National Health Expenditure Projections 2018-2027 Forecast Summary," Centers for Medicare & Medicaid Services, https://tinyurl.com/ya24kgbk; Bo Evans, "US companies saving money by sending employees overseas for healthcare," *The Denver Channel*, Feb. 14, 2020, https://tinyurl.com/vv6j4gj.

61. Phil Galewitz, "To Save Money, American Patients And Surgeons Meet In Cancun," *Kaiser Health News*, Aug. 12 2019, https://tinyurl.com/s6ja8up; Phil Galewitz, "A Mexican Hospital, an American Surgeon, and a $5,000 Check (Yes, a Check)," *The New York Times*, Aug. 9, 2019, https://tinyurl.com/yxtmosnr.

62. "Benchmark Employer Survey Finds Average Family Premiums Now Top $20,000," Kaiser Family Foundation, Sept. 25, 2019, https://tinyurl.com/y5qxkoj7.

63. "Visualizing Health Policy: US Statistics on Surprise Medical Billing," Kaiser Family Foundation, Feb. 11, 2020, https://tinyurl.com/w6sakak.

64. Josef Woodman, *Patients Beyond Borders: Everybody's Guide to Affordable, World-Class Medical Travel*, 4th ed. (2020), p. 9.

65. *Ibid.*, p. 40.

66. *Ibid.*, p. 25.

67. "Senate Bill Report SB6111," legislative summary, Washington state Senate, https://tinyurl.com/qrhpfe2.

68. Shelly Fagan, "Oh My God, You're Going To MEXICO For Medical Care?" *Medium*, Sept. 27, 2018, https://tinyurl.com/trou7w9.

69. "Global Level 4 Health Advisory—Do Not Travel," U.S. State Department, March 31, 2020, https://tinyurl.com/w9bm5b4.

70. "Covid-19 (Coronavirus Alert)," IndusHealth, https://tinyurl.com/sftaukq.

71. Julian Resendiz, "Medical tourism taking hit with border restrictions in place," *KTSM*, March 28, 2020, https://tinyurl.com/snyguj9.

72. *Ibid.*

73. "National Health Expenditure Projections 2018-2027 Forecast Summary," *op. cit.*

74. *Ibid.*

BIBLIOGRAPHY

Books

Becker, Elizabeth, *Overbooked: The Exploding Business of Travel and Tourism*, Simon & Schuster, 2013.
A former *New York Times* and *National Public Radio* journalist examines the development of medical tourism, especially in Southeast Asia.

Cohen, I. Glenn, *Patients with Passports: Medical Tourism, Law, And Ethics*, Oxford University Press, 2014.
A Harvard Law School professor offers a comprehensive analysis of global medical tourism and ethical issues.

Labonté, Ronald, and Arne Ruckert, *Health Equity in a Globalizing Era: Past Challenges, Future Prospects*, Oxford University Press, 2020.
Researchers from the University of Ottawa examine how wealthy, middle-income and poor nations interact in an increasingly connected global medical market.

Woodman, Josef, *Patients Beyond Borders: Everybody's Guide to Affordable, World-Class Medical Travel*, 4th ed., Calvander Communications, 2020.
A consultant offers practical guides about what research people should do before leaving their home countries for medical care.

Articles

Caulfield, Timothy, "What Does It Mean When Athletes Get 'Stem Cell Therapy'?" *The Atlantic*, Oct. 22, 2012, https://tinyurl.com/v842ebo.
An academic researcher looks at the reasons why athletes are seeking unproven therapies abroad to heal injuries.

Charo, R. Alta, "On the Road (to a Cure?)—Stem-Cell Tourism and Lessons for Gene Editing," *The New England Journal of Medicine*, Feb. 10, 2016, https://tinyurl.com/synmgjh.
An ethicist examines what kinds of regulations or other efforts might be needed to protect people from the risks of unproven stem cell therapies.

Galewitz, Phil, "A Mexican Hospital, an American Surgeon, and a $5,000 Check (Yes, a Check)," *The New York Times*, Aug. 9, 2019, https://tinyurl.com/yxtmosnr.
A reporter follows Americans to Cancún, Mexico, where they undergo orthopedic procedures.

Kirkner, Richard Mark, "Medical Tourism: Once Ready for Takeoff, Now Stuck at the Gate," *Managed Care Magazine*, March 28, 2018, https://tinyurl.com/wonn7mr.
A journalist details the recent history of optimistic projections and disappointing results for growth in medical tourism.

Labonté, Ronald, "Medical tourism isn't always a fair deal for developing countries," *The Conversation*, Feb. 25, 2015, https://tinyurl.com/s5ugfn9.
A professor of public health details the ways developing countries have diverted their limited public health resources to build networks intended to attract affluent medical tourists.

Nittle, Nandra, "A lack of insurance is leading more Americans to have weight loss surgery in Mexico," *Vox*, Oct. 18, 2018, https://tinyurl.com/t92ndsm.
A reporter uses the stories of a father and daughter who underwent weight loss surgery in Mexico as a lens to examine the risks and benefits of medical tourism.

Shah, Sonia, "Super-resistant Bacteria, Medical Tourism, and India's Poor: A Global Health Crisis in the Making," Pulitzer Center, Jan. 17, 2012, https://tinyurl.com/qrou8gr.
In a series of articles, a journalist examines the risks of medical tourism for patients and the diversion of health care investment away from the needs of poor people in India.

Reports and Studies

Ambagtsheer, Frederike, and Linde Van Balen, "'I'm not Sherlock Holmes': Suspicions, secrecy and silence of transplant professionals in the human organ trade," *European Journal of Criminology*, Jan. 18, 2019, https://tinyurl.com/tvhlo22.
Interviews with transplant specialists reveal that many fail to ask questions about the provenance of kidneys to be transplanted.

Mehta, Ambar, Seth D. Goldstein and Martin A. Makary, "Global trends in center accreditation by the Joint Commission International: growing patient implications for international medical and surgical care," *Journal of Travel Medicine*, September-October 2017, https://tinyurl.com/vwqs4x5.

Researchers detail rapid growth in positive ratings awarded by a well-known U.S. hospital oversight group to foreign hospitals.

Morris, Michele I., and Elmi Muller, "Infectious Complications of Transplant Tourism," *Current Infectious Disease Reports*, Aug. 31, 2019, https://tinyurl.com/rfyuxky.

Patients who obtain organ transplants abroad have a high risk of developing antibiotic-resistant infections that can pose public health risks when they return home, according to a study by two physicians.

Newscasts

"Birthstory," *Radiolab*, June 7, 2018, https://tinyurl.com/r33zz8h.

A radio program examines the ethical and financial issues surrounding international surrogacy.

Evans, Bo, "US companies saving money by sending employees overseas for healthcare," *Denver Channel*, Feb. 14, 2020, https://tinyurl.com/vv6j4gj.

A video newscast follows an employee of HSM, a North Carolina manufacturer, through his orthopedic procedure in Costa Rica.

THE NEXT STEP

Black Market

Glionna, John M., "Black-Market Medicine Pushers Are Targeting Latino Immigrants," *The Daily Beast*, Sept. 13, 2019, https://tinyurl.com/qk7rotp.

Black-market and counterfeit medication making its way into the United States from Mexico is mostly sold to Latino immigrants.

Neal, Will, "OORCP: International crackdown on black market medicine in Europe," *Kyiv Post*, March 11, 2020, https://tinyurl.com/um4bcgv.

A sting operation organized by a coalition of European countries seized 36 million units of black-market medical drugs over the course of several years.

Promchertchoo, Pichayada, "Kidney for sale: Inside Philippines' illegal organ trade," *Channel News Asia*, Oct. 19, 2019, https://tinyurl.com/y2dctwgt.

"Kidney hunters" in Manila earn commissions when they convince impoverished Filipinos to illegally sell a kidney.

Pharmacy Tourism

Gephardt, Matt, and Michelle Poe, "Americans are saving money on meds by traveling to Canada. Here's how it works," *KUTV*, Nov. 15, 2019, https://tinyurl.com/snhphfy.

The strength of the U.S. dollar versus the Canadian dollar and the high price of drugs in the United States create incentives for U.S. patients to fill prescriptions north of the border.

O'Dowd, Peter, "Utah Funds Public Employees Traveling to Mexico, Canada to Save Money on Costly Prescription Drugs," *WBUR*, Feb. 14, 2020, https://tinyurl.com/u2nrsnp.

A Utah Public Employees Health Program that covers the cost of travel to Canada or Mexico for the purchase of particularly expensive drugs is largely limited to members with serious chronic conditions.

Rashid, Raphael, "Thai medical tourism expands into new area: HIV prevention," *Nikkei Asian Review*, March 10, 2020, https://tinyurl.com/yx5pnt92.

South Korean and Taiwanese patients at a high risk of contracting HIV are seeking preventive treatment in Thailand in order to avoid stigma and take advantage of much lower costs than at home.

Regulations and Standards

Lee, Matthew, and Colleen Long, "US imposes visa rules for pregnant women on 'birth tourism,'" *The Associated Press*, Jan. 23, 2020, https://tinyurl.com/trnbnzb.

Under new rules introduced by the Trump administration, pregnant women traveling to the United States and planning to give birth must prove they are doing so for medical reasons.

Narayanan, Nayantara, "Nigerian man's Twitter complaint sparks discussion on lack of support for medical tourists in India," *Scroll*, April 30, 2019, https://tinyurl.com/y2msjrfw.

Medical tourists concerned about medical negligence in India are calling for more regulations and data collection.

Shieber, Jonathan, "Doctours offers packaged medical tourism for US customers," *TechCrunch*, July 9, 2019, https://tinyurl.com/y5t4s6hw.
An online platform for booking medical tourism trips says it ensures that all participating doctors are accredited by the Joint Commission International.

Surgery Abroad

Berr, Jonathan, "'I had my misgivings about going abroad,'" *BBC*, March 28, 2019, https://tinyurl.com/y222xv66.
Traveling abroad for surgery had become more common, especially among patients in developed countries.

Ho, Solarina, "Canadians sound alarm on dangers of cheap plastic surgery abroad," *CTV News*, Aug. 1, 2019, https://tinyurl.com/y6grpvpn.
Several Canadian women who contracted infections or developed complications after traveling to the Dominican Republic for cosmetic surgeries are warning others about the risks.

Varifanua, Tamara, "Medical tourism: the high price of a discount," *Fox 13* (Salt Lake City), Nov. 6, 2019, https://tinyurl.com/vkgs8ov.
A Utah woman who had weight loss surgery in Mexico developed severe complications, including a collapsed lung, when she returned to the United States.

For More Information

American Society of Plastic Surgeons, 444 E. Algonquin Road, Arlington Heights, IL 60005; 847-228-9900; plasticsurgery.org/patient-safety/dangers-of-plastic-surgery-tourism. Physician group that offers warnings about the risks of plastic surgery abroad.

American Medical Association, AMA Plaza, 330 N. Wabash Ave., Suite 39300, Chicago, IL 60611-5885; 312-464-4782; ama-assn.org/delivering-care/ethics/medical-tourism. Physician organization that provides general advice to patients considering treatment abroad.

Centers for Disease Control and Prevention, 1600 Clifton Road, Atlanta, GA 30329; 800-232-4636; cdc.gov/features/medicaltourism. Key federal agency in tracking efforts to prevent infections related to medical care provided abroad.

Declaration of Istanbul Custodian Group, The Transplantation Society, 505 Boulevard René-Lévesque Ouest, Suite 1401, Montréal, QC H2Z 1Y7, Canada; 514-874-1717; declarationofistanbul.org. Group of transplant specialists that aids in efforts to prevent organ trafficking.

Joint Commission International, 1515 W. 22nd St., Suite 1300W, Oak Brook, IL 60523; 630-268-7400; jointcommissioninternational.org/en. Organization that monitors the quality of hospitals in many nations. It is affiliated with the Joint Commission, which monitors U.S. hospitals.

SFU Medical Tourism Research Group, Simon Fraser University, 515 W. Hastings St., Vancouver, BC V6B 5K3, Canada; 604-782-2004; sfu.ca/medicaltourism. University group that researches different aspects of medical tourism and publishes information for consumers.

3

Pandemic Preparedness

Will the United States learn from its response to COVID-19?

By Bara Vaida

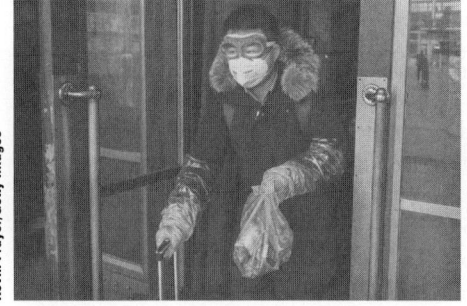

The day after the World Health Organization declared on Jan. 30, 2020, that the coronavirus outbreak, which first emerged in China, was a global public health emergency, a man wearing a protective mask and swim goggles exits a train station in Beijing. At the time, public health officials said the virus threat was low in the United States, but former Trump administration officials warned of gaps in the nation's pandemic preparedness plan.

From *CQ Researcher*,
September 4, 2020

THE ISSUES

On Feb. 12, members of the U.S. Senate Committee on Homeland Security and Governmental Affairs gathered around a large rectangular table in the Senate Dirksen Office Building for a hearing entitled: "Roundtable: Are We Prepared? Protecting the U.S. from Global Pandemics."

As the meeting convened, a new coronavirus causing pneumonia-like symptoms was quietly rolling across the world from Wuhan, China.

Although public health experts deemed the threat to the United States to be low at the time, two former Trump administration officials warned the panel that if the virus became a pandemic, there were worrisome gaps in the nation's readiness.

"We have fallen short in some very key areas, and they can't be overlooked," said Luciana Borio, the former director for medical and biodefense preparedness at the White House National Security Council. "We have neglected our health care system preparedness. . . . We have to assume that we are going to see a lot more cases here, and I really worry about the health care system preparedness. . . . We cannot afford to lose a minute in getting this health care system as ready as we can."[1]

Scott Gottlieb, the former head of the Food and Drug Administration, told the meeting that if the new virus had already been introduced into the United States undetected, as some people feared, the country would start seeing outbreaks of COVID-19, the disease caused by the coronavirus, "emerge sometime in the next two to four weeks." The country "should be leaning in very aggressively to try to broaden diagnostic screening right now," Gottlieb said, in order to identify infected people early enough to prevent the virus from spreading.[2]

Neither of their recommendations were carried out.

Despite repeated emerging infectious disease crises in recent years, U.S. political leaders from both parties have not prioritized pandemic prevention and response. They have invested in creating preparedness programs, but as each emergency ended, political priorities shifted, and the programs were cut back or defunded. Public health and political leaders say the COVID-19 crisis is the perfect time, given the public's heightened appreciation for the public health system, to push policymakers to boost pandemic preparedness among federal, state and local agencies.

"While we focus on the pandemic in front of us, we can't miss this opportunity to reflect on the lessons of COVID-19 and apply those lessons, so we are more prepared for the next pandemic or public health emergency," former U.S. Health and Human Services (HHS) Secretary Michael Leavitt testified to the U.S. Senate Committee on Health, Education, Labor and Pensions (HELP) on June 23.[3]

And public officials made plenty of mistakes early in the pandemic that should not be repeated, infectious disease experts say. In early February, when it was clear that the coronavirus was a highly contagious respiratory disease, the federal Centers for Disease Control and Prevention (CDC) botched the initial U.S. testing process, enabling the virus to spread silently and rapidly from coast to coast, experts say. And while some state health systems tried to prepare, there was no consistent guidance or urgency from the federal government to do so.

President Trump downplayed alarms about the virus, saying the pathogen was "under control," repeatedly pointing to the administration's Jan. 31 travel restrictions on non-U.S. citizens entering the United States. He

A street sign reminds New Yorkers gathered on Aug. 21, 2020, to mourn those who died from COVID-19 that they should get a flu shot to help prevent the public health system from having to deal with two viral epidemics at the same time this fall. By early September, U.S. COVID-19 deaths had surpassed 184,000, more than any other country.

reassured the public that all was going well, even after a CDC official told Americans, at the end of February, to prepare for the potential of widespread and "severe" disruptions to daily life due to the virus.[4]

Then, on March 11, the World Health Organization (WHO) declared COVID-19 a pandemic. Two days later, Trump declared a national emergency, closing the nation's borders and allowing states to enforce quarantines, essentially shutting down large sections of the U.S. economy.

By early September, however, the virus had killed more than 184,000, and infected over 6 million Americans—more than any other country, according to the Johns Hopkins University COVID-19 database. In other words, the United States has only 4 percent of the world's population but has nearly a quarter of the globe's coronavirus cases.[5]

"Boy, we weren't ready," said U.S. Rep. Donna Shalala, a Democrat from Florida and a former HHS secretary.[6]

But the United States should have been prepared, experts say. With an established public health infrastructure and a wealth of drugs, hospitals, health care providers and scientists, the United States seemed better equipped than almost any other country to combat a new virus.

Further, the United States had a comprehensive plan for responding to health emergencies, including data surveillance, testing, tracing the contacts of people carrying a contagious virus, hospital preparedness, distribution of medical supplies from a federal stockpile and federal guidance to state leaders and the public.

But when that plan needed to be activated earlier this year, the weaknesses experts had warned about became evident. The nation lacked enough public health staff, medical supplies or tests to stop the new virus from spreading. And it became clear that, to succeed, the plan needed clear, consistent federal leadership, experts say.

President Trump's critics say he has instead divided Americans along political lines over how to respond to the coronavirus and has frequently contradicted his own public health advisers.

Further, after the president's special coronavirus task force, headed by the president's son-in-law Jared Kushner, developed an aggressive nationwide COVID-19 testing plan in March, the White House never instituted it, allegedly because at the time the pandemic was affecting only "blue" states headed by Democratic governors. The president's advisers reportedly said it would make political sense to shift the responsibility for the pandemic's spread to those governors, according to an investigation by *Vanity Fair* magazine. White House spokesperson Kayleigh McEnany said the article was "completely incorrect in its assertion that any plan was stopped for political or other reasons."[7]

"We had plans, but the highest levels of government decided not to follow the plans," says Dr. Eric Toner, a senior scholar and senior scientist at the Johns Hopkins Bloomberg School of Public Health in Baltimore.

Trump's supporters say he did follow the plan, which they say gives state and local governments primary responsibility in a public health emergency. The strategy anticipated a localized event, like a bioterrorism attack or a hurricane, they say, not scenarios such as COVID-19 that require an all-government, societywide response.

"I think they did, operationally, follow the plan," says Kerry Weems, former acting administrator for the Centers for Medicare and Medicaid Services under President George W. Bush.

In June, two Senate committees began looking at lessons learned from the current pandemic, and legislators in both the House and Senate are considering establishing a bipartisan commission for the same purpose.[8]

Their work is urgent.

Public health experts worry that this fall and winter the nation could face two threats—COVID-19 and seasonal influenza—at the same time. And other pathogens potentially more deadly than the coronavirus lurk in the environment. On June 30, for instance, scientists said a new swine flu with pandemic potential has been detected in pigs in China.[9]

"We don't know even when a second surge is going to come . . . our second pandemic may come in about three months," former Senate Republican leader Bill Frist of Tennessee, who is himself a physician, said at the June 23 hearing before the Senate HELP Committee. "So, as much as we can do to prepare that [health care] infrastructure and the structure itself for the next pandemic, the next emerging threat, it will apply to what we are doing now."[10]

The world has seen repeated outbreaks of new viruses jumping from animals to humans in recent years, due in part to climate change, population growth and the destruction of forest habitats of virus-carrying animals, along with an increase in the ease and speed of global transportation that spreads disease-causing pathogens.[11]

Health experts say the solutions are well-known, based on lessons from past epidemics. Key ingredients include adequately investing in a public health system to catch early signals of an outbreak, ensuring that public and private laboratories work together in conducting tests, building a workforce to trace and quarantine people exposed to an infection, ensuring an adequate supply of hospital beds, health care staff and medical supplies and investing in a robust research and development infrastructure to quickly develop vaccines and treatments.

Previous pandemic preparedness plans called for many of those elements, but none were ever fully funded. Instead, Congress chose, over the past decade, to fund disease preparedness and response on a case-by-case basis. After each disease threat faded, so did the money.

"We call this the cycle of panic and neglect," says Carolyn Reynolds, co-founder of the Pandemic Action Network, which aims to build political support for long-standing investments in pandemic planning. "Essentially, there is a disease threat, you have a panic, then a flood of attention on it, then you throw money at it, you figure out lessons learned, then the outbreak disappears and the political will and the funding disappear."

While Congress is reviewing lessons learned from the coronavirus pandemic, the executive branch is not.

President Trump said on July 22 the administration's response to the pandemic is "working out"—and on Aug. 4 that the virus is "under control as much as you

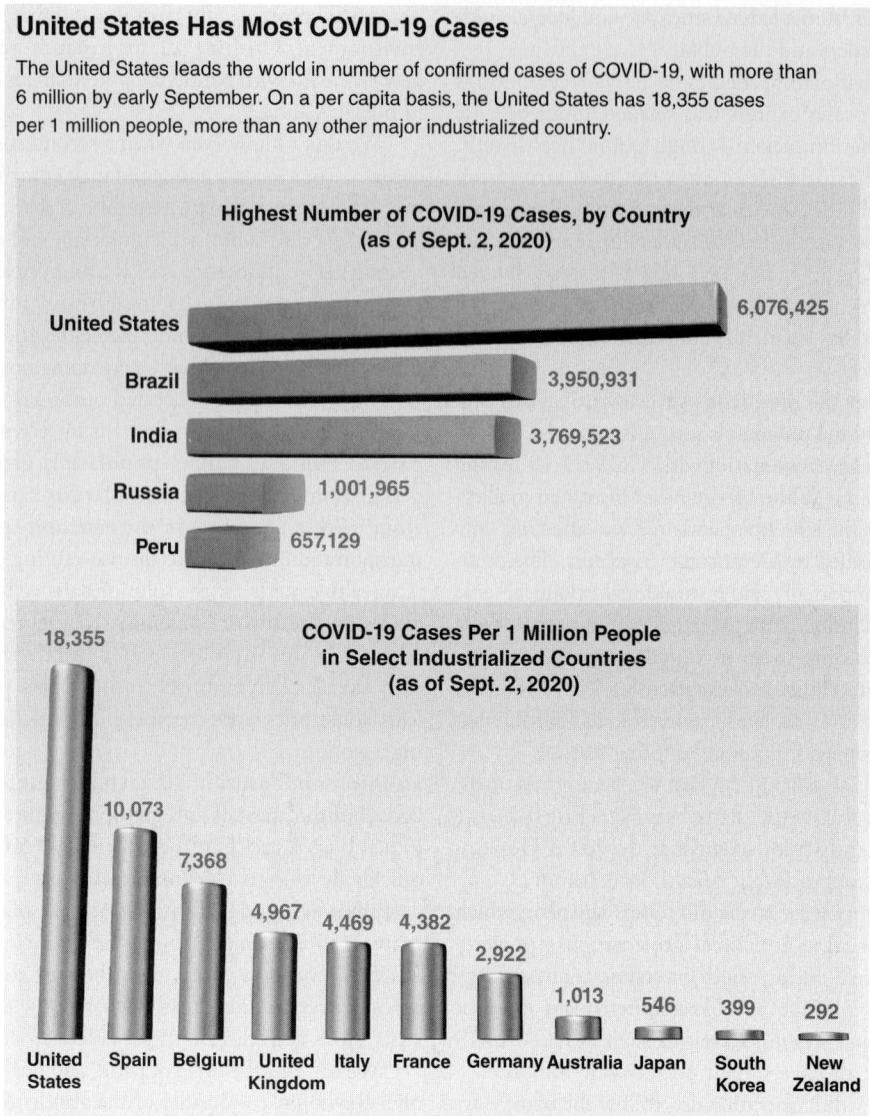

United States Has Most COVID-19 Cases

The United States leads the world in number of confirmed cases of COVID-19, with more than 6 million by early September. On a per capita basis, the United States has 18,355 cases per 1 million people, more than any other major industrialized country.

Highest Number of COVID-19 Cases, by Country (as of Sept. 2, 2020)

Country	Cases
United States	6,076,425
Brazil	3,950,931
India	3,769,523
Russia	1,001,965
Peru	657,129

COVID-19 Cases Per 1 Million People in Select Industrialized Countries (as of Sept. 2, 2020)

Country	Cases per 1 Million
United States	18,355
Spain	10,073
Belgium	7,368
United Kingdom	4,967
Italy	4,469
France	4,382
Germany	2,922
Australia	1,013
Japan	546
South Korea	399
New Zealand	292

Sources: "COVID-19 Dashboard," Center for Systems Science and Engineering, Johns Hopkins University, Sept. 2, 2020, https://tinyurl.com/rnjqnnh; "Coronavirus Pandemic (COVID-19) — the data," Our World in Data, Sept. 2, 2020, https://tinyurl.com/y6pvvurq

can control it," a fact belied by the spike in deaths that began in mid-July. And the president continued to blame China for the pandemic, saying "they should have stopped it, and they didn't."[12]

Indeed, China was slow to inform the world about the virus. Chinese officials told the WHO, the public health arm of the United Nations, on Dec. 31, 2019, about a cluster of illnesses of unknown origin, though the cases had begun spreading from a seafood and live animal market in Wuhan several weeks before.[13] China told the WHO around Jan. 11 that there was "no clear evidence" that the virus was being passed between humans.[14]

Less than two weeks later, cases of the virus had already spread to Thailand, South Korea and the United States, and China was forced to lock down Wuhan, a city of 11 million.[15] If China had acted even one to three weeks earlier to limit travel and implement social distancing measures, the outbreak might have been smaller, according to a study published in the scientific journal *Nature* on May 4.[16]

Trump blames the WHO for failing to prod China to be more forthcoming. In July, he began the yearlong process of formally withdrawing the United States from the organization, saying it is too "China-centric" and has not done enough to investigate why China was slow to respond to the pandemic.[17] (*See Pro/Con.*)

It is a move opposed by most global health experts.

"We need an organization that can work with the political leadership across all countries, and right now the WHO is the best option we have," says the Pandemic Action Network's Reynolds.

Whether U.S. leaders will use lessons from the current crisis to implement and fund pandemic response programs may well depend on who wins the November presidential election, Trump or former Vice President Joe Biden, the Democratic nominee.

Trump repeatedly has contradicted guidance from public health officials about the importance of social distancing—remaining at least 6 feet apart from other people—and wearing a mask in public. He has even retweeted comments from conspiracy theorists saying masks do more harm than good.[18] Experts say his behavior has helped sow public confusion over whether COVID-19 is a serious threat and has helped turn decisions on whether to wear a mask into a question of political loyalty.

Biden, meanwhile, has repeatedly called COVID-19 a public health crisis and voiced support for wearing a mask as a crucial tool in limiting its spread.[19]

"Any time there is politicization of an infectious-disease response, it makes it much harder to intervene," said Amesh Adalja, an infectious disease expert at the Johns Hopkins Center for Health Security. People are "less likely to actually listen to public health authorities on what are the best actions to take and how to take them because they think that everything has been politicized in that there is no truth—it's truth from Democrats or Republicans, rather than the truth."[20]

BACKGROUND
Constant Threat

Infectious diseases are a familiar enemy. Throughout history, viruses, bacteria and parasites have killed more humans than wars and natural disasters. In 1918, the Spanish flu, an influenza virus, killed an estimated 50 million to 100 million people globally.[21]

Nearly Four in 10 Americans Would Refuse Free COVID-19 Vaccine

Almost 40 percent of Americans surveyed by Gallup on Aug. 10-16 said they would refuse a hypothetical COVID-19 vaccine that had been approved by the U.S. Food and Drug Administration (FDA), even if it were offered for free.

Responses on accepting free FDA-approved COVID-19 vaccine:

- No 38%
- Yes 62%

Source: "Coronavirus Pandemic," Gallup, August 2020, https://tinyurl.com/y3fgakwg

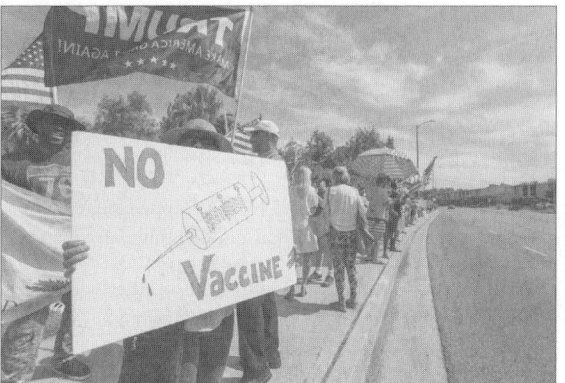

A protester holds a sign urging rejection of a coronavirus vaccine at a rally in May 2020 demanding the relaxation of pandemic restrictions in California. In August, a Gallup survey found that 38 percent of Americans would refuse a free vaccine against the virus, even as President Trump has said a vaccine would be ready "very soon."

CHRONOLOGY

1990s *U.S. government begins its modern pandemic planning.*

1995 The Centers for Disease Control and Prevention (CDC) establishes a program to help states track infectious diseases.

1996 Congress directs the U.S. Department of Health and Human Services (HHS) to develop a list of pathogens that pose a potential threat to national security.

1998 Congress appropriates funding to create the National Pharmaceutical Stockpile, which later becomes the National Strategic Stockpile, a federal warehousing system for critical medical supplies.

2000-2009 *Federal, state and local governments plan pandemic responses.*

2000 Congress passes Public Health Improvement Act to increase federal, state and local public health surveillance.

2001 After the Sept. 11 terrorist attacks on the World Trade Center and the Pentagon, and poisonings from anthrax powder sent through the U.S. mail, lawmakers realize they must boost planning for potential bioterror attacks.

2002 Congress enacts the Public Health Security and Bioterrorism Preparedness and Response Act, which provides grants to states to create pandemic preparedness plans, codifies the National Strategic Stockpile and creates a new office of the Assistant Secretary of Public Health Emergency Preparedness within HHS. . . . Congress creates the Department of Homeland Security.

2003-05 Department of Homeland Security creates the BioWatch program to create an early warning system for a bioterror attack in major cities. . . . Congress passes the Project BioShield Act and the Public Readiness and Emergency Preparedness Act, both designed to boost public and private coordination in responding to national emergencies.

2006 Congress passes the Pandemic and All-Hazards Preparedness Act, which codifies HHS as the lead federal agency for public health response to emergencies and creates the Biomedical Advanced Research and Development Authority, a program within HHS that aims to help get public health emergency drugs and vaccines to market.

2009 The first test of U.S. pandemic preparedness, the emergence of the swine flu from Mexico, generally goes well, with some challenges in testing and vaccine manufacturing.

2010-2020 *Emerging disease threats are on the rise as population growth and climate change destroy natural habitats, increasing the prevalence of new animal-borne viruses infecting humans.*

2013 Congress clarifies that the HHS assistant secretary for preparedness and response will lead responses to public health emergencies but must work with the Department of Homeland Security to minimize duplication efforts.

2014 Ebola virus outbreaks hit three West African countries and threaten to spread worldwide through global travel. The United States, working with the World Health Organization, creates the Global Health Security Agenda to boost health systems around the world.

2015 The Zika virus, a mosquito-borne illness, spreads from South America to Texas and Florida, highlighting the need for investment in vaccines for pathogens with pandemic potential.

2016 The 21st Century Cures Act includes measures intended to increase investments in research on pathogens with pandemic potential.

2017 H7N9 flu emerges among China's chicken farmers, reigniting worries about U.S. preparedness, but the threat fades as China gets the virus under control.

2018 President Trump merges White House National Security Council global health office into the council's office of counterproliferation and biodefense in order to streamline national security efforts, according to former security council adviser John Bolton.

2019 HHS conducts pandemic planning exercise called Crimson Contagion, demonstrating gaps in planning, but no further action is taken. . . . COVID-19, a pneumonia-like illness caused by a coronavirus, emerges in China's Wuhan province.

2020 As COVID-19 spreads across the globe, the World Health Organization declares it a pandemic. . . . In the United States, the need for renewed focus on pandemic preparedness becomes clear as the response to the outbreak is haphazard, with flawed test kits, limited contact tracing, insufficient protective equipment for health care workers and inconsistent messaging and enforcement of social distancing and mask-wearing requirements. . . . By late summer, the virus has infected more than 6 million Americans, more than any other country, and killed more than 184,000.

Development of vaccines, antibiotics and improved sanitation drastically reduced deaths from pathogens. As a result, experts say, the world has become more complacent about the threat posed by infectious diseases.

"Generally, the tendency [in human nature is] to have wishful thinking that a bad thing isn't going to happen," said Julie Gerberding, executive vice president and chief patient officer at drugmaker Merck and former director of the CDC.[22]

Still, every administration for the past 20 years has faced an infectious disease threat, either natural or human-made, including:

- Anthrax attacks using the U.S. mail in September and October 2001, which killed five people around the country. Federal officials linked the attacks to a government scientist who later committed suicide.[23]
- Severe acute respiratory syndrome (SARS), a coronavirus that jumped from a civet cat to humans. The disease, traced to a Chinese live animal food market, infected more than 8,000 people around the world and killed 774 in 2003.[24]
- Avian bird flu, which killed 74 people in southeast Asia in 2005.[25]
- The swine flu pandemic that originated in Mexico and killed 12,469 Americans in 2009.[26]
- Middle East respiratory syndrome (MERS), a coronavirus that jumped from camels to humans in Saudi Arabia in 2012 and killed more than 850 people in 27 countries by early 2020.[27]
- Ebola, a deadly virus that likely spread from bats to people and then into three West African nations in 2014 and killed 11,325 people in six countries before being brought under control in 2016.[28]
- Zika, a mosquito-borne virus that causes birth defects, which spread to more than 87 countries after emerging in 2015.[29]
- H7N9 avian influenza epidemic, which spread among chicken farmers in China and was brought under control in late 2017.[30]

In response to each of those infectious disease threats, the U.S. president at the time made plans to organize federal, state and local public health resources, only to have other priorities—such as war and financial crises—take precedence. That same pattern unfolded with each succeeding threat, right up until the virus from which COVID-19 emerged.[31]

The United States traces its modern pandemic planning to 1998, when President Bill Clinton, a Democrat, read a Richard Preston novel, *The Cobra Event*, about a fictional biological attack on the United States. With concerns that biological attacks aimed at disrupting the medical supply would occur during the new century, his administration pushed Congress to fund the National Pharmaceutical Stockpile (now part of the National Strategic Stockpile), a supply of life-saving medicine and equipment stored in secret locations around the country for use in an emergency. He also created a position in the National Security Council to focus solely on health threats.[32]

When Republican George W. Bush became president in 2001, he abolished the White House global health and security office, and later reinstated it after the 9/11 terrorist attacks and anthrax poisonings that same year. Bush also worked with Congress to build the interagency pandemic and biodefense infrastructure that exists today.[33]

Among the laws enacted during the Bush administration were the:

- Public Health Security and Bioterrorism Preparedness and Response Act, which codified the National Strategic Stockpile and created the HHS position of assistant secretary of public health emergency preparedness,
- Public Readiness and Emergency Preparedness Act, designed to coordinate public health emergency efforts with the private sector,
- Project BioShield Act, which authorized the federal government to secure medical countermeasures for health threats, and the
- Pandemic and All-Hazards Preparedness Act, which required the federal government to

Doomsday Prepping Goes Mainstream During Pandemic

"People realize the last few stable decades have been a fluke."

Michael Leavitt, who served as secretary of Health and Human Services (HHS) under President George W. Bush, is not someone most people would think of as a "prepper."

But in 2006, as a lethal avian flu was brewing in Southeast Asia, late-night television host Jay Leno mocked Leavitt for being one after he recommended that Americans consider picking up extra cans of tuna and powdered milk the next time they went to the grocery store, just in case there was a pandemic.[1]

"Secretary of Health and Human Services Michael Leavitt recommended that Americans store canned tuna and powdered milk under their beds for when bird flu hits," Leno said on the "Tonight Show." "What? . . . Powdered milk and tuna? How many would rather have the bird flu?"[2]

Fourteen years later, Leavitt's words do not seem so alarmist. In fact, prepping—stockpiling food or other essential items in case of a catastrophe—seems realistic now that the coronavirus pandemic has laid bare what many feared: federal, state and local governments cannot be relied upon to come to the public's rescue when there is wide-scale disaster.

"People are realizing the last few stable decades have been a fluke," said John Ramey, founder of the blog *The Prepared*. "It's the coronavirus now, but people have been watching climate change, inequality . . . [and] post-World War II systems falling apart. Our institutions have dropped the ball."[3]

Until the pandemic, many Americans did little to prepare for an emergency. In 2019, about 51 percent had no emergency plan in place for their family, and just 27 percent had a bag of emergency supplies on hand, according to a survey by Healthcare Ready, a nonprofit that represents health care supply chain companies.[4]

This past spring, Ready.gov, a website managed by the Department of Homeland Security, recommended that Americans stock up on masks, hand sanitizer, disinfectant wipes, prescription medications, pet food, infant formula and other supplies to help prevent the spread of the virus and other diseases.[5]

Now, businesses that sell emergency food and supplies are booming. The emergency management market—a $107 billion global industry—is expected to grow by about 40 percent over the next five years, according to Allied Market Research, an international business market analysis firm based in Portland, Ore.[6]

Companies that sell prepper supplies have even become fashionable. Retailers such as Pottery Barn and Nordstrom are offering survival system bags by a company named Preppi, while Hollywood personality Kim Kardashian is promoting an emergency kit called Judy. The bags include items such as dried food products and batteries.[7]

Some of these bags cost thousands of dollars, so they may be out of reach for many Americans, but public health experts have long recommended that individuals spend time thinking about how to prepare for a disaster.

"The federal government can't step in and buy a mask for everyone, and its ambition shouldn't be to do that," says Kerry Weems, an informal adviser to the Trump adminis-

develop and update a national plan for emergency health preparedness, appointed HHS as the lead coordinator during a public health emergency and established the Biomedical Advanced Research and Development Authority to oversee development of drugs and other countermeasures for health threats.[34]

While Congress initially funded all of these programs, they remained at the mercy of the annual federal budgeting process. Over time, lawmakers shifted money to other priorities, such as fighting the war in Iraq and coping with the aftermath of the 2007-09 financial crisis.

During Obama's presidency, a frugal Congress reduced per capita public health spending, adjusted for inflation, tration and the former acting administrator of the Centers for Medicare and Medicaid Services under Bush.

During the Obama administration, the federal government did consider, as part of a bioterrorism prevention measure, whether it should provide Americans with home medical kits containing antibiotics and other medical supplies. But the idea never made it beyond the discussion stage, according to Tevi Troy, former deputy secretary at HHS and author of the book *Shall We Wake the President?*[8]

"All of us can benefit by thinking about how the government responds to disaster," Troy wrote in his book. "This effort at the individual level begins with recognizing that the government is not always the best first responder."[9]

Certainly, Americans' individual actions will have a big impact on whether the public health system can tame COVID-19. Until there is a vaccine, medical experts say the three most important decisions people can make is to frequently wash their hands, wear a mask and maintain social distance. The virus transmits between people through respiratory droplets and aerosolized spray created by coughing, sneezing or talking, and a mask reduces the spread.[10]

During the summer, new cases of the virus surged to the highest levels since the beginning of the pandemic, mostly in the South, Midwest and West.

The increase occurred primarily in places where mask wearing was not mandatory and social distancing measures were relaxed or being ignored. Cases remained low in places such as the Northeast, which had not yet lifted as many restrictions.[11]

"We are an interconnected society," said Dr. Anthony Fauci, director of the National Institute of Allergy and Infectious Diseases at the National Institutes of Health, the federal government's medical research agency. "Anyone who is infected is part of the dynamic process of the outbreak.... You have an individual responsibility to yourself but [also] you have a societal responsibility because if we want to end this outbreak . . . the only way we are going to do it . . . is together."[12]

—*Bara Vaida*

---

[1] Bob Moen, "Leavitt urges people, institutions to take precaution against flu," *The Associated Press*, March 9, 2006, https://tinyurl.com/y3rntqme.

[2] Dan Diamond, "Inside America's 2-Decade Failure to Prepare for Coronavirus," *Politico*, April 11, 2020, https://tinyurl.com/tqyl962.

[3] Nellie Bowles, "I used to make fun of Silicon Valley preppers. Then I became one," *The New York Times*, April 24, 2020, https://tinyurl.com/y9c8wp9u.

[4] "Poll Reveals Lack of Preparedness in the Face of Increasingly Frequent Disasters," Healthcareready.com, May 29, 2019, https://tinyurl.com/y6lncxb7.

[5] "Build a Kit," Ready.gov, Department of Homeland Security, https://www.ready.gov/kit.

[6] "The end-of-the-world business is booming," *The Hustle*, March 28, 2020, https://tinyurl.com/y2mc2kxm.

[7] "The Preppi Go Box," https://tinyurl.com/yxbgbe4o; "Preppi the prepster 3 day emergency kit," https://tinyurl.com/y3ndt246; and Dan Hall, "Kitted out: Inside ultra-luxurious disaster survival kits where super rich can pay £4k for night vision goggles and posh chocolate," *The Sun*, May 21, 2020, https://tinyurl.com/yy4qkdxg.

[8] Tevi Troy, *Shall We Wake the President?* (2016), https://tinyurl.com/hss9g23.

[9] *Ibid.*

[10] "How does coronavirus spread?" *WebMD*, Aug. 21, 2020, https://tinyurl.com/rvoye2r.

[11] Josh Katz, Margot Sanger-Katz and Kevin Quealy, "A detailed map of who is wearing masks in the U.S.," *The New York Times*, July 17, 2020, https://tinyurl.com/yxfu375k; "Coronavirus in the U.S.: Latest Map and Case Count," accessed Aug. 29, 2020, https://tinyurl.com/t9j9fdw.

[12] "White House Coronavirus Task Force press briefing," *CNN*, June 26, 2020, https://tinyurl.com/y2dtxdsr.

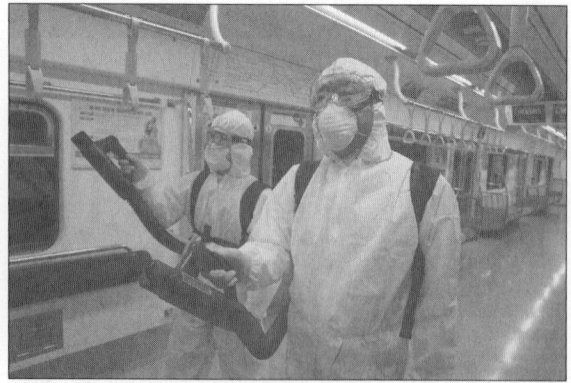

Workers clean the Seoul subway in June 2015 to help protect the public from Middle East respiratory syndrome, a coronavirus that jumped from camels to humans in Saudi Arabia and killed more than 850 people in 27 countries between 2012 and 2020. The United States began modern pandemic planning in 1998, but lawmakers often shifted money away from public health to other concerns.

by 9.3 percent from 2008 to 2016, according to the *American Journal of Public Health*.[35] The CDC's budget shrank 10 percent between 2010 and 2019, and its funding for state and local health preparedness dropped by one-third, according to the Trust for America's Health, a nonprofit public health advocacy group.[36]

"Public health has been malnourished over the course of the last almost 40 years," said Leavitt, the HHS secretary under Bush.[37]

During his term, Obama faced the swine flu, Ebola and Zika outbreaks. Each health threat tested the pandemic-response structure created by Bush and exposed gaps, demonstrating the need for steady federal investments that never materialized. Funding the response to Ebola and Zika, for instance, required individual emergency spending bills, after which those programs were set to expire during 2020—just as the current pandemic began.[38]

> "You're paying billions of dollars . . . to get the most worthless test results of any country in the world. No other country has this testing insanity."
>
> — Bill Gates
> Microsoft co-founder and
> head of a foundation dedicated to global health

Among other things, experts say, swine flu showed the need to invest more in diagnostics and testing, Ebola demonstrated the importance of financing global health security efforts, and Zika highlighted the need for investing in vaccine research on pathogens with pandemic potential. Ebola also showed the effectiveness of having a single voice coordinate the federal response to infectious disease outbreaks. Obama named attorney Ronald Klain as his point person on Ebola, which the public health community says created clarity about who was in charge.[39]

When Trump took office in 2017, his focus was on preventing terrorism. He merged the National Security Council's health security office into the office of counterproliferation, an office aimed at impeding the development of weapons of mass destruction, essentially reducing the focus on naturally occurring health threats. He did, in 2018, introduce a national biodefense strategy, the updated version of the national pandemic preparedness plan, as was required under the Pandemic and All-Hazards Preparedness Act. But by early 2020, many of the guidelines had not been fully implemented.[40]

CURRENT SITUATION
Federal Action

Almost nine months after the first case of COVID-19 was discovered in the United States, the disease continues to sicken thousands every day, indicating there is little chance Americans will return to their prepandemic lives anytime soon.

After a decline in new cases in May from a peak in April, the number of new COVID-19 cases and deaths surged during the summer, following weeks of civil rights protests across the country in response to the death of George Floyd at the hands of police, and the reopening of nonessential businesses in many states, especially in the South and Midwest.[41] Public health experts blamed the uptick on the lack of social distancing and the refusal by some Americans to wear a mask in public.

Senate HELP Committee Chairman Lamar Alexander, R-Tenn., said that now, while people are still focused on the pandemic, Congress should enact changes designed to respond to this and future pandemics. "We are in the midst of these problems, and our eyes will be clearer on what the solutions may be, and our wills will be better," Alexander said.[42]

He is circulating a detailed, 40-page proposal for a pandemic preparedness bill that he hopes will garner bipartisan support and pass this year. Alexander wants to boost funding for public health, clarify which officials should speak for the government in a health emergency, retool the critical medical supply system to emphasize domestic manufacturing and create incentives for drug companies to research pathogens with pandemic potential.[43]

His proposal also aims to strengthen testing, diagnostics and contact tracing—the basic tactics for containing infectious diseases. Federal budget cuts have hindered the ability of state and local public health departments to effectively do their work.

"We need about 300,000 additional public health workforce personnel in the coming months just to do contact tracing" and we don't have them, said Rep. Jason Crow, a Democrat from Colorado. "And that's not even to do the immunizations," and other public health measures.[44]

Countries that adopted such strategies, such as Australia, Germany, Japan, New Zealand and South Korea, have had far fewer COVID-19 cases than the United States, experts say.

"It seems like there's [already] a template that the successful nations have used to deal with COVID-19, and the template is aggressive early testing and contact tracing to find those who are ill, the isolation of people who have COVID-19, and immediate treatment of those folks," said Sen. Tim Kaine, D-Va., at a June 23 hearing of the Senate Committee on Health, Education, Labor and Pensions.[45]

Yet, as of early August, the United States remained one of the world's only developed countries without a national strategy for providing all citizens inexpensive tests that provide rapid results. Many Americans were having to wait more than a week to get their test results, during which time they could be infecting other people—a lag time that experts say makes the test results useless.

"You're paying billions of dollars in this very inequitable way to get the most worthless test results of any country in the world," said Microsoft co-founder Bill Gates, who now runs a foundation focused on global health issues. "No other country has this testing insanity."[46]

The Foreign Relations Committee is weighing a measure, the Global Health Security and Diplomacy Act, that would create a new coordinator for global health security at the State Department to work with foreign partners to limit the spread of pathogens that emerge overseas.[47]

Bars, Concerts, Big Church Services Carry High COVID Risk

Attending a large church service, sports event or concert or going to a bar are among the riskiest behaviors during the coronavirus pandemic, according to guidance from the Texas Medical Association. Opening the mail or getting takeout food carry low risk.

Activities by Level of Risk of Coronavirus Spread

Risk Level	Activities
Low Risk	Opening mail, getting takeout meal, pumping gasoline, tennis, camping
Low-Moderate Risk	Grocery shopping, walking/running/biking with others, golf, two-night hotel stay, sitting in doctor's waiting room, library/museum visit, outside restaurant eating, walking in busy downtown, spending an hour at a playground
Moderate Risk	Dinner/backyard barbecue at someone's house, going to beach, mall shopping, sending kids to school/camp/day care, working a week in an office building, swimming in public pool, home visit with elderly relative/friend
Moderate-High Risk	Visiting hair salon/barbershop or indoor restaurant, attending wedding/funeral, plane travel, playing basketball/football, hugging/shaking hands
High Risk	Eating at a buffet, gym workout, going to bar, movie theater, large concert, sports stadium, religious service with 500+ worshippers or amusement park

Source: "Know Your Risk During COVID-19," Texas Medical Association, July 8, 2020, https://tinyurl.com/yb5rm9ac

AT ISSUE

Should the United States withdraw from the World Health Organization?

YES David A. Ridenour
President, National Center for Public Policy Research

Written for CQ Researcher, September 2020

President Trump's move to pull the United States out of the World Health Organization (WHO) may give him the leverage to secure meaningful reform.

In its 1948 WHO membership resolution, Congress explicitly authorized withdrawal from the organization if the president provides one year's notice and U.S. current financial obligations are met.

Thus, President Trump's July 7 notification to the WHO was well-timed: He not only started the clock on U.S. withdrawal before incurring new obligations, but gave the agency ample time to show it is making good-faith efforts to reform before the U.S. exit.

No one questions whether the agency needs urgent reform. Its handling of every pandemic this century has been disastrous.

During the 2009 H1N1 pandemic, the WHO abruptly pulled its influenza pandemic guidelines from its website to avoid the embarrassment of an error, leaving the world without a roadmap for pandemic preparation.

The WHO also precipitated a world pork price collapse by initially designating the virus as a "swine flu"—implying that H1N1 was spread by animals—and then renaming it because the agency did not want Mexico, the origin of the virus, to suffer economic damage.

In 2014, the WHO was glacially slow in responding to the Ebola outbreak, in part because it was reluctant to challenge data provided by the West African countries at the virus' epicenter. Sound familiar?

The danger to world health comes not from President Trump's threatened withdrawal but from allowing the WHO to continue business as usual.

COVID-19 likely killed hundreds of thousands of people unnecessarily because the WHO refused to depart from China's party line. On Jan. 14, the WHO tweeted, "Chinese authorities have found no clear evidence of human-to-human transmission . . .," even though two weeks earlier, Taiwanese health authorities had warned the agency that the virus was spreading from person to person. Compounding this, the WHO put China's economic interests before public health by chastising countries that imposed travel restrictions on China to protect their populations.

The WHO's disastrous responses to H1N1 and Ebola triggered multiple investigations. Now, under member pressure, the agency is submitting to another one. But it does not need more investigation: It needs to implement past investigations' recommendations.

The organization needs greater transparency, better financial controls, a return to its core mission of contagious disease control and—most importantly—greater independence to "name and shame" countries that are jeopardizing world health.

President Trump's proposed withdrawal is the vehicle for achieving this.

NO Carolyn Reynolds
Co-Founder, Pandemic Action Network, and Senior Associate, Center for Strategic and International Studies

Written for CQ Researcher, September 2020

The administration's decision to withdraw the United States from the World Health Organization (WHO) would be ill-advised at any time. To do so as the world grapples with the mounting health and economic toll of the COVID-19 pandemic is unfathomable.

The WHO serves U.S. interests in several ways. First, as the pandemic has shown, infectious disease outbreaks anywhere in the world can quickly put American lives and livelihoods at risk. Until a vaccine exists, no country will be safe. Ending the pandemic requires a united global effort, in which WHO plays an indispensable role. Countries worldwide rely on WHO's expertise to lead the global response to the pandemic, from providing technical guidance on proven interventions to coordinating international efforts to accelerate research, development and universal access to a COVID vaccine and therapeutics.

Second, the WHO has led global efforts to combat a host of other infectious disease threats. The eradication in 1980 of smallpox, which killed an estimated 300 million people during the 20th century, is one of the agency's greatest achievements. With sustained WHO leadership, the world is now extremely close to eradicating polio, down to just 176 cases worldwide in 2019. U.S. political and economic support has been vital to this effort, and withdrawal could stall efforts to end this debilitating scourge. International efforts to fight influenza, HIV/AIDS, malaria, measles and tuberculosis also depend on the WHO for support.

Third, the agency provides the backbone for the world's infectious disease early warning system. Working closely with experts from the U.S. Centers for Disease Control and Prevention and the U.S. Agency for International Development, the WHO helps governments assess their preparedness gaps and mobilize early detection and response efforts. U.S. withdrawal will hobble that capacity and leave a major hole in the common global defense against growing pandemic threats.

The WHO—and the United States—have lessons to learn from this pandemic. While the WHO's emergency response capacity has improved considerably in recent years, all agree it can be strengthened. But scapegoating the WHO for COVID-19 is a political distraction. The agency, which lacks the ability to compel member states to act, is only as effective as its members—particularly its most powerful member and largest donor—will allow. Leaving the WHO will further erode U.S. influence on the global stage.

America needs the WHO, and the WHO needs America.

Protesters rally outside the state Capitol in St. Paul, Minn., on Aug. 1, 2020, to oppose a mandatory-mask order issued by Gov. Tim Walz. Experts say clear and consistent federal leadership on wearing masks would have helped prevent the coronavirus from spreading, but the Trump administration allowed states and local governments to set their own guidelines.

"In order to better detect, deter and contain infectious disease outbreaks before they become global pandemics, we need a strategically planned, carefully coordinated approach toward global health security that closes the gaps that threaten us all," said the committee chairman, Sen. James Risch, a Republican from Idaho, in a statement.[48]

Other lawmakers have taken a different approach. House Speaker Nancy Pelosi, D-Calif., created a bipartisan House Select Committee on the Coronavirus Crisis to investigate how the administration is utilizing emergency funding in response to the virus. Lawmakers in the House and Senate have introduced multiple measures to create a commission to document the federal government's response as the basis for potential legislation, similar to the congressional commission that investigated the Sept. 11, 2001, terrorist attacks.

The White House and Republican leaders in the House and Senate have not embraced a 9/11-style commission, and one is unlikely to emerge before November, according to Rep. Crow. "I'm not optimistic [a commission] will happen before the election," he said. "It's become . . . close to impossible to negotiate with this White House."[49] Rep. Jim Jordan, R-Ohio, ranking member of the House Oversight and Reform Committee, said the idea of setting up a 9/11-style panel was an "attack" on Trump's efforts to respond to the pandemic.[50]

As many American children and young adults return to school and college this month, either in person or online, it is unclear when students, parents and teachers will see a return to normal educational activities.

Trump continues to say his administration's response is going well, the federal government is making "tremendous progress" in research on a COVID-19 vaccine and treatments that will be ready "very soon."[51]

Health experts are more cautious than Trump about a vaccine. Though one is possible by early 2021, it likely will be available initially only to health care workers and individuals with higher risk of developing severe symptoms from COVID-19, according to Dr. Anthony Fauci, the head of the National Institute of Allergy and Infectious Diseases at the National Institutes of Health.[52]

In eyeing the future, Trump is focusing on the U.S. relationship with the World Health Organization and America's role in global health leadership. On July 6, Trump notified the WHO that the United States would formally withdraw from the organization and would allocate its $237 million in fees to other global health organizations. In September, he also said the United States would not join a global effort to speed up the development and deployment of a COVID-19 vaccine because the WHO is part of the effort.[53]

Global health experts say this go-it-alone strategy could make the United States less safe. The WHO has a global infectious disease surveillance network and is the primary mechanism for countries to work through an international public health emergency. Further, they say, by withdrawing from the organization, the United States risks ceding influence to China and other countries on future global health policies.

"I don't think the United States can be fully prepared for future outbreaks without being a part of the WHO," says Beth Cameron, vice president for global biological policy and programs at the Nuclear Threat Initiative, a group that works to strengthen global security.

OUTLOOK
Making the Connection

Many public health leaders hope Americans will embrace the need to improve the nation's pandemic preparedness and push Congress to make changes. They say that people who lose a relative or a job because of COVID-19 gain a personal, real-world understanding of the critical role of pandemic readiness.

"If you have never really seen widespread disease before, and you don't see people dying around you," it is harder to make changes in behavior aimed at disease prevention, says Rebecca Katz, director of the Center for Global Health Science and Security at Georgetown University Medical Center. "Once you have lived through something, then you are finally able to make the connections."

As of Aug. 30, 58.1 percent of Americans disapproved of President Trump's handling of the coronavirus, and 38.9 percent approved, a stark shift from Feb. 29, when 38 percent disapproved and 47.2 percent approved, according to the average of polls analyzed by FiveThirtyEight, a website that focuses on political polls and analyses.[54]

Democratic presidential nominee Biden has said that, if elected, he will implement many of the same recommendations that Alexander is promoting in the Senate, such as investing in a larger public health workforce.[55] Trump, meanwhile, maintains his administration's response has been "historic" and pledges he will make the United States safer by pressuring China to be more forthcoming about future brewing pandemic threats and by pressuring U.S. regulators to make therapeutics and a vaccine available before the November election.[56]

The election will be held just as the annual influenza season gets underway. Public health officials worry about the additional strain on the health care system from both diseases, so the CDC plans to push health providers and community leaders to promote the flu shot—another test of the country's ability to handle an infectious disease outbreak. Traditionally, about half of the U.S. population gets a flu shot, and about half a million Americans get sick enough from the flu to need hospitalization.

A group of nongovernmental organizations, led by the Rockefeller Foundation, has formed a coalition to create a nationalized COVID-19 testing system that would provide 30 million tests a week by this fall—up from the 5.5 million during the summer.[57]

Meanwhile, it is uncertain when and whether a COVID-19 vaccine will be approved. While Fauci says he is "cautiously optimistic" a vaccine will be available by early 2021, he also has said that there is no guarantee one will exist.[58]

Even if a vaccine is widely available, many public health experts worry that some Americans will not get one because a small but growing number of Americans are skeptical about vaccine safety in general. Many of the skeptics do not vaccinate their children for diseases such as measles and mumps, which led in 2019 to one of the largest U.S. measles outbreaks in decades.[59]

Now, with people dividing along political lines over pandemic response, there are questions about whether even more Americans will be afraid to trust the safety of vaccines, including one for COVID-19.

"If politicians get involved in vaccine decision-making, that is going to be tainted, because everything that politicians have touched so far in this pandemic has been compromised by their involvement in it," said Adalja, the infectious disease expert at the Johns Hopkins University.[60]

NOTES

1. "Roundtable: Are We Prepared? Protecting the U.S. From Global Pandemics," U.S. Senate Committee on Homeland Security and Governmental Affairs, Feb. 12, 2020, https://tinyurl.com/y26qjw8j.

2. *Ibid.*

3. Michael O. Leavitt, "Written Testimony," Hearing on COVID-19 Lessons Learned to Prepare for the Next Pandemic, U.S. Senate Committee on Health, Education, Labor and Pensions, June 23, 2020, https://tinyurl.com/yya97kr6.

4. Megan Thielking and Helen Branswell, "CDC expects 'community spread' of coronavirus, as top official warns disruptions could be 'severe,'" *STAT News*, Feb. 25, 2020, https://tinyurl.com/yyq2f5dz.

5. "COVID-19 Dashboard by the Center for Systems Science and Engineering," Johns Hopkins University, accessed Sept. 2, 2020, https://tinyurl.com/rnjqnnh; "United States Population," Worldometer, Aug. 25, 2020, https://tinyurl.com/y3xk2mes.

6. "COVID-19: Forewarned but not Forearmed," Bipartisan Commission on Biodefense, May 8, 2020, https://tinyurl.com/y2nzluhy.

7. Katherine Eban, "How Jared Kushner's Secret Testing Plan 'Went Poof Into Thin Air,'" *Vanity Fair*, July 30, 2020, https://tinyurl.com/yyr7ppz9.

8. "Casey, Feinstein, Klobuchar introduce bill to establish 9/11 style coronavirus commission," press release, Office of Sen. Bob Casey, July 10, 2020, https://tinyurl.com/y38pxtrk.

9. Bob Yirka, "New swine flu strain found in China poses threat of pandemic," *Medical Xpress*, June 30, 2020, https://tinyurl.com/y92ppztk.

10. "COVID-19 and U.S. International Pandemic Preparedness, Prevention, and Response," Committee on Foreign Relations, U.S. Senate, June 18, 2020, https://tinyurl.com/yxw7jr8j.

11. Sarah Glazer, "Zoonotic Diseases," *CQ Researcher*, June 26, 2020, https://tinyurl.com/hzu8ejr.

12. Grace Segers, "Trump says coronavirus response is 'working out,'" *CBS News*, July 23, 2020, https://tinyurl.com/y5nky6be; Sam Baker, "Trump: Coronavirus is 'under control,'" *Axios*, Aug. 4, 2020, https://tinyurl.com/y46mp6rm; "Remarks by President Trump in Press Briefing," White House, July 30, 2020, https://tinyurl.com/y6g728er; and Robin Foster and E.J. Mundell, "New coronavirus cases and deaths spike across America," *U.S. News & World Report*, July 13, 2020, https://tinyurl.com/yde9xnh4.

13. Bethany Allen-Ebrahimian, "Timeline: the early days of China's coronavirus outbreak and cover-up," *Axios*, March 18, 2020, https://tinyurl.com/u2ep55d.

14. "Novel coronavirus—China," World Health Organization, Jan. 12, 2020, https://tinyurl.com/uvqqk9g.

15. Allen-Ebrahimian, *op. cit.*

16. Lai Shengjie *et al.*, "Effect of non-pharmaceutical interventions to contain Covid-19 in China," *Nature*, May 4, 2020, https://tinyurl.com/y6plozzx.

17. Trump says 'China-centric' WHO 'really blew it' on coronavirus," *Reuters*, April 7, 2020, https://tinyurl.com/y4l6gmkn.

18. Dareh Gregorian, "Trump says 'I don't agree' with CDC director's mask message," *NBC News*, July 17, 2020, https://tinyurl.com/y4bxmaq7; Eliza Relman, "Trump shares tweet that argues face masks represent 'silence, slavery and social death,'" *Business Insider*, May 28, 2020, https://tinyurl.com/yafv4m4a.

19. Tommy Beer, "Biden says he would use federal power to mandate mask-wearing," *Forbes*, June 26, 2020, https://tinyurl.com/y5k9c42s.

20. Toluse Olorunnipa, Josh Dawsey and Yasmeen Abutaleb, "With Trump leading the way, America's coronavirus failures exposed by record surge in new infections," *The Washington Post*, June 27, 2020, https://tinyurl.com/y8q7jpfs.

21. Stacey Knobler *et al.*, "The threat of pandemic influenza: Are we ready? Workshop Summary," National Academies, 2005, https://tinyurl.com/shtmglp.

22. "Roundtable: Are We Prepared? Protecting the U.S. From Global Pandemics," *op. cit.*

23. "Timeline: How the anthrax terror unfolded," *NPR*, Feb. 15, 2011, https://tinyurl.com/y5t847bg.

24. "SARS Basics Fact Sheet," Centers for Disease Control and Prevention, Dec. 6, 2017, https://tinyurl.com/yx5zcuee; "Tracking SARS back to its source," University of California, Berkeley, July 2013, https://tinyurl.com/y772hmnz.

25. Robert Roos, "Year-end review: Avian flu emerged as high-profile issue in 2005," Center for Infectious Disease Research and Policy, Jan. 6, 2006, https://tinyurl.com/y4yebngb.

26. "CDC estimates of 2009 H1N1 influenza cases, hospitalizations and deaths in the United States," Centers for Disease Control and Prevention, June 24, 2014, https://tinyurl.com/uh9wfrs; "2009 swine flu pandemic originated in Mexico, researchers discover," *Science Daily*, June 27, 2016, https://tinyurl.com/jxnnqea.

27. "Middle East respiratory syndrome coronavirus," World Health Organization, November 2019, https://tinyurl.com/vznns6d.

28. "2014-2016 Ebola outbreak in West Africa," Centers for Disease Control and Prevention, March 8, 2019, https://tinyurl.com/yyygynoe.

29. "Zika epidemiology update," World Health Organization, July 2019, https://tinyurl.com/y4ahstdb.

30. Bara Vaida, "Pandemic threat: Is the world prepared for the next outbreak?" *CQ Researcher*, June 2, 2017, https://tinyurl.com/y2nlyjex.

31. Dan Diamond, "Inside America's 2-Decade Failure to Prepare for Coronavirus," *Politico*, April 11, 2020, https://tinyurl.com/tqyl962.

32. Ken Dilanian, Dan De Luce and Andrew W. Lehren, "From Clinton to Trump, 20 years of boom and mostly bust in preparing for pandemics," *NBC News*, April 13, 2020, https://tinyurl.com/y3fokutn.

33. Diamond, *op. cit.*

34. Sen. Lamar Alexander, "Preparing for the Next Pandemic," Committee on Health, Education, Labor and Pensions, U.S. Senate, June 9, 2020, https://tinyurl.com/yb35an39.

35. David Himmelstein and Steffie Woolhandler, "Public health's falling share of US health spending," *American Journal of Public Health*, January 2016, https://tinyurl.com/y3t5ctu4.

36. "The Impact of Chronic Underfunding of America's Public Health System: Trends, Risks, and Recommendations, 2019," Trust for America's Health, https://tinyurl.com/y38rtorq; "A Funding Crisis for Public Health and Safety," Trust for America's Health, https://tinyurl.com/y6okaf23.

37. "COVID-19 Lessons Learned to Prepare for the Next Pandemic," Committee on Health, Education, Labor and Pensions, U.S. Senate, June 23, 2020, https://tinyurl.com/yya97kr6.

38. Ronald Klain and Syra Madad, "A program protecting us from a deadly pandemic is about to expire," *The Washington Post*, Dec. 27, 2019, https://tinyurl.com/uv67m68/.

39. Rick Berke, "Former Ebola czar Ron Klain on Zika, pandemics, and the right way to respond," *STAT News*, Feb. 18, 2018, https://tinyurl.com/y6aupgpw.

40. Diamond, *op. cit.*; "National Biodefense Strategy: Opportunities and challenges with early implementation," Government Accountability Office, March 11, 2020, https://tinyurl.com/y43mdcm4; and "Partly false claim: Trump fired entire pandemic response team in 2018," *Reuters*, March 25, 2020, https://tinyurl.com/uauverg.

41. Lazaro Gamio, "How coronavirus cases have risen since states reopened," *The New York Times*, July 9, 2020, https://tinyurl.com/yb2tb78c.

42. "COVID-19 Lessons Learned to Prepare for the Next Pandemic," *op. cit.*

43. Alexander, "Preparing for the Next Pandemic," *op. cit.*

44. Rep. Jason Crow, "COVID Complexities: Converging Threats, Fractured Resources," Bipartisan Commission on Biodefense, July 14, 2020, https://tinyurl.com/y27w5drq.

45. "COVID-19 and U.S. International Pandemic Preparedness, Prevention, and Response," Committee on Foreign Relations, U.S. Senate, June 18, 2020, https://tinyurl.com/yxw7jr8j.

46. Yueqi Yang, "Bill Gates Says U.S. Virus Testing Has 'Mind-Blowing' Problems," *Bloomberg*, Aug. 9, 2020, https://tinyurl.com/yy7covdo.

47. Global Health Security and Diplomacy Act of 2020, https://tinyurl.com/yyhwvcjx.

48. "Risch, Murphy, Cardin introduce comprehensive global health bill to prevent future pandemics," press release, U.S. Senate Committee on Foreign Relations, May 28, 2020, https://tinyurl.com/y6szzwqg.

49. Crow, *op. cit.*

50. Lauren Egan, "Support grows in the House for a 9/11-style commission on coronavirus response," *NBC News*, April 3, 2020, https://tinyurl.com/y5awnaam.

51. "President Trump is leading a once-in-a-generation effort to ensure Americans have access to a COVID-19 vaccine," White House, July 27, 2020, https://tinyurl.com/y5lh5tle.

52. Stephanie Soucheray, "Fauci: U.S. COVID-19 vaccine likely by early 2021," Center for Infectious Disease Research and Policy, July 31, 2020, https://tinyurl.com/y4sfp4w4.

53. Pien Huang, "Trump and WHO: How much does the US give? What's the impact of a halt in funding?" *NPR*, April 15, 2020, https://tinyurl.com/tcvtn4u; Emily Rauhala and Yasmeen Abutaleb, "US says it won't join WHO-linked effort to develop, distribute coronavirus vaccine," *The Washington Post*, Sept. 1, 2020, https://tinyurl.com/yy6etnw7.

54. Aaron Bycoffe, Christopher Groskopf and Dhrumil Mehta, "How Americans View the Coronavirus Crisis and Trump's Response," FiveThirtyEight, Aug. 30, 2020, https://tinyurl.com/u26suq4.

55. "Combat Coronavirus (COVID-19) and Prepare for Future Health Threats," JoeBiden.com, https://tinyurl.com/qmk5svq.

56. "President Trump's historic coronavirus response," press release, White House, Aug. 10, 2020, https://tinyurl.com/y2b8y6rp; Nick Paul Taylor, "Trump pushes for preelection fast-tracked approval of AstraZeneca of COVID-19 vaccine: report," Fiercebiotech.com, Aug. 24, 2020, https://tinyurl.com/y4edptrw.

57. Eban, *op. cit.*

58. Bob Fredericks, "Anthony Fauci: 'No guarantee,' coronavirus vaccine will be ready by early 2021," *New York Post*, June 30, 2020, https://tinyurl.com/ybcjnhvf.

59. Stephen Collinson and Caitlin Hu, "What if they make a Covid-19 vaccine but Americans refuse to take it?" *CNN*, July 17, 2020, https://tinyurl.com/y5zr4m3y.

60. Nathaniel Weixel, "Experts fear political pressure on Covid-19 vaccine," *The Hill*, Aug. 2, 2020, https://tinyurl.com/y43tkr6n.

BIBLIOGRAPHY
Books

Barry, John, *The Great Influenza: The Epic Story of the Deadliest Plague in History*, Penguin Books, 2004.
A journalist writes the definitive story of the 1918 Spanish flu outbreak.

Osterholm, Michael T., and Mark Olshaker, *Deadliest Enemy: Our War Against Killer Germs*, Little Brown & Co., 2017.
The founder of the University of Minnesota's Center for Infectious Disease Research and Policy (Osterholm) and author Olshaker recount the history of pandemics and outline policies the United States should adopt to plan for them.

Troy, Tevi, *Shall We Wake the President? Two Centuries of Disaster Management From the Oval Office*, The Rowman & Littlefield Publishing Group, 2016.
A former U.S. Health and Human Services official and adviser to President George W. Bush provides an inside look at how the U.S. government plans for and responds to disasters.

Articles

Diamond, Dan, "Inside America's 2-Decade Failure to Prepare for Coronavirus," *Politico*, April 11, 2020, https://tinyurl.com/tqyl962.
A journalist describes the history of America's failure to sustain pandemic planning.

Fallows, James, "The 3 Weeks That Changed Everything," *The Atlantic*, June 29, 2020, https://tinyurl.com/ybzp59xs.
A journalist imagines how the United States could have better responded to the coronavirus pandemic.

McKenna, Maryn, "Covid Is Bad. But It May Not Be The 'Big One,'" *Wired*, June 17, 2020, https://tinyurl.com/yb6by4la.
A pandemic planning expert says another pathogen even worse than the coronavirus could be around the corner.

Osterholm, Michael T., and Mark Olshaker, "Chronicle of a Pandemic Foretold: Learning From the COVID-19 Failure—Before the Next Outbreak Arrives," *Foreign Affairs*, July/August 2020, https://tinyurl.com/yb9pr2xm.
The authors argue that, instead of relying on the private sector to ramp up production after an infectious disease outbreak, the government should treat the threat of such outbreaks as potential enemy combatants, establishing a military-style government procurement and production program with long-term funding to supply critical supplies, vaccines and treatments.

Quammen, David, "Why Weren't We Ready for The Coronavirus?" *The New Yorker*, May 4, 2020, https://tinyurl.com/yddo3mps.
A journalist who has worked on global health threats explains how the United States bungled its response to the coronavirus.

Yong, Ed, "How the Pandemic Will End," *The Atlantic*, March 25, 2020, https://tinyurl.com/ujqg3ze.
A journalist explains that the U.S. government's failed response to the coronavirus pandemic means the country must act quickly to rapidly supply health care workers with personal protective equipment, produce a massive number of COVID-10 tests and convince Americans to wear masks and practice social distancing.

Reports and Studies

Alexander, Lamar, "Preparing for the Next Pandemic: A White Paper," Senate Health, Education, Labor and Pensions Committee, 2020, https://tinyurl.com/yb35an39.
The Tennessee Republican who chairs the Senate Health, Education, Labor and Pensions Committee provides a history of modern U.S. pandemic planning and recommends how to stop the current pandemic and plan for the next one.

"Crimson Contagion 2019 Functional Exercise Key Findings," Office of the Assistant Secretary for Preparedness and Response, U.S. Department of Health of Health and Human Services, October 2019, https://tinyurl.com/qlhou26.
The New York Times posted this draft summary of an exercise from last fall that demonstrated holes in the U.S. government's pandemic preparedness plan.

Morrison, J. Stephen, Kelly Ayotte and Julie Gerberding, "Ending the Cycle of Crisis and Complacency in U.S. Global Health Security: A Report of the CSIS Commission on Strengthening America's Health Security," Center for Strategic and International Studies, November 2019, https://tinyurl.com/yxuj7odj.
A Washington think tank urges Congress and the federal government to plug holes in U.S. pandemic preparedness plans and boost funding for such programs.

"National Biodefense Strategy," Executive Office of the President of the United States, 2018, https://tinyurl.com/yd8txucy.
The U.S. government provides its most recent strategy for investing in public health infrastructure and coordinating a national response to a potential biological event, such as a pandemic.

"Playbook for early response to high-consequence emerging infectious disease threats and biological incidents," Executive Office of the President of the United States, 2017, https://tinyurl.com/y9rmjev6.
Outgoing President Barack Obama left this plan for dealing with pandemics for President Trump.

THE NEXT STEP
Administration Action

Bredemeier, Ken, "Trump Criticizes White House Coronavirus Adviser," *Voice of America*, Aug. 3, 2020, https://tinyurl.com/y5erhsd8.
President Trump tweeted criticism of a leading doctor on the White House coronavirus task force after she warned rural Americans about a rising numbers of cases.

Lemire, Jonathan, and Mike Stobbe, "Trump announces plasma treatment authorized for COVID-19," *The Associated Press*, Aug. 23, 2020, https://tinyurl.com/y52r6vva.
The White House authorized doctors to treat COVID-19 patients with convalescent plasma from patients who survived infection with the virus, but some scientists say questions remain about the treatment's effectiveness.

Lopez, German, "Trump asked for fewer COVID-19 tests. Now the CDC is recommending less testing," *Vox*, Aug. 26, 2020, https://tinyurl.com/y5g4lh5c.
The Centers for Disease Control and Prevention has stopped recommending a COVID-19 test for everyone who has been in close contact with an infected person.

Congressional Proposals

Brufke, JulieGrace, "GOP lawmaker introduces bill clamping down on hospital consolidation," *The Hill*, Aug. 26, 2020, https://tinyurl.com/y64b4lao.
Hoping to prevent the growth of monopolies profiting from the COVID-19 pandemic, an Indiana congressman introduced a bill to prevent hospitals from consolidating and raising prices.

Lambert, Lance, and Anne Sraders, "'There's going to be a selloff in the stock market' if Congress doesn't pass more stimulus," *Fortune*, Aug. 23, 2020, https://tinyurl.com/yxefr7qn.

Although Congress and the White House may feel less pressure to pass additional COVID-19 relief legislation because the stock market is doing well, economists warn that investors assume such a bill will be enacted and that not passing one could trigger a major stock sell-off.

North, Anna, "Elizabeth Warren calls for investigation into Trump's politicization of Covid-19," *Vox*, Aug. 26, 2020, https://tinyurl.com/y6r2ycma.

Democratic senators want to investigate whether the White House made major decisions about the nation's response to the COVID-19 pandemic based on political and partisan considerations.

International Response

"Covid-19: South Korea closes Seoul schools amid rise in cases," *BBC*, Aug. 25, 2020, https://tinyurl.com/y3t44wkk.

Schools closed in the South Korean capital as coronavirus cases spiked, but businesses remained open.

Lovelace, Berkeley, Jr. "WHO warns coronavirus vaccine alone won't end pandemic: 'We cannot go back to the way things were,'" *CNBC*, Aug. 21, 2020, https://tinyurl.com/y2sbowfx.

The World Health Organization told global leaders that countries will need to continue to test, trace and isolate potential COVID-19 cases, even after a vaccine has been developed.

Schmitz, Rob, "Germany Bans Prostitution During Pandemic. Sex Workers Say That Creates New Dangers," *NPR*, Aug. 26, 2020, https://tinyurl.com/yyv7bz2a.

Germany's ban on prostitution to limit the spread of the coronavirus remained in effect even after other parts of the economy reopened.

Vaccine

Bomey, Nathan, "Should employers force workers to get COVID-19 vaccine? Some experts say they should," *USA Today*, Aug. 26, 2020, https://tinyurl.com/y5weyueg.

Legal experts say companies can, and potentially should, require employees to receive a coronavirus vaccine when one becomes available.

Forgey, Quint, "'Nation of miracles': Pence pledges coronavirus vaccine by year's end," *Politico*, Aug. 27, 2020, https://tinyurl.com/y2ngf32j.

Vice President Mike Pence said the United States would produce the first effective and safe coronavirus vaccine in the world by the end of the year.

Lovelace, Berkeley, Jr. "Moderna says its coronavirus vaccine shows promising results in small trial of elderly patients," *CNBC*, Aug. 26, 2020, https://tinyurl.com/y5cpbcd2.

The pharmaceutical company Moderna says early trials of its COVID-19 vaccine have produced neutralizing antibodies in elderly adults, a group at higher risk of severe illness.

For More Information

Association of State and Territorial Health Officials, 2231 Crystal Drive, Suite 450, Arlington, VA 22202; 202-371-9090; astho.org. Represents public health agencies and professionals.

Center for Global Health Science and Security, Georgetown University Medical Center, 3900 Reservoir Rd., N.W., Washington, DC 20007; 202-687-9823; ghss.georgetown.edu. Works with policy leaders worldwide on global health security.

Center for Health Security, Johns Hopkins Bloomberg School of Public Health, 621 East Pratt St., Suite 210, Baltimore, MD 21202; centerforhealthsecurity.org. Works to help governments around the world prevent and respond to epidemics and health disasters.

Center for Infectious Disease Research and Policy, University of Minnesota, Academic Medical Center, 420 Delaware St., S.E. MMC 263, C315 Mayo, Minneapolis, MN 55455; 612-626-6770; cidrap.umn.edu. Provides research and news on infectious disease outbreaks and recommendations for policy responses.

Centers for Disease Control and Prevention, National Center for Emerging and Zoonotic Infectious Diseases, 1600 Clifton Rd., Atlanta, GA 30329; 800-232-4636; cdc.gov/ncezid. Lead federal agency for protecting and responding to U.S. health threats, including pandemics.

Infectious Diseases Society of America, 4040 Wilson Blvd., Suite 300, Arlington, VA 22203; 703-299-0200; idsociety.org. Organization for professionals specializing in infectious diseases.

Trust for America's Health, 1730 M St., N.W., Suite 900, Washington DC 20036; 202-223-9870; tfah.org. Public health advocacy group that issues reports on infectious disease outbreaks and other health issues.

4

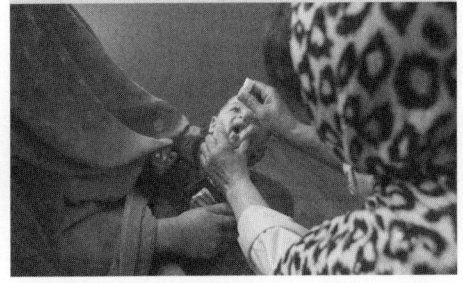

An Afghan child receives a polio vaccine at a USAID-funded clinic in 2011. Congress largely rebuffed the Trump administration's efforts to cut foreign aid, but COVID-19 may profoundly affect foreign assistance funding. (Getty Images/John Moore)

From *CQ Researcher*,
April 23, 2021

U.S. Foreign Aid

Will funding increase and priorities change under Biden?

By Zarrín Caldwell

THE ISSUES

In a visit to the Department of State in February just two weeks after his inauguration, President Biden laid out the main themes of his foreign policy. He promised to reclaim lost U.S. "credibility and moral authority," rebuild "alliances that have atrophied" and "catalyze global action on shared challenges."[1]

A key tool in pursuing these objectives will be international development aid. Biden has long supported such assistance and the U.S. Agency for International Development (USAID), which administers a significant chunk of it.[2] During his presidential campaign, Biden vowed to reprioritize development—along with defense, diplomacy and multilateral engagement—as core foreign policy themes.[3]

In his State Department appearance, Biden laid out a self-interested rationale for foreign aid. "When we invest in economic development of countries, we create new markets for our products and reduce the likelihood of instability, violence and mass migrations," he said.[4]

In an outline of his proposed budget for fiscal 2022, Biden requested a 12 percent increase in spending for international programs, including development aid.[5] His priorities include pandemic response, re-establishing U.S. leadership on climate change, countering China's and Russia's influence, advancing peace in the Middle East and fully funding United Nations peacekeeping responsibilities.[6]

U.S. Spends Proportionally Less on Aid Than Most OECD Countries

The United States spent the equivalent of 0.16 percent of its gross national income (GNI) on official development assistance in 2019, according to the Organisation for Economic Co-operation and Development (OECD). Of 29 OECD countries surveyed, only six spent less than the United States as a percentage of GNI.

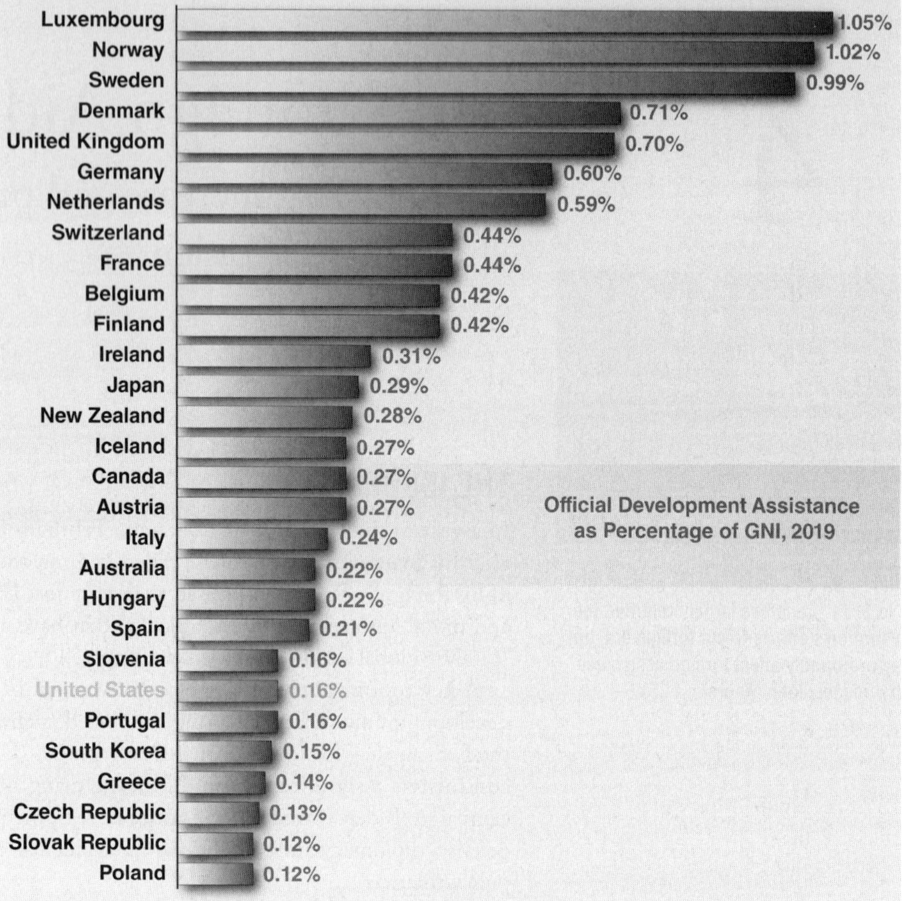

Official Development Assistance as Percentage of GNI, 2019

Country	%
Luxembourg	1.05%
Norway	1.02%
Sweden	0.99%
Denmark	0.71%
United Kingdom	0.70%
Germany	0.60%
Netherlands	0.59%
Switzerland	0.44%
France	0.44%
Belgium	0.42%
Finland	0.42%
Ireland	0.31%
Japan	0.29%
New Zealand	0.28%
Iceland	0.27%
Canada	0.27%
Austria	0.27%
Italy	0.24%
Australia	0.22%
Hungary	0.22%
Spain	0.21%
Slovenia	0.16%
United States	0.16%
Portugal	0.16%
South Korea	0.15%
Greece	0.14%
Czech Republic	0.13%
Slovak Republic	0.12%
Poland	0.12%

Source: "Aid by DAC members increases in 2019 with more aid to the poorest countries," Organisation for Economic Co-operation and Development, April 16, 2020, p. 7, https://tinyurl.com/2p4fnuut

Yet Biden will need to overcome many obstacles in pursuing his goals, despite his affinity for foreign affairs and personal relationships with many world leaders. For one thing, he faces significant challenges to American prosperity and cohesion following the disruptions to lives and livelihoods caused by the COVID-19 pandemic. That could make increased international aid a difficult sell in a divided Congress that is already being asked to authorize trillions of dollars in pandemic relief and infrastructure improvements, experts say.

The contrast between Biden's approach and that of former President Donald Trump could not be greater. Trump promoted an "America First" platform and sought to cut spending on foreign aid by about a third, vowing to send the money only to America's "friends."[7] However, Congress largely refused to go along, maintaining an average spending level of $46 billion per year from fiscal years 2018-2020 for military and economic aid, diplomatic initiatives and humanitarian assistance.[8]

International aid advocates called Trump's proposed cuts draconian and said they reflected a larger failure in his foreign policy: an absence of global leadership and a retreat from multilateral engagement.[9] "The reality is there has been a bipartisan consensus for a while that prioritizes U.S. leadership in the world on development, on humanitarian issues, and Trump has been an awful aberration from that," said Andrew Albertson, executive director of Foreign Policy for America, a group that advocates for principled American engagement in the world.[10]

Meanwhile, others have filled the void. China has invested billions in infrastructure projects globally, especially via its Belt and Road Initiative. Although China's investments are largely in the form of loans and do not reflect Western human rights and environmental standards, they still have offered an alternative development model.

U.S. allies and partners also stepped up during the Trump years. They continued to advance the United Nations' Sustainable Development Goals, 17 objectives adopted by U.N. members in 2015 that aim for a more sustainable future for people and the planet. These countries played a "great role in keeping the international spotlight on core development challenges in our absence," says Kristen Cordell, an adjunct fellow at the Center for Strategic and International Studies, a Washington think tank.

However, Trump's foreign aid record is more mixed than some of the criticisms would indicate. In 2018, his

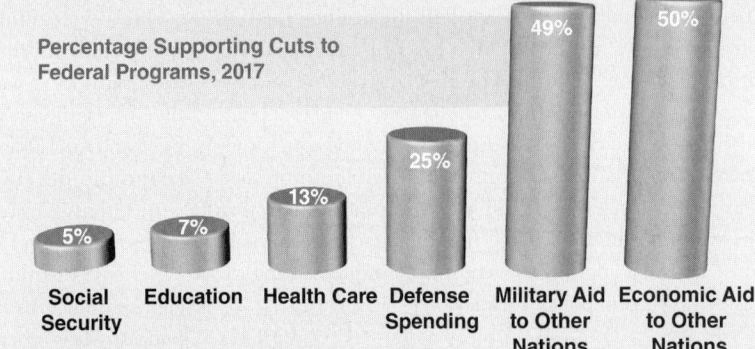

Most Favor Cuts to Foreign Aid

Fifty percent of American adults supported cutting economic aid to other nations in a 2017 survey by the Chicago Council on Global Affairs, and 49 percent backed reductions in military aid. Only 5 percent said Social Security should be cut.

Source: Lily Wojtowicz and Dina Hanania, "Americans Support Foreign Aid, but Oppose Paying for It," The Chicago Council on Global Affairs, November 2017, p. 2, https://tinyurl.com/9vt9jyjc

Mark Green, USAID's administrator during the Trump administration, won bipartisan praise for building partnerships and streamlining the agency's bureaucracy. After he left last year, critics alleged the White House appointed people to the agency who were not suited to its mission.

administration helped Congress create the U.S. International Development Finance Corporation, which aims to facilitate private investment in low- and middle-income countries. This new U.S. development bank—set up, in part, to compete with China—provides tools such as debt financing and investment funds. And in 2019 Trump signed the Global Fragility Act, which tasks select federal agencies with developing comprehensive, 10-year strategies to address violent conflict in fragile countries or regions.[11]

Mark Green, who served as USAID administrator from 2017 to 2020, won bipartisan praise for his largely successful efforts to build partnerships and streamline USAID's bureaucracy.[12] When he departed in April 2020, however, critics complained that the Trump White House and the State Department micromanaged the agency and that political appointees were slotted into positions for which they were unqualified. Media reports in 2020 left the impression of an agency in turmoil.[13] The Trump administration rejected such criticism, saying that the attacks were "malicious" and that appointees were simply implementing the president's foreign policy agenda.[14]

Supporters and Detractors

Looking at aid's moral underpinnings through the lens of the Cold War, David Lumsdaine, a professor of international affairs at Gordon College in Massachusetts, said these programs grew out of "an inclusive, humane internationalism, which . . . conceived of the world as an interdependent whole whose problems were the concern of all peoples."[15]

Under this vision, foreign aid has supported agricultural development, maternal and child health, vaccination campaigns, sanitation programs, education—especially for girls—and workforce development in developing countries.[16] It has also contributed to a significant decline in extreme poverty between 1990 and 2019, from 36 percent to 8 percent of the world's population.[17]

However, donor self-interest is also a big driver of foreign aid. "In the 21st century, we live in an incredibly interconnected world," said Samantha Power, the former U.S. ambassador to the U.N. who is Biden's nominee for USAID administrator. "As . . . we support the economic development of our partners around the world, that is an investment in our own security."[18]

Jessica Trisko Darden, a former fellow at the American Enterprise Institute, a Washington think tank, called foreign assistance an important foreign policy tool in a 2019 podcast. "It is inherently linked to the resources that diplomats at the State Department have at their disposal and the deals that can be cut," she said.[19]

Recent polls, such as one from Gallup in February 2019, show that almost 70 percent of Americans want the United States to play a strong role in world affairs.[20] But there are caveats. "When too many members of a society feel that their government is doing too little for its own people, when citizens feel left behind, any proclivity toward altruism becomes vulnerable to anxiety, anger, and a sense that there isn't enough to go around," two former aid officials, J. Alexander Thier and Douglas Alexander, wrote in 2019.[21]

A series of interviews on foreign affairs conducted by the Carnegie Endowment for International Peace in Nebraska—pre-COVID-19—showed that American families were, even then, anxious about maintaining a middle-class lifestyle. Interviewees still supported international trade and a pragmatic policy of bringing in foreign workers, but had concerns about meeting needs at home, and to whom and how international development aid was delivered.[22]

Most Americans think foreign aid expenditures are much larger

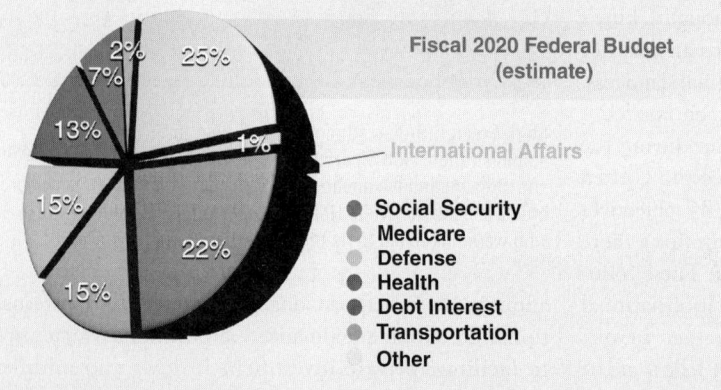

1 Percent of U.S. Budget Devoted to International Affairs

In fiscal 2020, only 1 percent of the federal budget was allocated to international affairs, which includes foreign aid and funding for the State Department and USAID. Social Security, at 22 percent, was the single largest component.

Source: "Department of State, Foreign Operations, and Related Programs: FY2021 Budget and Appropriations," Congressional Research Service, March 18, 2021, p. 2, https://tinyurl.com/2v972sxb

than they actually are. Estimates given to pollsters have ranged as high as 25 percent of the federal budget. In reality, it has hovered around 1 percent.[23]

Despite its small budgetary impact, there are frequent and intensely political battles in Washington over the level and distribution of foreign assistance. In his book *Why We Lie About Aid*, Pablo Yanguas, a research fellow at the University of Manchester in England, wrote that foreign aid has become a proxy for a much larger debate between "small-government conservatives and welfare-state progressives."[24]

Yanguas wrote that critics of foreign aid contend it does not work to address poverty, gets funneled into corruption and props up a self-serving bureaucracy. One such critic, economist William Easterly of New York University, argued that "expert approved" authoritarian approaches to development have not led to better lives for the poor, but, rather, to decades of human rights violations.[25]

Another critic, longtime development professional Thomas Dichter, asserts that aid systems are plagued by hubris. He argues that country ownership is key and the "whole notion of doing development for others is a ridiculous idea."

Who Benefits?

Analyzing the annual appropriations bill for the Department of State, Foreign Operations, and Related Programs (SFOPS) is the best way to understand the U.S. government's foreign assistance spending and priorities. Despite Trump's proposed cuts, spending for SFOPS from fiscal years 2018 to 2020 averaged about $46 billion per year.[26] In all of these years, around 70 percent of this spending went for economic aid and about 30 percent for military assistance.[27] Afghanistan, Israel, Jordan, Egypt and Iraq are among countries getting the most aid dollars—much of it via the Department of Defense.[28]

Many Americans—and American companies—benefit from aid contracts. A USAID report indicated that about 70 percent of the agency's $21 billion budget in 2020 was obligated in Washington, mostly on grants to consulting firms.[29] Putting Americans to work in this sector buttresses a small constituency for foreign aid and makes a case for funding, but it also raises questions about whom aid is really serving. (*See Pro/Con.*)

More than 20 federal agencies are involved in either funding or implementing foreign aid policy, according to James McBride, a deputy managing editor with the Council on Foreign Relations.[30] He added that this count does not include a plethora of other agencies such as the Millennium Challenge Corporation, which aims to develop more transparent and time-limited aid programs in which recipient countries must meet specific benchmarks, and the Peace Corps.

A "spaghetti chart" published by the Brookings Institution, a Washington think tank, in 2006 detailed that there were 48 pieces of legislation, 50 different objectives and 51 organizations involved in foreign assistance programs.[31] Fifteen years later, this is still "95 percent the same," says George Ingram, a senior fellow at Brookings' Center for Sustainable Development.

Ingram has called for giving USAID more independence and authority to ensure greater coherence in development policy. He said the current situation of uncoordinated and duplicative activities prevented the United States from presenting a unified position toward partner countries and in international forums, and also wasted valuable, scarce government human resources.[32]

Shock Waves

Foreign assistance and its development goals may be profoundly affected by COVID-19—not only by the pandemic's impact on global health systems, but also on battered economies. "The pandemic-induced recession threatens to throw decades of development into reverse and place hundreds of millions in desperate circumstances," said Stewart Patrick, a senior fellow at the Council on Foreign Relations.[33] This view is echoed by many international development professionals who have sounded alarms about what is coming.

"We're seeing the potential for a debt crisis among emerging economies and developing economies," said Secretary of State Antony Blinken during his Senate confirmation hearing in January. "We're seeing public health crises in country after country because COVID has made it more difficult to provide other health services. And we're seeing state fragility increase, not decrease, as a result of many of the challenges that COVID has exacerbated, or in some cases led to."³⁴

Debt distress is particularly serious, especially for lower-income countries. Public debt in developing nations swelled to more than 60 percent of gross domestic product last year because of lower economic growth and higher budget deficits, Reuters reported in April.³⁵

"Amid the COVID-19 pandemic, a growing number of poor countries are confronting an impossible fiscal choice between servicing greatly increased sovereign debt or spending more to protect the health, education, and livelihoods of their citizens," said Clemence Landers, a policy fellow at the Center for Global Development, a Washington think tank. She called for international action to avert defaults and what could be a "full-blown debt crisis" over the next few years.³⁶

While an influx of capital would help the debt situation, 2020 was a grim year for foreign direct investment; it fell by 42 percent, according to the U.N.'s Conference on Trade and Development.³⁷

In addition to economic shocks, a USAID report from August 2020 forecast "widespread increases in poverty, food and water insecurity, malnutrition, education gaps, other socioeconomic strains, and rising inequality" globally.³⁸ On hunger alone, David Beasley, executive director of the U.N.'s World Food Programme, indicated that acute food insecurity had doubled in 2020, from 135 million to 270 million people.³⁹

BACKGROUND
Cold War Origins

Foreign aid became a key part of U.S. foreign policy with the Marshall Plan in 1948. This effort pumped $12.5 billion into Western Europe to rebuild its economy after the devastation of World War II.⁴⁰ As the Cold War rivalry between the United States and the Soviet Union deepened in the late 1940s, President Harry Truman advocated providing political, military and economic assistance to "free peoples" in their "struggles against totalitarian regimes."⁴¹

President John F. Kennedy signed legislation in 1961 that created USAID and expanded programs to meet basic needs abroad, such as food, health care and education.⁴² Support for foreign aid dropped in the 1970s due, in part, to funding directed to military forces during the Vietnam War.⁴³

In the 1980s, President Ronald Reagan—as well as multilateral development banks—pushed aid recipients to adopt market-based reforms and "structural adjustment" policies. These approaches were mostly abandoned in the 1990s because of detrimental outcomes in many developing countries. Meanwhile, aid programs were coming under increased congressional scrutiny for alleged poor coordination and monitoring.

The Sept. 11, 2001, terrorist attacks were a turning point. Economic and military aid to countries, including Afghanistan, Pakistan and Iraq, was substantially increased. For example, aid to Afghanistan grew from $92 million in 2001 to a high of $13 billion in 2011. It was at $4.9 billion in 2019.⁴⁴

President George W. Bush holds a South African boy while his mother, who lives with AIDS, looks on during a 2007 White House event on the President's Emergency Plan for AIDS Relief (PEPFAR). The plan, created by the Bush administration, became one of the world's most successful health initiatives.

President George W. Bush's administration created the President's Emergency Plan for AIDS Relief (PEPFAR), which became one of the world's most successful health initiatives.[45] It also established the Millennium Challenge Corporation in 2004.[46]

Follow the Money

Although the U.S. provides more foreign assistance than any other country, it still ranks near the bottom of wealthy countries in the amount it provides as a percentage of its Gross National Product (GNP). "There is a broad international commitment that wealthy countries should provide annually 0.7 percent of GNP to assist poor countries," Brookings' Ingram wrote in 2019. "The average for all wealthy nations is around 0.3 percent. The U.S. ranks near the bottom at below 0.2 percent."[47]

Nonetheless, spending on U.S. foreign assistance has increased substantially over the past 20 years. According to USAID's Foreign Aid Explorer database, disbursements rose from $15 billion in fiscal 2001 to $45 billion in fiscal 2019, the last year for which all data were fully reported.[48]

These figures do not include so-called Overseas Contingency Operations, (OCO), which are not subject to discretionary budget limits and have largely supported temporary needs in conflict zones.[49] This spending—which is separate from a similar Defense Department program—peaked at more than $20 billion in fiscal 2017 and has been around $8 billion the last few years.[50] Some consider this money a safety valve for emergencies; others, such as Mick Mulvaney, acting White House chief of staff in the Trump administration, called it a "slush fund."[51]

Excluding security sector spending, USAID has been getting about 45 percent of U.S. foreign assistance dollars, or around $21 billion annually. "Since 2015, USAID's overall level of funding and percentage of the foreign assistance budget has remained relatively consistent," Pooja Jhunjhunwala, acting spokesperson, says. She adds that, over the past 15 years, 30 percent of USAID's programmatic budget has gone to global health.

Global health is, in fact, a core of USAID's work. The agency has been at the forefront of preventing child and maternal deaths, fighting infectious diseases such as malaria and tuberculosis and controlling the HIV/AIDS epidemic.[52]

Evaluation Reconsidered

USAID came under increased scrutiny in the 1990s for perceived lapses in monitoring and evaluating its programs.[53] There were calls in Congress to restructure or abolish the agency. Similar reform efforts have been ongoing ever since, particularly a push to move to measuring project results.

Former USAID Administrator J. Brian Atwood, who served under President Bill Clinton from 1993 to 1999, has argued that there has been an evolution in the approach to development assistance. He said it has become centered on separating aid from the financial interests of the donor, ensuring that aid is not creating dependency and focusing on local ownership and self-reliance.[54]

In line with this approach, Rajiv Shah, the agency's administrator from 2010 to 2015, launched the USAID Forward program. It aimed to "increase competition, expand its partner base and honor the U.S. government's aid effectiveness commitments to promote country ownership," says Jhunjhunwala. She adds that while the target at the time was to send 30 percent of funds to local actors, it never met that goal, reaching a peak of 18.6 percent in fiscal year 2015.

The Trump administration promoted similar principles. USAID'S Journey to Self-Reliance program, launched in 2017, aimed to support partners to lead their own development and, ultimately, to end the need for foreign assistance. Critics of this approach, such as Matthew Kavanagh, an assistant professor of global health at Georgetown University, said it failed to address inherent global inequities.[55] Others, such as policy researchers Sarah Rose and Erin Collinson at the Center for Global Development, acknowledged that it "found resonance both with some aid skeptics (at least to a degree) and aid advocates, with the latter keen to see USAID focus on building local capacity and getting results."[56]

CHRONOLOGY

1940s-1960s *As Cold War competition with the Soviets intensifies, U.S. international aid also grows.*

1948 With Europe devastated after World War II and divided into Western and Soviet blocs, the United States commits more than $12 billion under the Marshall Plan to help rebuild the continent.

1961 President John F. Kennedy signs the Foreign Assistance Act, which creates the U.S. Agency for International Development (USAID). . . . As Cuban leader Fidel Castro embraces Moscow, Kennedy initiates the Alliance for Progress, which aims to solidify U.S.-Latin American economic cooperation.

1980s *Reagan administration expands aid budget but focuses on military assistance and market-oriented approaches.*

1981 President Ronald Reagan announces the Task Force on Private Sector Initiatives, an aid program that aims to boost private enterprise in developing countries.

1984 Reagan administration halts aid to overseas health providers who discuss or provide abortions as an option in family planning, a provision that will be rescinded and then re-attached to U.S. aid by successive administrations.

1989 USAID focuses on helping to establish functioning democracies in Eastern Europe after the fall of the Berlin Wall.

1990s *Aid programs grow at government agencies and external partners as critics call for better evaluation of their effectiveness.*

1993 USAID Administrator J. Brian Atwood pushes for reforms and focuses on sustainable development, but faces a hostile Congress.

1995 Republican Sen. Jesse Helms of North Carolina, the Foreign Relations Committee chair, calls for the abolition of USAID, citing what he calls a bloated bureaucracy and money going to corrupt dictators.

1997 USAID remains in existence but must report to the U.S. Secretary of State.

2000-2006 *Foreign aid budgets increase substantially, focusing on programs related to anti-terrorism and global health initiatives.*

2003 President George W. Bush establishes the President's Emergency Plan For AIDS Relief (PEPFAR) to address the global HIV/AIDS epidemic.

2004 Congress creates the Millennium Challenge Corp., an independent federal agency that awards aid grants to developing countries that meet certain economic and political criteria.

2006 Secretary of State Condoleezza Rice establishes the Office of Foreign Assistance Resources within the State Department.

2010-Present *Obama administration builds on global health, climate change and nutritional programs, but Trump administration calls for significant cuts.*

2010 Secretary of State Hillary Clinton releases the first Quadrennial Diplomacy and Development Review, which outlines strategic priorities for USAID and the State Department. . . . Rajiv Shah, a physician and health economist, takes the helm as USAID administrator and focuses on a "USAID Forward" agenda, which aims for country-specific development strategies and more local ownership. . . . USAID establishes a Bureau for Policy, Planning and Learning in an effort to ground the agency's work in evidence and innovation.

2016 Congress passes the Foreign Aid Transparency and Accountability Act, which requires stronger monitoring and reporting of foreign aid's effectiveness.

2017 Trump administration releases executive order for all agencies to submit reorganization plans and proposes to cut USAID's budget by about a third, but Congress does not approve the cuts. . . . USAID Administrator Mark Green wins bipartisan support for streamlining USAID's bureaucracy.

2018 The federal government creates the U.S. International Development Finance Corp., which aims to facilitate investment in private sector projects in low- and middle-income countries.

2019 The Global Fragility Act, which requires 10-year coordinated government strategies for work in fragile states, is enacted.

2020-2021 The U.S. commits more than $17 billion in emergency funding to the global COVID-19 response.

2021 Incoming President Biden nominates Samantha Power to be the next USAID administrator (January). . . . Biden releases preliminary budget for fiscal 2022 requesting a 12 percent increase for the State Department and other international programs (April).

CURRENT SITUATION
The Next Cheerleader

Given Biden's competing priorities, most of the heavy lifting on development will likely fall to the USAID administrator. Biden has elevated this role to a seat on the National Security Council, which development professionals believe will give it more status.

Biden's nominee for this post, Power, was cleared for the role by a unanimous vote of the Senate Foreign Relations Committee on April 15. She comes to USAID with significant international experience and a record of advocacy on human rights issues. In addition to serving as Obama's U.N. ambassador, she has held high-level positions with the White House's National Security Council and at Harvard University.[57]

Development professionals have largely lauded Power's nomination and the stature it is expected to bring to USAID. But some have expressed concerns—usually not publicly—that she is too partisan politically and has little experience in either international development or in managing a large bureaucracy.[58] In her role at the U.N., she managed a staff of around 150.[59] USAID has a staff of nearly 10,000.[60]

In a statement submitted to the Senate Foreign Relations Committee prior to her March confirmation hearing, Power promised to work with lawmakers "on both sides of the aisle to ensure that taxpayer dollars are well spent. Guided by evidence, I will work with you to adapt or replace programs that are not delivering."[61]

Rose at the Center for Global Development says the next USAID administrator will need to be a "high level champion" of promoting an evidence-based agenda, especially when there are increasing needs due

Samantha Power, President Biden's nominee to head USAID, testifies at her Senate confirmation hearing on March 23, 2021. Power brings significant foreign policy experience to the job, but critics worry she is too partisan, has little background in international development and has never run a large bureaucracy.

to the pandemic and fewer resources. "It is imperative that aid money be effective in actually trying to alleviate some of this burden on global well-being," she says.

Aid in a Time of COVID

Besides restoring the U.S. relationship with the World Health Organization, Biden wants the United States to take a global lead in response to the COVID-19 crisis.[62] That will make the pandemic a top priority for the incoming USAID administrator.

Direct-Payment Aid Programs Attract Interest

"In this model, social protection is seen as a right."

Aid programs offering direct cash payments to the poor have assumed greater prominence over the past 25 years. There have been some successful programs, and some criticisms. CQ Researcher *freelance correspondent Zarrín Caldwell interviewed Sudhanshu Handa, a public policy professor at the University of North Carolina, Chapel Hill, who has evaluated several of these programs globally, to get his insights. The transcript has been edited for length and clarity.*

CQ Researcher: What are some of the main rationales behind these programs?

Handa: Distributing cash is an extremely low-cost thing to do in terms of development aid. Give Directly [a nonprofit working in this space] claims that they are able to distribute 90 cents for every dollar that is donated to them, for example. The overhead on heavy interventions that provide training or give people a suite of goods, like USAID provides, is around 30 to 40 percent. Cash transfers are very efficient in the administrative sense, and much cheaper than many other development programs.

CQR: When did the cash transfer concept start and why?

Handa: Mexico, Brazil and South Africa started giving cash on a large scale to poor citizens in, roughly, the mid-1990s. That really got people thinking and changed the mindset about the relationship between the state and citizens. The fact that these countries did it themselves—and paid for it themselves—was really influential. It wasn't about the World Bank or USAID lending money; it was the governments themselves financing these programs, which in turn influenced other countries.

CQR: What are some of the differences between conditional and unconditional cash transfers?

Handa: In Latin America, most of the large government programs—like the successful Bolsa Família program in Brazil—are almost all conditional. That means that parents, to get the cash, need to send their kids to school, they have to follow preventive health checkups, etc. In most of the rest of the world, the cash transfer programs run by governments are unconditional.

Significant U.S. "emergency" funding—above and beyond base funding for the foreign affairs account—has been devoted to the global COVID response. Money has gone to disease surveillance, infection prevention and strengthening laboratory systems in more than 100 countries.[63] The funding includes about $1.6 billion provided to the State Department and USAID last fall, another $4 billion to a program called Gavi, the Vaccine Alliance, to help get COVID-19 vaccines to poor countries, and an additional $10 billion in the $1.9 trillion COVID-19 relief bill that Biden signed in March.[64]

Kate Bernard, communications director at the U.S. Global Leadership Coalition, an advocacy group for foreign affairs budgets, says $17.46 billion of emergency funding for the 2020 and 2021 fiscal years has been committed to the international pandemic response. But even these amounts "do not begin to address the longer-term consequences of the pandemic that are essential for global economic recovery," said Kristin Lord, CEO of a development non-profit, and Ann Mei Chang, a fellow at Brookings.[65]

On the vaccine front, World Health Organization Director General Tedros Adhanom Ghebreyesus reported in late February that more than 210 million doses of COVID-19 vaccine had been administered

CQR: What is the justification for offering money with no strings attached?

Handa: In this model, social protection is seen as a right. It's the idea that everyone has a right to a minimum standard of living. Fundamentally, it's for the poorest and most vulnerable in a society. These families face severe food insecurity, cannot even send their kids to school, etc. Studies in Latin America show that the most vulnerable end up being excluded when there are conditions attached to cash transfers because the beneficiaries don't live near schools, health centers, etc.

CQR: Where have cash transfers worked successfully and why?

Handa: In addition to the Brazilian program—and a program called Progresa in Mexico—South Africa is a really fantastic case study. After apartheid, the government made a huge push to reduce inequality by ensuring there was a strong social safety net. They have a very sophisticated grants program for pensioners, the disabled and children. It's one of the most advanced social protection systems in the developing world. Their Child Support Grant reaches over 10 million children.

CQR: What are some of the main criticisms of cash transfers?

Handa: One of the benefits of cash transfers is that it allows people to choose and use the cash in a way that best fulfills their needs. The criticism is that people may waste the money, or spend it on alcohol. There is no evidence to support this, however, since the poor don't waste much. There is also the critique that handouts are far less useful than training. But the conditions of the poor in some of these developing countries are so onerous that they need help just to survive. The potential corruption of cash, and the fiduciary risk [the risk of improper use], is another criticism. Like all development programs, there is leakage, but less than in other programs because the level of scrutiny is so high, and systems like electronic payments can minimize fraud.

CQR: Are cash transfers providing short-term relief over long-term solutions?

Handa: Basic needs—related to food security for example—are fulfilled almost immediately. Second-order effects depend on context, like increased school attendance or buying livestock and fertilizer. But these programs don't leapfrog people into the middle class. There is often confusion about the objectives of cash transfers. It's not a productive investment to permanently boost everyone out of poverty. There are other educational and job training programs to do that.

Cash transfers will never be a substitute for a good road, piped water or a nice health facility. But people have genuine needs. They may not even be able to get to a health center, or need children to work rather than attend school. Cash can alleviate these basic constraints. Once people have a basic ability to survive and participate, then you can think about training.

---

globally, but that more than 80 percent of this had occurred in only 10 countries.[66]

He also called it "a catastrophic moral failure" that rich countries were funneling millions of vaccines to their own populations—often to young, healthy people—when vulnerable people in poor countries had received almost none.[67]

By early April, more than 38 million doses of vaccines had been delivered to 100 mostly lower-income economies, according to the World Health Organization.[68] Still, there is a "stark gap between vaccination programs in different countries, with many yet to report a single dose," wrote reporter Josh Holder in *The New York Times*.[69]

But money still seems to be flowing. According to a chart compiled by Devex, a media and business platform for the development community, more than $21 trillion in multi-year contracts are available for COVID-19 projects worldwide via governments, multilateral institutions, development banks, foundations and nonprofits.[70] Lisa Cornish, a reporter with Devex, says some of the proposed funds are going through multilateral channels, but "the largest part of government funding announcements are focused on their own domestic issues."

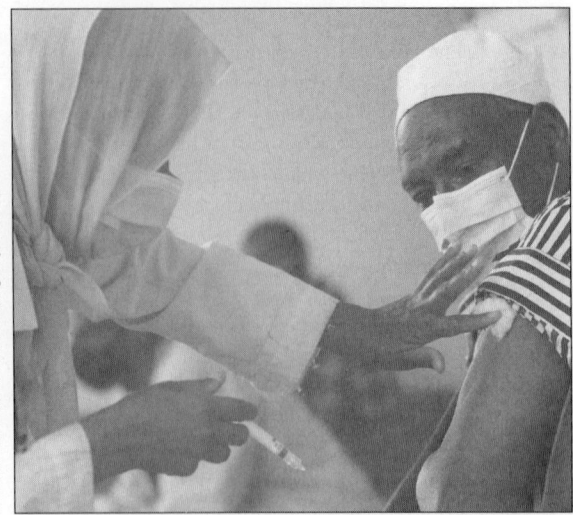

An Ethiopian man in Addis Ababa receives the AstraZeneca vaccine on April 14, 2021. The World Health Organization reported in late February that 210 million vaccine doses had been administered worldwide, with 80 percent going to people in 10 countries. By April more than 38 million doses had been delivered to 100 mostly lower-income economies.

Strategic Priorities Reconsidered

Given the urgent global health and humanitarian needs, it is unclear how much the next USAID administrator can, or will, focus on longer-term strategic planning.

The push and pull of short- versus long-term approaches is always present, says Dichter, the development professional. An anthropologist with more than 50 years of experience in development, he expresses disappointment that the field has been overtaken by "short-term quantification and non-results," a "blurring of lines" between humanitarian relief and long-term development and very little "hard thinking" on the latter. He says the "D" (for development) in USAID is gone and, because of COVID-19, "the chances of bringing that back anytime soon are pretty slim."

Author Yanguas voiced similar sentiments. "Aid has been forced to chase quick wins, instead of supporting the establishment of the kinds of sustainable institutions that underlie effective governments, free societies, and fair markets," he wrote.[71] Debates about aid, he said, are more about "value for money" and technical fixes than a larger and more fundamental discussion about the goals of development.

The growing prevalence of public-private partnerships has also changed the development debate, with some in the field arguing that they are a failed model.[72] Others, including Lord and Chang, make the case that international assistance money can be leveraged to draw in more private investors.[73]

Meanwhile, China has been gaining influence in development discourses. Both major U.S. political parties have pushed back against what they call China's authoritarian approach and disregard for human rights. Critics also say Chinese aid lacks transparency and leaves the recipient countries heavily indebted to China. Scott Morris, a senior fellow at the Center for Global Development, referenced China's $350 billion of outstanding claims on developing country governments, largely for infrastructure projects, as of December.[74]

"Countering China is the most critical national security effort of our day, and USAID has a pivotal role in addressing this challenge," said Bonnie Glick, a senior adviser at the Center for Strategic and International Studies. She pointed to existing USAID strategies that aim to counter China in digital, energy, infrastructure, governance and workforce development programs.[75]

U.S. policymakers view China with "deeper suspicion" and perceive an uneven economic playing field, added Morris. While he advised using the U.S. International Development Finance Corporation to better compete, he added that it is also a good time for the United States to cooperate with China to address a range of global challenges, such as pandemic preparedness and response, mitigating climate change and financial contributions to multilateral institutions.[76] It remains to be determined whether the Biden administration can walk these fine lines.

OUTLOOK
Funding Battles

Biden's fiscal 2022 budget request for a 12 percent increase for international programs would represent the largest boost in over a decade, according to the U.S. Global Leadership Coalition.[77]

Jason Gross, executive director of the coalition, says that these budgets have increased only slightly over the past few years despite growing needs. If Biden is to make good on his goal of reasserting U.S. leadership,

AT ISSUE

Will the Biden administration use international aid money effectively?

YES Lisa L. Peña
Director, Policy, Budget and Appropriations, InterAction

Written for *CQ Researcher*, April 2021

On the day of his swearing-in, President Biden had more experience in foreign affairs and diplomacy than any president in the 21st or 20th century. For 12 years, then-Sen. Biden served as the senior Democrat on the Senate Foreign Relations Committee, chairing the committee in 2001-03 and 2007-09. As vice president, he advised President Barack Obama on international issues and represented the United States in every region of the world.

Using his experience, President Biden has already started to build a robust platform to provide U.S. foreign assistance effectively and efficiently. He has nominated a talented team to lead the State Department and the U.S. Agency for International Development (USAID) and has taken critical early actions to elevate development and humanitarian programs.

In February, President Biden delivered remarks at the State Department, proclaiming, "America is back." He declared his commitment to countries' economic development, strengthening health systems around the world and defending equal rights of all people. As an early sign of keeping his promise of re-engaging with multilateral partners, the United States will provide $2 billion to the COVAX Facility, working to provide equitable access to a COVID-19 vaccine in developing countries.

Biden made clear his commitment to foreign assistance by nominating Samantha Power as USAID administrator in the first tier of nominations and elevating the position to the National Security Council. Power is a former U.S. ambassador to the United Nations and Cabinet member, with a long record on humanitarian issues, peacebuilding, and democracy. During her tenure as U.N. ambassador, Power was key in the creation of the sustainable development goals, defined by the United Nations as "the blueprint to achieve a better and more sustainable future for all." Her nomination sent a strong signal of the importance of development and humanitarian issues and granted the USAID administrator formal authority when crucial foreign policy decisions are made.

Antony Blinken, Biden's secretary of state, has worked in foreign affairs since 1994, serving with the Senate, the State Department and the White House. Serving as then-Vice President Biden's national security advisor and the Senate Foreign Relations Committee's staff director for six years, he has developed a close relationship with the president. Secretary Blinken's commitment to Biden's foreign policy vision was evident in a recent speech where he stressed the need to strengthen global health security and address the root causes of migration.

With experienced officials leading the charge, the Biden administration has committed to America stepping back into a global leadership position.

NO Matt Warner
President, Atlas Network

Written for *CQ Researcher*, April 2021

One consequence of President Donald Trump's infamous legacy is it threatens to lure us into thinking that a restoration of a pre-2016 status quo is progress. To wit, President Biden's first foreign policy speech since his inauguration can be summarized by his key message, "America is back." If getting foreign aid back to the way things used to be is the intention of this new administration, then we should not expect a sudden reversal in aid's efficacy.

In February the editorial board of *The New York Times* argued as much when it pointed out that our approach to making the world a better place is problematic. When donor countries use their wealth, privilege and value systems to design change for other people's communities, the result is too often disappointing—even harmful. It doesn't work.

As part of its promise to return to the way things used to be, the Biden administration is recommitting hundreds of millions of dollars to the usual suspects in the multilateral space, including the World Health Organization, the World Bank and the United Nations' International Fund for Agricultural Development. This, at a time when those organizations are reeling from the disruptions caused by the pandemic. The World Bank, in particular, is facing an existential crisis as it struggles to conduct its business with virtually no international travel.

Biden and his nominee to run USAID, Samantha Power, should take the opportunity this crisis has made ripe to accelerate a much-needed reimagining of donor country practices, not restore them to their previous state. The movement to "decolonize development" should compel all of us to reconsider the role of outsiders. It's a call for a principled fidelity to the human dignity—and practical utility—of self-determination. Outsider organizations can continue to gather and disseminate the latest data and research on development. Expertise and idea sharing are critical, but if we want to see donor country resources used effectively, we should defer to local vision for designing change.

In her 2019 memoir, *The Education of an Idealist*, Power reveals that her faith in America's paternalistic role in the world was tempered over time as she witnessed the complexities of foreign cultures. That's encouraging, and yet she also makes clear that she remains committed to outsider-led intervention.

Assuming she is confirmed, let's hope that Power, and Biden, will remain open to redefining America's role in the world so that our foreign aid tradition is not just "back," but better, too.

Gross says it will require "reversing the trend with meaningful funding increases across the entire account."

As for strategic planning, putting out fires may be more likely in the immediate term than any massive foreign aid overhauls. But if, and when, the next USAID administrator addresses the latter, development professionals are uncertain whether the administration should attempt a major restructuring or "just tinker around the margins" of existing reorganization efforts.[78]

In addition, aid agencies and organizations may have to confront larger questions in a world facing an onslaught of global challenges, including environmental ones. "As the effects of global warming worsen, human health, livelihood, food security, water supply, and economic growth will be jeopardized," Biden said during the campaign.[79]

USAID and other federal agencies have been doing some work to support international climate change resilience, but it has been "a relatively small portion of overall aid spending," says Rose from the Center for Global Development. That may change.[80]

Biden's discretionary budget request would provide $2.5 billion for international climate programs. In an executive order released on Jan. 27, Biden asked internationally focused federal agencies to detail how climate considerations could be integrated into their work.[81]

Whether that happens depends on the degree to which the final appropriations measure for foreign affairs reflects "the climate and, hopefully, broader environmental considerations," says Stewart of the Council on Foreign Relations. Either way, a more multilateral approach is likely, he says.

Power said as much during her confirmation hearing. "I will work every day to expand burden-sharing in the international system," she said, adding that the United States is "most powerful, effective, and efficient when it leverages the support that it offers . . . to get others to do more."[82]

NOTES

1. "Remarks by President Biden on America's Place in the World," The White House, Feb. 4, 2021, https://tinyurl.com/3mzsvnav.

2. "Remarks by Vice President Joseph Biden in Celebration of the 50th Anniversary of USAID," USAID, Nov. 4, 2011, https://tinyurl.com/35hcn6m9.

3. Michael Igoe, "Would Biden's foreign aid approach be progressive or bipartisan?" *Devex*, Nov. 2, 2020, https://tinyurl.com/jtvswcnu.

4. "Remarks by President Biden on America's Place in the World," *op. cit.*

5. "Recognizing Magnitude of Global Challenges, Budget Proposal Includes Critical Down Payment for International Affairs Needs," U.S. Global Leadership Coalition, April 9, 2021, https://tinyurl.com/yr72c4w.

6. "The President's FY2022 Discretionary Request," The White House, April 9, 2021, https://tinyurl.com/2hz926kj.

7. James McBride, "How Does the U.S. Spend Its Foreign Aid?" Council on Foreign Relations, Oct. 1, 2018, https://tinyurl.com/kv89ezsk.

8. Cory R. Gill, Marian L. Lawson and Emily M. Morgenstern, "Department of State, Foreign Operations, and Related Programs, FY2021 Budget and Appropriations," Congressional Research Service, March 18, 2021, https://tinyurl.com/2v972sxb.

9. Jennifer Rigby, Sarah Newey and Anne Gulland, "How Trump undermined US aid—but still spent billions in 'transactional' approach," *The Telegraph*, Oct. 31, 2020, https://tinyurl.com/59w2w2vb.

10. Igoe, *op. cit.*

11. Corinne Graff, *Addressing Fragility in a Global Pandemic: Elements of a Successful U.S. Strategy* (2020), https://tinyurl.com/jpbyuayj.

12. Robbie Gramer and Dan De Luce, "USAID Redesign Moves Forward, With No Drama," *Foreign Policy*, April 25, 2018, https://tinyurl.com/nc2sht5f.

13. Lara Jakes and Pranshu Verma, "At USAID, Juggling Political Priorities and Pandemic Response," *The New York Times*, Sept. 13, 2020, https://tinyurl.com/j5hky534.

14. "Statement from the Acting Administrator on Recent News Article Attacks on Political

Appointees," news release, USAID, June 8, 2020, https://tinyurl.com/3xcxh5cr.

15. David H. Lumsdaine, *Moral Vision in International Politics: The Foreign Aid Regime, 1949-1989* (1993).

16. J. Alexander Thier and Douglas Alexander, "How to Save Foreign Aid in the Age of Populism," *Foreign Policy*, Aug. 13, 2019, https://tinyurl.com/un52eevv.

17. George Ingram, "What every American should know about US Foreign Aid," The Brookings Institution, Oct. 15, 2019, https://tinyurl.com/2x357j3.

18. The White House, Twitter post, Jan. 13, 2021, https://tinyurl.com/weyr3x97.

19. Jessica Trisko Darden, "US foreign assistance policy with Jessica Trisko Darden," podcast, American Enterprise Institute, Dec. 19, 2019, https://tinyurl.com/5fv8r8v8.

20. V. Lance Tarrance, "Measuring the Fault Lines in Current U.S. Foreign Policy," Gallup, April 10, 2019, https://tinyurl.com/k7v7ds.

21. Thier and Alexander, *op. cit.*

22. Salman Ahmed, ed., "U.S. Foreign Policy for the Middle Class: Perspectives from Nebraska," University of Nebraska-Lincoln and Carnegie Endowment for International Peace, 2020, https://tinyurl.com/yxxz48zk.

23. Ingram, *op. cit.*

24. Pablo Yanguas, *Why We Lie About Aid: Development and the Messy Politics of Change* (2018).

25. William Easterly, *The Tyranny of Experts: Economists, Dictators, and the Forgotten Rights of the Poor* (2021).

26. Cory R. Gill, Marian L. Lawson and Emily M. Morgenstern, "Department of State, Foreign Operations, and Related Programs, FY2021 Budget and Appropriations," Congressional Research Service, March 18, 2021, https://tinyurl.com/2v972sxb.

27. "Foreign Aid Explorer," USAID, last updated Feb. 25, 2021, https://tinyurl.com/whc8tjk.

28. "Foreign Aid by Country: Who is Getting the Most—and How Much?" Concern Worldwide US, Jan. 2, 2021, https://tinyurl.com/8rcxse8r.

29. "Bureau for Management Office of Acquisition and Assistance Fiscal Year 2020 Progress Report," USAID, last updated March 1, 2021, https://tinyurl.com/uspc88tp.

30. McBride, *op. cit.*

31. Lael Brainard, "Security by Other Means," The Brookings Institution, 2006, https://tinyurl.com/scccj9c.

32. George Ingram, "Making USAID a premier development agency," The Brookings Institution, Feb. 17, 2021, https://tinyurl.com/r3jvr3pd.

33. Stewart Patrick, "Covid-19 Poses the Greatest Challenge Yet to the U.N. Humanitarian System," *World Politics Review*, Dec. 7, 2020, https://tinyurl.com/6p4brt3e.

34. Adva Saldinger, "What Antony Blinken's nomination hearing says about US foreign aid," *Devex*, Jan. 20, 2021, https://tinyurl.com/znty69tk.

35. Tom Arnold and Marc Jones, "Analysis: Poorest countries will follow a tricky path back to debt markets," *Reuters*, April 1, 2021, https://tinyurl.com/4tust6ht.

36. Clemence Landers, "A Plan to Address the Covid-19 Debt Crises in Poor Countries and Build a Better Sovereign Debt System," Center for Global Development, Dec. 3, 2020, https://tinyurl.com/7enscuhw.

37. "Global foreign direct investment fell by 42% in 2020, outlook remains weak," UNCTAD, Jan. 24, 2021, https://tinyurl.com/2c5bkbxs.

38. "Landscape Analysis: Over-the-Horizon Strategic Review," USAID, August 2020, https://tinyurl.com/tmfrkpr7.

39. "Amid Threat of Catastrophic Global Famine, Covid-19 Response Must Prioritize Food Security, Humanitarian Needs, Experts Tell General Assembly," United Nations, Dec. 4, 2020, https://tinyurl.com/2ysrc2bj.

40. Patrick Marshall, "Rethinking Foreign Aid," *CQ Researcher*, April 14, 2017, https://tinyurl.com/e7dv6enh.
41. "The Truman Doctrine, 1947," Office of the Historian, U.S. Department of State, https://tinyurl.com/2euv925d.
42. "USAID History," USAID, https://tinyurl.com/3admza4e.
43. Marshall, *op. cit.*
44. "Foreign Aid Explorer," *op. cit.*
45. David Pilling, "Why George W. Bush is Africa's favorite US President," *The Financial Times*, July 17, 2019, https://tinyurl.com/2a45mpz9.
46. Bradley Parks, "Where has the Millennium Challenge Corporation succeeded and failed to incentivize reform—and why?" The Brookings Institution, April 1, 2019, https://tinyurl.com/6u68vvb8.
47. Ingram, "What every American should know about U.S. foreign aid," *op. cit.*
48. "Foreign Aid Explorer," *op. cit.*
49. Emily M. Morgenstern, "Foreign Affairs Overseas Contingency Operations (OCO) Funding: Background and Current Status," Congressional Research Service, Feb. 10, 2021, https://tinyurl.com/5bn5u9nr.
50. Gill, Lawson and Morgenstern, *op. cit.*
51. Brendan W. McGarry and Emily M. Morgenstern, "Overseas Contingency Operations Funding: Background and Status," Congressional Research Service, Sept. 6, 2019, https://tinyurl.com/shr3y3w8.
52. "Global Health," USAID, last updated March 30, 2021, https://tinyurl.com/3beek8t2.
53. Marshall, *op. cit.*
54. J. Brian Atwood and Larry Garber, "USAID's policy voice should be heard," The Brookings Institution, Feb. 10, 2021, https://tinyurl.com/ys9e4abx.
55. Michael Igoe, "Q&A: Why 'self-reliance' is the wrong goal for US aid," *Devex*, June 17, 2019, https://tinyurl.com/4yr56apd.
56. Sarah Rose and Erin Collinson, "Mark Green's Legacy and Priorities for the Next USAID Administrator," Center for Global Development, April 10, 2020, https://tinyurl.com/5puum2xe.
57. "Samantha Power," Harvard Kennedy School, Harvard University, https://tinyurl.com/fuysbfk; "U.S. Senate committee backs Biden nominee Power to lead USAID," *Reuters*, April 15, 2021, https://tinyurl.com/j9y6bvut.
58. Michael Igoe and Adva Saldinger, "USAID officials prepare for higher-profile role under Samantha Power," *Devex*, Jan. 13, 2021, https://tinyurl.com/3w5a4fvw.
59. Samantha Power, *The Education of an Idealist: A Memoir* (2019).
60. "FY 2019 Agency Financial Report: Promoting a Path to Self-Reliance and Resilience," USAID, Nov. 19, 2019, https://tinyurl.com/5nd4fev7.
61. "Statement of Ambassador Samantha Power/Nominee To Be USAID Administrator/Senate Foreign Relations Committee," March 23, 2021, https://tinyurl.com/exw3643x.
62. "Fighting a Global Pandemic Requires a Global Response," U.S. Global Leadership Coalition, February 2021, https://tinyurl.com/s3knfner.
63. Kellie Moss, Stephanie Oum and Jennifer Kates, "U.S. Global Funding for Covid-19 by Country and Region," Kaiser Family Foundation, Oct. 23, 2020, https://tinyurl.com/yymc8z4h.
64. Gill, Lawson and Morgenstern, *op. cit.*
65. Kristin M. Lord and Ann Mei Chang, "The quiet revolution: What Congress should know about foreign assistance today," The Brookings Institution, Feb. 8, 2021, https://tinyurl.com/y6kac6rz.
66. "WHO Director-General's opening remarks at the Vaccines and Global Health Symposium," World Health Organization, Feb. 23, 2021, https://tinyurl.com/vxdxjeva; Moss, Oum and Kates, *op. cit.*; James Hacker, "US Congress Allocates $4b to Support Gave Vaccine Equity Plan," Health Policy Watch,

Dec. 12, 2020, https://tinyurl.com/4p66c4em; and Gill, Lawson and Morgenstern, *op. cit.*

67. "Covid vaccine: WHO warns of 'catastrophic moral failure,'" *BBC News*, Jan. 18, 2021, https://tinyurl.com/p36sxh3z.

68. "COVAX reaches over 100 economies, 42 days after first international delivery," World Health Organization, April 8, 2021, https://tinyurl.com/y5xmyy3d.

69. Josh Holder, "Tracking Coronavirus Vaccinations Around the World," *The New York Times*, April 17, 2021, https://tinyurl.com/9fun7pph.

70. Lisa Cornish, "Interactive: Who's Funding the Covid-19 response and what are the priorities?" *Devex*, https://tinyurl.com/5jb8hf89.

71. Yanguas, *op. cit.*

72. María José Romero, "Opinion: Public-private partnerships don't work. It's time for the World Bank to take action," *Devex*, April 19, 2018, https://tinyurl.com/xb4pbu4t.

73. Lord and Chang, *op. cit.*

74. Scott Morris, "China's Role in Developing Countries: Resetting US Policy with a '3 C's' Agenda," Center for Global Development, December 2020, https://tinyurl.com/nvxapeaa.

75. Bonnie Glick, "Memo to Incoming USAID Leadership in the Biden Administration," Center for Strategic and International Studies, Nov. 30, 2020, https://tinyurl.com/29vbz8f6.

76. Morris, *op. cit.*

77. "Recognizing Magnitude of Global Challenges, Budget Proposal Includes Critical Down Payment for International Affairs Needs," *op. cit.*

78. Adva Saldinger, "What would Biden's foreign aid policy look like?" *Devex*, Aug. 19, 2020, https://tinyurl.com/2bancv22.

79. "The Biden Plan for a Clean Energy Revolution and Environmental Justice," Biden-Harris, https://tinyurl.com/3rybejf4.

80. "International Climate Change Assistance: Budget Authority, FY2009-FY2019," Congressional Research Service, Nov. 25, 2019, https://tinyurl.com/4rxvkpcw.

81. "The President's FY 2022 Discretionary Request," *op. cit.*; "Executive Order on Tackling the Climate Crisis at Home and Abroad," The White House, Jan. 27, 2021, https://tinyurl.com/5h8hn2u3.

82. Michael Igoe, "Samantha Power shares vision for an elevated USAID," *Devex*, March 23, 2021, https://tinyurl.com/3apn8z63.

BIBLIOGRAPHY
Books

Bermeo, Sarah Blodgett, *Targeted Development: Industrialized Country Strategy in a Globalized World*, Oxford University Press, 2018.
An associate professor at Duke University's Sanford School of Public Policy shows how aid has shifted from addressing human well-being to benefiting donor states.

Honig, Dan, *Navigation by Judgment: Why and When Top-Down Management of Foreign Aid Doesn't Work*, Oxford University Press, 2018.
An assistant professor at Johns Hopkins University's School of Advanced International Studies draws on a database of 14,000 development projects to show how local management of aid projects increases effectiveness.

Power, Samantha, *The Education of an Idealist: A Memoir*, HarperCollins Publishers, 2019.
President Biden's nominee for administrator of the U.S. Agency for International Development (USAID) reflects on what she learned as a war correspondent in the Balkans, from her Pulitzer Prize-winning work on genocide and as U.S. ambassador to the United Nations.

Yanguas, Pablo, *Why We Lie About Aid: Development and the Messy Politics of Change*, Zed Books Ltd., 2018.
A professor at the University of Manchester and international development consultant argues a dysfunctional aid system mistakes short-term results for long-term transformation and that a different approach is needed.

Articles

Gramer, Robbie, and Dan De Luce, "USAID Redesign Moves Forward, With No Drama," *Foreign Policy*, April 25, 2018, https://tinyurl.com/s6ssf4w.
The authors examine the Trump administration's reorganization of USAID.

Igoe, Michael, "Would Biden's foreign aid approach be progressive or bipartisan?" *Devex*, Nov. 2, 2020, https://tinyurl.com/38e5uf7v.
A journalist analyzes how international aid may be positioned in a Biden administration.

Ingram, George, "What every American should know about US foreign aid," The Brookings Institution, Oct. 15, 2019, https://tinyurl.com/9xx4x2bb.
A senior scholar at the centrist think tank presents some big-picture perspectives on foreign aid and debunks some common misconceptions.

Lord, Kristin M., and Ann Mei Chang, "The quiet revolution: What Congress should know about foreign assistance today," The Brookings Institution, Feb. 8, 2021, https://tinyurl.com/cu5zdcb6.
Two development experts say new approaches to international aid have yielded fresh solutions and generated additional resources.

McBride, James, "How Does the U.S. Spend its Foreign Aid?" Council on Foreign Relations, Oct. 1, 2018, https://tinyurl.com/hr52ybwp.
A foreign affairs specialist describes how and where U.S. foreign aid is spent and makes arguments for and against it.

Rose, Sarah, and Erin Collinson, "Mark Green's Legacy and Priorities for the Next USAID Administrator," Center for Global Development, April 10, 2020, https://tinyurl.com/2fymez65.
Scholars at an international development think tank summarize former USAID Administrator Mark Green's accomplishments and forecast where the agency may go from here.

Thier, J. Alexander, and Douglas Alexander, "How to Save Foreign Aid in the Age of Populism," *Foreign Policy*, Aug. 13, 2019, https://tinyurl.com/jfm6mbrh.
Two development professionals argue for a new political narrative and policy framework for international development.

Reports and Studies

Gill, Cory R., Marian L. Lawson and Emily M. Morgenstern, "Department of State, Foreign Operations, and Related Programs: FY2021 Budget and Appropriations," Congressional Research Service, March 18, 2021, https://tinyurl.com/aj226pmp.
Foreign aid experts summarize for Congress the budget for the Department of State and Foreign Operations for fiscal 2021.

Ingram, George, "Covid-19 exposes a changed world: A prescription for renewing U.S. global partnership," The Brookings Institution, Jan. 12, 2021, https://tinyurl.com/9ph2kcyw.
A senior fellow at the institution's Center for Sustainable Development looks at how Covid-19 has affected development and offers recommendations for moving forward.

Kharas, Homi, Andrew Rogerson and Beata Cichocka, "Horizon 2025—End of the Beginning: Development Cooperation in the Pandemic Age," Center for Global Development, Nov. 30, 2020, https://tinyurl.com/2xtdxwx7.
Given the multiple stresses now facing development, three experts suggest that aid is putting more emphasis on what is happening within, rather than across, countries and call for a new development agenda in a post-pandemic world.

"Landscape Analysis: Over-the-Horizon Strategic Review," U.S. Agency for International Development, August 2020, https://tinyurl.com/292wnxft.
This short report examines the diverse development needs resulting from the COVID-19 pandemic and five trends arising from it.

Lawson, Marian L., and Emily M. Morgenstern, "Foreign Assistance: An Introduction to U.S. Programs and Policy," Congressional Research Service, April 20, 2020, https://tinyurl.com/4s87hjnr.
Experts in international aid provide an overview of U.S. foreign aid priorities and spending over time.

Morris, Scott, "China's Role in Developing Countries: Resetting US Policy with a '3 C's' Agenda," Center for Global Development, Dec. 3, 2020, https://tinyurl.com/2an2kpvm.
A China expert describes how the United States can confront, cooperate and compete with Beijing.

THE NEXT STEP

Biden Administration

"Biden administration to restore $235m in US aid to Palestinians," *BBC*, April 7, 2021, https://tinyurl.com/wsdcfwef.
The Biden administration plans to reinstate some of the economic and development assistance to the West Bank and Gaza that President Donald Trump had cut.

Detsch, Jack, and Christina Lu, "Assad Regime Continues Stonewalling U.S. Aid to Syria," *Foreign Policy*, April 13, 2021, https://tinyurl.com/6mnyzj8z.
The United States says the Syrian government is still blocking the delivery of humanitarian aid to Syrians.

Jakes, Lara, "After Backing Military Force in Past, U.S.A.I.D. Nominee Focuses on Deploying Soft Power," *The New York Times*, April 13, 2021, https://tinyurl.com/4hff738e.
To counter China and other rivals, Samantha Power, President Biden's choice to lead USAID, says she wants to advance human rights and democracy overseas instead of relying on military interventions.

Budget

"Catholic aid group praises Biden's proposed boost to foreign assistance," *Catholic News Agency*, April 12, 2021, https://tinyurl.com/yepat24j.
Catholic Relief Services praised Biden's proposed spending increase to fight poverty and infectious diseases internationally.

Hesson, Ted, and Matt Spetalnick, "U.S. considering cash payments to Central America to stem migration," *Reuters*, April 10, 2021, https://tinyurl.com/47fk2ady.
Biden called for $4 billion in development aid for Central American states, far more than the $500 million that was allocated the previous year, and might implement a cash transfer program to deter migration.

Lee, Matthew, "Biden rescinds abortion restrictions on US foreign aid," *The Associated Press*, Jan. 28, 2021, https://tinyurl.com/yhnjjzx4.
Biden restored funding to a United Nations program that President Trump alleged performed coercive abortions and involuntary sterilizations, which the agency running the program denies.

China

Cordell, Kristen A., "Chinese Development Assistance: A New Approach or More of the Same?" *Carnegie Endowment for Peace*, March 23, 2021, https://tinyurl.com/5u5ammhw.
A 2021 white paper by China says the country will use development assistance to take a more activist role in international rule-setting—but it is unclear how much influence the paper will have on Chinese officials who implement development projects.

Imran, Warda, "Is China using COVID aid to increase influence in Sri Lanka?" *DW*, April 8, 2021, https://tinyurl.com/t86pudhp.
China has shipped hundreds of thousands of COVID-19 vaccine doses to Sri Lanka, apparently in an attempt to bolster its influence in the region.

Nyabiage, Jevans, "Belt and Road Initiative: end of the line for China's Afristar rail firm in Kenya?" *South China Morning Post*, March 14, 2021, https://tinyurl.com/2w7sve47.
The Kenyan state railway manager will assume control of the Standard Gauge Railway from a Chinese firm sooner than anticipated.

Military Aid

Fredrick, James, "With Honduras' Narco Allegations, Pressure Rises To Sanction Its Leader," *NPR*, March 18, 2021, https://tinyurl.com/cxtu3tcb.
Calls to cut U.S. security aid to Honduras have increased as allegations of human rights abuses surrounding the country's leader, President Juan Orlando Hernández, mount.

Gramer, Robbie, and Jack Detsch, "U.S. Bucks Won't Stop in Afghanistan," *Foreign Policy*, April 15, 2021, https://tinyurl.com/97pdt46n.
President Biden intends to continue providing development and military aid to Afghanistan after the United States withdraws its remaining troops later this year.

Kelly, Laura, "Progressive lawmaker to introduce bill seeking more oversight of Israel assistance," *The Hill*, April 14, 2021, https://tinyurl.com/3m4dybjp.
Rep. Betty McCollum, D-Minn., plans to introduce legislation that would increase oversight of U.S. military assistance to Israel—but the bill will face bipartisan opposition and Biden has opposed the idea.

Discussion Questions

Here are some questions to consider regarding U.S. international assistance:

- What was the historic connection between the Cold War and U.S. foreign aid programs?

- How much of the federal government's budget is devoted to international programs?

- How will the goals and approach of American foreign policy change under President Biden's administration? How will Biden's approach to international affairs differ from that of President Donald Trump?

- Why has the COVID-19 pandemic set back development efforts in large parts of the developing world?

- Why do critics of aid programs say they are prone to corruption and are motivated more by the self-interest of donors than the needs of recipients? What is your assessment of these criticisms?

For More Information

American Enterprise Institute, 1789 Massachusetts Ave., N.W., Washington, DC 20036; 202-862-5800; aei.org. A think tank associated with free-market positions.

Brookings Institution, 1775 Massachusetts Ave., N.W., Washington, DC 20036; 202-797-6000; brookings.edu. A centrist think tank that addresses a variety of public policy issues.

Center for Global Development, 2055 L St., N.W., Washington, DC 20036; 202-416-4000; cgdev.org. A research organization that focuses on international development.

Congressional Research Service, 101 Independence Ave., S.E., Washington, DC 20540; 202-707-5000; loc.gov/crsinfo. Congress' research arm, providing lawmakers with reports and analysis on legislation and policy issues.

Council on Foreign Relations, 1777 F St., N.W., Washington, DC 20006; 202-509-8400; cfr.org. A think tank specializing in U.S. foreign policy and international affairs.

U.S. Agency for International Development, 1300 Pennsylvania Ave., N.W., Washington, DC 20004; 202-712-0290; usaid.gov. The federal government's primary agency for managing foreign development and humanitarian aid programs.

5

Supply Chains at Risk

Are tariffs and technology disrupting global trade routes?

By Rachel Layne

Employees line up for roll call before their shift starts at a Pegatron Corp. factory in Shanghai in 2016. Few other nations have the manufacturing scale and expertise China has developed over decades, with 100 million factory workers—equivalent to about a third of the total U.S. population.

From *CQ Researcher*, January 3, 2020

THE ISSUES

Headquartered near Pittsburgh and founded nearly a century ago, American Textile Co. is used to weathering big economic changes.

Today, its 1,200 employees, up from about 100 in 1991, work in four finishing plants in Georgia, Pennsylvania, Utah and Texas to make bedding for retailers and hotels. But like most textile companies, American Textile Co. keeps prices down by importing fabric and other components from around the world, including China and El Salvador.

So when President Trump began imposing tariffs on Chinese imports, which are paid not by China but by importers, and then tweeted that U.S. companies should abandon Chinese suppliers altogether, CEO Lance Ruttenberg grew alarmed.[1] It takes years to develop relationships with suppliers for quality components, he says, even for something as simple as a pillow.

Ruttenberg says the tariffs will cost his firm $1 million a month, eliminating any profit. "The average American—they can't in any way appreciate the complexity of a supply chain," he says, referring to the network of suppliers who provide the components and materials that go into a finished product. "And this administration, in my estimation, has made a very oversimplified case for why they're doing what they're doing."

Making 6,000 items for 40,000 stores, sourced from around the world, involves "an infinite amount of iterations that have to be considered in order to make things show up on the right shelf at the right time for the right retailer," Ruttenberg explains. "So . . . to oversimplify that by saying 'just move it' or 'just get a better price,' . . . it's just incorrect. It's wrong."

Trump's trade policy of using tariffs and other punitive measures as negotiating tools has upended norms and disrupted the flow of goods and services developed under a postwar system championed by the United States and later governed by the World Trade Organization (WTO). As U.S. companies scramble to find alternate suppliers and brace for lower profits, they warn that the cost of the tariffs eventually will trickle down to consumers in the form of higher prices. China has retaliated by imposing its own tariffs on U.S. products and halting purchases of American corn, soy and pork, triggering fears among some experts of a prolonged "cold" trade war between the United States and China, its biggest trading partner in 2018.[2]

Trump's new tariffs on steel and aluminum, washing machines and solar panels angered traditional political and trade allies. He also renegotiated the 25-year-old North American Free Trade Agreement (NAFTA) with Mexico and Canada, exited the 12-nation Trans-Pacific Partnership (TPP) in favor of negotiating with individual countries and threatened to tax all foreign-made cars and auto parts.[3] On Dec. 13, 2019, President Trump and Chinese authorities announced a partial deal to slow the trade war, with the United States holding back on tariffs that were to have been enacted two days later, mostly on consumer goods.[4]

If all the proposed tariffs had been implemented, virtually every Chinese-made item was slated to be taxed—paid not by China, as Trump has claimed, but by U.S. importers. Such measures have disrupted supply chains in both countries and around the world, as companies search for non-Chinese suppliers or move their factories out of China to avoid tariff-induced erosion of profits.[5]

In October, as a result of the trade tensions, the International Monetary Fund (IMF), which keeps tabs on economies across the globe, lowered its outlook for global economic growth in 2019. Some U.S. companies are cutting supply chain investments to prepare for a possible recession, just as new technologies that could further transform supply chains, such as 5G, the revolutionary fifth-generation cellular telecommunications technology, start to come online.[6]

These developments have alarmed experts who support the international system of ever-freer trade implemented worldwide after World War II. They fear a long trade war that could split global supply chains into one tied to China and another tethered to the United States.[7]

Henry Paulson, the Treasury secretary under Republican President George W. Bush during the global 2007-09 financial crisis, warned that there could be a "decoupling" of the world's two biggest economies. The stakes are much bigger than a trade war, he said, calling the potential divide an economic "iron curtain," referring to the political split that separated capitalist and communist countries from the 1940s to the late '80s.[8]

"This is a battle between two countries . . . to set the standards for the technologies of the future, the technologies which are going to bolster economic growth and competitiveness around the world," Paulson said.[9]

But some trade specialists argue Trump's approach may be working, at least in part. The U.S.-China partial deal announced Dec. 13, 2019, later earned Paulson's congratulations as a "hard fought" first step. On Dec. 23, 2019, China announced it was lowering tariffs on some 8,000 products including frozen pork, pharmaceuticals and some semiconductor products for all trading partners, starting on Jan. 1, 2020, ahead of a deal-signing with the United States.[10]

Employees work on the assembly line of Volkswagen's Tiguan model at the company's plant in Puebla, Mexico, in 2018. Importing products and parts from countries with lower labor costs holds down consumer prices and facilitates the consumer spending that drives U.S. economic growth. Mexican factory wages are one-fifth the U.S. average.

"It's important to understand that the president inherited a very difficult situation, one where we probably should have addressed some of these problems with China a lot sooner," said Stephen Vaughn, former general counsel for the U.S. trade representative under Trump. "But I think the president had great courage and wisdom to step up and realize that we really can start to make progress."[11]

The Trump administration's shift to protectionist policies seeks in part to rein in China, accused by U.S. officials, lawmakers and companies of stealing intellectual property—or patented inventions, designs, names and images—used in commerce and erecting other unfair trade barriers. "China is home to widespread infringing activity, including trade secret theft, rampant online piracy and counterfeiting," said a 2017 report from the U.S. Trade Representative's Office (USTR). Such practices are prohibited by WTO policies, and China denies the assertions.[12]

The Trump administration is not alone in leveling those charges. Several Democratic senators in February 2019 urged the administration to address such allegations in negotiations with China.[13]

Unfair trade practices, such as creating counterfeit goods, pirating software and trade secret theft, are estimated to cost the U.S. economy at least $225 billion each year and may reach $600 billion, according to a 2017 report by the Commission on the Theft of American Intellectual Property. Trade secret theft is estimated to cost between 1 percent and 3 percent of U.S. gross domestic product (GDP), or the total value of goods and services as measured in one year, the report said. The United States accounts for about a quarter of the world's $85.8 trillion in GDP; China accounts for about 16 percent.[14]

Trump's policies also are curbing foreign direct investment between the two countries, such as the construction of factories in the United States by Chinese companies, and vice versa. Such investment fell 60 percent in 2018, according to a report from the Rhodium Group, an economic research organization in New York City that specializes in the Chinese economy.[15]

"There's a lot of focus on production-worker jobs—where has the production gone and the assembly. And that's important," says Susan Helper, an economics professor at Case Western Reserve University and a former chief economist in the U.S. Department of Commerce during the Obama administration. "But it's also important where the design and engineering gets done. And China's policy in recent years has really focused on how they're going to get those jobs. [It's] how they're going to move up the value chain."

One way they hope to do that is by winning the race to develop and deploy 5G technology. Downloading data from the internet with 5G is expected to occur 100 times faster than with existing 4G technology, and 5G will reach more broadly and deeply into everyday life by expanding a hundredfold the use of wireless consumer products, from automobiles to drones to household appliances.[16]

Technological advances in manufacturing—including robotics, monitoring software and 3D printing of parts—are changing where and how companies procure components. Companies already use such technologies to make products ranging from rocket parts to blood vessels.[17] The speed and accuracy with which a product can be traced along the supply chain using tracking sensors and complex software are changing as well.

Strategies Dictate Where Manufacturing Moves

Manufacturers make decisions on where to locate their operations based on which strategic goals they are pursuing.

Where Manufacturing Is Moving and Why

Strategy	Example	Sourcing
Lowest cost	Apparel, most footwear	Most remain in China, but Vietnam/Bangladesh increasingly popular
Low cost and closer to demand	Aerospace parts, auto parts, some footwear	Moving to Mexico, Dominican Republic
Fast, responsive supply chain for low volume/high margin	High-end consumer goods	Slowly returning to the United States
Bound by huge existing supplier base	Consumer electronics	Staying in China

Source: "CTL.SC3x — Supply Chain Dynamics," Center for Transportation & Logistics, Massachusetts Institute of Technology, 2019, p. 56, https://tinyurl.com/m8msu3e

For example, Amazon, Walmart and Best Buy are introducing free next-day delivery for consumers—unthinkable without sophisticated supply chain software that tracks goods almost instantly. Soon, consumers will be able to see exactly how their food, such as fish, traveled from ocean to dinner plate. And U.S. consumers will increasingly communicate with freestanding electronic devices to regulate heat in their homes, turn off the lights or order dinner.[18]

Thus, to make fast decisions, American Textile Co. and other companies must be able to almost instantly track goods through every step in a supply chain. That includes all kinds of goods from textiles to electronics with hundreds of parts.

Changing technology, such as 3D printing, also can play a huge role in shortening supply chains and cutting costs. "If you can . . . print parts when you need it, maybe you don't have to be outsourcing them for the economics to faraway countries," says Kamala Raman, a senior director analyst at Gartner, a research and consulting firm in Stamford, Conn.

Even before the tariffs were imposed, rising labor costs in China were spurring some companies to shift production from China to places such as Vietnam. But leaving an established supplier can take years. And few places have the scale and expertise China developed over decades with a workforce of 100 million factory workers—equivalent to about a third of the U.S. population.[19]

As the trade discord escalated, corporate investment in everything from research and development to construction of new facilities fell to its lowest level in a decade during the third quarter of 2019, according to a survey of 100 CEOs by The Conference Board, a business think tank that measures their confidence in the economy.

"CEO confidence declined to its lowest level in a decade," said Lynn Franco, senior director of economic indicators at The Conference Board. "Tariffs and trade issues, coupled with expectations of moderating global growth, are causing a heightened degree of uncertainty."[20]

As manufacturers, importers and exporters, economists and trade specialists assess the impact on global supply chains of the U.S.-China trade war, here are some of the questions being discussed:

Are U.S. companies shifting supply chains out of China?

On Aug. 23, 2019, President Trump in a series of tweets urged U.S. companies to move their operations out of China: "The vast amounts of money made and stolen by China from the United States, year after year, for decades, will and must STOP. Our great American companies are hereby ordered to immediately start looking for an alternative to China, including bringing your companies HOME and making your products in the USA."[21]

In fact, rising manufacturing costs in China already had prompted some companies to consider looking elsewhere, such as to Vietnam, Malaysia, the Philippines, India and Mexico, for raw materials,

U.S. Imports from Vietnam Surge as Chinese Trade Declines

The total value of U.S. imports from Vietnam increased nearly 34 percent during the first nine months of 2019 compared to the same period in 2018. The value of imports from China declined 14.5 percent in that period, in part, experts say, due to new U.S. tariffs on a variety of Chinese imports.

Change in U.S. Imports from Major Trading Partners, Jan.–Oct. 2018 to Jan.–Oct. 2019

Vietnam	33.9%
Taiwan	20.1%
France	13.2%
Ireland	7.4%
Switzerland	6.8%
Italy	5.6%
India	5.5%
South Korea	5.2%
United Kingdom	4.8%
Mexico	4.0%
Japan	2.6%
Germany	1.9%
Malaysia	1.7%
Canada	0.7%
China	-14.5%

Sources: "Exhibit 4. Exports, Imports, and Trade Balance of Goods by Country and Area, Not Seasonally Adjusted: 2018," U.S. International Trade in Goods in Services (FT900): October 2018, Dec. 6, 2018, United States Census Bureau, https://tinyurl.com/trw3kjk; "Exhibit 4. Exports, Imports, and Trade Balance of Goods by Country and Area, Not Seasonally Adjusted: 2019," U.S. International Trade in Goods in Services (FT900): October 2019, Dec. 5, 2019, https://tinyurl.com/vq32l3x

semifinished and finished goods.²² But few cited the United States as a realistic alternative due to its comparatively high labor costs.

Some consumer product companies have announced they are moving from China. Action-camera maker GoPro opened a factory in Mexico earlier in 2019. And in October 2019, the maker of fitness tracker Fitbit said it is moving out of China by the end of the year due to the "ongoing threat of tariffs," though it did not say where it was headed. (Google announced it was buying Fitbit for $2.1 billion on Nov. 1.)²³

"We expect that effectively all trackers and smart-watches starting in January 2020 will not be of Chinese origin," Ron Kisling, Fitbit's chief financial officer, said on Oct. 9, 2019.²⁴

Keeping costs down is key to survival for smaller companies, said Nathan Resnick, who runs Sourcify, a company that pairs small and midsize companies with overseas factories. Last year, about 75 percent of Sourcify's partner factories were China-based. This year, that is down to 60 percent, Resnick said in June. The topic of companies moving out of China is mentioned in "pretty much every single conversation we have," Resnick said.²⁵

Chinese production costs are climbing as automation becomes more pervasive and education levels in the labor market rise. China is pushing for more complex manufacturing and research and development for its own high-tech products, so companies need high-skilled engineers and scientists rather than assembly line workers, says Jack Buffington, a University of Denver professor specializing in supply chain management.

"China grew as a supply chain power due to its low-cost labor market. So as more manufacturing becomes automated, labor rates in China increased," Buffington says. "There's increasing pressure on politicians to try to understand how a global supply chain can help their people, as opposed to hurt. I think a lot of the politics is superficial. Supply chains operate in an environment where there's always risk and there's always change."

Even before Trump's "hereby" tweet, about 50 companies, including HP Inc., Dell and Nintendo, had said they wanted to move at least some manufacturing outside of China, *The Nikkei Asian Review* reported.²⁶

"I would say, on the margin, I'm not aware of a single supplier who is not moving some form of manufacturing

Guests participate in a workout hosted by Fitbit in 2018 in Los Angeles. In October 2019, the maker of the fitness tracker said it is moving production out of China due to the "ongoing threat of tariffs."

outside of China," Ted Decker, the executive in charge of merchandise for Home Depot, said during an August conference call with analysts.²⁷

Apple, the biggest company in the United States by market value (a measure Wall Street calculates using stock price) of more than $1 trillion, considered moving up to 20 percent of its operations outside China, *The Wall Street Journal* reported on June 20, citing unnamed sources.²⁸

During a July 30, 2019, conference call with analysts, Apple CEO Tim Cook dismissed a report that Apple planned to move out of China. "I know there's been a lot of speculation around the topic of different moves and so forth," Cook said. "I wouldn't put a lot of stock into those, if I were you."²⁹

Apple arguably is the most visible U.S. company intertwined with China through its supply chain. It prints "Designed in California. Assembled in China" on its iPhones, a product that until 2018 accounted for more than half of its profit. And about 20 percent of Apple's sales are to Chinese consumers.³⁰

Apple is not alone among U.S. companies pursuing Chinese consumers. Even though China's economic growth rate for the first nine months of 2019 slowed to 6.2 percent—its lowest in 27 years—it is still growing faster than other large economies.³¹

Big multinational companies from the United States, Japan and Europe have long sought to tap that growth. In September 2019 Boeing raised its forecast for the number of planes China will need in the next 20 years. General Motors sells more cars in China than in the United States, though sales declined in 2019. Electric carmaker Tesla is opening a plant near Shanghai. And Caterpillar, the earth-moving equipment maker, makes up to 10 percent of its annual sales from China.[32]

Apple's top 200 suppliers span at least 17 countries. But it would take at least 18 months to move just 5 percent to 7 percent of iPhone production from China to India or Vietnam in a "best-case scenario," securities analyst Daniel Ives wrote in a note to clients on Aug. 13, 2019.[33]

Also in August 2019, the U.S.-China Business Council said only 13 percent of its 220 members operating in China—which include Apple, Boeing, Caterpillar, Coca-Cola and Walmart—planned to move or were already shifting some operations.[34] But only 3 percent planned to move some operations to the United States, a goal of Trump's.

"In short, there is little support for the view that large numbers of foreign firms are fleeing China," wrote Nicholas R. Lardy, a China specialist at the Peterson Institute for International Economics on Sept. 10, 2019. Annual investment in Chinese factories and other nonfinancial spending remain steady, at about $140 billion, rising at about 3 percent a year, Lardy wrote. "A handful of firms leaving China do not confirm a broad trend," he said.[35]

Can companies adjust their global supply chains to Trump's tariffs and still grow?

Trump's sudden trade policy changes are prodding companies to re-examine supply chains for new locations and what economists call resiliency—a way to quickly react to changes.

Researchers at the Massachusetts Institute of Technology, led by Jim Rice, director of the Supply Change Exchange Program, said that is not easy. "Within, say, one month, trade barriers may be erected and removed," the researchers wrote in a June 2019 blog post. "However, supply systems operate much more slowly; cycle times from source to the customer are often measured in months. Today's supply chains lack the agility required to keep pace with trade policy gyrations."[36]

That hurts business confidence and stifles investment, two things needed to keep the economy growing, says Michelle Casario, an assistant professor of economics at Villanova University. (*See Pro/Con.*)

But countries with lower labor costs, such as Vietnam, do not have as many workers or water, power and transportation systems as advanced as those in China. So, while Vietnam's exports to the United States rose nearly 34 percent through August 2019 and China's dropped 14.5 percent, the absolute amount of goods imported from China continues to dwarf that from Vietnam.[37]

"No one offers what China could offer if things were good," Casario says. "So everything seems to be a Plan B, a second best. Some of this is uncharted. Best case, if [companies] start moving supply chains, it could take two to three years" to find efficient and reliable non-Chinese alternative suppliers.

Importing unfinished and semifinished parts from countries with lower labor costs keeps prices down in places such as the United States, Canada and Europe, where consumer spending drives economic growth. And while wages in producing countries are rising, they remain far below those in the United States. Chinese factory workers earn about $5.78 an hour, compared with $4.66 in Mexico and $2.91 in Vietnam. The average manufacturing wage in the United States as of September was $23.65 per hour, according to the Bureau of Labor Statistics.[38]

So Trump's aim to bring traditional manufacturing jobs back to the United States is not likely to happen anytime soon on the scale he promised on the campaign trail in 2016.

Companies want to keep costs low to make their products more attractive to U.S. consumers, whose spending accounts for about 70 percent of economic growth (compared with China's 40 percent).[39] With unemployment in the United States hovering near its lowest level since World War II, consumers remain optimistic, according to a University of Michigan consumer sentiment survey, a measure closely watched by economists. Until September, most products imported from China subject to the tariffs were not sold directly to consumers, and prices had not yet climbed at the cash register.

Consumer sentiment, though down from earlier in the month, remained at very favorable levels, the survey showed. However, "The recent focus of consumers has been on income and job growth, while largely ignoring other news," said Richard Curtin, director of the survey.[40]

For example, The Conference Board, another sampler of consumer confidence, says it has dropped for four straight months and predicted that fourth-quarter economic growth will be weak.[41]

Growth in the U.S. manufacturing sector has officially slowed to a recessionary pace, and the International Monetary Fund predicted in October 2019 that global economic growth will fall to 3 percent in 2020—a pace not seen since the financial crisis a decade ago. It called the outlook "precarious."[42]

"The weakness in growth is driven by a sharp deterioration in manufacturing activity and global trade, with higher tariffs and prolonged trade policy uncertainty damaging investment and demand for capital goods," Gita Gopinath, director of the IMF's research department, wrote in a blog post explaining Census Bureau figures.[43]

Ultimately, U.S. companies will diversify and redesign their supply chains to better weather risk, says Gang Li, an associate professor of management at Bentley University, in Waltham, Mass. In the short term, however, the disruption from tariffs and other trade policies is "going to hurt, no question.

"But if we look at the long term, particularly if we look out five years, my estimate is our supply chain is strong enough to rebound from it," says Li, who expects economic growth to recover. "What doesn't kill you makes you stronger."

Will restrictions on Chinese technology giants protect U.S intellectual property?

From the outset, the Trump administration argued that slashing demand for Chinese exports would act as "an effective tool to pressure China to change its policies" regarding, among other things, the theft of intellectual property, according to a report from the Congressional Research Service.[44] But the White House also has used more direct tools, particularly when it comes to technology supply chains.

Perhaps the most intertwined technology supply chain—and the heart of the contentious trade battle between the United States and China—sits inside mobile phones. Since its inception, the Trump administration has focused on two Chinese telecommunications companies—Huawei and ZTE. To prevent intellectual property theft, Trump officials want the U.S. government to have detailed authority over what parts—such as semiconductor chips and software—are used in equipment made by such tech companies.

In January 2019, the Justice Department announced it was charging Huawei and its chief financial officer, Meng Wanzhou, with violating sanctions against Iran, stealing intellectual property and lying about it to U.S. banks. Meng, who was arrested in Vancouver, Canada, on a U.S. warrant, is fighting extradition.[45]

On May 15, 2019, the U.S. government added Huawei to a blacklist called the Entity List, which means the company cannot purchase or receive hardware, software and other supplies from U.S. firms without the federal government's permission. Later that day, Trump signed an executive order broadening the federal government's power to block transactions linked to information and communications technology (ICT) if those transactions would threaten national security. The move, experts say, was aimed at Huawei because the telecommunications giant's equipment depends heavily on parts from U.S. tech firms, including microchips made by Intel and Qualcomm, as well as mobile software from Google.[46]

Huawei in turn is important to U.S. technology companies because it is the world's biggest supplier of telecom equipment and the second-biggest phone maker, according to the tech website *CNet*.

The Trump administration has relaxed some rules and allowed companies to sell certain equipment to Huawei. About 130 companies applied for licenses to do so. On Dec. 17, 2019, *Bloomberg News* reported the Trump administration was weighing more Huawei restrictions, angering U.S. suppliers.[47]

"Once you take into account the supply chains underpinning Apple and Huawei and the enormous value American firms derive from them, it is easy to see why companies like Apple and Google, Broadcom and Qualcomm want the trade war to end," said Geoffrey Garrett, dean of the Wharton School at the University of Pennsylvania, in a Sept. 5, 2019, blog post.[48]

The quandary for U.S. technology suppliers is this: Can the United States balance the risk of the Chinese stealing technology contained in parts such as semiconductors with the economic boost derived from supplying those goods to China and other foreign customers?[49]

American restrictions may appear to protect U.S. technology, but they also may represent a step toward a "decoupling"—or separation—of the Chinese and U.S. technology supply chains, creating what former Treasury secretary Paulson warned could become an "economic iron curtain" between the two countries.

If the United States no longer has economic interests in China, the risk for more violent kinds of conflict, including military confrontation, increases, said Wharton's Garrett. So, in seeking to protect U.S. technology, a decoupling could "profoundly harm America's national security," he wrote.[50]

On Oct. 11, 2019, President Trump announced that the United States and China had reached "phase one" of a trade deal. On Dec. 13, 2019, the countries announced the broad outlines of the agreement. While it did not include some planned U.S. tariffs on consumer goods, most imports from China were still subject, on average, to tariffs of 19.3 percent, six times higher than before Trump began imposing the levies.[51]

Although the White House said the two sides made progress on some intellectual property issues, such as allegations that China forces U.S. companies to divulge some trade secrets before they can make or sell goods in China, the initial announcement did not address Huawei.[52] Huawei may need two to three years to make up for the damage caused by the U.S. trade ban, CEO Ren Zhengfei told *The Washington Post*.[53]

On Dec. 13, 2019, the United States and China said they would work on further agreements as both sides prepared a detailed version of "phase one." According to a summary from the U.S. trade representative, China will buy some $200 billion in goods over the next several years, including U.S. agricultural products. The agreement also covers technology-sharing requirements for U.S. companies doing business in China and addresses intellectual property concerns. China will also allow U.S. banks and credit card companies to do business in the Chinese consumer market.[54]

In 2018, Congress expanded the power of several administration agencies, working through an interagency body called the Committee on Foreign Investment in the United States, to determine whether foreign investment in a U.S. company poses a risk to national security. The idea is to protect, in addition to intellectual property, critical infrastructure such as electrical grids, ports and military designs.[55] The Commerce Department, through its Bureau of Industry and Security, is reportedly working on how tightly to control intellectual property for emerging and "foundational" technologies such as semiconductors.

The Trump administration is divided over how strictly to control those technologies. Some U.S. researchers and companies seeking to ultimately sell products and technology in China fear restrictions will be so tight that the United States will no longer be an attractive place to create new inventions, in part because the products that emerge will be prohibited for sale to Chinese companies and markets, according to *The New York Times*.[56]

Others, such as Derek Scissors, a China specialist at the conservative American Enterprise Institute think tank, favor decoupling, including as a means of protecting U.S. technology. Any new restrictions on doing business in China, he says, should have "explicit justification" that spells out potential consequences to the United States if such restrictions were not imposed.

The Trump administration pursued restrictions on intellectual property "because it has both economic and military applications," Scissors says. Trump then decided that tariffs were the best way to pressure China into changing its behavior on intellectual property theft.

"[But] we never got to the point of deciding what we should [target to better control intellectual property], so we ended up with across-the-board tariffs the next day, because that's what the president wanted," he says.

BACKGROUND
Shifting Trade Routes

Supply chains—and their disruption—stretch deep into human history.

East-West trade routes, collectively called the Silk Road, began emerging in 130 B.C. during China's Han dynasty. They enabled spices, gold, horses, camels, honey and textiles to travel between China and India, Persia and Europe.

When the Ottoman Empire blocked trade with the West in 1453, wealthy Europeans sent explorers to search for alternative sea routes to the East. After the explorations of Christopher Columbus and Vasco da Gama in the 1490s, an "intercontinental trade boom" ensued.[57]

But until the 1800s, most everyday goods came from a direct supply chain: a farmer grew wheat, took it to a gristmill or ground it at home and sold it nearby. Shipping goods took weeks, months or years. And countries imposed high tariffs to protect their fledgling industries from cheaper imported goods.[58]

During the Industrial Revolution, the steam engine and the telegraph revolutionized supply chains by speeding up trade. In the 1830s a ship took seven weeks to travel from Liverpool to New York, and the return could take more than five. By the 1840s, steam transport cut the trip to two weeks in either direction.

Some economists point to the cotton trade as a good example of how such breakthroughs—combined with the inventions of steel ship hulls, diesel engines and railways—enabled new, faster ways to transport goods. Raw materials, such as cotton, could be shipped to Liverpool's mills from places like the United States and India, refined into fabric and then sent back to be fashioned into finished goods.

But perhaps the most valuable breakthrough for global supply chains came in 1866 with the completion of the first transatlantic telegraph and, later, the telephone.[59]

"The information supplied by the telegraph was like a drug to businessmen, who swiftly became addicted," writes Tom Standage, the author of *The Victorian Internet*. "Suddenly, the price of goods and the speed with which they could be delivered became more important than their geographic location. Tradesmen could have several potential suppliers or markets at their disposal and were able to widen their horizons and deal directly with people whom it would have taken days to reach by mail."[60]

The technology, combined with faster overseas and continental transportation, made imports more common for a wider swath of the population and allowed suppliers to keep less inventory, because orders arrived faster. That freed up cash, making businesses more profitable and allowing increased investment.

In the cotton industry, the telegraph and telephone transformed supply chains, according to Wolfgang Lehmacher, head of the supply chain and transportation industries sections at the World Economic Forum in Geneva. "A broker could actually wire ahead and sell any cotton in transit, well before it arrived in port," Lehmacher wrote in his book *The Global Supply Chain*. "Liverpool became the center of the international cotton trade, connecting raw cotton producers in North and South America, Africa and Asia with manufacturers and consumers of finished goods."[61]

As industrialization spread across Europe, supply chains shifted with technological advances. In 1750, for example, India and China accounted for 73 percent of global manufacturing of finished goods made of cotton, silk and porcelain. By 1913, they accounted for just 7.5 percent, according to Richard Baldwin, a professor of international economics at the Graduate Institute Geneva and author of *The Great Convergence: Information Technology and the New Globalization*.[62]

In addition, from 1790 to 1913, the total value of global trade rose fiftyfold, raising living standards in Europe. "For the first time, products such as sugar, tea and cocoa became widely available," according to Lehmacher. "On the other hand, workers started to become more dependent on developments in other countries and the linkage in international trade."[63]

After the Civil War, the United States retained high tariffs implemented in the early 19th century to protect domestic industries, partly to raise revenue and rebuild U.S. industry decimated by the conflict. But the 1913 Revenue Act lowered the U.S. tariff rate on most imports from 41 percent to 27 percent.[64]

Meanwhile, U.S. manufacturing achieved a major breakthrough when the Ford Motor Co. opened its first moving assembly line in 1913. The Model T's 3,000 parts were grouped into 84 steps performed by different groups of employee as car bodies moved past, pulled by a rope. Assembling a vehicle now took 90 minutes instead of

Factory workers at a Ford Motor Co. plant assemble a Model T automobile in 1913. Henry Ford's creation of a moving assembly line that year was a major breakthrough for U.S. manufacturing. The time required to produce a vehicle fell from 12 hours to 90 minutes, and the car's price dropped from $850 to $300.

CHRONOLOGY

1800-1900 *Steam engines and the telegraph fuel an industrial revolution.*

1807 First commercially available steamboat travels from New York City to Albany, leading the way for commercial shipping by water routes.

1837 Samuel Morse is granted a patent for a telegraph machine.

Mid- to late 1800s Transportation by rail, ship and barge allows companies to obtain raw materials and ship products over longer distances, stoking demand for finished goods.

1910s-1930s *U.S. and Europe lower tariffs, reducing prices and expanding trade routes. Technology advances.*

1913 Revenue Act lowers tariff rates on most goods from 41 percent to 27 percent; Ford Motor Co. opens its first moving assembly line.

1927 Ford produces a Model T every 24 seconds.

1929 Stock market crashes in New York, triggering the deepest economic crisis in U.S. history, later known as the Great Depression.

1930 Republican President Herbert Hoover signs the Smoot-Hawley Tariff Act, raising tariffs on 900 products to protect U.S. industries; instead it helps usher in the Great Depression.

1934 To help jump-start the world economy, Democratic President Franklin D. Roosevelt signs the Reciprocal Trade Agreement Act, cutting tariffs on products from 34 countries that agree to reciprocate.

1940s-1960s *Logistics and intermodal containers standardize shipping as post-World War II economy booms.*

1947 The U.S. and Great Britain lead 23 nations in signing the General Agreement on Tariffs and Trade (GATT), a set of international rules lowering tariffs among participating countries.

1948 U.S. Army Master Sgt. Edward A. Guilbert creates a tracking system—the Electronic Data Interchange (EDI)—that uses radio-teletype, telephone or telex, an international telegraph system, to organize the Berlin airlift. It will be used to revolutionize supply chain management.

1961 The International Organization for Standardization sets standard shipping container sizes, boosting efficiency at ports.

1970s-1980s *The modern technology industry emerges, and China joins the world trading system.*

1971 Intel sells the first commercial microprocessor, shrinking space needed for data storage and calculation power.

1979 China and the United States establish diplomatic relations, eventually leading to mutual access to markets for goods and services.

1986 China's "open door" policy encourages foreign investment.

1990-2009 *The rise of the internet and "offshoring" allows companies to produce and track goods more cheaply, expanding global supply chains.*

1993 The European Organization for Nuclear Research puts its World Wide Web project in the public domain.

1994 The United States, Mexico and Canada sign the North American Free Trade Agreement (NAFTA), lowering tariffs among the three nations.

1995 The World Trade Organization (WTO) replaces GATT.

1998 Jack Welch, CEO of General Electric, says companies ideally should put "every plant you own on a barge to move with currencies and changes in the economy."

2001 China is admitted to the WTO.

2008 Lehman Brothers investment bank collapses, triggering worldwide financial crisis.

2009 The 3D printer patent expires, enabling entrepreneurs to develop parts on demand, from rocket engine blades to artificial blood vessels.

2010-Present *Financial crisis gives way to economic growth; a backlash against free trade develops as manufacturing moves out of the United States and robotics and artificial intelligence increasingly replace the need for workers.*

2012 Democratic President Barack Obama pursues free trade agreements, including continuing talks with 11 other Pacific Rim nations to craft a Trans-Pacific Partnership (TPP), begun under Republican President George W. Bush in 2008.

2016 Presidential candidates from both parties attack U.S. trade policy for allegedly eliminating U.S. jobs. . . . Republican Donald Trump wins election, promises to get tough with China and other trading partners, including traditional allies, whom he accuses of taking advantage of U.S. companies. . . . Technology companies test 5G wireless technology, dramatically shrinking download speeds.

2017 Trump withdraws from the TPP, threatens to pull out of NAFTA.

2018 Trump imposes tariffs on solar panels, steel and aluminum and, later, a slew of imported Chinese goods. . . . Negotiators sign an agreement replacing NAFTA called the U.S.-Mexico-Canada Agreement or USMCA (November).

2019 Trump's trade war with China escalates, culminating in plans to impose tariffs on nearly every Chinese-made product. . . . U.S. Trade Representative Robert Lighthizer submits draft agreement of the USMCA to Congress for ratification, but Democrats push for more labor, environmental protections (May). . . . Mexico ratifies the pact (June). . . . Canada says it will move "in tandem" with the United States in approving the deal. House Speaker Nancy Pelosi announces bipartisan changes to the agreement, and the House approves it (December). . . . Senate ratification is not expected until 2020.

12 hours. The price of the car fell from $850 to $300, making it affordable to a wider swath of Americans. Ford also instituted a "$5 workday" wage, up from about $2.25. By 1927, a Model T came off the line every 24 seconds, and Ford had sold 15 million worldwide.[65]

Then, in 1929 the U.S. stock market crashed. In an effort to prop up domestic industry, Congress passed the Smoot-Hawley Tariff Act of 1930, which raised tariffs by an average of 20 percent on 900 imported goods. Most economists say rather than boosting American industry, the law led other countries to implement similar tariffs, and international trade slowed dramatically. The global economy ground to a halt, helping to trigger the Great Depression. Prices of U.S. commodities plummeted by 75 percent and industrial production fell 25 percent during the 1930s; as millions lost their jobs, firms went out of business and demand dried up.[66]

In an attempt to restart the world economy, Democratic President Franklin D. Roosevelt in 1934 signed the Reciprocal Trade Agreement Act, in which 32 countries agreed to cut tariffs. But economic recovery did not really begin until the onset of World War II, when global military production skyrocketed.[67]

During the war the U.S. military made major strides in supply chain logistics, with some armed forces units and divisions developing systems to coordinate transportation, communication, medical services and supplies.[68]

In 1948, three years after the war's end, the Soviet Union cut off food, medicine and other supplies to the Allied-controlled areas of Berlin. A logistics group led by U.S. Army Master Sgt. Edward A. Guilbert created a tracking system using telex, radio-teletype or phone called the Electronic Data Interchange (EDI). It allowed businesses to swap documents such as purchase orders, inventory levels and invoices between mainframe computers. The method enabled what became known as the Berlin airlift—a 13-month effort to drop supplies into the city. Later, Guilbert further refined the EDI methods for use at DuPont, a chemical company, and other companies soon began using it widely.[69]

Tariffs on Cars Are Complicated for Suppliers

"There are really no 100 percent U.S.-built cars. Anywhere."

President Trump is using the broad threat of imposing tariffs on imported cars—invoking national security concerns under a 1962 law—as leverage in negotiating trade deals with Japan, South Korea, the European Union and other places.[1]

The administration wants to increase the percentage of cars and auto parts sold in the United States that are made in America. But the reality is complex.

About one in four vehicles assembled in the United States is made in a foreign-owned factory, says Kristin Dziczek, vice president of research at the Center for Automotive Research, a Michigan-based group that studies the auto industry. For instance, luxury German carmaker BMW's largest plant is in Spartanburg, S.C., where it employs 11,000 people. About 70 percent of the cars assembled there are exported.[2]

Trump's threat carries consequences: Tariffs could disrupt supply chains and slow sales and profits for vehicle and parts makers, potentially costing more than 368,000 factory jobs and another 77,000 jobs at dealerships, the center estimated. And U.S. consumers could pay an average of $2,800 more per car, with fewer model choices, according to the center.[3]

"If they do this, then we are all losers," BMW CEO Oliver Zipse said about the administration's tariff threat during an October automotive conference. "I have the impression [administration officials] are listening carefully. The export model sustains many jobs in the United States."[4]

Although BMW has not cut production at its Spartanburg plant, tariffs could change that, Zipse said.

The White House in November appeared to miss a legal deadline for imposing tariffs based on the 1962 law, first postponed in May. While Commerce Secretary Wilbur Ross said in December that negotiations with individual companies "may or may not" result in tariffs, he evaded questions about the administration's plans.[5]

As a result, the threat of auto tariffs hangs like a sword above negotiations with the Europeans over a broad trade treaty.[6] Tariffs also hover in the background of other negotiations, including a trade agreement with South Korea, signed in 2018, which did not specifically exempt South Korean cars from tariffs under the 1962 law.[7] A U.S.-Japan trade agreement, approved in December, also does not explicitly rule out potential auto tariffs.[8]

The U.S.-Mexico-Canada Agreement (USMCA), a replacement for the North American Free Trade Agreement (NAFTA) negotiated a quarter century ago, mandates that a higher percentage of parts for any vehicle produced in North America be made in one of the three countries.[9] The new agreement has yet to be fully ratified by Congress, but House Speaker Nancy Pelosi in December announced modifications that drew bipartisan approval, and the House passed the new version on Dec. 19. The Senate is expected to vote on the deal in 2020.[10]

Trump reportedly is prepared to hold off on a decision on auto tariffs, preserving the threat but avoiding opening another front in the trade wars. Even if the November deadline has lapsed, the threat remains, because the president could invoke other authority to impose tariffs on auto imports, according to Jennifer Hillman, a Georgetown law professor and former World Trade Organization official.[11]

That would be consistent with Trump's public stance since first threatening the action in 2018. "Auto tariffs are never off the table," Trump said in August. "If I don't get what I want, I'll have no choice but maybe to do that."[12]

Trump in May said he was seeking to protect U.S. automakers from what he characterized as unfair breaks granted to foreign-owned automakers, although industry experts disagree with Trump's characterization.[13]

Tariffs would present problems for auto and parts makers. About half the vehicles sold in the United States are imported, and half of those are made in Mexico or Canada by U.S. companies. At least 40 percent of the parts in most automobiles produced in the United States are made overseas.[14] And some parts, such as steering or braking systems, can cross the U.S.-Mexico border up to six times during the production phase as suppliers add components to pieces before final assembly.[15]

"There are really no 100 percent U.S.-built cars. Anywhere," says Dziczek.

Cars Made in the U.S. Contain Parts from Around the World

Auto manufacturers use parts made in several different countries and sometimes assemble cars in plants overseas. The share of parts coming from each country varies by company and model.

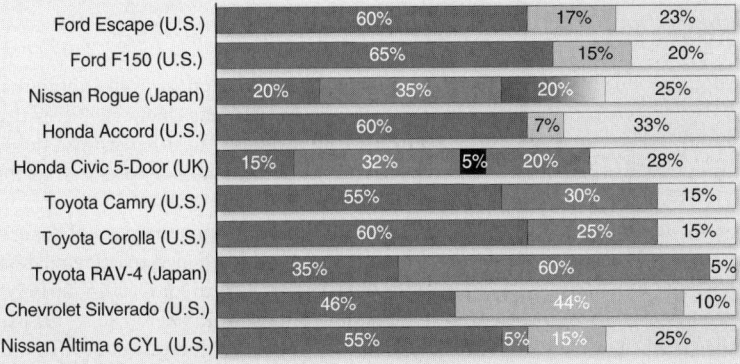

Source: Rachel Layne and Irina Ivanova, "The Trump trade war's hairpin curve: Autos," CBS News, https://tinyurl.com/y6py6kgb

much more decentralized global footprint."

— *Rachel Layne*

---

[1] "Adjusting Imports of Automobiles and Automobile Parts Into the United States," White House, Presidential Proclamation, May 17, 2019, https://tinyurl.com/y5cvjueq.

[2] BMW Group, https://tinyurl.com/s25ab7n.

[3] "Forging a New Path for North American Trade: The Auto Sector," Presentation by the Center for Automotive Research, Federal Reserve Bank of Chicago, Sept. 4-5, 2019.

[4] Edward Taylor, "BMW CEO says trade war could cost U.S. jobs," *Reuters*, Oct. 25, 2019, https://tinyurl.com/tk4q2x5.

[5] David Shepardson, "U.S. has not ruled out imposing tariffs on imported autos: Commerce chief," *Reuters*, Dec. 3, 2019, https://tinyurl.com/ukz4xkq.

[6] Josh Zumbrun, Ben Foldy and Emre Peker, "Threat of Auto Import Tariffs Remains Despite Lapsed Deadline," *The Wall Street Journal*, Nov. 21, 2019, https://tinyurl.com/wzz6xvd.

[7] Esha Dey, "Auto Industry Basks in a 'False Sense of Security' Over Trade," *Bloomberg*, Nov. 25, 2019, https://tinyurl.com/u4r6dy5; "U.S.-Korea Free Trade Agreement fact sheet," U.S. Trade Representative, https://tinyurl.com/vxzr8gz.

[8] Yuri Kageyama, "Trump's US-Japan trade deal wins Japan parliament approval," *The Associated Press*, Dec. 3, 2019, https://tinyurl.com/wgmuvul.

[9] "The United States-Mexico-Canada Agreement Fact Sheet: Automobiles and Automotive Parts," U.S. Trade Representative, https://tinyurl.com/y42voj32; "Proposed U.S.-Mexico-Canada (USMCA) Trade Agreement," Congressional Research Service, Dec. 17, 2019, https://tinyurl.com/t3bp4vf.

[10] Eric Marten, "Mexico's Senate Passes Changes to U.S., Canada Trade Deal," *Bloomberg*, Dec. 10, 2019, https://tinyurl.com/yxxvfbry; Erica Werner, "House passes reworked North American trade deal in victory for Trump, Democrats," *The Washington Post*, Dec. 17, 2019, https://tinyurl.com/sqqadpm.

[11] Jennifer Hillman, Twitter post, Nov. 21, 2019, https://tinyurl.com/rlhhhf4.

[12] Jeff Mason, Andrea Shalal and David Alexander, "Trump says auto tariffs are never off the table in European trade talks," *Reuters*, Aug. 2, 2019, https://tinyurl.com/y2mrj8v8.

[13] David Shepardson, "Trump declares some auto imports pose national security threat," *Reuters*, May 17, 2019, https://tinyurl.com/y6nt7vre.

[14] Rachel Layne and Irina Ivanova, "The Trump trade war's hairpin curve: Autos," *CBS News*, July 19, 2018, https://tinyurl.com/y6py6kgb.

[15] "Section 232 Auto Investigation," Congressional Research Service, June 17, 2019, https://tinyurl.com/y5n3vccv.

[16] *Ibid.*

Auto industry experts cite NAFTA as a major impetus for this trend. Under NAFTA, the free flow of parts, as well as the lower cost of labor in Mexico, made it more attractive for foreign companies to build vehicles for the U.S. market in the United States, Mexico or Canada rather than pay duties on imported finished cars. Since 1992, some 10 foreign-owned manufacturing plants opened in the United States, bringing the total to 17 in 2018. Because more factories were built and autos were more cost-effective to build in the United States, exports doubled.[16]

But because no trade tariffs exist between the three participating countries under NAFTA, it is difficult to determine a finished part's provenance, Dziczek says. "One company does this one piece, it gets sold to somebody else who does some other piece, and so on." So it is "really difficult to trace" an auto part's precise country of origin, she says.

If a tariff regime required automakers to trace their parts, suppliers could be forced to open distribution centers closer to the auto factories, says Charlie Chesbrough, the senior economist at Cox Automotive, an Atlanta-based company that researches the automotive industry and publishes the well-known Kelley Blue Book.

"They're going to have to have facilities and sales people and marketing people in every country where their [automaker] counterpart is going to be having operations," Chesbrough says. "So it probably means higher costs for them just to maintain this

Rising Supply Chain Costs Likely to Hit Consumers

"It is hard to predict how consumers will react to higher prices resulting from tariffs."

Economists predict that existing and proposed tariffs on Chinese-made imports, which range from bicycles to shoes to food, could mean higher prices for those at the end of the supply chain—U.S. consumers.

Although some prices already have gone up, manufacturers, distributors and retailers are scrambling to figure out how much extra the consumer will be willing to pay and how much of the higher costs retailers and suppliers will have to absorb by cutting expenses, such as workers.

"It is hard to predict how . . . consumers will react to higher prices resulting from tariffs," Best Buy CEO Corie Barry said during an Aug. 29, 2019, conference call with analysts.[1]

The Trump administration in August imposed $300 billion in tariffs on Chinese imports. Roughly half of the tariffs went into effect on Sept. 1 and the other half was delayed until Dec. 15, 2019, allowing some retailers to stock up on holiday inventory before the price hikes took effect.[2]

Companies are adopting a variety of strategies for dealing with the tariffs. Walmart, the nation's largest retailer, warned in a letter to the U.S. trade representative in September 2018, a year before the latest tariffs went into effect, that such tariffs would boost prices.

"The immediate impact will be to raise prices on consumers and tax American business and manufacturers," wrote Sarah F. Thorn, a senior director for global government affairs at Walmart.[3]

But Target, a Walmart competitor, told suppliers it would not accept increases in their wholesale prices tied to the tariffs on Chinese goods. In other words, Target expects suppliers to absorb the higher costs due to the tariffs.[4]

As part of the Dec. 13, 2019, announcement of the new trade deal, the administration postponed enacting the final round of tariffs previously scheduled for Dec. 15, 2019.[5]

Holiday sales this year are projected to rise as much as 4.2 percent from 2018, largely due to job growth and higher wages, according to the National Retail Federation, a lobby group for U.S. retailers. However, the group added, "considerable uncertainty" remains around trade issues.[6]

Import volume at the nation's most popular ports for retailers rose in August 2019, indicating that companies were stocking up on supplies ahead of the Sept. 1, 2019, tariffs, according to the National Retail Federation and Hackett Associates, which tracks U.S. port activity.[7]

Barry said the September 2019 tariffs will affect prices of smartwatches, televisions and headphones sold at Best Buy, and the December 2019 tariffs would affect prices of computers, mobile phones and gaming consoles. The company, which gets 60 percent of its goods from China, has lowered its 2019 revenue forecast and is working on "mitigation efforts" to provide a buffer against price increases tied to tariffs, she said.[8]

In 1957, the first ship carrying modified World War II metal containers for commerce landed in Miami from Port Newark, N.J. The containers, later modified and standardized for sea, rail and truck transport, made international trade even more efficient because a single size is easier to stack, maneuver and design equipment such as cranes to handle.[70]

New Trade Rule's

After World War II, the United States helped to create a free trade system among noncommunist countries, in part in reaction to Smoot-Hawley, which most economists and historians consider had been a major catalyst of the economic turmoil that helped give rise to extremist leaders such as Adolf Hitler and the outbreak of the war.

The Allied nations created postwar economic institutions and rules, culminating in 1944 in the creation of the International Monetary Fund and the World Bank. Discussions ultimately led to the 1947 signing of the General Agreement on Tariffs and Trade (GATT), a set of trade rules aimed at reducing tariffs between countries.[71]

Nearly 50 years later, the World Trade Organization (WTO) replaced the GATT. It promotes free trade by negotiating rules acceptable to its 164 member countries

About 91 percent of U.S. households have smartphones, three-quarters of which are imported from China, according to the Consumer Technology Association, a lobby group representing companies that range from chipmakers to cloud computing service providers. If the December tariffs had been imposed, cellphone prices would climb 14 percent, or about $70 per phone, the group said. Purchases could fall by 28 percent, the group estimated, with low-income households being disproportionately affected.[9]

The situation is starting to harm consumer confidence, an indicator of how consumers might behave in the future. The measurement fell in October to the lowest level since June, its third-straight decline.[10]

It is not just electronics prices that are rising. Some 70 percent of footwear sold in the United States comes from China, much of it subject to the September tariffs, according to the Footwear Distributors & Retailers of America. The industry group represents more than 500 companies, including Easy Spirit, Nike, Crocs and retailers such as DSW.

The group estimated in August that under the new tariffs, prices for a pair of canvas "skate" sneakers would rise from $49.99 to $60.98, while typical hunting boots would climb from $190 to $231.03. A pair of popular running shoes might rise to $193.75 from $150.[11]

Rick Helfenbein, the chief executive officer of the American Apparel and Footwear Association, a lobby group representing manufacturers of accessories, footwear and apparel, says he is concerned that recovery from the next economic downturn will not be as fast as from previous downturns, including the 2007-09 recession.

"In our industry, in retail and apparel, we're the first ones to go in, and we're the first ones to come out" of a recession, Helfenbein says. "What bailed us out in '08 and '09 was the low cost of goods from China. And you know, this time around we're not going to have that."

— *Rachel Layne*

[1] Khadeeja Safdar and Allison Prang, "Best Buy Lowers Sales Forecast, Citing Tariffs' Toll," *The Wall Street Journal*, Aug. 29. 2019, https://tinyurl.com/y6hq4wyv; "Best Buy Co. Inc. Q2 2020 Earnings Call Transcript," *Motley Fool*, Aug. 29, 2019, https://tinyurl.com/y4bukpp2.

[2] Ana Swanson, "U.S. Delays Some Tariffs Until Stores Stock Up for the Holidays," *The New York Times*, Aug. 13, 2019, https://tinyurl.com/y3qd3clb.

[3] Walmart letter to the U.S. Trade Representative, Regulations.gov, Sept. 6, 2018, https://tinyurl.com/y2jshs8f.

[4] William Mauldin and Sarah Nassauer, "Target Tells Its Suppliers to Handle Tariffs Costs," *The Wall Street Journal*, Sept. 4, 2019, https://tinyurl.com/y256t93f.

[5] "United States and China Reach Phase One Trade Agreement," press release, The United States Trade Representative, Dec. 13, 2019, https://tinyurl.com/yk3v5xvr.

[6] "NRF forecasts holiday sales will grow between 3.8 and 4.2 percent," press release, National Retail Federation, Oct. 3, 2019, https://tinyurl.com/y447z9fs.

[7] "Retail imports surging again ahead of more tariffs," press release, National Retail Federation, Sept. 10, 2019, https://tinyurl.com/y2nqn3cs.

[8] Safdar and Prang, *op. cit*.

[9] "Testimony to the U.S. Trade Representative," Consumer Technology Association, June 17, 2019, https://tinyurl.com/yxm6jl6b.

[10] Katia Dmitrieva, "U.S. Consumer Confidence Falls to Lowest Since June," *Bloomberg*, Oct. 29, 2019, https://tinyurl.com/yxg6yah3.

[11] "Pres. Trump's 10% Shoe Tariffs," press release, Footwear Distributors & Retailers of America, Aug. 13, 2019, https://tinyurl.com/tcvkl6v.

and adjudicates disputes that arise when members are accused of violating those regulations.[72] Until Trump's election in 2016, U.S. administrations mainly pursued free trade policies, using tariffs or quotas only occasionally, mostly to protect specific domestic industries.

As information and communications technology developed, the intricacy and speed of supply chains grew, along with multinational corporations.

While technology was advancing in the United States, China's new "open door" policy, adopted seven years after economic reforms began in 1979, encouraged the expansion of a labor pool that was paid more than the average Chinese but less than wages in developed nations. The policy, aimed at pulling China's population out of agrarian poverty, drew investment and business from around the world, including the United States.[73]

Also in the 1980s, foreign auto companies began building plants in the United States and integrating and expanding their supply chains across the globe—in part to avoid import quotas imposed by the Ronald Reagan administration. Japan-based Toyota introduced "just in time" manufacturing techniques to Americans, in which parts are delivered to the factory in time to be used on the day they are delivered. That made smaller factories possible and boosted profits.[74]

By 2019, Japanese companies had invested more than $50 billion in the U.S. auto industry and employed 170,000 Americans. European and South Korean makers had followed suit, and by 2018, some 17 foreign-owned car manufacturing plants were operating in the United States, up from seven in 1992.[75]

The supply chain—called the global value chain—became more closely coordinated, mostly by using special software. It allowed companies—ranging from suppliers of raw, semifinished and finished materials to people transporting those parts and, finally, those assembling the products in a plant—to coordinate their efforts.

Technological Advances

With the advent of the World Wide Web in 1993, businesses began using EDI, personal computing and the internet to produce profound change in global trade and supply chains. These advances helped usher in an ICT revolution, according to Baldwin, of the Graduate Institute in Geneva.[76]

Companies, especially in the world's most advanced economies—known as the Group of Seven (G-7)—saw an opportunity to improve efficiency by moving factories to developing nations. By 1998 Jack Welch, then-CEO of General Electric—the world's largest manufacturer of locomotives, power-plant turbines and jet engines—said the ideal situation would be for companies to put "every plant you own on a barge to move with currencies and changes in the economy."[77]

Just as the steam engine and telegraph had spurred an earlier wave of globalization, the ICT revolution unleashed the next. The supply chain became "denationalized," enabling ideas and factories to be moved across borders, Baldwin said on the podcast *Trade Talks*. "The key wasn't the investment or the offshoring of the jobs. It was know-how. The ICT revolution allows G-7 firms to take their technology, marketing, managerial logistics [and] know-how in manufacturing and move it to nearby developing countries."[78]

Initially, companies chose to make high-tech products in higher-wage G-7 countries, Baldwin said, but within two decades these products could be made anywhere. "The boundaries of competitiveness now become international supply chains, which can cross countries," he continued. "GM can take its technology and apply it in Mexico. They can apply the same technology in Thailand, or China, and thereby validate and increase the value of their knowledge."[79]

In 1994, the United States, Mexico and Canada entered into the North American Free Trade Agreement, which cut most tariffs among the three countries, and supply chains for every sector—from agriculture to manufacturing to consumer goods—spread across the continent.

Changes in the U.S. auto industry typify the impact NAFTA had on supply chains. By 2017 the United States was importing more than 4 million vehicles from Mexico, up from 1 million the year the pact was signed. In the same time period, exports of U.S. vehicles doubled.[80]

In addition, some parts, such as steering or braking systems, cross the border up to six times as plants in all three countries add parts. (*See Short Feature.*) About half the vehicles sold in the United States are imported, and half of those imports are made by U.S. companies in Mexico or Canada.[81]

Under Trump, NAFTA has been renegotiated to include a section on digital trade, an issue that didn't exist in the original treaty.[82]

The new pact, called the U.S.-Mexico-Canada Agreement (USMCA), has been revamped by congressional Democrats and Trump administration negotiators for more than a year, securing bipartisan support. USMCA now includes factory inspections by an international panel that will confirm adherence to new provisions for wages and the environment.[83]

The U.S. House of Representatives on Dec. 19 voted to approve the new version of the USMCA following Mexico's approval on Dec. 10. Senate approval may not come until 2020, and Canada has said it will follow the United States in ratifying the deal.[84] Earlier in December, some Republican senators said they felt cut out of the deal struck by the House and the Trump administration.[85]

Protectionist Backlash

China joined the WTO in 2001 with "most-favored nation" status, a controversial decision that allowed it to enjoy the lowest tariffs and the fewest trade barriers between member nations.[86]

The advent of the internet, plus inexpensive labor in China and India, prompted U.S. businesses to close U.S. factories and move the work overseas, a practice called offshoring. Nearly entire industries that are at the start of supply chains, such as textiles, migrated out of the United States.

In 1995, the United States produced 13 percent of the world's textiles, while China made 12 percent. By 2017, China produced 47 percent of global textile output while the United States produced only 3 percent, according to the consulting firm McKinsey & Co.[87]

Between 1999 and 2010, some 6 million manufacturing jobs left the United States. Some economists say the rise of automation and artificial intelligence will continue to exacerbate the loss, but others blame China's rise.[88]

Still, China's rapid growth was fueled by its transformation into the world's biggest exporter. China's share of the global economy, as measured by global gross domestic product (GDP), went from 2 percent in 2001 to 16 percent in 2018, according to McKinsey. Put another way, China went from being the world's 10th-largest exporter in 2000 to the world's biggest exporter in 2017.[89]

In response to China's alleged intellectual property theft and restrictive rules for foreign companies operating inside its borders, Trump began imposing tariffs on Chinese imports in 2018, as leverage to negotiate more-favorable trade agreements. If all the tariffs had been enacted, every import from China would have been subject to tariff levels not seen since the 1930s.

CURRENT SITUATION
Economic Uncertainty

Three years after Trump's election, worldwide trade alliances are in flux, triggering concern among some companies and economists of a looming global economic slowdown.

The vast majority of economists and trade experts oppose the Trump tariffs and predict slower growth as a result. Some numbers are starting to back up that concern. Global trade this year may slump to its slowest pace since the 2007-09 recession, according to the World Trade Organization. On Oct. 1, 2019, the WTO cut its economic growth forecast for 2020, calling it "discouraging but not unexpected."

"Beyond their direct effects, trade conflicts heighten uncertainty, which is leading some businesses to delay the productivity-enhancing investments that are essential to raising living standards," said WTO Director-General Roberto Azevêdo. "Job creation may also be hampered as firms employ fewer workers to produce goods and services for export."[90]

In September, U.S. manufacturing, which accounts for more than 10 percent of the economy and is often a harbinger of the broader economy, slipped into recession (officially measured as two consecutive three-month periods of slowing trade and industrial activity), according to the Institute for Supply Management, which polls purchasing executives.[91]

And the tariffs on goods imported from China alone probably cost some 300,000 U.S. jobs, Mark Zandi, Moody's Analytics' chief economist said in a September report. The figure could hit 900,000 by the end of 2020 if all tariffs are imposed as announced, he wrote.[92]

That is probably why the S&P 500—an index of the daily performance of 500 publicly traded companies—soared to a record on Oct. 28, 2019, when Trump announced his administration may be nearing at least a partial deal with China to end the trade war.[93]

According to the Dec. 13, 2019, announcements from China and the White House, the United States will hold off on tariffs scheduled for $160 billion in mostly imported consumer goods from China and reduce levies imposed in September 2019 from 15 percent to 7.5 percent.[94]

That same week, voters in the United Kingdom elected a government committed to the country's exit from the European Union, a strong signal the post-World War II era of global trade cooperation is ending, according to a *New York Times* analysis.[95]

For now, American consumers, who drive the U.S. economy, are still spending, as unemployment hovers at the lowest rate in half a century. The National Retail Federation, a lobby group for U.S. retailers, predicted on Oct. 3, 2019, that holiday sales will rise 4.2 percent over last year's holiday season but noted that "considerable uncertainty [exists] around issues including trade."[96]

Some retailers and their suppliers stockpiled goods ahead of tariffs that went into effect on Sept. 1, 2019, electing to accept the risk that the inventory may not sell rather than pay tariffs on imported Chinese goods, the retail federation said on Sept. 10, 2019. "Retailers are still

AT ISSUE

Can global supply chains adjust to Trump's tariffs and still generate economic growth?

YES Gang Li
Associate Professor, Operations Management, Bentley University

Written for *CQ Researcher*, January 2020

The pain caused by President Trump's tariffs is being felt by U.S. consumers and businesses alike. Consumers are seeing price hikes, while companies are busy stockpiling inventory, lowering profit expectations and cutting costs. In the long run, however, the growth of global supply chains will not stagnate, even if Trump's tariff policy continues.

I have spent many years studying the "bullwhip" effect in supply chains, which describes how a small disruption could profoundly impact their performance. True, global supply chains are prone to disruptions, and the disruption caused by high tariffs is by no means "small." However, preparing for the unpredictable and being agile in response to disruptions are requirements for successful supply chain management. Global supply chains have demonstrated their robustness and agility in confronting major disruptions in the past. They will prevail again.

Businesses will continue reshaping their supply chains in today's changing environment. In October, Samsung closed its last mobile phone factory in China and expanded its production capacity in India and Vietnam, while Tesla is fast building its first giant so-called gigafactory in China. Global supply chains have been "shortening" since the global financial crisis of 2008, in order to be closer to end consumers, to reduce complexity and, now, to avoid tariffs. In other words, although Trump's tariff policy is highly unpredictable, businesses have been preparing to prosper in such an environment since a decade ago.

Businesses will increase their investments in emerging technologies such as artificial intelligence, big data and business analytics. For example, Amazon is automating its fulfillment center operations by utilizing mobile robots and drones. Technologies like this help companies reduce operational costs and depend less on labor, thus responding agilely to disruptions. Meanwhile, technologies nurture new demands for global markets and talents, providing the engine for the continued growth of global supply chains. Trump's tariff policy might dampen but certainly cannot kill that trend.

Since the late 1940s, all U.S. presidential administrations, regardless of their political ideologies, have maintained essentially a zero-tariff policy and for good reason: It helps the American economy. Meanwhile, global supply chains have remained strong, despite various disruptions, such as Japan's earthquake and tsunami in 2011.

In summary, if we must put our trust in the continuation of one of them, global supply chains or Trump's tariff policy, which would we pick?

NO Michelle Casario
Assistant Professor, Economics, Villanova University, and Co-Faculty Director, Elenore and Robert F. Moran Sr. Center for Global Leadership

Written for *CQ Researcher*, January 2020

Global supply chains can and have adjusted to the Trump administration's tariffs, but these trade systems are highly integrated and complex, and the relocation process is slow and costly. The disruption of supply chains raises costs for producers, as firms scramble to relocate parts of their production outside of China.

In the long run, diversifying production will benefit U.S. firms, but in the short run, it is costly and inefficient. Firms, especially consumer electronics producers, have deep manufacturing roots in China, developed over decades. Replicating those networks elsewhere, without similar infrastructure, is difficult and could take years.

In addition, the uncertainty surrounding tariffs makes it difficult for firms to undertake long-term planning, forcing U.S. companies to delay investment and reduce capital expenditures. The cancellation of the fourth round of tariffs, scheduled for December 15th, which would have effectively covered all goods imported from China, was a welcome relief for businesses and investors. However, pre-existing tariffs remain in effect on $360 billion worth of Chinese goods, causing a continuous disruption of supply chains and a degree of business uncertainty. This level of prolonged uncertainty regarding trade policy is unprecedented, and firms are looking for clarity.

The recent partial agreement represents a truce in the trade war, but it does not address the main issue that prompted the war: China's subsidies to state-owned enterprises. Without a "phase-two" deal that addresses the fundamental differences between the United States and China, and as long as the threat of tariffs remain, business and investor confidence will not be restored. So, the tit-for-tat tariffs between the United States and China have hurt U.S. producers and consumers without making real progress on legitimate issues such as forced technology transfers and government subsidies.

The most significant consequence of a trade war between the world's two largest economies is the negative impact it has on global trade and growth. The costly disruption of supply chains and the reduction in business investment is showing up in global data. The latest World Trade Organization forecast on trade flows shows just 1.2 percent growth—the lowest annual increase in a decade. This is consistent with the International Monetary Fund's recently downgraded forecast for global growth: It will fall to its slowest rate since the 2007-09 financial crisis. Weaker global growth weighs on U.S. exports and investment spending, demonstrated by the decline in factory activity, which in September hit a 10-year low.

While there is broad agreement regarding China's unfair trade practices, few would argue that escalating trade wars are the solution.

trying to minimize the impact of the trade war on consumers by bringing in as much merchandise as they can before each new round of tariffs takes effect and drives up prices," said Jonathan Gold, the vice president for supply chains and customs policy for the National Retail Federation.[97]

Trump administration trade policy announcements can change within days, often communicated by a presidential tweet. On May 30, 2019, for example, Trump tweeted that he planned to impose a 5 percent tariff on all goods imported from Mexico unless it agreed to changes in immigration policy, an unprecedented link between trade and foreign policy. He rescinded the plan on June 7, 2019.[98]

"Even if there's a truce or deal, that could change," says Villanova's Casario. "It's really a tweet away from the president just saying, 'Nope, we're going to go ahead' with tariffs. There's nothing in this truce or this agreement that says they won't. That is what affects the laptops, the phone, the video game console. All of those [have] been spared up until now."

That kind of uncertainty can shake supply chain managers at companies such as the San Mateo, Calif.-based GoPro, which moved a plant out of China to Mexico in June 2019. "We have moved most of our U.S.-bound camera production to Mexico—Guadalajara to be specific," GoPro Chief Financial Officer Brian McGee said at an investor conference in September 2019. "We are continuing to move lines, and we've adjusted inventory levels ahead of tariffs . . . to effectively neutralize the impact."[99]

GoPro began planning the move in July 2018 after the Office of the U.S. Trade Representative announced some of the first tariffs on imported Chinese goods. The company is in "pretty good shape," but still had "a little bit more to do in 2020," McGee said.[100]

Preparing for Recession

It is unclear if or how the new partial agreement with China will crack down on a central reason Trump gave for the tariffs in the first place: alleged intellectual property theft and the forced transfer of technology for companies doing business in China.

When pressed by *CBS News*, U.S. Trade Representative Robert Lighthizer said the administration is "right where we hope to be," having gotten "tech transfer, real commitments, IP, real specific commitments" with China. "This is a real structural change. Is it going to solve all the problems? No. Did we expect it to?

No. Absolutely not." The full 86-page agreement is expected to be released in January 2020.[101]

Some U.S. companies are cutting investments in supply chains to prepare for a possible recession, just when investment in new technologies may be needed the most.[102]

One remedy under consideration is to blacklist more Chinese companies, particularly those that repeatedly steal intellectual property.[103]

"It's hard to overstate the complexity of supply chain challenges," Robert Mayer, co-chair of the U.S. Department of Homeland Security's Information and Communications Technology Supply Chain Risk Management Task Force, told Congress in October. "For both suppliers and buyers, the potential universe of supply chain vulnerabilities touches all aspects of information technology."[104]

The risk covers "any physical or logical element that can be used to generate, store, manipulate or transport data in digital form," he continued. "That means the billions of new connected objects coming online will expand the risk universe exponentially."[105]

Supply chain managers in North America are breathing a sigh of relief after an agreement was announced in December on terms for the USMCA trade deal.

Another unresolved trade issue involving supply chains concerns tariffs Trump has threatened to impose on every foreign-made automobile or auto part. Economists have warned such taxes could mean hundreds of thousands of layoffs in the United States alone.[106] The new USMCA agreement shields auto imports from Mexico and Canada. (*See Short Feature.*)

OUTLOOK
Rethinking Approaches

What will changes in trade and technology mean for supply chains, the U.S. consumer and the global economy?

No matter what happens with U.S. trade policy, companies will rethink their approach, says Gartner's Raman. That could mean moving 10 percent to 30 percent of their supply chains to a different location or using new technology such as 3D printing to create their own parts and materials closer to consumer markets, she says. "Companies that do business with China have excellent reasons to do so. They will continue doing so. But more and more companies will be forced to at least tweak a portion of their sourcing."

Still, most economists expect protectionist policies to weigh on the global economy this year and next. A survey conducted in September by the National Association for Business Economics predicted that global GDP growth would slip below 2 percent in 2020 and possibly even lower. Eighty-five percent of the economists said they had cut their forecasts because of the trade war.[107]

Despite the partial agreement announced on Dec. 13, 2019, some economists remain skeptical. For one thing, the bulk of tariffs already imposed on imported Chinese goods remain intact under the new deal.

It "remains to be seen if the deal will stick," wrote Julian Evans-Pritchard, a senior China economist at the firm Capital Economics. "China seems to have won larger-than-expected tariff rollbacks for relatively few concessions."[108]

As new technologies such as 5G get closer to widespread use and concerns around intellectual property and security coalesce, trade policy will play an increasing role in how the global economy evolves. If the U.S. and Chinese economies decouple, forcing other countries to take sides, it could even risk triggering military conflict, Wharton's Garrett wrote. Yet technology companies in both places are so intertwined that corporate clout should prevent such escalation, he wrote.

"Advocates promote decoupling in the name of national security. I believe the opposite would be true," Garrett said. "Decoupling would profoundly harm America's national security by reducing the [economic] costs of war with China, hence making military conflict more likely."[109]

He is not alone. The former prime ministers of Australia, New Zealand and Sweden wrote in a *New York Times* opinion piece on Oct. 11, 2019, that decoupling would "present a long-term threat to global peace and security."[110]

Amid the trade war, China is lowering tariffs for other countries while raising them on U.S. imports in retaliation, according to a Sept. 20 analysis from Chad Bown, a senior fellow at the Peterson Institute for International Economics. That encourages U.S. rivals to trade more with China and bolster supply chains and economic relationships that exclude the United States, Bown wrote.[111]

"Trump's provocations and China's two-pronged response mean American companies and workers now are at a considerable cost disadvantage relative to both Chinese firms and firms in third countries," Bown said.

"The result is one more eerie parallel to the conditions U.S. exporters faced in the 1930s."[112]

But advocates of decoupling, such as AEI's Scissors, say such predictions are exaggerated. Companies are struggling with relocating supply chains because while "they understand that the world of 2016 is probably gone," it is not yet clear if trade policy will sever the two economies or just invoke restrictions that limit profit growth.

The "short term efficiency losses of the supply chain disruption are extremely low," but in the longer-term the situation is likely to be resolved, Scissors says.

"I understand the distributional effects could be important," he continues. But, he added, "I don't remember the treaty where we promised you indefinite U.S.-China supply chains. There was an opportunity, you took advantage of it, hats off.

"Now the situation is shifting," he points out. "Sorry, that's the way it goes."

NOTES

1. Jeanne Whalen, Abha Bhattarai and Reed Albergotti, "Trump 'hereby' orders U.S. business out of China. Can he do that?" *The Washington Post*, Aug. 24, 2019, https://tinyurl.com/y6aehv7g.

2. "History of the multilateral trading system," World Trade Organization, https://tinyurl.com/y92sle2v; Kevin Rudd, Helen Clark and Carl Bildt, "Former World Leaders: The Trade War Threatens the World Economy," *The New York Times*, Oct. 11, 2019, https://tinyurl.com/y5aqk62x.

3. William Mauldin, "U.S. Tariffs Prompt Anger, Retaliation From Trade Allies," *The Wall Street Journal*, May 31, 2018, https://tinyurl.com/y4gq28ys.

4. William Mauldin, Lingling Wei and Alex Leary, "U.S., China Agree to Limited Deal to Halt Trade War," *The Wall Street Journal*, Dec. 14, 2019, https://tinyurl.com/vl5bjzd.

5. "Impact of U.S.-China Trade War Felt in Both Countries," "PBS News Hour," Sept. 28, 2019, https://tinyurl.com/y3x66qxs; Rachel Layne, "Who pays tariffs on imported goods: China or U.S. customers?" *CBS News*, Aug. 5 2019, https://tinyurl.com/yy64dpdr; Chad P. Bown, "U.S.-China

Trade War: The Guns of August," Peterson Institute for International Economics, Sept. 20, 2019, https://tinyurl.com/y47ayo9e; and Mark Mauer, "U.S. companies preparing for long-term 'confrontational relationship' with China," *The Wall Street Journal*, Oct. 22, 2019, https://tinyurl.com/yygas77g.

6. Josh Zumbrun, "Global Economy on Course for Weakest Growth Since Crisis," *The Wall Street Journal*, Oct. 15, 2019, https://tinyurl.com/yxlwfnoz; Vince Golle, "U.S. Recession Risk Creeps Higher Because of Weak Business Spending," *Bloomberg*, Sept. 17, 2019, https://tinyurl.com/y6lr5tk9; and Josh Chin, "The Internet, Divided Between the U.S. and China, Has Become a Battleground," *The Wall Street Journal*, Feb. 9, 2019, https://tinyurl.com/y52xf4ta.

7. Rudd, Clark and Bildt, *op. cit.*

8. Margaret Brennan, "Transcript: CBS Face The Nation," *CBS News*, May 12, 2019, https://tinyurl.com/yxu56hp2.

9. *Ibid.*

10. Henry Paulson, "Statement from Henry M. Paulson, Jr., Former U.S. Treasury Secretary and Chairman of the Paulson Institute," press release, The Paulson Institute, Dec. 13, 2019, https://tinyurl.com/ws98ek7; Grace Zhu and Chao Deng, "China to Cut Tariffs on Range of Goods Amid Push for Trade Deal," *The Wall Street Journal*, Dec. 23, 2019, https://tinyurl.com/udn5od2.

11. Tom Connors, Mike Byhoff, Jenny Leonard, "How Trump's Trade War Went From Method to Madness," *Bloomberg*, Dec. 5, 2019, https://tinyurl.com/tft27v5.

12. Grant Clark and Shelly Hagan, "QuickTake: What's intellectual property and does China try to steal it?" *Bloomberg News*, March 22, 2018, https://tinyurl.com/y9glysko; World Intellectual Property Organization, https://tinyurl.com/tegh7r8; "United States Trade Representative 2017 Special 301 Report," U.S. Office of the Trade Representative, p. 1, https://tinyurl.com/reexfgw.

13. "Senate Democrats press Trump for China IP, tech transfer commitments," *Reuters*, Feb. 13, 2019, https://tinyurl.com/rv4ya3a.

14. Dennis C. Blair and Jon M. Huntsman Jr., "Update to the IP Commission Report," Commission on the Theft of American Intellectual Property and the National Bureau of Asian Research, 2017, https://tinyurl.com/yyn62c9x; "Current GDP calculator," World Bank, https://tinyurl.com/y63ybe4e.

15. Thilo Hanemann *et al.*, "Two-Way Street: 2019 Update U.S.-China Direct Investment Trends," Rhodium Group, May 8, 2019, https://tinyurl.com/yy3xhwfh.

16. "The Race to 5G," CTIA, https://tinyurl.com/yxg4s65u.

17. Joshua Oliver, "How 3D Printing Will Transform Mass Production," *The Financial Times*, Oct. 6, 2019, https://tinyurl.com/yyxkfbu8; Daniel Oberhaus, "Massive AI-Powered Robots Are 3-D Printing Entire Rockets," *Wired*, Oct. 14, 2019, https://tinyurl.com/y3dybr4a.

18. Elly Cosgrove, "Best Buy follows Amazon, Walmart in next-day delivery push in time for the holidays," *CNBC*, Oct. 22, 2019, https://tinyurl.com/y5ezm9lc; Hiawatha Bray, "From ocean to table, via blockchain," *The Boston Globe*, Oct. 24, 2019, https://tinyurl.com/y4jj6njr; and Edward C. Baig, "Say thank you and please: Should you be polite with your Alexa and the Google Assistant?" *USA Today*, Oct. 10, 2019, https://tinyurl.com/y2qf4pp4.

19. "Manufacturing labor costs per hour for China, Vietnam, Mexico from 2016 to 2020 (in U.S. dollars)," Statista, https://tinyurl.com/y2jtst4; "Table B-8," press release, Bureau of Labor Statistics, Dec. 6, 2019, https://tinyurl.com/gwme9z8; Cissy Zhou, "Could robotic automation replace China's 100 million workers in its manufacturing industry," *The South China Morning Post*, Feb. 14, 2019, https://tinyurl.com/y2wefsv7; and Niharika Mandhana, "Manufacturers want to quit China for Vietnam. They're finding it impossible," *The Wall Street Journal*, Aug. 21, 2019, https://tinyurl.com/y48jw5wy.

20. "CEO Confidence Declined to Lowest Level in a Decade," press release, The Conference Board, Oct. 2, 2019, https://tinyurl.com/webx6h6.

21. Donald J. Trump, Twitter post, Aug. 23, 2019 https://tinyurl.com/yxwcjbnk.

22. Indermit Gill, "Future Development Reads: China's shifting manufacturing labor pool is creating global dreams—and nightmares," The Brookings Institution, Nov. 17, 2017, https://tinyurl.com/yc48t9tc.

23. Lauren Feiner, "Google to acquire Fitbit, valuing the smartwatch maker at about $2.1 billion," *CNBC*, Nov. 1, 2019, https://tinyurl.com/y2kkac5g.

24. "Fitbit Diversifies its Supply Chain Outside of China," press release, Fitbit, Oct. 9, 2019, https://tinyurl.com/y6ydxlyb.

25. Rachel Layne, "Trump's Mexico tariffs send companies packing—again," *CBS News*, June 5, 2019, https://tinyurl.com/y6h3q3ms.

26. Yoko Kubota and Tripp Mickle, "Apple examines feasibility of shifting some production out of China," *The Wall Street Journal*, June 20, 2019, https://tinyurl.com/y4bzvqd2.

27. "Home Depot Inc. Q2 (2019) Earnings Call Transcript," *The Motley Fool*, Aug. 20, 2019, https://tinyurl.com/y3ubz3um.

28. Kubota and Mickle, *op. cit.*

29. "Apple Q3 2019 Earnings Call Transcript," *The Motley Fool*, July 30, 2019, https://tinyurl.com/y4rvfsln.

30. Stephen Nellis, "Apple's data shows a deepening dependence on China as Trump's tariffs loom," *Reuters*, Aug. 28, 2019, https://tinyurl.com/y26dva8f; Ben Winck, "Apple surpasses Microsoft as the world's most valuable company," *Business Insider*, Oct. 18, 2019, https://tinyurl.com/y5nk7u4s; "Apple 10K filing for the year 2018," U.S. Securities and Exchange Commission, undated, p. 23, https://tinyurl.com/y4bx3bae; and Austen Hufford and Bob Tita, "Manufacturers move supply chains out of China," *The Wall Street Journal*, July 14, 2019, https://tinyurl.com/yy3dss88.

31. Anna Fifield, "China's Growth Slows to 27-Year Low, but Trump's trade war is only partly to blame," *The Washington Post*, Oct. 18, 2019, https://tinyurl.com/y2m3cag4.

32. Greg Waldron, "Boeing values 20-year Chinese market at $2.9 trillion," *Flight Global*, Sept, 17, 2019, https://tinyurl.com/y6bujqm3; "General Motors annual 10-K filing for 2018," Securities and Exchange Commission, p. 2, https://tinyurl.com/y5gltfvx; "GM's third-quarter China vehicle sales down 17.5%, as U.S. automakers cede ground," *Reuters*, Oct. 10, 2019, https://tinyurl.com/y4yec8ug; Dana Hull and Chunying Zhang, "Elon Musk Set Up His Shanghai Gigafactory in Record Time," *Bloomberg Businessweek*, Oct. 23, 2019, https://tinyurl.com/yxldvuxm; and Thomas Franck, "Two major companies—Caterpillar and Nvidia—on Monday Blamed China for poor earnings," *CNBC*, Jan. 28, 2019, https://tinyurl.com/y8okzgya.

33. "Apple Supplier List," Apple, https://tinyurl.com/ycphlg6q; Daniel Ives, "First Round of Tariffs Likely Absorbed by Cupertino; A Wild Card in FY20," Wedbush Securities, Aug. 13, 2019, https://tinyurl.com/trbeypb.

34. "Member Survey," U.S.-China Business Council, August 2019, https://tinyurl.com/yyjcxmm9.

35. Nicholas R. Lardy, "Are Foreign Companies Really Leaving China in Droves?" Peterson Institute for International Economics, Sept. 10, 2019, https://tinyurl.com/y3ndeuwz.

36. Jim Rice, Kai Trepte and Ken Cottrill, "Trade Policy Whiplash Is the New Norm. How Do Companies Maintain the Integrity of Their Supply Chains?" MIT Center for Transportation and Logistics, June 17, 2019, https://tinyurl.com/y2k5oa7h.

37. "Trade in Goods with China: 2019," U.S. Census Bureau, https://tinyurl.com/k5xumsy.

38. "Manufacturing labor costs per hour for China, Vietnam, Mexico from 2016 to 2020 (in U.S. dollars)," Statista, https://tinyurl.com/https-www-statista-com-stati.

39. "Consumer Spending," Bureau of Economic Analysis, https://tinyurl.com/y48dwxko.

40. "U-M Surveys of Consumers: Confidence depends on favorable job, income prospects," press release,

University of Michigan, Oct. 25, 2019, https://tinyurl.com/yycdpaz6.

41. Matt Ott, "Consumer Confidence still high despite November decline," *The Associated Press*, Nov. 26, 2019, https://tinyurl.com/uyz646l.

42. "November 2019 Manufacturing ISM Report On Business," Institute for Supply Management, Dec. 2, 2019, https://tinyurl.com/y285t5me; "World Economic Reports," International Monetary Fund, October 2019, https://tinyurl.com/y5xcnc7a.

43. Gita Gopinath, "The World Economy: Synchronized Slowdown, Precarious Outlook," *IMF blog*, Oct. 15, 2019, https://tinyurl.com/y2ffh9fc.

44. "U.S.-China Tariff Actions by the numbers," Congressional Research Service, Oct. 9, 2019, https://tinyurl.com/rcenlyk.

45. Ellen Nakashima and Devlin Barrett, "Justice Dept. charges Huawei with fraud, ratcheting up U.S.-China tensions," *The Washington Post*, Jan. 29, 2019, https://tinyurl.com/yxppnfr6; "Meng Wanzhou: Huawei CFO seeks halt to extradition after Trump comments," *The Guardian*, May 8, 2019, https://tinyurl.com/y354nx77.

46. Graham Webster, "It's not just Huawei. Trump's new tech sector order could ripple through global supply chains," *The Washington Post*, May 18, 2019, https://tinyurl.com/yym9jjtm; Jon Fingas, "Intel, Qualcomm and other chipmakers cut off supplies to Huawei," *engadget*, May 20, 2019, https://tinyurl.com/y4awaff3.

47. Ana Swanson, "Trump Green-Lights Some Sales to Huawei," *The New York Times*, Oct. 9, 2019, https://tinyurl.com/y6zbgk7n; Sean Keane, "Huawei ban: Full timeline as House bars US goverment from buying Chinese company's gear," *CNet*, Dec. 19, 2019, https://tinyurl.com/yytlvuhk; and Jenny Leonard and Ian King, "Tech Industry Shudders as U.S. Weighs New Limits on Huawei Sales," *Bloomberg*, Dec. 17, 2019, https://tinyurl.com/qlposec.

48. Geoffrey Garrett, "Why U.S.-China Supply Chains Are Stronger than the Trade War," Knowledge@Wharton, Sept. 5, 2019, https://tinyurl.com/y5sf2ty5.

49. Clinton Fernandes, "What's at stake in Trump's war on Huawei: Control of the global computer-chip industry," *The Conversation*, Oct. 1, 2019, https://tinyurl.com/y3aplqbl.

50. Garrett, *op. cit.*

51. Wei and Davis *et al.*, *op. cit.*; "United States and China Reach Phase One Trade Agreement," press release, The United States Trade Representative, Dec. 13, 2019, https://tinyurl.com/yk3v5xvr; and Chad Bown, Twitter post, Peterson International Institute for Economics, Dec. 17, 2019, https://tinyurl.com/rjfwvrv.

52. "Trump announces 'phase one' deal with China," *CBS News*, Oct. 11, https://tinyurl.com/yyopcxrc.

53. Jeanne Whalen and Anna Fifield, "China's Huawei may need two to three years to recover from U.S. trade ban, CEO says," *The Washington Post*, Dec. 12, 2019, https://tinyurl.com/t6kfpl2.

54. "United States and China Reach Phase One Trade Agreement," *op. cit.*

55. Martin Chorzempa, "New CFIUS Regulations: More Powerful, Transparent, and Complex," Peterson Institute for International Economics website, Oct. 10, 2019, https://tinyurl.com/vppxbfb.

56. Ana Swanson, "Trump Officials Battle Over Plan to Keep Technology Out of Chinese Hands," *The New York Times*, Oct. 25, 2019, https://tinyurl.com/y2neabru.

57. Kevin H. O'Rourke and Jeffrey G. Williamson, "After Columbus: Explaining Europe's Overseas Trade Boom, 1500-1800," *Journal of Economic History*, June 2, 2002, pp. 417-456, https://tinyurl.com/y5p3kqfn.

58. Wolfgang Lehmacher, *The Global Supply Chain: How Technology and Circular Thinking Transform Our Future* (2019), https://tinyurl.com/yy3rdzj4l.

59. "Impact of the Telegraph," Samuel F. B. Morse Papers at the Library of Congress, 1793 to 1919, Library of Congress, https://tinyurl.com/y5b6gegt.

60. Tom Standage, *The Victorian Internet: The Remarkable Story of the Telegraph and the Nineteenth Century's On-line Pioneers* (1998), pp. 166-167.

61. Lehmacher, *op. cit.*

62. Richard E. Baldwin, *The Great Convergence: Information Technology and the New Globalization* (2019), pp. 57-58, https://tinyurl.com/y4ropenw.
63. Lehmacher, *op. cit.*
64. "U.S Tariffs and Trade: A Timeline," International Trade Commission, https://tinyurl.com/ycduqwhl.
65. Kat Eschner, "One Hundred and Three Years Ago Today, Henry Ford Introduced the Assembly Line: His Workers Hated It," *Smithsonian.com*, Dec. 1, 2016, https://tinyurl.com/wumgf3w; "100 Years of the Moving Assembly Line," Ford.com, https://tinyurl.com/y4egurga.
66. "U.S. Tariffs and Trade: A Timeline," *op. cit.*; Lehmacher, *op. cit.*, p. 9.
67. "U.S. Tariffs and Trade: A Timeline," *ibid.*
68. Richard M. Leighton, "Logistics," *Encyclopedia Britannica*, https://tinyurl.com/y36kfze9.
69. Frank Hayes, "The Story So Far," *Computer World*, June 17, 2002, https://tinyurl.com/y53uu7hp.
70. "The birth of 'intermodalism,'" World Shipping Council, https://tinyurl.com/kpa5nbs.
71. "Milestones: 1937-1945," U.S. Office of the Historian, https://tinyurl.com/h3tc5cn.
72. "History of the Multilateral Trading System," World Trade Organization, https://tinyurl.com/y92sle2v.
73. "China Profile Timeline," *BBC*, July 29, 2019, https://tinyurl.com/y5u3kf57.
74. "Toyota production system," Toyota, https://tinyurl.com/y56frrx5.
75. "Section 232 Auto Investigation," Congressional Research Service, June 17, 2019, https://tinyurl.com/y5n3vccv.
76. Baldwin, *op. cit.*, pp. 79-82.
77. "Welcome Home: The outsourcing of jobs to far-away places is on the wane. But this will not solve the West's employment woes," *The Economist*, Jan. 19, 2013, https://tinyurl.com/yyhxpb3s.
78. Baldwin, *op. cit.*, pp. 83-84; Soumaya Keynes and Chad P. Bown, "Trade Talks, Episode 72: Richard Baldwin on Disruption, Technology and Trade," Peterson Institute for International Economics, Feb. 14, 2019, https://tinyurl.com/yxwfx6n9.
79. Keynes and Bown, *ibid.*
80. "Section 232 Auto Investigation," *op. cit.*
81. *Ibid.*
82. "USMCA Fact Sheet," Office of the U.S. Trade Representative, https://tinyurl.com/y4lddw2w.
83. Wei and Davis *et al.*, *op. cit.*
84. Werner, *op. cit.*
85. Seung Min Kim, "Trump's top trade official meets with GOP senators to soothe tensions over final USMCA deal," *The Washington Post*, Dec. 12, 2019, https://tinyurl.com/vsukxlk.
86. "Principles of the trading system," World Trade Organization, https://tinyurl.com/ycf4pbry.
87. Marco Beltrami *et al.*, "The state of fashion 2019," McKinsey & Co, December 2018, https://tinyurl.com/yymtcmgb.
88. Jill Lepore, "Are Robots Competing for Your Job? Probably, but don't count yourself out," *The New Yorker*, Feb. 25, 2019, https://tinyurl.com/y2labwpc; Jeffry Bartash, "China really is to blame for millions of lost U.S. manufacturing jobs, new study finds," *Marketwatch*, May 14, 2018, https://tinyurl.com/y2kosr4c.
89. "World Trade Statistical Review 2019," The World Trade Organization, https://tinyurl.com/y2kuhudl; Jonathan Woetzel *et al.*, "China and the World, inside the dynamics of a changing relationship," McKinsey Global Institute, July 2019, https://tinyurl.com/y6bqndsa.
90. "WTO lowers trade forecast as tensions unsettle global economy," World Trade Organization, Oct. 1, 2019, https://tinyurl.com/y3uenp42.
91. "November 2019 Manufacturing ISM Report On Business," *op. cit.*
92. Mark Zandi *et al.*, "Trade War Chicken: The Tariffs and the Damage Done," Moody's Analytics, September 2019, https://tinyurl.com/t8gdon5.
93. Thomas Heath, "S&P 500 hits all-time high on strong earnings, global trade optimism," *The Washington Post*, Oct. 28, 2019, https://tinyurl.com/t8gdon5.

94. "United States and China Reach Phase One Trade Agreement," *op. cit.*

95. Peter S. Goodman, "Brexit's Advance Opens a New Trade Era," *The New York Times*, Dec. 17, 2019, https://tinyurl.com/serss9g.

96. Patricia Cohen, "Hiring Slowed in September as Unemployment Rate Fell to a 50-Year Low," *The New York Times*, Nov. 1, 2019, https://tinyurl.com/yymtuogb; "NRF forecasts holiday sales will grow between 3.8 and 4.2 percent," press release, National Retail Federation, Oct. 3, 2019, https://tinyurl.com/y447z9fs.

97. "Retail imports surging again ahead of more tariffs," press release, National Retail Federation, Sept. 10, 2019, https://tinyurl.com/y2nqn3cs.

98. Annie Karni, Ana Swanson and Michael D. Shear, "Trump Says U.S. Will Hit Mexico With 5% Tariffs on All Goods," *The New York Times*, May 30, 2019, https://tinyurl.com/ub4cv7n; Michael D. Shear, Ana Swanson and Azam Ahmed, "Trump Calls Off Plan to Impose Tariffs on Mexico," *The New York Times*, June 7, 2019, https://tinyurl.com/txxqch2.

99. "GoPro Reiterates Plans to Move U.S. Bound Camera Production to Mexico," press release, GoPro, May 13, 2019, https://tinyurl.com/y2bb2ly5; "GoPro, Inc. (GPRO) CEO Nicholas Woodman presents at Citi 2019 Global Technology Conference," transcript, GoPro, Sept. 4, 2019, https://tinyurl.com/y3kmkxkw.

100. "USTR Issues Tariffs on Chinese Products in Response to Unfair Trade Practices," press release, Office of the U.S. Trade Representative, June 15, 2018, https://tinyurl.com/y52hunau; "GoPro, Inc. (GPRO) CEO Nicholas Woodman presents at Citi 2019 Global Technology Conference," *ibid*.

101. Margaret Brennan, "Transcript: Robert Lighthizer on 'Face the Nation,' December 15, 2019," *CBS News*, Dec. 15, 2019, https://tinyurl.com/wkorl8z.

102. Golle, *op. cit.*

103. Heather Long, "Trump administration considers blacklisting Chinese companies that repeatedly steal U.S. intellectual property," *The Washington Post*, Oct. 26, 2019, https://tinyurl.com/y4shc7d4.

104. Robert Mayer, written testimony before the House Committee on Homeland Security, Oct. 16, 2019, https://tinyurl.com/y48co4xy.

105. *Ibid.*

106. David Shepardson, "Automakers warn U.S. tariffs will cost hundreds of thousands of jobs, hike prices," *Reuters*, June 27, 2018, https://tinyurl.com/y93lp5f5.

107. "NABE Outlook Survey—October 2019," National Association for Business Economists, undated, https://tinyurl.com/yxg5vdkx.

108. Julian Evans-Pritchard, "US-China trade deal, infrastructure spending," Capital Economics, Dec. 13, 2019, https://tinyurl.com/tv6ttsu.

109. Garrett, *op. cit.*

110. Rudd, Clark and Bildt, *op. cit.*

111. Bown, "U.S.-China Trade War: The Guns of August," *op. cit.*

112. Chad P. Bown, Euijin Jung and Eva (Yiwen) Zhang, "Trump Has Gotten China to Lower Its Tariffs. Just Toward Everyone Else," Peterson Institute for International Economics, June 12, 2019, https://tinyurl.com/y3qv5h5e.

BIBLIOGRAPHY
Books

Baldwin, Richard, *The Great Convergence: Information Technology and the New Globalization*, Belknap Press, 2019.
An international economist explains the evolution of trade and supply chains, including breakthroughs in the 1990s that led to a shift in factories, jobs and intellectual property around the globe at a previously unseen pace.

Lehmacher, Wolfgang, *The Global Supply Chain: How Technology and Circular Thinking Transform Our Future*, Springer, 2019.
The head of supply chain and transport industries for the World Economic Forum in Geneva examines the role played by supply chains in the global economy.

Articles

Hufford, Austen, and Bob Tita, "Manufacturers Move Supply Chains Out of China," *The Wall Street Journal*, July 14, 2019, https://tinyurl.com/yy3dss88.

Some global companies are shifting supply chains out of China to avoid paying tariffs imposed in 2018 and 2019.

Kapadia, Shefali, "USMCA promises streamlined shipments and customs—if it passes," *SupplyChainDive*, Sept. 17, 2019, https://tinyurl.com/yypu5rtw.

A supply chain trade publication details changes in cross-border shipping rules proposed in the U.S.-Mexico-Canada Agreement.

Keane, Sean, "Huawei ban: Full timeline as House bars US government from buying Chinese company's gear," *CNet*, Dec. 19, 2019, https://tinyurl.com/yytlvuhk.

A technology publication provides a timeline of the Trump administration's regulation of Chinese telecommunications company Huawei.

Lardy, Nicholas R., "Are Foreign Companies Really Leaving China in Droves?" Peterson Institute for International Economics, Sept. 10, 2019, https://tinyurl.com/y3ndeuwz.

A trade and finance expert argues U.S. tariffs on imported Chinese goods are not slowing China's economy and raising its unemployment there, as President Donald Trump claims.

Webster, Graham, "It's not just Huawei. Trump's new tech sector order could ripple through global supply chains," *The Washington Post*, May 18, 2019, https://tinyurl.com/yym9jjtm.

A policy expert outlines the increased power gained by U.S. authorities over a wide swath of technology companies through new import policies aimed at Chinese suppliers such as telecom company Huawei.

Reports and Studies

Dollar, David, et al., "Global Value Chains Development Report 2019: Technological Innovation, Supply Chain Trade, and Workers in a Globalized World," World Bank Group et al., April 15, 2019, https://tinyurl.com/y5m76kjm.

Global trade and economic organizations and regulatory bodies examine the state of technology, supply chains, trade and labor in this annual report.

Kolb, Melina, "What Is Globalization? And How Has the Global Economy Shaped the United States," Peterson Institute for International Economics, 2019, https://tinyurl.com/y6gl87jc.

Economists outline how changes in supply chains, technology, labor and trade have shaped U.S. businesses, workers and consumers.

Schultz, Michael, et al., "U.S. Consumer & Economic Impacts of U.S. Automotive Trade Policies," Center for Automotive Research, February 2019, https://tinyurl.com/y233t9v8.

Experts detail what proposed and enacted U.S. trade policy changes may mean for the auto industry's reliance on complex, cross-border supply chains—and for the U.S. consumer.

Shikher, Serge, et al., "U.S.-Mexico-Canada Trade Agreement: Likely Impact on the U.S. Economy and Specific Industry Sectors," U.S. International Trade Commission, April 2019, https://tinyurl.com/y22323do.

The federal panel that oversees trade policy examines the potential effects of a pact among the United States, Canada and Mexico that, if approved, would replace the North America Free Trade Agreement implemented a quarter century ago.

Williams, Brock R., et al., "Trump Administration Tariff Actions (Sections 201, 232 and 301): Frequently Asked Questions," Congressional Research Service, Feb. 22, 2019, https://tinyurl.com/yxuf7f2g.

The research arm of the U.S. Congress looks at laws authorizing President Trump's tariff actions—and their potential consequences.

"World Development Report 2020: Trading for Development in the Age of Global Value Chains," World Bank Group, October 2019, https://tinyurl.com/yytmza5w.

The institution outlines current trade practices and policies tied to global supply chains.

Podcasts

Keyes, Soumaya, Chad Bown and Jenny Leonard, "Trump's Mini-Deal with China," *Trade Talks*, Oct. 14, 2019, https://tinyurl.com/y623gm8c.
An *Economist* editor (Keyes) and a senior fellow at the Peterson Institute for International Economics (Bown) join *Bloomberg* trade reporter Leonard to discuss a possible U.S.-China trade deal.

THE NEXT STEP

China and Intellectual Property

He, Laura, "China just signaled that it could reform its IP laws. That's good for trade talks," *CNN Business*, Nov. 25, 2019, https://tinyurl.com/qp9cyxd.
China released new, stronger guidelines on the protection of intellectual property, which could please the United States as trade negotiations continue.

Lynch, Colum, "China Bids to Lead World Agency Protecting Intellectual Property," *Foreign Policy*, Nov. 26, 2019, https://tinyurl.com/twn68lv.
China's drive to lead the United Nations' World Intellectual Property Organization has drawn criticism from trade experts, who cite that country's history of stealing intellectual property.

Zengerle, Patricia, "U.S. agencies lax as China stole intellectual property: Senate report," *Reuters*, Nov. 18, 2019, https://tinyurl.com/uw3rzcs.
A Senate subcommittee report found that federal agencies were slow to respond as China stole intellectual property from U.S. university laboratories and research institutions over the past two decades.

Potential Recession

Higgins, Sean, "Trade war presents lingering recession threat," *Washington Examiner*, Nov. 5, 2019, https://tinyurl.com/uz9z8ap.
While the ongoing U.S.-China trade war is unlikely to cause a recession on its own, economists say it is influencing business decisions that could ultimately slow U.S. economic growth.

Schulz, Bailey, "Recession in the near future is unlikely, economist says," *Las Vegas Review-Journal*, Dec. 3, 2019, https://tinyurl.com/u3cfmme.
Some economists predict economic growth will remain steady in the next two years, but they cite U.S. trade policy and an inverted yield curve—in which long-term interest rates fall below short-term rates—as potential warning signs.

Winck, Ben, "New study shows small businesses are the most optimistic on record, even as trade-war and recession fears swirl," *Markets Insider*, Dec. 4, 2019, https://tinyurl.com/qtej3tu.
Even though U.S.-China trade disputes are weighing down the U.S. manufacturing sector, small-business owners are the most optimistic about the economy.

Tariffs

Beech, Kai, "Metal scrappers say their industry is struggling since international tariffs hit," *ABC7 Denver*, Dec. 11, 2019, https://tinyurl.com/rr8vnbn.
Scrap metal prices dropped after the Trump administration's tariffs on steel and aluminum came into effect, hurting businesses that buy and sell those materials.

Groom, Nichola, "U.S. solar group says Trump tariffs killing jobs; White House says 'fake news,'" *Reuters*, Dec. 3, 2019, https://tinyurl.com/uf6ttpg.
A solar industry trade group warned that the Trump administration's tariffs on imported solar panels could cost the United States 62,000 jobs, a claim the White House disputed.

Thorbecke, Catherine, "Trump administration threatens tariffs of 'up to 100%' on certain French goods," *ABC News*, Dec. 3, 2019, https://tinyurl.com/wzawvyq.
After France levied a digital service tax affecting U.S. tech companies, the Trump administration said it would respond with tariffs of up to 100 percent on French products such as wine, cheese, beauty products and handbags.

Trade Deals

"Japan's parliament approves trade deal with U.S.," *Kyodo*, Dec. 5, 2019, https://tinyurl.com/s3yf4jg.
Japan's parliament passed a trade deal with the United States that will lower tariffs on U.S. farm goods in Japan

in exchange for a reduction in duties on Japanese industrial goods in the United States.

Leonard, Jenny, and Shuping Niu, "U.S., China Move Closer to Trade Deal Despite Harsh Rhetoric," *Bloomberg*, **Dec. 4, 2019, https://tinyurl.com/wzfv8ug.**
The United States and China appear close to agreeing on the first phase of a trade deal that would roll back tariffs, even as political disagreements over Hong Kong and China's treatment of the Uighur ethnic group persist.

Rowan, Lisa, "What the USMCA Trade Deal Means for You," *LifeHacker*, **Dec. 11, 2019, https://tinyurl.com/vdg73b5.**
The benefits of the United States-Mexico-Canada Agreement could include higher wages for autoworkers and quicker access to less expensive generic drugs for American consumers.

For More Information

American Enterprise Institute, 1789 Massachusetts Ave., N.W., Washington, DC 20036; 202-862-5800; aei.org. Conservative think tank promoting free trade and enterprise.

Brookings Institution, 1775 Massachusetts Ave., N.W., Washington, DC 20036; 202-797-6000; brookings.edu. Bipartisan think tank concerned with national and international policy.

Congressional Research Service, 101 Independence Ave., S.E., Washington, DC 20540; 202-707-5000; crsreports.congress.gov. The research arm of Congress that provides nonpartisan briefing papers on major issues.

MIT Center for Transportation and Logistics, 1 Amherst St., MIT E40, Fl 2, Cambridge, MA 02142; ctl.mit.edu. A university division devoted to supply chain management, research and technology.

National Bureau of Economic Research, 1050 Massachusetts Ave., Cambridge, MA 02138-5398; 617-868-3900; nber.org. Private nonpartisan organization that conducts economic research and disseminates the findings to academics, public policymakers and business professionals.

Office of the United States Trade Representative, 600 17th St., N.W., Washington, DC 20508; 202-395-3230; ustr.gov. Federal agency responsible for negotiating, coordinating and resolving trade disagreements, including those affecting U.S. imports and intellectual property protection issues.

Peterson Institute for International Economics, 1750 Massachusetts Ave., N.W., Washington, DC 20036; 202-328-9000; piie.com. Independent think tank that researches and analyzes global trade and economic issues.

U.S. Department of Commerce, 1401 Constitution Ave., N.W., Washington, DC 20230; 202-482-2000; commerce.gov. Federal department that promotes job creation and economic growth for the U.S. economy.

World Trade Organization, Rue de Lausanne, 154 Case Postale, 1211 Genève 2, Switzerland; +41 (0) 22 739 51 11; wto.org. Global organization that oversees international trade rules and resolves trade disputes.

6

China Rising

Will it soon be the world's dominant power?

By Jonathan Broder

Chinese President Xi Jinping is featured in a billboard on March 30, 2020, in Belgrade, Serbia, next to the words, "Thank you, brother Xi." China had sent six doctors to Belgrade earlier in the month to help Serbia battle COVID-19.

From *CQ Researcher*,
July 24, 2020

THE ISSUES

In March, after Chinese authorities had claimed victory in containing the country's coronavirus outbreak, fleets of Chinese jetliners carrying doctors and palettes of medical supplies began touching down at airports around the world to help struggling countries combat the deadly pandemic.[1]

Soon, images of a smiling President Xi Jinping appeared on billboards in Belgrade, Serbia, and on the front pages of newspapers in other virus-stricken countries, as leaders there thanked him for the assistance and hailed China as a model for the world to emulate.[2]

Already a regional military superpower with the world's largest population and second largest economy, China is now seeking additional laurels as a global health leader amid the worst pandemic in a century. Driving China's demand for greater global recognition, experts say, are two of Xi's top priorities: his insistence on claiming what he views as China's rightful place on the world stage, and his determination to bring about a new world order that rejects the rules and norms of the U.S.-led system and instead places Chinese values, both old and new, at its center.

As the United States and other advanced democracies challenge China's ambitions, the two rival powers are moving away from the economic integration that defined their relations for the past three decades. And as the U.S. and Chinese navies flex their muscles in the disputed waters of the South China Sea, some fear

Wide Gulf in Military Spending Still Separates China, U.S.

China's defense budget doubled over the past decade, from $91 billion in 2011 to $182.2 billion in 2020, according to the Chinese government. But its military spending still badly trails the United States', which totaled $713 billion in 2020, according to the Pentagon.

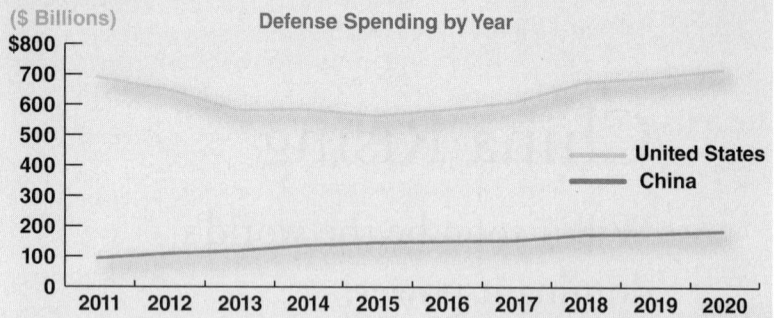

Sources: "Defense Budget Overview: United States Department of Defense Fiscal Year 2020 Budget Request," Office of the Undersecretary of Defense, March 2019, pp. 1-4, https://tinyurl.com/y579bon2; "Defense Budget Overview: United States Department of Defense Fiscal Year 2021 Budget Request," Office of the Undersecretary of Defense, March 2020, pp. 1-4, https://tinyurl.com/y8b6rmas; and Liu Xuanzun, "China slows defense budget growth to 6.6% in 2020," Global Times, May 22, 2020, https://tinyurl.com/y7a7mose

U.S. and China Make Up Nearly 40 Percent of Global Economy

The United States and China have by far the world's two largest economies: The U.S. accounted for 23.6 percent of global gross domestic production in 2019, and China accounted for 15.5 percent. Japan was a distant third at 5.7 percent.

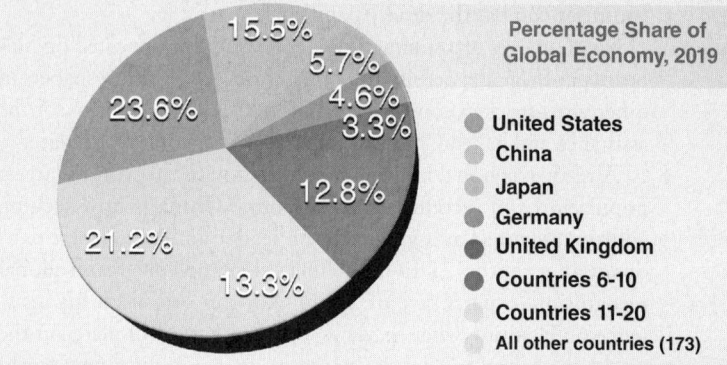

Source: Caleb Silver, "The Top 20 Economies in the World," Investopedia, March 18, 2020, https://tinyurl.com/y2f53utd

---

extent that it can start throwing its elbows around," says Jude Blanchette, an expert on China's ruling Communist Party at the Center for Strategic and International Studies (CSIS), a centrist think tank in Washington that focuses on global security issues.

Chinese officials used their elbows when they demanded that the leaders of countries receiving Chinese medical aid publicly praise Xi for his generosity, according to Wu Qiang, an independent political analyst in Beijing.[3]

After reports of an initial Chinese cover-up of the virus prompted President Trump to blame the pandemic on China and demand reparations, Beijing fired back by spreading false rumors that U.S. soldiers had brought the virus to China. And when the European Union (EU) and other industrialized democracies called for an independent investigation into the coronavirus' origins, China lashed out at its critics with a barrage of insults, threats and economic sanctions.[4]

China's initial mishandling of the coronavirus crisis, along with its belligerent response to criticism, has damaged Xi's standing in Washington and other Western capitals, analysts agree. But they are not so sure the damage will extend beyond the West's most advanced democracies.

Even though China's state-controlled capitalist economy contracted by 6.8 percent during the first quarter this year due to the pandemic, these analysts say that Beijing's economic weight is still simply too great for the leaders of many non-Western and developing countries to ignore, making their

a military confrontation over their increasingly irreconcilable differences.

"This is a much more aggressive China that is no longer willing to play second fiddle to the United States and now sees its own power as having increased to such an

praise for Xi a small price to pay for the Chinese aid. Recent surveys show China's economy is rapidly picking up steam, raising hopes for a full recovery this year as both its manufacturing and service sectors increase their activities.⁵

Experts said Beijing is not all that concerned about Western criticism. They point out that China's caustic rejoinders to its Western critics were never intended to change their minds. Rather, they say, they were meant to whip up nationalist pride at home and portray China to the non-Western world as a strong and self-assured power unafraid to stand up to the West.

"We think we're the audience, but we're not," says Nadège Rolland, a China expert formerly with the French Ministry of Defense and now with the National Bureau of Asian Research, an independent think tank in Washington.

Rolland and other analysts who study Xi's speeches and decisions say the 67-year-old leader believes the time has come to challenge the U.S.-led international order, reshape its liberal norms and establish a new order that reflects ancient Chinese values, such as benevolent autocratic rule and the people's fealty toward their authoritarian leaders.

The Chinese leadership has watched a number of events unfold over the past two decades that has convinced them the United States is a declining power, creating myriad opportunities for China, its autocratic form of governance and its state-controlled capitalism, the CSIS's Blanchette and other China analysts say.

Those events include the 2007-09 financial crisis, America's inconclusive wars in Afghanistan and Iraq and Trump's "America First" agenda that has harmed Washington's long-standing European and Asian alliances and has withdrawn the United States from foundational arms control treaties, the Paris climate accord and international organizations such as the World Health Organization (WHO).

Washington's increasing isolationism, these experts say, has allowed Beijing to exploit divisions among U.S. allies and assume leadership on climate change, global health and other weighty issues that Trump has shown little interest in pursuing. At the same time, they add, China has no interest in reprising the United States' performance as the world's policeman, except in East Asia, where Beijing sees itself as the dominant power.

Rolland says China's leadership is working toward a new order where China exerts what she calls "partial, loose and malleable hegemony" over countries that reject Western influence and liberal ideals, such as market-oriented capitalism, democratic rule and respect for human rights.

Under Beijing's vision of this new order, Rolland says, state-controlled capitalism is superior to its unrestrained version, which Chinese officials cite as the reason behind the financial crisis. She says China defines democracy not as a form of governance but as a reflection of a multipolar world. And, Rolland adds, China views human rights as the freedom of countries to pursue economic development, not in terms of individual freedoms.

Notably, she says, Chinese officials have not drawn the map of this sphere of influence along geographical or ideological lines but according to the degree of deference that countries are willing to give Beijing. "In other words, Beijing wants to create a modern version of its ancient tributary system," Rolland says.

Under the tributary system, which dates to the 2nd century B.C. and lasted until the fall of the Qing dynasty in 1911, the leaders of smaller East Asian lands acknowledged China's dominance by ritually kowtowing, or bowing, before the Chinese emperor and giving him symbolic gifts, or tribute, which opened the way for diplomatic and trade relations with their powerful neighbor.

Rolland says the contours of a 21st-century tributary system already have begun to emerge as a number of non-Western and developing countries scattered across South America, Eastern Europe, the Middle East, Central Asia and East Asia fall into China's orbit, drawn in by Chinese loans and investments and, in some cases, coerced by its growing military might.

But the Trump administration has portrayed China as an aggressive rising power that threatens both the United States and the U.S.-led world order. "This is a Chinese Communist Party that has come to view itself as intent upon the destruction of Western ideas, Western democracies [and] Western values," Secretary of State Mike Pompeo told *Fox News* in May. "It puts Americans at risk."⁶

Other countries have shown their willingness to abandon some Western ideals by defending China in international organizations.

For instance, after a state-owned Chinese shipping company bought a majority stake in Greece's busy Mediterranean port of Piraeus in 2016, Athens blocked the European Union the following year from delivering a statement to the United Nations that criticized

Beijing's human rights record. That record includes long prison sentences for dissidents and government critics, the detention and indoctrination of more than 1 million Uighurs, a Muslim, Turkic minority in far western Xinjiang province, and forced sterilizations of Uighur women violating China's strict two-child policy. A Greek official said the statement, which needed the agreement of all EU members for official release, amounted to "unconstructive criticism of China" that would have hindered its relations with the EU.[7]

At the United Nations itself, support for Beijing from many non-Western nations has helped Chinese nationals take control over four of the world body's 15 specialized agencies, where they have used their influence to advance China's interests, Western diplomats say. (See Short Feature.)

Chief among those interests is diplomatically isolating Taiwan, the self-governing island that Chinese leaders view as a renegade province that must be reunited with the mainland, preferably by peaceful means, but by force, if necessary. (See Short Feature.)

China also broadened its influence at the United Nations recently after Trump began withdrawing the United States from the WHO, the principal international agency fighting the coronavirus pandemic, over what the president charged was its complicity in Beijing's initial cover-up of the coronavirus outbreak. The WHO rejects the allegation.[8]

"We've ceded leadership to China," Bonnie S. Glaser, director of the China Power Project at CSIS, says of the U.S. pullout from the WHO. "And that plays to China's longer-term ambitions."

Beijing's assertive posture has alarmed ordinary Americans across the political spectrum. A recent Pew Research poll found that 68 percent of Republicans and 62 percent of Democrats regard China's power and influence as a major threat to the United States.[9]

A Harris poll in April showed similar results. "It's as much of a consensus issue as you can get in today's divided world," Harris Poll Chairman Mark Penn said. "Overall, there's very little trust for anything that the Chinese government says or does, especially its premier. Xi Jinping has less than half the credibility of President Trump in this poll."[10]

The public's distrust of China has led to a Trump re-election campaign that blames Beijing for the coronavirus pandemic, warns of its aggressive policies toward Hong Kong and India, and portrays the president's presumptive Democratic opponent, former Vice President Joe Biden, as weak on China.

But Biden has thrown those accusations back at Trump, citing the president's warm praise for Xi's leadership and allegations by former White House national security adviser John Bolton of Trump's efforts to enlist the Chinese leader in the president's re-election effort.

Meanwhile, administration hardliners are pushing to decouple parts of the U.S. and Chinese economies to eliminate America's dependence on some Chinese-made goods and bring manufacturing back to the United States.[11] And tensions are building in the South China Sea as the U.S. Navy sends more warships to the disputed waterway to match China's increased presence.

Many analysts say Sino-U.S. ties have now unraveled to their lowest point in decades, ushering in a new Cold War between the two world powers. As the U.S. election draws closer, they predict relations will only deteriorate further and most likely stay that way no matter who wins the November election.

Amid such tensions, here are some key questions analysts, politicians and others are asking about China's bid for global influence:

Has China's response to the coronavirus pandemic advanced its campaign for global leadership?

For several months now, China has been promoting its response to the coronavirus pandemic as both a model for other countries to follow in their own fight against the scourge and proof of the superiority of its autocratic system of governance as China tries to wrest key mantles of global leadership away from the United States.

A recent promotion came in a government report that detailed China's efforts to identify the virus, highlighted its strictly enforced lockdowns and quarantine measures that stopped its spread and underscored Beijing's warnings to other countries to prepare for outbreaks.[12]

Chinese officials and its state-run media often compare China's successful fight against the coronavirus with the United States' struggle to contain the pandemic.[13] Analysts say that Trump's heavily criticized performance has turned him into a perfect foil for the Chinese.

Moreover, they say, Trump's America First agenda, exemplified by his attacks on the WHO and his lack of

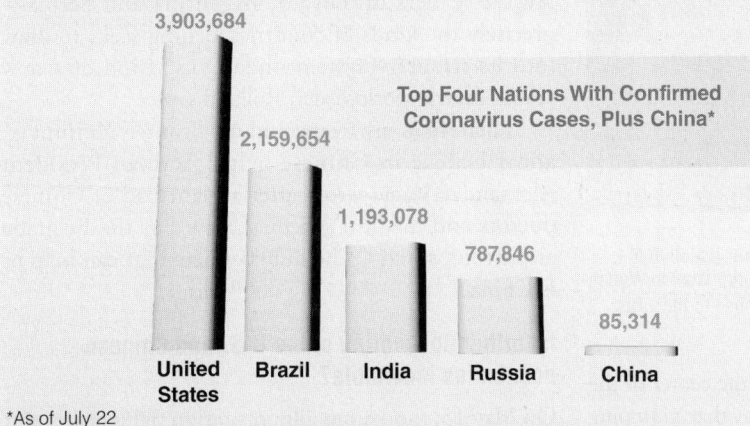

U.S. Leads the World in COVID-19 Cases

China, with the world's largest population at 1.4 billion, ranks 26th in the number of confirmed COVID-19 cases, at less than 86,000 as of July 22. The United States, with a population of 330 million, ranks first in cases, with more than 3.9 million as of that date. The pandemic began in China in late 2019.

Top Four Nations With Confirmed Coronavirus Cases, Plus China*

- United States: 3,903,684
- Brazil: 2,159,654
- India: 1,193,078
- Russia: 787,846
- China: 85,314

*As of July 22

Sources: "COVID-19 Dashboard by the Center for Systems Science and Engineering," Johns Hopkins University of Medicine, accessed July 22, 2020, https://tinyurl.com/rnjqnnh; "U.S. and World Population Clock," U.S. Census Bureau, July 15, 2020, https://tinyurl.com/pf8vpc8

interest in coordinating a global response to the pandemic, has left the door wide open for Beijing to fill the global health leadership vacuum. Indeed, soon after Trump announced he might withdraw from the WHO, Xi pledged more than $2 billion to the agency and promised to make any coronavirus vaccine that China develops available to the world.[14]

"Beijing has made the calculation that the international environment is tipping in its favor," says Scott Kennedy, an expert on China's economy at CSIS. "And one of the hallmarks of the Xi administration is pushing forward when it sees these opportunities arising."

But in the West, critics say Beijing's triumphant narrative involving the coronavirus makes no mention of the mistakes local Chinese officials made when the virus first appeared in the city of Wuhan late last year.

According to investigative accounts of China's initial response by both Chinese and Western journalists, local officials silenced doctors who warned of its dangers, withheld information from the public and played down the threat of further infections—all out of fear of delivering politically embarrassing news to their superiors.[15]

Only weeks later, after a respected Chinese epidemiologist had validated the public's mounting panic over the virulence of the virus killing their loved ones, did Xi order authorities to lock down Wuhan and other affected cities and enforce strict quarantine measures across the country. But by then, the virus had spread abroad.[16]

Bill Bishop, a business consultant who lived many years in China and now publishes his authoritative newsletter, *Sinocism*, says Chinese leaders in Beijing got caught between their own conflicting narratives explaining how they dealt with the outbreak—one meant for domestic consumption, the other for international audiences.

For the domestic audience that was already incensed over the Wuhan officials' misleading statements, "they had to blame the local officials for the cover-up," Bishop says. "So they allowed some very credible reporting by Chinese outlets that made it clear there were significant screw-ups at the beginning that allowed the virus to spread. But that narrative got picked up by the international media, which Trump used to blame Beijing for the pandemic."

Since then, China's reputation as breeding ground for dangerous diseases has grown. In June, the United States called on the country to shut down its markets that sell both live and dead animals and which health officials have identified as the source of several deadly viruses over the years.[17] Meanwhile, a recent study by the National Academy of Sciences said a new strain of the swine flu virus is spreading among pig farmers in China and urged immediate measures to avoid another pandemic.[18]

As a result, analysts say, China's standing as a trusted global leader—not only in health matters, but also on broader issues of governance, trade and respect for international law—has suffered, particularly among Western nations.

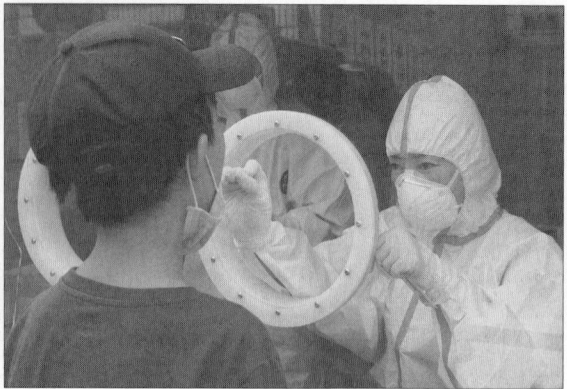

A health care worker tests for COVID-19 at a medical station in Beijing on July 14, 2020. The pandemic, which originated in Wuhan province, has aimed a spotlight on China's response to the virus.

"The pandemic has pushed China to the center of the international stage, but certainly not the way that Xi Jinping envisaged a while ago," says the National Bureau of Asian Research's Rolland. "Everybody's looking at China now, not for reasons of admiration or deference, but rather with anger and growing concerns about its actions."

Beijing's unusually pugnacious response to its critics—dubbed by the state-run media as "Wolf Warrior" diplomacy after two jingoistic Chinese films by that name—has only added to the West's anger toward China and its attempt to portray itself as the "responsible adult in the room," Rolland says.

Among the many examples of Beijing's new bare-knuckled statecraft, the Chinese Embassy in Paris provoked outrage across France in May after it alleged nursing homes in France had left elderly residents to die.[19] And when several Venezuelan legislators referred to the coronavirus as the "Chinese coronavirus," Chinese Embassy officials in Caracas accused them of suffering from a "political virus" and advised them to don their masks "and shut up."[20]

Beijing's Wolf Warriors reserved their strongest insults for Secretary of State Pompeo, whom they called "an enemy of humankind" in response to his repeated references to the pandemic as the "Wuhan virus."[21]

More than 110 countries have now called for a WHO investigation into the origins of the coronavirus. Xi has agreed to a probe, but only after the pandemic has been brought under control.[22]

But, says Rolland, China's campaign for recognition as a global health leader does appear to have gained traction among the non-Western and developing nations that received Chinese medical assistance. Among those who have offered fulsome praise to Xi for the assistance are the leaders of Turkey, Argentina and Serbia—precisely the kinds of countries Beijing seeks to draw into its tributary system under Xi's vision of a new China-centric world order, Rolland says.

"I believe in my friend and my brother, Xi Jinping, and I believe in Chinese help," Serbian President Aleksandar Vucic wrote after a planeload of Chinese doctors and medical supplies arrived at the Belgrade airport in March. "The only country that can help us is China."[23]

Is further decoupling of the U.S. and Chinese economies inevitable?

On May 15, the Trump administration tightened export restrictions on Huawei, the Chinese telecommunications giant, banning foreign chip manufacturers from supplying the company with advanced semiconductors designed with American equipment and software without a U.S. export license.[24]

The new regulation closed a loophole in earlier U.S. export controls that placed the same restrictions on U.S. chipmakers, but which Huawei managed to get around by buying the chips from manufacturers outside the United States that used American know-how.[25]

The May ruling was the latest in a series of measures Trump has ordered since taking office to decouple some of the complex supply chains that have defined the economic relationship between the United States and China for the past several decades.

Trump's decoupling efforts began in 2018 when he imposed tariffs on billions of dollars of Chinese imports. The tariffs sparked a trade war between the two countries, as China retaliated with its own levies on U.S. agricultural imports.[26]

Since then, the administration has placed export controls on a host of U.S. technologies that China could use for military purposes. It also has restricted the access of Chinese companies to U.S. telecommunications infrastructure and barred entry to Chinese graduate students and researchers in the fields of science and technology whose universities in China have ties to the Chinese military.[27]

In addition, the administration is pressuring NATO allies to keep Huawei's technology out of their military telecommunications infrastructure, warning the company will provide Beijing with a back door to spy on the alliance's communications—a charge Huawei denies.[28]

Analysts say another reason behind such measures is the administration's determination to prevent China from winning the race to master ultrafast 5G, or fifth-generation, telecommunications, artificial intelligence and quantum computing—advanced technologies that will determine global economic and military dominance for decades to come.

In December of last year, momentum toward an economic decoupling eased somewhat when U.S. and Chinese negotiators reached an interim trade agreement that required Beijing to buy $200 billion in U.S. products over 2017 levels during the next two years to help balance its trade surplus with the United States. The accord also required the Trump administration to gradually lift its tariffs as Beijing meets its purchase targets on schedule.[29]

But the damage the coronavirus has caused to the Chinese and global economy has set back that schedule. Of the $58 billion of U.S. goods that China should have purchased by the end of April, it bought just $26 billion, according to Chad Brown, a senior fellow at the Peterson Institute for International Economics, a nonpartisan Washington think tank.[30]

The United States will maintain 25 percent tariffs on approximately $250 billion of Chinese imports, as well as 7.5 percent tariffs on about $120 billion of Chinese imports, according to the Office of the U.S. Trade Representative. China has kept its own tariffs on $185 billion worth of U.S. goods.[31]

Most of these supply chains were established after China's 2001 accession to the World Trade Organization, which opened the door for U.S. companies to set up low-cost manufacturing plants in China. At the same time, Chinese companies such as Huawei grew to depend on U.S. supply chains for their high-tech needs.

Huawei has acknowledged the U.S. export controls pose a serious threat to the company's fortunes. "Survival is the keyword for us at present," company Deputy Chairman Guo Ping said in response to the latest measures.[32]

The export controls have drawn harsh Chinese threats of retaliation, along with the specter of further decoupling of the world's two largest economies.

"If the U.S. further blocks key technology supply to Huawei, China will . . . restrict or investigate U.S. companies such as Qualcomm, Cisco and Apple, and suspend the purchase of Boeing airplanes," tweeted Hu Xijin, editor-in-chief of the *Global Times*. The *Times* is published by the Communist Party's *People's Daily* and reflects the thinking of China's party leadership.[33]

Alex Capri, a supply chain expert at the National University of Singapore, said additional decoupling is virtually certain. "As the U.S. tightens the chokehold, tech companies in China and elsewhere will double-down on efforts to de-Americanize their supply chains," he told the *South China Morning Post*.[34]

Perhaps the strongest signal that more decoupling lies ahead, analysts say, is China's investment of hundreds of billions of dollars in its "Made in China 2025" initiative, which aims to manufacture its own advanced semiconductors and dominate key advanced technologies within the next five years.[35]

Yet China's vision of economic decoupling appears to run only in one direction, says the National Bureau of Asian Research's Rolland. While Beijing moves toward ending its reliance on U.S. technology, she says, it wants other countries to maintain their dependence on China's supply chains.

"What they want for themselves is not what they want for the outside world," she says. "They want others to remain coupled to China, even though they're decoupling themselves."

Many economists say that while a partial decoupling of the two economies may be underway, the economies of the United States and China have become so thoroughly integrated that a complete decoupling would be impossible without massive economic dislocation in both countries. Meanwhile, they add, Germany's willingness to ignore administration pressure does not bode well for the president's vision of a weakened China decoupled from the West.

"The chances that the U.S. will be able to isolate China is totally unrealistic," says CSIS' Kennedy. "The rest of the world is probably going to continue doing business with China, which means the only type of decoupling that the U.S. can realistically achieve is one that hurts both American companies and American interests."

Do U.S.-China tensions over the coronavirus increase the chances for a military clash between the two world powers?

When a coronavirus outbreak aboard two U.S. aircraft carriers earlier this spring forced them into quarantine at their home ports in Guam and Japan, China quickly sent one of its own carrier battle groups into the western Pacific.[36]

Independent military analysts say the appearance of the Chinese carrier *Liaoning* and five accompanying warships served as a reminder to neighbors of China's growing military power and a warning to the United States, East Asia's security guarantor since the end of World War II, that a changing of the guard is underway.

Military analysts say that the Chinese aircraft carrier and its accompanying frigates and destroyers are considered no match for the U.S. Navy. The *Liaoning*, for example, is a refit of a Soviet carrier that runs off old-fashioned steam-powered turbines and is much smaller than the biggest U.S. carriers, which are nuclear powered.

But these analysts also say that in any naval confrontation between the two powers in the western Pacific, China has the advantage of geographical proximity, while the closest U.S. naval bases are more than 1,000 miles away in Guam and Japan. The analysts add that China has hypersonic anti-ship missiles—missiles that exceed the speed of sound—that can sink a U.S. carrier.

As the Chinese warships steamed into the South China Sea, Beijing's state-controlled media brimmed with chest-thumping comparisons, including the claim that, unlike the hundreds of virus-stricken U.S. sailors from the two quarantined carriers, no Chinese sailors in its carrier battle groups had become infected.

"As the most powerful military force in the world, with the highest level of combat readiness, the U.S. military's failure to contain the virus has been disappointing," said Hu Bo, director of Peking University's Center for Maritime Strategy.[37]

One-upmanship aside, Rolland and other China experts say such displays of Chinese firepower are meant to underscore a nationalist message that Xi has repeatedly delivered in his speeches: After a century of humiliating foreign rule that lasted until the end of World War II, plus another 75 years during which the U.S. Navy has served as East Asia's maritime sheriff, a rich and powerful China will assume that role, whether the West likes it or not.

"They're saying, 'We will not back down from this Western arrogance. We will not bow,'" Rolland says.

Since then, however, both sides have increased their naval and air forces in the South China Sea and near Taiwan, adding an unpredictable layer of military tensions to the deteriorating political and economic ties between the two superpowers.

Reuters recently reported that China's Ministry of State Security, the country's top intelligence agency, presented a paper to China's leadership in April that said the nation faced a growing wave of Western hostility as a result of the pandemic and warned tensions could build into a military confrontation with the United States.[38]

To date, Xi has done little to reduce tensions, analysts say. If anything, they say, he has used the world's preoccupation with the pandemic to reinforce Beijing's claim to the South China Sea over Southeast Asian countries that have rival claims.

Over the past few months, Chinese paramilitary vessels have sunk a Vietnamese fishing boat in disputed waters and resumed their harassment of a Malaysian survey ship after a U.S. Navy escort left the area. And in different stretches of water claimed by the Philippines or by Vietnam, armadas of Chinese fishing boats, backed by Chinese naval vessels, have driven away fishermen from those countries.[39]

Such behavior, experts say, has left Southeast Asian nations caught between China, which wields both military and economic influence as their largest trading partner, and the United States, to whom they have been looking to temper China's behavior.

The Pentagon has stepped up the Navy's "Freedom of Navigation" operations in the South China Sea, sending U.S. warships and military aircraft into the area in a direct challenge to Beijing's territorial claims. According to sailors and airmen who have participated in these operations, Chinese officers routinely order the U.S. ships and aircraft to leave the area, which they eventually do, but only when their operations conclude.[40]

Daniel Blumenthal, director of Asian studies at the American Enterprise Institute, says these operations, along with closer U.S. military cooperation with Southeast Asian countries, such as Australia, the Philippines and Vietnam, will increase the geopolitical costs China will pay for its South China Sea territorial claim.

"Over time, as a result of the cooperation between the U.S. and its partners and allies, there will be an encirclement of the Chinese in the South China Sea, which is something the Chinese have been working to avoid for the better part of the 20th century," Blumenthal says.

But Gregory Poling, a senior fellow at CSIS and an expert on China's military, says the U.S. operations have accomplished nothing for the Southeast Asian countries.

"The Chinese continue to make it so Filipino fisherman can't fish, Vietnamese oil and gas operators can't drill, and Malaysian survey ships can't do their job," he says. Without greater political and diplomatic pressure on China, Poling expects China's Southeast Asian neighbors eventually will fall into Beijing's economic and political orbit.

"In short, China is now capable of controlling the South China Sea in all scenarios short of war with the United States," Adm. Philip S. Davidson told Congress just before taking up his post as head of the U.S. Indo-Pacific Command in 2018.[41]

Davidson's assessment still holds true, military analysts say.

Some experts say the U.S. military would quickly defeat Chinese forces in any confrontation over the South China Sea. But many others are not so sure.

Christian Brose, the former staff director of the Senate Armed Services Committee and national security adviser to the late Sen. John McCain, R-Ariz., argues that because of China's close proximity to the region, its huge arsenal of hypersonic and ballistic missiles and its new ultra-quiet diesel-powered submarines, the Chinese would inflict heavy losses on U.S. forces in the opening stages of any conventional war over the South China Sea.[42]

Other military experts agree with that grim scenario, adding such a conflict would quickly escalate.

"The U.S. either has to walk away if fighting starts, or the U.S. has to escalate very quickly to long-range [nuclear] missiles," Poling says. "And that's a big problem because in most cases, people are going to look at the South China Sea and say, 'This isn't worth nuclear war.'"

BACKGROUND
Turmoil in China

In 1911, Western-educated Chinese revolutionaries overthrew the country's Qing rulers after humiliating military defeats at the hands of European and Japanese armies, onerous reparations payments to the victors, internal rebellions and the ruling dynasty's refusal to implement modernizing reforms. The fall of the Qing dynasty marked the end of more than 2,000 years of imperial rule in China.[43]

In its place, the revolutionaries founded the Republic of China a year later. Inspired by the writings of America's Founders, they envisioned a constitutional democracy. But political differences among the leaders soon threw the infant republic into more than a decade of civil war.

Two rival groups emerged from the fighting as the strongest contenders for power: the internationally recognized government, headed by Chiang Kai-shek and his right-wing Kuomintang, or Nationalist Party, and the Chinese Communist Party (CCP), founded in 1921 amid widespread labor unrest and led by Mao Zedong.

Meanwhile, imperial Japan, hungry for raw materials, seized China's northeastern province of Manchuria in 1931. As Japanese forces began driving south in 1937 to capture more Chinese territory, Chiang's Nationalist troops and communist guerrillas temporarily shelved their bloody rivalry to team up against the invaders.[44]

But they were no match for the Japanese, who seized Beijing and the port of Tianjin. After capturing the eastern city of Nanjing, China's capital at the time, Japanese soldiers killed up to 300,000 mostly civilian Chinese in a weeks-long bloodbath meant to crush the country's will to resist.[45]

A Chinese family flees from the fighting in Shanghai after Japanese troops invaded the city in 1937.

CHRONOLOGY

1839-1912 *Opium wars and rebellions hasten the Qing dynasty's fall.*

1839-42 Britain goes to war against China's Qing dynasty after it bans the opium trade, Britain's most lucrative export; the victorious British gain Hong Kong and access to five mainland ports.

1850-64 Taiping rebellion leaves as many as 30 million dead, weakening Qing rule.

1858-60 In second opium war, Britain and France force Qing rulers to legalize trade of the drug and open several more ports to Western commerce and residence.

1894-95 China is defeated in Sino-Japanese war, making Japan the dominant power in East Asia.

1899-1901 Anti-foreigner Boxer Rebellion threatens Westerners in China; eight-nation force, including U.S. troops, defeats the rebels and their Imperial Army allies. Qing rulers are forced to pay the equivalent of $10 billion in reparations.

1911-12 Revolution topples the Qing dynasty, ending 2,000 years of imperial rule; the Republic of China is established.

1921-1949 *After long civil war, communists establish the People's Republic of China.*

1921 Amid widespread labor unrest, Mao Zedong forms the Chinese Communist Party.

1927 Civil war erupts between Nationalist government forces and communists.

1937 Government and communists join forces to fight Japanese troops after they invade the rest of China from occupied Manchuria; following the Japanese massacre of as many as 300,000 in Nanjing, the United States provides military aid to China's government.

1941-45 U.S. battles and eventually defeats Japan in World War II. . . . At conflict's end, Chinese civil war resumes.

1949 With the communists' defeat of government forces, Mao founds the People's Republic of China; Nationalists led by Chiang Kai-shek retreat to Taiwan, where they re-establish their government.

1950-1979 *After Korean War, Taiwan crises and Mao's disastrous economic policies, U.S. establishes relations with China.*

1950-53 Korean War pits Chinese and U.S. forces against each other as allies of North and South Korea, respectively; the war ends in stalemate.

1954 Fighting erupts across the Taiwan Strait; in defense of Taiwan, U.S. threatens China with nuclear attack, forcing Beijing to negotiate with Taipei over disputed islands.

1958 Negotiations falter and cross-strait fighting resumes; U.S. sends weapons and naval assistance to Taiwan and prepares nuclear strikes on major Chinese cities, forcing Beijing to back down.

1958-62 Under Mao's Great Leap Forward, amid an ill-prepared industrialization drive, agriculture is collectivized, resulting in as many as 45 million deaths from starvation.

1964 China explodes its first nuclear weapon.

1966-76 Mao's Cultural Revolution forces millions of city dwellers to move to the countryside, once again setting back the economy and leaving China a global backwater.

1972 President Richard M. Nixon visits China, beginning the process of normalizing relations between Washington and Beijing.

1976 Mao dies; two years later, Deng Xiaoping assumes power and institutes sweeping free market reforms.

1979 After President Jimmy Carter withdraws diplomatic recognition from Taiwan, the United States and China establish full relations.

1989-2011 *As China's economy grows, U.S. leaders overlook its human rights abuses.*

1989 Chinese students fill Beijing's Tiananmen Square and demand democracy, prompting communist leaders to send in troops and tanks, killing hundreds; Washington briefly imposes sanctions but signals it wants normal relations to continue.

1995-96 A third cross-strait crisis erupts, bringing Washington and Beijing to the brink of war; the crisis subsides after China makes an implicit nuclear threat against the United States.

2001 With U.S. support, China joins the World Trade Organization, ushering in a decade of economic integration in which American companies open factories in China and millions of American workers lose their jobs. With its exports of steel and cheap consumer goods, China's economy grows into the world's second largest.

2012-Present *U.S.-China relations unravel as Beijing challenges the U.S.-led world order.*

2012 Xi Jinping takes power, promoting Chinese nationalism.

2013 Xi launches his Belt and Road Initiative, using infrastructure projects to tie developing countries closer to China; Xi also asserts Chinese sovereignty over the South China and East China seas.

2016 Republican Donald Trump is elected U.S. president, promising to challenge China on trade.

2018 Trump imposes tariffs on an array of Chinese imports, sparking a trade war.

2019 The coronavirus breaks out in China and quickly spreads abroad.

2020 Trump blames China for the global pandemic and continues steps to decouple the U.S. and Chinese economies.... U.S. Navy challenges China's territorial claims over the South China Sea.... After the pandemic causes China's economy to contract by nearly 7 percent in the first quarter, its economy grows by 1.1 percent in second quarter as production slowly resumes.

Japan's atrocities outraged Americans. Over the next several years, President Franklin D. Roosevelt extended $100 million in credit to the Chinese government to buy war materiel.[46]

Roosevelt also imposed an oil embargo on Japan to hinder its Asian expansionism. In response, on Dec. 7, 1941, Japanese forces attacked the U.S. Navy's Pacific fleet at Hawaii's Pearl Harbor. The next day, Congress declared war against Japan, plunging the United States into World War II.

From then on, China's war against Japan became subsumed within the larger global conflagration. Despite the U.S. assistance, however, Japanese forces held nearly the entire eastern coast of China until the war ended in 1945 with Japan's defeat.[47]

Communist Victory

The war left China in ruins, with as many as 20 million dead and millions more displaced across a vast, war-ravaged landscape.[48] Without a foreign enemy to unite them, the alliance between the government and the communists crumbled and their civil war resumed.

In the United States, a group of influential Americans calling themselves the American China Policy Association pressured the Truman administration to continue U.S. support for Chiang.[49]

Still, despite $2 billion in U.S. aid to the Nationalists, Mao's communist forces defeated them in 1949 and founded the People's Republic of China, declaring its communist government the country's sole legitimate representative. Chiang and his Nationalist followers retreated to the island of Taiwan, where they reconstituted their Republic of China and staked a rival claim as China's sole legitimate sovereign.[50]

President Harry S. Truman shunned the communists on the mainland and recognized Chiang's Republic of China on Taiwan as China's legitimate government. This policy would keep Washington and Beijing estranged for years to come.

Americans' antipathy toward communism intensified when communist North Korea, backed by China and the Soviet Union, invaded South Korea in June 1950. The recently formed United Nations authorized an international force made up mostly of U.S. troops to aid South Korea. After three years of fighting that saw

China Is Locked in a Battle of Wills With Taiwan

Beijing increases pressure on what it calls a renegade province.

A Chinese H-6 nuclear-capable bomber and several fighter escorts penetrated Taiwan's air space recently before Taiwanese interceptors drove them off.[1] It was the latest in a series of Chinese violations this year as Beijing ramps up its efforts to intimidate and isolate the island and its pro-independence leader.

Beijing considers Taiwan a renegade Chinese province and its President Tsai Ing-wen a threat to Beijing's "One Country, Two Systems" framework. That formula states there is only one China, of which Taiwan is an inseparable part, but also stipulates that each side can define for itself what kind of China it represents.

Chinese officials say this means that, for now, Taiwan may retain its democratic governance while China is ruled by its authoritarian communist system. But eventually, China insists, the two parts of the country must be reunited under Beijing's rule—preferably by diplomatic means, but by force if necessary.

China has called this framework the "1992 Consensus" for the year it was negotiated with Taiwanese leaders. At the time, Beijing said that as long as Taiwan accepted this consensus, a peaceful status quo of cross-strait trade relations would continue.

Taiwanese leaders embraced the consensus until 2016. But when Tsai was elected that year, she rejected it, saying the People's Republic of China on the mainland and Taiwan (whose official name is the Republic of China) were two separate nations.[2] Taiwan split from the mainland in 1949 when anti-communist forces fled there after their defeat in a civil war.

In a speech before she was re-elected this year to a second four-year term, Tsai called reunification under the One Country, Two Systems framework "impossible." Her views have struck a chord with many in Taiwan, who have watched as Beijing's moves have eroded the semiautonomy granted to Hong Kong under the same framework and feared the same results if Taiwan accepted the One Country, Two Systems framework.[3]

Taiwanese officials say China's recent enactment of a national security law for Hong Kong that circumvented the city's Beijing-backed government has laid bare the hollowness of its One Country, Two Systems framework. And with China's intrusions into Taiwanese airspace and its warnings to Taipei not to shelter Hong Kong political refugees who have been arriving on the island in growing numbers, these officials fear Beijing may be poised to enforce its claim over Taiwan.

"Hong Kong has become less free, so our sense of fear has increased," said Chen Po-wei, a Taiwanese lawmaker who supports independence. "Because of China's nature, there is a high possibility of conflict."[4]

China also has accused Tsai of moving Taiwan toward independence—a charge she has done little to disprove. At a post-election news conference in January where a reporter asked if she would formally declare Taiwan's independence, Tsai replied that the country is "already independent," and therefore she saw no need to declare it so.[5]

Many analysts saw her remarks as a politically adroit way to reassure Taiwan's increasingly independence-minded voters while avoiding a military conflict with China. In 2005, Beijing adopted a law that authorizes the use of force against Taiwan if China judges it to have seceded from the mainland. President Xi Jinping and Chinese military leaders have repeatedly warned that a formal Taiwanese declaration of independence would mean war.

Infuriated by Tsai's refusal to accept the 1992 Consensus and her support for Hong Kong's pro-democracy movement, Beijing has cut all formal ties to her government since she took office and halted visits to Taiwan by Chinese tourists, delivering a painful blow to the island's economy. China also has wielded its political influence to exclude Taiwan's representatives from international forums and

---

Chinese and American troops battle each other, the war ended in a stalemate, with the two sides once again facing each other across the 38th parallel, the border between North and South Korea when the war started. In July 1953, they signed an armistice that ended the fighting.[51]

But tensions between the United States and China flared just a year later in what became known as the first

used its economic power to lure away more of Taiwan's few remaining diplomatic allies.

Since 2016, Beijing has pulled in seven of these countries, using billions of dollars in infrastructure loans as incentives to abandon Taiwan. The countries are the African nations of Burkina Faso and São Tomé and Principe; in Latin America, the Dominican Republic, El Salvador and Panama; and the tiny Pacific island nations of Kiribati and the Solomon Islands. The defections have whittled down the number of countries extending diplomatic recognition to Taiwan to 15, out of a total of 193 United Nations member states.[6]

Since Tsai's re-election in January, Beijing has added military threats to its pressure campaign.

Over the past several months, the Chinese military has conducted live-fire and amphibious military exercises on the mainland just across from Taiwan, sailed its two aircraft carrier battle groups through the Taiwan Strait that divides the island from the mainland, and repeatedly sent its bombers and warplanes into Taiwanese airspace in what analysts describe as both a deliberate exercise in intimidation and a test of Taiwan's air defenses in the event of a war.

After the first few intrusions, Tsai in April ordered the "forceful expulsion" of any Chinese military aircraft violating the country's airspace, prompting analysts to warn China's intrusions risked igniting yet another cross-strait clash that would most likely draw in the United States on Taiwan's side.[7]

On two consecutive days in February, U.S. military experts say, the violations involved large numbers of Chinese military aircraft. In one instance, a Chinese fighter jet locked its targeting radar onto a Taiwanese fighter—the last step before a pilot launches a missile at the aircraft. No shoot-down occurred, but Bonnie Glaser, a China expert at Washington's centrist Center for Strategic and International Studies, called the incident "very dangerous."

In June, the Trump administration sent a destroyer through the Taiwan Strait in a show of U.S. support for the island. Over the past few months, the United States has increased its naval patrols through the 100-mile-wide strait as a warning to Beijing not to use force against Taiwan.[8]

At the same time, Beijing has been sending conflicting signals regarding its intention to use force against Taiwan.

At the National People's Congress in May, the annual gathering of China's ever-compliant parliament, Premier Li Keqiang conspicuously omitted the word "peaceful" when he spoke about a future reunification of Taiwan with the mainland, analysts note. And Gen. Li Zuocheng, one of the country's most senior military officers, warned that China will "take all necessary steps to resolutely smash any separatist plots or actions. . . . We do not promise to abandon the use of force."[9]

But analysts also point out that Li Zhanshu, the third-highest-ranking leader of China's ruling Communist Party, called force against Taiwan "a last resort."

"As long as there is a slightest chance of a peaceful resolution, we will put in a hundred times the effort," Li said.[10]

— *Jonathan Broder*

---

[1] "Chinese bomber approaches Taiwan in latest fly-by near island," *Reuters, The Economic Times*, June 20, 2020, https://tinyurl.com/yahoxh2q.

[2] Charlotte Gao, "Was It Wise for Tsai Ing-wen to Reject the '1992 Consensus' Publicly?" *The Diplomat*, Jan. 4, 2019, https://tinyurl.com/ydgelaca.

[3] Chris Horton, "Taiwan's President, Defying Xi Jinping, Calls Unification Offer 'Impossible,'" *The New York Times*, Jan. 5, 2019, https://tinyurl.com/y836yg7o.

[4] Javier C. Hernández and Steven Lee Myers, "As China Strengthens Grip on Hong Kong, Taiwan Sees a Threat," *The New York Times*, July 1, 2020, https://tinyurl.com/y9j7lzwm.

[5] Nick Aspinwall, "Taiwan President Tsai Ing-wen Begins Her Second Term," *The Diplomat*, May 21, 2020, https://tinyurl.com/ya9uypun.

[6] Yimou Lee, "Taiwan says China lures Kiribati with airplanes after losing another ally," *Reuters*, Sept. 20, 2019, https://tinyurl.com/y5q4ulxf.

[7] Lawrence Chung and Liu Zhen, "Taiwan will forcefully expel PLA warplanes next time: Tsai Ing-wen," *South China Morning Post*, April 1, 2019, https://tinyurl.com/y6tjeat6.

[8] "US warship sails through Taiwan Strait on Tiananmen anniversary," *Reuters, Al Jazeera*, June 4, 2020, https://tinyurl.com/yalxthlu.

[9] "China general says force an option to stop Taiwan independence," *Reuters, Nikkei Asian Review*, May 29, 2020, https://tinyurl.com/yad3njyr.

[10] *Ibid.*

Taiwan Strait crisis. The roots of the crisis went back to the Nationalists' defeat in 1949. In addition to Taiwan, the Nationalists also had taken control of Quemoy and Matsu, two small islands located about 10 miles off China's southeastern coast. In the early 1950s, Chiang, determined to recover control of the mainland, used them to mount minor attacks against Chinese coastal positions.[52]

China's Influence at U.N. Grows

Experts say Beijing uses its clout to challenge the Western-oriented world order.

China had a problem. The United Nations was happy to provide a solution.

Beijing's marquee foreign policy effort, the Belt and Road Initiative (BRI), was pumping out $1 trillion in infrastructure funding to some 100 developing nations as part of an effort to expand China's global influence and generate business for its state-run construction firms. But many of the projects were causing serious environmental damage, according to experts.[1]

Facing mounting criticism from environmentalists, China looked for cover at the United Nations. It won the world body's endorsement for something Beijing called the Belt and Road Initiative International Green Development Coalition, a collection of environmental and financial institutions formed to advise China on sustainability.

U.S. officials say the U.N. stamp of approval has allowed Beijing to rebrand the Belt and Road program as a vehicle for environmentally conscious global development—despite critics' complaints that the coalition has so far been an exercise in greenwashing, or creating a false impression of environmentally sound practices.[2]

The success of Beijing's lobbying was another illustration of China's growing influence within the United Nations as a rising political and economic superpower, say experts who follow Beijing's activities at the world body.

With U.S. influence dwindling as President Trump voices his contempt for the U.N., these experts say China is using its diplomatic skills and economic clout to rewire the United Nations into a platform that advances China's economic and foreign policy interests—and moves away from the liberal democratic norms upon which the organization was founded in 1945.

China's campaign "aims to bend the arc of global governance toward a more illiberal orientation that privileges the interests of authoritarian actors," said Kristine Lee, a China expert at the Center for a New American Security, a centrist think tank in Washington.[3]

In a speech to the Chinese Communist Party Congress in 2017, President Xi Jinping declared his long-term plans for the United Nations when he said China will continue to "take an active part in reforming and developing the global governance system."[4]

Over the past few years, China, with the support of many developing nations, has placed its nationals at the head of four of the world body's 15 specialized agencies—more than any other country. And according to U.S. Rep. Michael McCaul of Texas, the ranking Republican on the House Foreign Affairs Committee, these officials have prioritized China's national interests over those agencies they chair.[5]

Zhao Houlin, formerly a senior official in China's Ministry of Posts and Telecommunications, serves as secretary-general of the U.N. International Telecommunication Union, where Western diplomats say he promoted Huawei, the Chinese telecom giant, as a global vendor of 5G telecommunications equipment.

The United States has labeled Huawei a national security threat and banned U.S. telecommunications companies from using its components out of concern they could provide the Chinese government a back door to spy on U.S. communications.

Fang Liu, head of the U.N. International Civil Aviation Organization, which regulates global air travel, has been accused of blocking Taiwan's access to COVID-19 protocols.[6]

Li Yong, who previously served as China's vice minister for finance, now heads the U.N. Industrial Development Organization (UNIDO), which helps member states develop sustainable industrial policies.

In dealing with the coronavirus pandemic, the agency's website said, "We are not an organization mandated to provide humanitarian or emergency response."[7]

Yet in February, during the early stages of the coronavirus outbreak, Li ordered UNIDO to fulfill Beijing's request for 100,000 medical masks and 20,000 protective suits to China. A UNIDO press release quoted Wang Qun, China's ambassador to the United Nations in Vienna, as calling the equipment "UNIDO's donation."[8]

In an email from UNIDO's Vienna headquarters, spokesman Stephan Sicars denied UNIDO showed any favoritism toward China. The agency, he says, normally does not provide emergency equipment to U.N. member states, but "exceptional times require exceptional actions, and . . . UNIDO has and will continue to provide the best possible support to the plight of its constituencies." He added that while China was not the only country to request emergency aid from UNIDO, China was the only country that received such assistance because Beijing paid for the protective equipment, as well as the agency's support costs. Sicars did not respond to a follow-up email asking to explain why Wang called the equipment a donation.

Last year, Qu Dongyu, formerly China's vice minister for agriculture, became director-general of the U.N. Food and Agriculture Organization (FAO) after trouncing the U.S.-backed candidate in a General Assembly election by a vote of 108-12.

But Western officials said China used bribes, economic threats and debt relief to win the election to the FAO, which helps direct food security policies worldwide and which China views as a vehicle for greater international influence.

According to an article in *Foreign Policy* magazine, rumors circulated widely among U.N. diplomats that Beijing paid for first-class plane tickets and posh hotel accommodations for officials from developing countries and their families as a way to encourage their U.N. delegations to support China's candidate. The article said China also threatened to block exports from several South American countries if they did not back Qu. And after China forgave $78 million of Cameroon's debt last February, the Cameroonian candidate for the FAO post withdrew from the race a month later, convincing many Western officials that a payoff had occurred.[9]

The Chinese and Cameroonian embassies in Washington did not respond to *CQ Researcher*'s requests for comment.

Earlier this year, China lost its bid to chair the U.N. World Intellectual Property Organization, which promotes the protection of intellectual property worldwide, after a U.S.-led campaign that alleged numerous instances of Chinese intellectual property theft. But it prevailed recently when Taiwan, facing strong Chinese opposition, withdrew its bid for observer status in the World Health Organization (WHO). China regards Taiwan, which is self-governing, as a "renegade province."[10]

Since taking office, Trump has withdrawn the United States from the U.N. Educational, Science and Cultural Organization (UNESCO) and the U.N. Human Rights Council, alleging they have an anti-Israel bias.

Earlier this year, Trump also began the process of pulling the United States out of the WHO, charging the U.N. agency echoed China's cover-up of the coronavirus' severity when it first appeared. China responded by pledging more than $2 billion to the WHO to make up for the loss of Washington's annual $550 million in funding.

Many experts say Trump's withdrawal from the WHO and other U.N. agencies plays into Beijing's hands by ceding U.S. influence to China. But the Center for New American Security's Lee said the United States can still regain the diplomatic ground it has lost by mobilizing its allies and challenging the Chinese at the United Nations. Trump, however, must be willing to change course, she said.

"If you want international organizations to perform to U.S. standards and reflect U.S. values, how much global leadership are you ready to take back . . . ?" Lee asked.[11]

— *Jonathan Broder*

---

[1] Sagatom Saha, "Is Belt & Road Destroying the World Environment?" *Belt & Road News*, Aug. 19, 2019, https://tinyurl.com/y7xah7kj; Hoong Chen Teo et al., "Environmental Impacts of Infrastructure Development under the Belt and Road Initiative," Multidisciplinary Digital Publishing Institute, June 2019, https://tinyurl.com/y8236gfu.

[2] "The Belt and Road Initiative International Green Development Coalition," United Nations Environmental Programme, https://tinyurl.com/y8xcc2vf; Jane Nakano, "Greening or Greenwashing the Belt and Road Initiative?" Center for Strategic and International Studies, May 1, 2019, https://tinyurl.com/y736zt6b.

[3] Kristine Lee, "It's Not Just the WHO: How China Is Moving on the Whole U.N.," *Politico*, April 15, 2020, https://tinyurl.com/ycglxgql.

[4] "Secure a Decisive Victory in Building a Moderately Prosperous Society in All Respects and Strive for the Great Success of Socialism with Chinese Characteristics for a New Era," *Xinhua*, Oct. 18, 2017, https://tinyurl.com/ybacqgow.

[5] Michael McCaul, "The United States Can't Cede the U.N. to China," *Foreign Policy*, Sept. 24, 2019, https://tinyurl.com/ybmw87gg.

[6] Lee, *op. cit.*

[7] "COVID-19 Response, Responding to the Crisis: Building a Better Future," United Nations Industrial Development Organization, April 2020, p. 5, https://tinyurl.com/yc7lqr3g.

[8] "UNIDO to provide emergency assistance to China to help contain the outbreak of coronavirus," press release, United Nations Industrial Development Organization, Feb. 14, 2020, https://tinyurl.com/ybb43946.

[9] Colum Lynch and Robbie Gramer, "Outfoxed and Outgunned: How China Routed the U.S. in a U.N. Agency," *Foreign Policy*, Oct. 23, 2019, https://tinyurl.com/yyvzltju.

[10] Nick Cumming-Bruce, "U.S.-Backed Candidate for Global Tech Post Beats China's Nominee," *The New York Times*, March 4, 2020, https://tinyurl.com/toulj9q; Jennifer Creery, "Taiwan postpones request for WHO observer status vote so members can focus on Covid-19 battle," *Hong Kong Free Press*, May 18, 2020, https://tinyurl.com/ybqt3v75.

[11] Lee, *op. cit.*

With U.S. troops already fighting the Chinese in Korea, Truman threw a U.S. naval blockade around Taiwan and its island possessions in 1951 to prevent the Korean conflict from spreading south. The move forced Chiang to halt his attacks on the mainland, but both the Nationalists and the communists continued to regard the islands as a potential launching pad for a Nationalist invasion, heightening their strategic importance.[53]

With the end of the Korean War in 1953, President Dwight D. Eisenhower lifted the blockade, and Chiang fortified Quemoy and Matsu with thousands of troops. In response, Chinese communist forces began shelling the islands in 1954, stoking Americans' concerns about further communist expansion. After Congress authorized the use of force to defend Taiwan in 1955, the United States threatened China with nuclear weapons unless it halted its artillery barrages. China, not yet a nuclear power, agreed to negotiate with the Nationalists.[54]

The negotiations, however, dragged on inconclusively for several years. In 1958, China resumed its shelling of the two islands, igniting the second Taiwan Strait crisis. Fighting erupted when Chinese communist forces tried to land on another small island nearby under Nationalist control. In response, the United States moved warships into the Taiwan Strait and supplied Nationalist forces with warplanes and other support.[55]

As the fighting escalated, U.S. military planners prepared to carry out nuclear strikes on several Chinese cities, including Shanghai. Once again, the communists backed down.

But the two Taiwan Strait crises fueled China's drive to develop its own nuclear weapons, which it did in 1964.[56]

Meanwhile, ideological differences between China and the Soviet Union had begun to corrode their communist alliance. Mao believed in prioritizing the collectivization of agriculture, rather than the industry-first approach favored by Moscow. Mao also took issue with Soviet leader Nikita Khrushchev's denunciation of Josef Stalin in the late 1950s. These differences led to a split that opened the door to a Chinese-U.S. rapprochement.[57]

The diplomatic dance between Beijing and Washington began with what the press called pingpong diplomacy. After U.S. and Chinese teams competed in the 1971 World Table Tennis Championship in Japan, Beijing invited the U.S. team to visit China, and Washington accepted. On the day the team arrived in Beijing, President Richard M. Nixon eased the U.S. trade embargo on China, imposed in 1950 after China entered the Korean War. Beijing reciprocated a few days later in a clear sign that both countries wanted friendlier relations.[58]

Nixon's historic 1972 visit to China ended 25 years of hostility between the two nations and opened the path for a U.S.-China alliance against the Soviet Union. The visit concluded with the Shanghai Communiqué, in which the two governments declared their intention to normalize diplomatic relations.[59]

Leadership changes in both countries hastened their rapprochement. Following the deaths of Mao and Premier Zhou Enlai in 1976, Deng Xiaoping became China's paramount leader in 1978, a year after President Jimmy Carter took office in Washington. Committed to the normalization of relations, Carter embraced Beijing's "One China" policy, which stipulated there is only one China and any country seeking diplomatic relations with Beijing could not maintain ties with Taiwan.[60]

Carter severed U.S. ties with Taiwan, and Beijing and Washington officially announced full diplomatic relations on Jan. 1, 1979.

Soon afterward, however, anti-China hawks in Congress pushed through the Taiwan Relations Act, which required the United States to sell Taiwan defensive military equipment and to regard any attack on the island with "grave concern."[61]

U.S. President Richard Nixon poses with Premier Zhou Enlai during Nixon's historic 1972 visit to China that normalized relations between the two countries after years of hostility.

Economic Revitalization

Deng undertook new policies to steer the country away from Mao's disastrous class-struggle policies—the so-called Great Leap Forward and the Cultural Revolution—which had left China impoverished. Under the banner of "reform and opening up," Deng implemented sweeping free market reforms as part of his nonideological approach to economic growth. "I don't care if the cat is black or white so long as it catches mice," Deng said.[62]

Successive U.S. administrations backed China's economic development, first by granting it "most favored nation" trading status and paving the way for its accession to the World Trade Organization in 2001, which allowed U.S. companies to open manufacturing plants in China.

Orville Schell, director of the Asia Society's Center on U.S.-China Relations in New York, said that Washington's policy of engagement with Beijing "neutralized the United States as an adversary at a time when it was most beneficial to Beijing." No longer facing the threat of war with a major power, China used the next three decades to strengthen its economy, build a modern infrastructure and play a greater role in international organizations, he said.[63]

During this period, Schell added, Washington consistently downplayed concerns over human rights in China. Though Deng had opened up the economy, China's Communist Party leaders were wary of any political liberalization, fearing democratic reforms would lead to chaos and the party's loss of power.

Even after the 1989 Tiananmen Square massacre, in which government troops killed hundreds of pro-democracy protesters in Beijing's central square, Washington still clung to its belief that China's economic liberalization would lead to greater political freedoms and China's respect for the rules governing the U.S.-led international order.

In 1995, however, Sino-U.S. tensions over Taiwan again erupted, bringing the two countries to the brink of war. The spark was a U.S. decision that had allowed then-Taiwanese President Lee Teng-hui to deliver a pro-Taiwanese independence speech at his alma mater, Cornell University.

Furious over Lee's remarks and what Beijing saw as a breach of an earlier U.S. promise not to allow Lee into the country, China responded by lobbing nuclear-capable ballistic missiles into the shipping lanes adjacent to Taiwan's two principal seaports.

Bound by the Taiwan Relations Act, which had been reaffirmed by President Ronald Reagan in 1982, President Bill Clinton responded to China's moves by sending two aircraft carrier battle groups into waters off Taiwan in the biggest show of U.S. military muscle in Asia since the Vietnam War. In tense face-to-face meetings, senior U.S. officials warned Chinese counterparts of "grave consequences" if their missiles hit Taiwan—a diplomatic euphemism that meant a U.S. military response.[64]

This time, however, the Chinese officials scoffed at the U.S. warning and implied they were prepared to use nuclear weapons against the United States, according to Chas W. Freeman Jr., a China specialist who had served as Nixon's interpreter during his 1972 China visit, the No. 2 diplomat at the U.S. Embassy in Beijing and an assistant secretary of Defense for East Asian affairs.

"I said you'll get a military reaction from the United States" if China attacks Taiwan, Freeman recalled telling top Chinese military officials, "and they said, 'No, you won't. We've watched you in Somalia, Haiti and Bosnia, and you don't have the will.'" Then, according to Freeman, a senior Chinese officer added: "In the 1950s, you three times threatened nuclear strikes on China, and you could do that because we couldn't hit back. Now we can. So you are not going to threaten us again because, in the end, you care a lot more about Los Angeles than Taipei."[65]

Tensions gradually subsided, and Sino-U.S. relations improved. For Beijing, however, the principal improvement was the change in Clinton's attitude toward China. Previously ambivalent about closer relations, Clinton emerged from the crisis with greater respect for China and became a full-throated supporter of greater U.S. engagement with Beijing, former aides say.

Xi's Accession

With Xi Jinping's rise to power in 2012, the tone of U.S.-China ties began to change. Under slogans such as "the Chinese dream," Xi projected an image of a far more rejuvenated, assertive and influential China.[66]

A fervent nationalist, Xi spoke often of his determination to reverse what he called China's "century of humiliation"—the period that stretched from the middle of the 19th century to 1945.

> "Beijing has made the calculation that the international environment is tipping in its favor."
>
> — Scott Kennedy
> Center for Strategic and International Studies

In pursuit of greater Chinese global influence, Xi hastened the buildup and modernization of China's military to near-parity with U.S. forces. He then built a string of heavily fortified naval and air bases on man-made islands in the South China Sea to strengthen China's longstanding territorial claim to the strategic waterway, through which a third of the world's maritime trade passes.[67]

Xi also asserted China's claim to the East China Sea, challenging Japan's counterclaim, and stepped up threats against Taiwan.[68]

He launched his signature Belt and Road Initiative in 2013, a trillion-dollar infrastructure program that drew scores of countries across Asia, Europe and Africa into China's economic and political orbit.

In a 2017 speech to party officials, Xi summed up his accomplishments by declaring that China had entered a "new era" in which it now wielded formidable economic, diplomatic and military power. Moreover, he said China could offer its autocratic communist-capitalist system as an effective model for developing countries and an alternative to messy Western-style democracy and free market capitalism.[69]

When Donald Trump took office in 2017, he abandoned Washington's accommodation policies with China, along with the Trans-Pacific Partnership (TPP) brokered by his predecessor, Barack Obama, that would have signaled a toughening U.S. trade policy toward China. The TPP was a free trade accord among 12 Pacific nations designed to create an economic bulwark against a rising China.

Free trade advocates say Trump's withdrawal from the TPP essentially ceded the field to China, which negotiated a trilateral trade agreement with Japan and South Korea and then drew the TPP's other members into Beijing's own version of a trade pact called the Regional Comprehensive Economic Partnership.

Meanwhile, Trump, angered by the growing U.S. trade deficit with China, Beijing's support for state-run enterprises and its closed markets, imposed tariffs on Chinese imports in 2018, igniting a trade war that signaled the beginning of a partial decoupling of the world's two largest economies.[70]

As diplomatic relations between the United States and China grew increasingly strained that year, both Xi and Trump ratcheted up their nationalist rhetoric. On Capitol Hill, Trump enjoyed bipartisan support for his tough China policies. By the time 2018 came to a close, U.S.-Chinese ties were rapidly deteriorating to their lowest point in decades.

CURRENT SITUATION
Western Response

The outlines of a common front against China are beginning to emerge among advanced industrialized democracies as they move to counter Beijing's increasing assertiveness on the world stage.

For several years, Western countries have been voicing concerns about China's forceful response to smaller Southeast Asian nations that have challenged its territorial claims in the South China Sea, as well as its weaponization of trade to punish uncooperative governments, its domination of cutting-edge technologies and its record of curtailing human rights.

But those concerns have deepened over China's bid to portray itself as a responsible leader in the global fight against the coronavirus pandemic.

Adding to those concerns are China's recent passage of a new national security law that threatens Hong Kong's semi-autonomous status; its latest attempts to intimidate Taiwan militarily; and a recent deadly clash between Chinese and Indian troops along their disputed border in the Himalayas.[71]

In March, China's growing influence within international organizations suffered a setback when it lost its bid to chair the U.N. World Intellectual Property Organization, which promotes the protection of intellectual property worldwide. The United States, which repeatedly has accused China of stealing intellectual property, waged an intense behind-the-scenes campaign at the United Nations to promote its preferred candidate, Singaporean Daren Tang, who won the internal election for the post.[72]

In April, Japan set aside $2.2 billion to help Japanese corporations bring home their manufacturing plants from China in a move to end Japan's dependence on Chinese supply chains. The European Union recently imposed tariffs as high as 30 percent on imports made by Chinese companies based outside China that are subsidized by Beijing and undercut EU competitors.[73]

And in June, a new international group was formed by senior Western politicians to find new ways to deal with an increasingly assertive China. Calling itself the Inter-Parliamentary Alliance on China, the group brings together more than 100 legislators across the political spectrum from more than a dozen countries, including the United States, Australia, Britain, Canada, the Czech Republic, Germany, Italy, Japan, Lithuania, Switzerland and the European Parliament.[74]

The group's mission, according to its website, is to help like-minded legislators craft strategic approaches to the challenges China poses to the rules-based international order, human rights, fairness in trade, regional security and sovereign integrity.[75]

"China, under the rule of the Chinese Communist Party, represents a global challenge," said Republican Sen. Marco Rubio of Florida. "We the Inter-Parliamentary Alliance on China stand together to coordinate the response to this great challenge."[76]

All of these measures come amid widespread acknowledgement in the West that it was mistaken to believe that China's economic rise would lead to greater political freedoms at home and to China's acceptance of the Western ruled-based international order.

Under Xi's leadership, China has grown more authoritarian over the past year, enacting a national security law that places the Hong Kong police under Beijing's direct control. China also has detained as many as 1 million ethnic Muslim Uighurs in prison-like "re-education camps" in the far-western Xinjiang province, where Beijing says they are taught about the dangers of Islamist extremism but where human rights groups allege they are indoctrinated to abandon Islam and adopt Chinese culture.[77]

China remains more aggressive abroad. Beijing and Iran are negotiating a 25-year strategic partnership that could involve about $400 billion in Chinese investment in the Iranian economy, including its railroads, ports and telecommunications. The agreement would also increase intelligence sharing and security cooperation

Taiwanese President Tsai Ing-wen speaks during a re-election rally in January 2020. Beijing regards Taiwan as a renegade province and considers Tsai a threat to its "One Country, Two Systems" framework.

among the two nations. Analysts say the deal would help Iran overcome punishing U.S. sanctions and bring two enemies of Washington closer together.[78]

In April, when Australia called for an independent investigation to determine the origin of the coronavirus, Beijing halted imports of Australian beef from four of its major abattoirs, slapped an 80.5 percent tariff on imported Australian barley and warned Chinese citizens not to travel to Australia. Amid the diplomatic row, China's nationalist *Global Times* newspaper called Australia "this giant kangaroo that serves as a dog of the U.S."[79]

Earlier this year, Beijing also threatened to hold back medical assistance from the Netherlands after it included the word Taipei, Taiwan's capital, in the new name of its unofficial representative's office in Taiwan. Beijing saw the name as a diplomatic gesture that violated its One China policy. Last year, Beijing also canceled a performance tour of China by the Prague Philharmonic Orchestra after the mayor of the Czech Republic's capital met with Taiwanese President Tsai Ing-wen.[80]

"What we once believed about China's rise no longer corresponds to reality," Shiori Yamao, an independent member of Japan's Diet and a member of the Inter-Parliamentary Alliance on China, said in a video released by the group.[81]

Meanwhile, as U.S.-China relations continued to deteriorate, the Pentagon sent two aircraft carrier battle groups into the South China Sea over the July 4 holiday

AT ISSUE

Should the United States demand compensation from China for its alleged responsibility for the coronavirus pandemic?

YES   **James Kraska**
Professor of International Law, Naval War College; Visiting Professor, Harvard Law School

Written for *CQ Researcher*, July 2020

As a champion of the rule of law in international diplomacy, the United States has become increasingly frustrated with China's departure from a rules-based order. China's violations of global norms in human rights, economics and security are destabilizing the international system at a time when international challenges require greater cooperation and integration.

Hence, when states fail to live up to their international obligations in a meaningful way—and indeed appear to have intentionally circumvented their commitments—the United States should consider legal recourse to induce compliance.

One of the most alarming of China's failures to comply with its international commitments is its past and ongoing omissions and commissions regarding the 2005 International Health Regulations. This legally binding treaty is designed to prevent the spread of disease. China is a state party to the treaty, but it failed to comply with its provisions under Articles 5-11 to notify and share information with the World Health Organization (WHO) that could have prevented or reduced the impact of the COVID-19 pandemic. China especially did not provide notification to the WHO within 24 hours of public health risks resulting from human-to-human transmission of the coronavirus, as required by Article 9 of the treaty.

While investigation continues into China's malfeasance, the public record is replete with either careless or purposeful breaches, including the Chinese government's decision to ban air travel from Wuhan to Beijing and Shanghai, while permitting hundreds of thousands of passengers from Wuhan to seed the rest of the world.

China should be held accountable, and the international law of state responsibility is an appropriate mechanism for doing so. State responsibility is a foundation of international law, and states may be held responsible for wrongful acts they have committed that harm other states. This area of law was developed through custom and state practice, is binding on all nations and has been codified by the United Nations' International Law Commission.

Injured states may lawfully take countermeasures against such violators to induce compliance and to fulfill reparations. Countermeasures permit injured states to suspend normal legal duties—in effect, take steps normally considered unlawful. For example, the United States might disregard the authoritarian

NO   **Robert S. Ross**
Professor of Political Science, Boston College; Non-Resident Fellow, Quincy Institute for Responsible Statecraft

Written for *CQ Researcher*, July 2020

China's response to the coronavirus outbreak in Wuhan was irresponsible and extraordinarily costly to the global community. During the first few weeks of the outbreak, China denied the world information about the disease, contributing to countless deaths and to the global recession.

China's record is clear. Given the price the United States incurred from Chinese policies, there are widespread calls for U.S. retaliation. But such calls reflect an atavistic reaction to a challenge to U.S. interests. The United States is no longer the world hegemon that can expect countries to appease America and cooperate with U.S. interests whenever the United States threatens punishment.

First, meaningful retaliation will not change Chinese behavior. China has not appeased U.S. interests in economic matters, in the competition in the South China Sea, in Middle East politics or in constraining nuclear proliferation in North Korea. It will be no more disposed to accommodate U.S. retaliation regarding its public health policies.

Second, U.S. retaliation will be ineffective because it will not receive the support of other countries. The European Union, South Korea and Australia have refused to participate in the U.S. politics of blame. U.S. retaliation against China's coronavirus policies would simply be the latest case of ineffective U.S. unilateralism.

Third, meaningful U.S. retaliation, rather than cheap talk, would require imposition of significant costs on China. But China will not simply acquiesce to U.S. retaliation. It is now a great power and will react in kind, imposing significant corresponding costs on the United States. Thus, at minimum, Chinese retaliation will undermine the U.S. economic recovery, without securing any U.S. benefit from changed Chinese policies.

Fourth, whereas the U.S. public health priority should be on reducing deaths from the coronavirus, retaliation would undermine U.S.-China cooperation, however limited, to contain the spread of the coronavirus and to develop and share a vaccine. Cooperation is already challenged by the U.S. trade, technology and ideological wars against China. U.S. retaliation would exacerbate conflict, delaying a vaccine for the American people and endangering more American lives.

management of pandemic information inside China and broadcast Taiwanese or Western media directly into the country concerning the coronavirus. States may take such action unilaterally without resort to lengthy international court proceedings. This approach offers the most powerful and economical approach to address China's breach of international law.

The views presented are those of the author and do not reflect the position of the Navy or the Department of Defense.

At best, retaliation against China would amount to nothing more than feel-good diplomacy. The only interest it would serve is President Trump's effort to mobilize his base in support of his re-election. At its worst, and far more likely, retaliation would exacerbate the U.S. health and economic crises. The American urge to retaliate is understandable, but good policy is pragmatic policy that serves U.S. interests. Retaliation, however emotionally satisfying, would harm those interests.

---

in a major demonstration of American military might. The U.S. Navy said the two carrier battle groups "conducted several tactical exercises designed to maximize air defense capabilities and extend the reach of long-range precision maritime strikes from carrier-based aircraft."[82]

A month before, a Navy destroyer sailed through the Taiwan Strait in another show of force as Chinese warplanes step up incursions into Taiwanese airspace as a warning against any move toward formal independence.[83]

The U.S. naval exercises in the South China Sea came soon after the Chinese navy conducted its own exercises in the same waters. China's *Global Times* dismissed the U.S. carriers as "nothing more than paper tigers on China's doorsteps" and warned that the China's hypersonic anti-ship missiles, known as "carrier killers," could easily defend Beijing's territorial claim.[84]

"Any US #aircraftcarrier movement in the region is at the pleasure of PLA," *Global Times* tweeted, referring to China's People's Liberation Army.[85]

U.S. Actions

The Trump administration has been urging allies and partners in Europe and Asia to rally behind its own efforts to contain China's technological advances, particularly by banning equipment made by Huawei for its new 5G networks. The campaign has had some success. In mid-July, the British government announced it would bar telecom companies from purchasing equipment from Huawei. Australia and New Zealand did the same in 2018. Germany, however, has indicated it will stay with the Chinese firm.[86]

In a major China policy paper released in May, the administration cast a critical eye on its predecessors, noting their policy of engagement with China over the past four decades had failed to produce a rules-abiding China. The policy paper said the Trump administration's policies on China would be based on "a clear-eyed assessment of the CCP's intentions and actions," referring to the Chinese Communist Party.[87]

Amid rising U.S.-China tensions, the Trump administration is taking a hard line against alleged Chinese intellectual property theft.

In late July, the U.S. Justice Department indicted two Chinese hackers said to be working with Beijing's intelligence services for a decade's worth of suspected computer breaches of American high-tech manufacturers, pharmaceutical companies and gaming firms, from whom they allegedly stole large amounts of proprietary data.

The indictment said the pair also targeted American and other biotech firms around the globe that are working to develop vaccines and therapeutic treatments for COVID-19.

The indictments are more symbolic than actionable. The indicted pair live in China, making it highly unlikely they will ever see the inside of a U.S. courtroom.[88]

But the State Department added teeth to the indictments, ordering the closure of China's consulate in Houston. State Department spokeswoman Morgan Ortagus said in a statement the closure order was issued "in order to protect American intellectual property and Americans' private information."

China's Foreign Ministry spokesman Wang Wenbin called the closure order "outrageous and unjustified" and vowed retaliation. The United States maintains five consulates in China.[89]

With the November election just a few months away, the centerpiece of Trump's China policy now appears to be his campaign's drive to blame the coronavirus pandemic on Beijing and to tie presumptive Democratic nominee Biden to what Trump calls the Obama administration's failed policies of engagement.

"I am TOUGH ON CHINA and Sleepy Joe Biden is WEAK ON CHINA," an April campaign email from Trump declared. Later that month, Trump tweeted, "China wants Sleepy Joe sooo badly," adding: "Joe is an easy mark, their DREAM CANDIDATE!"[90]

Biden's campaign responded with an ad that painted a hostile picture of China and included the president's fawning statements about Xi to suggest Trump was no hardliner on China.[91] Political analysts say the ad signals a tough U.S. policy toward China if Biden wins the November elections.

In his new memoir, former national security adviser Bolton paints a damning portrait of a divided White House where national security hawks and some hardline trade officials tried to develop tougher policies toward China, only to find themselves undermined by Trump, whose overriding concern, Bolton said, was nailing down a trade deal with Beijing that would help his re-election chances.[92]

To that end, Bolton said, Trump, in a dinner conversation with Xi at the 2019 G-20 meeting in Osaka, Japan, spoke approvingly of the internment camps for China's Uighurs and even pleaded with the Chinese leader to buy more U.S. agricultural products to bolster Trump's popularity among American farmers, a key political constituency for the president.[93]

Political analysts say Chinese officials are divided as to which U.S. presidential candidate they prefer for the next four years.

"Those people who want more predictability in the U.S.-China relationship, who think China would be able to resume at least some kind of cooperation with the United States on climate change, pandemics, things like that, want Biden to be president," says the CSIS' Glaser. "But there are other people looking more long-term who say Trump creates opportunities for China to increase its participation and role as a leader in the international community."

OUTLOOK
"Existential Threat"?

Most experts believe China's rise as a global superpower will continue economically, diplomatically and militarily in the years ahead, presenting an ever-growing strategic challenge to the United States.

While the World Bank expects the disruptions caused by the coronavirus to slow China's gross domestic product growth to 1 percent this year—the lowest rate since 1976—it predicts China's growth rate will rebound to 6.9 percent in 2021 as global economic activity returns to normal.[94]

Assuming Beijing avoids a second wave of the coronavirus outbreaks and trade tensions with the United States do not escalate, the bank forecasts China will have a gradual and sustained recovery in the years ahead.[95] Moreover, some economists predict China will provide the main engine for global economic growth in the coming years.

By contrast, the World Bank predicts U.S. GDP will contract by 6.1 percent in 2020, with a projected rebound of 4 percent growth in 2021.[96]

Analysts say Xi remains committed to his Belt and Road Initiative. But they add that he is concerned that corruption and unwise lending have sullied the BRI's reputation, and they expect the program will slow in the coming years as Beijing scrutinizes more carefully to whom it is loaning money and their ability to pay it back.

Meanwhile, economists say Beijing is banking on the success of its "Made in China 2025" initiative to establish China's global dominance over the United States and other Western competitors in the manufacture and sale of 5G telecommunications, artificial intelligence and electric vehicles.

The new technologies will have military applications, making some aspects of Xi's military modernization program dependent on China's domestic chip production now that the Trump administration has placed export controls on its advanced semiconductors, analysts who study China's armed forces say. But even with lower-quality, home-produced chips, these analysts say China's armed forces will likely be fully modernized by 2035 and reach parity with the U.S. military as a first-tier force in another 15 years after that.

In the meantime, experts expect the standoff between U.S. and Chinese forces in the South China Sea to intensify under either a second-term Trump presidency or a Biden administration. Both countries are deploying an increasing number of warships and military aircraft in the area, raising the odds that a mistake or a miscalculation by either side could spark a military confrontation.

Others believe China has no interest in a military conflict with the United States at this time and would go out of its way to avoid one.

But no matter who wins the U.S. presidential election, political analysts say U.S.-China relations are likely to remain on a downward spiral until Washington adopts a policy of peaceful coexistence with China.

"But right now, it looks like the U.S. sees China as an existential threat," says CSIS' Kennedy. "And that means that one way or another, both Republicans and Democrats are going to be tough on China."

NOTES

1. Lily Kuo, "China sends doctors and masks overseas as domestic coronavirus infections drop," *The Guardian*, March 18, 2020, https://tinyurl.com/u2l7p72.
2. Steven Lee Myers, "China's Aggressive Diplomacy Weakens Xi Jinping's Global Standing," *The New York Times*, April 17, 2020, https://tinyurl.com/yddtqg3s.
3. *Ibid.*
4. Vivian Wang, "China's Coronavirus Battle Is Waning. Its Propaganda Fight Is Not," *The New York Times*, June 17, 2020, https://tinyurl.com/ya85hxbd; Henry Austin and Alexander Smith, "Coronavirus: Chinese officials suggests U.S. Army to blame for outbreak," *NBC News*, March 13, 2020, https://tinyurl.com/sex253a.
5. Jonathan Cheng, "China's Economy Regains Strength After Strict Coronavirus Measures," *The Wall Street Journal*, July 3, 2020, https://tinyurl.com/yaygxc5k.
6. Guy Taylor, "Mike Pompeo blasts China's Communist Party: 'Intent upon the destruction of Western ideas,'" *The Washington Times*, May 31, 2020, https://tinyurl.com/y3r9n2oo.
7. Robin Emmott and Angeliki Koutantou, "Greece blocks EU statement on China human rights at U.N.," *Reuters*, June 18, 2017, https://tinyurl.com/yxh8nqgm.
8. Brianna Ehley and Alice Miranda Ollstein, "Trump announces U.S. withdrawal from the World Health Organization," *Politico*, May 29, 2020, https://tinyurl.com/y7dllfxj.
9. Jacob Poushter and Moira Fagan, "Americans See Spread of Disease as Top International Threat, Along With Terrorism, Nuclear Weapons, Cyberattacks," Pew Research Center, April 13, 2020, https://tinyurl.com/y5cshpfa.
10. Josh Rogin, "The coronavirus crisis is turning Americans in both parties against China," *The Washington Post*, April 8, 2020, https://tinyurl.com/wxcctkl.
11. Grady McGregor, "Trump's demand that China pay coronavirus reparations evokes an ugly history," *Fortune*, May 7, 2020, https://tinyurl.com/yc4pzcxp; Keith Johnson and Robbie Gramer, "The Great Decoupling," *Foreign Policy*, May 14, 2020, https://tinyurl.com/y9p7ulu6.
12. "Fighting COVID-19: China in Action," State Council Information Office, People's Republic of China, June 7, 2020, https://tinyurl.com/y5xm7n6h.
13. Wang, *op. cit.*
14. Gerry Shih, Emily Rauhala and Josh Dawsey, "China's Xi backs WHO-led review of covid-19 outbreak," *The Washington Post*, May 18, 2020, https://tinyurl.com/y5k2cn3f.
15. Chris Buckley and Steven Lee Myers, "As New Coronavirus Spread, China's Old Habits Delayed Fight," *The New York Times*, Feb. 7, 2020, https://tinyurl.com/u3t8ryc.
16. *Ibid.*
17. R. Scott Nolen, "United States seeks ban on China's wildlife wet markets," American Veterinary Medical Association, June 10, 2020, https://tinyurl.com/yo9vpf2.
18. Mike Ives, "Scientists Say New Strain of Swine Flu Is Spreading to Humans in China," *The New York Times*, June 30, 2020, https://tinyurl.com/y97omz2e.
19. Chun Han Wong and Chao Deng, "China's 'Wolf Warrior' Diplomats Are Ready to Fight," *The Wall Street Journal*, May 19, 2020, https://tinyurl.com/y3a5uhb4.

20. *Ibid.*
21. Anna Fifield, "China wasn't wild about Mike Pompeo before the virus. It's really gunning for him now," *The Washington Post*, April 30, 2020, https://tinyurl.com/yb9rv7vc.
22. Tom Porter, "More than 110 countries are backing a motion for WHO to investigate the origins of the coronavirus outbreak, despite China's objections," *Business Insider*, May 18, 2020, https://tinyurl.com/y83ll4of; Shih, *op. cit.*
23. Vuk Vuksanovic, "China Has Its Eyes on Serbia," *Foreign Policy*, April 8, 2020, https://tinyurl.com/yy8cyzqe.
24. Alex Fang and Yifan Yu, "US pushes China decoupling, wiping billions off Apple and Boeing," *Nikkei Asian Review*, May 16, 2020, https://tinyurl.com/yymrgprq.
25. *Ibid.*
26. "A quick guide to the U.S.-China trade war," *BBC News*, Jan. 16, 2020, https://tinyurl.com/y4v4tlz6.
27. James Politi, "Export controls emerge as way to curb China's rise," *Financial Times*, Jan. 29, 2020, https://tinyurl.com/y2bqkkfz; Arjun Kharpal, "Trump administration seeks ban on China Telecom in US citing 'unacceptable' national security risks," *CNBC*, April 12, 2020, https://tinyurl.com/uyq8mdq; and Yifan Yu, "US to suspend entry of Chinese students with military ties," *Nikkei Asian Review*, May 30, 2020, https://tinyurl.com/ybck2b35.
28. David E. Sanger et al., "In 5G Race With China, U.S. Pushes Allies to Fight Huawei," *The New York Times*, Jan. 26, 2019, https://tinyurl.com/ycqt7grc.
29. William Mauldin, Lingling Wei and Alex Leary, "U.S., China Agree to Limited Deal to Halt Trade War," *The Wall Street Journal*, Dec. 14, 2019, https://tinyurl.com/valkla5.
30. Josh Zumbrun, "China a Bright Spot for U.S. in Gloomy Global Trade Picture," *The Wall Street Journal*, June 14, 2020, https://tinyurl.com/yygjjx4l.
31. "United States and China Reach Phase One Trade Agreement," press release, Office of the U.S. Trade Representative, Dec. 13, 2019, https://tinyurl.com/qrxu8ut; Dorcas Wong and Alexander Chipman Koty, "The U.S.-China Trade War: A Timeline," Dezan Shira and Associates, May 13, 2020, https://tinyurl.com/y2suzjkc.
32. Rita Liao, "Huawei admits uncertainty following new US chip curbs," *TechCrunch*, May 18, 2020, https://tinyurl.com/y6atgrea.
33. Fang and Yu, *op. cit.*
34. Finbarr Bermingham, "US-China decoupling to be accelerated by tightening of technology export controls, experts say," *South China Morning Post*, April 29, 2020, https://tinyurl.com/y8cxvehb.
35. Elsa Kania, "Made in China 2025, Explained," *The Diplomat*, February 2019, https://tinyurl.com/yxrjtxkh.
36. Tom O'Connor, "Chinese Aircraft Carrier Sails into Pacific as State Media Mock U.S. Navy's Coronavirus Troubles," *Newsweek*, April 13, 2020, https://tinyurl.com/y9rwx8sl.
37. *Ibid.*
38. "Exclusive: Internal Chinese report warns Beijing faces Tiananmen-like global backlash over virus," *Reuters*, May 4, 2020, https://tinyurl.com/y7oaldqr.
39. Zachary Williams, "China's Tightening Grasp in the South China Sea: A First-Hand Look," *The Diplomat*, June 10, 2020, https://tinyurl.com/y5sxavoe; Gregory Poling, "China's Hidden Navy," *Foreign Policy*, June 25, 2019, https://tinyurl.com/y665qvsa.
40. Hannah Beech, "China's Sea Control Is a Done Deal, 'Short of War With the U.S.,'" *The New York Times*, Sept. 20, 2018, https://tinyurl.com/y8f3mmcp.
41. *Ibid.*
42. Christian Brose, *The Kill Chain: Defending America in the Future of High-Tech Warfare* (2020), pp. 4-6.
43. David Pong, "The Fall of the Qing, 1840-1912," Oxford Bibliographies, June 8, 2017, https://tinyurl.com/y2peo4du.
44. "Second Sino-Japanese War," Encyclopaedia Britannica, March 14, 2019, https://tinyurl.com/y6rdkgjb.

45. *Ibid.*
46. "Chronology of U.S.-China Relations, 1784-2000," Office of the Historian, U.S. Department of State, https://tinyurl.com/y3mbfw5o.
47. Erin Monroe, "U.S.-China Relations: A Brief Historical Perspective," U.S.-China Policy Foundation, August 2014, https://tinyurl.com/yyx8geds; Mark Witzke, "How much of China did Japan control at its greatest extent?" Pacific Atrocities Education, July 24, 2017, https://tinyurl.com/y28oa6wu.
48. "Research Starters: Worldwide Deaths in World War II," National World War II Museum, https://tinyurl.com/ybgpwr88.
49. Niels Bjerre-Poulsen, *Right Face: Organizing the American Conservative Movement 1945-65* (2002), p. 105.
50. Robert P. Newman, "The Self-Inflicted Wound: The China White Paper of 1949," *Prologue: Journal of the National Archives*, Fall 1982, pp. 141-56.
51. "Chronology of U.S.-China Relations, 1784-2000," *op. cit.*
52. "The Taiwan Straits Crises: 1954-55 and 1958," Office of the Historian, Foreign Service Institute, U.S. Department of State, https://tinyurl.com/l8bbzbv.
53. *Ibid.*
54. "First Taiwan Strait Crisis: Quemoy and Matsu Islands," Global Security, https://tinyurl.com/y4on5zv7.
55. "Second Taiwan Strait Crisis: Quemoy and Matsu Islands, 23 August 1958-01 January 1959," Global Security, https://tinyurl.com/y3g24mt4.
56. *Ibid.*
57. Monroe, *op. cit.*
58. Carroll Kilpatrick, "U.S. Ends Ban on China Trade; Items Are Listed," *The Washington Post*, June 11, 1971, https://tinyurl.com/y42qzngn.
59. Monroe, *op. cit.*
60. *Ibid.*
61. "United States-Taiwan Relations Act," U.S. House of Representatives, March 8, 1979, https://tinyurl.com/y62l2z3s.
62. "The Great Pragmatist: Deng Xiaoping," *The Guardian*, Dec. 17, 2008, https://tinyurl.com/y48u5b2k.
63. Orville Schell, "The Ugly End of Chimerica," *Foreign Policy*, April 3, 2020, https://tinyurl.com/rxfazqu.
64. Barton Gellman, "U.S. and China Nearly Came to Blows in '96," *The Washington Post*, June 21, 1998, https://tinyurl.com/y32oy8gq.
65. *Ibid.*
66. Jeffrey A. Bader, "How Xi Jinping Sees The World . . . And Why," Brookings Institution, February 2016, https://tinyurl.com/y7tly6xr.
67. *Ibid.*
68. *Ibid.*
69. "Xi Jinping: 'Time for China to take centre stage,'" *BBC*, Oct. 18, 2017, https://tinyurl.com/y25zekvm.
70. "A quick guide to the U.S.-China trade war," *op. cit.*
71. Chris Buckley, Keith Bradsher and Tiffany May, "New Security Law Gives China Sweeping Powers Over Hong Kong," *The New York Times*, June 29, 2020, https://tinyurl.com/y9n94msy; Erin Hale, "In shadow of coronavirus, China steps up manoeuvres near Taiwan," *Al Jazeera*, April 23, 2020, https://tinyurl.com/y4w4a7bc; and Jeffrey Gettleman, Hari Kumar and Sameer Yasir, "Worst Clash in Decades on Disputed India-China Border Kills 20 Indian Troops," *The New York Times*, June 16, 2020, https://tinyurl.com/yamuhf7r.
72. Mary Hui, "The US is relieved that Singapore beat out China's nominee as the new UN IP agency head," *Quartz*, March 4, 2020, https://tinyurl.com/y439ugpp.
73. Isabel Reynolds and Emi Urabe, "Japan to Fund Firms to Shift Production Out of China," *Bloomberg*, April 8, 2020, https://tinyurl.com/rrtferj; Jonathan Stearns, "EU Challenges China's Trade Expansion With Landmark Tariff," *Bloomberg*, June 15, 2020, https://tinyurl.com/y8awwleb.
74. Benedict Rogers, "Parliamentarians From Around the World Unite to Discuss the China Challenge," *The Diplomat*, June 6, 2020, https://tinyurl.com/y4n9sc4x.

75. Inter-Parliamentary Alliance on China, https://tinyurl.com/y5h6j8be.
76. Ibid.
77. Lindsay Maizland, "China's Repression of Uighurs in Xinjiang," Council on Foreign Relations, June 30, 2020, https://tinyurl.com/yxb5r8zx.
78. Ishaan Tharoor, "Trump's two main foreign foes plan a major pact," *The Washington Post*, July 14, 2020, https://tinyurl.com/yybnryzv.
79. Greg Ip, "A United Front on China Starts to Take Shape," *The Wall Street Journal*, June 17, 2020, https://tinyurl.com/y2yb2eyh.
80. Steven Erlanger, "Global Backlash Builds Against China Over Coronavirus," *The New York Times*, June 17, 2020, https://tinyurl.com/y4nr77ko; Elizabeth Shim, "China takes aim at Czech mayor with cancelled orchestra tour," *UPI*, May 2, 2019, https://tinyurl.com/y5mlktno.
81. Inter-Parliamentary Alliance on China, *op. cit.*
82. Brad Lendon, "Tensions heat up in South China Sea as US makes significant show of force," *CNN*, July 6, 2020, https://tinyurl.com/ycvfd3wm.
83. "US warship sails through Taiwan Strait on Tiananmen anniversary," Reuters, *Al Jazeera*, June 4, 2020, https://tinyurl.com/yalxthlu.
84. Lendon, *op. cit.*
85. Ibid.
86. Stephen Fidler and Max Colchester, "U.K. to Ban Huawei From Its 5G Network Amid China-U.S. Tensions," *The Wall Street Journal*, July 14, 2020, https://tinyurl.com/y5gotsy9; Robert Fife and Steven Chase, "New Zealand becomes third Five Eyes member to ban Huawei from 5G network," *The Globe and Mail*, Nov. 29, 2018, https://tinyurl.com/y9yc3h98; and Janka Oertel, "Germany Chooses China Over the West," *Foreign Policy*, Oct. 21, 2019, https://tinyurl.com/yy2uxarf.
87. "United States Strategic Approach to the People's Republic of China," The White House, May 20, 2020, https://tinyurl.com/y79g6wus.
88. Ellen Nakashima and Devlin Barrett, "U.S. accuses China of sponsoring criminal hackers targeting covid-19 vaccine research," *The Washington Post*, July 21, 2020, https://tinyurl.com/yxgm5w4y.
89. Edward Wong, Lara Jakes and Steven Lee Myers, "U.S. Orders China to Close Houston Consulate, Citing Efforts to Steal Trade Secrets," *The New York Times*, July 22, 2020, https://tinyurl.com/yyuca49e; "US Ratchets Up China Tensions, Closing Houston Consulate," *The Associated Press, The New York Times*, July 22, 2020, https://tinyurl.com/y2ke3xav.
90. Lauren Gambino, "Trump plots new election strategy: tie Biden to China—and attack them both," *The Guardian*, April 27, 2020, https://tinyurl.com/yxrbwueu.
91. Eli Stokols and Janet Hook, "Trump and Biden clash over China in dueling ads," *Los Angeles Times*, April 17, 2020, https://tinyurl.com/y4qatrfy.
92. Josh Dawsey, "Trump asked China's Xi to help him win reelection, according to Bolton book," *The Washington Post*, June 17, 2020, https://tinyurl.com/y829q7hr.
93. Ibid.
94. "Global Economic Prospects," World Bank, June 2020, https://tinyurl.com/yxmeg4ve.
95. Ibid.
96. Ibid.

BIBLIOGRAPHY
Books

Fang, Fang, *Wuhan Diary: Dispatches from a Quarantined City*, HarperCollins, 2020.
One of China's most acclaimed writers gives a first-person account of life and death in Wuhan during the coronavirus outbreak.

Lee, Kai-Fu, *AI Superpowers: China, Silicon Valley, and the New World Order*, Houghton Mifflin Harcourt, 2018.
A technology expert focuses on the rivalry between the United States and China to master artificial intelligence and how it will affect the workplace in both countries.

Mattis, Peter, and Matthew Brazil, *Chinese Communist Espionage: An Intelligence Primer*, Naval Institute Press, 2019.
Two China experts outline the range of China's spying and the intricate web of government and military agencies that carry it out.

Osnos, Evan, *Age of Ambition: Chasing Fortune, Truth, and Faith in the New China*, 2014.
A *New Yorker* correspondent profiles the collision of ordinary Chinese citizens' aspirations for wealth and the authoritarian government they live under.

Articles

Campbell, Kurt M., and Rush Doshi, "The Coronavirus Could Reshape Global Order," *Foreign Affairs*, March 18, 2020, https://tinyurl.com/vfv599q.
A former senior U.S. diplomat (Campbell) and a China expert (Doshi) discuss how the Trump administration's heavily criticized response to the coronavirus pandemic and China's narrative of victory over the outbreak could spell the end of the U.S.-led world order.

Cheng-Chia, Tung, and Alan H. Yang, "How China Is Remaking the UN In Its Own Image," *The Diplomat*, April 9, 2020, https://tinyurl.com/yas6pdsz.
Two Taiwanese researchers explore how China's growing influence within the United Nations is helping Beijing advance its foreign and economic policies.

Harshaw, Tobin, "Emperor Xi's China Is Done Biding Its Time," Belfer Center for Science and International Affairs, March 3, 2018, https://tinyurl.com/y6vthxev.
A senior fellow at a Harvard University research center interviews former Australian Prime Minister Kevin Rudd about where Chinese President Xi Jinping's nationalist policies are taking China.

Johnson, Keith, and Robbie Gramer, "The Great Decoupling," *Foreign Policy*, May 14, 2020, https://tinyurl.com/y9p7ulu6.
Two journalists explore the political tensions between Washington and Beijing that are pulling the world two largest economies apart.

Myers, Steven Lee, "China's Aggressive Diplomacy Weakens Xi Jinping's Global Standing," *The New York Times*, April 17, 2020, https://tinyurl.com/yddtqg3s.
A *New York Times* correspondent based in China says Beijing's pugnacious response to foreign critics of Xi's policies is hurting the Chinese leader's reputation in Western capitals.

Wang, Vivian, "China's Coronavirus Battle Is Waning. Its Propaganda Fight Is Not," *The New York Times*, April 8, 2020, https://tinyurl.com/ya85hxbd.
A *New York Times* correspondent in Hong Kong describes how Chinese propaganda portrays the country as a global health leader, omitting its initial mishandling of the coronavirus crisis.

Reports and Studies

Chen, John, *et al.*, "China's Internet of Things," SOS International, October 2018, https://tinyurl.com/ycbxsu69.
A report prepared for Congress' U.S.-China Economic and Security Review Commission explores the challenges the United States faces from China in the fields of artificial intelligence, 5G telecommunications and quantum computing.

"China's National Defense in the New Era," State Council Information Office of the People's Republic of China, July 2019, https://tinyurl.com/y8emkfd4.
A Chinese government white paper describes the country's national defense strategy and explains the reasoning behind Beijing's military buildup.

Ratner, Ely, *et al.*, "Rising to the China Challenge: Renewing American Competitiveness in the Indo-Pacific," Center for New American Security, December 2019, https://tinyurl.com/ydd9fct5.
A group of independent strategic thinkers and China experts discusses the military, diplomatic and technological challenges facing the United States as it competes against China to maintain dominance in the Indo-Pacific region.

Rolland, Nadège, "China's Vision for a New World Order," National Bureau for Asian Research, January 2020, https://tinyurl.com/ycme37gm.
A China expert examines the ideological themes behind Beijing's vision for a new world order and the policies it is enacting to make it a reality.

THE NEXT STEP

Economy

Cheng, Evelyn, "China's jobs problem runs deeper than the coronavirus," *CNBC*, July 7, 2020, https://tinyurl.com/ycuq5pty.
An aging workforce, combined with employers' preferences for younger workers, may lead to higher unemployment in China.

"Coronavirus: Chinese economy bounces back into growth," *BBC*, July 16, 2020, https://tinyurl.com/y9m7jot2.

China's economy mostly rebounded in the second quarter after a steep drop in the first quarter due to the coronavirus outbreak.

Standaert, Michael, "As China's economy rebounds, dangers lurk beneath the surface," *Al Jazeera*, July 15, 2020, https://tinyurl.com/y9nrgjqo.

China faces worsening trade tensions with the United States along with lower domestic consumer demand following the COVID-19 outbreak.

Pandemic Response

McGregor, Grady, "China's military approves coronavirus vaccine for its own use," *Fortune Magazine*, June 29, 2020, https://tinyurl.com/ybyzur27.

Chinese troops will be among the first to receive doses of the leading coronavirus vaccine candidate under trial in the country.

Wen Liu, Tracy, "China's Second Wave of Coronavirus Censorship Is Here," *Foreign Policy*, July 7, 2020, https://tinyurl.com/ydydfxjj.

China has made it difficult for hospital staff to speak about the initial outbreak of the virus and the government's response, even after cases dropped dramatically throughout the nation.

Yee, Isaac, and James Griffiths, "As coronavirus spikes in US, China locks down 400,000 people . . . over 18 cases," *CNN*, June 29, 2020, https://tinyurl.com/y74wapzw.

China is aggressively trying to prevent a second outbreak with a massive lockdown in a country 90 miles to the south of Beijing.

Taiwan

Hernández, Javier C., and Steven Lee, "As China Strengthens Grip on Hong Kong, Taiwan Sees a Threat," *The New York Times*, July 1, 2020, https://tinyurl.com/y2y3mgw4.

The implementation of a tough new security law in Hong Kong has further eroded Taiwanese support for unification with China.

McFall, Caitlin, "China places sanctions on Lockheed Martin over arms sales to Taiwan," *Fox News*, July 15, 2020, https://tinyurl.com/y8dnbxpx.

China slapped sanctions on Lockheed Martin after the arms manufacturer sold missiles to Taiwan in a sale approved by the U.S. government.

Suliman, Adela, "Taiwan conducts major annual military exercise amid rising China tensions," *NBC News*, July 16, 2020, https://tinyurl.com/ycmlxjeo.

Taiwan showcased its military in an annual event, as China increased its military activity around the island, which China considers a renegade province.

U.S. Policy

Hansler, Jennifer, Kylie Atwood and Michael Conte, "US announces visa restrictions for employees of Huawei and other Chinese tech companies," *CNN*, July 15, 2020, https://tinyurl.com/ydgmzjcc.

Secretary of State Mike Pompeo announced visa restrictions on employees of Chinese tech companies but did not say which employees would be targeted, and he hinted at further action against the companies.

Mason, Jeff, "Trump administration action on risks posed by TikTok likely 'in weeks': official," *Reuters*, July 15, 2020, https://tinyurl.com/y8n3w2cx.

The Trump administration is studying the national security risks of Chinese social media apps, including TikTok and WeChat, and could decide to ban the apps in coming weeks.

Wertime, David, "The decaying U.S.-China relationship will change each of our lives," *Politico*, July 16, 2020, https://tinyurl.com/yb344mem.

Foreign policy experts discuss the potential decoupling of the United States and China and the effect it could have on American companies and consumers.

For More Information

American Enterprise Institute, 1789 Massachusetts Ave., N.W., Washington, DC 20036; 202-862-5800; aei.org. Conservative think tank that created and regularly updates the China Global Investment Tracker, the only U.S. database that monitors China's Belt and Road developments.

Australian Institute of International Affairs, Stephen House, 32 Thesiger Court, Deakin ACT 2600, Canberra, Australia; +61 (02) 6282-2133; internationalaffairs.org.au. Leading Australian think tank for China policy and regional security issues; produces research papers and holds briefings.

Center for Strategic and International Studies, 1616 Rhode Island Ave., N.W., Washington, DC 20036; 202-887-0200; csis.org. Centrist research institute with strong China- and Asia-related programs; publishes papers and reports and holds symposia featuring senior current and former officials.

China Foreign Affairs University, 24 Zhanlanguan Road, Xicheng District, Beijing 100037, People's Republic of China; +86 10 6832 3367; en.cfau.edu.cn/. China's top school for diplomats, administered by the Ministry of Foreign Affairs; website takes questions from researchers.

Global Public Policy Institute, Reinhardtstr. 7, 10117, Berlin, Germany; +49 30 2759 59 75-0; gppi.net. Independent think tank whose China research focuses on security and human rights issues; produces papers and reports in partnership with leading universities and research institutions.

Heritage Foundation, 214 Massachusetts Ave., N.E., Washington, DC 20002; 202-546-4400; heritage.org. Conservative think tank that provides analytical papers, reports and books on Asia- and China-related issues.

Mercator Institute for China Studies, Klosterstrasse 64, 10179 Berlin, Germany; (49) 30 3440 999-0; www.merics.org. Liberal think tank that produces studies and reports analyzing China's political, economic and social developments and their consequences for Europe; advises European decision-makers on Chinese politics, business and society.

National Bureau of Asian Research, 1819 L St., N.W., Ninth Floor, Washington, DC 20036; 202-347-9767; nbr.org. Nonpartisan think tank that offers papers, books and reports on Asian regional and national security issues, as well as briefings.

7

The Natural Gas Industry

Will LNG transform the global energy market?

By Sara Toth Stub

Farmland surrounds a fracking site in Scenery Hill, Pa., in October 2020. Plans to transport LNG by rail from Pennsylvania have encountered pushback from environmentalists and local communities worried about accidental explosions.

From *CQ Researcher*, January 01, 2021

THE ISSUES

In Gibbstown, N.J., residents worry that trains carrying highly flammable liquefied natural gas (LNG) will soon pass regularly through their town to a port on the Delaware River, where the fuel will be exported overseas.

Critics of the project, which includes building a facility in Pennsylvania to liquefy natural gas from nearby fracking fields and then transporting it overland, call the rail cars "bombs on wheels" due to the risk of explosions. The project was approved in December, a decision that could open the door for the now-banned railway transport of LNG nationally.

"It's so dangerous," said resident Dave Rogers of the project. "I've got to sell my house. I've got to move away," said Rogers, who has lived in Gibbstown in southern New Jersey for decades.[1]

But the project's supporters say it will provide jobs and increased flexibility in the LNG sector, which has enjoyed rapid growth in recent years and has enabled the United States to become a major gas exporter. The nation was on track in 2020 to be a net energy exporter for the first time in more than 70 years.[2]

In its gaseous form, natural gas—a major fossil fuel, along with oil and coal—can be transported only via pipelines, which are

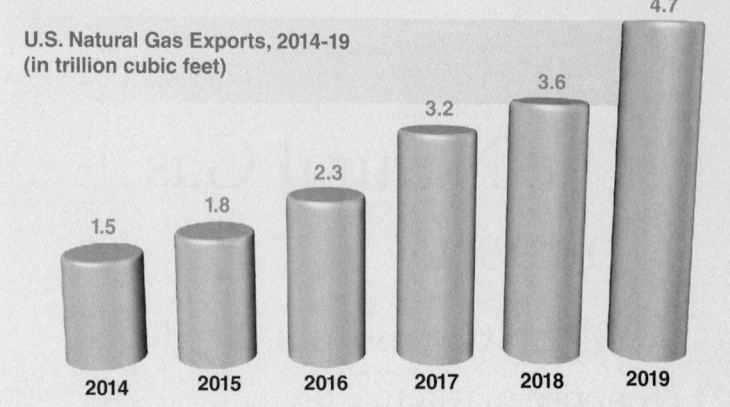

U.S. Natural Gas Exports Rising Rapidly

In 2019, the United States exported 4.7 trillion cubic feet of natural gas, more than three times as much as in 2014. Gas exports increased by more than 1 trillion cubic feet from 2018 to 2019 alone.

U.S. Natural Gas Exports, 2014-19 (in trillion cubic feet)

- 2014: 1.5
- 2015: 1.8
- 2016: 2.3
- 2017: 3.2
- 2018: 3.6
- 2019: 4.7

Source: "U.S. Natural Gas Exports and Re-Exports by Country," U.S. Energy Information Administration, Nov. 30, 2020, https://tinyurl.com/y9gjan65

A natural gas and oil refinery lights up the early morning sky in Bismarck, N.D. Large gas discoveries in North Dakota and other states allowed the United States to become an energy exporter in recent years.

limited by distance and geography. But LNG—natural gas that has been cooled to at least minus 260 degrees Fahrenheit, reducing its volume by about 600 times—can be transported long distances, usually on ships. Regasification facilities turn it back into its gaseous state upon arrival at its destination, where it is distributed over local pipeline networks.[3]

The debate in Gibbstown is emblematic of the promise and perils in the natural gas industry. Increasing demand for cleaner-burning energy, more gas discoveries and improved extraction technology that includes fracking—drilling thousands of feet underground and injecting a mixture of chemicals to extract oil and gas—have driven sharp growth in both LNG and the gas sector over the past decade.

Gas is also playing a larger role in the global energy market, economy and politics. But the sector is currently suffering a downturn in both price and demand because of the COVID-19 pandemic, and it faces an uncertain future with a growing number of countries adopting or considering policies that favor renewable energy over fossil fuels.

In the United States, President-elect Joe Biden has vowed to put the country on a path to achieve net-zero carbon emissions by 2050. He has said he will strengthen the limits on methane, a greenhouse gas, emitted during the production and transportation of natural gas.[4]

But at the same time, natural gas is emerging as the fuel of choice to provide backup power at wind and solar plants when the wind is not blowing or the sun is not shining—a solution until better storage systems are developed for renewables.[5]

"Overall, gas is very abundant and has proved to be a good all-around fuel, although it's not as cheap as coal and it's not as clean as renewables," says Patricia Roberts, managing director of LNG-Worldwide Ltd., a London-based industry consulting firm. "But there are a lot of unknowns at the moment, and you have massive uncertainty about future energy transitions."

Until the pandemic hurt demand, the natural gas sector had grown impressively:

- It was the fastest-growing fossil fuel in 2019, and the only one expected to see growth beyond 2035.[6]

- Natural gas is on track to overtake coal as the second most popular energy source after oil by 2030, largely because it is a cleaner option than coal: It produces up to 60 percent less carbon dioxide than coal for generating electricity and between 15 percent and 20 percent less greenhouse gases than gasoline-powered cars.[7]

- The world has enough known natural gas reserves to last another 53 years, compared with 51 years for oil.[8]

LNG, meanwhile, has created a more interconnected and competitive marketplace for gas. Countries with large reserves of natural gas, including the United States, Qatar and Australia, are increasingly finding overseas markets for excess gas and selling it as LNG—especially to China, South Korea and Japan.[9] The United States is the world leader in gas production.[10]

LNG, as a result, experienced rapid growth in recent decades:[11]

- The volume of LNG traded globally quadrupled between 1996 and 2016, resulting in a more competitive market worldwide.

- The number of countries importing LNG totaled 43 in 2019, up from 23 in 2009; Qatar alone exports more LNG than all countries combined did in 1995.[12]

- About half of the LNG produced globally in 2019 went to make electricity; nearly a quarter was used to power vehicles.[13]

- The United States is on track to become the world's leading LNG exporter by 2024, with a record $65 billion committed to new LNG liquefaction facilities in 2019. In 2015, the nation's LNG production was near zero.[14]

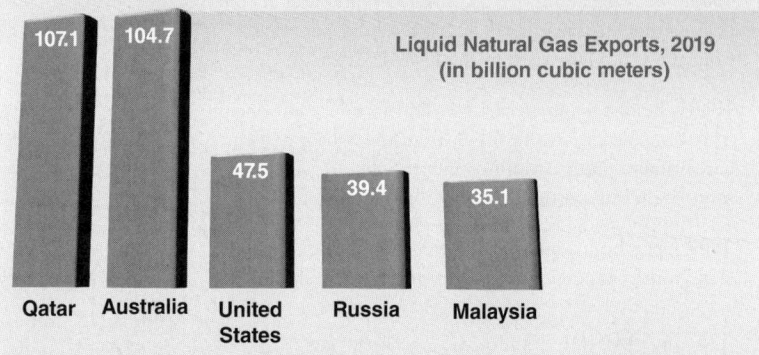

Qatar Is Largest LNG Exporter

Qatar exported 107.1 billion cubic meters of liquid natural gas (LNG) in 2019, nearly matched by Australia, which exported 104.7 billion cubic meters, according to a report from BP. The United States, Russia and Malaysia filled out the top five.

Liquid Natural Gas Exports, 2019 (in billion cubic meters)

Source: "Statistical Review of World Energy: 2020," BP, 2020, p. 42, https://tinyurl.com/y93mc5yc

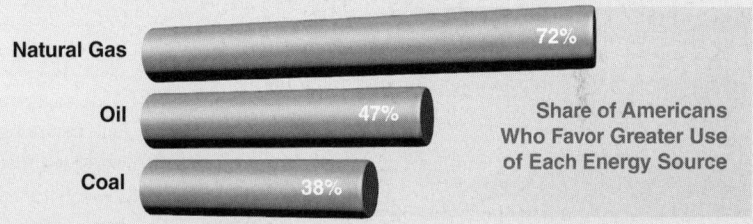

Most Americans Support Greater Use of Natural Gas

More than 7 in 10 Americans favor expanding the use of natural gas as a source of energy, according to a survey by the Pew Research Center. Some 47 percent support greater use of oil, while 38 percent favor using more coal.

Share of Americans Who Favor Greater Use of Each Energy Source

Source: Brian Kennedy, Alison Spencer and Cary Funk, "Natural gas viewed more positively than other fossil fuels across 20 global publics," Pew Research Center, Oct. 19, 2020, https://tinyurl.com/yase33l9

The increase in trade has been driven in part by improved technology, such as floating regasification and storage terminals, which can anchor in ports and connect temporarily to local gas grids, eliminating the need for building permanent onshore LNG facilities.[15]

"Demand can be [met] much quicker than it was done in the past," said Melissa Lindsay, CEO of Emsurge, an online LNG trading platform.[16]

These developments have "raised the profile and importance of LNG in international relations," says Steven Miles, a nonresident fellow at the Baker Institute's Center for Energy Studies at Rice University.

CHRONOLOGY

1950s-1960s *Liquefied natural gas industry emerges.*

1959 The *Methane Pioneer*, a converted World War II ship, delivers the first transatlantic liquefied natural gas (LNG), from the U.S. Gulf Coast to the United Kingdom.

1964 The first commercial LNG liquefaction plant opens in Arzew, Algeria, to ship LNG from the Sahara to France and Britain; North African countries, including Libya, soon begin transporting LNG to Europe by sea.

1969 Japan begins importing LNG from Alaska, starting a shift from coal-powered electricity to reduce pollution.

1970s-1980s *LNG industry grows as the world struggles with energy security.*

1971 Massachusetts-based Distrigas receives first shipment of LNG from Algeria, launching a decade of increased American imports of LNG.

1972 Brunei, in southeast Asia, becomes the fourth country to export LNG, mainly supplying Japan.

1973 OPEC imposes an oil embargo on the United States and other countries that support Israel in the 1973 Mideast war; the disruption spurs more research on fuel-efficiency and alternative-energy resources.

1975 The U.S. bans petroleum exports.

1979 U.S. LNG imports peak, making up about 1.3 percent of all natural gas consumed nationally that year. . . . The Islamic revolution in Iran contributes to a decline in global oil production and a price spike, boosting interest in energy efficiency and independence in the United States.

1980s-1990s *U.S. moves away from LNG imports, but the industry grows in Asia.*

1980 President Jimmy Carter signs the Energy Security Act, offering incentives for research into renewable energy such as solar and biomass and discouraging coal use.

1982 An LNG terminal in Lake Charles, La., shuts down shortly after opening as LNG prices rise and demand drops.

1986 U.S. imports of LNG drop to zero.

1989 Australia builds its first gas liquefaction facility and begins regional exports.

1997 The large Qatar gas liquefaction facility opens in Qatar, which becomes a major LNG exporter, boosting its economy and strategic importance.

2000-2010 *U.S. sees a major jump in gas supply.*

2000 U.S. natural gas prices hit a new high.

2002 LNG imports into the U.S. begin rising, and the federal Energy Information Administration forecasts the trend will continue to meet American energy needs.

2005 President George W. Bush calls for more LNG imports to secure supply amid worries about shortages and record-high prices, but other policymakers raise concerns about safety and overreliance on foreign energy. . . . U.S.-based Excelerate Energy builds and deploys the world's first floating storage and regasification unit off the coast of Louisiana.

2007 U.S. energy companies increase gas extracted by hydraulic fracturing from shale (known as fracking), sparking a decline in prices.

2011-Present *U.S. becomes a major global energy supplier as environmental concerns about fossil fuels increase.*

2011 Nord Stream gas pipeline opens to bring Russian gas to Germany under the Baltic Sea, bypassing Ukraine, which is increasingly in conflict with Russia.

2016 Most nations, including the U.S., sign the Paris Agreement on climate change to reduce carbon emissions. . . . The U.S. exports its first LNG shipment abroad, to Brazil, as it begins its shift to becoming a net energy exporter. . . . Republican Donald Trump wins the presidential election; his administration encourages more fracking, and he withdraws the U.S. from the Paris accord.

2017 China becomes the world's second-largest importer of LNG as government policies favor gas over coal.

2019 U.S. places sanctions on Nord Stream 2 project, a pipeline to bring more Russian gas to Germany. . . . U.S.-China trade tensions halt Chinese purchases of American LNG.

2020 The coronavirus pandemic cuts global demand for natural gas (March). . . . Democrat Joe Biden wins the presidency after campaigning on a platform to cut U.S. carbon emissions and to end fracking on federal land (November).

"LNG exports are an important tool in the U.S. government's toolkit."

For example, the State Department has referred to LNG exports to Europe as "freedom gas," because they could reduce the continent's reliance on gas from Russia, a political rival.[17] Miles says that American LNG also offers an alternative to the coal plants that China is building outside its borders as part of its infrastructure projects known as the Belt and Road Initiative.

LNG's enhanced role globally has raised the stakes in the United States over fracking—formally known as hydraulic fracturing—and other environmental aspects of the natural gas industry. While fracking has been largely responsible for the increase in U.S. gas production, opponents of the process say it damages the environment by causing earthquakes, contaminating water supplies and harming air quality.[18]

But its proponents say fracking is critical to the economy and to energy security. Analysts estimate the fracking industry was worth $28.13 billion in 2019. Banning fracking would eliminate 4 million jobs in 2021 and 19 million jobs by 2025, according to the U.S. Chamber of Commerce's Global Energy Institute.[19]

Many scientists say the environmental effects of fracking are unclear. "This is one of those issues where there's just so much gray," said Sam Ori, executive director of the Energy Policy Institute at the University of Chicago.[20]

The Trump administration has been a vocal supporter of fracking, especially in electoral battleground states with large fracking industries, including Pennsylvania and Ohio. But Biden has sent mixed messages on the issue, denying he would prohibit it outright while suggesting he might institute a ban on new fracking projects on federal land. Some liberal Democrats are pushing for a total ban on fracking and halting exports of all fossil fuels.[21]

"It is unlikely that Biden would actively try to damage the gas industry during an economic crisis," says Henning Gloystein, director of energy, climate and resources at the Eurasia Group, a political risk and consulting firm, explaining that the ongoing COVID-19 pandemic and a potentially divided Congress would likely prevent immediate steps against fracking or other parts of the oil and gas industry. Biden's presidency "will raise green energy policy support and slow fossil fuel momentum," says Gloystein.

With concerns about climate change accelerating, the gas sector faces other questions about its environmental impact. Although it burns cleaner than coal, natural gas still made up about 33 percent of the total carbon dioxide emissions in the U.S. energy sector in 2019.[22] State-level policies mandating lower carbon emissions in the energy sector could reduce the use of gas in favor of renewable sources. And the falling cost of renewables, including solar, could make them more attractive to consumers and industries than natural gas.

Some projections, as a result, see natural gas starting to decline in the coming decade, in favor of cleaner, and eventually cheaper, renewable sources.[23]

"Gas is not going anywhere at the moment," says Nikos Tsafos, deputy director and senior fellow at the energy security and climate change program at the Center for Strategic and International Studies, a Washington think tank. "But carbon constraints will eventually hit gas, even if in the short term gas may benefit because it is replacing coal."

BACKGROUND
Early Days

Natural gas, often a byproduct of oil drilling, was long relegated to being a "poor relation" of the energy

Natural Gas Fields Shake Up Mideast Diplomacy

"Washington is keen to encourage regional economic cooperation."

In October, officials from Israel and Lebanon, along with U.S. mediators, met at a United Nations border post to discuss the exact location of their maritime boundary in the Mediterranean Sea, where large amounts of potentially valuable natural gas have been found in recent years.

It was the first time the two countries, still technically at war, met to talk about nonmilitary issues—and it only happened after much U.S. prodding, the details of which remain classified.[1]

"This is a win-win, if you can get the deal," former U.S. Ambassador to Israel Dan Shapiro said, adding that the gas could help revive the struggling Lebanese economy. The gas reserves could be worth $6 billion annually.[2]

Although the talks stalled in November, the negotiations demonstrate how large gas finds are shaping cooperation—and raising tensions—in the region. The United States is watching developments closely, as gas from the region could be exported to Europe, providing an alternative to the Continent's heavy reliance on Russia for energy.[3]

"Washington is keen to encourage regional economic cooperation," says Simon Henderson, a research fellow specializing in energy at the Washington Institute for Near East Policy, a pro-Israeli think tank.

Energy companies began finding large deep-water gas reserves in the region in the mid-2000s, with the largest discoveries off Israel, Cyprus and Egypt. In the past few years, some of those discoveries have entered the production phase, including two large fields off Israel, Tamar and Leviathan. Israel is now selling gas to Egypt and Jordan, in addition to supplying about 63 percent of its domestic electricity production.[4]

"The gas has been very important for Israel," says Sarit Zehavi, CEO and founder of the Alma Research and Education Center, an Israeli think tank located near the country's border with Lebanon. "Israel has become independent in energy sources, and now even has others depending on it."

Egypt, Israel and the Palestinian Authority, along with Greece, Italy and Cyprus, recently formed the East Mediterranean Gas Organization to cooperate on development of the industry and to transport the gas to Europe by underwater pipeline.[5]

"Today is an historic moment," said Egypt's oil minister, Tarek el-Molla, at the signing in September. "Once the organization is up and running, we will soon see important projects that add value to all our countries."[6]

But this cooperation has elevated tensions between Greece and Turkey, which is not part of the gas organization. Turkey recently carried out naval exercises and gas drilling in waters claimed by Greece, and it could mount costly international legal battles over gas rights. Turkey also has angered gas forum members by signing a deal with the Government of National Accord in civil-war-plagued Libya to cooperate on offshore gas exploration, as most members of the forum support the opposing side in the Libyan conflict. The European Union has recently suggested placing sanctions on Turkish companies and their partners who are drilling off Cyprus, in waters claimed by Greece.[7]

Analysts have warned the situation could turn violent, and they are calling for the United States and gas forum members to be more flexible toward Turkish membership.[8] The presence of Greece and Cyprus in the forum, and their ongoing disputes with Turkey over general border issues and control of parts of Cyprus, have helped keep Turkey out.

In exchange for forum membership, "Turkey should contain its regional ambitions, bearing in mind that an armed conflict between these Mediterranean powers would

industry, according to research fellow Jonathan Stern and energy economist Adi Imsirovic. Energy companies mainly sold gas to the local market or left it in the ground if it was too far or expensive to ship to potential consumers.[24]

It was only upon discovering several large but remote reserves of natural gas in the late 1950s and '60s, and facing political pressure to diversify fuel sources, that European and U.S. energy companies began the first projects liquifying gas for transport to broader markets.[25]

be catastrophic," writes Federica Saini Fasanotti, a nonresident senior fellow at the Brookings Institution, a Washington think tank.[9]

While tensions between Turkey and some of its neighbors continue, the Israeli-Lebanese border issue remains unresolved. Neither country, as a result, can harvest the gas reserves in the disputed area, which is about 330 square miles. The lack of an agreement affects Lebanon, which has no other gas fields, more than Israel, which has several offshore fields.[10]

Israel and Lebanon have long been foes, most recently fighting a war in 2006. Lebanon's fragile government has the support of Hezbollah, an Iranian-backed group accused of being a terrorist organization.

But, initially, some analysts thought the countries could solve the border dispute, citing Lebanon's struggling economy, the continued economic and political fallout from a powerful chemical explosion in Beirut's port that killed hundreds in August, and increased U.S. pressure. The Trump administration imposed sanctions on Hezbollah's ally in parliament, the Amal party, which agreed to the talks despite the fact that it does not recognize Israel.

"Hezbollah is being cornered, even by its own allies," said Nadim Koteich, a Lebanese political columnist and host on *Sky News Arabic*. But when the Lebanese side began asking for more territory, new land borders and access to more gas fields, Israel halted the negotiations, at least for now, with Israel's energy minister calling Lebanese demands "a provocation."[11]

Zehavi, the Israeli think tank head, says that Israel also worries about Hezbollah profiting from the gas and using the revenue to fund its terrorist activities against Israel.

"This money will end up in the wrong hands," she says. "And we could eventually end up with a stronger Hezbollah."

Israel recently deployed a naval ship to guard its offshore gas rigs, with some officials citing threats from Hezbollah.[12]

But even if the political tensions dissipate and cooperation increases, some analysts still doubt the feasibility of harvesting enough Mediterranean gas to export to Europe, especially with gas prices falling globally.

"The amounts of gas so far discovered are not large compared with other parts of the Middle East and would have limited impact on European demand," says Henderson, the energy analyst. "The pipeline proposal doesn't currently make commercial sense."

—*Sara Toth Stub*

[1] Ben Hubbard, "Israel and Lebanon Begin Talks on Sea Border, with U.S. as a Mediator," *The New York Times*, Oct. 14, 2020, https://tinyurl.com/y6eqndtp.

[2] Joshua Mitnick, "How a Maritime Deal With Israel Could Ease Lebanon's Woes," *Foreign Policy*, Oct. 13, 2020, https://tinyurl.com/y87886e5.

[3] "Israel Accuses Lebanon of Changing Stance on Maritime Border," *Agence France-Presse, Barron's*, Nov. 20, 2020, https://tinyurl.com/yaol5k53; John Psaropoulos, "Why Greece is key to US plans to sell more natural gas to Europe," *Al Jazeera*, Jan. 7, 2020, https://tinyurl.com/y9rye4hg.

[4] Selcan Hacaoglu, "How Turkey Is Spoiling Its Neighbors' Big Gas Plans," *Bloomberg Businessweek*, Dec. 10, 2019, https://tinyurl.com/trt459f; "Israel-Energy," U.S. International Trade Administration, Dec. 3, 2019, https://tinyurl.com/yd3mqkoc.

[5] Hacaoglu, *ibid*.

[6] Salma El Wardany and Mirette Magdy, "Egypt, Greece, Cyprus Form Six-Member Mediterranean Gas Group," *Bloomberg*, Sept. 22, 2020, https://tinyurl.com/y7ty8wzp.

[7] Laura Pitel and David Sheppard, "Turkey fuels regional power game over Mediterranean gas reserves," *Financial Times*, July 19, 2020, https://tinyurl.com/y4mh2ngs; Stuart Elliott and David O'Byrne, "EU leaders pave way for additional limited sanctions on Turkey over gas drilling," S&P Global, https://tinyurl.com/ybqqlvpc.

[8] Federica Saini Fasanotti, "The new, great dangerous game in the Eastern Mediterranean," Brookings Institution, Aug. 28, 2020, https://tinyurl.com/y27rw6sz.

[9] *Ibid*.

[10] Timour Azhari, "Lebanon's first offshore gas drill is a huge disappointment," *Al Jazeera*, April 27, 2020, https://tinyurl.com/y8peghcs.

[11] Mitnick, *op. cit.*; "Israel-Lebanon maritime border talks postponed, both sides say," *Reuters, The Jerusalem Post*, Nov. 30, 2020, https://tinyurl.com/y4tuewya.

[12] "Israel gets missile boat to defend gas rigs, 'dramatically' help counter Iran," *Agence France-Presse, The Times of Israel*, Dec. 2, 2020, https://tinyurl.com/y7hkt5jn.

But because of the large investment needed to build infrastructure, including liquefaction and regasification facilities, and the reliance on long-term contracts, LNG did not immediately transform gas into a commodity like oil.[26]

Anti-pollution laws in Japan in the late 1960s boosted the nascent global trade of LNG, with Japan importing large amounts from Alaska.[27]

Around the same time, the United States began to import LNG from Algeria to make up for shortfalls in

Motorists wait in line to buy gasoline in New York City during OPEC's 1973 oil embargo. The embargo spurred the United States to seek alternative energy sources.

gas supply during peak winter use along the East Coast, which was served poorly by pipelines from gas-producing regions.[28]

Through the 1970s, American imports of LNG increased and large energy companies invested in the specialized infrastructure needed to receive it and turn it back into gas. The rise was driven by worries about dwindling local gas supplies and global energy uncertainty in the years following the 1973 oil embargo by Middle East producers and other events.[29]

Federal policy, however, began to discourage LNG imports and treat them as an option of last resort, due to worries about imported gas pushing up local prices. The nation's LNG imports, as a result, dwindled in the 1980s. Meanwhile, LNG demand continued to grow steadily in the Pacific region, with Japan and South Korea, which lack significant local gas reserves, increasing imports for generating electricity and powering industrial plants. These imports mainly came from others in the region, including Australia, Indonesia and Brunei.[30]

Discovery of Large Reserves

It was only in the late 1990s and early 2000s, when giant gas reserves were discovered in the Persian Gulf country of Qatar, that the industry began to see significant growth. Rising concerns about carbon emissions from coal-fired power plants, combined with dropping costs for producing and transporting LNG, resulted in more demand globally. With Qatar exporting to both Europe and Asia, prices in geographically distant and separate LNG markets began to converge, and competition increased.[31]

During this time, the United States feared its domestic gas supply was insufficient, and President George W. Bush began a controversial campaign to ramp up LNG imports. Many opposed the plan, citing the potential for explosions in ports receiving the fuel and increased exposure to supply disruptions from foreign policy disputes.[32]

However, large domestic gas and oil discoveries later that decade, mainly from fracking in states such as Colorado and North Dakota, quickly eliminated the need for imports. Between 2006 and 2016, U.S. natural gas production grew almost 50 percent and prices fell by half.[33]

This abundant and cheap gas spurred electricity generation plants to switch from coal to cleaner-burning gas, with more than 500 coal-fired plants closing in the United States between 2010 and 2019. The closures contributed to an overall drop in carbon emissions.[34]

The United States began exporting gas in its liquified state, able to reach distant markets at decent returns due to abundant and cheap production. Flooding a rapidly expanding global market with supply, the United States became the world's third-largest gas exporter by 2019. This expansion has put U.S. gas in direct competition with Russia, the world's second-largest gas producer, and provided another source of natural gas to rapidly growing markets in Asia.[35]

"The United States has been responsible for significantly increasing world gas and LNG supply," says John Madigan, analyst at market research firm IBISWorld.

CURRENT SITUATION
Falling Prices, Demand

In the global gas sector, the coronavirus pandemic is exacerbating three pre-existing problems: falling prices, oversupply and challenges in how LNG is sold.[36]

Global gas demand is on track to fall about 3 percent in 2020, its biggest drop in at least 50 years, due mainly to the effects of the virus. The pandemic-related recession has slowed parts of the world economy, such as manufacturing, that are powered by gas.[37] Gas prices are also low, hit both by the drop in demand and the supply glut.

"We've got demand and supply moving in opposite directions," says Madigan. "But it does mean we are seeing more motivation to switch from coal to gas now that gas is cheap."

Rather than grow slightly, as expected before the pandemic, the volume of LNG shipped in 2020 will be

AT ISSUE

Is natural gas an environmentally sustainable long-term major energy source?

YES Dave Schryver
President and CEO, American Public Gas Association
Written for CQ Researcher, January 2021

Natural gas is a critical part of our nation's energy future. Thanks to its abundant and growing domestic supply, paired with its safe, reliable and efficient delivery system, natural gas is environmentally sustainable and a key piece to a balanced energy infrastructure in the long term.

As distribution networks have expanded over the past few decades, natural gas utilities and their customers have led the charge in reducing greenhouse gas emissions. This unprecedented expansion of the nation's gas infrastructure, along with continuous efficiency increases and advancements in renewable energy sources, have led to energy-related carbon dioxide emissions hitting 25-year lows. And, since 1970, gas utilities have added more than 30 million residential customers with virtually no increases in emissions, providing customers across the country with energy that is three times as efficient as electricity at just one-third of the cost.

With greater efficiency bringing gas from the source to the user—92 percent compared with just 32 percent for electricity—the direct use of natural gas in the home for heating and cooking represents an opportunity to give customers nationwide access to a low-cost, clean-energy source while providing a pathway to continue reducing greenhouse gas emissions.

While natural gas has contributed to reductions in global greenhouse gas emissions using new technologies, the industry continues to innovate ways to be even more efficient and sustainable, such as converting waste streams from landfills or agricultural sites to a usable energy source in residential and commercial applications.

Natural gas' reliability and resiliency also provide clean and readily available energy when disasters strike—which is critically important for first responders, hospitals and senior living facilities. And while environmental factors often limit the reach of renewable resources, natural gas provides energy to homes when the sun isn't shining and the wind isn't blowing.

Additionally, Americans' preference for natural gas underscores the need to include it in a balanced energy future. According to the Energy Solutions Center, an organization of energy utilities and equipment makers, nearly 70 percent of new homeowners nationwide prefer natural gas to meet their home energy needs over electric appliances. The reliability, safety and affordability of the direct use of natural gas make it an appealing option for residential customers, especially as households with all-electric appliances pay over $900 a year more than those using a traditional mix of gas and electric.

Natural gas is an efficient, resilient and affordable energy source that is fundamental to achieving a diversified and sustainable energy future.

NO Robert B. Jackson
Earth System Science Professor, Stanford University, and Chair, Global Carbon Project
Written for CQ Researcher, January 2021

Natural gas has many advantages as an energy source. It is abundant and is cheaper and cleaner than coal. Its use in power plants produces only half the carbon dioxide per unit of energy that coal produces, and little of the mercury, nitrogen and particulate pollution that kills millions of people each year. Natural gas is unabashedly the "cleanest fossil fuel."

Being the cleanest fossil fuel is no longer enough, though. To make natural gas an environmentally sustainable energy source, progress is needed in several areas.

First, methane emissions from the extraction and use of natural gas need to be much lower than they are today. Methane, which makes up the bulk of natural gas, is 30 times more potent than carbon dioxide over a century. It isn't fair to take credit for all the carbon dioxide savings in switching from coal to natural gas but not acknowledge the higher methane emissions we're bearing as a result. The natural gas supply chain is unnecessarily and dangerously leaky.

Second, natural gas use is growing rapidly. Despite being cleaner than coal, natural gas still yields greenhouse gases when burned—more than 7 billion tons of carbon dioxide pollution a year. Natural gas use is growing at $2\frac{1}{2}$ percent annually. We can't reach the net zero emissions needed for a habitable planet by burning *more* fossil fuels.

One way we could continue to burn some fossil fuels for power would be to capture their carbon dioxide emissions and store them underground. Unfortunately, costs and technological and social concerns have kept carbon capture and storage (CCS) from the marketplace. We need many more demonstration projects to convince people that widespread CCS is feasible.

Third, we need more work on renewable natural gas, such as the "biogas" generated from landfills, agricultural waste and other sources. In theory, natural gas can be produced from excess capacity generated by renewable sources such as solar power, although the large scale needed is daunting. Why bother to do this? Because keeping some gas in the system would allow for large-scale energy storage in underground reservoirs during "dunkelflaute," the dark power doldrums of winter.

That is a long list, and it is why many environmentalists and energy experts believe sufficient progress is unlikely to happen fast enough to warrant the investments needed, especially when even cleaner and cheaper renewables are already available.

Workers install a natural gas pipeline in Berthoud, Colo. A boom in gas production has meant that "we've got demand and supply moving in opposite directions," says John Madigan, analyst at market research firm IBISWorld.

about the same as in 2019, says Roberts, managing director of LNG-Worldwide. Previously signed long-term contracts and strong demand in Asia, where the pandemic has not stunted demand as sharply as in other regions, has prevented a decline, Roberts says.

"LNG volumes have stood up quite well, but the margins have been quite affected as prices have fallen dramatically," she says. Oversupply and low prices are further accelerating trends in how LNG is sold. Roberts says sellers are facing increased pressure to abandon traditional long-term contracts that led to higher and more stable prices in favor of spot trading. "Buyers are starting to have more power, which is normal as an industry grows," she says.

Globally, the LNG industry is seeing the fastest growth in demand in Asia, especially in China, where government policies to reduce reliance on coal are creating more demand for gas, at least in the short term. China is expected to surpass Japan to become the world's largest buyer of LNG by 2022.[38]

But an ongoing trade war, started in 2018 when the Trump administration slapped tariffs on some Chinese goods, causing China to retaliate, is keeping the United States from selling large amounts of LNG to China. With Biden's election as president, there is still uncertainty but also some hope: U.S.-based Cheniere Energy signed a deal in November to supply the first American LNG to China in more than a year.[39]

"The U.S. may play a role in China if bilateral relations between Beijing and Washington improve," says the Eurasia Group's Gloystein. "If they don't improve, China will be reluctant to increase its energy reliance on a geopolitical rival."

Meanwhile, the United States continues to oppose the Nord Stream 2 pipeline under construction in Europe that will bring Russian natural gas to Germany. Washington is trying to stall the project by threatening economic sanctions—approved recently by Congress in a bipartisan initiative pushed by Ukrainian lobbyists—on companies that work on the pipeline. The United States is reluctant to let Russia, which has already been sanctioned for invading Ukraine, control key energy sources of American allies in Europe.[40]

Environmental Challenges

The gas industry is facing growing pressure to reduce its environmental impact, with recent studies showing that gas extraction and distribution emit much more methane than thought. This comes after researchers concluded that more than 2 percent of the methane-rich natural gas harvested by fracking leaks into the atmosphere during the process, and scientists studying Arctic ice cores have traced more methane emissions to the oil and gas production industry.[41]

"When you factor in methane emitted during the extraction and distribution of natural gas, climate advantage shrinks substantially," says Robert Jackson, an earth system science professor at Stanford University and the chairman of the Global Carbon Project, an international research group focused on greenhouse gases and climate change.

Some analysts say natural gas production is now at its peak, with more than half of U.S. states, many European countries and China adopting legal or voluntary measures to reduce carbon output.[42]

"The image of gas has changed, especially in the progressive wing of the Democratic party," says the Center for Strategic and International Studies' Tsafos.

As with coal and oil, views on natural gas often "reflect broader political divides in the debate over climate and energy issues," says Brian Kennedy, senior researcher focusing on society and science at the Pew Research Center, a nonpartisan Washington think tank. Republicans generally support fracking while many Democrats do not.

THE NATURAL GAS INDUSTRY

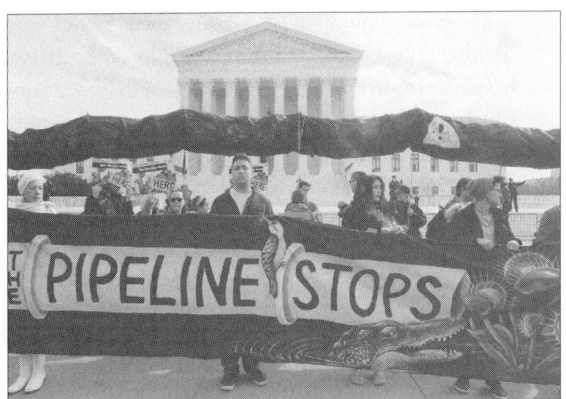

Climate activists gather outside the Supreme Court in February 2020 to protest plans to build a natural gas pipeline underneath the Appalachian Trail in Virginia. The court ruled that the pipeline could proceed, but the companies involved canceled the project, citing litigation costs.

In the LNG sector, multinational companies Total and Siemens are launching a project to develop technology to more cleanly produce LNG through more efficient equipment, heat-recovery technology and use of renewable energy. Some LNG sales contracts, including those involving divisions of Royal Dutch Shell, are starting to include the purchase of carbon offsets—investments in reforestation or renewable energy projects that will remove carbon from the atmosphere to make up for carbon created through the production and transportation of LNG.[46]

OUTLOOK
A Slow Rebound

In the short term, the International Energy Agency expects demand for gas, including LNG, to recover when the coronavirus pandemic fades. A cold winter could also boost prices in the Northern Hemisphere.[47]

Trade in LNG, according to a recent International Energy Agency forecast, will likely grow about 21 percent through 2025, boosted mainly by growing demand in Asia, where fast-growing economies in India, China and elsewhere will need more gas as they transition from coal to meet carbon reduction targets. As renewable energy plays a bigger role in power production, that development will also increase the use of gas, as it is seen as the best backup fuel to use at solar and wind plants—at least in the short term.[48]

"Gas is an essential part of the transition," said Rachel Kyte, former U.N. special representative for sustainable energy.[49]

But the recovery and growth of the LNG sector will no longer depend solely on the control of gas supplies and other factors, energy analysts say. Carbon reduction, lowering costs by developing better technology and investment in power plants and pipelines will also be critical.[50]

"What will separate winners from losers will be an adaptive business model," says the LNG-Worldwide's Roberts.

Another source of growth for the LNG industry will likely come from the shipping sector, with more gas-fueled vessels expected to come online as the industry seeks to reduce oil use and cut carbon emissions.[51]

Eventually, many forecasters see gas consumption peaking at some point in the next three decades, as more governments commit to reducing carbon output and the use of fossil fuels.[52]

Environmentalists' complaints about fossil fuel production are having an impact. Large power provider Dominion Energy, for example, is selling off its natural gas infrastructure amid worries that the company could be subject to lawsuits if the government dictates growing use of renewables, and major gas turbine makers are increasingly working to make hydrogen-burning equipment.

"Investment in gas transmission and storage has become increasingly litigious, uncertain and costly," said Tom Farrell, Dominion's executive chairman. "This trend, though deeply concerning for our country's economic growth and energy security, is a new reality, which threatens the pace at which we intended to grow these assets."[43]

Two major energy companies this summer canceled a gas pipeline that would have run underneath the Appalachian Trail in Virginia, citing ballooning litigation costs.[44]

And despite receiving approval in December, the proposed LNG terminal in New Jersey, which would also require overland transport of gas from fracking fields in the region, still faces opposition from environmental groups over safety and environmental questions.

"We will continue to fight," said Jeff Tittel, director of the New Jersey Sierra Club. "People of the region and Puerto Rico [where some of the LNG could go] don't want this disastrous project."[45]

But Tsafos of the Center for Strategic and International Studies says that much uncertainty about how and when this could happen remains, because some of the biggest uses for natural gas, including powering factories and heating buildings, do not have clear replacements that are cleaner.

"We don't really know what we will do without gas," Tsafos says. "It will take a lot of effort to replace it."

NOTES

1. Samantha Maldonado, "How South Jersey Became Ground Zero in Feds' Push for New Way to Transport LNG," *Politico*, March 16, 2020, https://tinyurl.com/ydfuq2gz; "Delaware River commission approves Gibbstown, New Jersey, LNG terminal," *Reuters*, Dec. 9, 2020, https://tinyurl.com/y9v78vgz.

2. Joanna Marsh, "Environmental Groups Appeal Permits For LNG Export Facility in New Jersey," *FreightWaves*, Oct. 15, 2020, https://tinyurl.com/y72bcyf8; Tom DiChristopher, "US to become a net energy exporter in 2020 for first time in nearly 70 years, Energy Dept says," *CNBC*, Jan. 24, 2019, https://tinyurl.com/ya6l2cjr; and "LNG at the crossroads: Identifying key drivers and questions for an industry in flux," Deloitte Center for Energy Solutions, https://tinyurl.com/y9uddmyx.

3. "Liquefied Natural Gas," Office of Fossil Energy, U.S. Department of Energy, https://tinyurl.com/ych48j9j.

4. "World Energy Outlook 2019," International Energy Agency, November 2019, https://tinyurl.com/y8qt55kr; "The Biden Plan for a Clean Energy Revolution and Environmental Justice," Biden-Harris Campaign, https://tinyurl.com/y3agqq6p; and Ben Lefebvre, "How Biden may save U.S. gas exports to Europe," *Politico*, Nov. 27, 2020, https://tinyurl.com/yylq757l.

5. Giorgio Bresciani *et al.*, "The future of liquefied natural gas: Opportunities for growth," McKinsey & Company, Sept. 21, 2020, https://tinyurl.com/ybvp4v8a.

6. "Global Gas and LNG Outlook to 2035," McKinsey & Company, Sept. 4, 2019, https://tinyurl.com/y5vqogq5.

7. Anjli Raval, "Majors Back Gas in Power Switch as a 'Bridge Fuel,'" *Financial Times*, Nov. 28, 2018, https://tinyurl.com/y79glu23; "World Energy Outlook, 2018," International Energy Agency, November 2018, https://tinyurl.com/y9tkezeg; and "Environmental Impacts of Natural Gas," Union of Concerned Scientists, June 19, 2014, https://tinyurl.com/y8ydvk69.

8. Hannah Ritchie and Max Roser, "Fossil Fuels," Our World in Data, https://tinyurl.com/yavf9upv.

9. "LNG Market Trends and Their Implications," International Energy Agency, June 2019, https://tinyurl.com/y7zpyal6.

10. Drew Desilver, "Renewable Energy is Growing Fast in the U.S., but Fossil Fuels Still Dominate," Pew Research Center, Jan. 15, 2020, https://tinyurl.com/y3qfonky.

11. "LNG at the crossroads," Deloitte Center for Energy Solutions, https://tinyurl.com/y9uddmyx.

12. Bresciani *et al.*, *op. cit.*

13. "Liquefied Natural Gas Market Size, Share and Trends Analysis," Grand View Research, July 2020, https://tinyurl.com/y9kta4xg.

14. Sean O'Brien and Antonio Erias Rodriguez, "Record year for gas liquefaction investment lights a path towards market flexibility," International Energy Agency, Feb. 19, 2020, https://tinyurl.com/s9ulh9s.

15. Bresciani *et al.*, *op. cit.*

16. "Digital LNG Trading," "Redefining Energy," July 2020, episode 30, https://tinyurl.com/ybdt9f47.

17. Sam Meredith, "Russian energy minister ridicules Rick Perry's idea of US 'freedom gas,'" *CNBC*, Oct. 2, 2019, https://tinyurl.com/y4ggce43.

18. Umair Irfan, "The best case for and against a fracking ban," *Vox*, Oct. 7, 2020, https://tinyurl.com/yapeyofv.

19. "Oil & Gas/Hydraulic fracturing market," Fortune Business Insights, September 2020, https://tinyurl.com/yd42azhw; "What if hydraulic fracturing was banned?" Global Energy Institute, 2020, p. 6, https://tinyurl.com/tdm7y77.

20. Irfan, *op. cit.*
21. Lisa Friedman, "Trump's 'Frack' Attack on Biden Seems to Be Falling Short," *The New York Times*, Oct. 13, 2020, https://tinyurl.com/y3jkv49z; Lefebvre, *op. cit.*
22. "Energy and the environment explained," U.S. Energy Information Administration, https://tinyurl.com/y39wlws8.
23. Naureen Malik *et al.*, "Peak Gas Is Coming to the U.S. Sooner Than Anyone Expected," *Bloomberg*, Oct. 22, 2020, https://tinyurl.com/y4vculrr.
24. Jonathan Stern and Adi Imsirovic, "A Comparative History of Oil and Gas Markets and Prices: Is 2020 just an extreme cyclical event or an acceleration of the energy transition?" Oxford Institute for Energy Studies, April 2020, pp. 1, 7, https://tinyurl.com/yxdtyqns.
25. "Liquefied Natural Gas (LNG)," Royal Dutch Shell, https://tinyurl.com/yyogbbhy.
26. James T. Jensen, "The Development of a Global LNG Market," Oxford Institute for Energy Studies, 2004, p. 2, https://tinyurl.com/yanrhcdz.
27. Philip R. Weems and Nina M. Howell, "Japan's pivotal role in the global LNG industry's 50-year history," King & Spalding LLP, https://tinyurl.com/y8xbb96b.
28. "LNG Trade: Past, Present, Future (?)," U.S. Department of Energy, 1995, p. ii, https://tinyurl.com/yb94e288.
29. Jensen, *op. cit.*, p. 8.
30. *Ibid.*
31. *Ibid.*, pp. 8, 11, 12; "Global LNG Fundamentals," U.S. Department of Energy, 2017, p. 9, https://tinyurl.com/ycqgny37.
32. Simon Romero, "Demand for Natural Gas Brings Big Import Plans, and Objections," *The New York Times*, June 15, 2005, https://tinyurl.com/y8km775j.
33. "Can the United States sustainably export LNG at competitive prices?" Deloitte Center for Energy Solutions, 2016, p. 1, https://tinyurl.com/y95fah9n.
34. "More U.S. coal-fired power plants are decommissioning as retirements continue," U.S. Energy Information Administration, July 26, 2019, https://tinyurl.com/y3mprktr; Nicholas Kusnetz, "U.S. Emissions Dropped in 2019: Here's Why in 6 Charts," *Inside Climate News*, Jan. 7, 2020, https://tinyurl.com/teqr8eo.
35. "U.S. liquefied natural gas exports have declined by more than half so far in 2020," Energy Information Agency, June 23, 2020, https://tinyurl.com/ybngz875; Bresciani *et al.*, *op. cit.*; and Tatiana Mitrova and Tim Boersma, "The Impact of US LNG on Russian Natural Gas Export Policy," Columbia Center on Global Energy Policy, December 2018, pp. 7, 32-33, https://tinyurl.com/y8pr94ny.
36. Bresciani *et al.*, *ibid.*
37. "IEA nudges up 2020 gas demand forecast, but still sees record fall," *Reuters*, Oct. 12, 2020, https://tinyurl.com/y66sspbg.
38. Aaron Sheldrick, "China could top Japan's LNG imports in 2020 as coronavirus cuts demand," *Reuters*, June 18, 2020, https://tinyurl.com/ybd98ct6.
39. "China Inks First Term Deal for US LNG Since Trade War Erupted," *Bloomberg News*, Nov. 7, 2020, https://tinyurl.com/y3e78twr.
40. Brett Forrest, "U.S., Russia Race to Outflank Each Other on Russian Pipeline," *The Wall Street Journal*, Nov. 29, 2020, https://tinyurl.com/y43pap5g; "U.S. Sanctions on Russia: An Overview," Congressional Research Service, March 23, 2020, https://tinyurl.com/y389htrb.
41. Alejandra Borunda, "Natural gas is a much 'dirtier' energy source than we thought," *National Geographic*, Feb. 19, 2020, https://tinyurl.com/y2p2o27q.
42. Malik *et al.*, *op. cit.*
43. *Ibid.*
44. Ivan Penn, "Atlantic Coast Pipeline Canceled as Delays and Costs Mount," *The New York Times*, July 5, 2020, https://tinyurl.com/y926obnl.
45. "Delaware River commission approves Gibbstown, New Jersey, LNG terminal," *op. cit.*

46. Mirza Duran, "Siemens, Total to work on 'green' LNG production," *Offshore Energy*, June 12, 2020, https://tinyurl.com/yapxweu9; "LNG carbon offsetting: fleeting trend or sustainable practice?" International Group of Liquefied Natural Gas Importers, June 18, 2020, pp. 4, 5, https://tinyurl.com/ydapmxe4.

47. "Gas 2020," International Energy Agency, June 2020, https://tinyurl.com/y7k3t6nx; Vanessa Dezem, Rachel Morison and Anna Shiryaevskaya, "Wintry Weather Arriving in Europe Boosts Power and Gas Prices," *Bloomberg*, Dec. 1, 2020, https://tinyurl.com/y96to6nn.

48. "Gas 2020," *ibid.*; Bresciani *et al.*, *op. cit.*

49. Karl Matthiesen, "Transition 2020: Moniz defends natural gas as climate transition fuel," *Politico Pro*, Dec. 3, 2020, https://tinyurl.com/y894mlqu.

50. Bresciani *et al.*, *op. cit.*

51. Molly Burgess, "Hyundai unveils world's first LNG-powered container ship," *Gas World*, Aug. 24, 2020, https://tinyurl.com/yat5qpz7.

52. Simon Flowers, "Decarbonisation and Peak Gas Demand," Wood Mackenzie, July 31, 2020, https://tinyurl.com/yatmbyc3.

BIBLIOGRAPHY

Books

Jensen, James T., *The Development of a Global LNG Market*, Oxford Institute for Energy Studies, 2004.
An academic at a British research institute offers a rare in-depth history of the liquefied natural gas (LNG) industry.

Rhodes, Richard, *Energy: A Human History*, Simon & Schuster, 2018.
A Pulitzer Prize-winning writer, historian and journalist outlines energy transformations throughout history, including the shifts from wood to coal and then to oil and gas.

Yergin, Daniel, *The New Map: Energy, Climate and the Clash of Nations*, Penguin Press, 2020.
An energy expert and economic historian analyzes the relationship between technology, energy resources and geopolitics.

Articles

Aizhu, Chen, and Muyu Xu, "China on course for record LNG imports as industries recover, expand," *Reuters*, Sept. 25, 2020, https://tinyurl.com/y65zzy8x.
Two journalists provide an in-depth look at China's increased demand for liquefied natural gas.

Borunda, Alejandra, "Natural gas is a much 'dirtier' energy source than we thought," *National Geographic*, Feb. 19, 2020, https://tinyurl.com/y2p2o27q.
Recent studies show that the distribution of natural gas results in high levels of methane emissions.

Fasanotti, Federica Saini, "The new, great, dangerous game in the eastern Mediterranean," Brookings Institution, Aug. 28, 2020, https://tinyurl.com/y27rw6sz.
A think tank analyst explains some of the political issues involved in harvesting deepwater gas reserves in the Middle East.

Forrest, Brett, "U.S., Russia Race to Outflank Each Other on Russian Pipeline," *The Wall Street Journal*, Nov. 29, 2020, https://tinyurl.com/y43pap5g.
A journalist looks at U.S. attempts to stop a Russian project to export more gas to Europe.

"IEA nudges up 2020 gas demand forecast, but still sees record fall," *Reuters*, Oct. 12, 2020, https://tinyurl.com/y66sspbg.
The International Energy Agency reports on how the coronavirus pandemic has dampened gas demand.

Malik, Naureen, *et al.*, "Peak Gas Is Coming to the U.S. Sooner Than Anyone Expected," *Bloomberg*, Oct. 22, 2020, https://tinyurl.com/y4vculrr.
The business news site examines how greener energy policies could reduce gas use.

Tabuchi, Hiroko, and Brad Plumer, "Is This the End of New Pipelines?" *The New York Times*, July 8, 2020, https://tinyurl.com/y7gywkum.
Two journalists report on how environmental groups and policies favoring reduced emissions are making it more difficult to build gas and oil infrastructure.

Reports and Studies

"Global gas and LNG outlook to 2035," McKinsey & Company, Sept. 4, 2019, https://tinyurl.com/y5vqogq5.

The consulting firm looks at how the growing supply of gas is affecting price and other market fundamentals.

"Global Gas Report 2020," Snam, International Gas Union and BloombergNEF, August 2020, https://tinyurl.com/y6ykq4la.

A report examines recent trends and future projections for gas demand and trade around the world.

Mitrova, Tatiana, and Tim Boersma, "The Impact of US LNG on Russian Natural Gas Export Policy," Columbia Center on Global Energy Policy, December 2018, https://tinyurl.com/y8pr94ny.

Two analysts examine how U.S. exports of liquid natural gas are creating competition for Russia.

Stern, Jonathan, and Adi Imsirovic, "A Comparative History of Oil and Gas Markets and Prices: is 2020 just extreme cyclical event or an acceleration of the energy transition?" Oxford Institute for Energy Studies, April 2020, https://tinyurl.com/yxdtyqns.

Two academics look at aspects of the gas market, including pricing, national strategic policies and the role of monopolies.

"World Energy Outlook 2020," International Energy Agency, October 2020, https://tinyurl.com/y295vglk.

The international agency reviews recent developments, including the coronavirus pandemic, and how they will influence the energy mix and demand in the near future.

THE NEXT STEP
Environmental Concerns

Germanos, Andrea, "ExxonMobil Lambasted Over 'Grossly Insufficient' Emissions Reduction Plan," *EcoWatch*, Dec. 15, 2020, https://tinyurl.com/y95366rw.

ExxonMobil will phase out flaring, or controlled burning, of natural gas by the end of the decade, but other aspects of its emission reduction plan disappointed environmental activists.

Leber, Rebecca, "These Ladies Love Natural Gas! Too Bad They Aren't Real," *Mother Jones*, Dec. 14, 2020, https://tinyurl.com/yda5s6vr.

A natural gas advocacy group funded by energy companies used fake testimonials, stock photos of women and a humorous Instagram account to push back against environmental concerns and negative perceptions of natural gas.

Morison, Rachel, Will Mathis and Jess Shankleman, "U.K. Targets Gas in Next Fight Against Fossil Pollution," *Bloomberg Green*, Dec. 14, 2020, https://tinyurl.com/yd6hr9yf.

To cut carbon emissions, the United Kingdom is considering burning more hydrogen gas to power the national electric grid.

Exports

Gardner, Timothy, "U.S. senator warns France's Macron over gas exports deal delay," *Reuters*, Nov. 2, 2020, https://tinyurl.com/yb9hxe5w.

French President Emmanuel Macron stepped in to delay the signing of a 20-year import contract between a French energy company and an American natural gas producer because of his concerns about the Trump administration's environmental rollbacks.

Lefebvre, Ben, "How Biden may save U.S. gas exports to Europe," *Politico*, Nov. 27, 2020, https://tinyurl.com/yylq757l.

If President-elect Joe Biden brings American gas regulations in line with stricter European standards, U.S. natural gas shipments could become more palatable to Europe.

Saefong, Myra P., "Natural Gas Prices Outpaced Oil in 2020. Here's Why They Could Keep Rising," *Barron's*, Dec. 11, 2020, https://tinyurl.com/yc4yzabx.

Natural gas prices rose as U.S. production slowed during the COVID-19 lockdowns and could rise further, as economists predict overseas demand for liquid natural gas will continue to surge next year.

Federal Policy

Pager, Tyler, and Zack Colman, "Biden to tap former Michigan Gov. Granholm to lead Energy Department," *Politico*, Dec. 15, 2020, https://tinyurl.com/y984e9by.

President-elect Biden's pick for Energy secretary signals a focus on reducing carbon emissions and a shift away from the push by the current secretary, Rick Perry, to increase natural gas exports.

Roth, Sammy, "The 'war on coal' is over. The next climate battle has just begun," *Los Angeles Times*, Nov. 17, 2020, https://tinyurl.com/ydy26ak4.
Biden campaigned on 100 percent climate-friendly electricity by 2035, a goal that could knock natural gas off the power grid in 15 years.

Sanicola, Laura, "U.S. oil industry group pledges to fight possible Biden fracking limits," *Reuters*, Nov. 23, 2020, https://tinyurl.com/y8rh7u7o.
A fossil fuel group plans to use legal action to combat any Biden move to ban on fracking on federal lands.

Mideast

Foxman, Simone, "Qatar Set for Biggest Budget Deficit Since Gulf Spat in 2017," *Bloomberg*, Dec. 10, 2020, https://tinyurl.com/y7w6uer4.
Sagging energy prices will force Qatar, the world's largest exporter of natural gas, to run a budget deficit this year, despite recent annual surpluses.

"IS claims Egypt-Israel gas pipeline blast that caused fire, but little damage," *The Times of Israel*, Nov. 20, 2020, https://tinyurl.com/y8o5akz3.
Gas pipelines are frequent targets of radical groups in the Middle East.

Peshiman, Gibran Naiyyar, and Jessica Jagnathan, "Qatar Petroleum Trading participates in Pakistan LNG tender for first time," *Reuters*, Dec. 11, 2020, https://tinyurl.com/y7m4j3dk.
A Qatari company negotiated the sale of natural gas to Pakistan for the first time, a task the government usually takes up.

For More Information

American Public Gas Association, 201 Massachusetts Ave., N.E., Suite C-4, Washington, DC 20002; 202-464-2742; apga.org/home. Trade organization representing publicly owned natural gas distribution systems in the United States.

Center for Liquefied Natural Gas, 900 17th St., N.W., Washington, DC 20006; 202-289-2253; lngfacts.org. Organization of six major liquefied natural gas (LNG) suppliers and others in the industry that advocates for policies favorable to LNG.

Columbia Center on Global Energy Policy, 1255 Amsterdam Ave., New York, NY 10027; 202-853-2475; energypolicy.columbia.edu. University research center on energy and climate change.

Global Carbon Project, CSIRO Oceans and Atmosphere, GPO Box 1700, Canberra, ACT 2601, Australia; +61-2-6246 5631; globalcarbonproject.org/index.htm. International group of scientists researching greenhouse gases and the human effects on the climate.

International Energy Agency, 9 rue de la Fédération, Paris, Cedex 15, France, 75739; +33 (0)1 40 57 65 00; iea.org. Global organization tracking energy data and government energy policies; also advises governments on energy efficiency.

International Group of Liquefied Natural Gas Importers, 8 rue de l'Hôtel de Ville, Neuilly-sur-Seine, France, 92200; + 33 1 56 65 51 60; giignl.org. Nonprofit organization promoting development of the LNG sector.

U.S. Energy Information Administration, 1000 Independence Ave., S.W., Washington, DC 20585; 202-586-8800; eia.gov. Federal agency that collects and analyzes energy data and information to support policymaking and public information.

8

K-pop

Can it sustain its global following?

By Lorna Collier

BTS is considered the Beatles of Korean pop music and is the most successful K-pop band to hit the United States. The fast-growing K-pop industry generates billions for South Korea's economy.

From *CQ Researcher,*
May 21, 2021

THE ISSUES

Last Aug. 21, David Roberts took the afternoon off from his job in Milwaukee. The 25-year-old project manager had an important task: to watch a new video by his favorite band, BTS, over and over again. Roberts, like other BTS fans worldwide, hoped to help boost the band's "Dynamite" music video on YouTube to a viewing record. "And we did it! We got 101 million views in 24 hours!" Roberts says.

Why give up half a day to help seven South Korean musicians he had never met? For the same reason that Roberts is planning a two- to three-week trip to South Korea to see BTS-related sites. Or for the same reason he has spent close to $1,000 since 2018 on albums, concert tickets, shirts and other BTS merchandise.

BTS' music and its performing style got Roberts hooked. Led by 26-year-old RM, BTS is known for its well-crafted songs, semi-androgynous appearance and precision choreography. *Rolling Stone* magazine recently praised band members for their "magical levels of charisma, their genre-defying, sleek-but-personal music, even their casually nontoxic, skin-care-intensive brand of masculinity."[1]

However, Roberts says the biggest reason he is a fan is the connection to the band he feels from watching countless behind-the-scenes videos and live fan chats. "You get to feel like you're almost friends with them," Roberts says.

BTS — the Beatles of Korean popular music, aka K-pop — is the most successful South Korean band to hit the United States and arguably the world. With a *Billboard*-topping four No. 1 albums in less than two years, the group has filled stadiums, both in-person (during COVID) and virtually (during COVID). In October, BTS' two-day online show sold nearly 1 million tickets.[2]

BTS is not the only K-pop group or artist riding a wave of South Korean music popularity. K-pop sold 40 million albums worldwide last year, including 9.1 million from BTS.[3] U.S. record companies increasingly are pairing with K-pop music agencies and artists to produce music, while U.S. consumers are turning to South Korea to buy its products or plan visits. Indeed, K-pop has become both a business and cultural phenomenon, benefiting the South Korean economy while driving the U.S. music industry to adopt some of its fan-focused and high-tech approaches — especially important during a global pandemic that has shuttered most concert venues.

Challenges remain, among them: Critics say K-pop music is guilty of cultural insensitivity and allege that some music agencies exploit their band members, while U.S. radio and record labels remain resistant to Korean-language recordings, which could limit future success.

So far, though, the K-pop phenomenon shows no signs of slowing down. K-pop has helped boost South Korea's economy, both in direct music sales as well as in indirect revenues from sales of related products, such as food, cosmetics and clothes.

"I always say K-pop is not just the music," says Jeff Benjamin, who writes about K-pop for *Billboard*, the music industry magazine and website. "It really is about this kind of culture. People are definitely getting interested in Korean food, Korean fashion, Korean television."

K-pop also benefits Korea's tourism industry. Before the government imposed COVID-19 restrictions, about 800,000 people visited South Korea for BTS-motivated reasons — 7.6 percent of all foreign tourists, the Korean Foundation for International Cultural Exchange found. The Seoul-based Hyundai Research Institute has estimated that BTS alone is worth $4.65 billion annually to the South Korean economy.[4]

And K-pop has helped make South Korea the world's fastest-growing music market, up 44.8 percent from 2019 to 2020, according to the International Federation of the

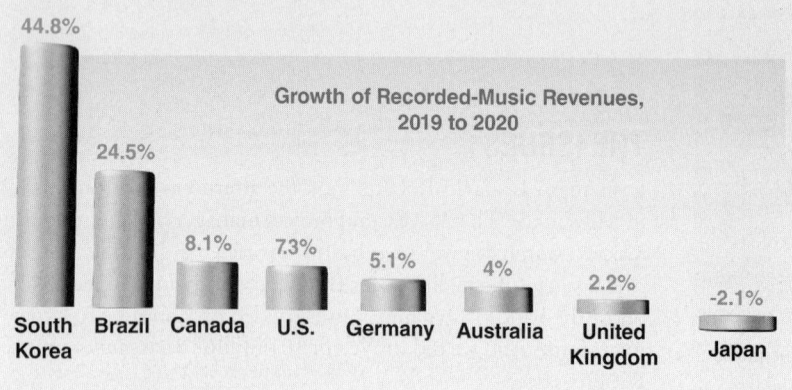

K-pop Fuels Music Boom in South Korea

A record-breaking year in K-pop helped South Korea become the fastest-growing music market in the world, according to the International Federation of the Phonographic Industry (IFPI). Korea's revenues from recorded music grew 44.8 percent from 2019 to 2020. Brazil was second with 24.5 percent growth.

Growth of Recorded-Music Revenues, 2019 to 2020

- South Korea: 44.8%
- Brazil: 24.5%
- Canada: 8.1%
- U.S.: 7.3%
- Germany: 5.1%
- Australia: 4%
- United Kingdom: 2.2%
- Japan: -2.1%

Source: "Global Music Report 2021," IFPI, p. 14, https://tinyurl.com/sew7t48s

Fans cheered for BTS as it performed in New York City's Central Park in May 2019. K-pop's popularity is leading the U.S. music industry to adopt some of its fan-focused, high-tech approaches.

Phonographic Industry (IFPI).[5] This compares to an overall growth rate of 7.4 percent for all markets.[6] The IFPI does not release sales figures, but it ranks South Korea sixth behind the United States, Japan, the United Kingdom, Germany and France. The top four K-pop music companies reported combined sales of $1.5 billion in 2020.[7]

Partnerships

U.S. music companies have noticed — and recently formed partnerships or merged with K-pop entities. In April BTS' management company, Hybe (formerly Big Hit Entertainment), bought Ithaca Holdings, owned by U.S. music manager Scooter Braun. Acquiring a stable of Ithaca's superstar artists, who include Justin Bieber and Ariana Grande, will likely further K-pop's expansion and influence in the United States.[8]

K-pop's popularity comes at a time when the U.S. music industry has been on an upswing, as it adjusted to the shift to streaming: Retail music revenues reached $12.2 billion in 2020, up from $9.7 billion in 2018, according to the Recording Industry Association of America. However, the pandemic hurt revenues due to the loss of concert ticket sales.[9]

"K-pop has been quite smart and innovative with how they handled the pandemic," *Billboard*'s Benjamin says, pointing to strategies such as selling club memberships and CDs bundled with photo books and other merchandise. Also, he says, South Korea's technological advantages — faster, better Wi-Fi and the development of streaming platforms — helped create fan bases accustomed to receiving content in this fashion, which helped mitigate the loss of touring revenue.

Digital connection has been especially important during the pandemic, according to Jenna Gibson, a doctoral student in political science at the University of Chicago. K-pop artists have held virtual concerts, often featuring augmented reality. "The artists are dancing and then the background will fall away, and it looks like they're on a mountaintop," Gibson says. "It's like 3D — it's very cool."

K-pop appeals to a diverse group of Americans, experts say, but demographic data are limited. Miranda Larsen, a Ph.D. candidate who studies Japanese popular culture at the University of Tokyo and has attended numerous "KCONs" (K-pop conventions) as a panelist, says that in recent years, "the attendees have skewed BIPOC [Black, Indigenous and people of color]."

Crystal S. Anderson, who researches Korean popular music and culture at George Mason University in Fairfax, Va., says the fan base is "overwhelmingly female," as well as ethnically and socioeconomically diverse.

Benjamin says he has seen a growing number of minority and LGBTQ fans. "I do think there's a lot of connection" between those who may see themselves as "underdogs and seeing something that they can connect with — regardless of language," he says.

Besides BTS, other K-pop artists to achieve Western success include the "girl group" Blackpink, which has

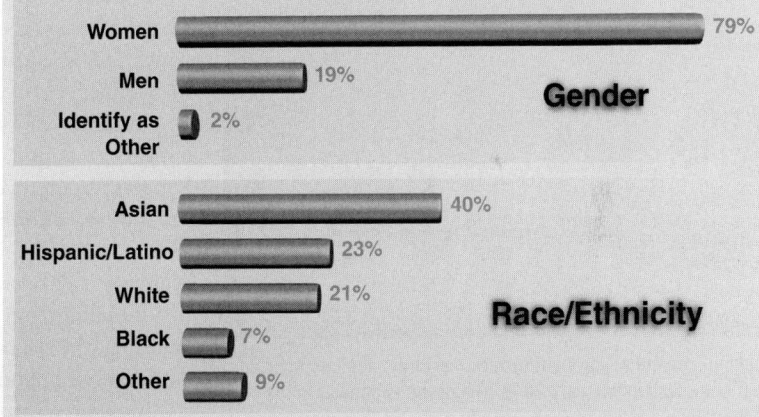

Most U.S. K-pop Convention Attendees Are Women

Seventy-nine percent of attendees at U.S. K-pop conventions (known as "KCONs") in 2019 were female. The attendees' racial and ethnic makeup was diverse: 40 percent were Asian, 23 percent were Hispanic or Latino, 21 percent were white and 7 percent were Black. The conventions were held in New York and Los Angeles.

KCON Attendees in U.S., 2019

Gender:
- Women: 79%
- Men: 19%
- Identify as Other: 2%

Race/Ethnicity:
- Asian: 40%
- Hispanic/Latino: 23%
- White: 21%
- Black: 7%
- Other: 9%

Source: "A Flourishing Fan Base," Billboard, accessed May 12, 2021, https://tinyurl.com/pp2y2px5

had a string of *Billboard* hits and is ranked by *Bloomberg* as the No. 11 most powerful pop star (BTS is No. 9). The all-male band SuperM hit No. 2 on *Billboard*'s album chart last October with its first full-length album.[10] The biggest K-pop artist before BTS was Psy, who released his megahit "Gangnam Style" in 2012.

K-pop uniquely mixes styles and genres, such as hip hop, R&B and traditional Korean music, says Anderson, who has written a book about Black influences on K-pop.

Although BTS' "Dynamite" was in English, as is its newest single, "Butter," debuting May 21, most K-pop songs are largely sung in Korean.[11] The lack of English has limited K-pop on radio. But in today's YouTube and Spotify era, that has not seemed to matter, says Inkyu Kang, an associate professor of digital journalism at Pennsylvania State University. Fans can overcome language barriers via technologies, such as automatic captioning and translation apps.

They also respond to messages that address universal concerns, such as bullying, depression and self-hate, which are prominent themes in BTS songs and particularly appeal to young people, Kang says. Benjamin agrees, noting that BTS' meaningful lyrics "became a trend in the larger K-pop scene," influencing other groups to similarly craft deeper lyrics and themes. In "Life Goes On," for example, BTS sang about the pandemic's impact on people's lives: "One day, the world stopped/Without any warning/Spring didn't know to wait."

K-pop's Impact

The South Korean government began supporting K-pop in the late 1990s as part of its effort to promote the export of Korean arts and culture, an endeavor called Hallyu or Korean Wave. The government has spent millions on concert venue construction, holographic technology and subsidies for artists appearing outside Korea, says Gibson. In March, the government announced plans to build and run a $17.8 million K-pop online concert hall, so that musicians without deep pockets could put on high-tech virtual shows.[12]

The investments are part of a "soft power" strategy that South Korea hopes will help it internationally, Gibson says. "It is about creating friendly alliance ties, where you don't have to force anybody to do anything," she says. "Ultimately, the goal is to support Korean policies on the international stage."

Gibson says it is unclear whether the strategy will work. So far, the government has not pushed any particular policies, she says. "But I could see a universe in which they tried to tap into this potential resource of so many fans."

South Korea's return on its investment in Hallyu appears to be paying off, says Anderson, adding that K-pop's importance transcends numbers. A chart posted on Statista, an online data portal, found that at $4.65 billion annually, BTS' contribution to the national economy is 0.3 percent. This amount has been updated to $4.9 billion, but it still is dwarfed by 13.1 percent for Samsung, the electronics giant, which has annual sales of almost $212 billion.[13] However, Anderson says, beyond its budgetary impact, "K-pop introduces people to Korean culture in a way that your Samsung cellphone does not."

Blackpink, one of K-pop's girl groups, performs at a Los Angeles artist showcase in February 2019. The group is popular in the West and has a string of *Billboard* hits to its credit. K-pop lyrics are largely in Korean, which some say could limit the genre's reach in U.S. markets.

K-pop idols are seeking to exert social influence. Blackpink urged action to prevent climate change, for example. BTS supported UNICEF's campaigns to end child poverty and donated to Black Lives Matter.[14]

In March, BTS denounced anti-Asian hate, citing its own members' examples of being discriminated against.[15]

Fans have at times taken their "idols" — the term for K-pop stars — to task for cultural insensitivity and misappropriation, both of Black and South Asian cultures. Blackpink featured the statue of a Hindu god in a video, which drew criticism from fans and was withdrawn. The group Mamamoo wore blackface while performing a parody of Bruno Mars' "Uptown Funk" in 2017.[16]

American singer and former K-pop idol Alexandra Reid, the first African American in such a role, calls for K-pop companies to employ cultural liaisons to educate artists and agencies about such concerns. She said that from her time spent in South Korea, "I see how a lot of it isn't malicious and they truly don't know better."[17]

However, Larsen says, Black fans who speak out — such as herself — have been criticized, called the "N" word and doxed (had personal information revealed) by non-Black fans on social media.

Former trainees and idols allege K-pop's agency training model has led to eating disorders, stress and suicides. Other problems: low wages and exorbitant penalties for trying to leave a group.[18] The South Korean government responded in 2017 by seeking to end "slave contracts" and other harmful practices, and experts say the actions have helped reduce mistreatment.[19]

"The K-pop management system has been far from perfect in the past," said Bernie Cho, a South Korean music executive whose agency provides digital media and marketing help to K-pop artists. But, he said, the new regulations along with oversight by fans and stock market investors have reduced much of the problem. "The days of overbearing, overly controlling and overtly exploitative K-pop management situations are becoming less the rule and more the exception," Cho said.[20]

Others defend rigorous training regimens for young people. "What makes K-pop K-pop is its training systems," says Kang, the Penn State professor, who compares it to the Bolshoi Ballet.

Aside from these controversies, K-pop at its best offers joy to audiences, says Jung-Min Mina Lee, an instructor of Asian and Middle Eastern studies at Duke University.

"I was at a basketball game at Duke when 'Gangnam Style' came on," Lee recalls. "It was so amazing, as a Korean person. All these people were not knowing the lyrics, but they're all dancing together in the stadium and having so much fun. And I think that's what K-pop offers."

BACKGROUND

Early Influences

K-pop's roots largely date to Japan's 35-year occupation of Korea that began in 1910, when Japan tried to assimilate Koreans into its culture.[21] Koreans were influenced by Japanese "Enka" music, which mixed Western and Japanese musical styles; the Koreans then added elements and began producing their own version, called "trot," named after the foxtrot dance. Trot rhythms eventually found their way into K-pop.[22]

Following the 1950-53 Korean War in which the United States led a U.N. effort to defend South Korea from a North Korean invasion, many South Koreans heard U.S. popular music for the first time via Armed Forces radio and TV. South Korean musicians entertaining at U.S. military bases learned to blend the Western music favored by American soldiers — such as rock, hip-hop and R&B — with traditional Korean pop, says Kang.

In 1992, the Korean group Seo Taiji and Boys performed a song on a TV talent show that blended hip-hop and dance with Korean pop — a performance that is considered the start of modern K-pop's first wave. The group lost the competition, but its song topped Korean music charts for the next 17 weeks.[23]

South Korea shifted from rule by the military, which had censored Western-style music, to democracy in the late 1980s and artistic freedom grew. In 1996, the boy band H.O.T. released its first hit single, while studios began building idol groups.[24]

A financial crash in 1997-98 prompted the South Korean government to launch its Hallyu strategy. K-pop groups such as Super Junior started becoming popular in other countries, mostly in Asia. In 2009, Japan was the largest importer of K-pop music, accounting for 70 percent, followed by Southeast Asia with 21 percent and China with 8 percent.[25]

CHRONOLOGY

1910s-1980s *Korean musicians are introduced to Japanese, American music.*

1910-1945 Japan's occupation of the Korean Peninsula exposes Koreans to Japanese "Enka" music, which helps form Korean trot, an influence in today's popular music known as K-pop.

1950s In the aftermath of the Korean War, South Korean musicians entertaining at U.S. military bases learn to blend rock, hip-hop and R&B favored by American soldiers.

1979 South Korean President Park Chung-hee is assassinated in a coup that installs Chun Doo-hwan as president; the regime imposes martial law and music censorship.

1987 South Korea adopts democracy, allowing for more musical freedom.

1990s-2009 *K-pop experiences its first and second waves of growth.*

1992 Seo Taiji and Boys perform live on a TV music talent show, mixing rap with traditional Korean music to create a signature sound; music historians consider this the birth of modern K-pop.

1995 Lee Soo-man, who develops an agency model to find, train and control "idols" (or stars), founds SM Entertainment.

1996 Yang Hyun-suk, a former member of Seo Taiji and Boys, launches YG Entertainment.

1997 J.Y. Park, a singer, songwriter and record producer, founds JYP Entertainment, the third major music company to be established in South Korea.

1997-98 Asian financial crisis rocks the South Korean economy, leading the government to promote the export of Korean culture, including K-pop.

2005 Big Hit Entertainment, the future home of K-pop super band BTS, is founded.

2008 Government establishes a Ministry of Culture, Sports and Tourism, with a department for promoting the globalization of K-pop.

2009 Wonder Girls' English-language version of "Nobody" is the first K-pop single to appear on *Billboard*'s Hot 100 song chart.

2010-Present *From Psy to BTS, K-pop becomes popular in the United States.*

2012 Psy's "Gangnam Style" video earns 100 million views on YouTube within 51 days of its release, making it the first major U.S. K-pop hit.

2013 BTS debuts with a song called "No More Dream."

2017 BTS becomes the first group with a primarily Korean-language song, "DNA," to make the *Billboard* 100. . . . South Korea's Fair Trade Commission sets new rules protecting K-pop trainees, aimed at breaking "slave" contracts.

2018 BTS' "Love Yourself: Tear" becomes the first K-pop album to debut at No. 1 on the *Billboard* 200 chart.

2019 Several K-pop singers are accused of participating in the drugging of women for sex.

2020 "How You Like That" — a single recorded by K-pop girl group Blackpink — sets a record for the biggest YouTube music video debut with 86.3 million views. . . . BTS' online concert draws nearly 1 million paying attendees. . . . Big Hit goes public. . . . South Korean government gives BTS a two-year extension on mandatory military service, as oldest member turns 28.

2021 Big Hit announces a partnership with Universal Music Group; as part of the deal, a new label is in the works (February). . . . International Federation of the Phonographic Industry (IFPI) releases a report showing South Korea is the world's fastest-growing music industry (March). . . . Big Hit, now known as Hybe, acquires Ithaca Holdings' stable of U.S. pop stars in a $1 billion deal (April).

Music companies worked to increase their appeal to Western markets by downplaying Korean references and creating "hook songs with English lyrics that didn't make much sense a lot of the time," says Duke University's Lee.

The first big U.S. crossover K-pop song was Psy's 2012 comic hit "Gangnam Style," featuring a "horse-riding" dance video that was the first to hit 1 billion YouTube views (now more than 4 billion).[26] Yet Psy is not typical of most K-pop artists, who tend to be toned, polished and, for men, near-androgynous. He did show, though, that U.S. audiences would be receptive to Korean-language music and that "being more culturally true" could sell in the West, says Lee. "That was a turning point in K-pop."

A third K-pop generation arose in 2013 that expanded the fusion of musical genres and styles while retaining its Koreanness. BTS debuted in 2013 and Blackpink in 2016.[27] These and other artists were able to take advantage of streaming services and social media to reach audiences worldwide and increasingly in the United States.

K-pop in recent years has targeted Japan, the world's second-largest music market after the United States, by including more Japanese members in K-pop groups, which industry officials say is key to success in the insular Japanese market. Some Japanese K-pop members make Japanese-only content.[28]

North Korea

In 2016, South Korea retaliated against North Korea's nuclear weapons testing by blasting K-pop — including Big Bang's song "Bang Bang Bang" — over loudspeakers set up near the demilitarized zone between the two countries. North Korea's government forbids K-pop, although residents reportedly access it via smuggled flash drives.[29]

North Korea's all-female Moranbong — the Communist regime's answer to South Korean K-pop bands — performs in Pyongyang in May 2016. The group plays more traditional music and wears less skimpy costumes than are seen in South Korea.

South Korea has broadcast K-pop, along with pro-democracy messages, at its northern neighbor off and on over the years, sometimes riling North Korea enough to threaten war if Seoul did not turn the music down.[30] A more pleasant exchange occurred during a period of détente in 2018, when South Korean pop stars, such as the girl group Red Velvet, performed in North Korea for its leader, Kim Jong Un, who reported being "deeply moved." However, North Koreans could only watch smuggled footage of the concert, because consuming South Korean music remains a crime that can result in imprisonment.[31]

Kim has instead offered North Koreans an alternative: girl band Moranbong, formed in 2012, with members and setlists chosen by the supreme leader. The group plays more traditional music and wears less skimpy costumes than its South Korean K-pop counterparts.[32]

North Korea has continued its rhetorical attacks on K-pop and foreign cultural influences. In December, the country passed a law forbidding the spread of "anti-socialist ideology." In March, it called BTS and Blackpink victims of "slave-like exploitation."[33]

Digital Musicians Are Taking the Stage in K-pop

Use of AI technology garners praise — and worries.

The opening shot features five girls in pink cheerleader skirts. "I'm real," one croons, a half-smile on her face. "Let's awake a real girl." Images of the girls in various costumes and settings flash past, singing and dancing. "Not an illusion! Not a fake!" they rap.

Don't believe them.

Eternity is a new K-pop group made up of "girls" who are all digital creations. In other words, not real. The virtual group was launched in March by a South Korean artificial intelligence company, Pulse9, which said the band members were made using deepfake technology it had developed called Deep Real AI, with faces created from synthesized images. No word on who is doing the singing, although it too is likely computer-generated.[1]

The video "I'm Real" had garnered more than 550,000 views in its first two months on YouTube, along with comments such as: "Sorry, it's the scariest thing of K-pop I have ever seen. No hate, but it's soooo creepy."[2]

Pulse9 says the band has 11 members, although only five appear in group shots on the video. Plans are for members to release solo songs and work as market influencers and brand models, the company says. One has already appeared in a brokerage firm ad.[3]

Eternity is not K-pop's first virtual singing group. In November, SM Entertainment, one of the top musical agencies in the genre, debuted girl group Aespa with four human members and four avatar versions of themselves to share performing and publicity duties. Aespa's name is a combination of "avatar," "experience" and "aspect." Aespa's avatars, though, do not look as human as the Eternity girls do. Their faces have a cartoonish, anime quality that makes them distinguishable from the real thing, even in videos posted online.[4]

Lee Soo-man, founder and chairman of SM Entertainment, said Aespa is "the beginning of the future of entertainment," with celebrity avatars fitting into peoples' lives "like a living person, like a friend."[5]

Fans also will be able to generate avatars for themselves and interact in a virtual world, using a smartphone app called SYNK.

Aespa and Eternity have "some ties to the wider virtual idol movement that's really popular in Japan and China," says Miranda Larsen, a Ph.D. candidate in information technology and Asian society at the University of Tokyo who studies fan culture.

Larsen has attended concerts put on by Japan's famous virtual singer, Hatsune Miku, who started performing via projection screen in 2009 and opened for Lady Gaga during her 2014 concert tour. Miku, who sings via computer generation, is beamed in as a hologram, surrounded by excited fans waving light sticks and singing along to her hits.[6]

"I was like, that's an amazing projection," says Larsen, who was surprised by how real Miku seemed.

Potential for Misuse?

Larsen, however, says she is skeptical about Aespa, especially if fans use augmented reality technology in their homes to interact with the avatars.

"It becomes very questionable about what's allowed and what's not," she says, raising the specter of simulated sexual activity. "When I first saw the images for Aespa and saw the [real members] standing side by side with the [virtual ones], I went, 'Oh, no.' Especially with the release statement about how the virtual verson would allow greater intimacy with the fan. . . . It was so shady."

Others, too, are concerned that some fans might use the avatars for deepfake pornography. "Because these are virtual idols [or stars], they are not legally protected from digital sex crimes or sexual harassment," said Lee Hye Jin, a

CURRENT SITUATION

Mergers and Acquisitions

Big Hit Entertainment went public in October, making the BTS members, who had each been given about 68,500 shares, multimillionaires — a reward for the band generating 88 percent of Big Hit's sales in 2020 and 97 percent in 2019. The company was originally valued at about $8.5 billion, although stocks have fluctuated since the initial public offering.[34]

clinical assistant professor at the Annenberg School for Communication and Journalism at the University of Southern California.[7]

Female K-pop stars have long been used in deepfake pornography, said Thomas Baudinette, a lecturer in international studies at Macquarie University in Sydney. "The idea underlying Aespa's virtual idols leaves them open to the possibility of problematic use."[8]

Eternity and Aespa are not the only K-pop groups with virtual members. Another female virtual idol group, K/DA, debuted in 2018 as a video game offshoot, featuring anime-like members based on League of Legends characters. They "sing" using the voices of real-life singers and have collaborated with members of the K-pop group (G)-IDLE.[9]

Last year, K-pop girl group Blackpink partnered with an augmented reality app, Zepeto, to create personalized avatars of the group members, as well as with their "Ice Cream" song collaborator, Selena Gomez. In one event, fans could interact with the avatars via the app and collect virtual autographs and other prizes.[10]

Will the virtual K-pop idol trend continue?

Entertainment companies will likely see economic benefits from such a practice. AI idols can do superhuman work — seeing many more fans, for example. They do not sleep or eat, get sick or generate scandals that can ruin their careers and cost their managers money, says Larsen.

"I do think this is part of K-pop's impulse to innovate," says Crystal S. Anderson, a K-pop scholar at George Mason University in Virginia. "It might work in Japan and in other places in East Asia, but it may not work anywhere else. Or it could be that this is the next big thing that's going to circulate around the world, and we'll see virtual artists popping up all over the place. It's not really clear — it's so new."

However, Anderson says she is concerned about how the music — which should be K-pop's primary emphasis — is presented. If it is subpar or is a machine-created afterthought, with the music taking a backseat to visual effects, then she says she is not a fan of using avatars.

"I do not think that's in the best interest of K-pop, because that is not what spread K-pop around the world," Anderson says.

— *Lorna Collier*

---

[1] Eunice Dawson, "New Girl Group Eternity Composed Entirely of AI Members Attracts Attention + To Debut This March," *KPopStarz*, March 17, 2021, https://tinyurl.com/8dmm5wjm; Queenie Lastra, "Cool or creepy? AI Korean girl group Eternity debut with 'I'm Real' music video," *Giz Guide*, March 25, 2021, https://tinyurl.com/ev89pdn5.

[2] "Eternity — I'm Real M/V," YouTube, March 22, 2021, https://tinyurl.com/34mueebc.

[3] Suzanne Sng, "Deep-fake idols for new K-pop group," The Straits Times, March 19, 2021, https://tinyurl.com/2b93t5ra.

[4] Kendrea Liew, "Future of entertainment? Avatars could be K-pop's next superstars," *CNBC*, Jan. 10, 2021, https://tinyurl.com/3ua35emj.

[5] Ibid.

[6] Egan Loo, "Hatsune Miku Virtual Idol Performs 'Live' Before 25,000," Anime News Network, Aug. 23, 2009, https://tinyurl.com/4ffju98t; "Hatsune Miku Full Opening For Lady Gaga, May 20, 2014, St. Paul MN," *YouTube*, May 22, 2014, https://tinyurl.com/4a2dj4w4; and Mika Fukuda, "Japan's biggest pop star is not human," *Japan Today*, April 2, 2014, https://tinyurl.com/49we5pxr.

[7] Liew, op. cit.

[8] "New K-pop girl group Aespa's virtual members cause fears over dehumanisation of K-pop stars," *Today*, updated March 1, 2021, https://tinyurl.com/8sjmnsn9.

[9] Trilby Beresford, "'League of Legends' Virtual Pop Group K/DA Return With New Track," *Billboard*, Aug. 28, 2020, https://tinyurl.com/4jv4b6p6.

[10] Joey Alarilla, "'Ice Cream' dance video, fansign event via Zepeto app," *Digital Life Asia*, Sept. 3, 2020, https://tinyurl.com/2fvyh2vd; Alicia Valley, "Blackpink To Hold 'World's First Virtual Fansign' Through Zepeto," *Koreaboo*, Sept. 1, 2020, https://tinyurl.com/eecnecmf.

In February, Big Hit — renamed Hybe in April — announced a partnership with Universal Music Group, the world's largest music company. Universal's artists will take advantage of Hybe's Weverse social platform to better connect with fans, following the K-pop mold of closer, more personal interactions. The deal, the companies announced, will include a newly created label.[35]

"One of the things they talked about was making a joint venture label based in the U.S. with Korean oversight," says *Billboard*'s Benjamin. He says it will be

AT ISSUE

Does K-pop rely too heavily on cultural appropriation?

YES Miranda Ruth Larsen
Ph.D. Candidate, Graduate School of Interdisciplinary Information Studies, University of Tokyo

Written for *CQ Researcher*, May 2021

The answer to this question is yes, but not for the reasons you may think. K-pop has its standout moments of cultural appropriation, particularly around Black hairstyles, fashion modes and posturing. (Some examples: BTS, G-DRAGON and Zico.)

There are even more examples of cultural misappropriation in K-pop, less insidious infractions that add up to a bigger sting. The systemic issues with this entertainment form are far more wide-reaching, however.

First, K-pop's problem lies in its branding as a K-product; this branding, coupled with the obfuscation of labor in the industry, attempts to package and market K-pop as somehow solely Korean. Do we consider a music video solely Korean because of the performers and the main language used? What if the melody and lyrics are written by Black creators, as so many K-pop songs are? What if the production design team is Japanese? Does the "Koreanness" come from the K-pop idol, many of whom are now not even Korean or raised in Korea?

The industry's answer is that the *system of production* itself is the Korean element, but even that falls short when we consider K-pop's origins as a hybrid of Black American sound and the Japanese idol system. (K-pop is, after all, a deliberate answer to J-pop.)

Second, K-pop has a "concept" addiction. The industry is built around comebacks and charting, with extended plays (EPs) and mini-albums leading to frequent media appearances, concert tours, endorsements and cycles of promotion. Individual music videos and the more frequent music releases usually have a "concept," something akin to film studies' mise-en-scène.

This makes instances of cultural appropriation/misappropriation hurt more deeply, because things like hairstyles, sacred imagery and stereotypical representations become costumes and decoration. (Watching a few music videos of Blackpink, CL and early BTS illustrates how "concept" fades into the outright offensive). There's little time to delve into a performer's awareness of particular symbols with this fast-paced system that portrays groups using a few supposedly intrinsic traits.

Finally, K-pop and K-pop fandoms don't recognize the problematic. The chain of command is often erased, as is the below-the-line work that makes a music video or album happen. The K-product branding and "concept" format encourages fans toward toxic behavior where fair criticism somehow becomes "anti" and "hate" against the artist. K-pop is far more problematic than the industry and fans want to admit.

NO Crystal S. Anderson
Affiliate Faculty, Korean Studies, George Mason University

Written for *CQ Researcher*, May 2021

K-pop is criticized for using elements of foreign cultures and ignoring the original context of those cultures, or for using foreign cultures in ways that demean or mock the original culture. To be sure, there are instances when K-pop misappropriates a culture, using elements of it in ways that are contrary to the original culture or in ways that mock or demean, such as incorporating sacred objects or engaging in negative racial performances such as blackface.

However, many erroneously describe K-pop's use of foreign cultures as cultural appropriation, using the term to describe all instances where K-pop draws on a different culture. Doing so equates normal cultural interaction with cultural theft, mockery or disparagement. Cultural appropriation was originally an academic term used to describe the inevitable impact that one culture may have on another culture as they come into close contact. So, cultural appropriation critiques tend to generalize how K-pop interacts with other cultures.

Contemporary use of the term *cultural appropriation* fails to recognize how K-pop represents cultures in an authentic way. For example, some may compare the way K-pop artists draw on African American popular music to how white musicians covered songs by Black musicians in the 1950s and 1960s. These white artists produced watered-down versions of these songs, devoid of the Black musical aesthetics that made them unique. They never referenced the original versions or recognized the established music tradition from which they came.

On the other hand, K-pop artists render Black music aesthetics authentically in ways that are recognized by fans as well as Black creatives familiar with the culture. K-pop artists often talk about their musical influences. Song credits reveal the creative personnel on tracks, including African American producers and composers.

The critique of cultural appropriation in K-pop also distorts all cultures involved. Such a critique ignores how musical traditions work and overlooks the nuances of those traditions. For example, Black popular music is a hybrid tradition made up of elements from different cultures. While Black songwriters, composers and artists have created a unique music tradition that draws on the experiences of African Americans, they have also reached across racial lines to work with white creatives to create that music.

K-pop emulates this tradition of hybrid music. K-pop creatives work with Black popular music genres and artists and, at the same time, bring unique Korean production and creative strategies to the creation of K-pop music.

interesting to see whether American artists will be able to work within the rigorous K-pop training and development system, possibly becoming part of a band that could contain more members than are typical with a U.S. band.

Hybe then announced in April a billion-dollar deal to acquire Ithaca Holdings, the entertainment agency that represents many top U.S. artists. The deal makes Hybe one of the biggest globally focused music entertainment companies in the world.[36]

Bang Si-Hyuk, Hybe chairman and CEO, said the merger should help the two companies "transcend borders and break down cultural barriers."[37]

Lee Gyu-tag, a professor of cultural studies at George Mason University's Korean campus, said the deal could give greater opportunity to other, less well-known Hybe bands such as Enhypen, Seventeen and GFriend, and "will benefit from the new promotion and distribution channels and also gain more notice in the U.S. and international market."[38]

Another K-pop industry deal took place in March between JYP Entertainment, a major music company that represents girl group Twice and boy band 2PM, and Chinese firm Tencent Music Entertainment Group. The two firms formed a partnership featuring joint marketing and promotional events, with JYP providing music by its artists to Tencent — and thereby to "hundreds of millions of music fans in China," Tencent said in a statement.[39]

China had banned K-pop and other Korean cultural imports in 2016, after South Korea allowed a U.S. missile defense system to be built on its soil. However, in March, China appeared open to softening this stance, when it announced that a Chinese film will feature a member of the EXO K-pop group. K-pop is reportedly popular in China through pirate channels.[40]

Besides the mergers and acquisitions, two K-pop audition shows are in the works. One deal involves SM Entertainment and MGM Worldwide Television Group, headed by "Survivor" producer Mark Burnett, and would have a U.S. team of contestants go to South Korea to train to become a K-pop idol in the NCT-Hollywood boy band.[41]

HBO Max also announced a similar program, but featuring Latin American contestants who would train in Seoul.[42]

Such moves among K-pop companies and other music enterprises demonstrate the "synergy that can result from joining complementary approaches to music and entertainment," says Hae Joo Kim, assistant chair of professional music at the Berklee College of Music in Boston. K-pop is well-positioned to meet the growing demand for content "beyond 'just music'" in today's increasingly digitized music world, she says.

A poster of Big Hit Entertainment artists, including BTS, decorates the lobby of a Seoul brokerage firm as investors in October 2020 wait to get in on the initial public offering of the entertainment company.

Military Service for BTS?

Hybe's deal with Ithaca Holdings should help it weather what otherwise could be a big setback — losing its most popular band for 18 months as members fulfill their commitments to South Korea's military.

BTS' seven members range in age from 23 to 28, making them all subject to South Korea's law requiring men to serve in the military once they turn 28, if they have not done so already. Oldest BTS member Jin turned 28 in December, while Suga hit that milestone in March. In early December, parliament approved a bill allowing pop stars such as BTS members to defer their service to 30. The legislation specified that the criteria for the exemption would be decided through a presidential order, and the subsequent regulation decreed that individuals must have received the Order of Cultural Merit and permission from the minister of culture — criteria that in pop music only BTS could meet.[43]

Some music companies called the legislation unfair, saying it was created with BTS in mind and that their K-pop artists should be considered for exemptions and deferments, too. In April, the Korea Music Content Association, which has on its board of directors representatives from Universal Music Group, YG Entertainment and Hybe, filed a complaint over the situation.[44]

It is uncertain when BTS members will enter the military. In response to rumors that all the members would enlist together in 2022, Hybe said in April that it had nothing to add, beyond what BTS members had already said. Jin previously had commented: "If the nation calls me to do my military service, I will respond whenever that time is."[45]

Whenever they go, said Gyu-tag, the George Mason professor, "the gap between new album releases will likely become longer in the future," leaving open the question of how Big Hit and BTS' fans will fare, as well as the South Korean economy.[46]

OUTLOOK
"It Kept Evolving"

Berklee's Kim says she used to be a K-pop skeptic. In the early to mid-2000s, she says, she kept wondering whether K-pop would attract only a small fringe audience — or, worse, was just a passing fad. Kim says she no longer thinks this.

"It kept being vibrant, kept alive by incredible fandoms, and it kept evolving," she says. Now, "it's here, it's arrived" and will not be fading any time soon.

"The only constant in K-pop is change," says George Mason's Anderson. She expects its innovations to continue, including more multinational groups such as the Z-Girls and Z-Boys — a pop group formed by a Korean music company, featuring members from Asian nations outside South Korea.

Billboard's Benjamin also expects continued partnerships between U.S. and South Korean music entities. But he predicts these will occur earlier in an artist's career, so that the U.S. label will offer more "support from the get-go."

The University of Chicago's Gibson anticipates that within five years, U.S. radio "will get with the times and take these groups more seriously," finally airing songs even if the lyrics are in Korean. Benjamin disagrees, suggesting that radio moves so slowly that this change is likely to take 10 to 15 years.

Gibson warns K-pop could face a backlash as it grows more successful. She points to anti-Asian comments directed at BTS as an example: "We need to be prepared for that."

Pop audiences also can be fickle. "There is no guaranteed way to keep them satisfied," says Penn State's Kang. But he says K-pop's ability to evolve will keep it relevant. For example, K-pop agencies used to carefully control entertainers to maintain the images they crafted for them, Kang says. Now, agencies allow fans and idols to connect. "The success of BTS and Blackpink would not have been possible without a strong bond with their fans," he says.

Gibson agrees. "There's a level of loyalty and community among fans that I think is part of K-pop's great success and also part of the longevity of a lot of these groups."

NOTES

1. Brian Hiatt, "The Triumph of BTS," *Rolling Stone*, May 13, 2021, https://tinyurl.com/zxys7nj9.

2. Eryn Murphy, "BTS Just Achieved Their Fourth No. 1 Album in Less Than 2 Years," *Showbiz Cheat Sheet*, March 2, 2020, https://tinyurl.com/euuyhfr2; Glenn Rowley, "BTS' Virtual Map of the Soul ON:E Concert Garnered Nearly 1 Million Viewers Across the Globe," *Billboard*, Oct. 12, 2020, https://tinyurl.com/t33tmbve; and Tamar Herman, "BTS Sell Out 'Love Yourself: Speak Yourself' Stadium Dates in England, France & U.S.," *Billboard*, March 1, 2019, https://tinyurl.com/kmz3m7w5.

3. YeEun Kim, "K-pop Records Biggest Growth In History, Selling Over 40 Million Albums In 2020," *Hypebae*, Dec. 24, 2020, https://tinyurl.com/yt4pzdvc.

4. "How K-pop band BTS generates billions of dollars for South Korea," *CNBC*, July 15, 2019, https://tinyurl.com/ej4fdrax.

5. Mark Sutherland, "The Power of BTS and K-Pop, the Problem With Streaming's 20% Growth, and Other Notes From IFPI's Global Music Report," *Variety*, March 23, 2021, https://tinyurl.com/y2z2s2bm.

6. "Global Music Report 2021," IFPI, https://tinyurl.com/4j5hhkv6.

7. Victoria Marian Belmis, "'Big 4' Emerges: HYBE Corporation, YG, JYP, and SM Entertainment Tops K-Pop Industry," Korea Portal, April 1, 2021, https://tinyurl.com/ke4urbtp.

8. Shirley Halperin and Patrick Frater, "BTS Label Owner HYBE Merges With Scooter Braun's Ithaca Holdings for $1 Billion (EXCLUSIVE)," *Variety*, April 2, 2021, https://tinyurl.com/y4c6zknx.

9. "Year-End 2020 RIAA Revenue Statistics," Recording Industry Association of America, 2020, https://tinyurl.com/5e3sp5jz.

10. Lucas Shaw, "Hold on, Taylor Swift: Justin Bieber Is the Biggest Pop Star in the World," *Bloomberg*, April 21, 2021, https://tinyurl.com/nap33ejv; "SuperM's 1st studio album debuts at No. 2 on Billboard 200," Yonhap News Agency, Oct. 5, 2020, https://tinyurl.com/8vkj3d34.

11. Angie Orellana Hernandez, "What did BTS' livestream reveal? Sizzling, melting butter and a possible summer hit," *Los Angeles Times*, April 27, 2021, https://tinyurl.com/eny6ttyf.

12. Lim Chang-won, "S. Korea to build state-run K-pop concert hall for unaffordable online performances," *Aju Business Daily*, March 3, 2021, https://tinyurl.com/p7xhrsmf.

13. Katharina Buchholz, "How Much Money Does BTS Make for South Korea?" Statista, Nov. 5, 2019, https://tinyurl.com/3fx6ckde; Anita Elberse and Lizzy Woodham, "Big Hit Entertainment and Blockbuster Band BTS: K-Pop Goes Global," Harvard Business School Case 520-125, June 2020, https://tinyurl.com/3vcr9rb9.

14. Anna Kusmer, "Can K-pop stars wield their celebrity to influence climate action?" *The World*, April 1, 2021, https://tinyurl.com/c6bupdf7; Alison Choi, "BTS' #EndViolence Campaign and the Link Between Poverty and Violence," Borgen Project, Sept. 25, 2020, https://tinyurl.com/6v7bdpsx; and Jeff Benjamin, "BTS and Big Hit Entertainment Donate $1 Million to Black Lives Matter," *Variety*, June 6, 2020, https://tinyurl.com/32pr8tz6.

15. Eric Todisco, "BTS Shares Experiences of Racism as They Denounce Anti-Asian Attacks: 'We Feel Grief and Anger,'" *People*, March 30, 2021, https://tinyurl.com/5xezxftw.

16. Chang Dong-woo, "Reckoning with cultural diversity imperative in K-pop moving beyond: observers," Yonhap News Agency, May 7, 2021, https://tinyurl.com/4w8r56ka; Tiffany May and Su-Hyun Lee, "Hindu God in a Music Video? A K-Pop Band Runs Afoul of Fans," *The New York Times*, July 11, 2020, https://tinyurl.com/k63tea4c.

17. Dong-woo, *ibid*.

18. Valentina Pegolo, "How K-Pop's Record Labels Exploit Its 'Idols,'" *Jacobin*, July 13, 2020, https://tinyurl.com/7884uwdz; "'I could have been a K-pop idol — but I'm glad I quit,'" *BBC*, Feb. 13, 2020, https://tinyurl.com/24cebfs9; and Nancy Matsumoto, "How the Asian Pop Culture Boom Is Feeding Eating Disorders," *Psychology Today*, Sept. 16, 2014, https://tinyurl.com/zmbf69jj.

19. Sonia Kil, "Korean Talent Agencies Ordered to End Slave Contracts," *Variety*, March 9, 2017, https://tinyurl.com/shtmuxw.

20. Marian Lu, "The branding genius of K-pop band BTS," *The Washington Post*, Jan. 30, 2020, https://tinyurl.com/kbhe23j9; Bernie Cho," *SparkLabs*, https://tinyurl.com/hsuxp2ku.

21. Dana, "Trot: The Original K-pop," Seoul Beats, Aug. 10, 2012, https://tinyurl.com/wwpbsdrj; Erin Blakemore, "How Japan Took Control of Korea," *History*, July 28, 2020, https://tinyurl.com/4wpsxnw6.

22. "Trot Is Hot Again: How The Music Genre Made A Comeback In Korea," *Creatrip*, 2021, https://tinyurl.com/9hjbtydn.

23. Aja Romano, "A beginner's guide to K-pop," *Vox*, May 20, 2020, https://tinyurl.com/euc5kwcv.

24. Joshua Keating, "K-Pop Has Always Been Political," *Slate*, June 26, 2020, https://tinyurl.com/xwfbrpxp; Aja Romano, "A beginner's guide to K-pop," *Vox*, May 20, 2020, https://tinyurl.com/euc5kwcv.

25. Kim Yoon-mi, "K-pop's second wave," *The Korea Herald*, Aug. 21, 2011, https://tinyurl.com/5znyvkxc.

26. Lorraine Murray, "PSY," Britannica, last updated Dec. 27, 2020, https://tinyurl.com/5a8ub2vt.

27. Erica Gerald Mason, "Blackpink: What You Need to Know About K-pop's Biggest Girl Group," *People*, Dec. 14, 2020, https://tinyurl.com/2wxawttf; Fatima Farha, "BTS celebrates 6 years and global reach, with Army at its back," *USA Today*, June 12, 2019, https://tinyurl.com/8uwbwtbx.

28. Park Ji-won, "K-pop groups rush to target Japanese market," *The Korea Times*, May 8, 2021, https://tinyurl.com/t74c6pt6.

29. "Bang bang bang! The K-pop songs being blasted into North Korea," *The Guardian*, Jan. 8, 2016, https://tinyurl.com/23y6952w.

30. Victoria Ho, "North Korea to South Korea: Turn off your loudspeakers or it's war," *Mashable*, Aug. 21, 2015, https://tinyurl.com/4fvx5xs2.

31. "Red Velvet Perform for North Korean Leader Kim Jong-Un in Rare Pyongyang Concert," *The Associated Press*, Billboard, April 2, 2018, https://tinyurl.com/4an6fu2n; Simon Denyer and Min Joo Kim, "How K-pop is luring young North Koreans to cross the line," *The Washington Post*, Aug. 22, 2019, https://tinyurl.com/2ypjy553.

32. "Meet Kim Jong-un's own state-approved girlband," *The Guardian*, Dec. 13, 2015, https://tinyurl.com/572vt5dk.

33. Joshua Berlinger and Yoonjung Seo, "North Korea blasts K-pop industry as 'slave-like exploitation' amid crackdown on foreign media," *CNN*, March 17, 2021, https://tinyurl.com/znppp3v2.

34. Shalini Nagarajan, "K-Pop band BTS became multi-millionaires minutes after their record label's hit IPO doubled on its stock market debut," *Markets Insider*, Oct. 15, 2020, https://tinyurl.com/axe-afee8; Halperin and Frater, *op. cit.*

35. Jem Aswad, "Big Hit Entertainment, Home of BTS, and Universal Music Unveil Expanded Partnership, Including New Label," *Variety*, Feb. 17, 2021, https://tinyurl.com/8h8st7kh.

36. Halperin and Frater, *op. cit.*

37. *Ibid.*

38. Yim Hyun-Su, "Hybe: Breaking down K-pop giant's aggressive expansion," *The Korea Herald*, April 4, 2021, https://tinyurl.com/4d6atyex.

39. Yonhap, "K-pop agency JYP to ink partnership with China's Tencent," *The Korea Herald*, March 24, 2021, https://tinyurl.com/axx8m6a5.

40. Patrick Frater, "China Poised to Give Korean Content a Boost After Three Year Boycott," *Variety*, March 3, 2021, https://tinyurl.com/53rby5vw.

41. Rebecca Sun, "MGM Television Teams With Korea's SM Entertainment for U.S. K-Pop Competition Show," *The Hollywood Reporter*, May 6, 2021, https://tinyurl.com/5sfrkx76.

42. Peter White, "K-Pop Latin American Boy Band Competition Series In The Works At HBO Max," *Deadline*, May 5, 2021, https://tinyurl.com/kj55vzur.

43. Rhea Mogul, "K-pop group BTS can defer military service after South Korea passes new law," *CNN*, Dec. 2, 2020, https://tinyurl.com/rapckr53; Ben Beaumont-Thomas, "K-pop stars BTS extend career by two years after military service law change," *The Guardian*, Dec. 1, 2020, https://tinyurl.com/2hjbsyw7; and Dylan Smith, "South Korean Lawmakers Face Criticism Over 'Unrealistic and Unfair' BTS Military-Deferment Terms," *Digital Music News*, April 12, 2021, https://tinyurl.com/y8t2fy7x.

44. Smith, *ibid.*

45. Suman Priya Mendonca, "Will BTS Members Enlist in Military Together in 2022? Big Hit Music Reacts," *International Business Times*, April 21, 2021, https://tinyurl.com/549njyru.

46. Yim Hyun-Su, "Hybe: Breaking down K-pop giant's aggressive expansion," *The Korea Herald*, April 4, 2021, https://tinyurl.com/4d6atyex.

BIBLIOGRAPHY

Books

Anderson, Crystal S., *Soul in Seoul: African American Popular Music and K-pop,* **University Press of Mississippi, 2020.**
A Korean studies scholar at George Mason University in Virginia explores the critical impact Black music has had on the development of K-pop, the globally popular musical genre.

Lee, Hark Joon, and Dal Yong Jin, *K-Pop Idols: Popular Culture and the Emergence of the Korean Music Industry,* **Lexington Books, 2019.**
A journalist (Lee) and communications professor at Simon Fraser University in Canada (Jin) examine the underside of the K-pop idol system by following the band Nine Muses.

Articles

Bell, Crystal, "For K-pop Fans, Learning Korean Is About Connection," *MTV***, April 7, 2020, https://tinyurl.com/yvt34eyk.**
A writer finds that more K-pop fans are seeking to learn Korean, and that Korean language enrollment at U.S. universities jumped 13.7 percent between 2013 and 2016.

Bruner, Raisa, "BTS's Parent Company Is Going Public. Here's How the Music Industry Could Replicate Its Massive Success," *Time***, Oct. 14, 2020, https://tinyurl.com/784znss2.**
A journalist shows how the music agency Big Hit's method of grooming talent rather than bidding for "the next kid with the latest TikTok hit" might be a better strategy for others to follow.

Collins, Hattie, "'No One Else Wanted To Be Openly Gay. So I Stood Up.' K-pop Star Holland Explains Why He Had To Come Out," *Vogue***, Feb. 20, 2020, https://tinyurl.com/4az7cvz2.**
One of the first openly gay K-pop artists describes his quest for acceptance.

Gibson, Jenna, "How South Korean Pop Culture Can Be a Source of Soft Power," *Carnegie Endowment for International Peace***, Dec. 15, 2020, https://tinyurl.com/2wvk5t96.**
A doctoral student in political science at the University of Chicago finds that by supporting cultural exports, South Korea is changing its image and increasing its global influence, potentially helping its political goals.

"'I could have been a K-pop idol — but I'm glad I quit,'" *BBC***, Feb. 13, 2020, https://tinyurl.com/uuvrnap7.**
One-time K-pop trainee Euodias describes her decision to quit her grueling K-pop training, begun at age 10, after she was told she would need plastic surgery to win a band slot.

Kim, Regina, "K-Pop Is Only Half the Story of Korean Pop Music," *Rolling Stone***, Dec. 9, 2020, https://tinyurl.com/p8p7cw8n.**
A music writer says other types of Korean music exist besides K-pop, including trot (an updated version of the foxtrot dance).

Kirk, Mimi, "K-Pop Makes the Scene in Seoul," *Bloomberg CityLab***, Aug. 9, 2016, https://tinyurl.com/5ysnf384.**
With a study showing that South Korea gets back $5 for every $1 invested in K-pop, the government decided to subsidize a Seoul neighborhood to support the music genre.

Lu, Marian, "The branding genius of K-pop band BTS," *The Washington Post***, Jan. 30, 2020, https://tinyurl.com/89k29yba.**
A reporter explores the economic impact of BTS, the leading K-pop band, on products and how it generates billions of dollars of sponsorships.

Pegolo, Valentina, "How K-Pop's Record Labels Exploit Its 'Idols,'" *Jacobin Magazine***, July 2020, https://tinyurl.com/ervt9ppc.**
A doctoral candidate in international relations says old-school K-pop management companies dehumanize their stars and are thus an example of "capitalism on steroids."

Reports and Studies

"Global Hallyu Trends, 2020: Diagnosing the present and future of Hallyu across the world," Korean Foundation for International Cultural Exchange, 2020, https://tinyurl.com/4fu4jkur.

A cultural exchange group provides an in-depth analysis of Korean cultural export trends, including K-pop, and how they have been affected by the pandemic.

Lin, Xi, and Robert Rudolf, "Does K-pop Reinforce Gender Inequalities? Empirical Evidence From a New Data Set," Research Institute of Asian Women, Dec. 31, 2017, https://tinyurl.com/6tsuez36.
Korea University researchers studied 6,317 K-pop fans from 100 countries and found that the industry as promoted by the Korean government includes elements that might be bolstering a sexist culture and traditional gender roles, thus harming women's fight for equality.

THE NEXT STEP
Business of K-pop

Cao, Steffi, "How Korean Pop Groups Are Formed — An Introduction To The K-Pop Trainee Process," *BuzzFeed*, May 13, 2021, https://tinyurl.com/p3myxcsz.
In the competition to create K-pop stars known as idols, music companies seek out rappers, dancers and visually attractive performers.

Garcia, Tonya, "McDonald's to launch BTS meal in collaboration with K-pop band in the U.S. in May," *MarketWatch*, April 20, 2021, https://tinyurl.com/eywrnzkz.
McDonald's collaboration with BTS, the leading K-pop band, will mark the first time a celebrity meal will be available globally.

Sajnach, Paulina, "The Korean Wave: From PSY to BTS — The Impact of K-Pop on the South Korean Economy," Asia Scotland Institute, Jan. 22, 2021, https://tinyurl.com/ztjhfwjs.
K-pop's expansion has benefited the South Korean economy in myriad ways, in some cases through direct collaboration between bands and the government to drive tourism.

Controversies

Liew, Kendrea, "Future of entertainment? Avatars could be K-pop's next superstars," *CNBC*, Jan. 10, 2021, https://tinyurl.com/w4zn5n5f.
Virtual K-pop stars who never age could lead to impossibly high beauty standards for human stars, and the technology could also be used to create deepfakes, critics say.

Yeo, Gladys, "Korean music labels file complaint over new military deferment law," NME, April 9, 2021, https://tinyurl.com/52tf225t.
In a lawsuit against the defense ministry, a South Korean music association calls new rules on military deferments unrealistic, as well as unfair for nearly all K-pop musicians.

Yun, Hyeong, "Inside the Bullying Scandal Cancelling South Korean Celebrities," *Vice*, March 11, 2021, https://tinyurl.com/n2z6rsey.
Former classmates have accused several K-pop stars of bullying, and some of the performers apologized for their behavior before they became idols.

Pandemic

Manson, Destine, "How K-pop groups create community during COVID-19," *Washington Square News*, April 12, 2021, https://tinyurl.com/ys2mav7n.
Because live performances cannot take place during the COVID-19 pandemic, young K-pop fans have created dance videos and online content to maintain a sense of community.

"'Not during Ramadan!' Fans disappointed as K-Pop's BTS announce virtual concert during Holy month," *Arab News*, April 13, 2021, https://tinyurl.com/yavu2udm.
BTS' decision to hold a virtual concert during Ramadan, the month-long Islamic holiday, upset some Muslim fans.

Park, Juwon, "BTS, Blackpink are gaining momentum, but lesser-known K-pop bands are struggling amid the pandemic," *USA Today*, Dec. 15, 2020, https://tinyurl.com/yen5jmsp.
Most new K-pop groups fail, and the pandemic has made the odds of success even steeper.

United States

Guy, Jack, "K-pop stars BTS share racial discrimination they faced," *CNN*, March 30, 2021, https://tinyurl.com/2psnvry7.
BTS has weighed in on American social issues on multiple occasions, speaking out against a wave of violence

against Asian Americans and donating to Black Lives Matter.

McIntyre, Hugh, "K-Pop Powerhouses SHINee Command Almost 30% Of The Top 10 On The World Songs Chart," *Forbes*, April 20, 2021, https://tinyurl.com/38pzsjvd.
The K-pop group SHINee simultaneously debuted three songs on a global Top 10 digital sales list, a rare achievement that is in part due to its growing popularity in the United States.

Siegler, Mara, "Justin Bieber to collaborate with K-pop superstars BTS on new song," *Page Six*, May 12, 2021, https://tinyurl.com/jta4kd93.
An upcoming collaboration between pop icon Justin Bieber and BTS seems to be the result of the merger between their record companies.

Discussion Questions

Here are some questions to consider regarding K-pop:

- What accounts for its great popularity? What makes K-pop so distinctive?
- Can K-pop sustain its growth rate? Or is it a passing fad?
- Do you think the training of K-pop "idols" is exploitive? Why or why not?
- What do you think about the use of avatars? What are the drawbacks to using fake musicians? What are the upsides?
- Do you feel K-pop artists are insensitive to other cultures in their videos, choreography and use of lyrics?

For More Information

Asia Society Korea, 212-288-6400; asiasociety.org/korea; facebook.com/askoreacenter/. Nonprofit educational institution with U.S. locations in Houston, Los Angeles, New York and Washington, as well as offices in Asia; produces email newsletter on Korean culture, including information on K-pop webinars.

Association for Korean Music Research, https://tinyurl.com/9dnw3rx7; facebook.com/groups/574453839275652. A community of scholars and performers affiliated with the Society for Ethnomusicology who promote, exchange and advance the study of Korean music. Many of its scholars work on K-pop as a primary research area.

Bangtan Scholars, 600 Cleveland St., Suite 300, Clearwater, FL 33755; bangtanscholars.com. Research-oriented fan site, co-founded by Ph.D. students who organize gatherings to share research on BTS, the leading K-pop group.

KCON, 3333 Redondo Ave., Stage 19, Manhattan Beach, CA 90266; 213-355-1600; kconusa.com. Events group that organizes fan celebrations of Korean culture, music and K-pop, held in 24 locales over four continents; in the United States, KCONs are staged in Los Angeles and New York.

Korea Creative Content Agency, 5509 Wilshire Blvd., Los Angeles, CA 90036; 323-935-5001; kocca.kr/en/main.do. South Korean governmental agency that, among other things, recruits rising musicians and provides concert support.

U.S. BTS Army, usbtsarmy.com; usbtsarmy@gmail.com. Unofficial fan club for BTS; provides information, schedules and other information on the K-pop band.

Weverse, Weverse.io; Contact@benx.co. Korean social platform that provides a sign-up to the official BTS fan club; also offers a store and ways for fans to connect with BTS via video.

A supporter of ousted President Evo Morales faces off against police during a protest in Cochabamba, Bolivia, in November 2019. Demonstrations for and against Morales were part of a worldwide wave of protests in 2019.

From *CQ Researcher*,
May 1, 2020

9

Global Protest Movements

Can they lead to lasting change?

By Bill Wanlund

THE ISSUES

Enraged Lebanese took to the streets last Oct. 18, 2019, when their government announced a $6-a-month tax on calls made via WhatsApp and other online apps. One of the protesters in Beirut, Rayya Haddad, says, "As I was walking to my parents' house, a friend texted me about the demonstrations starting, so I went. There were blocked streets, burning tires—all the country was up in revolt."

Within hours, the Cabinet scrapped the tax proposal, which was supposed to help ease a lingering economic crisis and rescue Lebanon's ailing telecommunications industry. But the demonstrations continued, and the "WhatsApp tax" protests morphed into what Haddad and her fellow protesters began calling a revolution.

On Oct. 29, 2019, 11 days after the protests began, Prime Minister Saad Hariri resigned—but even that did not satisfy anti-government demonstrators, who had swelled into the hundreds of thousands. "The protests . . . continued because people are fed up with government corruption and incompetence," Haddad says.

Lebanon's protests bear many of the characteristics of those that roiled the world last year: Seemingly mundane local events, like a WhatsApp tax, spark demonstrations, which in turn unleash anger about more fundamental grievances such as government incompetence or social and economic inequality. A report by the Center for Strategic and International Studies, a Washington think tank, found that more than 37 countries experienced massive

187

Protests Worldwide Grew More Frequent

During the decade between 2009 and 2019, the number of protests increased worldwide by 11.5 percent annually, according to an analysis by the Center for Strategic and International Studies. Protests increased the most in sub-Saharan Africa, by just under 24 percent.

Increase in Protests Annually, 2009–19

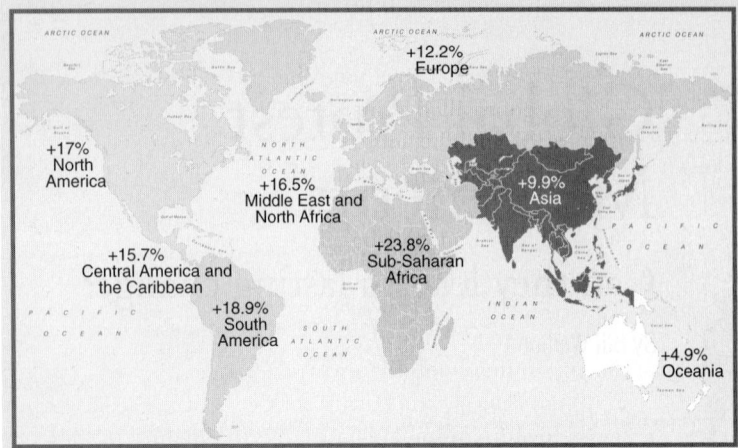

Source: Samuel J. Brannen, Christian S. Haig and Katherine Schmidt, "The Age of Mass Protests," Center for Strategic and International Studies, March 2020, https://tinyurl.com/wgceft8

anti-government movements in the last few months of 2019 alone. This continued a decade-long trend, during which mass political protests increased by an annual average of 11.5 percent, the center reported.[1]

"Protesters have taken to the streets to speak out about corruption, economic injustices, environmental questions, repression and a range of particular local issues," Richard Youngs, a senior fellow at Carnegie Europe, a part of the Carnegie Endowment for International Peace think tank, wrote last fall. "Several protests have driven political leaders out of office; some have triggered draconian government reprisals. Mass mobilizations have occurred in democracies and nondemocracies and advanced and developing economies alike. They are now a major feature of global politics."[2]

Maria Stephan, director of the Program on Nonviolent Action at the U.S. Institute of Peace in Washington, puts it this way: "We are probably living in the most contentious time in recorded history."

But early this year, as the deadly coronavirus spread rapidly around the world and governments instituted social distancing requirements and bans on public gatherings to limit the contagion, the mass street demonstrations that had characterized the protest wave largely came to an end. Many movements turned to other means of expressing dissent, such as strikes, boycotts or virtual protests on the internet, to keep their grievances before the public.[3]

Protesters generally acknowledge that the measures taken by governments have been necessary to protect public health. However, some also fear that authoritarian governments are using the coronavirus breakout as an excuse to exert powers to quash legitimate dissent. "We could have a parallel epidemic of authoritarian and repressive measures [closely] following . . . a health epidemic," said Fionnuala Ní Aoláin, the United Nations special rapporteur on counterterrorism and human rights.[4]

Lebanon's protests followed a predictable pattern. Demonstrations often progress from small, discrete issues to larger, more encompassing ones, says Kai Thaler, a professor of global studies at the University of California, Santa Barbara. The movements "start out with small causes. Then, some people make the case for wider protests, and other people see the opportunity to express their own grievances, and things snowball."

Recent examples include:

- France's *gilets jaunes* (yellow vests) protests, named for the high-visibility safety jackets that French motorists must carry, were triggered by a proposed increase in the national fuel tax in 2018. The tax was abandoned in April 2019.[5] The size of the protests dwindled, but they continued as part of a wider anti-government movement.
- Protests erupted in Hong Kong in March 2019 when many citizens felt the city's limited autonomy from mainland China was threatened by a proposed extradition law in the Hong Kong Legislature. After five months of protests, the bill

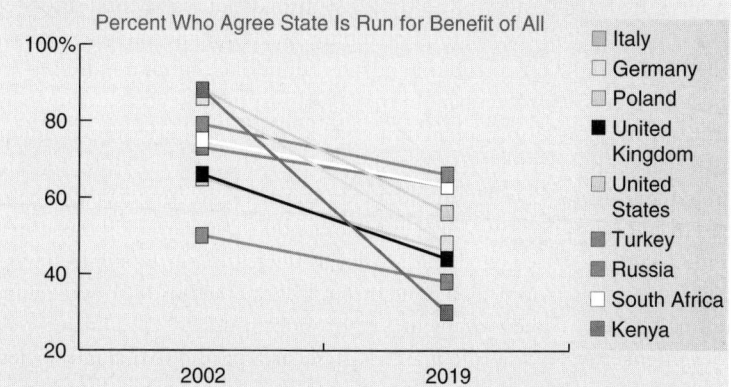

Fewer Believe State Benefits All Citizens

The view that the state is run for the benefit of everyone is losing popularity in many countries, according to polling by the Pew Research Center. In Italy, the proportion holding this view fell from 88 percent in 2002 to 30 percent last year. In the same period, the share in the United States dropped from 65 percent to 46 percent.

Source: Richard Wike and Shannon Schumacher, "Democratic Rights Popular Globally but Commitment to Them Not Always Strong," Pew Research Center, Feb. 27, 2020, https://tinyurl.com/y9yjlhm4

was withdrawn—but protests continued, with expanded demands for democratic guarantees.[6] The emergence of the coronavirus diminished the size of the demonstrations, although movement participants vow to continue pressing their demands.[7] (*See Short Feature.*)

- Bolivians took to the streets in October to protest once-popular President Evo Morales' extralegal effort to seek a fourth term in office. After three weeks, Morales fled the country, but demonstrations continued against his conservative interim successor, Jeanine Áñez, until coronavirus safety measures suspended street protests.[8]
- In Chile, student demonstrations in October over a 30-peso (4-cent) rise in rush-hour subway fares mushroomed into a protest against economic mismanagement and inequality that drew a million participants.[9] The national Congress agreed to call a referendum (now postponed) in April on the question of creating a new constitution, meeting a key protester demand. President Sebastián Piñera promised to increase pensions. Demonstrations continued, however, amid complaints of harsh repressive tactics by police: According to press reports at least 30 demonstrators have been killed, though no official figure is available.[10] The Office of the U.N. High Commissioner for Human Rights reported some 28,000 were jailed.[11]
- In November, increased fuel costs triggered protests in Iran. Then, in January, the government's lack of transparency over its reporting of the downing of a Ukrainian airliner led to another nationwide protest. Security forces quelled both; neither protest led to noticeable change in government policies.[12]

Experts see the trend toward more protests as signaling an erosion of faith in governments' ability to solve problems, and even in democracy itself. "More people are motivated to engage in nonviolent mobilization because of a seeming inability of governments around the world to address major challenges of our time," says Erica Chenoweth, a professor of human rights and international affairs at Harvard University's Kennedy School of Government. "People believe our political institutions are not equipped to address national problems that also affect people locally."

Chenoweth adds, "There's also a rising tide of authoritarianism. There are fewer democracies in the world than there were 10 years ago, and more democracies at risk today than in a very long time. People are resisting this authoritarian march."

Although the number of protests has increased dramatically, there is no guarantee that they will achieve their objectives. Political analyst Youssef Cherif, deputy director of Columbia University's Global Center in Tunisia, said, "Staging [demonstrations] is no longer the difficult part. The problem is what to do after the protests, how to make your point and achieve the goals you're protesting for. . . . You can break off part of a system, but it's very hard to break the whole structure . . . of institutions and networks."[13]

Authoritarian regimes often resort to violence to end opposition protests.

In Iran, which is controlled by a theocratic Islamist regime, the human rights group Amnesty International said it had seen credible reports that security forces killed at least 208 protesters during last year's protests.[14] The U.S. State Department, pointing to unspecified "international media reports," put the number killed at approximately 1,500.[15]

Hadi Ghaemi, executive director of the New York-based Center for Human Rights in Iran, believes repression will not stop the protests. "The future of Iran is completely tied to whether the government will represent the people's interests or try to suppress them," he says. "If they continue to kill and to refuse to tolerate any dissent, we're sure to see more dissent and more violence in the future."

And even nominally democratic governments, such as Chile's, can adopt harsh measures. Alexa Schaeffer Quintero, an American working in Santiago, who took part in some of the protests there, says, "As the weeks passed, the police's repressive tactics got worse—the police used rubber and metal bullets that caused hundreds of flesh wounds and eye injuries. During protests the water tanks sprayed a yellowish water that caused a burning sensation. . . . My fear was never of the actions of other protesters, only of the police and their excessive and unnecessary use of force."

Today, as in earlier times, there is lively debate over whether violent acts can advance the goals of protesters or will prove counterproductive.

Thaler, the University of California scholar, said violence can help further a movement's cause. "In Chile, protesters' willingness to fight with police and burn buildings, in addition to nonviolent tactics, helped push the government to make serious concessions," he said. And violent protests pushed Bolivia's Morales to step down "amid unhappiness with his ignoring the results of a referendum and allegations of electoral fraud."[16]

Stephan, of the U.S. Institute of Peace, says any benefits violence might lend to an otherwise nonviolent movement are short-lived. "If you add violence," she says, "in the short term you get more media covering it, or you may get a morale boost, but over time you may see participation levels decrease, more people staying home. That, at the end of the day, ends up weakening the movement."

While many protests are specific to a single society and its problems, some issues catalyze far-flung cross-border protests. Two examples are climate change and violence against women.

Millions of students around the world have rallied to demand climate action in both physical and online protests. Many were inspired by Greta Thunberg, the Swedish teenager who called for action to end climate-damaging practices in high-profile appearances at the United Nations and the World Economic Forum in Davos, Switzerland.[17]

A movement against femicide—gender-based killing of women—has spread across Latin America and to other continents as well. According to the United Nations, some 87,000 women and girls were murdered worldwide in 2017—50,000 by a spouse, partner or close family member.[18]

As nations and their citizens confront both rising social tensions and a virulent virus, here are some of the questions they are asking:

Is the current protest wave a sign that democracy is failing?

It is no coincidence that the wave of protests has occurred at a time when there is also an upsurge in authoritarian regimes and rulers and increasing skepticism about democratic governance, Stephan says.

"This resurgent authoritarianism is probably linked to growing global inequality and sense of disenfranchisement," she says. "People orient to those populist leaders

To protest police use of pellet guns, Chilean demonstrators hold placards depicting eyes in Santiago in December 2019. The pellets caused numerous eye injuries during anti-government protests last fall.

who say they have the solutions to the problem. They're giving up on the traditional legislative and judicial processes that are seen to be ineffective, and look to the autocratic strongman to bring solutions."

Some recent studies echo these views. According to the latest survey by Freedom House, a Washington-based organization that researches issues pertaining to democracy, last year 64 countries experienced a deterioration in political rights and civil liberties while just 37 experienced improvements. "The unchecked brutality of autocratic regimes and the ethical decay of democratic powers are combining to make the world increasingly hostile to fresh demands for better governance," the group said.[19]

And a 2020 Pew Global Research study found "considerable dissatisfaction with the way democracy is working in many countries." Across the 34 nations polled, 52 percent of respondents said they were dissatisfied with how their democracy was functioning. The biggest complaint was the feeling that political leaders were out of touch; Pew found that 64 percent "believe elected officials do not care what people like them think." In the United States, 71 percent feel that way. Overall, the Pew study found that 59 percent of Americans are dissatisfied with the way democracy is working in the United States.[20]

"I think we're living through an anti-establishment wave, and public frustration is at play," says Chenoweth of Harvard's Kennedy School. "A lot of people think the electoral system isn't as representative as it should be, or perhaps as it used to be, and that institutions aren't responsive to urgent issues."

She adds, "There's also a sense of gridlock, that public polarization has infected government institutions in ways that keep them from moving. The public is divided, so the institutions are divided, so much so that there's no wiggle room."

Another gloomy assessment comes from the University of Cambridge in England. Its 2020 "Global Satisfaction with Democracy" report, which reviewed dozens of international surveys between 1995 and this year, found that "dissatisfaction with democracy has risen over time, and is reaching an all-time global high." It said last year represented "the highest level of democratic discontent on record."

The report marks 2005 as the high point for global satisfaction with democracy. Since then, it said, "democratic institutions around the world have faced setbacks ranging from military coups, to domestic crises, to the election of populist or authoritarian leaders willing to use their office to erode the independence of parliament, courts and civil society."[21]

The Cambridge study's principal author, Roberto Foa, a lecturer in politics and public policy, says global democracy is in "a state of deep malaise." He says, "In transitional democracies in Africa, Latin America, parts of Asia, many of the hopes and expectations that were raised during the democratic transition—better delivery of public services, better rule of law, more control over corruption—have been disappointed."

In developed democracies, Foa says, "it's more to do with the consequences of the [2007-09] financial crisis and the eurozone crisis and the economic frustrations that created, and the feeling of being left behind without a voice."

But Monica de Bolle, director of Latin American studies and emerging markets at the Johns Hopkins University School of Advanced International Studies, says there is no evidence that democracy is dying.

"Nothing is linear," she says. "We make progress, we take a step back, we make progress. To infer that democracy and democratic institutions are going away on the basis of what's been going on in the past very few years is overly pessimistic, even irresponsible."

Democracy is complicated, de Bolle says. "Institutions need to be modernized, and they will modernize when there's discontent with what's happening. That's what will move things forward."

Erica Frantz, a Michigan State University political science assistant professor, believes government institutions are falling short of their promise. "On one hand, it's cause for optimism that people are hitting the streets and protesting," she says. "At the same time, the underlying cause of their frustration is that they don't feel their governments are delivering. If there is some sort of ideological battle between democracy and authoritarianism at the moment, it's up to these democratic governments to prove they can provide, and do all those things democracies are supposed to do."

Haddad, the protester in Beirut, describes Lebanon as a "schizophrenic" democracy. "We have an open, free press," she says. "That's why the government didn't put a blackout on the internet, it would have been unconstitutional. But we don't really have free speech—people have been imprisoned for criticizing the president."

Support for Free Speech Rising in Many Nations

Support for the view that people should be able to say what they want without government censorship rose between 2015 and 2019 in most countries surveyed by the Pew Research Center. The biggest increase was in Turkey, where support jumped 22 percentage points. Israel and India experienced declines.

Share Who Say Free Speech Is Very Important

Country	2015	2019	Change
Turkey	43%	65%	+22
France	67%	83%	+16
Hungary*	74%	87%	+13
United Kingdom	57%	68%	+11
Argentina	77%	87%	+10
Mexico	65%	73%	+8
Indonesia	29%	37%	+8
United States	71%	77%	+6
Philippines	50%	56%	+6
Israel	58%	51%	-7
India	44%	32%	-12

* Hungary was polled in 2016.

Source: Richard Wike and Shannon Schumacher, "Democratic Rights Popular Globally but Commitment to Them Not Always Strong," Pew Research Center, Feb. 27, 2020, https://tinyurl.com/y9yjlhm4

Thomas Carothers, founder and director of the Democracy and Rule of Law Program at the Carnegie Endowment for International Peace, says the surge of protests "is not a crisis of democracy per se, though a lot of democracies are facing pressure from their citizens—as are a lot of autocracies. Part of the paradox of governing is, the more you satisfy [citizens], the more demands they have. Sometimes good performance leads to high expectations, and you fail to meet them. It isn't a straight line between bad performance and failure to meet expectations."

And for all the turmoil and discontent, Stephan sees the protests as a sign of democracy's health. "People finding voice and employing it in institutional, extralegal ways is arguably very good for democracy—people believing they can bring about change through collective action," she says. "That's a hopeful aspect of what we're seeing around the world: an exertion of agency."

Is social media responsible for the recent wave of protests?

One thread linking recent mass protests is the use of social media as a recruitment and organizing tool.

Haddad, who participated in the WhatsApp tax protests in Lebanon, says social media played a huge role.

"It unites the people, people send flyers and documents, tell where the next protest is, when to meet, where people are gathering, what to bring," she says. "People share stories, or photos. It's much more accurate than TV or other traditional media for following what's happening."

Most scholars agree that social media has played an important part in modern movements, but add that there are limits to its value. "There's no question that social media is an accelerator of protest, but I wouldn't point to it as an original cause," says Carothers of the Carnegie Endowment. "I think it's an accelerator of underlying causes."

Social media has played an important role in the Hong Kong protests, activist and lawyer Angeline Chan says. Two platforms that have been especially important are Telegram, a Dubai-based messaging app that describes itself as heavily encrypted, and a Hong Kong forum, LIHKG, she says.

"These platforms are where people can come together and brainstorm and make plans," Chan says. "They can get people together from all districts of Hong Kong, for example to form a human chain, or to start online petitions, for circulating posters—they're really the place to go for information."

Michigan State's Frantz, who studies authoritarianism, says that "access to new technologies facilitates more protests and helps reduce barriers to collective action. Protests are on the increase, and there's good evidence that it's due to the rise of social media."

At the same time, she says, "dictatorships are using this technology to repress dissent—shutting down the internet, for example, or surveilling people online."

And Frantz says that reliance on social media may, perversely, be undermining the ultimate success of protests.

"The logic behind this is that, before social media, to organize a protest you had to work hard to develop your organization and get feet on the ground," she says. "Now, because it's easier to spread the word about a protest, the organizations that are backing them are weaker and less cohesive than in the past. . . . Opposition movements could become more resilient by strengthening their organizations offline and mimicking opposition movements of the past that didn't rely on social media to get going."

Under an authoritarian regime, it can be difficult to use the internet to facilitate protests. That is the case in Iran, says Garrett Nada, program officer at the U.S. Institute of Peace's Center for the Middle East & Africa. In order to communicate more safely, he says, Iranian protesters must use a virtual private network, which allows a user to make an encrypted connection to a public network to block monitoring and bypass censorship.

"Most popular foreign social media platforms are banned, such as Telegram, Facebook, YouTube and Twitter," Nada says. "During the November 2019 protests, the regime resorted to shutting down the internet for five days to limit communications."

At the same time, social media can create a diffusion of inspiration, ideas and tactics across borders—a "global contagion," in the words of David Gordon, senior adviser in the Washington office of the International Institute for Strategic Studies, a research organization. "Seeing protests in other places motivates people to be willing to go to the streets in their own countries," Gordon said.[22]

But Dawn Brancati, a research scholar at Yale University's MacMillan Center for International and Area Studies, says pro-democracy protests in one nation are unlikely to be replicated in adjoining countries, because protests arise primarily from unique domestic conditions such as fraudulent elections or economic crises.

"Democracy protests can even dampen prospects for protests in neighboring countries," Brancati says. "After all, national leaders watch the same regional developments that activists do, and can take steps to block protests in their own countries, like shutting down internet access and pre-emptively arresting activists."

The 2011 Arab Spring, a wave of pro-democracy uprisings across the Arab world, began in Tunisia. The protests, widely shared on Facebook and other social media, led within weeks to the resignation of the country's president and, subsequently, to democratic elections. Tunisia has been cited as an example of how a successful protest in one country can, thanks to social media, inspire similar events in another.

"The protests that brought down Tunisia's leader had an immediate impact—people in other Arab countries said, 'Wow, we can do the same thing,'" says Kurt Weyland, professor of government at the University of Texas at Austin.

But while the unrest soon spread to Egypt, Libya, Syria, Yemen and other countries in the region, it ultimately failed to achieve its fundamental goal of a democratic transformation in the Arab world.

"If change is not inspired by a country's own domestic reasons, then that change isn't likely to succeed," Weyland says. "The Arab Spring brought democratization to one country: Tunisia. In the others it didn't succeed. Diffusion is a prediction of probable failure."

Can protests bring about lasting change?

Several of 2019's protests have led to major changes. In Algeria, Sudan, Lebanon, Iraq and Bolivia, leaders were forced out. Governments in Chile, France, Ecuador and Hong Kong made significant concessions in response to demonstrators' initial demands.

However, most of these protests have yet to produce the fundamental changes many protesters had sought. Bolivia's Morales was ousted for suspected election corruption, but replaced by an unpopular right-wing politician; new elections were scheduled for May but then postponed over coronavirus concerns. The Hong Kong extradition legislation, which would have allowed mainland China to extradite criminal defendants, was withdrawn, but the protesters' wider demands for greater democracy remain unfulfilled. Demonstrators' success in overthrowing Sudan's longtime dictator, Omar al-Bashir, has been thrown into question by repressive tactics on the part of the interim military government that succeeded Bashir.[23]

Youngs of Carnegie Europe believes what activists do after an action can determine the movement's success or failure. "What happens in the immediate aftermath of a protest is just as crucial as what occurs during the protest," he said. "It is a major factor in determining whether mass protest becomes a force to restructure politics or ultimately remains a dramatic yet ineffective interlude in the status quo."

Sudanese protesters wave the national flag in Khartoum in February 2020. Demonstrations last year toppled President Omar al-Bashir, but repressive tactics by an interim military government have sparked new protests.

Youngs is the editor of "After Protest: Pathways Beyond Mass Mobilization," a Carnegie Europe report in which educators and other experts analyze 10 major recent domestic conflicts and how the choices made by the activists affected the outcomes.[24]

In Egypt, Youngs wrote, activists were ready for revolution but not prepared to govern in the aftermath. "Civic activist strategies after the 2011 revolution that ousted President Hosni Mubarak became highly polarized around a division between secularists and Islamists," and a repressive authoritarian government filled the vacuum, he wrote.

Ukrainians, on the other hand, generally chose to work—albeit warily—with their new government after toppling President Viktor Yanukovych in 2014. Activists "moved into new roles of supporting the formally democratic [new] government but also sought ways to resist the government's growing reluctance to reform fully," said Youngs. "The largest activist group has focused on local-level volunteering and community-organizing. . . ."[25]

Whether a protest movement will succeed is difficult to forecast. "Nonviolent popular uprisings are among the least predictable events we see in humankind," says Harvard's Chenoweth.

Stephan of the Institute of Peace says successful movements typically share a few central attributes. She says the key questions are: "Is the protest growing and bringing in new participants from different parts of society? How are they dealing with violent repression? Can they maintain nonviolent discipline? Are there loyalty shifts among key pillars of regime support, such as workers and security forces?"

In addition, she says, a successful protest will display "innovative, dispersed and coordinated use of tactics—more than just street protests, for example."

Stephan notes one striking trend: "The overall success rate of nonviolent campaigns has decreased noticeably. Twenty years ago, about 70 percent of nonviolent campaigns succeeded in achieving their goals. Starting in the 2000s, that rate dropped to 30 percent. That's a staggering decline," she says, one she attributes to an increase in authoritarian governments, which tend to use repressive tactics against protesters.

George Lakey, a retired professor in peace and conflict studies at Swarthmore College, says one thing is certain: A single protest is not sufficient to bring about change.

"In a one-off demonstration, your opponent knows perfectly well at the end of the day you're going to go back home, so the next day they continue doing what they've been doing," says Lakey.

As a case in point, Lakey—who is also a longtime activist in support of progressive causes—recalls the massive Feb. 15, 2003, global protest against U.S. plans to go to war against Iraq. Perhaps as many as 11 million people gathered in at least 650 cities around the world—the largest one-day protest in history.[26]

But the demonstrations ultimately had no impact on the Bush administration's war plans, because other actions did not follow, he says.

"It was an amazing expression of public opinion, and it had very little impact," Lakey says. "The one-off may persuade more people to agree with the protesters' point of view, but the newly convinced don't have a place to go without a campaign—a sustained series of actions."

BACKGROUND
Peasants and Protestants

For centuries, social and economic inequality has been at the heart of protest. England's Peasants' Revolt of 1381 challenged the conditions of serfdom—heavy taxes, bondage to the land and a government-enforced income cap. The nobility quelled the uprising, but because the revolt demonstrated peasants' potential power, historians say it helped break down England's feudal system.[27]

The Protestant Reformation, sparked in 1517 by German monk Martin Luther, challenged the authority of the Roman Catholic Church (and gave "protest" its modern meaning). Luther questioned the church's right to define Christian practice. The Reformation, supported by princes seeking to replace the church's authority with their own, spread through much of Europe, resulting in Protestant dominance of much of the northern part of the continent by 1648.[28]

By preaching the leveling notion of a "priesthood of all believers," Luther unintentionally inspired discontented agrarian workers to challenge social and political hierarchies, leading to another rebellion, the German Peasants' War of 1524-25. Like England's, it sprang from the social and economic inequality that were hallmarks of feudalism—and, like England's, it was put down by nobles' armies.[29]

In the late 18th century, colonists in British North America also chafed under what they regarded as unequal treatment, in that they were heavily taxed by Parliament but had no political representation in England. As taxes and trade restraints on the colonies increased, so did American resentment. Battles between British troops and American militias broke out in 1775 and the 13 colonies formally declared their independence in 1776. Britain's superiority in manpower and materiel was negated by its long, unreliable supply lines and the hemorrhaging effects of the rebels' guerrilla tactics. With the Treaty of Paris in 1783, the United States had secured its independence.[30]

Encouraged by the American example but motivated by their own grievances, French citizens rose up against their monarchy in 1789. Social inequality and onerous taxation were core concerns. In a bloody revolution, French citizens eliminated the absolute monarchy and the feudal system, adopting a new constitution in 1791. However, the ensuing government, inefficient and corrupt, was overthrown in 1799 in a coup d'état led by Napoleon Bonaparte, who crowned himself emperor in 1804.[31]

Expanding literacy helped spread the writings of political thinkers and philosophers throughout Europe, and by 1848 the idea of revolution had taken hold throughout the continent. In January, Sicilians threw out the ruling Bourbon monarchy; revolutions in the states of the Italian peninsula erupted later that year. In February, the French overthrew their constitutional monarchy and replaced it with the Second Republic under Louis-Napoléon, nephew of Bonaparte. Revolution spread to the German states and to Austria, Denmark and Hungary in March.

The revolutions of 1848 enjoyed limited success; the dethroned monarchs soon returned to power. However, the upheavals resulted in some victories: Hungary gained autonomy within the Hapsburg Empire, the Italian states made progress toward a unified government, Austria ended the feudal system and abandoned press censorship and the German state of Prussia established an elective assembly.

Other European countries avoided 1848's revolutionary turmoil. Some had undergone earlier revolutions or civil wars and enacted reforms.[32] Others pre-emptively instigated reforms demanded elsewhere and successfully avoided violent unrest; in the Netherlands, King William II voluntarily authorized a new constitution, including direct elections, and ceded royal authority.[33]

Birth of Nonviolent Resistance

Mohandas Gandhi, a 24-year-old Indian-born lawyer, moved to Natal, a British colony in present-day South Africa, in 1893. There, he quickly discovered the discrimination against people of Indian descent. When Indians lost the right to vote in 1894, he led protests against the colonial government.

Gandhi developed satyagraha, a philosophy of nonviolent resistance, and in 1915 brought it home to India. Although the British imprisoned him several times, he was instrumental in winning support for India's independence, and eventually became known as mahatma, or great soul. Gandhi, although himself a Hindu, was assassinated in January 1948 by a Hindu extremist because of his tolerance of India's Muslims, five months after India became independent from Great Britain.[34]

Gandhi's nonviolent philosophy and the struggle for racial equality came together in the U.S. civil rights movement. Martin Luther King Jr., an admirer of Gandhi, became a dominant figure in the movement, which sought full political, economic and social rights for African Americans. King's nonviolent strategy and powerful oratory helped build sympathy for the

CHRONOLOGY

14th Century *Peasants unite to seek better life.*

1381 English peasants march on London seeking relief from serfdom.

18th-19th Centuries *An age of revolutions opens.*

1776 Protesting "taxation without representation," American colonists declare independence from Britain.

1783 After a long war, Britain recognizes American independence.

1789 Revolution topples the French monarchy, establishes a republic three years later.

1848 Revolutions sweep across Europe, toppling monarchs; most return to power, but with concessions to demands. . . . The Seneca Falls Declaration asserts U.S. women's right to full citizenship.

1894 Mohandas Gandhi leads Indian-rights protests in South Africa.

1915-1945 *Nonviolent protests arise.*

1915 Gandhi brings nonviolent resistance to India's campaign for independence from Britain.

1930 Gandhi leads a "salt march," a civil disobedience protest over British colonial treatment of India; he and 60,000 other protesters are arrested.

1945 As World War II ends, the Soviet Union begins to expand its influence in Eastern Europe. . . . Vietnamese communists and other nationalists declare their country independent from France, triggering conflict with French forces.

1950s-1970s *Racism and war take people into the streets.*

1954 The U.S. Supreme Court rules racial segregation in schools is unconstitutional. . . . Nationalists defeat French forces in Vietnam; Geneva Accords ending the war result in division of the country into a communist-controlled North and noncommunist South.

1955 Rosa Parks, a black activist, is arrested for refusing to yield her seat to a white bus rider in Montgomery, Ala., touching off a monthslong boycott in protest. . . . United States sends 700 military advisers to train South Vietnamese forces, the beginning of a commitment in which more than 2.7 million service members would serve in Vietnam by war's end.

1960 Security forces at Sharpeville, South Africa, massacre 69 black demonstrators, spotlighting the injustice of South Africa's rigid system of racial separation known as apartheid.

1963 The Rev. Martin Luther King Jr. leads a civil rights March on Washington and delivers "I have a dream" speech to 250,000 at Lincoln Memorial.

1964 President Lyndon B. Johnson signs Civil Rights Act, guaranteeing full citizenship rights to black Americans.

1965 Johnson orders bombing of North Vietnam and sends U.S. combat troops to South Vietnam in an effort to help defeat North Vietnamese and Vietcong forces. The war, popular at first, becomes increasingly controversial as casualties rise.

1968 King is assassinated in Memphis, touching off riots and rebellions in hundreds of cities. . . . Anti-war protesters battle police outside Democratic convention in Chicago. . . . Anti-government student protests paralyze France. . . . Soviet military invasion of Czechoslovakia ends brief Prague Spring liberalization. . . . Mexico City police kill dozens of students demonstrating for greater freedoms.

1970 An estimated 20 million Americans observe the first Earth Day to call attention to the environment; Congress authorizes creation of the Environmental Protection Agency.

1980s-1990s *Democracy takes center stage.*

1989 Pro-democracy demonstrations at Tiananmen Square in Beijing call attention to Chinese desire for democracy, but end in bloody suppression. . . . Soviet bloc convulses as Berlin Wall falls. The following year, communist East Germany disappears and Germany reunites.

1991 Soviet Union dissolves, and its constituent republics become independent nations.

1999 Anti-globalization demonstrators disrupt World Trade Organization meeting in Seattle.

2000-Present *New voices speak out against political, economic and social grievances.*

2003 As many as 11 million people take part in a worldwide protest against the impending U.S. invasion of Iraq, the largest single-day protest in history; the United States invades anyway.

2011 Pro-democracy Arab Spring protests sweep the Middle East. . . . Occupy Wall Street protests against economic inequality emerge in New York, spread across the United States and overseas.

2013 Black Lives Matter movement organizes to protest police killings of African Americans.

2017 Marches around the country, sparked by Donald Trump's comments about women, protest his inauguration as president.

2018 Students protest gun violence after a mass shooting at a Florida high school. . . . Swedish teenager Greta Thunberg's protests calling for greater action against climate change engage millions of students around the world.

2019 Protests against the lack of democracy or persistent social grievances engulf dozens of countries, ranging from Lebanon to France and Hong Kong.

2020 Government stay-at-home orders to diminish the coronavirus threaten to halt global protest movements. . . . As economic pressure tightens, protests to end government lockdown restrictions erupt in dozens of U.S. states.

---

movement, as did the tactics employed by its participants, including acts of civil disobedience such as sit-ins—peaceful occupation by blacks of whites-only facilities—along with marches, boycotts and letter-writing campaigns.

Violence, or at least the fear of it, was also present in the movement, embodied by Malcolm X, who sought a separate society for African Americans. In 1964 he urged blacks "to fight whoever gets in our way . . . and bring about the freedom of [people of African descent] by any means necessary."[35] He was assassinated in 1965 while giving a speech in Harlem. Three members of the Nation of Islam, a group that Malcolm X once helped lead but had split from, were convicted of his murder. Many years later, amid doubts about the case, New York authorities reopened the investigation into his death.[36]

The Black Panther Party, formed in 1966, supported black nationalism, socialism and "armed self-defense."[37]

Civil rights activism played a key role in bringing about several laws enacted in the 1960s to protect the rights of black Americans. The Civil Rights Act of 1964 outlawed racial segregation in schools, at the workplace and in facilities such as stores, restaurants and hotels that

Young civil rights demonstrators in Birmingham, Ala., in 1963 are flattened against a wall by fire hoses. The images of police brutality against the marchers created widespread sympathy for their cause.

served the general public.[38] In 1965, the Voting Rights Act made it illegal to deny the right to vote based on race and set up a system of federal registrars to ensure that blacks could vote.[39] The Fair Housing Act of 1968 outlawed racial discrimination in the sale, rental or financing of housing.[40]

King was assassinated in 1968; a white man with a racist past, James Earl Ray, was convicted of the crime.[41]

Hong Kong Protesters Confront Beijing's Power

"They're fighting because they feel they have no choice."

In 2018, a Hong Kong teenager visiting Taiwan, Chan Tong-kai, allegedly killed his girlfriend. He then returned to Hong Kong. Chan subsequently confessed to police, but Hong Kong has no extradition treaty with Taiwan, a separately-governed island off the Chinese mainland, so the killing could not be prosecuted.[1]

This tawdry murder case set off a chain of events that led to an eruption of dissent among Hong Kong citizens who feared the encroachment of the People's Republic of China and its authoritarian government. The result has been massive and at times violent street demonstrations, a significant electoral victory for the protesters, but also lingering questions about what they have ultimately achieved as the coronavirus and its restrictions now force protesters off the streets.

The year after the killing, the Hong Kong government cited Chan's case when it proposed legislation permitting case-by-case extradition to countries with which it does not have formal agreements—including the People's Republic.[2] This triggered alarm that such a law could lead to arbitrary imprisonment of Hong Kong residents who dissent against the Chinese government. Pro-democracy activists responded by organizing protests against the proposed law.

The dispute was rooted in the laws that govern relations between Hong Kong and the mainland. The 1,108-square-mile Hong Kong Special Administrative Region enjoys special economic, political and legal status until at least 2047, the result of the agreement by which Great Britain ceded Hong Kong to China in 1997. Under the agreement, which applies a principle called "one country, two systems," Hong Kong has maintained the free-market economic system that makes it an important world financial center, and its citizens enjoy civil and political rights unheard of in mainland China.[3]

"Extraditing people from Hong Kong into China would break down the 'one country, two systems' firewall," says Angeline Chan, a Hong Kong lawyer who took part in the pro-democracy movement that opposed the legislation.

The protests peaked on June 9 with a crowd estimated by police at 240,000 and by organizers at more than 1 million.[4] The protests continued during the summer.

On Sept. 4, 2019, Hong Kong Chief Executive Carrie Lam withdrew the extradition bill, saying she was doing so "to eradicate the worries of [the] people" of Hong Kong.[5] But her move came too late to quell the movement. By that time the protesters had broadened their demands and hardened their position.

They said they would not end the demonstrations until the government met four other demands in addition to withdrawing the extradition bill: cease defining the protests as rioting, grant amnesty for arrested protesters, conduct an independent inquiry into police violence and give Hong Kong citizens more say in choosing their government. At present, residents elect a territorial council with limited authority, but the powerful chief executive is chosen by an electoral council made up of 1,194 representatives of various sectors of Hong Kong society who are approved by Beijing.[6]

Protesters criticized Hong Kong's security forces for using unreasonable force. "We've seen police violence used regularly—tear gas, beanbag rounds, pepper spray, batons, with hardly any police held to account," Chan says. "The focus of the protests has shifted from the extradition bill to the fact that the police are acting with impunity."

But protesters too have used violence. During a standoff at Hong Kong Polytechnic University in November 2019, barricaded students used firebombs and bows and arrows against police—who themselves had used tear gas, rubber bullets and water cannons.[7]

The protesters can claim some credit for a major political shift in Hong Kong. In November 2019's territorial council elections, pro-democracy candidates won 389 of

452 seats; previously they held 124. Pro-Beijing candidates took just 58 seats, down from 300.[8] "This election [was] totally a de facto referendum for the protests," said Samson Yuen, an assistant professor of political science at Hong Kong's Lingnan University.[9]

A survey by the Hong Kong Public Opinion Research Institute taken March 17-20, 2020, indicated substantial public support for protesters' demands, with those backing the protests outnumbering opponents by 58 percent to 28 percent.[10]

But Richard Bush, a China specialist and senior fellow in foreign policy at the Brookings Institution, a centrist Washington think tank, says the movement is probably failing in fulfilling its objectives.

"If the goal is to get Beijing to create a more democratic system, then it has failed," he says. "If the goal was to deal with the extradition bill and then return to more normal circumstances, it failed by following up with unreasonable demands that would lead Beijing, the Hong Kong government and the Hong Kong elite to conclude the movement really didn't want a mutually acceptable solution."

However, he adds, "if the goal is to keep Hong Kong in a permanent state of instability, the movement succeeded, and will probably be back for more once the coronavirus subsides."

Without a doubt, the pandemic is complicating the pro-democracy movement. Hong Kong's first coronavirus death was confirmed Feb. 4, and the city instituted quarantines and other preventive measures. Since then, demonstrations have been sporadic, and smaller.[11]

Albert Ho, a pro-democracy leader, said authorities appear to be using the respite to prevent large demonstrations, including rounding up protest organizers. "They have to do everything to deter the social organizers from continuing to organize marches and demonstrations on a big scale," Ho said.[12]

The coronavirus outbreak may dampen enthusiasm for street demonstrations, but in the long run it could help fuel the protest movement, whose leaders see the government's failure to cope with the virus as an opportunity to rally support.

"Street protests are just a part of the movement," said Eric Lai Yan-ho, deputy convener of the Civil Human Rights Front. Yan-ho's group, which organized rallies, also helped gather more than 35,000 online signatures in a city-wide campaign to protest the government's handling of the virus crisis. Unions added to the pressure by engaging in Hong Kong's largest-ever medical strike.[13]

Chan, the lawyer-activist, says the cause is vital to Hong Kong residents. "A lot of the protesters I come into contact with feel that if they don't resist, the way of life we know in Hong Kong will disappear," she says. "They're fighting because they feel they have no choice."

—*Bill Wanlund*

---

[1] Cindy Sui, "The murder behind the Hong Kong protests: A case where no-one wants the killer," *BBC*, Oct. 23, 2019, https://tinyurl.com/y8fjl24o.

[2] Daniel Victor and Tiffany May, "The Murder Case That Lit the Fuse in Hong Kong," *The New York Times*, June 15, 2019, https://tinyurl.com/y6qz8cx3.

[3] Eleanor Albert, "Democracy in Hong Kong," Council on Foreign Relations, Sept. 20. 2019, https://tinyurl.com/ybw2yd7r.

[4] Eric Kleefeld, "Hundreds of thousands attend protest in Hong Kong over extradition bill," *The South China Morning Post*, June 9, 2019, https://tinyurl.com/y2pmzr65.

[5] "Hong Kong: Carrie Lam withdraws controversial extradition bill," *Deutsche Welle*, Sept. 4, 2019, https://tinyurl.com/y967uqfw.

[6] "How Hong Kong picks its chief executives," *The Economist*, March 21, 2017, https://tinyurl.com/y7fp2723.

[7] Edward Wong *et al.*, "Hong Kong Violence Escalates as Police and Protesters Clash at University," *The New York Times*, Nov. 17, 2019, https://tinyurl.com/voa6lwq.

[8] Keith Bradsher, Austin Ramzy and Tiffany May, "Hong Kong Election Results Give Democracy Backers Big Win," *The New York Times*, Nov. 24, 2019, https://tinyurl.com/qk33gms.

[9] Casey Quackenbush, "Hong Kong democrats score historic victory amid ongoing protests," *Al-Jazeera*, Nov. 24, 2019, https://tinyurl.com/uzr3v9w.

[10] Felix Tam and Clare Jim, "Exclusive: Support for Hong Kong protesters' demands rises even as coronavirus halts rallies: poll," *Reuters*, March 27, 2020, https://tinyurl.com/y87z8vsp.

[11] James Griffiths, "Hong Kong appeared to have the coronavirus under control, then it let its guard down," *CNN*, March 23, 2020, https://tinyurl.com/ws6xhhq.

[12] Helen Davidson, "Hong Kong: with coronavirus curbed, protests may return," *The Guardian*, March 15, 2020, https://tinyurl.com/s664gyy.

[13] Natalie Wong and Tony Cheung, "A new strain of resistance? How the coronavirus crisis is changing Hong Kong's protest movement," *The South China Morning Post*, Feb. 10, 2020, https://tinyurl.com/yddyq8t3.

Parkland Protesters Meld Power of Youth, Social Media

"People are caring a lot more about what young people want."

On Feb. 14, 2018, a gunman killed 17 people at Cameron Kasky's high school. Almost immediately, Kasky, then 17, became one of the leaders of a national movement to end gun violence.

"One Wednesday everything changed," says Kasky. "And by Sunday we were living a completely different life that had a different structure to it."

The shooting at Marjory Stoneman Douglas High School in Parkland, Fla., was neither the first nor the most lethal in a string of recent mass shootings in the United States, but it inspired the largest protests against gun violence nationwide.

Exactly one month after the Parkland shooting, thousands of students across the country walked out of class in a coordinated protest against gun violence. Ten days after that, hundreds of thousands of protesters descended on Washington for the March for Our Lives, which became the name of an organization that continues to organize against gun violence.

"To the leaders, skeptics and cynics who told us to sit down, stay silent and wait your turn, welcome to the revolution," Kasky told the protesters.[1]

David S. Meyer, a professor of sociology and political science at the University of California, Irvine, says it is not unusual for political movements to take off after a push from younger people. And he says the Parkland students were in a kind of sweet spot: young enough so they had no political background that opponents could attack, but old enough to be able to speak for themselves—unlike the students at Sandy Hook Elementary School in Newtown, Conn., where 20 first graders and six staffers died in a 2012 shooting.

In addition, Meyer says, "these kids went to one of the best-funded schools in Florida." Because they were more likely to be children of professionals, they had access to resources that others in their situation might not have had, he says.

Despite his rhetoric at the Washington march, Kasky says he does not want to fan the flames of generational resentment. "It always made me upset when people made things a generational battle," he says.

In the two years that have followed the initial burst of activism, the Parkland activists have compiled a mixed record of achievements. Their demands for new federal gun laws remain unfulfilled, and some movement leaders, such as David Hogg and Kasky, became targets for criticism themselves. Their critics say they ignore the constitutional rights of gun owners and unfairly ascribe illegitimate motives to their opponents.

"The student activists presume that there is a ready solution to mass shootings that everyone knows, and the only reason why someone might not act on this universally accepted policy is malice or corruption," wrote Rich Lowry, editor of *National Review*, a conservative publication.[2]

They have had more success at the state level and in the private sector, and participation by younger voters—one of the organization's goals—has recently increased. In the 2018 midterm elections, turnout among 18-to-29-year-olds surged to almost 36 percent from 20 percent in 2014.[3]

From the start, the young Parkland survivors relied heavily on social media to tell their stories, spread the hashtag #NeverAgain and inspire others to join them.[4]

"The March for Our Lives movement started using social media during the shooting itself," says Errol

King's assassination sparked riots and rebellions in nearly 200 cities across the United States.[42]

Also in 1968, protests against the U.S. war in Vietnam swept the world. That was the year when the number of American troops in Vietnam peaked, and also when American public opinion turned against the war.[43] Tens of thousands of mostly young demonstrators protested the war at the Democratic Party's national convention in Chicago. Violence outside the convention—later termed a "police riot" by the head of an investigating commission—and rancor and confusion within the hall crippled the Democrats and helped Republican nominee Richard Nixon win the presidency in November.[44]

Salamon, a postdoctoral teaching associate in media and popular culture at the University of Minnesota who attended the 2018 Washington march. "And they were using tools on social media that people could identify with."

Salamon says the consistent use of Twitter was essential to the movement's growth. But while the methods of communication may be new, youth activism has been a staple of American politics for decades, he says.

"Young people have long been in protest movements, and this extends back as far as the countercultural movement of the 1960s," Salamon says.

While the Parkland movement did not persuade a Republican-controlled Congress to enact gun laws such as a new assault weapons ban, the movement has had lasting effects in other ways. Several state legislatures have taken up the issue of gun control, passing laws designed to prevent another Parkland.[5]

Florida raised the legal age to purchase a firearm to 21 shortly after the shooting. (The Parkland gunman was 19.)[6] Several states, including Colorado, Nevada and Hawaii, have passed "red flag" laws, which allow police or family members to petition a state court to temporarily remove firearms from someone who may pose a danger to themselves or others.[7]

Kasky says federal action is still needed to prevent potential perpetrators of gun violence from buying weapons in other states. "We can pass strong gun laws in one state, but there are always going to be people taking advantage of that," he says.

Despite the lack of new federal legislation, Kasky says the movement and its message have motivated some businesses to take action in order to appear socially responsible in the eyes of younger consumers. "People are caring a lot more about what young people want and what young people have to say," Kasky says.

One company that changed its policy was Dick's Sporting Goods, which stopped selling the type of semi-automatic rifle used in the Parkland shooting and raised the age required to purchase any firearm at its stores to 21. The chain's CEO, Ed Stack, said he was personally moved by the Parkland tragedy and the young survivors' response.[8]

But it may be hard to maintain momentum during the coronavirus pandemic. In the current era of social distancing, in-person protests may be dangerous, frowned upon or even illegal.

Parkland survivors believe their movement can adjust, because many activists have been sharing their message on social media for years. "It's very much online already right now," Kasky says.

Yet while the movement may have spread on Twitter early on, Salamon says it is unlikely it would have gotten so far without a physical presence. "It could not have just been a hashtag movement," he says. "People needed to be there in person."

—*Brock Hall*

---

[1] Ray Sanchez, "Student marchers call Washington's inaction on gun violence unacceptable," *CNN*, March 23, 2018, https://tinyurl.com/y8qrjf8s.

[2] Rich Lowry, "The Teenage Demagogues," *National Review*, March 27, 2018, https://tinyurl.com/y8vj7adv.

[3] Tara Golshan, "Young people, women, voters in cities: how Democrats won in 2018, by the numbers," *Vox*, April 26, 2019, https://tinyurl.com/y6yxz8k4.

[4] "Timeline: How the #NeverAgain Movement Gained Momentum After Parkland," *NBC Philadelphia*, Feb. 14, 2019, https://tinyurl.com/y9gza2u8.

[5] Rep. David N. Cicilline, "H.R. 5087—Assault Weapons Ban of 2018," Congress.gov, Feb. 26, 2018, https://tinyurl.com/ydcl9uv3; Steven Melendez, "Here's a list of gun control laws passed since the Parkland shooting," *Fast Company*, Feb. 14, 2019, https://tinyurl.com/y83juh79.

[6] Patricia Mazzei, "Florida Governor Signs Gun Limits Into Law, Breaking With the N.R.A.," *The New York Times*, March 9, 2018, https://tinyurl.com/ybu7f4mu.

[7] Jonathan Levinson and Lisa Dunn, "What is a Red Flag Law?" *WAMU*, Aug. 5, 2019, https://tinyurl.com/y8vsh6jg.

[8] Alina Selyukh, "Soul-Searching After Parkland, Dick's CEO Embraces Tougher Stance On Guns," *NPR*, Feb. 12, 2019, https://tinyurl.com/ybo8fv8s.

Other events led some observers to compare 1968 to 1848 in the global sweep of the protests:

- In May, much of France shut down as tens of thousands of students, later joined by millions of workers, protested capitalism, consumerism and the Vietnam War.[45]

- Soviet troops invaded Czechoslovakia in August to end the Prague Spring, the government reforms instituted by Czech leader Alexander Dubček. Thousands of Czechs protested, but the Soviet military prevailed.[46]

- That summer, inspired in part by the French protests and the anti-Vietnam War demonstrations, students in Mexico City protested for greater freedom. At a rally on Oct. 2, just days before Mexico hosted the Summer Olympics, soldiers fired into a crowd of thousands of students. Dozens died; the actual number killed is still in dispute. The protests and the violent reaction of the authorities are often cited as a key moment in the development of Mexican democracy.[47]

A Democratic Moment

By the late 1980s, two decades after the Soviet crackdown in Prague, demands for political change were again rising within the communist world. This hunger for democratic reforms underpinned two major events in 1989.

In China, pressure was building for greater freedoms and an end to government corruption. That spring, protesters began gathering in Beijing's Tiananmen Square—perhaps as many as 1 million at one point. After weeks of internal Communist Party debate about how to handle the protests, the Chinese military forcibly cleared the square with tanks and troops. The government estimated the death toll at 200 civilians and several dozen security personnel; other casualty estimates ranged as high as 10,000.[48] The Tiananmen Square events failed to democratize China, and they remain a sensitive issue for the authorities to this day—government internet censors still block content related to the protest.[49]

Also in 1989, Soviet leader Mikhail Gorbachev, who had come to power four years earlier pledging greater openness, began loosening Moscow's control over its Eastern European satellites. Seeing an opportunity for independence, trade unions in Poland negotiated free elections. In November, after months of protests in Soviet-dominated East Germany, the wall separating communist East Berlin from democratic West Berlin was breached; Czechoslovakia overthrew its pro-Moscow government and, in the coming months, other Soviet allies broke away. In December 1991, the Soviet Union itself ceased to exist and its constituent states became independent.

Arab Spring and Grassroots Protests

In December 2010, police forbade a 26-year-old Tunisian street vendor to sell his produce because he had no official permit. Unable to make a living, the man, Mohamed Bouazizi, publicly immolated himself. Sympathy demonstrations evolved into nationwide anti-government protests that toppled the regime of longtime President Zine el-Abidine Ben Ali. It marked the start of the Arab Spring, a wave of pro-democracy demonstrations around the Middle East.[50]

When the Arab Spring ended, Tunisia's rebellion was the only clear success. Although the protests also brought about the downfall of leaders in Egypt and Libya, their successors proved no more democratic. Protests led to bloody civil wars in Libya, Syria and Yemen.[51] The Arab Spring showed the power of social media to communicate, organize and mobilize, but also its limits in sustaining a movement.[52]

In 2007 a financial crisis brought about by risky practices by U.S. financial institutions spawned a global recession that lasted until 2009, the deepest slump since the Great Depression of the 1930s. In the United States, a plummeting stock market, mortgage foreclosures and widespread unemployment contributed to the rise of populist movements on both the left and right in opposition to the political elite.[53]

In 2009 fiscally conservative Americans formed the Tea Party movement. Rallies in many states voiced opposition to what participants called big government and wasteful economic policies. In the 2010 midterm elections, the Tea Party helped end Democratic control of the House of Representatives and pushed the Republican Party further to the right, widening political polarization, fostering distrust of the federal government and helping to enable Donald Trump's election as president in 2016.[54]

On the left side of the spectrum, on Sept. 17, 2011, hundreds of demonstrators marched into a small park in New York City to protest what they called corporate greed and economic inequality. The Occupy Wall Street movement spread to other cities across the United States; it also had a presence in Canada, Europe, Australia and elsewhere. While it did not produce major structural changes, it made economic and social equality a part of the national political debate and helped fuel support for the 2016 and 2020 presidential campaigns of Sen. Bernie Sanders of Vermont, a self-described democratic socialist.[55]

Other grassroots protest movements arose in the United States during and after the presidency of

Democrat Barack Obama, who served from 2009 to 2017. The Black Lives Matter movement was founded in 2013 in response to the acquittal of George Zimmerman, a white man accused of killing Trayvon Martin, a 17-year-old African American who Zimmerman said was acting suspiciously.[56] By publicizing shootings of unarmed blacks by white police officers, the movement has "forced [America] to confront its deep-rooted problems with race and inequality," said a World Economic Forum report.[57]

Trump's 2016 election angered many who were upset by what they regarded as his demeaning attitude toward women.[58] A Women's March on Jan. 21, 2017, the day after Trump's inauguration, drew hundreds of thousands of protesters to Washington and large crowds to events in other cities.[59] Subsequent annual rallies were held, although the number of participants steadily declined.[60] However, the movement is credited with encouraging women to run for political office; a record 117 women were elected to Congress in 2018.[61]

Frightened and angered by shootings in U.S. schools and frustrated by the lack of legislative action to prevent them, students began to protest. The March For Our Lives movement was started by students at Marjory Stoneman Douglas High School in Parkland, Fla., who were galvanized into action after a gunman walked into their school on Feb. 14, 2018, and killed 17 classmates and faculty members. The organization tries to maintain public attention through group protests and student walkouts.[62] (*See Short Feature.*)

Gun owners and enthusiasts also have taken a stand. The National Rifle Association (NRA) and other gun-rights groups have lobbied with considerable success against state and federal legislation that would restrict and regulate gun ownership.[63] After Virginia's state elections in 2019 gave control of the Legislature to Democrats, and lawmakers then proceeded to enact stricter gun laws, a large crowd of pro-gun-rights protesters gathered at the state Capitol in Richmond on Jan. 20, 2020. The demonstration was peaceful.[64]

CURRENT SITUATION
Coronavirus Impact

The wave of protests in 2019 had been expected to continue and even expand as protesters dug in, and new movements formed, to press demands for government action on corruption, economic reform and other issues.

But the emergence of the coronavirus altered the landscape. While government responses to protesters' demands have blunted some protests and refocused others, public fear of the coronavirus and strictures imposed by governments as disease preventative measures have led to a decline in protesters' participation and enthusiasm.

In the Middle East, during what the Carnegie Endowment's Middle East expert Michele Dunne calls "the second wave of the Arab Spring," pro-democracy protests in 2019 toppled longtime dictators Abdelaziz Bouteflika in Algeria and Bashir in Sudan and forced the resignations of prime ministers Hariri of Lebanon and Adel Abdul-Mahdi in Iraq.

Despite these apparent successes, demonstrations continued because "the sense lingers of a job left unfinished," said Bobby Ghosh, former editor of New Delhi's *Hindustan Times*, who writes about the Middle East. "The political systems in all four countries remain largely intact, in the hands of the elites that enabled the misrule protesters were hoping to end."[65]

But in March, amid the threat of the coronavirus and strictly enforced government restrictions on public gatherings, the protests in the Middle East were largely suspended. Algerians ended their string of Friday protests after 56 consecutive weeks.[66]

On March 10, 2020, Lebanese protesters formed a human chain around the Palace of Justice in the capital of Beirut, but they wore masks and gloves and kept a distance from one another. On March 21, 2020, the government ordered security services to enforce social distancing and stay-at-home measures and to "prevent gatherings."[67] Since then, virtual outreach has replaced physical demonstrations: Activists livestream information sessions, stage social media campaigns and solicit funds.

Protests in other regions also were affected by the coronavirus. In Chile, protests over economic inequities, which ebbed at the end of 2019, resumed in early March, only to be dampened weeks later by the pandemic. "Plaza Dignidad, a place that has been the point of congregation for daily protests in Santiago since October 19th, is now completely empty," says Schaeffer Quintero in Santiago.

On March 15, 2020, President Sebastián Piñera declared a 90-day "state of catastrophe," giving the govern-

AT ISSUE

Is violence an effective tool for protest?

YES **Benjamin Ginsberg**
David Bernstein Professor of Political Science, Johns Hopkins University

Written for *CQ Researcher*, May 2020

Violence is the driving force of politics. The importance of violence derives from the dominance it usually manifests over other forms of political action, from its destructive and politically transformative power and from the capacity of violence to serve as an instrument of political mobilization. These three factors explain why Chinese leader Mao Zedong was correct in his assertion that political power emanated from the gun barrel.

Political forces willing and able to employ violence to achieve their goals will generally best their less bellicose adversaries, overturning the results of elections, negating the actions of parliamentary bodies and riding roughshod over peaceful expressions of political opinion. Indeed, the mere threat of violence is often enough to instill fear in, and compel acquiescence by, those unwilling or unable to forcefully defend themselves. Violent groups can usually be defeated only by adversaries able to block their use of mayhem or to employ superior force against them. Those who cannot or will not make use of violence seldom achieve their goals over the opposition of those who are not similarly constrained. As Machiavelli observed, things have seldom turned out well for unarmed prophets.

Much attention, of course, is given to the putative effectiveness of nonviolence as a political method. In actuality, though, far from being nonviolent, the protest tactics—strikes, boycotts, demonstrations and the like—employed by such leaders as Mahatma Gandhi and Dr. Martin Luther King were designed to produce economic and social disruption and, in some instances, to actually provoke violent responses from their opponents. Violent attacks on apparently peaceful protesters would, it was hoped, elicit sympathy for the innocent victims of bloodshed and perhaps encourage powerful external forces to intervene on their behalf. Their success was predicated upon the availability of allies who could be drawn into the fray.

In the United States, nationally televised images of the violence unleashed upon peaceful protesters generated enormous sympathy for the civil rights cause and helped create the setting for enactment of the 1965 Voting Rights Act, which sent an army of federal law enforcement officials into the South with the power to suppress white resistance to the registration of black voters. In essence, nominally nonviolent protest succeeded because the protesters' allies had an even greater capacity for violence than their foes. Where, as in the case of China's Tiananmen Square in 1989, powerful allies are not available to deploy or at least threaten the use of force, nonviolent protest is almost always doomed to failure.

NO **Jonathan Pinckney**
Program on Nonviolent Action, U.S. Institute of Peace

Written for *CQ Researcher*, May 2020

To answer whether violence is an effective tool for protest, one needs to first ask how protest works. Public protests are only one of a broad set of tactics employed by social movements such as strikes or boycotts. Protest is effective when it is strategically deployed alongside these additional tactics to undermine an opponent's power by prompting defections from their supporters. This defection process varies. A movement against a polluting company, for instance, might convince investors to divest, or customers to boycott. A pro-democracy movement might convince security forces to disobey orders to violently crack down.

Does violence help this process? While the impact of violence varies across cases, on average there are strong reasons to believe that it cannot.

First, violence tends to increase and legitimize government repression. Violent protests face much higher levels of government violence in response. While violent government repression of nonviolent protesters may spark backlash and condemnation, government repression of violent protesters is more likely to be seen as legitimate. Governments more easily paint violent protests as dangerous to social order and worthy of state violence in return. This tends to demobilize movements, leading to lower effectiveness.

Second, violence reduces who can reasonably participate in protests and other social movement tactics. Protest violence is overwhelmingly the province of young men, and when movements turn to violence their size and diversity tend to drop precipitously. This further undermines the protesters' legitimacy, as well as their potential points of connection with regime supporters. Without these points of connection, inducing defection among the opponent's supporters becomes more difficult.

Third, on average violence undermines mobilization of and external support for a movement. Numerous studies in political science and social psychology have shown that when movements use more violence, observers become less sympathetic and less likely to join or support them. This mobilization disadvantage is likely to undermine movements' attempts to achieve their goals.

There are certainly exceptions to these general trends. Some studies indicate that large social movements may have sufficient momentum that they are unaffected by peripheral incidents of violence. And in some specific cases, violence may have a highlighting effect, drawing attention to otherwise neglected causes. But when looking at movements as a whole, there are few good reasons to believe that violence is an effective tool, and many good reasons to believe that it directly undermines movements' effectiveness.

ment powers to restrict freedom of movement and secure supply lines for food and medical supplies.[68] The government also postponed for six months the scheduled April 26, 2020, referendum on whether to write a new constitution—a key protester demand—because of the virus.[69]

In Bolivia, elections to choose the successor to Morales had been scheduled for May 3, 2020, but the government postponed them, citing coronavirus concerns. The Bolivian electoral tribunal has proposed new dates between June 7 and Sept. 6.[70]

In Hong Kong, protests waned after the coronavirus arrived in the city. Organizers are exploring alternate ways of pressuring the government for change. (*See Short Feature.*) However, protesters began to defy the government's pandemic-related ban on public gatherings of more than four people. On April 24, 2020, 100 pro-democracy activists demonstrated at a Hong Kong shopping mall; on April 26, 300 demonstrators targeted another mall.[71]

Yellow vest protesters in France—which is among the nations hit hardest by the coronavirus—defied a government public health ban on gatherings of more than 100 people to demonstrate on March 14, 2020, the eve of local elections.[72] Prime Minister Edouard Philippe banned yellow vest protests on the Champs-Élysées in central Paris and in two other cities after 18 weeks of violent demonstrations.[73]

Lebanese activists suspect their government is using the virus as an excuse to suppress dissent. They say the emergency measures enacted March 15, 2020, that mandated stay-at-home restrictions and closed offices and businesses failed to include basic practices to safeguard public health.

"The government activated criminal laws to arrest and charge people [but] did not stop flights from [coronavirus] epicenters like Iran and ignored taking necessary measures to protect the people," said activist Jad Yateem.[74] The government eventually stopped airline flights from Iran, some three weeks after Lebanon's first reported coronavirus victim—who had returned from Iran.[75]

Global Climate Campaign

The coronavirus also has affected the global movement to fight climate change undertaken by Swedish teenager Thunberg. The Fridays for Future (FFF) movement she inspired, in which students took Fridays off from school to agitate for cutting greenhouse gas emissions, had drawn millions of protesters to demonstrate in cities around the world.

But the pandemic has closed schools and driven the campaign indoors, robbing it of publicity, draining its influence and forcing its leaders to change tactics. FFF in many countries has suspended public demonstrations, instead using social media and the internet to get its message out.[76] On March 13, 2020, Thunberg, who said she believed she had the virus, tweeted, "In a crisis we change our behaviour and adapt to the new circumstances for the greater good of society."[77]

With public demonstrations off the table in most countries, a coalition of environmental organizations held a three-day continuous livestream "mobilization to stop the climate emergency" called Earth Day Live, April 22-24, 2020. The event included teach-ins, musical performances and a voter registration drive for U.S. audiences. The Future Coalition, an organizer of Earth Day Live, said 2.75 million people viewed the event.[78]

One online tactic is the "digital strike," in which activists post a picture of themselves and a sign bearing a slogan on social media. Joe Hobbs, 17, a student and FFF-United States activist from Columbia, Md., says, "Before [the virus struck] we would have physical strikes—protesting at the White House or the Capitol or the Library of Congress—once a month, and once a week we'd strike digitally, on social media. Now, we're going for all-digital strikes."

A student in Davos, Switzerland, participates in a January 2020 school strike demanding action against climate change. Inspired by teenage Swedish activist Greta Thunberg, students around the world have joined climate demonstrations.

Dana Fisher, a professor of sociology at the University of Maryland who researches activism, said social media campaigns "end up . . . amplifying within an echo chamber, which is really different from what the movement wants." Twitter hashtags do not get the visibility and publicity that large public demonstrations do, she said. However, she acknowledged that the young climate-change protesters are skilled at using social media to advance their cause.[79]

Hobbs says that "a digital strike, like a physical strike, raises awareness among your followers and anyone else who sees it." He says, "A lot of people thought that, because of the coronavirus, our numbers [of supporters] would go down, but actually they've gone up—more people are staying at home and able to interact with us online."

But online protests have drawbacks. Akshaya Kumar, director of crisis advocacy at Human Rights Watch, sees "a huge issue with . . . the digital divide—questions about who's able to get online and the bandwidth limitations for people based on their economic situation." She added, "It's certainly not as [accessible] as participating in a street protest, which is available to people regardless of their socioeconomic status."[80]

The coronavirus has had profound effects on the global economy. Stock market values have plunged, as have industrial production and retail sales, and unemployment has soared. The disease and governments' attempts to combat it have themselves become the target of protesters as the desire to slow the rate of infection conflicts with citizens' fears that the economic slowdown will leave them unable to make a living.[81] In Kenya, police killed 12 people while enforcing a dusk-to-dawn curfew that began March 27, 2020—more than the 11 that had been officially reported killed by the virus itself as of April 16.[82]

In the United States, hundreds protested in state capitals against stay-at-home measures and other safeguards imposed by governors, arguing the restrictions were no longer necessary and infringed on constitutional liberties. President Trump had declared the preventative measures to be the province of the state governors rather than the federal government, but he also encouraged the protests by criticizing governors for obstructing the nation's economic recovery, saying they've "gone too far." Targeted governors responded that they lacked the data that would justify relaxing the measures.[83] *The Washington Post* reported that the state protests, though appearing spontaneous, had actually been orchestrated in a Facebook campaign by far-right activists.[84]

Between mid-March and mid-April, 2020, more than 22 million Americans filed for unemployment benefits, a record number.[85] As of April 25, the U.S. Centers for Disease Control and Prevention was reporting 928,619 coronavirus cases, with 52,459 deaths from the disease.[86]

Foreign Protests and U.S. Policy

Trump won the gratitude of the Hong Kong protesters when he signed legislation allowing the United States to levy sanctions on those who violate human rights in the city. Protesters draped themselves in American flags and waved pro-Trump banners in demonstrations celebrating the president's Nov. 27, 2019, signing of the Hong Kong Human Rights and Democracy Act, which also requires the State Department to conduct an annual review of Hong Kong's special trade status.[87]

The Chinese Foreign Ministry called the law "a severe interference in Hong Kong affairs, which are China's internal affairs. It is also in serious violation of international law and basic norms governing international relations."[88]

Another new law forbids U.S. companies to sell rubber bullets, pepper spray, tear gas and other crowd management munitions to Hong Kong police.[89]

Trump also inserted himself into Iran's January 2020 protests over the downing of a Ukrainian airliner when, in a series of tweets, he expressed solidarity with the demonstrators and warned the government, "DO NOT KILL YOUR PROTESTERS."[90] In response, Iranian Supreme Leader Ali Khamenei tweeted, "The villainous US [government] repeatedly says that they are standing by the Iranian [people]. They lie. If you are standing by the Iranian [people], it is only to stab them in the heart with your venomous daggers."[91]

Joseph Nye, former dean of Harvard's Kennedy School of Government and former chair of the U.S. National Intelligence Council, which provides long-term strategic analysis to government officials, says supporting protests in other countries "is useful if it's in the context of a general advancement or protection of human rights. But if it's seen as a weapon used against some countries but turning a blind eye to similar events in other countries, then it's viewed as hypocrisy."

"If President Trump wants to defend protesters in Iran, he has to reconcile that with his excusing the dismemberment of [Jamal] Khashoggi in the Saudi Arabian consulate in Istanbul," Nye says, referring to the Saudi dissident and *Washington Post* columnist who was murdered there. "Those responses don't fit together very well."

Frantz of Michigan State University says, "Both mainland China and the Iranian regime are very adept at putting forth the narrative that the U.S. is an agent provocateur. In some ways any U.S. involvement is just fodder for these regimes to put out this propaganda and help them withstand the [protesters'] challenge. If the U.S. is not willing to put up the resources to back up its words, it's empty rhetoric."

OUTLOOK
Democracy in Peril?

As the coronavirus spreads rapidly around the world, governments have imposed strict social distancing requirements and limitations on public gatherings to mitigate the impact of the virus and protect public health. But some protesters and civil liberties advocates fear governments might also use the new laws to suppress dissent and that autocratic leaders could assume dictatorial powers that do not expire when the virus threat subsides.

"The pandemic may well lead to a serious decline in democracy around the world," said Florian Bieber, professor of Southeast European history and politics at the University of Graz in Austria.

"Emergency laws or declared states of emergency [are] a tactic autocrats can use to consolidate power," Bieber said. He acknowledged that restricting gatherings and postponing elections are valid public health practices, noting that "French municipal elections held on March 15 might have accelerated the spread of the coronavirus." But he added: "Postponing elections for months might deprive governments of their legitimacy and allow autocrats to" strengthen their power.[92]

Democracy experts Crothers and David Wong of the Carnegie Endowment for International Peace wrote that "some governments are capitalizing on the crisis to enhance their ability to quash protest." But despite this challenge, they said, "the global protest wave is by no means moribund. Government responses to the virus have already sparked a spate of new protests. Prisoners in Lebanon and Italy have rioted over unsanitary conditions and overcrowding, and Brazilian and Colombian citizens have banged pots and pans from their windows to protest their leaders' public health response."

Moreover, they said, "the unfolding economic devastation resulting from the virus and the governance crises it has triggered may also sow the seeds for future protests. By exposing governments' incompetence in key areas such as public health and socioeconomic justice, the global pandemic could reinvigorate existing protests or even ignite demonstrations in new contexts."[93]

Hong Kong may be a case study for the theory. While the coronavirus has stalled public protests, a survey by the independent Hong Kong Public Opinion Research Institute found that three-quarters of Hong Kong residents believe the city did not do enough to stop the illness.[94] "The handling of the crisis by the government has been extremely poor," said activist Nathan Law. "[P]ublic anger is still growing and . . . the movement will revive when the outbreak is ended."[95]

Dunne of Carnegie believes many more protests are in store for the Middle East, too. "The whole economic structure of the region is crumbling," she says. "World energy markets are changing. There's a lot of oil and gas in the region, but it's not worth what it was."

Yet as the region's economic situation worsens, its population is growing and its people are increasingly aware of inequality, Dunne says. "I would say virtually every country in the region is vulnerable."

Stephan of the U.S. Institute of Peace says the future for peaceful protest movements is cloudy. "It's very disconcerting when considering the future of nonviolent movements," she says. "My worst fear is that we will see a strengthening of authoritarianism and a backsliding of democracies around the world."

But, she adds, "My optimistic side says people know how to organize and push back, and they can learn from each other. There's a competition going on between democracy and authoritarianism, and it remains to be seen who prevails."

NOTES

1. Samuel J. Brannen, Christian S. Haig and Katherine Schmidt, "The Age of Mass Protests: Understanding

an Escalating Global Trend," Center for Strategic and International Studies, March 2020, https://tinyurl.com/wgceft8.

2. Richard Youngs, ed., "After Protest: Pathways Beyond Mass Mobilization," Carnegie Europe, Oct. 24, 2019, https://tinyurl.com/y938awr4.

3. Jonathan Pinckney and Miranda Rivers, "Nonviolent Action in the Time of Coronavirus," U.S. Institute of Peace, March 25, 2020, https://tinyurl.com/y93qxzdo.

4. Selam Gebrekidan, "For Autocrats, and Others, Coronavirus Is a Chance to Grab Even More Power," *The New York Times*, March 30, 2020, https://tinyurl.com/yd4xfrp9.

5. James McAuley, "'Yellow vest' anniversary: What happened to the movement that shook France?" *The Washington Post*, Nov. 16, 2019, https://tinyurl.com/u8599be.

6. Tara John, "Why Hong Kong is protesting: Their five demands listed," *CNN*, Aug. 30, 2019, https://tinyurl.com/y2prgjze.

7. Brian C.H. Fong, "Where Does Hong Kong's Protest Movement Stand Amid Coronavirus Fears?" *The Diplomat*, Feb. 24, 2020, https://tinyurl.com/ycgyjud2.

8. Lucien Chauvin and Anthony Faiola, "As the U.S.-backed government in Bolivia unleashes a wave of political persecution, the Trump administration remains silent," *The Washington Post*, March 6, 2020, https://tinyurl.com/yarmjdfj.

9. Charis McGowan, "Chile protests: What prompted the unrest?" *Al-Jazeera*, Oct. 30, 2019, https://tinyurl.com/yypf9obg.

10. "Violence resurgence in Chile: three deaths, looting and torched supermarkets," *MercoPress*, Feb. 1, 2020, https://tinyurl.com/ycprltzp.

11. J. Patrice McSherry, "Chile's Struggle to Democratize the State," North American Congress on Latin America, Feb. 24, 2020, https://tinyurl.com/yb6fvokz.

12. Andy Gregory, "'They are killing us slowly': Iranian security forces used 'unlawful force against plane protesters,'" *The Independent*, Jan. 15, 2020, https://tinyurl.com/ycstf6s7.

13. Michael Safi *et al.*, "Protests rage around the world—but what comes next?" *The Guardian*, Oct. 25, 2019, https://tinyurl.com/yxjdm74k.

14. "Iran: Death toll from bloody crackdown on protests rises to 208," Amnesty International, Dec. 2, 2019, https://tinyurl.com/y7pbyakj.

15. "Iran 2019 Human Rights Report," U.S. Department of State, March 2020, https://tinyurl.com/ya6u7mb7.

16. Kai Thaler, "Violence Is Sometimes the Answer," *Foreign Policy*, Dec. 5, 2019, https://tinyurl.com/ya7xpcsb.

17. Shola Lawal, "Coronavirus Halts Street Protests, but Climate Activists Have a Plan," *The New York Times*, March 19, 2020, https://tinyurl.com/r4nm8bv.

18. "Femicide: A global scourge," *Agence France-Presse*, Nov. 19, 2019, https://tinyurl.com/yaoo75bc.

19. Sarah Repucci, "A Leaderless Struggle for Democracy," Freedom House, 2020, https://tinyurl.com/qwh9ek8.

20. Richard Wike and Shannon Schumacher, "Democratic Rights Popular Globally but Commitment to Them Not Always Strong," Pew Research Center, Feb. 27, 2020, https://tinyurl.com/y9yjlhm4.

21. R.S. Foa *et al.*, "The Global Satisfaction with Democracy Report 2020," University of Cambridge, January 2020, https://tinyurl.com/vcof6j3.

22. Robin Wright, "The Story of 2019: Protests in Every Corner of the Globe," *The New Yorker*, Dec. 30, 2019, https://tinyurl.com/v5ptgme.

23. Danna Takriti, "Sudan just took a step backward on its path to democracy," *Vox*, Feb. 21, 2020, https://tinyurl.com/yadm8sok.

24. Youngs, *op. cit.*

25. *Ibid.*

26. Paul Blumenthal, "The Largest Protest Ever Was 15 Years Ago. The Iraq War Isn't Over. What Happened?" *Huffpost*, March 17, 2018, https://tinyurl.com/y89as2hj.

27. Kim Milone, "The English Peasants' Revolt of 1381," *Loyola University Student Historical Journal 1986-87*, https://tinyurl.com/y9wx6azz.

28. Tara Isabella Burton, "The Protestant Reformation, explained," *Vox*, Nov. 2, 2017, https://tinyurl.com/y742lygk.
29. "The Reformation," History.com, https://tinyurl.com/yb9pk6xq.
30. Robert Longley, "The Road to the American Revolution," ThoughtCo., Jan. 14, 2019, https://tinyurl.com/ybbx62xv.
31. "French Revolution," History.com, Feb. 21, 2020, https://tinyurl.com/ybvhnauh.
32. "Revolutions of 1848," *Encyclopedia Britannica*, Jan. 20, 2019, https://tinyurl.com/y5ctwqkl.
33. "William II: King of the Netherlands," *Encyclopedia Britannica*, March 13, 2020, https://tinyurl.com/y7bcb5zt.
34. Erin Blakemore, "How Mahatma Gandhi changed political protest," *National Geographic*, Sept. 27, 2019, https://tinyurl.com/y6rp2hae.
35. "Malcolm X's Speech at the Founding Rally of the Organization of Afro-American Unity," *Blackpast*, Oct. 15, 2007, https://tinyurl.com/y7d5j3gu.
36. John Leland, "Who Really Killed Malcolm X?" *The New York Times*, Feb. 6, 2020, https://tinyurl.com/ychcls9q.
37. "The Black Panther Party," National Archives, https://tinyurl.com/r963yzu.
38. "Transcript of Civil Rights Act (1964)," National Archives, https://tinyurl.com/s5yev7x.
39. "Transcript of Voting Rights Act (1965)," National Archives, https://tinyurl.com/ycmpcm3t.
40. "Fair Housing Act," U.S. Department of Justice, https://tinyurl.com/y72pxabo.
41. "The Assassination of Martin Luther King, Jr.," Stanford University, https://tinyurl.com/yawhf47c.
42. Lorraine Boissoneault, "Martin Luther King Jr.'s Assassination Sparked Uprisings in Cities Across America," *Smithsonian Magazine*, April 4, 2018, https://tinyurl.com/yawab8aa.
43. Daniel S. Levy, "Behind the Anti-War Protests That Swept America in 1968," *Time*, Jan. 19, 2018, https://tinyurl.com/y9ycgrsw.
44. Joel Achenbach, "'A party that had lost its mind': In 1968, Democrats held one of history's most disastrous conventions," *The Washington Post*, Aug. 24, 2018, https://tinyurl.com/y7h6s584.
45. Alissa J. Rubin, "May 1968: A Month of Revolution Pushed France Into the Modern World," *The New York Times*, May 5, 2018, https://tinyurl.com/y7j7onro.
46. Robert Tait, "Prague 1968: lost images of the day that freedom died," *The Guardian*, Aug. 19, 2018, https://tinyurl.com/y4vplqzk.
47. Elizabeth Malkin, "50 Years After a Student Massacre, Mexico Reflects on Democracy," *The New York Times*, Oct. 1, 2018, https://tinyurl.com/y78w7gen.
48. "Tiananmen Square: What happened in the protests of 1989?" *BBC*, June 4, 2019, https://tinyurl.com/y8ujo2fr.
49. Cate Cadell, "China's internet censors are on high alert ahead of the anniversary of the Tiananmen Square protests," *Reuters, Business Insider*, May 26, 2019, https://tinyurl.com/y9h4oz7e.
50. "The Arab Spring: A Year Of Revolution," *National Public Radio*, Dec. 17, 2011, https://tinyurl.com/ybxw7ggh.
51. Erin Blakemore, "What was the Arab Spring and how did it spread?" *National Geographic*, March 29, 2019, https://tinyurl.com/yy4ae9eh.
52. Jessi Hempel, "Social Media Made the Arab Spring, But Couldn't Save It," *Wired*, Jan. 26, 2016, https://tinyurl.com/yag4o99f.
53. Gautam Mukunda, "The Social and Political Costs of the Financial Crisis, 10 Years Later," *Harvard Business Review*, Sept. 25, 2018, https://tinyurl.com/y7n5ykzj.
54. Jeremy W. Peters, "The Tea Party Didn't Get What It Wanted, but It Did Unleash the Politics of Anger," *The New York Times*, Aug. 28, 2019, https://tinyurl.com/y2gfhafq.
55. Megan Leonhardt, "The Lasting Effects of Occupy Wall Street, Five Years Later," *Money*, Sept. 16, 2016, https://tinyurl.com/y8pn4p7y; Emily Stewart, "We are (still) the 99 percent," *Vox*, April 30, 2019, https://tinyurl.com/y4qk58wz.

56. "Herstory," Black Lives Matter, https://tinyurl.com/t7r4x8b.

57. Alem Tedeneke, "The Black Lives Matter movement explained," World Economic Forum, Aug. 11, 2016, https://tinyurl.com/y42dadhu.

58. Ritu Prasad, "How Trump talks about women—and does it matter?" BBC, Nov. 29, 2019, https://tinyurl.com/s2rzvrh.

59. Anemona Hartocollis and Yamiche Alcindor, "Women's March Highlights as Huge Crowds Protest Trump: 'We're Not Going Away,'" The New York Times, Jan. 21, 2017, https://tinyurl.com/jb5ouxu.

60. Austa Somvichian-Clausen, "After low attendance, is the Women's March still relevant?" The Hill, Jan. 22, 2020, https://tinyurl.com/yah6o7fe.

61. Li Zhou, "A historic new Congress will be sworn in today," Vox, Jan. 3, 2019, https://tinyurl.com/yc3a56sr.

62. "We Want Change!" March for our Lives, https://tinyurl.com/yaz2fsxa.

63. Dominic Rushe, "Why is the National Rifle Association so powerful?" The Guardian, May 4, 2018, https://tinyurl.com/y7bxcd4o.

64. Alan Suderman and Sarah Rankin, "Pro-gun Rally by Thousands in Virginia Ends Peacefully," The Associated Press, Jan. 20, 2020, https://tinyurl.com/ueg4zp3.

65. Bobby Ghosh, "Coronavirus blunts momentum of second Arab Spring," The Eagle, March 27, 2020, https://tinyurl.com/y8y4ffuk.

66. "Coronavirus: Algeria protests called off for first time in a year," BBC, March 20, 2020, https://tinyurl.com/yc6eyeht.

67. "Lebanon calls in army to enforce coronavirus lockdown," Agence France-Presse, March 3, 2020, https://tinyurl.com/ycu7sht2.

68. Dave Sherwood, "Chile's Pinera Declares 90-Day State of Catastrophe Over Coronavirus Outbreak," Reuters, March 18, 2020, https://tinyurl.com/y7pabzpt.

69. Charis McGowan, "Chile moves to postpone constitutional referendum amid coronavirus crisis," The Guardian, March 19, 2020, https://tinyurl.com/u2v9oak.

70. Sergio Limachi, "Bolivia election body proposes June-to-September window for coronavirus-delayed vote," Reuters, March 26, 2020, https://tinyurl.com/yc35rjcf.

71. Julia Fioretti and Iain Marlow, "Hong Kong Police Disperse Protesters Gathered at City Mall," Bloomberg, April 26, 2020, https://tinyurl.com/y957oph6.

72. John Irish and Marine Pennetier, "Teargas, clashes in Paris as Yellow Vests' protesters defy coronavirus ban," Reuters, March 14, 2020, https://tinyurl.com/sef5dul.

73. Victoria Albert, "France's Prime Minister Edouard Philippe Bans Yellow Vest Protests After Saturday Riots," The Daily Beast, March 18, 2019, https://tinyurl.com/yaeqcgxf.

74. Nisan Ahmado, "Lebanese Activists Fear Hezbollah-led Government Is Using Coronavirus to Solidify Power," Voice of America, March 30, 2020, https://tinyurl.com/y8638ocw.

75. "Hezbollah Shifts Attention From Syria Fight to Battle Virus," The Associated Press, March 30, 2020, https://tinyurl.com/yd22f6my.

76. Paul Hockenos, "Shifting Gears: The Climate Protest Movement in the Age of Coronavirus," Yale Environment 360, March 26, 2020, https://tinyurl.com/yc8xe85e.

77. Greta Thunberg, Twitter post, March 20, 2020, https://tinyurl.com/ydfdpup4.

78. "Earth Day Live," https://tinyurl.com/ydbpdf4c; Anna Belle Peevey, "Video: Covid-19 Drives Earth Day Anniversary Online, Inspiring Creative New Tactics For Climate Activists," Inside Climate News, April 26, 2020, https://tinyurl.com/y9eje4s5.

79. Lawal, op. cit.

80. Max de Haldevang, "Coronavirus has crippled global protest movements," Quartz, April 1, 2020, https://tinyurl.com/y86rfg7e.

81. Liz Sly, "Stirrings of unrest around the world could portend turmoil as economies collapse," The Washington Post, April 19, 2020, https://tinyurl.com/yay7vnab.

82. Rael Ombuor and Max Bearak, "'Killing in the name of corona': Death toll soars from Kenya's curfew crackdown," *The Washington Post*, April 16, 2020, https://tinyurl.com/yccp6kg2.
83. Brett Samuels, "Trump: Some governors have gone too far on coronavirus restrictions," *The Hill*, April 19, 2020, https://tinyurl.com/y8ct9py9.
84. Isaac Stanley-Becker and Tony Romm, "Pro-gun activists using Facebook groups to push anti-quarantine protests," *The Washington Post*, April 19, 2020, https://tinyurl.com/yahe9k6h.
85. Heather Long, "U.S. now has 22 million unemployed, wiping out a decade of job gains," *The Washington Post*, April 16, 2020, https://tinyurl.com/yby2yet3.
86. "Cases of Coronavirus Disease (COVID-19) in the U.S.," U.S. Centers for Disease Control and Prevention, accessed April 25, 2020, https://tinyurl.com/qqt3aq6.
87. Deanna Paul and Shibani Mahtani, "Hong Kong protesters wave 'Swole Trump' posters at Thanksgiving rally," *The Washington Post*, Nov. 29, 2019, https://tinyurl.com/vecjv74.
88. "Statement of the Ministry of Foreign Affairs," People's Republic of China, Nov. 28, 2019, https://tinyurl.com/y83jfupp.
89. David Brunnstrom, "Trump approves legislation backing Hong Kong protesters," *Reuters*, Nov. 27, 2019, https://tinyurl.com/y7thythp.
90. Donald Trump, Twitter post, Jan. 11, 2020, https://tinyurl.com/yx82xbea; Donald Trump, Twitter post, Jan. 12, 2020, https://tinyurl.com/y8lj72gkl; and Donald Trump, Twitter post, Jan. 13, 2020, https://tinyurl.com/yczu63rt.
91. Ali Khamenei, Twitter post, Jan. 17, 2020, https://tinyurl.com/ycpt2ezp.
92. Florian Bieber, "Authoritarianism in the Time of the Coronavirus," *Foreign Policy*, March 30, 2020, https://tinyurl.com/ycohshj8.
93. Thomas Carothers and David Wong, "Misunderstanding Global Protests," Carnegie Endowment for International Peace, April 1, 2020, https://tinyurl.com/yc8fbkp2.
94. "Coronavirus widens Hong Kong anger at government, China," *Reuters*, Feb. 21, 2020, https://tinyurl.com/y8bhl8k8.
95. Dawn Brancati, "Coronavirus and the Hong Kong Protests," *Political Violence at a Glance*, Feb. 20, 2020, https://tinyurl.com/ybwccury.

BIBLIOGRAPHY
Books

Brancati, Dawn, *Democracy Protests: Origins, Features, and Significance*, **Cambridge University Press, 2016.**
A scholar at Yale University's MacMillan Center for International and Area Studies examines why major protests get started and how economic crises can trigger them.

Chenoweth, Erica, and Maria Stephan, *Why Civil Resistance Works: The Strategic Logic of Nonviolent Conflict*, **Columbia University Press, 2011.**
Two political scientists use statistical analysis and case studies to explain why some protest movements succeed and others fail, concluding that nonviolent campaigns have a better record than violent ones.

Kendall-Taylor, Andrea, Natasha Lindstaedt and Erica Frantz, *Democracies and Authoritarian Regimes*, **Oxford University Press, 2020.**
Three scholars look at the challenges facing democracy today, including populism and the rise of authoritarian regimes.

Articles

"COVID-19 and Conflict: Seven Trends to Watch," International Crisis Group, March 24, 2020, https://tinyurl.com/spu4kzy.
Analysts from a foreign affairs think tank discuss the coronavirus and its potential impact on world political events even after the danger of contagion has passed.

Karam, Zeina, "The New Mask: Wave of Global Revolt Replaced by Virus Fear," *The Associated Press*, **March 12, 2020, https://tinyurl.com/rlsylp3.**
Journalists for a global news agency report on how the coronavirus put 2019's wave of political protests on hold.

Kendall-Taylor, Andrea, Erica Frantz and Joseph Wright, "The Digital Dictators: How Technology Strengthens Autocracy," *Foreign Affairs*, **March-April 2020, https://tinyurl.com/yaz9x3f6.**

The director of the trans-Atlantic security program at the Center for a New American Security (Kendall-Taylor) and two political science professors explain how artificial intelligence, social media and other technologies are helping authoritarian leaders stay in power.

Kennon, Isabel, and Grace Valdevitt, "Women protest for their lives: Fighting femicide in Latin America," Atlantic Council, Feb. 24, 2020, https://tinyurl.com/qvnk5zj.

Two intern-researchers at the Atlantic Council examine gender-based violence directed at women and what governments are doing about it, and provide recommendations for more action.

Wright, Robin, "The Story of 2019: Protests in Every Corner of the Globe," *The New Yorker*, **Dec. 30, 2019, https://tinyurl.com/v5ptgme.**

In a pre-coronavirus report, a joint fellow at the U.S. Institute of Peace and the Woodrow Wilson Center discusses the protests that spanned the world last year.

Reports and Studies

Brannen, Samuel J., Christian S. Haig and Katherine Schmidt, "The Age of Mass Protest: Understanding an Escalating Global Trend," Center for Strategic and International Studies, March 2, 2020, https://tinyurl.com/y86cm553.

Researchers from a Washington foreign affairs think tank examine the causes and outcomes of the current global wave of protests and why it is likely to continue and expand.

Foa, R.S., *et al.*, **"The Global Satisfaction with Democracy Report 2020," Centre for the Future of Democracy, Bennett Institute for Public Policy, January 2020, https://tinyurl.com/vcof6j3.**

In this survey of surveys, researchers from the United Kingdom's University of Cambridge found global dissatisfaction with democracy in 2019 reached the highest level since measurements began 25 years ago.

Repucci, Sarah, "Freedom in the World 2020: A Leaderless Struggle for Democracy," Freedom House, https://tinyurl.com/y743l3xn.

In its most recent annual report on political rights and civil liberties, the research and advocacy organization finds democracy in decline around the world for the 14th straight year.

Youngs, Richard, ed., "After Protest: Pathways Beyond Mass Mobilization," Carnegie Endowment for International Peace, 2019, https://tinyurl.com/ydhbzqkk.

Local experts in civic activism analyze protests in 10 countries to explain what happens to protesters after their movement has ended.

Websites

Chenoweth, Erica, and Christopher Wiley Shay, "List of Campaigns in NAVCO 1.3," Harvard University, last updated March 17, 2020, https://tinyurl.com/y7ugzjhz.

Harvard researchers identify 622 major resistance campaigns, violent and nonviolent, from 1900 to 2019, by name, location, date, objective and outcome.

"Global Protest Tracker," Carnegie Endowment for International Peace, last updated April 1, 2020, https://tinyurl.com/ybrgyaee.

A Washington think tank launched an interactive site in April that provides details on causes, triggers, duration and sizes of protests around the world since 2017.

THE NEXT STEP
Coronavirus-Related Protests

Dougherty, Conor, and John Eligon, "Protesting Without Gathering, Tenant Organizers Get Creative," *The New York Times*, **April 23, 2020, https://tinyurl.com/yc6c4jmz.**

Housing activists are decorating their cars in support of a protest movement that wants rents canceled during the pandemic.

Selyukh, Alina, "Amazon Workers Stage New Protests Over Warehouse Coronavirus Safety," *NPR*, **April 21, 2020, https://tinyurl.com/ydym9b32.**

Hundreds of Amazon warehouse workers staged a nationwide walkout to protest the lack of paid sick leave and to support further measures to protect employees from contracting the coronavirus.

Wang, Vivian, Maria Abi-Habib and Vivian Yee, "'This Government Is Lucky': Coronavirus Quiets Global Protest Movements," *The New York Times*, April 23, 2020, https://tinyurl.com/y888ly69.

Millions of protesters are forced to stay at home worldwide because of the coronavirus, but dissent over some pandemic-related restrictions could lead to future demonstrations.

International Protests

Davidson, Helen, "China to prosecute first foreign national over Hong Kong protests," *The Guardian*, April 24, 2020, https://tinyurl.com/y97aev5h.

China is prosecuting a Belizean national for his participation in the 2019 Hong Kong protests.

McGowan, Charis, "How quarantined Chileans are keeping their protest movement alive," *Al-Jazeera*, April 14, 2020, https://tinyurl.com/y7cm8ont.

Chilean protesters bang pots and create virtual art to continue protesting inequality during the coronavirus pandemic restrictions.

Saleh, Walid, "Lebanon cities erupt against economic hardship, one protester killed in Tripoli," *Reuters*, April 27, 2020, https://tinyurl.com/yagj83y4.

One demonstrator was killed as protests erupted in Lebanon over worsening economic hardship.

Social Media

Overly, Steven, "Republicans attack Facebook as network shuts down anti-lockdown protests," *Politico*, April 20, 2020, https://tinyurl.com/y72ou2vt.

Facebook is blocking anti-quarantine protesters from organizing on their platform because they say the protests will violate states' stay-at-home orders, and some conservatives are criticizing the move.

Serhan, Yasmeen, "The Common Element Uniting Worldwide Protests," *The Atlantic*, Nov. 19, 2019, https://tinyurl.com/y767qppt.

Social media allows movements to operate in a decentralized way, which can benefit protesters facing suppression.

Tucker, Margaret, "A Guide to Chile's Revolutionary Social Media Slang," *Slate*, Dec. 17, 2019, https://tinyurl.com/qtxfe2w.

Chilean protesters have developed online slang and jokes to needle the government, such as dubbing President Sebastián Piñera, who was seen eating pizza shortly before ordering a crackdown, "El Pizza."

U.S. Protests

Gabbatt, Adam, "US anti-lockdown rallies could cause surge in Covid-19 cases, experts warn," *The Guardian*, April 20, 2020, https://tinyurl.com/y7per7jq.

Some health care workers are worried that anti-quarantine protests could allow the virus to spread faster.

Hauck, Grace, and Chris Woodyard, "Outraged Americans condemn US actions in Iraq and Iran: 'Enough with this nonsense,'" *USA Today*, Jan. 4, 2020, https://tinyurl.com/sey3dyz.

Protests against the Trump administration's killing of an Iranian general took place across the United States in an effort to prevent war with Iran.

Vogel, Kenneth P., Jim Rutenberg and Lisa Lerer, "The Quiet Hand of Conservative Groups in the Anti-Lockdown Protests," *The New York Times*, April 21, 2020, https://tinyurl.com/ycj3k39r.

Political groups founded during the Tea Party protests a decade ago are helping organize demonstrations against states' stay-at-home orders.

For More Information

Belfer Center for Science and International Affairs, 79 John F. Kennedy St., Cambridge, MA 02138; 617-495-9858; belfercenter.org. A center at Harvard University's Kennedy School of Government that performs research and training in international security and diplomacy and environmental and resource issues.

Carnegie Endowment for International Peace, 1779 Massachusetts Ave., N.W., Washington, DC 20036-2103; 202-483-7600; carnegieendowment.org. Independent think tank that researches and reports on issues pertaining to world peace.

Center for Security and International Studies, 1616 Rhode Island Ave., N.W., Washington, DC 20036; 202-887-0200; csis.org. Think tank examining trends and developments in international security.

Centre for the Future of Democracy, Bennett Institute for Public Policy, Department of Politics and International Studies, Alison Richard Building, 7 West Road, Cambridge, CB3 9DT England; +44-(0)1223-767233; bennettinstitute. cam.ac.uk. Part of England's University of Cambridge, the center conducts research into challenges facing democracy and democratic societies.

Peterson Institute for International Economics, 1750 Massachusetts Ave., N.W., Washington, DC 20036-1903; 202-328-9000; piie.com. Research institution dealing with economic aspects of current and emerging international issues.

United States Institute of Peace, 2301 Constitution Ave., N.W., Washington, DC 20037; 202-457-1700; usip.org. Congressionally funded independent organization that researches and promotes nonviolent conflict resolution and mitigation.

Woodrow Wilson Center, One Woodrow Wilson Plaza, 1300 Pennsylvania Ave., N.W., Washington, DC 20004-3027; 202-691-4000; wilsoncenter.org. Nonpartisan think tank conducting research into, and disseminating information about, international issues and U.S. policy.

10
The Abraham Accords
Will they transform the Middle East?
By Jonathan Broder

The skyline of Dubai, the most populous city in the United Arab Emirates (UAE), creates a glittering spectacle at night. The oil-rich UAE, which signed a normalization deal with Israel in August 2020, has become a major player in the Middle East.

THE ISSUES

In 1993, Benjamin Netanyahu, then leader of Israel's right-wing opposition Likud Party, backed a hard-line doctrine to address the Israeli-Palestinian conflict called "peace for peace."

That year, Israel's centrist government and the Palestinians had signed the Oslo Accords, a framework for negotiations that raised hopes for an eventual comprehensive settlement through Israel's withdrawal from the West Bank, the establishment of an independent Palestinian state and peace between Israel and all Arab countries.

That was not how Netanyahu saw things. He insisted that he also sought a genuine peace with the Palestinians—but he opposed any West Bank withdrawal to achieve it. In exchange for peace with Palestinians and Arab states, Netanyahu proposed giving peace in return—and no more.

Critics in Israel, the Arab world and the United States called this a fantasy. They noted that ever since Israel captured the West Bank in 1967, the principle undergirding all diplomacy to end the Israeli-Arab conflict was a "land for peace" formula that required Israel's withdrawal from occupied Arab lands in exchange for Arab recognition.

Twenty-seven years later, after the failure of successive U.S. and international efforts to broker peace between Israelis and

Palestinians on the basis of land for peace, the scorned peace-for-peace approach has unexpectedly come through for Israel's relations with Arab states. At a White House ceremony in September, Netanyahu, now Israel's longest-serving prime minister, and the foreign ministers of the United Arab Emirates (UAE) and Bahrain signed separate bilateral agreements normalizing full relations between their countries. A month later, Sudan moved to recognize Israel, and on Dec. 10, President Trump announced that Morocco had also agreed to normalize relations with the Jewish state.[1] President Trump said the agreements, collectively named the Abraham Accords, marked "the dawn of a new Middle East."[2]

The quartet of Arab countries are the first to recognize Israel since Jordan signed a peace treaty with the Jewish state in 1994. Their accords require no Israeli withdrawal from the West Bank. Netanyahu's only concession, at the insistence of the Emiratis, was the suspension of his plan to annex nearly a third of the West Bank. The texts of the Abraham Accords gloss over the Palestinian issue, briefly mentioning a negotiated solution as an aspiration for the region.[3] The lasting significance of the accords, experts agree, is the death of the decades-old status quo that had put the Palestinians' plight at the center of the larger Arab-Israeli conflict and ruled out any Middle East peace until Israel agreed to give them their own state in the West Bank.

"We have broken this terrible and dangerous doctrine, and I am proud of it," Netanyahu said in August, after the first of the normalization agreements between Israel and the UAE was announced.[4]

The Palestinians have denounced the accords as a "stab in the back" by their purported Arab allies. Their leaders have found themselves more isolated and with far less leverage, a toxic combination that could spark more violence against the Israeli occupation, says Steven A. Cook, a Middle East expert at the Council on Foreign Relations, a centrist think tank in Washington.

For Israel and its newest Arab friends, however, the Abraham Accords are very good news. Former U.S. officials say the agreements are an important diplomatic achievement that advances Israel's decades-long quest for Arab acceptance. Experts add that the accords also have produced a strategic realignment in the Middle East to challenge the regional ambitions of Iran, whose nuclear program and proxy militias in Lebanon, Syria, Iraq and Yemen threaten both Israel and the Persian Gulf states.

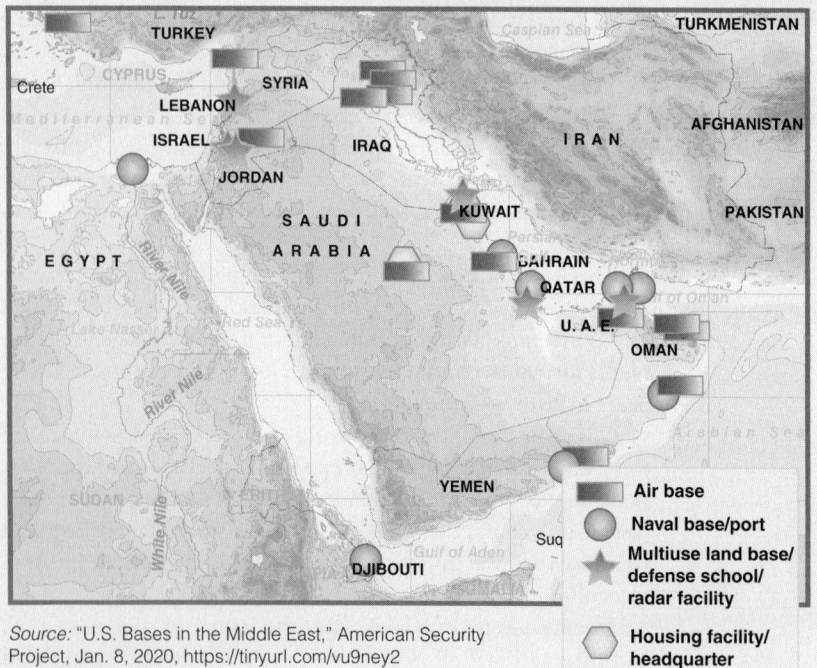

U.S. Has Military Facilities Throughout the Middle East

The United States maintains multiple military installations in the Middle East and Persian Gulf region, including one air base and one naval port in the United Arab Emirates, one air base and one radar facility in Israel and three military facilities in Bahrain.

U.S. Military Facilities in Middle East, January 2020

Source: "U.S. Bases in the Middle East," American Security Project, Jan. 8, 2020, https://tinyurl.com/vu9ney2

And Israel and the Gulf countries can expect commercial and economic rewards from normalized relations. So will Sudan if its as yet unformed parliament ratifies its accord.

Of the four Arab countries that recognized Israel, "the UAE is by far the most significant," says Aaron David Miller, who served as a senior Middle East adviser to six U.S. administrations, both Republican and Democratic. Though it has operated for years in Saudi Arabia's shadow, the UAE, with a population of just 10 million, has quietly become a major regional player, Miller and other Middle East experts say.

The UAE's oil wealth has bought it influence in Egypt, Libya and the Eastern Mediterranean as part of its twin battles against the politicization of Islam and Turkey, which supports Islamist political organizations such as the Muslim Brotherhood.

Though the UAE views Iran and its radical Shiite regime as a threat, it has maintained a policy of balanced pragmatism toward Tehran. After what U.S. officials charged were Iranian attacks on oil tankers and Saudi oil installations last year in response to Trump's sanctions on Iran's oil exports, the Emirates reached out to Tehran to discuss maritime security. Earlier this year the UAE provided the Islamic Republic with aid to help it fight the COVID-19 pandemic. And after Iran's leading nuclear scientist, Mohsen Fakhrizadeh, was assassinated last month in an operation Iran blamed on Israel, both the UAE and Bahrain condemned the killing, while urging Middle Eastern countries to avoid actions that inflame tensions.[5]

But the UAE also maintains a well-trained and competent military. And although it has discreetly swapped intelligence with Israel for years on both Iran and terrorist threats, their open alliance now broadens their cooperation to include cybersecurity and possibly even joint military exercises, experts say. They add that the timing of the agreement is also significant, coming when the United States is reducing its military footprint in the Middle East.

"The Middle East isn't as important to Washington as it used to be," says Miller, now a senior fellow at the Carnegie Endowment for International Peace, a centrist foreign-policy think tank in Washington. "As a consequence, the Emiratis have got to hedge their bets. And one of those hedges is Israel."

Though Bahrain still has strategic importance to the United States as the home port for the U.S. Navy's Fifth Fleet, the tiny island kingdom has far less strategic value to Israel. Israeli officials say it could serve as an Iran listening post and also has commercial value as a market for Israeli technology and software exports. But one Israeli official says Bahrain's biggest value to Israel has been political, serving as a bellwether for Saudi thinking on normalization.

"So Bahrain is effectively a Saudi vassal state," says the official, speaking on condition of anonymity in accordance with Israeli regulations. "The Saudis pay their [Bahraini] bills, take final responsibility for their security and decide its foreign policy. Bahrain never would have made relations with us if the Saudis hadn't first given them the go-ahead. So that tells us the Saudis like the idea [of normalizing relations] and may do it some other time."

Several analysts have expressed concerns that the new Israel-Gulf partnership could further destabilize the region. Some said Tehran's furious reaction to the Abraham Accords—which included direct threats against the UAE's ruling royal family—exposed Tehran's strategic concerns that Israel, once a distant enemy, will gain a foothold in the Persian Gulf. Iran's top general warned that if even the smallest sign of a national security threat emerges, he will hold the UAE responsible.[6]

Hussein Ibish, a senior scholar at the Arab Gulf States Institute in Washington, a think tank funded by the Saudis and UAE, cautioned that pending congressional approval for the Trump administration's proposed sale of up to 50 advanced F-35 stealth warplanes to the Emirates could spark an arms race with Iran. Now that a United Nations arms embargo on Iran ended in October, "Russia and China are eager to supply it with advanced jets, tanks and missiles," Ibish said.[7] (*See Short Feature.*)

Such concerns, along with fears of popular protests on behalf of the Palestinians, have made the leaders of several Arab countries think twice before giving in to American pressure to join the accords. Despite such entreaties, Saudi Arabia and Oman—both countries that have had contacts with Israel over the years—remain on the sidelines, and Arab diplomats say they do not appear to be moving in the direction of normalization anytime soon.

Saudi Arabia, the grand prize of normalized relations because of its wealth and role as guardian of Islam's holy places, is also withholding recognition, in part because of a generational split within the ruling family, experts say. King Salman says he will recognize Israel only after the Palestinian issue has been resolved. But the king's son, Crown Prince Mohammed bin Salman—known by his initials, MBS—regards the Israeli-Palestinian conflict as intractable and views Israel as a valuable ally against Iran and an attractive business partner, according to Bruce Riedel, a Saudi expert at the Brookings Institution think tank.

Riedel and other experts say normalized relations between Saudi Arabia and Israel are unlikely before the ailing Salman, 84, dies. Other have speculated that MBS, the kingdom's de facto ruler, may want to offer recognition of Israel as an olive branch to President-elect Joe Biden once he takes office. The aim would be to improve the kingdom's image, badly tarnished after MBS's lieutenants murdered and dismembered self-exiled Saudi journalist Jamal Khashoggi at the Saudi consulate in Istanbul last year. Biden has called Saudi Arabia a "pariah" and vowed to reassess U.S. relations with the kingdom.

In the meantime, MBS has continued to pursue his own relations with Israel. Saudi advisers confirm he met face-to-face last month with Netanyahu for talks that many experts believe were aimed at presenting a united anti-Iran front to Biden, who has said he wants to rejoin the 2015 Iran nuclear accord that Trump withdrew from two years ago. When Trump did so, Israel and Saudi Arabia applauded the move.[8]

Political graffiti and murals cover a section of the Israeli-built security wall separating Israel and the West Bank near the Palestinian-administered city of Bethlehem. An Israeli government plan to annex nearly one-third of the West Bank was suspended to facilitate Israel's normalization agreement with the UAE.

As Israel, the UAE and Bahrain move to appoint ambassadors and open embassies in each other's countries, both Israeli and Arab diplomats acknowledge they are only at the beginning of a still-undefined diplomatic relationship. As their respective governments move to shape the contours of their ties, they say some big questions remain unanswered.

Perhaps the most discomfiting question is what impact Netanyahu's legal problems could have on the normalization process. The answer will go a long way in determining how relations develop, Israeli observers say.

Netanyahu is under indictment in Israel for bribery, fraud and breach of trust, charges he has denied but which could send him to prison if convicted. He now leads a unity government of ideologically disparate parties under an agreement that requires him to turn over the premiership next year to his defense minister, Benny Gantz, a political rival. That transfer of power would lift the immunity from prosecution that the prime minister's position has afforded Netanyahu so far.

Gilead Sher, an attorney who served as Israel's chief negotiator with the Palestinians, says Netanyahu has only one way to retain that immunity: dissolve parliament and call for new elections in hopes of securing the parliamentary majority he would need to stay in power.

Sher, who has observed the political maneuvers that Netanyahu has used to win five successive elections since 2009, says Netanyahu would have no qualms about reviving his original West Bank annexation plan as part of a campaign to prevent his political base from defecting to even more right-wing political parties.

"If putting annexation back on the table means the difference between staying in power and going to jail, I have absolutely no question he would do it and think about the [Abraham] agreement later," Sher says.

Amid such uncertainties, here are some key questions that analysts, former officials and others are asking about the Abraham Accords:

Are the Abraham Accords as historically significant as the Trump administration claims?

At the signing ceremony for the accords, President Trump declared: "We're here this afternoon to change the course of history. After decades of division and conflict, we mark the dawn of a new Middle East." The U.S.-brokered accords, he said, not only normalize relations between Israel and the UAE and Bahrain, but also "will serve as the foundation for a comprehensive peace across the entire region."[9]

John Hannah, the former national security adviser to Republican Vice President Dick Cheney, described the accords as a "genuine historic accomplishment that's unambiguously good for the United States." It will bolster Israeli security, contribute to broader Middle East stability by forestalling Israeli annexation of the West Bank, give the Gulf states full access to the Israel economy and help isolate Iran, Hannah said. "And it reaffirms Washington's still-unrivaled ability to serve as a force for good in alleviating some of the world's most intractable conflicts," a role no other county could have played, he added.[10]

The accords have won accolades across the U.S. political spectrum. Biden welcomed them as a "historic step to bridge the deep divides of the Middle East" in August.[11]

Even some of the administration's harshest critics have given credit to Trump's so-called "outside-in" approach to Middle East peacemaking, which ignored the playbook of previous administrations that prioritized resolving the Israeli-Palestinian conflict. Instead, the Trump administration produced a Middle East peace plan that was heavily slanted in Israel's favor and then focused on winning agreements between the Arab states and Israel as a way to isolate the Palestinians and pressure them to accept the peace plan.

"We basically got this wrong," acknowledges Miller, the former Middle East adviser. "We assumed all along that normalization would have to follow meaningful progress, if not a solution, between Israelis and Palestinians."

But Miller and other Middle East experts say the administration and its supporters have hyped the significance of the accords. First, they point out, they are not all peace agreements, since the UAE, Bahrain and Morocco were never at war with Israel. Sudanese troops did fight against Israel in the 1967 war, the critics say—but in recent years, Sudan and Israel have quietly cooperated on security and intelligence matters.

Second, these experts note Israel, Morocco and the Gulf states have conducted their own discreet relations since the early 2000s, driven largely by mutual concerns over Iran. But the changing attitudes and priorities among Gulf leaders also played a role, the experts say. Far removed from the Israeli-Palestinian conflict, these leaders came to see Israel not only as an ally against Iran but also a potential business partner and a source for advanced technologies in cybersecurity, agriculture and medicine.

Beginning with intelligence cooperation, these relations grew over the years to include business deals

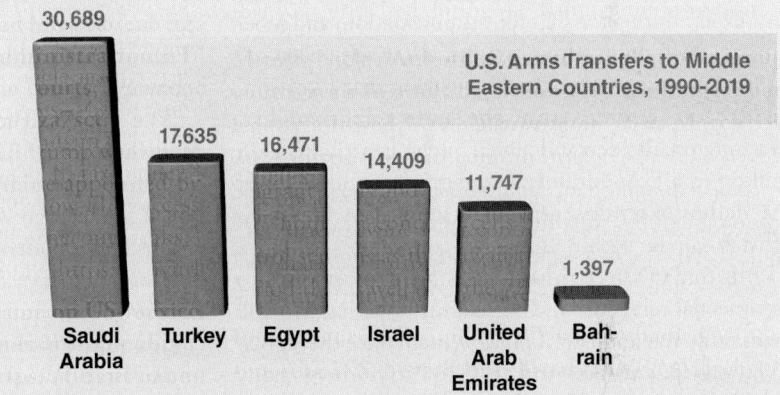

Saudis Received Greatest Share of U.S. Arms Sent to Middle East

Since 1990, Saudi Arabia has been the biggest purchaser of U.S. weapons sold in the Middle East, according to data collected and analyzed by the Stockholm International Peace Research Institute (SIPRI), a Swedish research group. Turkey, Egypt and Israel have also been major arms recipients.

U.S. Arms Transfers to Middle Eastern Countries, 1990-2019

Saudi Arabia	Turkey	Egypt	Israel	United Arab Emirates	Bahrain
30,689	17,635	16,471	14,409	11,747	1,397

Note: These numbers reflect a unit of measure developed by SIPRI called Trend Indicators Value, which is based on known production costs. It allows for comparison of transfers of major conventional weapons using a common measurement. It is not a reflection of the weapons' financial value.

Sources: "Importer/Exporter TIV Tables," Stockholm International Peace Research Institute, accessed Dec. 1, 2020, https://tinyurl.com/y3zvm7cr; "Sources and Methods," Stockholm International Peace Research Institute, https://tinyurl.com/y42c6atp

conducted through third parties and increasingly public displays of deepening ties. In the two decades before the Abraham Accords were signed, officials from Bahrain, Mauritania, Oman, Qatar, Saudi Arabia and the UAE quietly met individually with Israeli officials, and some Arab countries even opened Israeli trade missions. In 2018, Saudi Arabia publicly acknowledged Israel's right to exist.[12]

"No, this was not a paradigm-shifting peace agreement like Israel's peace agreements with Egypt and Jordan," says Cook, of the Council on Foreign Relations. "The UAE, Bahrain and Israel already had been moving quite publicly toward normalization for several years. So the Abraham Accords essentially made official the things that already were happening."

"Right now," adds Miller, "these are transactional arrangements based on a narrow coincidence of interests between Israel, the Emirates, Bahrain, Sudan and the Americans."

For Sudan, experts agree that recognizing Israel was the only practicable way to relieve its dire economic circumstances. Though the Sudanese last year toppled autocratic leader Omar al-Bashir and replaced him with a civilian-military ruling council, the country remained on a U.S. list of countries that supported terrorism, making it ineligible to receive desperately needed American and international aid.

According to Brian Katulis, who served as a Middle East expert during the Clinton administration, and other experts, the Trump administration effectively "coerced" Sudan into recognizing Israel by making that a key condition for removal from the state terrorism list. Washington also demanded that Sudan contribute $335 million to a U.S.-administered compensation fund for the victims of terrorist attacks, in several of which U.S. officials say the Bashir regime was complicit.[13]

But Sudan's recognition of Israel only extends to commercial relations, and the country's parliament still must ratify the normalization agreement once the legislative body is created. And in a country where many strongly sympathize with the Palestinians, parliamentary approval is not guaranteed, says Lucy Kurtzer-Ellenbogen, director of the Israeli-Palestinian conflict program at the U.S. Institute of Peace, a congressionally funded think tank in Washington.

"Sudan is a place where its civil society is not as ready to welcome the agreements as the Emiratis," she says.

Several of Netanyahu's Israeli critics say the Abraham Accords actually came about as an unintended consequence of Trump's Middle East peace plan, which gave Netanyahu a green light to annex nearly a third of the West Bank. These critics say it was only after the UAE conditioned normalization on Netanyahu's vow to scrap annexation that Trump, eager to score a foreign policy victory for his re-election bid, pivoted away from his own peace plan and pressured Netanyahu to accept the UAE's condition.

"Trump didn't intend it that way, but we can generously credit him at least indirectly for the cancellation of a disastrous [annexation] move by Israel that he had first encouraged," said Yossi Alpher, who served in a senior post in the Mossad, Israel's foreign intelligence service.[14]

Have Arabs abandoned the Palestinians?

The diplomatic recognition that the United Arab Emirates extended to Israel was not the only shock that lay in store for the Palestinians.

At a meeting in Cairo a few weeks after the announcement of the Israel-UAE deal, the Arab League not only refused a Palestinian demand to condemn the agreement, but its top official also scolded the Palestinians for attempting to bully its members.

"It is the indisputable right of each country to have sovereignty in conducting its foreign policy in the way it sees fit," Secretary-General Ahmed Aboul Gheit said. "This is something that this council respects and approves."[15]

The Arab League's response was a far cry from the days when a 1975 United Nations resolution recognizing "the inalienable rights of the Palestinian people" served as the Arab world's unifying trope. Middle East experts said it underscored just how far Palestinian political fortunes have fallen since 2002, when the Arab League gave its full-throated endorsement to a Saudi-crafted Arab Peace Initiative that offered Arab recognition to Israel in exchange for withdrawal from the West Bank and the establishment of a Palestinian state.

"The Palestinians always held a weak hand against the Israelis, but the [2002] Arab peace plan strengthened their leverage because all the Arab countries were behind it," says the U.S. Institute of Peace's Kurtzer-Ellenbogen. "This has been a wake-up call to the Palestinian leadership that they cannot rely on that any longer."

Many analysts, including some prominent former Middle East officials, say the Palestinian issue lost its urgency for many Arab leaders after decades of U.S.-mediated negotiations between the Israelis and Palestinians went nowhere, largely because the Palestinians refused to budge from their maximalist demands. They say Arab leaders also grew tired of the corruption inside the West Bank's Palestinian Authority, its expectation of limitless funding from the rich-oil states and its political differences with the Islamist militants of Hamas in the Gaza Strip that effectively paralyzed decision-making. (Hamas took control of Gaza in 2007, dividing the Palestinian territories into two antagonistic political entities.)

"The Palestinian cause is a just cause, but its advocates are failures," Prince Bandar bin Sultan, the former Saudi ambassador to the United States, said recently in an unusually blunt interview with *Al-Arabiya*, a Saudi-owned television network with wide viewership across the Middle East.[16]

Katulis, the Clinton administration expert, adds that the internal problems plaguing the Palestinian leadership coincided with "tectonic changes" that the Middle East was going through.

These included the 2003 U.S. invasion of Iraq, which shifted the regional balance of power in neighboring Iran's favor. Using Shiite militias and political parties in Iraq, Lebanon and Yemen as proxies, Shiite-ruled Iran was able to spread its influence deep into the Sunni heartland. Then came the 2011 Arab Spring uprisings that toppled regimes in Egypt, Libya, Tunisia and Yemen and ignited a savage civil war in Syria that strengthened Islamist groups. Most recently, the Gulf states have experienced a decline in oil prices and the slow but steady withdrawal from the region of U.S. forces, once the guarantor of their security.

For many Arab leaders, the combination of such momentous developments and the challenges they presented simply overshadowed the Palestinian issue, Katulis says. And as Gulf states sought alternative ways to protect their countries and their thrones, Israel's military, technological and scientific expertise became increasingly attractive, he adds.

Emirati and Bahraini officials say they have not betrayed the Palestinians. To the contrary, the Emiratis

An Iranian military unit marches in a parade to celebrate National Army Day in 2019. Both the UAE and Israel view Iran as a security threat, one of the factors that brought them together.

argue their success in getting Netanyahu to shelve his annexation plan clears the path for a resumption of Israeli-Palestinian peace talks, which collapsed in 2014.[17] Bahrain has echoed the UAE's calls for a Palestinian return to the negotiating table.

At the same time, these Arab officials made it clear they have lost patience with the bitter infighting between the moderate secular leadership in the West Bank and Hamas in Gaza. They say the Palestinians' inability to unify around a single ruling authority has led them to reject every peace offer since the Oslo Accords. As a result, the Gulf officials say they are no longer willing to wait for the Palestinians to resolve their differences before seizing the benefits that recognizing Israel will provide to their own countries.

"If something is in the interest of the UAE, we will pursue it," said the Emirates' Minister of State for Foreign Affairs, Anwar Gargash. "We cannot be also prisoners of [hard-line Palestinian] . . . rhetoric, and at the same time, stagnation and inaction on the Palestinian issue."[18]

Dennis Ross, a senior Middle East adviser to both Republican and Democratic U.S. presidents, said the Palestinians can now use the precedent that the Emiratis established in conditioning normalized relations on an Israeli annexation freeze to link any future Arab normalization overtures with Israel's behavior toward the Palestinians.

"Instead of insisting on a maximal position of no steps toward Israel without complete Israeli withdrawal—something that is not going to happen—why not engage Arab states in a discussion in which Palestinians suggest a menu of actions that Israel should take in response to Arab public outreach to the Jewish state," said Ross, now counselor at the Washington Institute for Near East Policy, a pro-Israel thank tank.[19]

But so far the Palestinians are not biting. They see such arguments as part of a coordinated campaign by the Trump administration, Israel and pro-Israeli Americans such as Ross to persuade the Palestinians to accept Trump's peace plan, which offers far less territory than the 2002 Arab Peace Initiative, including limited autonomy in several noncontiguous West Bank enclaves. Trump's plan also would provide $50 billion in aid to revive the struggling West Bank and Gaza Strip economies.

Diana Buttu, a former legal adviser to the Palestinian negotiating team, accused Trump and Netanyahu of ignoring the Palestinians and "arrogantly telling us that we should simply accept whatever crumbs are thrown our way and be grateful for those crumbs."[20]

In a recent commentary that ran in *Arab News*, Saudi Arabia's largest English-language daily, editor-in-chief Faisal Abbas counseled that if the Palestinians ever decide to negotiate again, they would be wise not to repeat their maximalist demands and for once be prepared to consider something less.

"When will they learn that every time they turn away from the negotiating table, the pie only gets smaller?" he wrote.[21]

Does the new Israel-Gulf Arab coalition threaten Iran?

When the first of the Abraham Accords—the Israel-UAE normalization—was announced in August, the reaction from top Iranian leaders was predictably fierce for a country that claims the mantle of the Palestinians' most dedicated ally.

But analysts noted their diatribes included remarks that pointed to the leaders' deep apprehension about the threats to Iran arising from the agreement.

In its statement, the Islamic Revolutionary Guard Corps, the country's ideological shock troops, threatened a "dangerous future" for the UAE's leadership. President Hassan Rouhani said that if the Emiratis "allow Israel a foothold in the region, they will be treated differently."[22]

According to some experts on Iran, driving such threats is Tehran's concern that the UAE's alliance with Israel could spell the unraveling of what has been one of Iran's most reliable security bulwarks, namely Arab hostility toward Israel. With the UAE's recognition of Israel, these experts say, Iranian policymakers fear a domino effect of more Arab countries embracing relations with the Jewish state. The analysts said Iranian leaders worry that the final domino to fall will be the anger and distrust of Israel that Arabs and Iranians shared, leaving Iran more vulnerable to Arab, Israeli and American military and cyberattacks, as well as espionage operations.

The argument that the Israel-UAE agreement presents Iran with a new strategic nightmare is laid out in an analysis that appeared in the online journal *Foreign Policy*. It was co-authored by Maysam Behravesh, a former Iranian intelligence analyst and national security adviser now with the Washington-based geopolitical risk consultancy Gulf State Analytics, and Hamidreza Azizi, an Iran expert at the German Institute for International and Security Affairs in Berlin.[23]

Ever since the 1979 Islamic revolution brought the mullahs to power in Iran, the Arabs' hatred of Israel has provided Tehran with an "organic security buffer" that kept Israel out of Iran's Persian Gulf neighborhood while allowing Iran to train and arm Shiite Arab militias, such as Hezbollah in Lebanon and Syria, extending Iran's military reach right up to Israel's borders, Behravesh and Azizi argue.

The UAE-Israel normalization, they continue, "spells systematic security cooperation and intelligence-sharing between the two partners against their common adversary," which will erode Iran's natural buffer with Israel. The result, they said, will be an Iran that is more exposed to cloak-and-dagger operations, such as Israel's 2018 theft of half a ton of top-secret Iranian nuclear documents from a Tehran warehouse and Fakhrizadeh's assassination.[24]

An example of Israeli-UAE strategic cooperation since they reached their normalization agreement is their reported joint work in building an intelligence base on the island of Socotra in the Arabian Sea, near the Bab el-Mandeb Strait, which serves as the southern entrance to the Red Sea. From there, it would be possible to monitor and inspect shipping suspected of ferrying Iranian weapons to Houthi rebels in Yemen, and to Bedouin in Egypt's Sinai Peninsula who then smuggle the arms into the Gaza Strip for Hamas militants.

However, in a recent Columbia University online forum focusing on Middle East issues, James Spencer, a former British infantry commander and now an independent London-based security consultant, questioned why the UAE's formalized ties with Israel would constrain Iran, particularly in the event of a war between Israel and Iran.

"I'm still struggling to see the defense benefit to the Arabs from this accord," Spencer said. He noted that Israel is more than 1,200 miles and several flying hours from the UAE, with no capacity to airlift ground forces to the Emirates on short notice.

In the event of an Israeli decision to conduct airstrikes against Iran's nuclear facility, Israeli pilots could theoretically launch their sorties from UAE air bases. But because Israel, the UAE, Bahrain and the United States have other options for such an operation, Spencer questioned the wisdom of a UAE-based Israeli attack.

"Are the Emiratis really going to allow the Israelis to launch airstrikes against Iran from Emirati air bases, and then fly home, leaving the Emiratis alone in the crosshairs?" Spencer asked.

Meanwhile, Congress is now weighing the Trump administration's approval of a $23 billion arms package for the UAE that could include 50 F-35 fighter jets, 18 Reaper drones and other precision weapons. Israel is also expected to receive another infusion of U.S. weaponry, including an additional squadron of F-35s, bringing Israel's total to 75.[25]

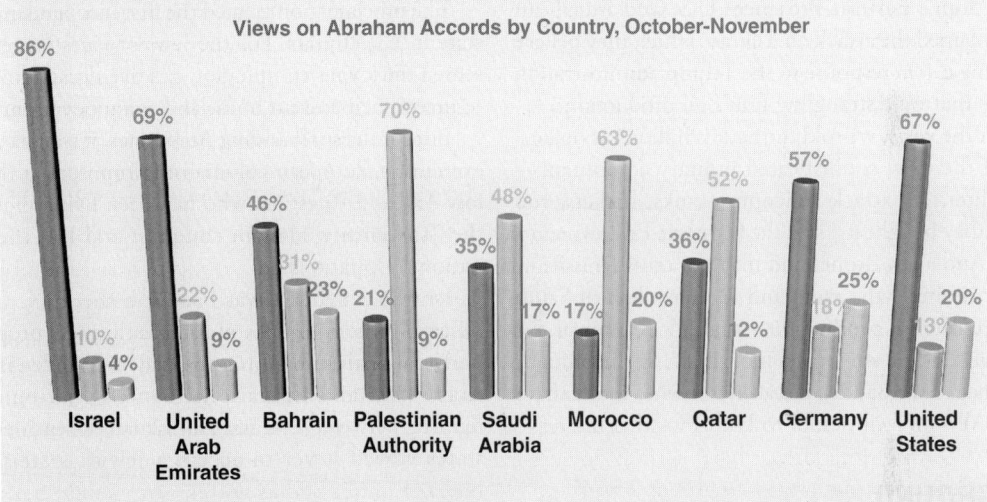

Accords Are Popular in Participating Nations, but Others in Region Are Cool

Some 86 percent of Israelis, 69 percent of Emirati citizens and 46 percent of Bahraini citizens support the Abraham Accords, according to an October poll by two research organizations. Americans and Germans also largely approve of the pacts. However, 70 percent of Palestinians and 48 percent of Saudi Arabian citizens oppose the agreements.

Views on Abraham Accords by Country, October-November

Note: Polls conducted in the UAE, Bahrain, Saudi Arabia and Qatar include data from citizens only.
Source: Alexander Brakel and Mitchell Barak, "Measuring the Attitudes of Citizens in Israel, UAE, Bahrain, Palestinian Authority, Saudi Arabia, Qatar, Morocco, United States, and Germany Towards the Israel-UAE-Bahrain Peace Accords," Konrad Adenauer Stiftung and Keevoon Global Research, Nov. 11, 2020, p. 17, https://tinyurl.com/y5u8yezc

Among the reasons for the arms-buying spurt, analysts say, are concerns in Washington, Israel and the Gulf that since the expiration of the United Nations arms embargo against Iran in October, Tehran is eager to upgrade its military with big purchases of Russian and Chinese advanced warplanes, tanks and missiles.

Some analysts have raised the specter of a runaway arms race in the Gulf that will add more deadly firepower to sectarian and proxy wars already underway in the region.

But there is another view that maintains despite UAE and Israeli military superiority over Iran, the Islamic Republic still poses a dangerous threat, particularly to coastal Gulf Arab cities and their oil production facilities, thanks to state-of-the-art targeting and guidance systems Iran has acquired for its huge arsenal of homemade missiles and drones. Iran says it has built three underground "missile cities" along its Persian Gulf coast, concealing hundreds of missiles ready to launch from under five levels of protective concrete.[26]

The immense disruptive power of this asymmetrical strategy was driven home last September when an estimated 10 drones attacked Saudi Arabia's state-owned Aramco oil processing facility at Abqaiq and Khurais in the kingdom's Eastern Province. U.S. and European officials blamed the attack on Tehran, which they believe was lashing out in response to the Trump administration sanctions that were strangling Iran's oil production.

"Over the years, we sold the Saudis billions of dollars' worth of the most sophisticated military equipment—F-16 fighter jets, attack helicopter, tanks, rockets, you name it, they bought it," says the Carnegie Endowment's Miller. "And a few drones and maybe a cruise missile or two flew in under the radar and took out half of Saudi Arabia's entire oil production—that's 5 percent of the world's oil production—for a month. . . . If the Iranians can do that to the Saudis, just think of what they can do to the UAE's oil facilities, or to Dubai for that matter."

BACKGROUND
Birth of Israel

On May 14, 1948, the day when British rule over Palestine ended, Jewish Agency Chairman David Ben-Gurion, a small man with unruly white hair, rose to speak at the Tel Aviv Museum, where a small audience had gathered.

Jewish leader David Ben-Gurion proclaims the establishment of the state of Israel on May 14, 1948. Six Arab nations reacted to the proclamation by invading the new state, but were defeated by Israel in a 10-month war that caused some 700,000 Palestinians to flee or to be expelled from their homes, becoming refugees.

Reading slowly from a document, Ben-Gurion said, "By virtue of the natural and historic right of the Jewish people and by resolution of the General Assembly of the United Nations, we hereby proclaim the establishment of a Jewish state in Palestine, to be called Israel."[27]

The proclamation created the first independent Jewish state in 2,000 years. For the Jews of Palestine, it represented the joyous culmination of a five-decade struggle to resurrect their ancient homeland as a modern nation.

But for the surrounding Arab states, it was yet another exercise in European colonialism, imposed on their fellow Arabs in Palestine, who had been living there since the 7th-century Muslim conquest and had their own national aspirations.

Israel's statehood was based on the U.N. General Assembly's adoption six months earlier of a proposal to partition Palestine into two states, one Jewish, one Arab, with an international zone for Jerusalem. As fighting between Jews and Palestinians intensified, Arab states vowed never to accept a Jewish state in their midst.[28]

The same night that Ben-Gurion, later Israel's first premier, issued his proclamation, Egyptian planes bombed Tel Aviv. The next morning, the first Arab-Israel war broke out as units from six Arab armies invaded, determined to crush the Jewish state in its infancy.

After 10 months, the fighting ended with an Israeli victory. When an armistice was signed on March 10, 1949, the Israelis held all the territory allotted under the U.N. partition plan, plus more than half of the proposed Arab state, including the western half of Jerusalem. In the process, some 700,000 Palestinians fled or were expelled from Israeli-controlled areas, scattering across the Jordanian West Bank, the Egyptian-controlled Gaza Strip, Lebanon and Syria. The Palestinians called their displacement the "nakba," or catastrophe, which marked the birth of the Palestinian refugee problem.[29]

Israel and Arab states went to war again in June 1967. In a period of only six days, the Israel Defense Forces defeated Egyptian, Syrian and Jordanian armies, capturing the West Bank, the Gaza Strip, Egypt's Sinai Peninsula and the Syrian Golan Heights. Israel also captured and annexed Arab East Jerusalem, in a move no other country recognized. Another 300,000 Palestinians, many refugees for the second time, fled into Jordan, where they ended up in sprawling refugee camps.

Three months later, the Arab League, an umbrella organization representing 22 Arab states, approved a resolution that became known as "the three no's": no negotiations, no recognition and no peace with Israel.[30]

Israelis paid little heed. Nationalist and religious Jews saw the victory as a divine miracle. They were particularly elated over the capture of the West Bank, which held many Jewish biblical sites. Over the following years, they pressed for Jewish settlements in the West Bank. The victory also ingrained in many Israelis a swaggering overconfidence, fueled by a sense of military superiority over the Arabs.

Israelis would come to regret that mindset just six years later.

In October 1973, the third Arab-Israeli war erupted when Egyptian and Syrian forces launched simultaneous offensives across the Suez Canal and the Golan Heights, catching the Israelis by surprise. After suffering heavy losses, the Israelis mounted counteroffensives on both fronts. They cut off Egyptian forces on the Israeli side of the Suez Canal, drove the Syrians off the Golan Heights and brought the Israelis within 35 miles of the Syrian capital of Damascus. A ceasefire ended the war three weeks later.[31]

Because the Egyptians had managed to hold a thin band of recaptured Sinai territory until the war's end, Egyptian President Anwar Sadat declared victory, announcing that Arab honor had been restored after the humiliating 1967 defeat. He then began making public overtures to Israel for peace talks, which Israel at first refused to take seriously.

In 1977, Sadat stunned the world by flying to Israel to declare his readiness to make peace. So extraordinary was Sadat's gesture that when his plane, bearing the red, white and black Egyptian flag, touched down at Ben-Gurion Airport outside Tel Aviv, many Israelis compared his arrival to the landing of an alien spacecraft.

But Sadat was sincere in his call for peace, and his visit led to the U.S.-brokered 1979 Israel-Egypt peace treaty, the first between Israel and an Arab foe. The United States underwrote the agreement, providing both Israel and Egypt with billions of dollars in foreign assistance.

For Israel, the treaty's strategic significance was immense: It removed the Arab world's most powerful military from the Israeli-Arab conflict. But Sadat's efforts to win Israeli concessions for the Palestinians failed. Israeli Prime Minister Menachem Begin offered the Palestinians only limited autonomy, which the Palestinians refused. Israel continued to build Jewish settlements on West Bank land, deepening Palestinian resentment.

Iranian Revolution

That same year, another political earthquake rocked the Middle East. A revolution in Iran toppled the country's shah and brought to power radical Shiite Muslim clerics who blamed the United States and Israel for supporting the shah's authoritarian rule.

The Iranian revolution awakened the West for the first time to the power of Islam as a political force, a lesson that was dramatically underscored again in 1981, when Islamists in the Egyptian army gunned down Sadat as punishment for making peace with Israel.

That same year, Israel unilaterally annexed the Golan Heights in another move that went unrecognized by the international community. In 1982, Israel invaded Lebanon with the objective of destroying the Palestine Liberation Organization (PLO), the umbrella political group that claimed sole representation of the Palestinians. The PLO had its headquarters in Beirut, where its fighters had carved out what many observers described as a state within a state in Lebanon. The invasion was the brainchild of Israeli Defense Minister Ariel Sharon, a

CHRONOLOGY

1917-1949 *Jews and Arabs fight over British-controlled Palestine, leading to Israel's birth.*

1917 British troops conquer Palestine in World War I.

1920-1939 Communal violence between Jews and Arabs intensifies; Britain limits Jewish immigration to Palestine to 10,000 annually.

1940s Despite the Nazi Holocaust, Britain maintains immigration quota; armed Jewish groups fight both Palestinian Arabs and British authorities.

1947 Britain hands the Palestine problem to the United Nations, which votes to divide Palestine into Jewish and Arab states. Jews accept the partition, Arab states reject it.

1948-49 Israel declares independence; Arab armies invade, sparking the first Arab-Israeli war. An armistice leaves Israel with more territory than the partition allotted, including West Jerusalem; some 700,000 Palestinians are expelled or flee to neighboring Arab states.

1950-1973 *Israel and Arab states fight three more wars.*

1956-57 Israel seizes the Sinai Peninsula as part of secret Britain-French military operation to wrest control of the Suez Canal from Egypt. Under U.S. pressure, Israeli, French and British forces withdraw.

1957 Israel builds a large nuclear reactor in the Negev desert, fueling the country's officially unconfirmed nuclear weapons program.

1967 Another war erupts; in six days Israel occupies Egypt's Gaza Strip and Sinai Peninsula, the Syrian Golan Heights and the Jordanian West Bank, humiliating the Arab world.

1973 Egypt and Syria launch coordinated attacks against Israel in the occupied Sinai and Golan Heights. Israel eventually prevails, but a ceasefire leaves Egyptian troops holding a narrow strip of Sinai territory. Egypt's President Anwar Sadat declares Arab honor has been restored.

1977-1994 *Israel signs peace treaties with Egypt and Jordan, begins negotiations with the PLO and opens a secret relationship with the United Arab Emirates (UAE).*

1977-79 Sadat visits Jerusalem and offers peace; two years later, Israel and Egypt sign the first peace treaty between Israel and an Arab state.

1982 Israel invades Lebanon to destroy the Beirut-based Palestine Liberation Organization (PLO); the embattled PLO leadership relocates to Tunis.

1987 Palestinians in the West Bank and Gaza revolt against the Israeli occupation in what becomes known as the first intifada.

1993 Israel and the PLO sign Oslo Accords, creating the Palestinian Authority, which exercises limited autonomy in a small portion of the occupied territories; Palestinian "rejectionists" opposed to the accords launch deadly suicide bombings inside Israel. . . . Israel and the United Arab Emirates secretly begin to share intelligence on what they see as the growing Iranian threat to the region.

1994 Jordan signs a peace treaty with Israel.

1995-2002 *An assassination spells the death of the Israeli-Palestinian peace process.*

1995 A right-wing Israeli assassinates Israeli Prime Minister Yitzhak Rabin. A year later, Benjamin Netanyahu takes office and slows further concessions to the Palestinians over the next four years.

2000 Palestinians in the occupied territories revolt a second time; the violence leaves thousands dead and halts the peace process. Two years later, Israel builds separation barriers around the occupied territories.

2002 Arab League endorses a Saudi peace plan that offers Israel peace in exchange for a Palestinian state in the West Bank and Gaza.

2009-Present *Israel expands contacts with Gulf Arab states, culminating in normalization of ties with three Arab countries.*

2009 As security cooperation with the UAE deepens, Israel opens a secret embassy in Bahrain to handle official contacts and growing business conducted through third parties.

2011 Arab Spring protests topple autocratic regimes in Egypt, Tunisia, Yemen and Libya and spark civil war in Syria.

2015 UAE allows Israel to open a diplomatic office in Abu Dhabi; Gulf states and Israel oppose an accord signed by Iran, the United States and European countries aimed at curbing Iran's nuclear program.

2018 President Trump withdraws from Iran nuclear deal and imposes crippling economic sanction on Tehran.

2020 The UAE, Bahrain and Sudan normalize relations with Israel.

hero of the 1973 war who believed that eliminating the PLO would give Israel a free hand to impose its autonomy plan in the occupied territories.

The invasion forced the expulsion of PLO fighters and their leadership to Tunisia, moving them far away from the West Bank and Gaza. But in 1987, the territories erupted in a grassroots intifada, or uprising, against the Israeli occupation, which the PLO soon began directing from afar, marking the organization's return to the political fray.

The deteriorating security situation in the occupied territories prompted several left-wing Israeli academics to reach out to the PLO in a bid to find common ground. Those initial contacts led to secret official negotiations in Norway, and in 1993, Israeli Prime Minister Yitzhak Rabin and PLO leader Yasser Arafat signed the Oslo Accords, which created a governing Palestinian Authority in Gaza and a small enclave around the West Bank town of Jericho.[32]

The accords established security cooperation between Israeli and Palestinian police as the two sides implemented additional economic agreements and Israel turned over more designated West Bank land to be administered by the Palestinian Authority. In 1994, Jordan signed a peace treaty with Israel.[33]

Around this time, secret contacts began between Israel and the United Arab Emirates, initially over the UAE's request to buy F-16 warplanes from the United States. The Emiratis were aware that Israel could mobilize its supporters in Congress to block the sale, so it sought to assure the Israelis that the aircraft would never be used against them. After several meetings, Israel said it would not stand in the way of the arms sale.

In subsequent secret meetings, Israeli and Emirati officials found they shared similar concerns over the

Ayatollah Ruhollah Khomeini led a 1979 revolution that toppled Iran's shah from power and established an Islamic Republic.

growing threat from Iran, which not only supported anti-Israel groups such as Hamas, but also called for the overthrow of the Sunni monarchies that ruled the Gulf countries. Israel and the UAE began sharing intelligence to keep a closer eye on Iranian activities in the region.[34]

In 1995, a right-wing Israeli assassin killed Rabin at a Tel Aviv peace rally in an effort to halt what he saw as a peace process that inevitably would lead to a Palestinian state in the West Bank and Gaza. Shimon Peres took over as prime minister, vowing to continue the peace talks. But Hamas, which opposed any negotiations with Israel, launched a campaign of devastating suicide bombings inside Israel that deeply shook the public's confidence in the peace process.

The following year, Netanyahu came to power at the head of a right-wing Israeli government that slow-walked the negotiations and stepped up the establishment of Jewish settlements on West Bank lands the Palestinians sought for their state, leaving the Oslo peace process hanging by a thread.

Normalization Accords May Spark New Mideast Arms Race

Israelis fear a "potential domino effect."

Israeli Prime Minister Benjamin Netanyahu has praised his country's normalization of ties with the United Arab Emirates (UAE), Bahrain and Sudan for enlarging what he calls "the circle of peace" in the Middle East. But the agreements also have set off what experts fear is a new arms race in the region.

The spark, these experts say, was the Trump administration's authorization of an arms package for the UAE worth $23 billion that includes up to 50 F-35 stealth fighters, widely regarded as the world's most advanced multirole warplanes, plus 18 Reaper drones and precision munitions.[1]

Congress must still approve the deal, the final step in the foreign arms sale process. In the past, when Israel feared that proposed U.S. arms sales to enemy Arab states would threaten its military superiority in the region, it has succeeded in blocking most of the deals with the support of friendly lawmakers. But Israel has said it will not oppose the sale to its new Gulf partner, and congressional aides say it is likely lawmakers will approve the arms package, which would make the UAE the first Arab country to receive the F-35.

Israel's approval did not come without strings. Citing a U.S. law that requires the United States to maintain Israel's qualitative military edge over the Arabs, Defense Minister Benny Gantz flew to Washington with an $8 billion shopping list that includes another 25 F-35 fighters, which would add to the 50 Israel already has. It is also seeking additional F-15 warplanes and KC-46A tanker airplanes for in-flight refueling.[2]

"Gantz tried to limit the damage," said retired Maj. Gen. Amos Gilad, a former senior Israeli defense ministry official and now executive director of the Institute for Policy and Strategy, an Israeli national security think tank. "The problem isn't the Emirates, but with what the other Arab countries are going to get."[3]

Saudi Arabia and Qatar also have asked to buy F-35 warplanes. And Middle East experts say it is likely that other Arab states, including Egypt and Jordan, will request them too.

"This potential domino effect is exactly what the Israelis fear and have warned Washington about," said Bilal Y. Saab, a political and military analyst at the Middle East Institute, a Washington think tank that focuses on the region.[4]

Such additional Arab requests for U.S. arms sales, which have been welcomed by President Trump, are likely to encounter a different response from the incoming Biden administration. During his presidential campaign, Democratic nominee Joe Biden said he will reassess relations with Saudi Arabia and end U.S. support for the Saudi war in Yemen against Iran-backed Houthi rebels, which according to the United Nations has caused a severe humanitarian disaster in the country.[5]

After nearly six years of fighting, however, Saudi Arabia now appears to be looking for an exit. In high-level back-channel talks with the Houthis, the Saudis have offered to accept a United Nations-proposed nationwide ceasefire if the Houthis agree to a buffer zone along the Saudi-Yemen border, *Reuters* reported in November. The U.N. has been working to end the conflict by the end of 2020.[6]

Saeb Erakat, the late chief Palestinian negotiator, once compared the peace talks with Israel to a negotiation over a pizza in which one side is eating the pie as it negotiates.

In 2000, President Bill Clinton corralled Arafat and Netanyahu's successor, Prime Minister Ehud Barak, at Camp David for an all-or-nothing push for a final settlement. According to U.S. officials, Barak was far more forthcoming than Arafat, who stuck to his opening positions. After two weeks of marathon negotiations, the talks collapsed. By then, the West Bank was a tinderbox of communal tensions, primed to explode.[35]

The blowup came when right-wing Israeli politician Sharon showed up at Jerusalem's Temple Mount, the holiest site in Judaism, to underscore Israel's sovereignty

But the Trump administration's plan to designate the Houthis as a foreign terrorist organization before Trump leaves office in January could torpedo both the Saudi offer and the United Nations' efforts to end the war, U.N. officials say. Such a designation, they say, would make it harder to negotiate with the Houthis and deliver international aid to civilians in Houthi-controlled areas.

Middle East experts say that if the Biden administration restricts U.S. weapons sales, Arab states could turn to Russia, which has sold arms to Saudi Arabia, the UAE, Kuwait, Jordan and Egypt and would be happy to sell them more. China is also eager to play in the Middle East arms market. Last year, a Chinese manufacturer and an Emirates defense firm agreed to open a plant in the UAE, which will manufacture drones and other weapons.[7]

Russia and China are also hoping to sell their military hardware to Iran, which is looking to modernize its armed forces since the October expiration of a 10-year U.N. arms embargo that was imposed amid concerns over its nuclear program. An Arab diplomat, who asked not to be identified, says one of the reasons the UAE requested the F-35 warplanes was out of fear that Iran, no longer bound by the U.N. embargo, would go on a weapons-buying spree in Russia and China. He says other Gulf countries share those concerns.

But many experts say that Iran, economically crippled by the sanctions Trump has imposed, is in no position now to purchase large quantities of weapons from Russia and China unless it can obtain extremely favorable terms.

In the meantime, says Hussein Ibish, the senior scholar at the Saudi-funded Arab Gulf States Institute in Washington, the real threat to the Gulf Arab states is the state-of-the-art precision targeting and guidance systems on Iran's locally manufactured missiles and drones. This technology "can help Iran inflict more damage than planes and tanks," he said.[8]

Meanwhile, concerns on Capitol Hill over Iran's continuing nuclear program are causing some lawmakers to press for even more weapons sales for Israel. In October, two U.S. lawmakers introduced a bill that would allow the United States to provide Israel with the 30,000-pound GBU-57 "bunker buster" bomb if Iran pursues nuclear weapons. The bomb can penetrate heavily fortified underground targets.

"There should be absolutely no doubt that our ally Israel must be prepared for every contingency if Iran seeks . . . a nuclear weapon," one of the measure's sponsors, Rep. Josh Gottheimer, D-N.J., told reporters in a conference call after the bill's introduction.[9]

—*Jonathan Broder*

---

[1] Mark Mazzetti, "Administration Proposes Arms Deal for U.A.E., but Some in Congress Already Object," *The New York Times*, Nov. 10, 2020, https://tinyurl.com/y2r5z9vs.

[2] Arie Egozi, "Israel Seeks $8B Arms Deal At White House: F-35s, V-22s, KC-46s," *Breaking Defense*, Sept. 15, 2020, https://tinyurl.com/y6gfzfq8.

[3] Tom Bateman, "Could Israeli-Arab peace deals spark an arms race?" *BBC*, Nov. 2, 2020, https://tinyurl.com/y496yby8.

[4] Bilal Y. Saab, "The Coming F-35 Fiasco," *Defense One*, Oct. 8, 2020, https://tinyurl.com/y6ht54wr.

[5] Abubakr Al-Shamahi, " 'Relationship reassessed': Joe Biden and Saudi Arabia relations," *Al-Jazeera*, Nov. 11, 2020, https://tinyurl.com/y622gxvv.

[6] Aziz El-Yaakoubi, "Saudis seek buffer zone with Yemen in return for ceasefire—sources," *Reuters*, Nov. 17, 2020, https://tinyurl.com/y5fk42se.

[7] Nicolas Parasie and Robert Wall, "Russia and China Target Middle East Arms Deals," *The Wall Street Journal*, April 6, 2019, https://tinyurl.com/y487u63n.

[8] Hussein Ibish, "Arab States Should Avoid an Arms Race With Iran," *Bloomberg*, Oct. 22, 2020, https://tinyurl.com/y3q4s8sn.

[9] Connor O'Brien, "Lawmakers push to send bunker-busting bombs to Israel," *Politico*, Oct. 27, 2020, https://tinyurl.com/yyvch5mw.

---

over the compound. The area is also home to the Al-Aqsa Mosque, the third holiest site in Islam. Sharon's visit sparked armed clashes between Palestinians and Israeli security forces that quickly spread across the occupied territories into what became known as the second intifada. Over the next five years, some 3,200 Palestinians and 1,000 Israelis were killed.[36]

Sharon was elected prime minister in 2001. After several years in office, he concluded the Gaza Strip had no strategic value and ordered the full withdrawal of Israeli troops and settlers from the territory in 2005. He was widely expected to win re-election in 2006, but he suffered a severe stroke that year that left him in a coma until his death in 2014.[37]

Jewish Revival in UAE and Bahrain Follows Diplomatic Deals

"The agreement changes everything."

A few weeks after the August announcement that Israel and the United Arab Emirates (UAE) had agreed to normalize relations, Abu Dhabi's Department of Culture and Tourism sent an unprecedented order to all the hotels in the capital city.

"To ensure certain foods are available for all visitors and tourists in the emirate of Abu Dhabi, please note that all hotel establishments are advised to include kosher food options on room service menus and at all food and beverage outlets in their establishments," the order said. It was issued in anticipation of Israeli tourists and business people arriving to explore the Persian Gulf country and its potential for sales and investments.[1]

In tweets just before Rosh Hashana in September, the foreign ministers of both the UAE and Bahrain wished Jews "Shana Tova"—Happy New Year in Hebrew. Meanwhile, the Emirate's largest English-language daily, *The Khaleej Times*, published a supplement including kosher recipes and an explanation of the Jewish New Year's religious significance. And for the first time, Rosh Hashana services were held at a synagogue in Dubai for a small but growing Jewish community there.[2]

In Abu Dhabi, the Emiratis are building another synagogue as part of an interfaith complex that includes a mosque and a church, all connected by gardens. The complex is called the Abrahamic Family House in deference to the biblical patriarch considered the father of the Jews, Muslims and Christians. It is intended as a symbol of religious tolerance in a part of the world better known for an austere brand of Islam that views all non-Muslims as infidels.[3]

One of the least noticed results of the agreement between the UAE and Israel is what Steven A. Cook, a Middle East expert at the Council on Foreign Relations think tank, called "the normalization of Jews and Judaism in an Arab and Muslim society."

"That is a big deal," he said.[4]

Cook should know. He is a Jewish American who has lived in Egypt, Syria, Turkey, the West Bank and Israel during his studies of the Middle East, which earned him a master's degree from the Johns Hopkins School of Advanced International Studies and a doctorate in political science from the University of Pennsylvania. He speaks Arabic and Turkish and returns to the Middle East several times a year.[5]

In a candid personal essay published recently in the online magazine *Foreign Policy*, Cook wrote that while living in the Middle East, he was not surprised by Arabs' rejection of Zionism, the movement for Jewish self-determination that resulted in the state of Israel. What did strike him, he said, was the anti-Semitism "that was part of the cultural discourse."[6]

Cook said he learned that in Saudi Arabia, children are taught that Jews are the descendants of pigs and apes. As a student in Damascus during the summer of 1994, he recalled an evening when Syrian officials recited for him a long list of anti-Semitic canards because they felt it was necessary to provide the truth about Jews that he was not being taught in the United States.

"I don't remember any of these narratives making any distinction between Israelis and Jews," he said. Cook added that this blurring of national and religious identities, which continues in many Arab states today, undermines the view among some "apologists" for Palestinians and Arab regimes "that there is a sharp distinction between criticism of Israel's conduct and the grotesque image of Jews that is all too common in the region."[7]

At the same time, the Arab League held a summit in Beirut in 2002 where it adopted the Arab Peace Initiative that offered Israel full recognition and peace in exchange for its complete withdrawal from occupied territories and the establishment of a Palestinian state in the West Bank and Gaza Strip. The plan was the Arab League's first peace proposal since its "three no's" resolution after the 1967 war. Israel rejected the plan, saying it would leave Israel

And that is what makes the UAE's normalization of relations with Israel so different from the peace treaties that Israel signed with Egypt in 1979 and Jordan in 1994, say Middle East experts.

Despite those treaties, which have been focused almost entirely on security coordination among the Israeli, Egyptian and Jordanian militaries, the peace is a cold one, diplomats from all three countries agree. Since their signing, few Egyptian or Jordanian tourists have visited Israel, and few Israelis visit Egypt, according to Israeli officials.

Many Israelis each year do visit the red-hued second-century B.C. city of Petra, just across the Israeli border in southwestern Jordan. But in the Jordanian capital, Amman, Israelis report some bookstores still sell copies of *The Protocols of the Elders of Zion*, an anti-Semitic forgery fabricated in czarist Russia at the turn of the 20th century that purports to reveal Jewish plans for world domination.

The UAE is far more tolerant of different religions than Saudi Arabia, which allows no other faiths to practice on its soil.

Although Islam is the UAE's official religion, the UAE's laws guarantee freedom of worship provided it does not violate public policy or morals. The ruling family has donated land for Hindu and Sikh temples and Christian churches. An estimated 15 percent of the UAE's 10 million people are non-Muslims. Around 120 Jews live in the UAE, concentrated in Abu Dhabi and Dubai, says the UAE's Canadian-born chief rabbi, Yehuda Sarna.

The UAE, however, does not permit proselytizing by non-Muslims or conversion from Islam to another religion. The government also has outlawed the Muslim Brotherhood, branding the Middle East's oldest and largest Islamist political organization a terrorist group. UAE authorities also carefully vet imams and impose strict guidelines for their Friday sermons.[8]

A Jewish revival is also underway in Bahrain in the wake of its normalization of ties with Israel.

The tiny Jewish community in Bahrain's capital of Manama, numbering about 60, is made up of the descendants of Jewish families who migrated to the tiny Gulf island in the 19th century from Baghdad. Most left for Israel after it became a state in 1948. In the turbulent years that followed, the synagogue in Manama was burned down and its Torah scroll damaged.

Still, those who remained thrived under the protection of Bahrain's royal family. In 2008, Houda Nonoo became Bahrain's ambassador to the United States, the first Jew to serve as an ambassador representing any Arab country and only the third woman in Bahrain to attain ambassadorial rank.[9]

Today, following Bahrain's normalization of ties with Israel, the country's Jews are rebuilding the synagogue and looking for a rabbi, said the community's leader, Ebrahim Nonoo, Houda Nonoo's brother.

"The agreement changes everything," he said.[10]

—*Jonathan Broder*

---

[1] Emily Judd, "How the UAE is 'keeping kosher' for Jewish tourists after Israel deal," *Al-Arabiya*, Sept. 9, 2020, https://tinyurl.com/yy52vu5e.

[2] Rachel Wolf, "UAE, Bahrain send out Rosh Hashanah wishes," *The Jerusalem Post*, Sept. 18, 2020, https://tinyurl.com/y22sxf27.

[3] Sophie Tremblay and Jessie Gretener, "Mosque, church and synagogue to share home in Abu Dhabi," *CNN*, Sept. 26, 2019, https://tinyurl.com/r3qfvgx.

[4] Steven A. Cook, "The Arab World Is Having a Jewish Revolution," *Foreign Policy*, Sept. 27, 2020, https://tinyurl.com/yxzgkbkj.

[5] "Steven A. Cook," Foreign Policy Research Institute, https://tinyurl.com/y5vddeko.

[6] Cook, "The Arab World Is Having a Jewish Revolution," *op. cit.*

[7] *Ibid.*

[8] Tamer el-Ghobashy, "Five things to know about religious freedom in the United Arab Emirates," *The Washington Post*, Feb. 5, 2019, https://tinyurl.com/y67g4rsx.

[9] Menachem Wecker, "The Arab World's Jewish Ambassador," *GW Today*, Feb. 1, 2010, https://tinyurl.com/yxqpke6t.

[10] Emily Judd, "After Israel deal, Bahrain's Jews seek to revive community with new rabbi, synagogue," *Al-Arabiya*, Sept. 14, 2020, https://tinyurl.com/y246x2aw.

---

only nine miles wide at its narrowest point, a short march to the Mediterranean Sea for any invading Arab armies.

Netanyahu returned to power in 2009. Under his direction, the Jewish settler population in Arab East Jerusalem and the West Bank grew by 25 percent, reaching a total of 656,000 by the beginning of 2014. Palestinians in the West Bank numbered 2.7 million.[38]

AT ISSUE

Do the Abraham Accords represent an historic sea change in the Middle East's strategic balance?

YES — Varsha Koduvayur
Senior Research Analyst, Foundation for Defense of Democracies

Written for *CQ Researcher*, December 2020

The Abraham Accords represent a fundamental shift in the region's strategic balance. Brought together by the signatories' mutual antipathy to Iran and the Muslim Brotherhood, the accords reflect the open and public embrace of Israel by countries that have historically been ideologically opposed to the Jewish state. And they reflect a dramatic shift in the Gulf states' approach to the Palestinian issue.

The accords have effectively shattered the old pan-Arab consensus that normalization hinged on peace between Israel and Palestinians. The United Arab Emirates' and Bahrain's deals are a clear sign that the Gulf states are no longer willing to give the rejectionist, obstructionist Palestinian leadership veto power over regional diplomacy, security coordination and economic development. Through these deals, the UAE and Bahrain have positioned themselves to exert a moderating influence on Palestinian politics and society, marginalizing the actors that stoke Palestinian rejectionism. Indeed, it was this rejectionism that exacerbated the Gulf states' frustration and Israel's hesitation to offer concessions to the Palestinians.

The accords also establish a new paradigm for a warm peace with Arab states, built on people-to-people ties. This focus is the accords' single most important point of distinction, setting them apart from Israel's previous—and historic—deals with Egypt and Jordan, which fell far short of expectations. Both are best described as a cold peace, limited to transactional diplomacy, security cooperation and some economic cooperation.

By contrast, Emirati and Bahraini leaders have energetically stated their intent to foster a warmer peace and multisector cooperation—which in turn could have ripple effects throughout the region. As regional business hubs, the UAE and Bahrain host large populations of expatriate workers from the Arab and Islamic world whose home countries view Israel as an enemy. The deals have the potential to facilitate interpersonal interactions between Israeli visitors and these expat populations, creating a space for both sides to interact as humans in a supportive environment—thus planting the seeds for a societal and generational transformation.

If Israel's deals with Jordan and Egypt—the "first act" of Israel's regional recognition—represent a grudging tolerance of the Jewish state, the "second act" marked by the Abraham Accords represents a more open embrace of Israel. The accords reflect an understanding that Israel is an important and permanent regional actor, one that Arab leaders need for security, technology and diplomacy. With sustained momentum, this will have a transformational impact on the region's strategic balance.

NO — Steven A. Cook
Eni Enrico Mattei Senior Fellow for Middle East and Africa Studies, Council on Foreign Relations

Written for *CQ Researcher*, December 2020

The Abraham Accords are an important step in widening the circle of peace in the Middle East. The agreements between Israel and the United Arab Emirates and Israel and Bahrain deserve the near-universal praise they have received. Yet despite the fanfare of a White House signing ceremony last September, the accords do not represent a fundamental change in the regional strategic balance. Instead, they are a public affirmation of the prevailing diplomatic, political and military order in the Middle East.

As important as the Abraham Accords may be, they do not compare to Israel's peace treaties with Egypt and Jordan, both of which fundamentally altered the Middle East. With the famous three-way arm grasp on the White House lawn among President Jimmy Carter, Egyptian President Anwar Sadat and Israeli Prime Minister Menachem Begin in 1979, the era of regional Arab-Israeli wars came to an end. Without Egypt and its large army, there was no longer a coalition of Arab states that could threaten Israel's security. This was a paradigm shift that contributed to regional stability. It also capped an American effort dating back to the October 1973 war to peel Egypt away from the Soviet Union—a significant setback for Moscow in the Middle East.

The impact of the peace treaty between Jordan and Israel was different, but also represented a significant shift in the geostrategic environment. The agreement not only ended the state of war between the two countries, but also affirmed (albeit implicitly) that a resolution to the conflict between Israel and the Palestinians hinged on the establishment of a Palestinian state. With the treaty, ideas such as a Jordanian-Palestinian confederation and "Jordan is Palestine"—an idea the Israeli right championed—became politically untenable for all but the most diehard believers in annexation and ethnic cleansing of the West Bank. The two-state solution has never materialized, of course, but the Jordan-Israel peace treaty institutionalized this idea, which has guided American policymaking ever since.

In contrast, the Abraham Accords—as important as they are—reinforce an existing regional order. The agreements shine a light on developments that were widely known but never officially acknowledged: i.e., Israel and Gulf countries have shared strategic interests. They have merely layered onto this fact an openness to trade, tourism, technology and cultural exchange. This may make a broader peace—including Palestinians—possible in the long run, but the strategic environment in the Middle East has not changed.

Improving Gulf Ties

As the Israeli-Palestinian conflict festered, Israel's secret ties with the UAE and other Gulf countries deepened. In 2009, Israel began operating a diplomatic mission disguised as a business consultancy in Bahrain. The mission facilitated hundreds of commercial deals between Israeli and Bahraini firms while also serving as an official channel between the two governments.[39]

A key focus of these discreet ties was Iran's growing influence in the region as a result of its support for Shiite proxy militias in Lebanon, Syria, Iraq and Yemen. There were also growing concerns that Iran was trying to develop a nuclear weapon.

By 2015, with Arab attitudes toward the Palestinians cooling, the UAE no longer bothered to cloak its relations with Israel in secrecy. Officials gave Israel permission to open diplomatic offices in Abu Dhabi to handle the growing number of Israeli experts and businessmen who were arriving there.[40]

Following Trump's election as president in 2016, his son-in-law and adviser Jared Kushner began visiting Gulf states to push for normalization of relations with Israel as part of the administration's larger diplomatic effort to develop a Middle East peace plan. He found Emirati leaders had lost patience with the Palestinians and were eager to recognize Israel.[41]

Meanwhile, Trump, in a bid to appeal to U.S. evangelical Christians who saw support for Israel as a necessary component of their vision for world redemption, abandoned past U.S. policies that had preserved Washington's role as an honest broker in the Israeli-Palestinian conflict. He recognized Israeli sovereignty over all of Jerusalem and moved the U.S. embassy there from Tel Aviv. Later, he shuttered the Palestinian diplomatic office in Washington and cut all bilateral U.S. aid to the Palestinians, including U.S. contributions to a U.N. agency that provides relief to Palestinian refugees.

Trump also reversed long-standing U.S. policy by declaring Israel's West Bank settlements were not illegal, despite international law that forbids an occupying power from moving portions of its population into the occupied territory.[42]

In June 2019, Kushner unveiled the economic portion of his peace plan at what the administration called a "Peace to Prosperity" conference in Manama, the capital of Bahrain. The $50 billion plan consisted of an investment and infrastructure proposal, with the projected creation of at least 1 million new jobs for Palestinians if they agreed to the political component of the plan, which was not publicized at the time. The Palestinian leadership opposed the plan and did not attend the conference, although several Palestinian business executives showed up.[43]

Trump unveiled the political part of his plan in January 2020. It gave Israel a green light to annex 30 percent of the West Bank. It made no mention of a two-state solution, offering the Palestinians limited self-governance in several noncontiguous West Bank enclaves. Palestinian President Mahmoud Abbas rejected the plan out of hand, calling it a "conspiracy deal."[44]

Kushner said the plan presents "a big opportunity for the Palestinians" and urged them to accept it and "stop posturing." He added: "They have a perfect track record of missing opportunities."[45]

UAE Ambassador to the United States Yousef al-Otaiba said the plan was "a serious initiative that addresses many issues raised over the years." But Robert Malley, a former Middle East adviser in previous U.S. administrations, told *The New York Times*, "The message to the Palestinians, boiled down to its essence, is 'You've lost. Get over it.'"[46]

Kushner's initiative delighted Netanyahu, who announced in May he would annex 30 percent of the West Bank in July. The UAE, however, feared such a move would provoke a backlash across the Arab world that would derail its hopes of normalizing ties with Israel. Otaiba, the UAE ambassador, published an op-ed in Israel's largest-circulation Hebrew-language daily, saying Israel could have normalization with the UAE or annexation, but not both.[47]

"In the UAE and across much of the Arab world, we would like to believe Israel is an opportunity, not an enemy. We face too many common dangers and see the great potential of warmer ties," Otaiba said. "Israel's decision on annexation will be an unmistakable signal of whether it sees it the same way."[48]

According to American and Israeli officials, Otaiba's appeal prompted a flurry of diplomatic traffic between Jerusalem, Abu Dhabi and Washington. The result of those deliberations emerged with great fanfare in August, when Trump announced that Israel and the UAE had agreed to fully normalize relations in exchange for Netanyahu's suspension of his annexation plan.[49]

CURRENT SITUATION
Open for Business

Emiratis, Bahrainis and Israelis are wasting no time in laying down the legal, bureaucratic and trade infrastructure that will translate their newly normalized relations into investment and business deals.

Ofir Akunis, Israel's minister of regional cooperation, said he expects Israel and its new partners will sign deals worth $500 million annually, and he projects investments and trade totaling "billions of dollars" for each country in the coming years.[50]

"The opportunities that have been opened up in the Arab markets for Israeli firms are huge and could dramatically boost Israel's exports to the UAE, and via them, to other Arab countries," the Israeli business publication *Globes* said.[51]

Although Israel has maintained quiet trade ties with the UAE and Bahrain through third parties for several years, the normalization agreements bring those connections into the open, legitimizing business transactions and making them easier to conduct, experts say.

Israeli agricultural technology companies say they have been receiving inquiries from the UAE and Bahrain regarding Israel's expertise in water desalination and recycling, along with related technologies for hydroponic farming and measuring the moisture in soil—attractive opportunities for Gulf states that need to overcome chronic water shortages to grow more of their own food. The UAE currently imports 80 percent of its food.[52]

Since the signing of the normalization accords in September, the three countries have been busy finalizing the bilateral agreements and memoranda of understanding needed to lay the groundwork for trade, investment, scientific cooperation and technology transfers.

Under a transportation agreement, the UAE's flydubai airline began flying twice daily from Dubai to Tel Aviv last month. Israel's El Al Airlines will operate a similar schedule along the same route, starting on Dec. 13. The Emirates' Etihad airline has said it will begin daily flights between Abu Dhabi and Tel Aviv in March. Saudi Arabia has granted permission to all flights between Israel and the UAE to pass through Saudi airspace.[53]

To encourage and protect investment, the UAE and Israel also reached a preliminary agreement on avoiding double taxation and signed other accords granting most-favored-nation trade status to each other and providing protection of investments from noncommercial risks, such as nationalization, confiscation and freezing of assets.[54]

In one of the most significant collaborations, Dubai port operator DP World has signed a memorandum of understanding with the Israeli conglomerate DoverTower, indicating an intention to establish a direct trading route between Dubai's Jebel Ali port and the Israeli port of Eilat on the Red Sea, which DoverTower owns.[55]

At the same time, a joint Emirati-Israeli venture has signed a memorandum of understanding with Israel's state-owned Europe-Asia Pipeline Company to pipe UAE oil from Eilat to a terminal in the Israeli Mediterranean port of Ashkelon, allowing UAE oil headed for Europe to skirt the Suez Canal and its heavy transit fees.[56]

In other business developments, the Dubai Diamond Exchange and the Israel Diamond Exchange have signed an agreement under which each company will establish representative offices in the other's bourses, the Dubai Multi Commodities Center, which owns the Dubai exchange, said in a statement. The two diamond exchanges will share expertise, promote bilateral trade opportunities and partner on exhibitions and conferences to boost the growth of the global diamond industry, the statement said.[57]

An Israeli company that makes women's pajamas and lingerie took advantage of normalized ties to stage a photo shoot in the UAE desert featuring top Israeli model May Tager and an Emirati model holding hands to symbolize the new friendly relations between their countries.

Out of consideration for the UAE's conservative mores, the women modeled only pajamas.

"We respect the rules here," said Tager.[58]

Palestinians on Defensive

Middle East experts agree that the Palestinians find themselves in their weakest position since the 1993 Oslo Accords gave them limited autonomy in the West Bank and Gaza Strip.

Within the Arab world, the Abraham Accords have knocked the Palestinian issue from its perch at the core of the Arab-Israeli conflict.

The Palestinian Authority's relations with the West are shaky at best. In 2018, after the Palestinians severed contacts with the Trump administration in response to its recognition of Israeli sovereignty over all of Jerusalem, Trump cut off all U.S. funding and closed their diplomatic offices in Washington.[59] Normally supportive European powers have been too busy with the COVID-19 pandemic and the economic problems it has caused to make up for the funding shortfall, according to European Union diplomats.

Palestinian Authority President Abbas also has been struggling with a financial crisis since May, when he severed all contact with Israel because of Netanyahu's West Bank annexation plan.

Abbas' move to distance the Palestinians from Israel included rejecting the taxes that Israel collects on their behalf and remits to the Palestinian Authority every month, because he opposed Israel's practice of deducting the total amount of stipends Abbas pays to the families of Palestinians killed or jailed by the Israelis.[60]

And finally, despite what had appeared to be recent progress toward patching up the long-standing feud between the Palestinian Authority and Hamas in the Gaza Strip, the rift remains as deep as ever, shelving for now the prospect of a unified Palestinian leadership speaking with a single voice in any future peace negotiations.[61]

"Their options are very few," says the Carnegie Endowment's Miller. "One is a major round of violence, a third intifada, the last two of which only made their situation worse. The other is some sort of diplomatic re-engagement under a more sympathetic Biden administration."

> **"These are transcational arrangements based on a narrow coincidence of interests between Israel, the Emirates, Bahrain, Sudan and the Americans."**
>
> — *Aaron David Miller*
> *Carnegie Endowment for International Peace*

In hopes of reviving the peace process with Biden playing a more balanced role, the Palestinian Authority in November said it would resume cooperating with the Israelis on security and civil matters.

Ever since Oslo, Israelis and Palestinians have worked together to maintain a semblance of normal life in the West Bank. Their security forces have thwarted terrorist attacks and other disturbances. With the resumption of contacts, Israel transferred over $1 billion in taxes and customs fees earlier this month to the beleaguered Palestinian Authority. The tax and customs payments make up more than 60 percent of the Palestinian government's budget.[62]

Abbas has repeatedly rejected calls for another violent uprising sanctioned and directed by the PLO, as the last two intifadas were.

Palestinian officials have pinned their hopes on a shift in policy by the Biden administration that will reverse the Trump administration's acceptance of Israel's settlement activity in the West Bank and revive talks for a two-state solution that are not based on Trump's peace plan.

But Biden has said he will keep the U.S. Embassy in Jerusalem, even though he criticized Trump's decision to move it there as "short-sighted." Members of Biden's foreign policy team say a renewed push for two-state solution is not at the top of the president-elect's agenda, given the urgent need to address the United States' health and economic crises caused by the COVID-19 pandemic.[63]

Unless it is resolved, the problem of the Palestinians' divided leadership in the West Bank and Gaza Strip will continue to loom over any resumption of the peace process, Palestinian officials say.

"The big elephant in the room is the Palestinian-Palestinian conflict," says Bashar Azzeh, a member of the Palestine National Council, the Palestinian parliament. "We Palestinians need to unify."

New Rivalry

Emirati officials say that in addition to the UAE's concerns about Iran, the normalization with Israel also serves the country's need to broaden its circle of allies to confront Turkey and its Islamist-driven ambitions in the region.

Indeed, some experts say the contest for regional power and influence between the UAE and Turkey has become the Middle East's newest fault line as their assertive and headstrong leaders clash over ideology, energy and alliances.

Emile Hokayem, a Middle East expert at the International Institute for Strategic Studies in London, said the fierce competition between the UAE's Crown

Prince Mohammed bin Zayed and Turkish President Recep Tayyip Erdogan is fueling tensions that are playing out across a wide front that includes the Persian Gulf, the Horn of Africa, the Libyan civil war and the Eastern Mediterranean.

Hokayem called the UAE-Turkey rivalry "the struggle defining the politics of the Middle East at the moment."[64]

At its core, Hokayem and other experts say, is the incendiary issue of politicized Islam, which Erdogan embraces and Crown Prince Mohammed, along with other Gulf monarchs, views as a threat to regional stability, not to mention their thrones.

"For quite some time . . . the goal of the Erdogan government was to turn the country into a hegemonic regional power," said Soli Özel, an expert on Turkey at the Carnegie Middle East Center in Beirut, a branch of Washington's centrist Carnegie Endowment for International Peace. Özel added that Turkey's push for regional dominance stems from a combination of nationalism and the Islamist strategic vision of Erdogan's ruling AKP Party.[65]

Under Erdogan, Turkey has signed defense cooperation agreements with Gulf countries Kuwait and Qatar, the latter another rival of both the UAE and Saudi Arabia because of its financial support for Islamists across the Middle East. Soon after Abu Dhabi and Riyadh slapped an embargo on Qatar in 2017 as punishment for its pro-Islamist policies and other complaints, Turkey responded by deploying more troops to a garrison it established in Doha, Qatar, two years earlier.[66]

The UAE-Turkey rivalry has extended to the Horn of Africa, with its location near the southern entrance to the Red Sea, a strategic waterway for oil tankers sailing from the Middle East to the West through the Suez Canal. In 2017, Turkey opened a large military base in the Somali capital of Mogadishu. A year later, the UAE established its own military base in the autonomous region of Somaliland.[67]

Meanwhile, the UAE has joined with Cyprus, Greece, Israel, Italy, Jordan and the Palestinian Authority in a bloc called the East Mediterranean Gas Forum to challenge Turkey's claim to natural gas resources under the Eastern Mediterranean.[68]

The UAE also has been fighting a proxy war against Turkey in Libya, where Ankara backs the internationally recognized government in Tripoli, whose armed forces include several Islamist groups.

Together with Egypt, Russia, France and Israel, the UAE has provided money and weapons to the army of renegade Libyan Gen. Khalifa Haftar, who is fighting to depose the Tripoli government. Earlier this year, Haftar's forces were poised to take the city when Turkey rushed in with advisers, Syrian mercenaries, missiles and armed drones. With Ankara's assistance, government forces broke Haftar's siege and drove his army back to eastern Libya, where it is now regrouping.[69]

But Hokayem says it will be difficult for Turkey to sustain its presence there against Russian mercenaries and air support, French political cover and the UAE's deep pockets.

Add to that the bloc of countries challenging Turkey's claims in the Eastern Mediterranean, and Erdogan is facing a tightening vise of opposition to his quest for political influence in North Africa and the Mediterranean, Hokayem said.

"For Erdogan," Hokayem said, "being surrounded in the Mediterranean is no longer a distant possibility, but an unfolding reality."[70]

OUTLOOK
Revival of Annexation?

In the near term, Middle East experts say Israel's normalized ties with the UAE and Bahrain can be expected to develop and grow smoothly. But if Netanyahu decides to take his West Bank annexation plan off the shelf and use it as a carrot to secure his right-wing political base, relations could turn frosty.

And if he follows through with the annexation, normalized ties could be in jeopardy. Some experts think the UAE and Bahrain could rescind recognition. But many others believe that, while annexation almost certainly would precipitate a diplomatic crisis, the UAE and Bahrain have too much invested in the new relationship to cut ties altogether. They say a slowdown in relations is more likely.

The future of the Palestinians depends on numerous factors. The most critical is how the Biden administration approaches its relations with Israel and the Palestinians. Biden is a long-standing friend of Israel, but the liberal wing of his Democratic Party has grown vocally critical of Israel's treatment of the Palestinians, and Biden will have to take its views into consideration, political analysts say.

According to Vice President-elect Kamala Harris, Biden will restore U.S. aid to the Palestinians and resume contributions to a United Nations agency that looks after Palestinian refugees, both of which Trump cut. Biden also opposes Israel's settlement policy in the West Bank, and sources close to him say he is likely to reinstate Washington's pre-Trump policy that views the settlements as illegal under international law. But Biden is unlikely to launch a new peace process anytime soon.[71]

Meanwhile, Abbas will face continuing difficulties resolving differences with Hamas leaders to produce a single voice that speaks for the Palestinians. If he succeeds without Hamas abandoning its call for Israel's destruction through armed struggle, Israel will not sit down with any unified Palestinian negotiating team.

Perhaps the biggest factor that will affect U.S. relations with both Israel and the Gulf Arab states will be how Biden goes about fulfilling one of his main campaign promises: to rejoin the Iran nuclear accord, which Trump scrapped in 2018.

Experts say a recent United Nations report that Iran has stockpiled 12 times the amount of low-enriched uranium as was allowed under the nuclear agreement is just one of the hurdles that Biden must overcome to pull off such a feat.

In addition to renegotiating the facts on the ground that have been created over the past two years, Iran says it deserves compensation from the United States for the economic punishment it has endured from renewed U.S. sanctions.

And Biden will have to find a way to deal with Israel and Gulf Arab states, who will object to anything less than an end altogether to Iran's nuclear program. Israel has tremendous political influence on Capitol Hill and can make it exceedingly difficult, and politically costly, for Biden to rejoin the nuclear accord.

"That's why the Arab Gulf states are looking to the region, not beyond the region, to shore up their security," says the U.S. Institute of Peace's Kurtzer-Ellenbogen. "They're hedging their bets against a very uncertain future."

NOTES

1. Lara Jakes *et al.*, "Trump Announces Sudan Will Move to Normalize Ties With Israel," *The New York Times*, Oct. 23, 2020, https://tinyurl.com/yye3vzgl; Matthew Lee, "Trump announces Israel-Morocco to normalize relations," *The Associated Press*, Dec. 10, 2020, https://tinyurl.com/y6hcs2qt.

2. "Remarks by President Trump, Prime Minister Netanyahu, Minister bin Zayed and Minister Al Zayani at the Abraham Accords Signing Ceremony," The White House, Sept.15, 2020, https://tinyurl.com/y5wz6cye.

3. "The Abraham Accords," U.S. Department of State, Sept. 15, 2020, https://tinyurl.com/y4xvznvd.

4. Cody Levine, "Netanyahu: 'Land for Peace' formula ineffective for Middle East peace," *The Jerusalem Post*, Aug. 16, 2020, https://tinyurl.com/y58z3lna.

5. Parisa Hafezi, "Rivals Iran and UAE to hold maritime security talks," *Reuters*, July 30, 2019, https://tinyurl.com/yxd4llzc; "UAE Sends Additional Aid to Iran in Fight against COVID-19," UAE Government, June 27, 2020, https://tinyurl.com/y557xw6y; and Zainab Fattah, "UAE Condemns Iranian Scientist's Slaying as Threat to Peace," *Bloomberg*, Nov. 30, 2020, https://tinyurl.com/yx9qd8ck.

6. Maysam Behravesh and Hamidreza Azizi, "Israel's Peace Deals Are a Strategic Nightmare for Iran," *Foreign Policy*, Sept. 14, 2020, https://tinyurl.com/y5xoc78w.

7. Hussein Ibish, "Arab States Should Avoid an Arms Race With Iran," *Bloomberg*, Oct. 22, 2020, https://tinyurl.com/y2ykfoqx.

8. Felicia Schwartz and Summer Said, "Israel's Netanyahu, Saudi Crown Prince Hold First Known Meeting," *The Wall Street Journal*, Nov. 23, 2020, https://tinyurl.com/y6f6kqhu.

9. "Remarks by President Trump, Prime Minister Netanyahu, Minister bin Zayed and Minister Al Zayani at the Abraham Accords Signing Ceremony," *op. cit.*

10. John Hannah, "The Israel-UAE Deal Is Trump's First Unambiguous Diplomatic Success," *Foreign Policy*, Aug. 14, 2020, https://tinyurl.com/yxc5cdb3.

11. Joe Biden, "My Statement on the Agreement between Israel and the United Arab Emirates," medium.com/@JoeBiden, Aug. 13, 2020, https://tinyurl.com/y2cgkzg4.

12. Dion Nissenbaum, "Secret Ties Between U.A.E. and Israel Paved Way for Diplomatic Relations," *The Wall Street Journal*, Aug. 14, 2020, https://tinyurl.com/y3kkkqym; Barak Ravid, "Israel's secret embassy in Bahrain," *Axios*, Oct. 21, 2020, https://tinyurl.com/y6tyamgk; and "Israel Among the Nations: Middle East & North Africa," Israel Ministry of Foreign Affairs, https://tinyurl.com/y5p38lfb.

13. Andrew Restuccia and Courtney McBride, "Trump to Remove Sudan From List of Countries That Sponsor Terrorism," *The Wall Street Journal*, Oct. 19, 2020, https://tinyurl.com/y4lb56gp.

14. Yossi Alpher, "Hard Questions, Tough Answers," Americans for Peace Now, Oct. 12, 2020, https://tinyurl.com/y5ojts69.

15. Aaron Boxerman, "In blow to Palestinians, Arab League refuses to condemn Israel-UAE deal," *The Times of Israel*, Sept. 9, 2020, https://tinyurl.com/y5994uwv.

16. "Full Transcript: Prince Bandar bin Sultan's interview on Israel-Palestine conflict," *Al-Arabiya*, Oct. 5, 2020, https://tinyurl.com/yyy6bhw4.

17. William Booth and Ruth Eglash, "Kerry's nine-month quest for Middle East peace ends in failure," *The Washington Post*, April 29, 2014, https://tinyurl.com/y3d5jurn.

18. "Transcript: A Conversation with H.E. Anwar Gargash, UAE Minister of State for Foreign Affairs," Atlantic Council, Aug. 20, 2020, https://tinyurl.com/y5kbahaf.

19. Dennis Ross, "The Middle East is changing. Will Palestinians be left behind?" *The Washington Post*, Sept. 13, 2020, https://tinyurl.com/yxkf6k6l.

20. Diana Buttu, "Trump and Netanyahu's big fat fake peace deal," *Haaretz*, Sept. 16, 2020, https://tinyurl.com/yyz5rfbr.

21. Sarah Dadouch, "Saudi media softens tone on normalization, offering clue to kingdom's thinking on Israel," *The Washington Post*, Oct. 13, 2020, https://tinyurl.com/y2j5ty5r.

22. Behravesh and Azizi, *op. cit.*

23. *Ibid.*

24. *Ibid.*

25. Mark Mazzetti, "Administration Proposes Arms Deal for U.A.E., but Some in Congress Already Object," *The New York Times*, Nov. 10, 2020, https://tinyurl.com/y2r5z9vs; Arie Egozi, "Israel Seeks $8B Arms Deal At White House: F-35s, V-22s, KC-46s," *Breaking Defense*, Sept. 15, 2020, https://tinyurl.com/y6gfzfq8.

26. Lee Steed, "Hidden Threat: Iran has secret underground 'missile cities' hiding rockets ready to strike under five layers of concrete," *The Sun*, Jan. 12, 2020, https://tinyurl.com/yxpgy88u.

27. "Declaration of Independence of the State of Israel (English subtitles)," YouTube, posted Feb. 4, 2010, https://tinyurl.com/mxrjd2c.

28. "State of Israel Proclaimed," *History*, May 12, 2020, https://tinyurl.com/yydlbjnd.

29. "1947-1949 Palestine war," Military.wikia.org, https://tinyurl.com/yx9xn8mq.

30. "Six-Day War," *History*, Aug. 21, 2018, https://tinyurl.com/y7bsft6x.

31. "Yom Kippur War," *History*, Aug. 21, 2018, https://tinyurl.com/yxjet3yf.

32. "War in Lebanon," *Encyclopaedia Britannica*, https://tinyurl.com/y2ptgbkh; "The Oslo Accords," *Encyclopaedia Britannica*, https://tinyurl.com/y3fnr54b.

33. "The Oslo Accords and the Arab-Israeli Peace Process," Office of the Historian, U.S. Department of State, https://tinyurl.com/j6mydw6.

34. Adam Entous, "Donald Trump's New World Order," *The New Yorker*, June 11, 2018, https://tinyurl.com/ybtjkabf.

35. Jonathan Freedland, "The assassination of Yitzhak Rabin: 'He never knew it was one of his people who shot him in the back,' " *The Guardian*, Oct. 31, 2020, https://tinyurl.com/y4xyb6gz; Jane Perlez, "Impasse at Camp David: The Overview; Clinton Ends Deadlocked Peace Talks," *The New York Times*, July 26, 2000, https://tinyurl.com/y2q3tnod.

36. Zack Beauchamp, "What were the intifadas?" *Vox*, May 14, 2018, https://tinyurl.com/yc6dheja.

37. "Ariel Sharon," Jewish Virtual Library, https://tinyurl.com/yyajlyjh.
38. Ishaan Tharoor, "Map: The spread of Israeli settlements in the West Bank," *The Washington Post*, Dec. 22, 2014, https://tinyurl.com/y5woqlwc; "Estimated Population in Palestine Mid-Year by Governorate, 1997-2021," Palestinian Central Bureau of Statistics, 2020, https://tinyurl.com/y4tdhfcr.
39. Ravid, *op. cit.*
40. Barak Ravid, "Exclusive: Israel to Open First Diplomatic Mission in Abu Dhabi," *Haaretz*, Nov. 26, 2015, https://tinyurl.com/y4b92ytw.
41. Entous, *op. cit.*
42. "President Donald J. Trump Keeps His Promise To Open U.S. Embassy In Jerusalem, Israel," The White House, May 14, 2018, https://tinyurl.com/y9zr2wr8; David Brunnstrom, "Trump cuts more than $200 million in U.S. aid to Palestinians," *Reuters*, Aug. 24, 2018, https://tinyurl.com/ya54aslt; and Karen DeYoung *et al.*, "Trump administration says Israel's West Bank settlements do not violate international law," *The Washington Post*, Nov. 18, 2019, https://tinyurl.com/uj2oxwb.
43. Matt Spetalnick and Steve Holland, "Exclusive: White House's Kushner unveils economic portion of Middle East peace plan," *Reuters*, June 22, 2019, https://tinyurl.com/y3zajy8u.
44. Michael Crowley and David M. Halbfinger, "Trump Releases Mideast Peace Plan That Strongly Favors Israel," *The New York Times*, Jan. 28, 2020, https://tinyurl.com/vdv64dc.
45. CNN, Twitter post, Jan. 28, 2020, https://tinyurl.com/y5338kvz.
46. David E. Sanger, "A Deal That Has Two Elections, Rather Than Mideast Peace, as Its Focus," *The New York Times*, Jan. 28, 2020, https://tinyurl.com/yyazzg2n.
47. "Netanyahu: 'We will annex 30% of the West Bank area to Israel,'" *Middle East Monitor*, May 30, 2020, https://tinyurl.com/y8ob8xgt.
48. Yousef al-Otaiba, "Annexation will be a serious setback for better relations with the Arab world," *YNetNews*, June 12, 2020, https://tinyurl.com/y69n4b9q.
49. Peter Baker *et al.*, "Israel and United Arab Emirates Strike Major Diplomatic Agreement," *The New York Times*, Aug. 13, 2020, https://tinyurl.com/y67bj8p4; Michael Crowley and David M. Halbfinger, "Bahrain Will Normalize Relations With Israel, in Deal Brokered by Trump," *The New York Times*, Sept. 11, 2020, https://tinyurl.com/y4ek88yh; and Mohammed Alamin, "Sudan announces normalization ties with Israel," Anadolu Agency, Oct. 24, 2020, https://tinyurl.com/yysx6rtt.
50. Simeon Kerr, "Israel expects $500m in deals with Bahrain and UAE," *Financial Times*, Sept. 14, 2020, https://tinyurl.com/y3m94nya.
51. Dan Zaken, "Pact with UAE opens entire Arab world to Israeli business," *Globes*, Aug. 14, 2020, https://tinyurl.com/y3hmz2us.
52. Sara Toth Stub, "Fields of dreams: UAE farmers want Israeli sensors that let crops ask for water," *The Times of Israel*, Oct. 20, 2020, https://tinyurl.com/y5bhchpy.
53. Steven Scheer, "Israel's El Al Airlines to fly 14 weekly flights to Dubai," *Reuters*, Nov. 23, 2020, https://tinyurl.com/y2gs8la3.
54. Tuqa Khalid, "UAE, Israel reach agreement on double taxation avoidance to encourage investment," *Al-Arabiya*, Oct. 15, 2020, https://tinyurl.com/y23dd6mt.
55. Steven Scheer, "Israel Shipyards, DP World jointly bid in Haifa Port privatisation," *Reuters*, Oct. 29, 2020, https://tinyurl.com/y46hjtb2.
56. "Israeli firm signs deal to pipe UAE oil to Europe," *The Times of Israel*, Oct. 21, 2020, https://tinyurl.com/y54fou7j.
57. "DMCC's Dubai Diamond Exchange and Israel Diamond Exchange Sign Landmark Agreement to Boost Regional trade," press release, DMCC, Sept. 17, 2020, https://tinyurl.com/y4k7dusz.
58. "Israel-UAE deal inspires new cooperation on pajamas," *Israel Hayom*, Sept. 8, 2020, https://tinyurl.com/y2ynmw8w.
59. David Brunnstrom, "Trump cuts more than $200m in U.S. aid to Palestinians," *Reuters*, Aug. 24, 2018, https://tinyurl.com/ya54aslt.

60. Adam Rasgon and Mohammed Najib, "Palestinians Rejected Tax Money to Slap Israel. It's Not Israel That's Hurting." *The New York Times*, Sept. 11, 2020, https://tinyurl.com/yytl948w; "Palestinian Authority rejects UAE aid sent via Israeli airport," *Al-Jazeera*, May 21, 2020, https://tinyurl.com/y2cuhrxx.
61. "Palestinian Authority to resume coordination with Israel," *Al-Jazeera*, Nov. 17, 2020, https://tinyurl.com/y5evpl2m.
62. Rasgon and Najib, *op. cit.*; "Israel transfers $1b to cash-strapped Palestinian Authority," *The Associated Press*, Dec. 2, 2020, https://tinyurl.com/yxk69zt6.
63. Bill Barrow, "Joe Biden says he'd leave US embassy in Jerusalem if elected," *The Associated Press*, April 29, 2020, https://tinyurl.com/yxsdqtf9.
64. Andrew England *et al.*, "UAE vs Turkey: the regional rivalries pitting MBZ against Erdogan," *Financial Times*, Oct. 26, 2020, https://tinyurl.com/y2lu-3mus.
65. Michael Young, "The Lure of Regional Hegemony," Carnegie Middle East Center, July 27, 2020, https://tinyurl.com/yyxd9y2u.
66. "Turkey sends more troops to Qatar," *Al-Jazeera*, Dec. 27, 2017, https://tinyurl.com/y4nmn727.
67. Abdirahman Hussein and Orhan Coskun, "Turkey opens military base in Mogadishu to train Somali soldiers," *Reuters*, Sept. 30, 2017, https://tinyurl.com/y35vuups; Alexander Cornwell, "UAE to train Somaliland forces under military base deal: Somaliland president," *Reuters*, March 15, 2018, https://tinyurl.com/yxpp98c9.
68. "A row between Turkey and Greece over gas is raising tension in the eastern Mediterranean," *The Economist*, Aug. 20, 2020, https://tinyurl.com/y6ef9p5e.
69. Emile Hokayem, "Libya: a cauldron for Mediterranean power politics," International Institute for Strategic Studies, July 6, 2020, https://tinyurl.com/y39wzlod.
70. *Ibid.*
71. Emily Judd, "If elected, Biden to restore Palestinian aid, reopen PLO office in Washington: Harris," *Al-Arabiya*, Nov. 3, 2020, https://tinyurl.com/y5nsgv5s.

BIBLIOGRAPHY
Books

Friedman, Thomas L., *From Beirut to Jerusalem*, **Farrar, Straus and Giroux**, 1989.
Although three decades have passed since this book's publication, the headlines confirm that the dynamics guiding events in Lebanon, Israel and the Palestinian territories have not changed—and few explain those forces better than Friedman, a Pulitzer Prize-winning *New York Times* correspondent.

Ghattas, Kim, *Black Wave: Saudi Arabia, Iran, and the Forty-Year Rivalry That Unraveled Culture, Religion, and Collective Memory in the Middle East*, **Henry Holt and Company**, 2020.
A veteran Middle East correspondent details the cross-Gulf, Sunni-Shiite rivalry between Saudis and Iranians that has defined Middle East politics for a generation.

Hubbard, Ben, *MBS: The Rise to Power of Mohammed bin Salman*, **Tim Duggan Books**, 2020.
The New York Times' Beirut bureau chief provides a fresh and often unflattering assessment of the ambitious, rules-breaking crown prince who is upending Saudi life and society and producing real, if uncertain, change.

Worth, Robert, *A Rage for Order: The Middle East in Turmoil, from Tahrir Square to ISIS*, **Farrar, Straus and Giroux**, 2016.
A former *New York Times* correspondent provides a smart overview of the Arab Spring protests across the Middle East and what they wrought.

Articles

Behravesh, Maysam, and Hamidreza Azizi, "Israel's Peace Deals with UAE and Bahrain Are a Strategic Nightmare for Iran," *Foreign Policy*, Sept. 14, 2020, https://tinyurl.com/y2yomx34.
A former Iranian intelligence analyst who is now a geopolitical risk consultant in Washington teams up with an Iranian Middle East expert at a German think tank to explain why Tehran's furious reaction to the Israel-Gulf normalization deal is not just rhetorical.

Crowley, Michael, and David M. Halbfinger, "Trump Releases Mideast Peace Plan That Strongly Favors Israel," *The New York Times*, Jan. 28, 2020, https://tinyurl.com/vdv64dc.

Two reporters, one covering foreign policy at the White House and the other *The Times*' Jerusalem correspondent, provide a thorough analysis of the Trump Middle East peace plan.

Dadouch, Sarah, "Saudi media softens tone on normalization, offering clue to kingdom's thinking on Israel," *The Washington Post*, Oct. 20, 2020, https://tinyurl.com/y2j5ty5r.
A reporter analyzes the signals Saudi Arabia's de facto ruler, Crown Prince Mohammed bin Salman, has sent to indicate his approval of the U.S.-brokered Abraham Accords, while his father, King Salman, refuses to recognize Israel until the Palestinian issue is resolved.

"Full Transcript: Prince Bandar bin Sultan's interview on Israel-Palestine conflict," *Al-Arabiya*, Oct. 5, 2020, https://tinyurl.com/yyy6bhw4.
In rejecting Palestinian criticism of the Abraham Accords, Prince Bandar, a former Saudi ambassador to Washington, delivers a brutally frank critique of the poor choices Palestinian leaders have made at critical times in their history.

Hannah, John, "The Israel-UAE Deal Is Trump's First Unambiguous Diplomatic Success," *Foreign Policy*, Aug. 14, 2020, https://tinyurl.com/y5vqq8l3.
The former national security adviser to Vice President Dick Cheney cites all the national security and economic pluses of the Abraham Accords.

Nissenbaum, Dion, "Secret Ties Between U.A.E. and Israel Paved Way for Diplomatic Relations," *The Wall Street Journal*, Aug. 14, 2020, https://tinyurl.com/y3kkkqym.
A reporter based in Beirut recounts the intelligence ties between Israel and the UAE going back to 1993.

Ravid, Barak, "Israel's secret embassy in Bahrain," *Axios*, Oct. 21, 2020, https://tinyurl.com/y6tyamgk.
An Israeli reporter with knowledgeable sources in Israel's intelligence community breaks the story of Israel's secret relations with Bahrain going back a decade.

Spetalnick, Matt, and Steve Holland, "Exclusive: White House's Kushner unveils economic portion of Middle East peace plan," *Reuters*, June 22, 2019, https://tinyurl.com/y3zajy8u.
Two veteran Washington reporters reveal the economic part of President Trump's peace plan, which was unveiled before the political portion as a $50 billion carrot to entice the Palestinian leadership. With no sense at that point to indicate what the plan would cost politically, the Palestinians took a pass.

"Transcript: A Conversation with H.E. Anwar Gargash, UAE Minister of State for Foreign Affairs," *Atlantic Council*, Aug. 20, 2020, https://tinyurl.com/y6rqyfyc.
Appearing before the Atlantic Council, a Washington foreign policy think tank, the senior United Arab Emirates (UAE) official explains his country's strategic thinking behind its decision to normalize relations with Israel without waiting for a solution to the Palestinian issue.

Reports and Studies

Page, Matthew, and Jodi Vittori, "Dubai's Role in Facilitating Corruption and Global Illicit Financial Flows," *Carnegie Endowment for International Peace*, July 7, 2020, https://tinyurl.com/y9c2dokg.
Two money-laundering experts explore the role Dubai plays in illicit financial flows, but note that law enforcement agencies and policymakers face complex challenges in halting the emirate's activities.

Sharp, Jeremy M., *et al.*, "Israel's Qualitative Military Edge and Possible U.S. Arms Sales to the United Arab Emirates," *Congressional Research Service*, Oct. 26, 2020, https://tinyurl.com/yxlzwnl5.
A team of Middle East experts at Congress' in-house think tank examines the impact of a proposed sale of the F-35 Joint Strike Fighter and other advanced weaponry to the UAE.

Thomas, Clayton, "Arms Sales in the Middle East: Trends and Analytical Perspectives for U.S. Policy," *Congressional Research Service*, Oct. 11, 2017, https://tinyurl.com/yxe4662o.
This report analyzes state-to-state arms sales in the Middle East with a focus on U.S. transfers.

Ulrichsen, Kristian Coates, and Giorgio Cafiero, "Oman plays it safe on Israel," *Middle East Institute*, Oct. 27, 2020, https://tinyurl.com/y5a6ubsu.
Two geopolitical risk analysts examine why Oman has not joined its Gulf neighbors, the United Arab Emirates and Bahrain, in normalizing relations with Israel.

THE NEXT STEP

Arms Sales

Ahronheim, Anna, "No deal between Israel & Saudi Arabia yet, but expect more weapons sales," *The Jerusalem Post*, Nov. 26, 2020, https://tinyurl.com/yxczmqqg.
Saudi Arabia could purchase additional arms from the United States if it agrees to normalize ties with Israel.

Stone, Mike, "U.S. arms sales to UAE draw fire from 29 rights groups," *Reuters*, Nov. 30, 2020, https://tinyurl.com/y6yblt7d.
Human rights groups asked Congress to block the sale of weapons to the United Arab Emirates (UAE) due to the country's involvement in conflicts in Yemen and Libya.

Zengerle, Patricia, and Mike Stone, "U.S. senators seek to stop Trump's $23 billion in arms sales to UAE," *Reuters*, Nov. 18, 2020, https://tinyurl.com/y4j8x9d3.
Sens. Robert Menendez, D-N.J., Chris Murphy, D-Conn., and Rand Paul, R-Ky., will introduce separate resolutions of disapproval of President Trump's plans to sell drones, aircraft and missiles to the UAE.

Saudi Arabia and Israel

Roos, Meghan, "As Iran Vows to Avenge Slain Scientist, Saudi-Israel Peace Talks Reportedly Break Down," *Newsweek*, Nov. 27, 2020, https://tinyurl.com/yyncntkc.
Although normalization talks between Israel and Saudi Arabia apparently have paused, the Saudis have hinted they would be willing to resume negotiations once President-elect Biden assumes office on Jan. 20.

"Saudis okay Israeli use of airspace on way to UAE, hours before maiden flight," *The Times of Israel*, Nov. 30, 2020, https://tinyurl.com/yy84tko2.
Saudi Arabia allowed an Israeli airline to use Saudi airspace for flights to the United Arab Emirates, but the move is good for only four days.

"A secret, high-level meeting suggests Israel and Saudi Arabia are hedging their bets on Biden," *Business Insider*, Nov. 30, 2020, https://tinyurl.com/y489v3ej.
Israel and Saudi Arabia might reduce their reliance on U.S. cooperation and diversify their international relationships out of fear that a Biden administration will adopt a moderate approach to Iran.

Turkey

"Greece, UAE sign political, defense agreements," *Al-Monitor*, Nov. 18, 2020, https://tinyurl.com/y3tm7scj.
Greece and the UAE are developing closer ties as their mutual tensions with Turkey continue.

Soylu, Ragip, "Turkey seeking to repair Saudi relations with high-level contacts," *Middle East Eye*, Nov. 27, 2020, https://tinyurl.com/yyokvg9j.
Turkey appears ready to move past its falling-out with Saudi Arabia after the murder of journalist Jamal Khashoggi in the Saudis' Istanbul consulate.

Zaman, Amberin, "Turkey opens secret channel to fix ties with Israel," *Al-Monitor*, Nov. 30, 2020, https://tinyurl.com/yxwpbvyk.
The chief of Turkey's international intelligence service has initiated secret talks with Israeli officials to improve relations after a 2018 disagreement over Gaza and the movement of the U.S. Embassy to Jerusalem.

U.S. Politics and Israel

Fenenbock, Michael, "Why Joe Biden's Middle East and Israel policy is not Obama's," *The Jerusalem Post*, Dec. 2, 2020, https://tinyurl.com/y55uga2k.
An American political strategist suggests President-elect Biden's view of Israel is less critical than former President Barack Obama's, and that the Middle East is not at the top of Biden's agenda.

Ravid, Barak, and Dave Lawler, "Biden speaks with Israeli leaders Netanyahu and Rivlin," *Axios*, Nov. 17, 2020, https://tinyurl.com/y3jtf3sn.
Biden called Israel's prime minister and president a few days after his victory became evident.

Zilber, Neri, "Israel Is the Wrench in Biden's Iran Policy," *Foreign Policy*, Nov. 30, 2020, https://tinyurl.com/y24kefdk.
Analysts and intelligence officials say the assassination of an Iranian nuclear scientist, widely attributed to Israel, may have been timed as a last-chance opportunity to strike a blow against Iran before Biden attempts to return to the nuclear agreement negotiated by the Obama administration.

For More Information

Arab Gulf Institute in Washington, 1050 Connecticut Ave., N.W., Washington, DC 20036; 202-768-9522; agsiw.org. Think tank funded by Saudi Arabia and the United Arab Emirates that provides analysis of the social, economic and political dimensions of the Gulf Arab states and key neighboring countries.

Carnegie Endowment for International Peace, 1779 Massachusetts Ave., N.W., Washington, DC 20036; 202-483-7600; carnegieendowment.org. Independent think tank with Middle East experts in Washington and its Middle East Center in Beirut that publishes books and papers on the region and holds online conferences.

Foundation for the Defense of Democracies, 1800 M St., N.W., Washington, DC 20036; 202-207-0190; fdd.org. Nonpartisan think tank that focuses on U.S. foreign policy and national security with a strong pro-Israel, anti-Iran viewpoint. Produces policy briefs, podcasts and videos of its experts testifying before Congress.

Institute for National Security Studies, Chaim Levanon St. 40, Tel Aviv-Yafo, Israel; +972 3-640-0400; inss.org.il. Independent Israeli think tank providing high-quality research and analysis of Israel's national security challenges through books, papers, strategic assessments and online conferences.

International Institute for Strategic Studies—Bahrain, Bahrain Financial Harbour, 14th Floor, GBCorp Tower, 4626, Bahrain; +973 1718-1155; iiss.org. International research institute providing objective expertise on military, political and economic developments in the Middle East. Hosts the annual Manama Dialogue, the region's premier security summit, which attracts senior officials from around the world.

Middle East Institute, 1763 N St., N.W., Washington, DC 20036; 202-785-1141; mei.edu. Nonpartisan think tank providing policy papers and webinars with expert analysis of the Middle East's political, military and social issues. Also offers regional language courses and a forum for the region's arts and culture.

Palestinian Center for Policy and Survey Research, Sharia Off Irsal, PO Box 76, Ramallah, Palestine; +970 2-296-4933; pcpsr.org. Independent Palestinian think tank providing research and analysis of Palestinian Authority policy and foreign policy, West Bank and Gaza public opinion polls and conferences.

U.S. Institute of Peace, 2301 Constitution Ave., N.W., Washington, DC 20037; 202-457-1700; usip.org. Congressionally funded institution that sends experts to the Middle East's most troubled areas to provide training, expertise and analysis to those working to prevent or reduce violent conflict. Publishes the *Iran Primer*, a book explaining the Islamic Republic's political and military institutions.

Washington Institute for Near East Policy, 1111 19th St., N.W. #500, Washington, DC 20005; 202-452-0650; winep.org. Nonpartisan think tank closely associated with the pro-Israel lobbying group American Israel Public Affairs Committee. The Washington Institute offers expert analysis, policy briefs and webinars focusing on Middle East developments that affect Israel's national security.

11
Immigration Overhaul

Would a border crisis derail efforts to make U.S. policy more welcoming?

By Val Ellicott

Honduran migrants clash with Guatemalan security forces in Vado Hondo, Guatemala, on Jan. 17, 2021. Former President Donald Trump had conditioned aid to El Salvador, Guatemala and Honduras on their taking aggressive action to curb northward migration.

From *CQ Researcher*, March 19, 2021

THE ISSUES

The families began trickling out of a bus station in Honduras on Jan. 14, first in small groups and later in massive waves. By the next day, they had formed a caravan numbering in the thousands, all headed on foot, in cars or on packed buses to the border with Guatemala and, in the coming weeks, to what they hoped would be a new life in the United States.[1]

Within a week, most were back where they started. Guatemalan security forces, acting on public health concerns related to the coronavirus and on Trump administration demands to do more to stop migrants heading north, used tear gas, batons and riot shields to break up the caravan and send most of the would-be migrants home.[2]

But smaller groups continued making their way north in January and February, driven by increasingly desperate conditions in Central America's Northern Triangle—Honduras, Guatemala and El Salvador—where poverty, gang violence and political instability have worsened due to the coronavirus and two devastating tropical storms in November.[3]

"There is no work in Honduras, especially after the two cyclones and the pandemic," Dixón Vázquez, 29, said on Jan. 17. "Our goal is to reach the United States."[4]

He and other caravan members said they see new hope in President Biden's vow to treat migrants—including asylum-seekers fleeing persecution and violence in their home countries—humanely after former President Donald Trump's four-year effort to sharply reduce options for both legal and undocumented immigrants.[5]

The expectations created by Biden's promise, however, threaten to create a new humanitarian crisis at the Southern border, as new waves of migrants flow northward from Central America and Mexico. Homeland Security Secretary Alejandro Mayorkas said on March 16 that the government expects to encounter more migrants at the border in 2021 than in any year in the past two decades. The increasingly unmanageable situation led Biden, in an interview with ABC News the same day, to tell would-be migrants, "don't come" until his administration sets up policies and procedures to handle the new arrivals.[6]

Biden's long-term goal is to dismantle Trump's immigration programs while pursuing policies that acknowledge the "tremendous economic, cultural and social value" immigrants contribute. But the president faces major hurdles. Experts say the centerpiece of Biden's immigration agenda—legislation that offers millions of undocumented immigrants a path to citizenship but does not contain the enforcement provisions Republicans typically demand—stands little chance of passage in a closely divided, highly polarized Congress.[7]

"In its current form, it's a nonstarter," says Lora Ries, a senior research fellow for homeland security at the Heritage Foundation, a conservative think tank in Washington.

Other changes Biden wants to make through executive orders or rule changes likely will run into legal or logistical challenges, as immigration competes with the coronavirus and the economy for the president's attention. In one early setback, a federal judge granted a request from Texas to block one of Biden's first immigration actions: suspension of most deportations for 100 days.[8]

Immigration experts say growing chaos along the U.S.-Mexico border poses an even bigger threat to Biden's immigration agenda. Apprehensions of migrants at the border—including unaccompanied children—have spiked in recent months, alarming immigration officials and testing Biden's ability to maintain order while demonstrating compassion.

"If there is another humanitarian crisis at the border, it would . . . lessen the likelihood of getting Republican support in the future for bigger immigration legislation," said Ariel Ruiz Soto, a policy analyst at the Migration Policy Institute, a think tank in Washington.[9]

Republicans increasingly view deteriorating conditions at the border as a powerful weapon in their 2022 midterm election strategy. During a trip to the U.S.-Mexico border on March 15, House GOP leader Kevin McCarthy of California described the new waves of migrants as "a Biden border crisis."[10]

Trump, aided by his top immigration adviser, Stephen Miller, used his executive power to make more than 400 changes to immigration policy. Biden can use his own executive power to immediately reverse some of those changes, but others are deeply embedded in federal regulations, experts say.[11]

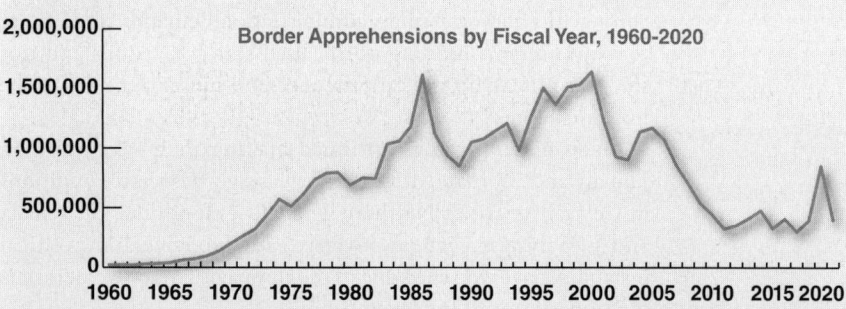

Border Apprehensions Peaked in 2000

Apprehensions at the Southwest border, which surged in the 1980s and '90s after Congress passed major immigration reforms in 1965 and 1986, have totaled less than 1 million per year since 2007.

Border Apprehensions by Fiscal Year, 1960-2020

Sources: "Total Illegal Alien Apprehensions by Fiscal Year," U.S. Border Patrol, accessed March 11, 2021, https://tinyurl.com/3758h7vy; "Southwest Border Migration FY2020," U.S. Customs and Border Protection, Nov. 19, 2020, https://tinyurl.com/2mav8zaj

"It's policy after policy layered on top of each other," said Stephanie Leutert, director of the Central America & Mexico Policy Initiative, a research program at the University of Texas at Austin. "Each one is going to take a very long series of steps to unwind responsibly."[12]

Further complicating Biden's plans, many of the country's 240,000 border and immigration agents remain loyal to Trump, immigration advocates say. And Miller is actively working to undermine Biden's immigration agenda, partly by encouraging GOP members of Congress to attack it.[13]

Despite such obstacles, Biden already has reversed some of his predecessor's most significant immigration changes. He has halted work on Trump's signature project, a wall along the Southern border; reversed Trump's ban on travel to the United States from some Muslim-majority and African countries; scrapped a ban on new permanent residency permits, or "green cards"; and ordered a review of Trump's restrictive asylum policies and other barriers to legal immigration, with the goal of eventually ending them.[14]

Among other things, Biden's executive orders, proclamations and memos on immigration aim to:

• Create a task force to reunite hundreds of children forcibly separated from their parents at the Southern border, mostly due to Trump's "zero tolerance" policy that ramped up prosecutions of migrants caught crossing the border without permission. Department of Homeland Security officials rescinded the zero-tolerance policy on Jan. 26.[15]

• Stop enforcing Trump's "public charge" rule denying a green card to foreigners deemed likely to rely on public benefits such as housing assistance or Medicaid.[16]

• Suspend Trump's "safe third country" deals with El Salvador, Guatemala and Honduras, which allowed U.S. officials to immediately return asylum-seekers to the region if they failed to seek asylum there before arriving at the U.S.-Mexico border. Biden also wants to spend billions to help Northern Triangle countries attack the crime and poverty that lead people to migrate northward.[17]

• Reaffirm that about 645,000 "Dreamers," undocumented immigrants brought to the United States as children, remain shielded from deportation under the Obama-era Deferred Action for Childhood Arrivals (DACA) program. A Supreme Court ruling last June blocked Trump's 2017 attempt to scrap the program, but it faces other court challenges.[18]

• Review the Migration Protection Protocols policy, known as Remain in Mexico, which requires asylum-seekers to wait south of the border while their requests for entry into the United States are processed. Homeland Security officials halted new enrollments under the policy on Jan. 20, and in February authorities began allowing Remain in Mexico asylum-seekers into the United States while their cases are reviewed.[19]

• Raise the annual cap on refugee admissions to 125,000 for fiscal 2022, which begins Oct. 1. Trump had reduced the cap to a record-low of 15,000 for this fiscal year. Refugees—those fleeing persecution in their home countries—are people whose requests to move to the United States have been screened and approved by U.S. officials, unlike asylum seekers, whose requests have not yet received such approval.[20]

During last year's presidential campaign, Biden had promised to immediately rescind Remain in Mexico and other Trump border policies. In December, he revised that timeline to six months, saying that acting too quickly could put "2 million people on our border." More recently, Biden has encouraged Mexico and

Hundreds rally outside the U.S. Supreme Court in 2019 as the court hears arguments on the legality of the Deferred Action on Childhood Arrivals program, which prevents the deportation of more than 600,000 people brought to the U.S. as children.

Guatemala to continue preventing Central American migrants from reaching the United States, and his administration has warned potential asylum-seekers against traveling to the border right now, saying the vast majority will be turned away.[21]

"I can say quite clearly: Don't come," Biden said in the ABC interview. "We're in the process of getting set up, don't leave your town or city or community."[22]

But Biden is taking other actions that experts and even some of the president's fellow Democrats say are creating confusion and encouraging further migration to the border. Besides allowing Remain in Mexico migrants into the country, for example, administration officials plan to convert migrant family detention centers in South Texas into processing facilities that will quickly screen families seeking asylum and release them into the United States within 72 hours.[23]

"As you move people faster (into the United States), that provides an incentive to keep the pipeline of people from Central America to continue coming," Rep. Henry Cuellar, D-Tex., said on March 6.[24]

Biden continues to enforce Trump's coronavirus emergency order—known as Title 42—that requires immigration officials to summarily expel migrants who arrive at the border without documents. But he has exempted unaccompanied children from the order, even as immigration facilities strain to accommodate new waves of unaccompanied children and other asylum seekers.

During the first five months of fiscal 2021, border officials reported 396,958 "encounters" with migrants at the Southern border, which includes detentions of those trying to cross without legal permission, often repeatedly, and expulsions under Title 42. That is almost double the number from the same period last year. In February, officials reported 100,441 encounters, more than five times last year's low of 17,106 in April. Detentions and expulsions remain below mid-2019 levels, but the recent buildup risks further burdening an immigration court system already facing a record-setting backlog of 1.3 million cases.[25] (*See Short Feature.*)

"We need to prepare for border surges now," Timothy Perry, chief of staff at U.S. Immigration and Customs Enforcement (ICE), the agency responsible for apprehending undocumented immigrants in the country's interior, cautioned in a Feb. 12 email to other ICE officials. "We need to begin making changes immediately."[26]

Increasing encounters involving unaccompanied migrant children are proving especially problematic. During the first five months of fiscal 2021, such encounters were up 74 percent compared to the same period last year, and rose 61 percent, to 9,457, between January and February. *The New York Times* reported that the number of unaccompanied children detained along the border tripled in the two-week period ending March 9.[27]

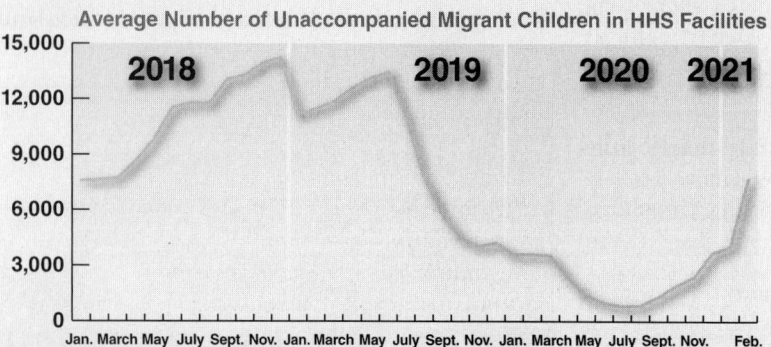

Unaccompanied Minors Overwhelm Immigration Shelters

After declining through most of last year during the coronavirus epidemic, the number of unaccompanied children arriving at the U.S.-Mexico border—mostly teenagers—is rising to early-2018 levels. The surge coincides with a shortage of beds in government shelters due to the virus and is forcing the Department of Health and Human Services (HHS) to open makeshift tent facilities around the country to house the children while observing social distancing guidelines.

Sources: "Latest UC Data — FY2018," U.S. Department of Health and Human Services, Feb. 1, 2021, https://tinyurl.com/296jzpme; "Latest UC Data — FY2019," U.S. Department of Health and Human Services, Feb. 1, 2021, https://tinyurl.com/3pea778n; "Latest UC Data — FY2020," U.S. Department of Health and Human Services, Feb. 1, 2021, https://tinyurl.com/mjthfux6; "Latest UC Data — FY2021," U.S. Department of Health and Human Services, March 2, 2021, https://tinyurl.com/85km9w87; "Fact Sheet: Unaccompanied Children (UC) Program," U.S. Department of Health and Human Services, March 1, 2021, https://tinyurl.com/tachwfmw; and Nick Miroff, Andrew Ba Tran and Leslie Shapiro, "Hundreds of minors are crossing the border each day without their parents. Who are they?" *The Washington Post*, March 11, 2021, https://tinyurl.com/2b5vvmr5

Construction crews work on a new section of a wall near Tijuana along the Southern California border with Mexico. President Biden halted work on the Trump administration's plan to extend the wall.

On March 15, border officials were holding more than 4,000 children—a record—in adult detention facilities as federal health officials struggled to find space for the children in shelters with restricted capacity due to the pandemic. Federal law requires that migrant children be transferred to the Department of Health and Human Services within 72 hours, but many of the youths had been held longer than that. In February, officials reopened a Trump-era shelter in Texas to house hundreds of unaccompanied migrant children, sparking criticism from immigration advocates.[28]

"It goes absolutely against everything Biden promised he was going to do," said Linda Brandmiller, an immigration attorney in San Antonio, Texas.[29]

Authorities are considering housing some unaccompanied children at Fort Lee, a military base in Virginia. In March, Biden deployed the Federal Emergency Management Agency (FEMA) to the Southern border to help care for unaccompanied migrant children, a sign that the number of those children is reaching crisis levels. FEMA planned to use a Dallas convention center as a temporary shelter for thousands of migrant teens.[30]

Border officials also are struggling to cope with migrants who have tested positive for the coronavirus. Authorities in at least one border community say immigration agents failed to notify them before releasing infected migrants into their area.[31]

Meanwhile, officials also have issued temporary guidelines for ICE agents, directing them to prioritize national security threats, recent border-crossers and criminals with aggravated felony convictions who might pose a threat to public safety. The number of arrests by ICE agents has fallen sharply since Biden became president.[32]

Groups that advocate for migrants have praised most of Biden's immigration moves, but they also say he should act more quickly to dump Trump's policies, including the Title 42 order.[33] "The Biden administration has done a lot through executive action, but there are still many policies in place that are harming immigrant communities," says Jorge Loweree, policy director at the American Immigration Council, a Washington advocacy group for immigrants.

Conservatives and former Trump officials counter that Biden's moves ignore the previous administration's success in deterring mass migration at the Southern border and combating what they say are asylum-seekers' often fraudulent claims of "credible fear" of persecution or torture back home. Trump called such claims "a big fat con job."[34]

Speaking at the Conservative Political Action Conference in Orlando, Fla., on Feb. 28, Trump said Biden has "triggered a massive flood of illegal immigration into our country, the likes of which we have never seen before."[35]

Already, conservatives are attacking Biden's legislative proposal, which would create an eight-year path to citizenship for the about 11 million undocumented immigrants living in the United States and would allow Dreamers to apply for citizenship after just three years. Ries says Biden's proposal shows he is taking direction from "a radical left that will not give up on just opening the border—and doing it now."

Despite such criticism, public opinion appears to be shifting in Biden's favor on at least some immigration issues. A Quinnipiac University poll conducted between Jan. 28 and Feb. 1 found that 65 percent of respondents supported allowing undocumented immigrants to remain in the United States and eventually apply for citizenship. And most respondents said they backed Biden's decisions to halt construction on Trump's border wall (54 percent) and reverse Trump's travel ban (57 percent).[36]

Last year, in a first for a Gallup survey, the share of Americans supporting more immigration exceeded those who opposed it. The survey found that 34 percent supported more immigration, up from 27 percent the year before, while the percentage favoring decreased immigration fell to a new low of 28 percent.[37]

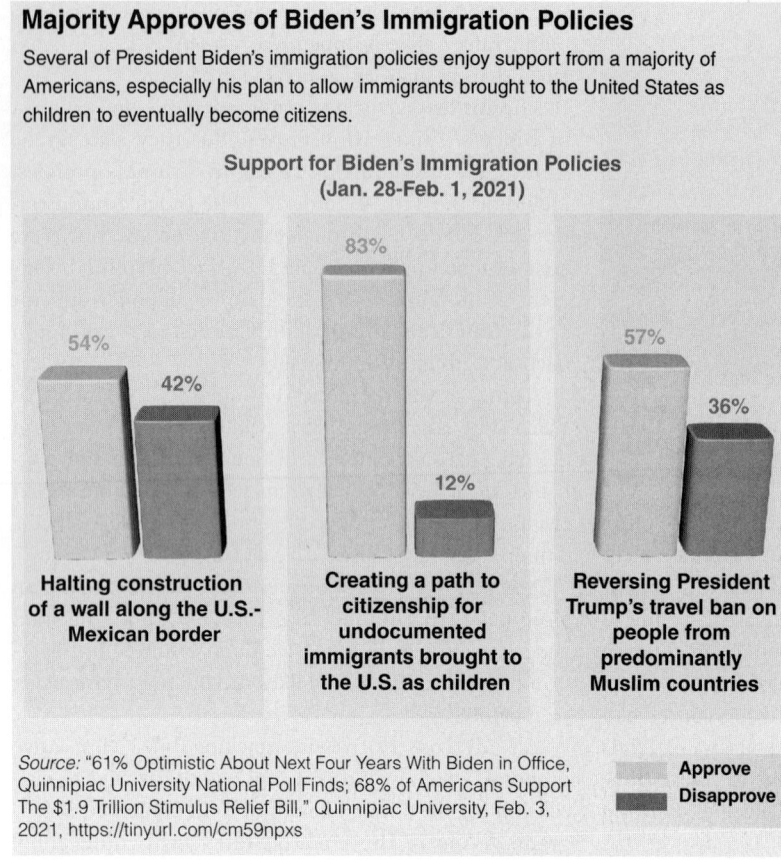

Majority Approves of Biden's Immigration Policies

Several of President Biden's immigration policies enjoy support from a majority of Americans, especially his plan to allow immigrants brought to the United States as children to eventually become citizens.

Support for Biden's Immigration Policies
(Jan. 28-Feb. 1, 2021)

- Halting construction of a wall along the U.S.-Mexican border: Approve 54%, Disapprove 42%
- Creating a path to citizenship for undocumented immigrants brought to the U.S. as children: Approve 83%, Disapprove 12%
- Reversing President Trump's travel ban on people from predominantly Muslim countries: Approve 57%, Disapprove 36%

Source: "61% Optimistic About Next Four Years With Biden in Office," Quinnipiac University National Poll Finds; 68% of Americans Support The $1.9 Trillion Stimulus Relief Bill," Quinnipiac University, Feb. 3, 2021, https://tinyurl.com/cm59npxs

Biden hopes to build on that support by reminding Americans that immigrant scientists "are on the frontlines of research" to develop coronavirus vaccines and treatments. And immigration advocates note that many of those providing essential services during the COVID-19 pandemic—from delivery drivers to hospital workers — are undocumented immigrants.[38]

"There's more support for immigrants in the U.S. than ever before," Loweree says. "If there was ever a moment when immigration reform actually should pass in Congress, this is it."

BACKGROUND

Early Trends

The demographic trends that helped Donald Trump win election in 2016 on a hard-line, anti-immigrant platform began taking shape more than 50 years ago, after President Lyndon B. Johnson signed the Immigration and Nationality Act of 1965.[39]

The law focused on family reunification and attracting skilled workers and ended discriminatory quotas first enacted in the 1920s that had favored immigrants from Northern Europe. But, in a classic case of unintended consequences, illegal immigration from Western Hemisphere countries, which had not previously been subject to quotas, and legal immigration from Asia and Africa surged. Over the next three decades, more than 18 million legal immigrants moved to the United States, more than triple the number admitted over the preceding 30 years.[40]

"Inadvertently, the 1965 legislation created the perfect conditions for an explosive growth in undocumented immigration from Latin America," says Julia Young, an associate professor of history at The Catholic University of America in Washington.

Immigration policy dramatically shifted again in 1986, when President Ronald Reagan signed the Immigration Reform and Control Act, combining tougher border enforcement with provisions that eventually allowed 2.7 million undocumented immigrants already in the United States to become legal permanent residents.[41]

Other comprehensive immigration reform measures failed in 2006 and 2013 after running into fierce opposition from House Republicans because they would have provided a path to citizenship for additional undocumented immigrants.[42]

President Barack Obama created DACA in 2012, preventing about 800,000 young undocumented immigrants from being deported. But he also deported about 2.8 million undocumented immigrants, more than any other administration—including Trump's. The Obama administration also began detaining migrant families in 2014 until courts halted the practice a year later.⁴³

Trump Policies

Trump began reshaping immigration policy immediately after taking office in 2017, authorizing construction of additional sections of a wall along the Southern border, banning travelers from some Muslim-majority countries and expanding the criteria for deportations.⁴⁴

Trump pursued what he called a "merit-based" plan for admitting highly skilled, financially secure immigrants while excluding most other foreigners. But Congress was unenthusiastic about taking up the plan, at least partly because it did not address the DACA program and because some Republicans opposed its restrictions on legal immigration. So, Trump resorted to executive action.⁴⁵

"He stuck to his guns and said, 'Well, I'll do it myself,'" said Theresa Cardinal Brown, director of immigration and cross-border policy at the Bipartisan Policy Center, a think tank in Washington.⁴⁶

Immigration measures stalled in Congress during Trump's tenure. The Senate emphatically rejected a 2018 White House-backed proposal to provide $25 billion for Trump's border wall and restrict legal immigration while offering a path to citizenship to 1.8 million Dreamers. The House passed legislation the following year giving Dreamers a chance at citizenship, but the Senate never considered it.⁴⁷

Central American migrants, mostly from Honduras, are crammed into a truck in 2018 as part of a caravan traveling through Mexico to seek asylum in the United States. The Trump administration sought to deter them by making them ineligible for asylum if they crossed the border illegally, but a judge struck down the proposal.

During his administration, Trump slashed refugee admissions to record-low levels, sharply limited access to asylum and permanent residency, ended Temporary Protected Status for immigrants from some countries plagued by civil war or natural disasters and made it more difficult for lawful permanent residents to become citizens.⁴⁸

Other Trump policies included:

• Widespread use of family separation at the Southern border to deter migration, first as a pilot program in 2017 and later as part of Trump's zero tolerance policy, announced in April 2018. More than 5,000 families were torn apart before Trump ended the practice two months later in response to public and congressional outrage, but the separations continued on a limited basis. When Trump left office, the whereabouts of about 600 of the children remained unknown.⁴⁹

• An effort in 2017 to end DACA, while calling on Congress to devise a strategy for protecting Dreamers.⁵⁰

• Announcement of the public charge rule in September 2018. The Supreme Court had agreed to review the rule, but those cases were dismissed in March at the request of the Biden administration and groups challenging the rule.⁵¹

• The January 2019 imposition of the Remain in Mexico policy, which resulted in about 69,000 migrants being forced to wait in Mexico—often in squalid, crime-infested camps—while their asylum requests were processed. When Biden took office, about 25,000 migrants were still waiting in such camps.⁵²

• A February 2019 declaration of a national emergency at the border to divert already appropriated Pentagon money and other government funds for a border wall, circumventing Congress' power of the purse.⁵³

• Suspension of $450 million in foreign aid to Northern Triangle countries in June 2019 on grounds they were not acting aggressively enough to curb northward migration. Critics assailed the move as counterproductive, saying the money was used to mitigate the poverty and crime that spurred migration. The Trump administration later restored some of the aid, citing "great progress" by Northern Triangle countries in containing migration.⁵⁴

CHRONOLOGY

1800s-1900s *Congress moves toward restrictive immigration policy.*

1882 The Chinese Exclusion Act, the first significant U.S. law restricting immigration based on nationality, bars immigration by Chinese laborers.

1890 The country's 9.2 million immigrants make up 14.8 percent of the population, the largest share ever.

1891 Congress creates an Immigration Bureau to process legal immigrants and enforce immigration restrictions.

1924 Immigration Act adopts quotas based on nationality to limit immigration from southern and eastern Europe. . . . Congress creates Border Patrol to monitor the northern and southern borders.

1942 Bracero Agreement recruits Mexicans to enter on temporary labor permits to work in agriculture and other industries during World War II.

1965 Immigration and Nationality Act, passed with strong bipartisan support by Congress and signed by Democratic President Lyndon B. Johnson, ends the 1924 quotas and refocuses immigration policy on family reunification and attracting skilled workers. Immigration surges.

1986 Republican President Ronald Reagan signs the Immigration Reform and Control Act, which penalizes employers who hire undocumented immigrants, boosts funding for immigration enforcement and grants legal status to about 2.7 million undocumented immigrants who had arrived before 1982.

1990 Immigration Act, signed into law by President George H.W. Bush, retains focus on family reunification, more than doubles employment-related immigration and creates a lottery system to admit immigrants from "underrepresented" countries.

1996 Illegal Immigration Reform and Immigrant Responsibility Act boosts enforcement of immigration restrictions but is hampered by lack of funding.

2000-*Present* *Reform proposals founder in Congress; President Donald Trump reshapes policy through executive orders. President Biden reverses Trump's changes.*

2006 Secure Fence Act authorizes 700 miles of fencing along U.S.-Mexico border. About 650 miles are completed by 2017.

2012 President Barack Obama creates the Deferred Action for Childhood Arrivals (DACA) program to prevent the deportation of undocumented immigrants brought to the country as children.

2013 Comprehensive immigration reform crafted by a bipartisan "Gang of Eight" senators passes Democratic-controlled Senate, but Republican-controlled House refuses to consider it because it allows undocumented immigrants to eventually apply for citizenship.

2017 After campaigning on restricting immigration, Trump orders construction of additional barriers along the Southern border, ramps up interior immigration enforcement, bans travel from some Muslim-majority and African countries and moves to end legal protections for DACA recipients.

2018 Trump's "zero tolerance" policy ramps up criminal prosecution of undocumented migrants caught crossing the Southern border, resulting in the separation of thousands of migrant children from their parents. . . . Trump announces he will implement "public charge" rule denying permanent resident status ("green cards") to immigrants deemed likely to rely on public benefits.

2019 Administration announces Migration Protection Protocols policy, also known as Remain in Mexico, requiring asylum seekers at the Southern border to wait in Mexico while their requests are processed. . . . Number of migrants apprehended or declared inadmissible at the Southern border reaches a 13-year monthly high of 144,116. . . . Administration cuts aid to El Salvador, Guatemala and Honduras for failing to control migration to the U.S. . . . Lawyers describe inhumane conditions for migrant children held in detention centers. . . . Trump says border officials will deny asylum to migrants who did not apply for asylum in a country they passed through while traveling to the U.S.-Mexico border. . . . Number of legal and undocumented immigrants in the U.S. reaches a record 45 million.

2020 Citing the coronavirus, Trump begins summarily expelling all undocumented migrants at border crossings. . . . To protect U.S. workers from job competition during the coronavirus pandemic, Trump temporarily stops issuing green cards to foreigners. . . . Supreme Court prevents Trump from ending DACA. . . . Trump expands green-card suspension to include some highly skilled and seasonal guest workers, while exempting farm workers, and extends it for the rest of 2020. . . . Trump sets fiscal 2021 refugee cap at 15,000—a historic low.

2021 President Biden sends legislation to Congress that would create a pathway to citizenship for the country's nearly 11 million undocumented immigrants; he also takes executive action to reverse Trump's travel ban affecting people from seven Muslim-majority countries, reaffirm DACA protections and halt construction of border barriers (January). . . . Biden administration suspends deportations for 100 days, but a federal judge blocks the move (January). . . . Biden creates task force to reunite migrant families separated at the Southern border by the Trump administration, announces plans to raise cap on refugee admissions, begins process of ending Remain in Mexico policy, rescinds green-card suspension and orders review of public charge rule (February). . . . Apprehensions along U.S.-Mexico border jump sharply, raising fears that surging numbers of migrant families and unaccompanied children will overwhelm immigration facilities; in response, Biden officials reopen a Trump-era holding facility for migrant children and announce they will release migrant family members seeking asylum into the United States within 72 hours of their arrival (March).

- A July 2019 policy disqualifying Central American migrants from asylum unless they first applied for relief in one of the countries they had passed through on their way north. A U.S. district judge struck down the policy in July 2020.[55]

In early 2019, a rising tide of asylum-seekers created what federal officials described as a humanitarian and security crisis at the Southern border. But in response to the administration's hard-line policies, encounters at the border dropped 76 percent between May 2019 and March 2020.[56]

By then, the coronavirus was spreading throughout the country, and Trump accelerated his anti-immigration actions on the grounds that he was protecting public health. In March 2020, he directed officials to immediately deport without

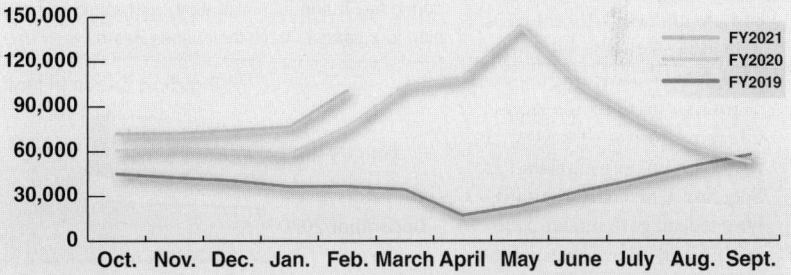

Border Entry Attempts on the Rise Again

The number of people attempting to enter the United States at the Mexican border plummeted last spring, after President Donald Trump closed the border due to the COVID-19 pandemic. However, by the last quarter of 2020 — the beginning of fiscal 2021 — such attempts were higher than during the same period in recent years.

Source: "Southwest Border Migration," U.S. Customs and Border Protection, March 10, 2021, https://tinyurl.com/44pjamr6

Swamped Immigration Court System Hinders Biden's Goals

The backlog of pending cases more than doubled under Trump.

"Chaotic, crowded and confusing." That was how Associated Press reporters summed up what they observed while visiting immigration courts around the country in November 2019.[1]

The reporters found some immigration judges handling nearly 90 cases a day in a losing battle to keep pace with a massive, systemwide backlog of cases. And many migrants were waiting years for a hearing in their effort to avoid deportation, only to have the hearing postponed due to an overcrowded docket or because no interpreter could be found.

"It's been more difficult to get my client's case heard than to litigate [it]," W. Paul Alvarez, an immigration attorney in Mount Kisco, N.Y., said. "It's kind of crazy."[2]

Today, the backlog of cases in immigration courts is even worse, after more than doubling during former President Donald Trump's tenure. Courts in California and Texas face the largest caseloads. Immigrants targeted for deportation, who are overwhelmingly from Guatemala, Honduras, Mexico and El Salvador, now wait an average of more than four years just to have their case heard.[3]

The backlog poses a serious challenge to President Biden as he works to erase Trump's hard-line immigration policies and fulfill a campaign promise to "preserve the dignity of immigrant families, refugees and asylum-seekers."[4]

"Even if the administration halted immigration enforcement entirely, it would still take more than . . . Biden's entire first term in office—assuming prepandemic case completion rates—for the cases now in the active backlog to be completed," according to the Transactional Records Access Clearinghouse (TRAC), a research organization at Syracuse University that analyzes federal government data.[5]

Already, Biden has significantly narrowed the criteria for deportation. But he also has begun allowing thousands of migrants—required under a Trump-era policy to wait in Mexico while their asylum claims were processed—to enter the United States, a move that will add to the immigration court backlog.[6]

The nation's 69 immigration courts and their 520 judges handle civil cases in which undocumented immigrants apprehended by immigration authorities at the border or inside the country are fighting deportation, often without an attorney. Such proceedings do not occur until any criminal prosecution for illegal entry has been completed. Many people appearing in immigration court are seeking asylum, claiming they would be in danger if returned to their home country. Others request cancellation of deportation orders, or even legal permanent residency, for various reasons, such as having strong family ties to a legal U.S. resident.[7]

When Trump became president in 2017, the immigration court system faced 542,411 pending cases. That increased to almost 1.3 million during Trump's four-year focus on expanding deportations of undocumented immigrants, combined with temporary courtroom closures due to the coronavirus pandemic. Although the budget for the Executive Office for Immigration Review, which manages the immigration court system, rose 53 percent between fiscal 2017 and fiscal 2020, that was not enough to keep pace with the growing workload.[8]

Court Backlog Doubled During Trump Administration

The number of unresolved cases pending in U.S. immigration courts more than doubled during the Trump administration, with would-be immigrants waiting an average of more than four years to have their cases heard.

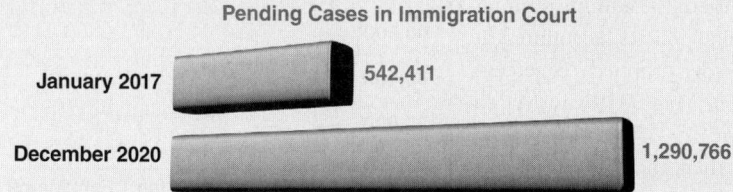

Pending Cases in Immigration Court

January 2017: 542,411
December 2020: 1,290,766

Source: "The State of the Immigration Courts: Trump Leaves Biden 1.3 Million Case Backlog in Immigration Courts," TRAC Immigration, Jan. 19, 2021, https://tinyurl.com/7sajk5dj

Biden has promised to double the number of immigration judges and wants Congress to restore those judges' "discretion to review cases and grant relief to deserving individuals," something advocates for immigrants say was almost nonexistent under Trump. In January, Biden replaced James McHenry, Trump's director of the Executive Office for Immigration Review, with Jean King, the agency's former general counsel, naming her acting director.[9]

McHenry defended his agency's work in November 2019, telling Congress that while cases were seriously backed up, the immigration court system had made "considerable progress . . . restoring its reputation as a fully-functioning, efficient and impartial administrative court system fully capable of rendering timely decisions consistent with due process."[10]

Trump said in 2018 that he would prefer to make immigration courts unnecessary, arguing that undocumented immigrants should be immediately sent back to their home countries "with no judges or court cases." But that would violate the Constitution's guarantee of due process for every "person" in the country, a guarantee the Supreme Court has said extends to undocumented immigrants.[11]

Judicial discretion is not a certainty in the immigration court system, as it is in other courts, because the system is part of the executive branch.[12] "The Department of Justice controls the immigration courts," says Greg Chen, senior director of government relations for the American Immigration Lawyers Association, a Washington group that advocates for improved immigration laws.

Advocates for immigrants said Trump's administration appointed immigration judges who favored deportation and pressured judges to resolve cases quickly rather than fairly, partly by setting quotas for closing cases. The rate at which judges denied asylum increased from about 55 percent to 72 percent under Trump, according to TRAC.[13]

About 300 judges appointed by Trump "demonstrated highly biased viewpoints against asylum seekers and other people . . . appearing before the court," Chen says.

In a December 2019 lawsuit, six immigrants' rights groups accused Trump administration officials of manipulating the courts "to serve an anti-immigrant agenda." Trump's former attorney general, Jeff Sessions, who served from February 2017 to November 2018, said reforms were needed to root out bogus asylum claims.[14]

Turnover among immigration court judges increased significantly under Trump, with many judges retiring in response to what they viewed as the administration's attacks on due process. "Judges are going to other federal agencies and retiring as soon as possible," said A. Ashley Tabaddor, then-president of the National Association of Immigration Judges, the union representing immigration court judges. "They just don't want to deal with it. It's become unbearable."[15]

The union and many immigration experts want Congress to establish an independent immigration court system outside the Justice Department's control.[16]

"We won't see progress in immigration courts until we create a court system that is not as subject to political influence as it is today," says Austin Kocher, a research associate professor in communications at Syracuse University who works on TRAC.

—*Val Ellicott*

---

[1] Kate Brumback, Deepti Hajela and Amy Taxin, "AP visits immigration courts across US, finds nonstop chaos," *The Associated Press*, Jan. 19, 2020, https://tinyurl.com/1l0fc8j7.

[2] *Ibid.*

[3] "The State of the Immigration Courts: Trump Leaves Biden 1.3 Million Case Backlog in Immigration Courts," Transactional Records Access Clearinghouse, Jan. 19, 2021, https://tinyurl.com/65mrqnz9; Julián Aguilar, "President Biden's early immigration overhaul has overlooked one growing problem: A massive court backlog," *The Texas Tribune*, Feb. 4, 2021, https://tinyurl.com/46kg9nnu.

[4] "The Biden Plan for Securing Our Values as a Nation of Immigrants," Biden Harris Campaign, undated, https://tinyurl.com/kbn6e8nn.

[5] "The State of the Immigration Courts," *op. cit.*

[6] Nick Miroff and Maria Sacchetti, "New Biden rules for ICE point to fewer arrests and deportations, and a more restrained agency," *The Washington Post*, Feb. 7, 2021, https://tinyurl.com/4oaz5vlc; Elliot Spagat, "Biden to slowly allow 25,000 people seeking asylum into US," *The Associated Press*, Feb. 12, 2021, https://tinyurl.com/4mk2r62l.

[7] "Executive Office for Immigration Review (EOIR)," U.S. Department of Justice, undated, https://tinyurl.com/4lqu327g; "Executive Office for Immigration Review Announces Investiture of 20 New Immigration Judges, Resulting in a 70 Percent Expansion of the Immigration Judge Corps Since 2017," U.S. Department of Justice, Oct. 9, 2020, https://tinyurl.com/5fsh9r4r; "Access to Counsel," National Immigrant Justice Center, undated, https://tinyurl.com/duc2zb3e; "The Trump Administration's 'Zero Tolerance' Immigration Enforcement Policy," Congressional Research Service, Feb. 2, 2021, https://tinyurl.com/runu63el; and "Executive Office for Immigration Review: An Agency Guide," U.S. Department of Justice, December 2017, https://tinyurl.com/1omoofxh.

[8] "The State of the Immigration Courts," *op. cit.*; Cristobal Ramón and Lucas Reyes, "Interior Enforcement Under the Trump Administration by the Numbers: Immigration Courts," Bipartisan Policy Center, April 27, 2020, https://tinyurl.com/rbez9ksx.

[9] "Fact Sheet: President Biden Sends Immigration Bill to Congress as Part of His Commitment to Modernize our Immigration System," The

(*Continued*)

> (Continued)
>
> White House, Jan. 20, 2021, https://tinyurl.com/3cw4ja2f; Josh Gerstein and Sabrina Rodriguez, "Biden administration replaces top immigration court official," *Politico*, Jan. 27, 2021, https://tinyurl.com/129ab6we.
>
> [10] "Executive Office for Immigration Review Director James McHenry Testifies Before the Senate Committee on Homeland Security and Governmental Affairs," U.S. Department of Justice, Nov. 13, 2019, https://tinyurl.com/hdkozmz5.
>
> [11] Salvador Rizzo, "President Trump's misconceptions about immigration courts and law," *The Washington Post*, June 26, 2018, https://tinyurl.com/vcuz6c2e.
>
> [12] "Report on the Independence of the Immigration Courts," New York City Bar, October 2020, https://tinyurl.com/yixt05xp.
>
> [13] Amy Taxin, "Trump puts his stamp on nation's immigration courts," *The Associated Press*, July 23, 2019, https://tinyurl.com/1tdv4yzy;

a hearing all migrants who showed up at land borders without documentation. Later that year, he halted issuance of new green cards for family members of U.S. citizens and highly skilled workers hoping to emigrate to the United States. He also canceled routine visa appointments and suspended naturalization ceremonies.[57]

During his first three years in office, Trump's anti-immigration efforts resulted in record-low caps on refugee admissions. But the impact of his policies was less dramatic in other areas. "At the end of the day, he was not that successful in making huge changes," says Muzaffar Chishti, a senior fellow at the Migration Policy Institute.

The number of green cards issued between 2017 and 2019, for example, declined only slightly and was in line with previous trends. Grants of asylum dropped from 2019 to 2020 but actually rose over the three-year period, even though immigration judges increasingly denied requests.[58] "He pushed the immigration court system to push out more [asylum] cases," Chishti says. "The more cases you push out, the more cases get approved."

The pandemic, however, "brought about a dramatic reduction in immigration, unlike anything seen in years," said the Migration Policy Institute. As U.S. consulates closed, immigrant visas issued abroad fell 45 percent in fiscal 2020, and temporary work visas declined 54 percent, the institute said.[59]

CURRENT SITUATION
Dramatic Shift

Biden's legislative proposal on immigration—the U.S. Citizenship Act of 2021—would be the most significant overhaul of immigration policy since 1986.[60]

It would allow an estimated 11 million undocumented immigrants who pass background checks and were in the country as of Jan. 1 to apply for a green card after five years of temporary legal status. They could then apply for citizenship three years later. Currently, it takes five years to obtain citizenship after receiving a green card. A separate group composed of Dreamers, Temporary Protected Status recipients and undocumented farmworkers could apply for a green card immediately, followed by the same three-year path to citizenship.[61]

Biden's measure also would:

- Allow certain immigrants deported during the Trump administration to seek permission to reunite with family or to re-enter for other humanitarian reasons.[62]

- Raise caps on employment-based and family visas and begin reducing a backlog of green card applicants.[63]

- Authorize a four-year, $4 billion program to help Northern Triangle countries address government corruption, poverty and other problems, and establish facilities in Central America where people could apply to resettle in the United States. The bill also would revive an Obama-era program allowing at-risk Central American children to reunite with U.S.-based family members.[64]

- Offer community-based alternatives to immigrant detention and change the term "alien" to "noncitizen" in immigration laws.[65]

- Expand technology at the Southern border for detecting illegal drugs and boost training in cultural

"Asylum Denial Rates Continue to Climb," Transactional Records Access Clearinghouse, Oct. 28, 2020, https://tinyurl.com/q75mkkel.

[14] "Case 3:19-cv-02051-SB," U.S. District Court, District of Oregon, Portland Division, Dec. 18, 2019, https://tinyurl.com/fyjavc5t; Tom Dart, "Jeff Sessions accused of political bias in hiring immigration judges," *The Guardian*, June 16, 2018, https://tinyurl.com/i1gplhc2; David K. Li, "The up-and-down relationship between Jeff Sessions and Donald Trump," *NBC News*, Nov. 7, 2018, https://tinyurl.com/e3hbxv8u.

[15] "More Immigration Judges Leaving the Bench," Transactional Records Access Clearinghouse, July 13, 2020, https://tinyurl.com/smdraw8r; Alexandra Kelley, "Immigration judges are quitting and retiring early due to job stress," *The Hill*, Jan. 27, 2020, https://tinyurl.com/24qyetcc.

[16] Ernie Smith, "Independent Immigration Courts Needed, Legal Groups Say," *associations now*, July 15, 2019, https://tinyurl.com/syjdeb99.

awareness, ethics, community policing and other areas for ICE agents and U.S. Customs and Border Protection (USCBP) officials, who are responsible for securing the Northern and Southern borders.[66]

- Hire new immigration judges and expand their discretion in providing asylum and other relief.[67]

Sen. Bob Menendez, D-N.J., who is leading the fight for Senate passage of the administration's proposal, said voters handed Biden a mandate that includes "fixing our immigration system, which is a cornerstone of Trump's hateful horror show." But he acknowledged that getting the measure adopted "will be tough."[68]

In the House, Democrats can afford to lose just five votes in their caucus if Republicans are united in opposition. In the evenly divided Senate, Vice President Kamala Harris could cast tie-breaking votes—but passing most major legislation requires 60 votes to overcome the threat of a filibuster, so Biden will need support from at least 10 Senate Republicans. It is unclear that support exists, especially since the GOP became more anti-immigrant under Trump.[69]

Senate Republican Leader Mitch McConnell, R-Ky., and Sen. Marco Rubio, R-Fla., described the Biden proposal as "blanket amnesty" for people in the country illegally, and Sen. Tom Cotton, R-Ark., claimed it showed "no regard for the health or security of Americans, and zero enforcement."[70]

Democrats have not settled on a strategy for advancing Biden's priorities. Some, including Congressional Progressive Caucus Chair Pramila Jayapal, D-Wash., favor breaking the proposal into separate pieces and passing some measures using a process called budget reconciliation, which requires only 51 votes in the Senate. Other Democrats, including Menendez, want to move forward with a single bill. Democrats also could fold individual immigration proposals into other high-priority bills or move to eliminate the filibuster. Biden has said he opposes doing away with the filibuster but would support making it more difficult to use.[71]

Meanwhile, House Democratic leaders are moving ahead with smaller bills that would offer a pathway to citizenship to Dreamers and Temporary Protected Status recipients and would offer green cards to undocumented farmworkers.[72]

Biden will feel intense pressure to compromise on his proposal, even as progressives oppose any concessions and have urged the new president to abolish ICE and make illegal entry a civil rather than a criminal offense.

President Biden and Homeland Security Secretary Alejandro Mayorkas meet virtually on March 1, 2021, with Mexican President Andrés Manuel López Obrador to discuss immigration challenges along the U.S.-Mexico border.

AT ISSUE

Should Congress approve a path to citizenship for the nation's 11 million undocumented immigrants?

YES — Nithya Nathan-Pineau
Policy Attorney and Strategist, Immigrant Legal Resource Center

Written for *CQ Researcher*, March 2021

The goal of immigration reform should be to create a system that welcomes immigrants, recognizes their full humanity, treats everyone with dignity and provides a path to citizenship. Pushing immigrants into the shadows, forcing them to live in constant fear of being separated from their families and basing immigration policy on hatred and alarm has brought the U.S. immigration system to its current state. The only path forward is an entirely new framework built on inclusion and recognition of the contributions made by immigrant communities.

While the executive branch has broad powers to influence and affect immigration policy, Congress must act to dismantle the harm inflicted on immigrant communities and create a pathway to citizenship. For the vast majority of immigrants in the United States without legal status, no path to citizenship exists. This inexcusable travesty must be addressed immediately. Rather than forcing immigrants to live in fear and denying them health care, the right to work and other basic necessities, Congress must create an accessible, inclusive path to citizenship that does not create barriers, such as excessive fees or extensive criminal carveouts based on previous contacts with the criminal justice system. Such barriers will exclude many people and continue perpetuating injustice.

Congress' program must include a broad, inclusive path to citizenship, because only as citizens do immigrants have the full rights and responsibilities enjoyed by their American-born family members. Temporary programs leave immigrant families and their futures up to the whims of future administrations, do not provide a pathway to permanent status and do not allow family members to apply for entry on behalf of other family members living in dangerous situations back home.

In 2020, the United States witnessed a reckoning with racial inequity and police brutality, founded in white supremacy, built into our government structures—including the immigration system. This has led to the criminalization and demonization of immigrants, culminating in the racist and xenophobic rhetoric and policies adopted by President Donald Trump.

As public awareness of how racial bias infects our legal system grows, we will continue to push policymakers to reject immigration outcomes that rely on that system. And we have the American public on our side. Polls show overwhelming support for transforming the immigration system.

The forces against us are white supremacy and racism. Which side would you want to be on in this fight?

NO — Lora Ries
Senior Research Fellow for Homeland Security, The Heritage Foundation

Written for *CQ Researcher*, March 2021

No, Congress should not pass legislation to legalize the millions of individuals illegally present in the United States. Congress has an obligation to enact and enforce laws that lead to an orderly immigration system for our sovereign nation and for the American people.

Over the past three decades, any discussion of legislation to give green cards to those here illegally has consistently triggered increases in the number of migrants from Central America, Mexico and elsewhere, inducing them to journey to the United States in the hope of obtaining green cards. Illegal immigration at the border is rising again, as migrants seek to benefit from President Biden's campaign promise of amnesty. Within just the first few weeks of the new administration, the Border Patrol is reporting more than 3,500 daily encounters, up from around 1,000 a day. These are crisis numbers—the very opposite of an orderly immigration system.

The rise shows that the Biden administration has done enough damage to border security by suspending the effective "Remain in Mexico" program and declaring an end to the safe third-country agreements with the governments of El Salvador, Guatemala and Honduras. Congress should not perpetuate or encourage even more illegal immigration by negotiating or debating a legalization program for illegal aliens in the United States.

The administration claims the number of illegal residents eligible for green cards is 11 million. Yet a Yale-MIT study estimates the number to be more than 22 million. Notably, the left has purposely stymied gathering accurate data on the number of those illegal immigrants through the U.S. census and other means of data sharing. It would be the height of irresponsibility for Congress to pass amnesty legislation when it has no idea how many people are truly eligible for the benefit.

Passing amnesty in the 1986 Immigration Reform and Control Act did not end illegal immigration. It merely generated the next cycle of illegal immigration, which has grown into numbers that dwarf the 3 million who applied under the 1986 amnesty. A new amnesty will perpetuate this cycle, rendering our immigration laws, passed by Congress, meaningless.

The Remain in Mexico program and safe third-country agreements demonstrated that enforcing our immigration laws prevents illegal immigration. Congress should build on that success, rather than repeating past, failed amnesty legislation, particularly with an unknown applicant population size and cost. Americans want law and order, not more immigration chaos.

Discussion Questions

Here are some questions to think about regarding immigration reform:

- Did President Donald Trump have a significant impact on immigration?

- Is Congress likely to enact President Biden's immigration reform package, in whole or in part? If in part, which elements are most likely to achieve passage?

- Does the current immigration system reflect U.S. values?

- How did the 1965 and 1986 immigration reform packages affect the influx of people from Latin America?

- Would Biden's plan to enable undocumented immigrants brought to the U.S. as children to eventually attain citizenship spur further influxes of undocumented immigrants?

- Imagine you are a parent with young children living in Central America. You hear from a relative living in the U.S. that there are job opportunities in the relative's community and that you could stay with your relative temporarily. Would you risk taking your children north and trying to enter the U.S.? Why or why not?

- Now imagine that you are a local official in a U.S. community near the U.S.-Mexican border. How would you feel about Biden's efforts to make immigration policy less restrictive?

Biden pledged on the campaign trail to rein in ICE but not eliminate it. Mayorkas, the first Latino to head the Department of Homeland Security, has said he opposes abolishing ICE, which is part of the agency. Both ICE and USCBP are currently run by temporary heads, and Biden has yet to nominate replacements.[73]

Progressives already are angry that some Democrats sided with Republicans in voting to deny coronavirus stimulus payments to undocumented immigrants.[74] Biden also faces trust issues with some Democrats and advocacy groups due to his association with Obama's immigration policies when he was vice president.

"Family detention was used widely in the Obama administration," says Nithya Nathan-Pineau, an attorney and strategist for the Immigrant Legal Resource Center, an advocacy organization in San Francisco. "There were a lot of things that happened during the Obama administration that advocates have not forgotten."

Family Reunification

Biden will have a similarly difficult task reuniting families separated at the border. The location of more than 600 children remains unknown after their parents were detained or deported and the children were sent to shelters, foster homes or relatives in the United States.

"There's no central database with information on where the parent and child went," says Nathan-Pineau.

Even assuming the parents can be found, Biden must decide whether to allow the reunited families to remain in the United States and, if so, under what conditions. His executive order creating the reunification task force raises the possibility the families will receive legal status.[75]

The American Civil Liberties Union (ACLU), which has been working with other groups to find the children's parents, says Biden needs to offer legal status to all 5,500 families who were separated. "Given what the . . . families have been through, they deserve to be reunited and given safe refuge in the United States," said Lee Gelernt, deputy director of the ACLU's Immigrants' Rights Project.[76]

Immigrant advocates want Congress to criminally punish Trump officials responsible for the separations. They point to a report released in January by the inspector general at the Homeland Security Department that says then-Attorney General Jeff Sessions told U.S. attorneys in May 2018, "We need to take away children" in order to deter migrant families from seeking asylum at the border.[77]

OUTLOOK

Investment Choices

Biden's success in moving his immigration priorities through Congress depends largely on keeping large waves of asylum-seekers away from the Southern border, experts on both sides of the immigration debate say. Numerous family groups of migrants, including some from Haiti and Africa who have come up from South America, continue flowing toward the Southern border, according to reports from Mexico.[78]

"It would undermine most of (Biden's) plans," Alex Nowrasteh, director of immigration studies at the Cato Institute, a libertarian think tank in Washington, said of the possibility that new arrivals could overwhelm immigration facilities. "American voters want order on the border."[79]

The Migration Policy Institute's Chishti and other experts say avoiding such a crisis will require cooperation from Mexico and the Northern Triangle countries.

After meeting on March 1, Biden and Mexican President Andrés Manuel López Obrador affirmed their commitment to cooperating on migration issues, but it was unclear whether Biden can count on Mexico's help in keeping migrants from the border.[80]

Growing pressure at the border also will test Biden's theory that helping Northern Triangle countries combat poverty and gang violence will be more effective than Trump's approach of withholding aid as a penalty for increased migration. Ries at the Heritage Foundation says Trump was right to condition U.S. aid on efforts by Northern Triangle countries to control their own borders.

"The U.S. has poured foreign aid into that area for decades," she says. "If it's not tied to anything, history has shown that money goes wasted."

Chishti agrees that trusting Northern Triangle countries to make their own decisions on spending U.S. aid would be a mistake. But if Biden requires that the aid be earmarked for job, education and anti-corruption programs, he says, "that may pay more dividends."

NOTES

1. Reuters and Adry Torres, "Caravan of at least 3,000 Hondurans is marching to the US-Mexico border in time for Biden to take over as president," *Daily Mail*, Jan. 15, 2021, https://tinyurl.com/2z22hly5.

2. Kirk Semple and Nic Wirtz, "Migrant Caravan, Now in Guatemala, Tests Regional Resolve to Control Migration," *The New York Times*, Jan. 17, 2021, https://tinyurl.com/2uxrxtc2.

3. Isabel Mateos and María Verza, "Migrants on the move again in Mexico and Central America," *The Associated Press*, Feb. 18, 2021, https://tinyurl.com/s6jhve6z; "Guatemala buses more migrants back to Honduras; small groups press on toward Mexico," *The Associated Press/Fox News*, Jan. 2021, https://tinyurl.com/39nfl4pg.

4. Semple and Wirtz, *op. cit.*

5. "'No choice except to flee': After back-to-back hurricanes, Central Americans go north," *NBC News*, Dec. 4, 2020, https://tinyurl.com/7dbspc2a; "The Biden Plan For Securing Our Values As A Nation Of Immigrants," Biden Harris campaign, undated, https://tinyurl.com/2c99s4ry.

6. Matthew Impelli, "Read Homeland Security Chief Mayorkas' Full Statement on Migrant Situation at Border," *Newsweek*, March 16, 2021, https://tinyurl.com/3927nsz9; Maegan Vazquez and Kate Sullivan, "Biden tells migrants not to come to US: 'Don't leave your town,'" *CNN Politics*, March 16, 2021, https://tinyurl.com/nhhrc87x.

7. "The Biden Plan For Securing Our Values As A Nation Of Immigrants," *ibid.*; Cecilia Vega and Quinn Owen, "Democrats introduce Biden's immigration reform bill," *ABC News*, Feb. 18, 2021, https://tinyurl.com/1f4hymum; Adam Shaw, "Marco Rubio rejects Biden immigration bill, calls it 'blanket amnesty,'" *Fox News*, Jan. 20, 2021, https://tinyurl.com/lh0rbfw1.

8. Chuck Lindell, "Judge blocks Biden's 100-day deportation pause in nationwide order," *Austin American-Statesman*, Feb. 24, 2021, https://tinyurl.com/vumcw9c5.

9. Daniel Gonzalez and Rafael Carranza, "Biden pushing for major immigration reforms, but another humanitarian crisis at the border could derail his agenda," *Arizona Republic*, Jan. 29, 2021, https://tinyurl.com/1hf8z3kj.

10. Sean Sullivan and Nick Miroff, "Biden faces growing political threat from border upheaval," *The

Washington Post, March 15, 2021, https://tinyurl.com/pvtay6z6.

11. Sarah Pierce and Jessica Bolter, "Dismantling and Reconstructing the U.S. Immigration System: A Catalog of Changes under the Trump Presidency," Migration Policy Institute, July 2020, https://tinyurl.com/1axy7kij; Muzaffar Chishti and Jessica Bolter, "The 'Trump Effect' on Legal Immigration Levels: More Perception than Reality?" Migration Policy Institute, Nov. 20, 2020, https://tinyurl.com/1h8nr3d5; and Arelis R. Hernández and Kevin Sieff, "Unwinding Trump's asylum policy will be major challenge for Biden," *The Washington Post*, Dec. 2, 2020, https://tinyurl.com/1w4mvm94.

12. Hernández and Sieff, *ibid.*

13. Zolan Kanno-Youngs and Michael D. Shear, "Trump Loyalists Across Homeland Security Could Vex Biden's Immigration Policies," *The New York Times*, Feb. 18, 2021, https://tinyurl.com/pdvsr6u4; Maria Sacchetti and Nick Miroff, "Biden squeezed on immigration policy, bracing for border crisis," *The Washington Post*, Feb. 24, 2021, https://tinyurl.com/2p9jphch.

14. Victor Reklaitis and Robert Schroeder, "All of President Biden's key executive orders—in one chart," *MarketWatch*, March 9, 2021, https://tinyurl.com/y9mqduou; Nicole Narea, "Biden's next executive actions address family separations, legal immigration, and asylum," *Vox*, Feb. 2, 2021, https://tinyurl.com/4n5omeeu; and Michael D. Shear, "Biden Revokes Trump's Pause on Green Cards," *The New York Times*, Feb 24, 2021, https://tinyurl.com/yem8uc5y.

15. Dartunorro Clark and Julia Ainsley, "Biden signs immigration executive orders to address 'moral failing' of Trump's policies," *NBC News*, Feb. 2, 2021, https://tinyurl.com/3b94sjay; Michael D. Shear and Zolan Kanno-Youngs, "Biden Issues Orders to Dismantle Trump's 'America First' Immigration Agenda," *The New York Times*, March 11, 2021, https://tinyurl.com/1ror1bt9; and Justine Coleman, "DOJ rescinds 'zero tolerance' border policy behind family separations," *The Hill*, Jan. 26, 2021, https://tinyurl.com/22bsnsth.

16. Camilo Montoya-Galvez, "Biden administration stops enforcing Trump-era 'public charge' green card restrictions following court order," *CBS News*, March 10, 2021, https://tinyurl.com/4wman987.

17. "Biden administration suspends Trump asylum deals with El Salvador, Guatemala, Honduras," *Reuters*, Feb. 6, 2021, https://tinyurl.com/pxhg4t0p; Rebecca Beitsch, "Biden immigration policy looks beyond reversing Trump," *The Hill*, Feb. 7, 2021, https://tinyurl.com/acsajbpd; and Jasmine Aguilera, "Joe Biden's Immigration Bill Aims to Address the Root Causes of Migration. Will it Work?" *Time*, Feb. 18, 2021, https://tinyurl.com/4s4e3su3.

18. Julián Aguilar, "Joe Biden to pause border wall construction, issue protections for DACA recipients and roll back other Trump immigration policies," *The Texas Tribune*, Jan. 20, 2021, https://tinyurl.com/2ojmwcvy.

19. James Gordon, "Asylum seekers who Trump banned from the US stream across Gateway International Bridge from Mexico after Biden relaxed rules—with 500 expected by end of the week," *Daily Mail*, Feb. 28, 2021, https://tinyurl.com/yp7226h4.

20. Abigail Hauslohner, "Biden seeks to restore 'badly damaged' refugee resettlement program," *The Washington Post*, Feb. 5, 2021, https://tinyurl.com/1n6reat4; "Definitions: Refugee, Asylum Seeker, IDP, Migrant," Hebrew Immigration Aid Society, undated, https://tinyurl.com/srncmcc.

21. Nick Miroff and Maria Sacchetti, "Biden says he'll reverse Trump immigration policies but wants 'guardrails' first," *The Washington Post*, Dec. 22, 2020, https://tinyurl.com/pvcnxo5u; Matthew Brown and Rebecca Morin, "White House says most migrants at border to be rejected, says administration needs time develop 'humane' process," *USA Today*, Feb. 10, 2021, https://tinyurl.com/gnvqqye7; and Laura Gottesdiener, Frank Jack Daniel and Ted Hesson, "Tough migration enforcement south of border key to Biden plans," *Reuters*, Feb. 12, 2021, https://tinyurl.com/ysxehat3.

22. Vazquez and Sullivan, *op. cit.*

23. Maria Sacchetti, Nick Miroff and Silvia Foster-Frau, "Texas family detention centers expected to transform into rapid-processing hubs," *The Washington Post*, March 4, 2021, https://tinyurl.com/bvkaht2v.
24. "Transcripts," *CNN*, March 6, 2021, https://tinyurl.com/zxj4n84b.
25. "Southwest Land Border Encounters," U.S. Customs and Border Protection, March 10, 2021, https://tinyurl.com/munkzj7b; "The State of the Immigration Courts: Trump Leaves Biden 1.3 Million Case Backlog in Immigration Courts," Transactional Records Access Clearinghouse, Jan. 19, 2021, https://tinyurl.com/1bqevsnp.
26. Miroff and Sacchetti, "Biden squeezed on immigration policy, bracing for border crisis," *op. cit.*
27. "Southwest Land Border Encounters," *op. cit.*; Zolan Kanno-Youngs, "A surge in migrant children detained at border is straining shelters," *The New York Times*, March 9, 2021, https://tinyurl.com/4ydhz8ma.
28. Priscilla Alvarez, "More than 4,000 unaccompanied migrant children in Border Patrol custody," *CNN*, March 15, 2021, https://tinyurl.com/6prk364e; Nick Miroff, "At border, record number of migrant youths wait in adult detention cells for longer than legally allowed," *The Washington Post*, March 10, 2021, https://tinyurl.com/253x3czy; and Silvia Foster-Frau, "First migrant facility for children opens under Biden," *The Washington Post*, Feb. 22, 2021, https://tinyurl.com/5fs4mvdc.
29. Foster-Frau, *ibid.*
30. Ted Hesson, "Exclusive: U.S. considering use of Virginia military base to house migrant children," *Reuters*, March 5, 2021, https://tinyurl.com/yfz79umw; Sacchetti, Miroff and Foster-Frau, *op. cit.*; Nick Miroff, "Biden will deploy FEMA to care for teenagers and children crossing border in record numbers," *The Washington Post*, March 13, 2021, https://tinyurl.com/fsahrand; and Nick Miroff, "Biden administration will use Dallas convention center to shelter migrant teen boys," *The Washington Post*, March 15, 2021, https://tinyurl.com/y76ud67c.
31. Jon Gerberg and Maria Sacchetti, "A border community, ICE at odds over release of detainees with covid," *The Washington Post*, March 14, 2021, https://tinyurl.com/3j8emxwc.
32. Nick Miroff and Maria Sacchetti, "Immigration arrests have fallen sharply under Biden, ICE data show," *The Washington Post*, March 9, 2021, https://tinyurl.com/8tvj4uzc.
33. Suzanne Monyak, "Despite travel ban repeal, Trump orders still keep immigrants out," *Roll Call*, Jan. 28, 2021, https://tinyurl.com/2r2qw2qe; Will Weissert and Nomaan Merchant, "Immigrants, activists worry Biden won't end Trump barriers," *The Associated Press*, Feb. 8, 2021, https://tinyurl.com/c25veyun; and Isabela Dias, "The Biden Administration Is Telling Asylum Seekers They Still Have to Wait," *Mother Jones*, Feb. 10, 2021, https://tinyurl.com/yu7swkxw.
34. Donica Phifer, "Donald Trump Calls Asylum Claims a 'Big Fat Con Job,' Says Mexico Should Stop Migrant Caravans From Traveling to U.S. border," *Newsweek*, March 29, 2019, https://tinyurl.com/c56ajsai.
35. Adrian Carrasquillo, "Trump, Miller Think Road to 2022 Victory Is Immigration, Democrats See It as a Failed Playbook," *Newsweek*, March 1, 2021, https://tinyurl.com/d8hm5rsw.
36. "61% Optimistic About Next Four Years With Biden In Office, Quinnipiac University National Poll Finds; 68% Of Americans Support The $1.9 Trillion Stimulus Relief Bill," Quinnipiac University Poll, Feb. 3, 2021, https://tinyurl.com/mbz2w96g.
37. Mohamed Younis, "Americans Want More, Not Less, Immigration for First Time," Gallup, July 1, 2020, https://tinyurl.com/2cwl66ou.
38. "Executive Order on Restoring Faith in Our Legal Immigration Systems and Strengthening Integration and Inclusion Efforts for New Americans," The White House, Feb. 2, 2021, https://tinyurl.com/w7gzxxng; Nicole Prchal Svajlenka, "Protecting Undocumented Workers on the Pandemic's Front Lines," Center for American Progress, Dec. 2, 2020, https://tinyurl.com/1lfv84wv.
39. "Immigration and Nationality Act of 1965," History, Art & Archives, U.S. House of Representatives, https://tinyurl.com/mkyth9u3.

40. *Ibid.*; Douglas S. Massey and Karen A. Pren, "Unintended Consequences of US Immigration Policy: Explaining the Post-1965 Surge from Latin America," Population and Development Review, 2012, https://tinyurl.com/2ntcb3zr.

41. Ingrid Rojas, "The 1986 Immigration Reform Explained," *ABC News*, May 5, 2013, https://tinyurl.com/3chl2v2u.

42. Miriam Valverde, "Did Senate pass immigration bills in 2006, 2013 and House failed to vote on them?" *Politifact*, Jan. 26, 2018, https://tinyurl.com/4v2hrksg.

43. Amanda Sakuma, "Obama Leaves Behind a Mixed Legacy on Immigration," *NBC News*, Jan. 15, 2017, https://tinyurl.com/2deatfye; "Judicial Rulings Ending the Obama Administration's Family Detention Policy: Implications for Illegal Immigration and Border Security," U.S. Senate Committee on Homeland Security and Governmental Affairs, Jan. 10, 2019, https://tinyurl.com/6484fhhk.

44. Avalon Zoppo, Amanda Proença Santos and Jackson Hudgins, "Here's the Full List of Donald Trump's Executive Orders," *NBC News*, Oct. 17, 2017, https://tinyurl.com/jdunm2ql; "Trump administration widens net for immigrant deportation," *BBC News*, Feb. 21, 2017, https://tinyurl.com/1icxdps5www.

45. Catherine E. Shoichet, "What 'merit-based' immigration means, and why Trump keeps saying he wants it," *CNN Politics*, May 16, 2019, https://tinyurl.com/4zmnzty3; Maegan Vazquez, Kevin Liptak and Lauren Fox, "Trump unveils new (likely doomed) immigration plan," *CNN Politics*, May 16, 2019, https://tinyurl.com/1boxp6x4; and Jill Colvin and Astrid Galvan, "Trump offers confusion, contradictions on immigration order," *The Associated Press/The Washington Post*, July 20, 2020, https://tinyurl.com/fdj9s384.

46. Miriam Valverde, "Donald Trump's immigration promises: failures and achievements," *Politifact*, July 27, 2020, https://tinyurl.com/3mesyduj.

47. Burgess Everett, "McConnell: Senate will 'probably not' vote on Dreamers bill," *Politico*, June 5, 2019, https://tinyurl.com/463fq592; Sheryl Gay Stolberg and Michael D. Shear, "Senate Rejects Immigration Plans, Leaving Fate of Dreamers Uncertain," *The New York Times*, Feb. 15, 2018, https://tinyurl.com/ij1u8l1s; and Billy Binion, "House Tries to Give 'Dreamers' a Path to Citizenship, but Mitch McConnell Won't Even Consider the Bill," *Reason*, June 6, 2019, https://tinyurl.com/3e8f6vnv.

48. Peniel Ibe, "Trump's attacks on the legal immigration system explained," American Friends Service Committee, Blog, April 23, 2020, https://tinyurl.com/4tju43ds.

49. David Shepardson, "Trump says family separations deter illegal immigration," *Reuters*, Oct. 13, 2018, https://tinyurl.com/xhgz3wr9; Nila Bala and Arthur Rizer, "Trump's family separation policy never really ended. This is why," *Think*, July 1, 2019, https://tinyurl.com/yzn8tl5u; Nicole Narea, "The Trump administration knew exactly what it was doing with family separations," *Vox*, Oct. 7, 2020, https://tinyurl.com/3v87ay8c; and Daniel Gonzalez, "628 parents of separated children are still missing. Here's why immigrant advocates can't find them," *Arizona Republic/USA Today*, Dec. 11, 2020, https://tinyurl.com/vc7h3e4s.

50. Tal Kopan, "Trump ends DACA but gives Congress window to save it," *CNN Politics*, Sept. 5, 2017, https://tinyurl.com/3kka9992.

51. Miriam Jordan, "Trump's 'Public Charge' Immigration Rule Is Vacated by Federal Judge," *The New York Times*, Nov. 2, 2020, https://tinyurl.com/nw749aje; Amy Howe, "Cases testing Trump's 'public charge' immigration rule are dismissed," SCOTUSblog, March 9, 2021, https://tinyurl.com/durs5hya.

52. Gordon, *op. cit.*

53. Peter Baker, "Trump Declares a National Emergency, and Provokes a Constitutional Clash," *The New York Times*, Feb. 15, 2019, https://tinyurl.com/42blxhcg.

54. Deirdre Shesgreen, "In shift, Trump administration says it will restore some U.S. aid to Central America," *USA Today*, Oct. 16, 2019, https://tinyurl.com/7fgy32gt.

55. Spencer S. Hsu, "Federal judge strikes down Trump asylum rule targeting Central Americans," *The Washington Post*, July 1, 2020, https://tinyurl.com/you7wuqp.

56. "Southwest Border Migration," *op. cit.*; "Illegal Immigration Hits 12-Year High; More than 76,000 Migrants Cross in February," U.S. Department of Homeland Security, March 6, 2019, https://tinyurl.com/sxlztpgh.

57. Zolan Kanno-Youngs and Kirk Semple, "Trump Cites Coronavirus as He Announces a Border Crackdown," *The New York Times*, March 27, 2020, https://tinyurl.com/4x33ggns; Danilo Zak, "Immigration-related Executive Actions During the COVID-19 Pandemic," National Immigration Forum, Nov. 18, 2020, https://tinyurl.com/4aopdbpb; and Danilo Zak, "President Trump's Proclamation Suspending Immigration," National Immigration Forum, June 23, 2020, https://tinyurl.com/1o3fw5qt.

58. Chishti and Bolter, *op. cit.*; Ryan Baugh, "Refugees and Asylees: 2019," U.S. Department of Homeland Security, September 2020, https://tinyurl.com/crs5uv8s; Justin Fox, "Trump Didn't Actually Accomplish Much on Immigration," *Bloomberg Opinion*, Feb. 2, 2021, https://tinyurl.com/sz4qrqf8; "Table 1. Persons Obtaining Lawful Permanent Resident Status: Fiscal Years 1820 to 2019," U.S. Department of Homeland Security, Oct. 27, 2020, https://tinyurl.com/s0txeqm1; and "Asylum Denial Rates Continue to Climb," Transactional Records Access Clearinghouse, Oct. 28, 2020, https://tinyurl.com/q75mkkel.

59. Chishti and Bolter, *op. cit.*

60. Nicole Narea, "Biden's sweeping immigration bill, explained," *Vox*, Jan. 20, 2021, https://tinyurl.com/12pil023.

61. *Ibid.*

62. Camilo Montoya-Galvez, "Democratic lawmakers unveil Biden-backed immigration overhaul bill," *CBS News*, Feb. 18, 2021, https://tinyurl.com/4f7e4qua.

63. Camilo Montoya-Galvez, "Biden plan would offer legal status to farmworkers, 'Dreamers' and other undocumented immigrants," *CBS News*, Jan. 20, 2021, https://tinyurl.com/2lnxoav7.

64. *Ibid.*

65. "Senate Bill: U.S. Citizenship Act," American Immigration Lawyers Association, Feb. 18, 2021, https://tinyurl.com/l1rc28jq.

66. *Ibid.*

67. *Ibid.*

68. "Biden's Immigration Plan Would Offer Path to Citizenship for Millions," *The New York Times*, March 8, 2021, https://tinyurl.com/ga10rkew; "Biden's Bold Immigration Overhaul May Face a Republican Wall in Congress," *Reuters/U.S. News and World Report*, Jan. 21, 2021, https://tinyurl.com/3nuybght.

69. Eliza Relman, "Republican voters have become more xenophobic as Trump has normalized racist rhetoric," *Business Insider*, July 18, 2019, https://tinyurl.com/iaeod1k2.

70. Jordain Carney, "Biden reignites immigration fight in Congress," *The Hill*, Jan. 30, 2021, https://tinyurl.com/1t39tvhj; Alan Fram, Lisa Mascaro and Bill Barrow, "Biden immigration plan opposed by GOP, conservative groups," *The Associated Press*, Jan. 19, 2021, https://tinyurl.com/4nosjfw4.

71. Laura Barrón-López, Heather Caygle and Anita Kumar, "Biden's immigration bill lands on the Hill facing bleak odds," *Politico*, Feb. 18, 2021, https://tinyurl.com/j14k01a2; Laura Barrón-López, Anita Kumar and Sabrina Rodriguez, "Biden open to breaking his immigration bill into pieces," *Politico*, Jan. 26, 2021, https://tinyurl.com/fnrnhkve; and Kate Sullivan, "Biden says he supports bringing back the Senate's talking filibuster rule," *CNN*, March 16, 2021, https://tinyurl.com/6mjr6jwn.

72. Seung Min Kim, "Next Biden agenda items on immigration and infrastructure already running into trouble," *The Washington Post*, March 11, 2021, https://tinyurl.com/8y9zwt22.

73. Sabrina Rodriguez, "Biden wants to undo Trump's family separation legacy. It won't be easy," *Politico*, Jan. 31, 2021, https://tinyurl.com/7ru5909s; Nick Miroff and Maria Sacchetti, "New Biden rules for

ICE point to fewer arrests and deportations, and a more restrained agency," *The Washington Post*, Feb. 7, 2021, https://tinyurl.com/3xc8nb74; Adam Shaw, "Biden DHS nominee Mayorkas says ICE should not be defunded, despite liberal calls," *Fox News*, Jan. 19, 2021, https://tinyurl.com/1dsxap6u; Alana Wise, "Senate Makes Alejandro Mayorkas First Latino Head of Homeland Security," *NPR*, Feb. 2, 2021, https://tinyurl.com/15w2pesq; "Leadership/Organization," U.S. Customs and Border Protection, Feb. 5, 2021, https://tinyurl.com/ttevwkk6; and "ICE Leadership," U.S. Immigration and Customs Enforcement, accessed March 11, 2021, https://tinyurl.com/49xb8mh3.

74. Burgess Everett and Marianne Levine, "Dems split as progressives rage over immigration vote," *Politico*, Feb. 8, 2021, https://tinyurl.com/mlq7nupg.

75. Elliot Spagat and Josh Boak, "Biden signs immigration orders as Congress awaits more," *The Associated Press*, Feb. 2, 2021, https://tinyurl.com/1xr756s3.

76. Rick Jervis, "Biden's effort to reunite Trump-era separated families is trickiest immigration challenge," *USA Today*, Jan. 25, 2021, https://tinyurl.com/krxsi6h9.

77. Nicole Narea, "What Biden could do about family separations," *Vox*, Dec. 28, 2020, https://tinyurl.com/1gani6fa; "Review of the Department of Justice's Planning and Implementation of Its Zero Tolerance Policy and Its Coordination with the Departments of Homeland Security and Health and Human Services," U.S. Department of Justice, January 2021, https://tinyurl.com/xs2pbh34.

78. Todd Bensman, "Aspiring Immigrants, Foregoing Caravan Tactic, Are Massing in Northern Mexico on Biden Promises," Center for Immigration Studies, Feb. 19, 2021, https://tinyurl.com/2vuk589n.

79. Gonzalez and Carranza, *op. cit.*

80. Anne Gearan *et al.*, "Biden meets with Mexican president amid growing pressure on immigration," *The Washington Post*, March 1, 2021, https://tinyurl.com/2rh4tdn4.

BIBLIOGRAPHY

Books

Goodman, Adam, *The Deportation Machine: America's Long History of Expelling Immigrants*, **Princeton University Press, 2020.**
An assistant professor of history at the University of Illinois, Chicago, recounts the troubling history of efforts by public officials at all levels of government to single out immigrants for expulsion.

Hirschfeld Davis, Julie, and **Michael D. Shear,** *Border Wars: Inside Trump's Assault on Immigration*, **Simon & Schuster, 2020.**
An editor (Davis) and a reporter (Shear) at *The New York Times* detail how former President Donald Trump and his top immigration adviser, Stephen Miller, worked to shut the nation's doors to asylum-seekers, refugees and other migrants while conditioning Americans to view immigration as a threat to national security.

Salam, Reihan, *Melting Pot or Civil War? A Son of Immigrants Makes the Case Against Open Borders*, **Sentinel, 2018.**
A magazine editor and the U.S.-born son of Bangladeshi immigrants argues that unlimited immigration encourages income inequality and social injustice and recommends that U.S. immigration policy prioritize high-skilled workers in order to avoid "a new populist revolt."

Yang, Jia Lynn, *One Mighty and Irresistible Tide: The Epic Struggle Over American Immigration, 1924-1965*, **W.W. Norton and Co., 2020.**
The national editor at *The New York Times* looks at the activists, presidents and others who worked to abolish the discriminatory nationality quotas of the 1920s, setting the stage for the 1965 law that opened the country's doors to millions of immigrants.

Articles

Narea, Nicole, "**Progressives are getting ready to push Biden on immigration reform,**" *Vox*, **Dec. 11, 2020,** https://tinyurl.com/1dk3ccky.
An immigration reporter says some Democrats in Congress will demand that President Biden take aggressive action on immigration that includes creating

alternatives to deportation and expanding immigrants' access to health care.

Reklaitis, Victor, and **Robert Schroeder,** "All of President Biden's key executive orders—in one chart," *MarketWatch*, Feb. 18, 2021, https://tinyurl.com/yrza7ja9.
The authors provide a concise summary of Biden's executive orders, proclamations and memoranda on immigration and other issues since taking office in January.

Shear, Michael D., "Democratic Lawmakers Introduce Biden's Immigration Overhaul in House," *The New York Times*, Feb. 18, 2021, https://tinyurl.com/e9s1zkoh.
A reporter explains the key provisions of Biden's legislation to chart a new course for U.S. immigration policy and undo the actions taken by former President Donald Trump.

Wise, Alana, "Biden Team Unveils New Asylum System To Replace Trump's 'Remain In Mexico,'" *NPR*, Feb. 12, 2021, https://tinyurl.com/187hyv8i.
In allowing entry by asylum seekers forced to wait in Mexico under previous U.S. policy, the Biden administration faces a difficult challenge in avoiding a rush of migrants to the U.S.-Mexico border.

Reports and Studies

Loweree, Jorge, Aaron Reichlin-Melnick and **Walter Ewing,** "The Impact of COVID-19 on Noncitizens and Across the U.S. Immigration System," American Immigration Council, Sept. 30, 2020, https://tinyurl.com/1o6ar8py.
An immigrant advocacy group catalogs the Trump administration's coronavirus-related policies on legal and illegal immigration.

Pierce, Sarah, and **Jessica Bolter,** "Dismantling and Reconstructing the U.S. Immigration System: A Catalog of Changes under the Trump Presidency," Migration Policy Institute, July 2020, https://tinyurl.com/1axy7kij.
A pro-immigration think tank analyzes President Donald Trump's more than 400 actions taken to reshape asylum policies, refugee programs, deportation priorities and other aspects of immigration.

Ries, Lora, "President Trump and Joe Biden: Comparing Immigration Policies," Heritage Foundation, Oct. 21, 2020, https://tinyurl.com/56vf3j5a.
A senior research fellow at a conservative think tank breaks down the policy differences between Biden and his predecessor on immigration policy, including the border wall, asylum programs and protections for undocumented immigrants brought to the United States as children.

"The State of the Immigration Courts: Trump Leaves Biden 1.3 Million Case Backlog in Immigration Courts," Transactional Records Access Clearinghouse, Jan. 19, 2021, https://tinyurl.com/zyz1v3h1.
A Syracuse University research center analyzes the backlog of immigration court cases hindering President Biden's efforts to reverse his predecessor's immigration legacy.

THE NEXT STEP
Biden's Plans

Ferris, Sarah, Heather Caygle and **Laura Barrón-López,** "'Not quite ready yet': Democrats won't take up Biden immigration plan this month," *Politico*, March 4, 2021, https://tinyurl.com/5xrdahfy.
House Democrats reportedly do not have enough votes yet to pass President Biden's comprehensive immigration bill.

Kumar, Anita, "Biden yet to act on overturning some Trump immigration policies," *Politico*, March 9, 2021, https://tinyurl.com/ykju7zaw.
The Department of Homeland Security may ask courts to overturn Trump-era immigration policies, rather than replace them through the time-consuming process of issuing new regulations.

Min Kim, Seung, "Next Biden agenda items on immigration and infrastructure already running into trouble," *The Washington Post*, March 11, 2011, https://tinyurl.com/hf4827hk.

Facing dissension within their ranks about Biden's proposed immigration package, congressional Democrats may try to pass smaller pieces of the measure separately, such as creating a path to citizenship for undocumented immigrants brought to the United States as children and permanent residency permits for farm workers without legal status.

Immigration Courts

Brache, Laura, "A Day With A Charlotte Immigration Attorney Inside One Of The Nation's Toughest Courts," *WFAE*, March 11, 2011, https://tinyurl.com/5btendn4.

A reporter follows an immigration attorney in Charlotte, N.C., where more than 80 percent of asylum cases end in deportation.

Frost, Amanda, "Deportation Without Disclosure: Immigration Courts Need Transparency," *Bloomberg Law*, Feb. 23, 2021, https://tinyurl.com/6sxn3jje.

A law professor argues that all immigration court rulings should be made public, after the U.S. Court of Appeals for the Second Circuit ruled that only the nation's highest immigration court must disclose its opinions.

Levinson, Reade, **Kristina Cooke** and **Mica Rosenberg**, "Special Report: How Trump administration left indelible mark on U.S. immigration courts," *Reuters*, March 8, 2021, https://tinyurl.com/ffza7sct.

Judges appointed by President Donald Trump were more likely to deny asylum claims than those appointed by other presidents.

Remain in Mexico

Alvarez, Priscilla, "Infamous tent camp on US-Mexico border drawn down after Biden ends Trump policy," *CNN Politics*, March 7, 2021, https://tinyurl.com/rysvzzsu.

Temporary migrant camps in Mexico are emptying as the Biden administration allows an estimated 25,000 migrants who have active asylum cases to cross the border into the United States to wait for their cases to be adjudicated.

Kocher, Adam, "Biden ends policy forcing asylum-seekers to 'remain in Mexico'—but for 41,247 migrants, it's too late," *The Conversation*, March 10, 2021, https://tinyurl.com/57k9ajud.

Most of the asylum seekers forced to remain in Mexico during the Trump administration were denied asylum.

Smith, Michael, and **Naureen S. Malik**, "Biden Ends Trump's 'Remain in Mexico' Rule, and a Border Camp Empties," *Bloomberg*, March 1, 2021, https://tinyurl.com/ypvuauzk.

Migrants living in border camps in Mexico faced harsh and unhealthy conditions as they waited for their asylum claims to be processed.

Unaccompanied Minors

Blitzer, Jonathan, "Biden Has Few Good Options for the Unaccompanied Children at the Border," *The New Yorker*, March 9, 2021, https://tinyurl.com/3y223mas.

The Biden administration began accepting unaccompanied children claiming asylum at the border, reversing a Trump policy, but as space in shelters runs out, the new rule has led to decisions to use adult holding facilities that were criticized during the Trump administration.

Miroff, Nick, "At border, record number of migrant youths wait in adult detention cells for longer than legally allowed," *The Washington Post*, March 10, 2021, https://tinyurl.com/5h3nw9j6.

Migrant teens and children are spending an average of 107 hours in concrete cells built for adults in Border Patrol stations as they await transfer to a shelter, a time period that is well over the 72-hour legal limit.

Romo, Vanessa, "Number Of Unaccompanied Minors Entering U.S. Soared In February," *NPR*, March 11, 2011, https://tinyurl.com/2thre58n.

The number of unaccompanied minors and families seeking to enter the United States through the Southwest border more than doubled from January to February.

For More Information

American Civil Liberties Union, 915 15th St., N.W., Washington, DC 20005; 212-549-2666; aclu.org/issues/immigrants-rights. Civil rights group that defends immigrants' rights and is working to locate migrant children separated from their families at the Southern border.

Federation for American Immigration Reform, 25 Massachusetts Ave., N.W., Suite 330, Washington, DC 20001; 202-328-7004; fairus.org. Policy group that advocates for limiting immigration "to manage growth, address environmental concerns and maintain a high quality of life."

Migration Policy Institute, 1400 16th St., N.W., Suite 300, Washington, DC 20036; 202-266-1940; migrationpolicy.org. A think tank that analyzes immigration data, recommends policies and tracks trends.

Transactional Records Access Clearinghouse, 215 University Place, Suite 360, Newhouse II, Syracuse University, Syracuse, NY, 13244; 315-443-3563; trac.syr.edu. Research group that analyzes and disseminates data on federal policies affecting immigration and other issues.

U.S. Citizenship and Immigration Services, 111 Massachusetts Ave., N.W., Washington, DC 20529; 800-375-5283; uscis.gov. Department of Homeland Security agency that oversees the country's immigration system.

U.S. Customs and Border Protection, 1300 Pennsylvania Ave., N.W., Washington, DC 20004; 877-227-5511; cbp.gov. Homeland Security agency that enforces immigration laws at the country's borders.

12

Targeted Killings
Is taking out terrorists beyond the battlefield a legitimate tactic?

By Sara Toth Stub

Yemeni children pray over the graves of relatives killed during a nearly decade-long war between Yemeni rebels and Saudi Arabia and its regional allies, which are seeking to restore Yemen's government to power. U.S. drone strikes in Yemen have killed many civilians, including members of a wedding party.

From *CQ Researcher,*
April 9, 2021

THE ISSUES

In December 2013, a missile from an American drone struck a wedding procession in Yemen, killing several members of the al-Ameri and al-Taisy families, according to witnesses. Over the next several years, these families say that at least 34 of their relatives were killed in drone strikes during U.S. counterterrorism operations.

Now these families, who say they were never involved in terrorism, have filed a petition with the Inter-American Commission on Human Rights—an independent body affiliated with the Organization of American States—demanding that the United States stop targeting them and release its criteria for killing suspected terrorists. It is the first time a human rights body is investigating an American drone strike, after U.S. courts have declined to hear such cases.

Although any ruling or injunction issued by the commission is not legally binding, those who filed the petition say it is bringing long-needed attention to the United States' secretive targeted killing program, launched in the wake of the terrorist attacks on New York City and the Pentagon on Sept. 11, 2001.[1]

"The initial aim is to halt further strikes against the family," says Jennifer Gibson, a lawyer with the London-based nongovernmental organization Reprieve, which helped the families file the petition. "But we also need a real public debate about a program that has operated in the shadows."

Pioneered by Israel, the targeted killing of nonstate actors, such as members of militant or terrorist organizations, has become a more common tactic of warfare and security for the United States and other countries, including the United Kingdom, France and other democracies.

The rise of targeted killings, often with armed drones and other precision weapons, is changing the nature of warfare and military operations. States can now participate remotely in years-long operations against enemies. Thirty-nine militaries around the world have armed drones, and 12 countries have used these drones to target and kill individuals.[2]

In drone strikes between 2010 and 2020, the United States killed up to 16,900 people—including as many as 2,200 presumably innocent civilians, according to the Bureau of Investigative Journalism, a U.K.-based nonprofit that is one of the few organizations that has tracked drone strikes in the absence of official government data.[3]

The practice has raised ethical and legal questions. International law governs the use of lethal force in warfare, but targeted killings often happen outside of defined battlefields, with little accountability. This lack of accountability, especially when government officials are targeted, such as the U.S. killing of Iranian Gen. Qassim Soleimani in January 2020, could lead to a dangerous escalation, said Agnes Callamard, the United Nations' special rapporteur investigating extrajudicial and summary executions.

"If you have a few more countries moving in that direction, the real risks of global conflagration are becoming very high," Callamard said.[4]

The International Committee of the Red Cross defines targeted killings as a nation's or armed group's use of lethal force against pre-selected individuals, including suspected terrorists, who are not in one's physical custody either during or outside of an armed conflict. The past three U.S. administrations have used the method to varying degrees in Iraq, Afghanistan, Syria, Yemen, Somalia, Libya, Pakistan and elsewhere.[5]

Only one targeted killing has been reported so far in the 11 weeks since President Biden took office, and his administration has reportedly tightened requirements for carrying them out, but the White House has issued no official public comment or policy change on the matter.[6]

"The war on terror created the drone campaigns," says David Sterman, senior policy analyst at the think tank New America. "Still today, it creates a willingness to use force in this way."

The Trump administration carried out at least 340 drone strikes in Yemen, Somalia and Pakistan alone in the past four years. The Obama administration tallied 563 drone strikes in these countries in eight years, up from 57 strikes under the George W. Bush administration, according to the Bureau of Investigative Journalism.[7] While the Trump administration reduced troop levels in Afghanistan, where the United States declared war against the Taliban and its allies in 2001, it carried out more than 11,000 drone strikes there since 2017.[8]

The use of targeted killings has its defenders. Some experts and government officials say assassinating key individuals can stop imminent terrorist attacks, limit the power of terrorist organizations and, in the case of Iran, slow its development of nuclear weapons.

"The deterrent element is especially important," wrote David

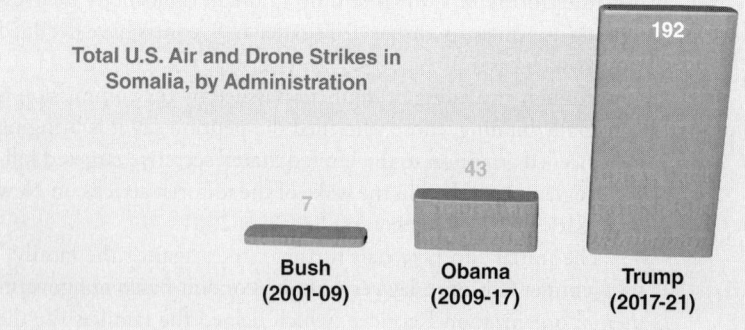

U.S. Strikes in Somalia Escalated Under Trump

During Donald Trump's four years as president, the United States conducted 192 air strikes, including drone strikes, in Somalia — far outstripping the number under the previous two administrations. Presidents George W. Bush and Barack Obama authorized seven and 43 strikes, respectively, while holding office for twice as long as Trump.

Total U.S. Air and Drone Strikes in Somalia, by Administration

- Bush (2001-09): 7
- Obama (2009-17): 43
- Trump (2017-21): 192

Source: "The War in Somalia," New America, March 23, 2021, https://tinyurl.com/7khwmvz9

Deptula, a retired U.S. Air Force lieutenant general and the dean of the Mitchell Institute of Aerospace Studies, in support of the Trump administration's 2020 decision to assassinate Soleimani. "Killing Soleimani sent a particularly powerful message because he is not replaceable in the short term. He was Iran's top terrorist, a leader of its revolutionary ideology and an important strategic thinker."[9]

President Barack Obama argued that drones hold significant advantages over other military options. "Conventional airpower or missiles are far less precise than drones and are likely to cause more civilian casualties and more local outrage," Obama said in 2013. "And invasions of these territories lead us to be viewed as occupying armies, unleash a torrent of unintended consequences, are difficult to contain, result in large numbers of civilian casualties and ultimately empower those who thrive on violent conflict."[10]

Critics, however, question the effectiveness of targeted killings in preventing terrorism or achieving other military and defense goals. They argue such strikes actually can empower terrorist groups by creating momentum for their cause.

"My work has not found convincing evidence that targeted killings carried out by the U.S. have reduced terrorism perpetrated by the global jihadist movement," says Jennifer Carson, associate professor of criminal justice at the University of Central Missouri, who has conducted one of the few empirical studies about the effects of targeted killings of suspected terrorists in Iraq and Afghanistan by the United States.

Targeted killings are gaining public support in the United States. A 2019 poll by the Chicago Council on Global Affairs, for instance, found that 48 percent of Americans felt that drone strikes on targets abroad make the United States safer.[11]

"The public has become almost inured to these killings," says Claire Finkelstein, director of the Center for Ethics and the Rule of Law at the University of Pennsylvania Carey Law School. The United Kingdom, France and others have also engaged in the practice, sometimes in coordination with the United States or with American weapons.[12] In a few cases, Britain and the United States have targeted their own citizens overseas, suspecting them of being involved in terrorism.[13]

"States that employ targeted killing have also started to abandon their policies of denial and to hesitantly engage in public justification," says Jodok Troy, a political science professor at the University of Innsbruck in Austria. "So targeted killing has moved from the fringes of undercover activity to the very core of policymaking in national security."

Israel continues to use targeting killings against Palestinians and, according to analysts, has recently expanded them in places such as Syria and Iraq, partly to hinder Iran's nuclear weapons development program. Experts have attributed to Israel the November 2020 killing of Mohsen Fakhrizadeh, an Iranian military officer, physicist and senior official in the country's nuclear program. Israel has carried out at least 2,300 targeted killing operations since its establishment in 1948, with most of those happening since 2000, according to investigative journalist Ronen Bergman.[14]

Meanwhile, many European countries, including Germany, continue to debate whether they should arm drones.[15]

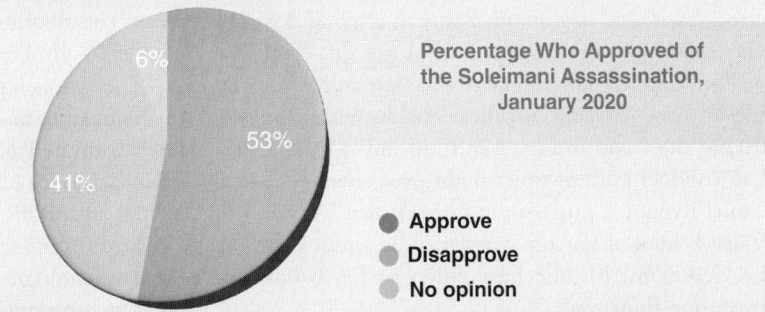

Majority Backed Soleimani Killing

A majority of Americans approved of the U.S. drone strike that killed Iran's top military commander, Gen. Qassim Soleimani, in January 2020, according to a poll taken shortly after the assassination. The Trump administration said Soleimani was targeted because he was responsible for attacks on U.S. troops and civilian contractors in Iraq.

Percentage Who Approved of the Soleimani Assassination, January 2020

- Approve: 53%
- Disapprove: 41%
- No opinion: 6%

Source: "Washington Post-ABC News poll, Jan. 20-23, 2020," The Washington Post, Jan. 28, 2020, https://tinyurl.com/4c5fx6ck

"I believe that what makes countries willing to engage in such killings is their perception of the level of threat," says Daniel Statman, a philosophy professor at the University of Haifa in Israel, who has studied the moral, legal and practical dimensions of the topic. "If any of the countries who are now against targeted killings faced a terror threat, and saw no other way to respond, I would put my money on that they would accept this tactic."

The relatively low financial and human cost on the side of those carrying out these attacks with drones is driving the trend to target and kill individuals rather than conduct raids or other traditional operations, says Daniel Byman, a professor at Georgetown University's Walsh School of Foreign Service and a senior fellow at the Center for Middle East Policy at the Brookings Institution think tank.

"Even if the drones are shot down or crash, the pilot always lives," Byman says. "It enables missions that would not take place otherwise."

But many analysts say the use of armed drones carries important ethical costs that are changing the nature of warfare.

"Armed drones vastly increase the asymmetry of the battlefield," Sterman says. In addition to preventing casualties on the side carrying out the attack, he says, drone warfare means that targets cannot surrender as they could, in theory, to human troops.

Drones can also loiter for hours waiting for the right moment to fire at the target, giving them "a persistence that manned aircraft don't possess," said Sophy Antrobus, a research associate at the Freeman Air and Space Institute at King's College London and an honorary research fellow at the University of Exeter.[16]

This, plus the lack of casualties among those who carry out the strikes, helps targeted killing missions stay secret, contributing to the long-lasting nature of current conflicts, Antrobus said.[17]

"They are being used outside of wars and expanding the boundaries of wars," says Michael Merryman-Lotze, director of the Palestine-Israel program at the American Friends Service Committee, one of many nongovernmental organizations that oppose targeted killings.

In addition, experts and policymakers say drones' rapid technological advances—including the development of autonomous drones or even swarms of drones that can find and attack targets—will alter warfare even more dramatically. The extent of human responsibility for the actions of these machines will need to be considered and defined, they say.[18]

"The weapon illustrates the need to carefully consider what risks the United States is willing to accept," said Zak Kallenborn, author of a recent report on such drones for the U.S. Air Force Center for Strategic Deterrence Studies.[19]

Despite these perils, most experts expect targeted killings to continue. "The scope or rules of engagement may change slightly," Byman says. "But this tactic is now ingrained in an entire generation of military intelligence officers."

As military analysts, government officials, human rights advocates and others debate the legality and effectiveness of targeted killings, here are some of the questions they are asking:

Are drone strikes outside war zones legal?

As targeted killings using drones have proliferated, a debate has emerged about when—if ever—they are within the bounds of law. Top officials in the Bush, Obama and Trump administrations have said killing members and leaders of terrorist organizations overseas is legal, based on a document drawn up after 9/11 that declared the right to target those acting on behalf of al Qaeda and similar groups.

Going back to the George W. Bush administration, the United States has viewed such people as combatants

A soldier guards a Reaper drone at the French air base in Niamey, the capital of Niger, during a French-led campaign against Islamist insurgents across five African countries. Armed drone technology has spread to 39 nations.

who can be killed in self-defense under the laws of war rather than treated as civilian criminals, who would require arrest. But unclassified American documents also state conditions that need to be met for the United States to kill someone out of self-defense, mainly that they present an imminent threat and cannot be apprehended, and that civilian deaths are to be avoided.

"America does not take strikes to punish individuals; we act against terrorists who pose a continuing and imminent threat to the American people, and when there are no other governments capable of effectively addressing the threat," Obama said in a now-famous 2013 address to the National Defense University in Washington. The speech was the first official public disclosure of the targeted killing program.[20]

But this definition of imminent threat is flexible and does not necessarily mean immediate, making the targeting of many suspected terrorists legal, says Georgetown's Byman.

"What imminence is about is [whether] there is any evidence of someone plotting attacks, whether it's for tomorrow or next year," Byman says. "If you know an attack is coming at some point, it doesn't matter when, that target is legitimate." This is what made the strike on Iranian Gen. Soleimani legitimate, he says, because the force he commanded was providing general training for terrorist attacks.

Most of the policy debates about targeted killings in the United States have occurred in closed meetings and classified memos. In Israel, which has carried out more targeted killings than any other Western country, the country's highest court ruled in 2006 that targeted killings are legal if they meet certain criteria, including that targets are participating in ongoing hostilities; the government has reliable information for identification; it has no other way to deal with the person; and the attack avoids harm to surrounding civilians and is proportional.[21]

"This case gave legitimacy to the principle of targeting killings," says the University of Haifa's Statman.

He says that when Israel or any country is dealing with a terrorist group that presents a threat, it is impossible to meet the group on a battlefield, so legally and morally it is acceptable to find and target their members while they are home or anywhere else.

"The only way to defend yourself is by killing their fighters," he says.

In January 2020, mourners in the holy Iraqi city of Karbala carry the coffins of Iranian military commander Qassim Soleimani and eight others killed in a U.S. drone strike. The attack intensified the debate over whether such killings are legal.

But others disagree and say that targeted killings outside of war are not lawful.

"Lethal force outside of armed conflict violates international human rights law," says Hina Shamsi, director of the National Security Project at the American Civil Liberties Union and a lecturer at Columbia University's School of Law. Under the rules of self-defense, only someone who presents a direct and imminent threat—meaning timely and immediate—can be killed, she says. And most targeted killings do not meet these narrow criteria, Shamsi says, including that of Soleimani.

The University of Pennsylvania's Finkelstein argues the bar is high to kill an individual: It is not enough that someone was involved in past attacks, is expressing a desire to carry out a future attack or is considering joining a group whose objective is to attack the United States.

"The use of lethal force must be preventative in all cases, and it must prevent something imminent," she says. For example, Finkelstein says, the killing of Soleimani was illegal because the United States did not provide proof that he was planning an immediate attack—an argument the United Nations also makes.

"Absent an actual imminent threat to life, the course of action taken by the U.S. was unlawful," said Special Rapporteur Callamard about the assassination of Soleimani.[22]

Shamsi adds that a targeted killing must also be an act of last resort and prevent an event that would have had a "significant cost of human life."

In addition, the burden of proof that such killings actually do eliminate immediate threats lies on the U.S. government, she says, something it has failed to provide in most cases.

"We have virtually never seen the backup and evidence for anything that meets this scenario," Shamsi says. "A fundamental problem is not only the letter violation of the law, but also the secrecy. It has become an internal bureaucratized system, without any judicial review."

Regarding Israel, Shahaf Rabi, former founding director of the Israeli Center for the Study of Targeted Killings at the University of Massachusetts, says that Israel often does not follow all of the guidelines set out by the 2006 high court ruling that made targeted killings legal. Rabi, along with colleague Avery Plaw, wrote that "the state's compliance with the safeguards set out in the 2006 targeted killing judgments remains doubtful, especially with regards to the independent ex-post targeted killing investigative committee," to look into civilian deaths.[23]

Do targeted killings reduce civilian and other casualties?

Some analysts argue that targeted killings by drone or airstrike reduce civilian casualties because they are precise and avoid the use of ground troops, who can encounter resistance and use violence against people other than the targets. But others disagree, saying many civilians have been killed by accident during drone strikes, especially in Yemen, Pakistan and Afghanistan.[24]

New America's Sterman concedes that thousands of civilians have died in America's targeted killing campaign, but says that drone strikes often present less risk to bystanders than alternatives such as special forces operations.

"They actually often are a relatively precise tool," Sterman says. "It definitely depends on the specifics, but a ground operation involves a lot more risks and are less often called off when they run into challenges the way drone strikes are." He pointed out that special forces raids and operations in Yemen under President Donald Trump killed many bystanders.[25]

Michael O'Hanlon, director of research on foreign policy at the Brookings Institution, says that when the United States needs to act, killing via drone strikes is often the least threatening option when it comes to hurting local civilians.

"The precision can be quite impressive," he says. "They are seen as the least bad option for handling some types of threats."

Yahli Shereshevsky, a postdoctoral researcher on international law at Hebrew University, says that the remote nature of drones and the fact that a pilot's life is not at risk can help reduce civilian casualties because the drone will only fire at a well-defined target and does not need to fire out of self-defense.

"In the battlefield, fighters make mistakes because of pressure, so they sometimes kill out of fear," he says. "But with drones you can say this is not the case, so you use less force, and it can be more precise."

But others argue that targeted killings carried out with drones are more likely to kill or injure civilians than other methods, mainly because intelligence is sometimes wrong. For example, a U.N. report that analyzed classified information said drone attacks in Afghanistan in 2010 and 2011 were 10 times more likely to result in civilian casualties than airstrikes by planes or helicopters.[26]

"The biggest misnomer is that it's targeted," Reprieve's Gibson says. "The missile may hit X, but if the intelligence is wrong, then it's the wrong X. [And it's the] wrong people that are killed."

She argues that nations are more likely to make mistakes with unmanned drones.

"If you need to put a pilot in a plane, you will think twice if it's really worth it," Gibson says. "But your risk calculation changes dramatically with drones."

For those living in areas where the United States and others have carried out targeted killings by drone, the fear over pending strikes is constant, and many who witness strikes suffer emotionally.

"It's not only those who die that are affected," Gibson says. "There are entire communities that are traumatized, either from seeing strikes, hearing them, or losing relatives or others they know, in them," she says. "You have communities that live with drones overhead, and they don't know if it will strike today or tomorrow."

Andrea Prasow, deputy Washington director at Human Rights Watch, says the debate over which counterterrorism methods—whether targeted killings or

Drone Technology Spreads Worldwide

Thirty-nine countries have acquired armed drones, and 12 of those countries have conducted drone strikes, according to the Washington think tank New America. Countries on every continent except South America and Australia have acquired drones.

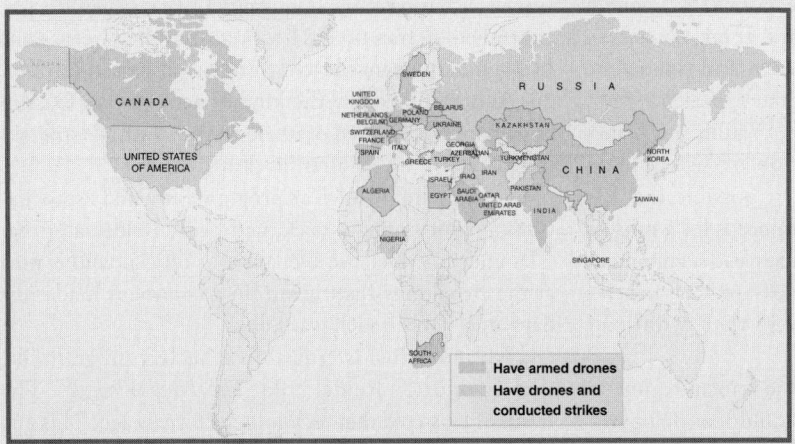

Countries That Have Acquired Armed Drones and Conducted Strikes

Source: "Who Has What: Countries that have Conducted Drone Strikes," New America, March 23, 2021, https://tinyurl.com/8cweyjcw

military operations such as invasions and arrest raids—kill fewer civilians is in itself not constructive or conclusive.

"It's impossible to know if a particular drone strike results in fewer casualties than a ground operation would," she says. A larger problem, Prasow says, is that the secretive nature of the United States' targeted killing program helps hide the actual human cost. Since 2019, when Trump revoked an Obama-era regulation to annually report the number of civilians killed in drone strikes outside of war zones, the United States does not even report the number of deaths in most strikes.[27]

"What we do know is that targeted killings have caused significant numbers of civilian casualties, and that the harm is often compounded by the fact the strikes are often unacknowledged and survivors receive little or no redress," Prasow says.

Are targeted killings effective in combating terrorism or Iran's nuclear weapons program?

Supporters of targeted killings say assassinating individuals can prevent imminent terrorist attacks, disrupt terrorist organizations and, in Iran's case, slow its efforts to develop nuclear weapons. But others say such strikes can draw the United States and other nations deeper into conflicts, empower terrorist groups, raise the risks of retaliation and decrease political clout in any negotiations. And they say killing Iranian officials and scientists will not make a difference in the nuclear program because the know-how is already there.[28]

Georgetown's Byman argues that targeted killings—and the threat of targeted killings—limit the power and abilities of terrorist groups. Killing their leaders or other senior members is especially effective in limiting their ability to carry out attacks and grow as a group.

"These groups don't have an infinitely deep bench of leaders," Byman says. "Experience matters, and if you keep losing experienced people on a regular basis it degrades an organization." He also points out that the constant threat of being taken out by an armed drone or airstrike hampers the abilities of terrorist leaders to effectively lead, because they are forced to hide and limit all phone, internet and other communications.

"Everything they do makes them vulnerable, so they can't really communicate or organize," Byman says. "So they lose the ability to control their organization."

New America's Sterman cites evidence from terrorist groups themselves, including intercepted and recovered statements from Qaeda personnel in Pakistan lamenting the difficulties of operating there under the threat of drone strikes.

"These drone attacks have knocked out the ability of al Qaeda to plot from Pakistan," Sterman says. "And there is a pretty good case to make that drone strikes in Yemen have been somewhat effective at putting holes in al Qaeda in the Arabian Peninsula." But he added that the actual likelihood or ability of these groups to attack American targets is often questionable.

"So whether these killings actually translate into broader strategic success is less clear," Sterman says.

Regarding Iran, Amos Yadlin and Assaf Orion at the Institute for National Security Studies at Tel Aviv University argue that the assassination of Iranian nuclear scientists damages leadership and morale in the nuclear weapons program, setting it back, even if remaining scientists retain the knowledge and know-how.

"The damage to the nuclear weapons effort, which experts consider to be very significant, is not necessarily due to the loss of scientific knowledge, but due to the loss of project leadership, managerial experience, and access to Iran's top political echelon," Yadlin and Orion wrote shortly after the assassination of lead Iranian nuclear scientist Fakhrizadeh. "It is possible that his departure will lengthen the time Iran needs for a nuclear weapons breakout.... Those with such leadership, management, and professional abilities are few and far between, and their loss leaves a void that is difficult to fill."

It could also make it harder for the Iranian regime to recruit additional scientists, who would fear being targeted and killed, they argue.[29]

Other experts say targeted killings do not achieve such goals and could actually strengthen groups by stirring up animosity toward the United States and others, which helps them recruit members.[30]

"The backlash effects have superseded any possible deterrence or incapacitation effects," says the University of Central Missouri's Carson. She says high-profile targeted killings, especially, can lead to more support for terrorist groups.

"While I cannot speak to the individual motivations of terrorists, there is anecdotal evidence that the killing of certain individuals has the ability to rally additional support for a cause," she says.

Merryman-Lotze, of the American Friends Service Committee, says that even if terrorists who were planning attacks are killed, that often does not solve the bigger problem.

"The cost of carrying these operations out is often the stability of the country," he says, pointing to places such as Yemen and Libya. "There's a lot of repercussions that we need to consider. The terrorist may be killed, but it could lead to further trauma in the place."

Sterman echoes some of these concerns: "The U.S. drone efforts, although they took out individuals, may have also contributed to the broader breakdown in Yemen."

On the one-year anniversary of the Soleimani assassination, National Public Radio's international news editor, Greg Myre, said the killing has not changed Iranian-U.S. relations or altered the region.

"The U.S. and Iran are still in this tense standoff," Myre said. "And we really have a perfect example here. Just in recent days, an Iraqi militia that's believed to be controlled by Iran fired 21 rockets into the Green Zone in Baghdad, where the U.S. Embassy is based on Dec. 20. And that's exactly the kind of activity that Qassim Soleimani was accused of orchestrating. And it's still taking place now a year after his death."[31]

As far as Iran's nuclear program, targeted assassinations are not setting it back, said Bruce Reidel, a former CIA and U.S. Defense Department official who is now at the Brookings Institution, in a comment made just days after Fakhrizadeh was killed.[32]

"No individual is crucial in a nuclear program like this anymore," Reidel told *The New Yorker*. "The Iranians mastered that technology 20 years ago. This guy was important, no question, but he was not crucial to it. Nobody is crucial to it anymore. That's why describing this as a devastating blow is nonsense."

BACKGROUND
The Hague Conventions

While philosophers and religious leaders have long debated the morality of war and lethal force, it was not until the mid-19th century that nations began formulating a body of law to govern military action. After a number of international meetings, often spearheaded by czarist Russia, the Hague peace conferences in 1899 and 1907 drew dozens of countries, including the United States, to meet and formalize for the first time modern multinational agreements on the laws and conduct of war.[33]

But these agreements, which came to be known as the Hague Conventions, dealt only with conflicts that took place between states, leaving civil war and other nonstate fighting unaddressed.[34]

Meanwhile, beginning in the 1910s, armed Zionist movements began to target Arab officials for assassination in Palestine, then part of the Ottoman Empire, often in revenge for violent attacks. They also targeted other Jewish community leaders who did not support establishing a Jewish state. David Ben Gurion, the future Israeli prime minister who emerged as the political leader of the Zionist movement in the 1920s, when Palestine became a British-ruled area, at first opposed such methods and even punished those who tried to carry them out.35

But after World War II and the Holocaust, in which more than 6 million Jews and others were murdered, members of the Haganah Zionist militia in 1946 killed several leaders of the German Templer community in Tel Aviv, who had fought for the Nazis in the war in Europe and then returned to their homes in the Holy Land. Ben Gurion's views, as a result, changed—perhaps because of targeted killings' apparent effectiveness.

The killing of the Templers "had an immediate effect," said Rafi Eitan, who participated in those assassinations as a teenager and soon after founded the targeted killing unit of the Mossad, Israel's international intelligence agency. "The Templers disappeared from the country, leaving everything behind, and were never seen again," he said. The Templers' abandoned Tel Aviv neighborhood became the headquarters of the military and intelligence service of the state of Israel, which was formally established in 1948; these institutions remain there today.36

"Jus ad Bellum"

After World War II and the formation of the United Nations in 1945, formalized principles of international human rights law and regulations outlining the appropriate interstate use of force began to emerge.

These use-of-force rules were known as "jus ad bellum." Article 51 of the U.N. charter required that any lethal force a country takes outside its borders in self-defense must be directed against an "imminent threat"; meets standards of "necessity," meaning that the nation has no available alternative course of action, and that the attack be in "proportionality," meaning that force can only be used to the extent needed.37

The Geneva Conventions, which outline human rights during war, were also updated and finalized in 1949. They prohibit, even during war, the premeditated killing of individuals for what they have done or may do on the battlefield—another concept along with jus ad bellum that critics later used to argue that targeted killings violate international legal norms.38

In the 1950s and '60s, Israel continued to engage in targeted killings, often relying on undercover

Patrice Lumumba, the first popularly elected president of the Democratic Republic of Congo, was assassinated in 1961, a killing that some historians believe the CIA helped carry out.

missions to kill individual militants in neighboring Egypt and Jordan who organized continuing violence against the Israeli military and civilians, despite an armistice agreement signed between their governments in 1949.

Israel also killed Egyptian officials associated with these attacks, and later carried out complex operations against German scientists suspected of helping Egypt develop advanced missiles; this operation resulted in the killing of at least one of the scientists. In addition, Israel targeted leaders of the emerging Palestinian national movement, which began carrying out attacks against Israeli civilians by the mid-1960s.39

By this point, undercover missions in enemy territory, including targeted killings, became a key component of national security policy. But it remained a secretive practice, and the government did not officially acknowledge the organization—or even the existence—of the institutions involved, including the Mossad, the Shin Bet domestic intelligence agency and various military spy units that controlled the special forces that carried out the operations.40

The CIA, the U.S. intelligence agency founded in 1947, began targeting foreign officials in the 1950s and 1960s, most famously Cuban leader Fidel Castro. Many historians and analysts have also attributed the 1961 murder of Patrice Lumumba, the first elected president of the Democratic Republic of Congo, at least partially to the CIA. But many of these attempts, including the

CHRONOLOGY

1890s-1940s *Laws governing armed conflicts begin to emerge.*

1899-1907 Dozens of countries discuss laws and norms for governing warfare between nations at the Hague peace conferences.

1917 Ottoman Empire loses its grip on the Middle East, eventually dissolving in 1922. . . . Britain occupies Jerusalem and in 1920 receives an international mandate to rule Palestine.

1920 The Haganah, a Jewish militia, forms in Palestine to defend the local Jewish community. It uses violence and sabotage against the British and local Arab authorities in an attempt to establish an independent state.

1945 The Charter of the newly created United Nations outlines "jus ad bellum," defining when countries can use lethal force outside their borders.

1946 The Haganah Zionist militia in Palestine kills leaders of the local German Templer community who had fought for the Nazis in Europe during World War II; the mission's success leads the emerging Jewish state, which is founded in 1948, to embrace a policy of targeted killings.

1949 Geneva Convention finalizes guidelines for behavior during armed conflict, including protections for civilians.

1950s-1980s *As Israel relies on targeted killing, the U.S. explores assassinations.*

1952 A West German general meets with CIA officials who discuss, but ultimately pass on, assassinating the leader of Communist East Germany; the idea sparks a years-long debate among U.S. intelligence officials about targeting foreign leaders.

1962 CIA launches unsuccessful efforts to assassinate Cuban dictator Fidel Castro. . . . Israel's intelligence agency, Mossad, kills at least one of several targeted German scientists helping Egypt develop surface-to-surface missiles.

1975 U.S. Senate investigates CIA attempts to assassinate foreign leaders, including Castro and others who are aligned with the USSR during the Cold War.

1976 Republican President Gerald Ford issues an executive order banning assassinations but does not define the term.

1986 U.S. troops bomb a residence of Libyan leader Moammar Gadhafi, hoping to kill him.

1989 U.S. military legal adviser Hays Park issues a memorandum stating that airstrikes against suspected terrorists are not assassinations and are therefore legal; earlier, Secretary of State George P. Shultz argued that fighting terrorism could require "preventative or pre-emptive actions" against terrorism suspects.

1990s-Present *With international terrorism rising, governments begin to embrace the use of drones for assassinations of terrorist leaders.*

2000 After Qaeda leader Osama bin Laden issues a fatwa, or formal ruling under Islamic law, against the United States and his followers bomb U.S. embassies in Kenya and Tanzania, a surveillance drone spots him in Afghanistan. But U.S. officials cannot launch missiles in time to kill him; the failure leads the U.S. to arm drones.

2001 After attacks on the U.S. kill nearly 3,000 Americans on Sept. 11, Congress issues an order authorizing the use of force against al Qaeda and associated groups. . . . The first U.S.-armed drone mission unsuccessfully targets Afghan Taliban leader Mullah Omar, who is accused of harboring bin Laden, mastermind of the 9/11 attacks.

2002 U.S. carries out the first successful armed drone operation, in Yemen, against Qaeda members suspected of planning the attack on the *USS Cole*, a guided missile destroyer, in 2000.

2004 A U.S. drone kills Taliban leader Nek Muhammad in Pakistan, the first of hundreds of strikes there against suspected Taliban and Qaeda members as part of the so-called U.S. war on terrorism. The killing is a clear expansion of such operations into areas outside war zones.

2008 Israel kills Iranian-backed Hezbollah military chief Imad Mughniyeh in Damascus, Syria, kicking off a series of plots against people connected to Iran, including nuclear scientists.

2010 Security cameras expose a Mossad operation to kill an official of the militant Palestinian group Hamas in Dubai, United Arab Emirates, revealing how the team used forged foreign passports, amateurish disguises and prepaid credit cards.

2011 The U.S. renews drone strikes targeting suspected terrorists in Yemen, including cleric Anwar al-Awlaki, a U.S. citizen.

2013 Democratic President Barack Obama gives the first public speech on drone strikes and promises more transparency on the matter.

2016 Obama issues an executive order to release annual reports on drone strikes and casualties. Over eight years, his administration carried out at least 563 strikes in Yemen, Pakistan and Somalia, about 10 times the number that his predecessor, Republican George W. Bush, used in these places. Up to 807 civilians died in strikes, according to independent estimates.

2019 Republican President Donald Trump revokes Obama's order on reporting drone strikes.

2020 The U.S. kills Iranian Gen. Qassim Soleimani in a drone strike in Iraq, saying he was responsible for attacks on U.S. troops and civilian contractors in Iraq. The Trump administration also increased drone strikes, carrying out at least 2,243 during his first two years in office, compared with 1,878 during Obama's two terms. . . . The killing of top Iranian nuclear scientist Mohsen Fakhrizadeh is attributed by Iran and experts to Israel.

2021 President Biden pauses drone strikes while he re-evaluates U.S. military plans. As of late March, he had not yet announced any policy changes on targeted killings.

---

ones on Castro, failed. Many U.S. officials were appalled at the idea of targeted assassinations, and after a series of congressional investigations into the CIA's alleged killings and assassination attempts, Republican President Gerald Ford issued an executive order in 1976 banning assassinations.[41]

The order, however, did not define an assassination.[42]

This ambiguity left the door open for U.S. intelligence officials to occasionally target, or to discuss targeting, individuals, especially as terrorism emerged as a global threat in the 1980s. Secretary of State George P. Shultz, who served from 1982 to '89 during the Reagan administration, argued that fighting terrorism could require "preventative or pre-emptive actions" against terrorism suspects before they strike, an idea the United States only fully embraced two decades later.[43]

But several missions began to test this approach, including Operation El Dorado Canyon, when in 1986 the CIA, with the help of Israeli intelligence, bombed a residence of Libyan leader Moammar Gadhafi, who they accused of orchestrating terrorist attacks on Americans, hoping to kill him and his family.[44]

A few years later, Hays Parks, the top official in the U.S. Army's legal department, wrote a memorandum arguing that targeting suspected terrorists in certain situations, "where such individuals or groups pose an immediate threat to United States citizens or the national security of the United States," did not amount to assassination, and therefore did not violate Ford's executive order or international law.[45]

These arguments provided a basis for future justifications for targeted killings.[46] The United States then went on to target (unsuccessfully) Iraqi President Saddam Hussein and Qaeda leader Osama bin Laden under the George H.W. Bush and Clinton administrations. But such actions were controversial, with many officials denying their existence at the time.[47]

Post-9/11 Targeted Killing Program

Until 2001, U.S. officials also voiced disapproval of Israel's targeted killing program. It was the only acknowledged one in the Western world and had accelerated with the outbreak in 2000 of the Second Intifada, or Palestinian uprising, during which Israel killed more than 200 suspected Palestinian terrorists, mainly with bombs from helicopters and airplanes, over four years.[48]

"They are extrajudicial killings, and we do not support that," U.S. Ambassador to Israel Martin Indyk said in July 2001.[49]

But after al Qaeda's attacks on Sept. 11, 2001, which killed nearly 3,000 people, Congress passed the Authorization for Use of Military Force against terrorism. Combined with a series of memos and other

U.S. Faces Growing Drone Competition

"The idea that this can be kept in a box is done."

Armed unmanned aerial vehicles (UAVs)—better known as drones—are changing the nature of warfare and leading to what some experts warn is an arms race, with the United States facing increasing competition from China, Turkey and other countries.

"It's a rapidly expanding type of weapon," says Seth Frantzman, an Israeli-based journalist and the author of the forthcoming book *Drone Wars*. "While just a handful of countries admit to having them, many others want to get them. It's a logical evolution of a military platform because it's basically a missile that can hover around."

The global military drone market is growing more than 12 percent a year, with analysts expecting it to be worth $24 billion by 2027. More than 100 countries have military drone programs, and 39 have armed drones.[1]

In addition to carrying out targeted killings, drones are used to gather intelligence and attack strategic positions, enemy troops or weapons caches. These unmanned weapons can be deployed quickly and for long periods of time without endangering pilots, according to experts and critics alike.

"The existence of this tool makes certain forms of endless war possible," allowing countries to carry out anti-terrorism and other operations without risking soldiers' lives, says David Sterman, senior policy analyst at the New America think tank.

The world's leading drone-makers are mainly in the United States, Europe and Israel, and they sell this technology to militaries that are already strong and advanced.[2]

"Drones are part of the larger trend of military disparity" between stronger and weaker nations, says Daniel Byman, professor at Georgetown University's Walsh School of Foreign Service.

For years, as part of the Missile Technology Control Regime—an informal agreement among 35 nations to limit the proliferation of missiles—the United States refrained from exporting missile-carrying drones, such as the Reaper and the Predator, even to allies. The restriction was born of fear that such drones could fall into the wrong hands, be used on civilians for political reasons or erase Israel's military advantage over its rivals in the Middle East.

But in 2020, the Trump administration reinterpreted the agreement, opening the door to selling drones to allies. Due to this change, a U.S. deal to sell Reaper drones to the United Arab Emirates is pending, as the new Biden administration reviews it.[3]

In addition, other countries, such as Turkey and China, are now producing or buying armed drones.[4]

"The idea that this can be kept in a box is done," Frantzman says. "We are still waiting to see who really becomes the superpower in this; the United States could fall behind."

In fact, this threat of competition was one reason the Trump administration liberalized the drone export policy, a policy first initiated but not finalized under President Barack Obama, Frantzman says. For years, American allies, including Saudi Arabia and Jordan, have been buying drones from China, which began exporting armed drones in 2014.[5]

---

documents, it backed a practice of killing members of terrorist organizations if they could not be captured.[50]

The post-9/11 targeting killing program has relied on drones for up to 95 percent of its operations. The first reported successful drone strike against a suspected Qaeda-affiliated terrorist occurred in Yemen on Nov. 3, 2002, shortly after the United States had declared Yemen an additional battleground against al Qaeda. (The strike killed six suspected terrorists.)[51]

Before this attack, the United States used drones solely for surveillance. The United States undertook a program to arm drones after a spy drone spotted bin Laden in 1998 but forces could not unleash cruise missiles on his location with confidence because they were not sure if he remained there.[52]

Nevertheless, considerable internal disagreement remained over how and when to use these deadly drones, with the CIA ultimately controlling the drones everywhere except inside the war zones of Iraq and Afghanistan, where the military operated them.[53]

Obama expanded the use of targeted killings during his eight years in office. From 2009 to 2017, his

> "UAVs are a cheap man's air force. They are a much more economical way to fight wars'."
>
> — Franz-Stefan Gady
> International Institute for Strategic Studies

As far back as 2017, the Pentagon expressed worry about this development: "China faces little competition for sale of such systems, as most countries that produce them are restricted in selling the technology," said a Pentagon statement.[6]

In addition to improving the ability of advanced militaries to fight from afar, drones are an increasingly attractive option for poorer countries, because they are cheaper than planes, says Franz-Stefan Gady, a research fellow for cyber, space and future conflict at the London-based International Institute for Strategic Studies. He noted that Azerbaijan, due largely to drones purchased from Israel and Turkey, dominated Armenian forces in a 44-day conflict over the disputed territory of Nagorno-Karabakh that ended with a cease-fire in November.[7]

Nonstate actors, including alleged terrorist groups such as Hezbollah in the Middle East and the Houthis in Yemen, are also using more drones.[8]

"UAVs are a cheap man's air force," Gady says. "They are a much more economical way to fight wars. However, they are no panacea to every tactical problem. For example, a key vulnerability are the data links of UAVs that can be jammed. And they can still only carry a fairly limited amount of munitions that are not effective for every target."

Although experts expect armed drones to proliferate quickly, they say the bigger challenge and next area for growth—mainly among wealthy nations—is developing defense systems against drones. Success, however, is far from certain, they say.

"Often the problem is, you cannot put systems in enough places, and because drones can be small and move slowly, it's hard for defensive systems to pick them up," Frantzman says. "So for now, the drone seems to be doing better than defense systems against them. Countries will need to invest a lot in this."

—*Sara Toth Stub*

---

[1] "Military Drone Market Size to Hit USD 23.78 Billion by 2027," *Fortune Business Insights*, Nov. 11, 2020, https://tinyurl.com/23z6s648; Nick Cumming-Bruce, "The Killing of Qassim Suleimani Was Unlawful, Says U.N. Expert," *The New York Times*, July 9, 2020, https://tinyurl.com/3uxj9sew.

[2] "Military Drone Market Size to Hit USD $23.78 Billion by 2027," *ibid*.

[3] "UAE confident F-35 jets sale will go through, says ambassador," *Al Jazeera*, Feb. 2, 2021, https://tinyurl.com/n7rbk9s.

[4] Sébastien Roblin, "Cheap drones from China, Turkey and Israel are fueling conflicts like Armenia and Azerbaijan's," *NBC News*, Oct. 14, 2020, https://tinyurl.com/d8zh7bx9.

[5] Jeremy Page and Paul Sonne, "Unable to Buy U.S. Military Drones, Allies Place Orders With China," *The Wall Street Journal*, July 17, 2017, https://tinyurl.com/fvckh3us.

[6] *Ibid*.

[7] Robyn Dixon, "Azerbaijan's drones owned the battlefield in Nagorno-Karabakh—and showed future of warfare," *The Washington Post*, Nov. 11, 2020, https://tinyurl.com/8u6bsp9f.

[8] Dan De Luce, "Iranian-backed Houthi rebels in Yemen ramp up drone, missile attacks on Saudi Arabia," *NBC News*, March 12, 2021, https://tinyurl.com/z8cke4y6; "Hezbollah claims to fly drone into Israel undetected, film border bases," *The Times of Israel*, Dec. 5, 2020, https://tinyurl.com/4akxwxts.

---

administration carried out at least 563 drone strikes in Yemen, Pakistan and Somalia, up from 57 in these countries under Republican George W. Bush. Obama officials, after 2010, also began leaking information to the media hinting at the existence of the program and its operations, which had long been kept secret from the public.[54]

One killing immediately revealed to the public was that of bin Laden, who was shot dead by Navy SEALs in a 2011 raid in Pakistan. Government lawyers had worked for weeks before the raid to craft documents outlining why it was legal to kill rather than arrest bin Laden. The authorization to use force against those behind the 9/11 attacks, limiting innocent civilian casualties and knowing for certain whether bin Laden was dead were among the reasons cited for making it a mission to kill rather than capture. The legal team also wrote that the United States could legally violate Pakistan's sovereignty to carry out the operation without telling them by relying on an exception to sovereignty based on the argument that Pakistan may not be able or willing to quash the threat posed by bin Laden.[55]

Assassinations of Iranians Draw Criticism and Praise

"Sporadic eliminations are worth nothing."

In November, Iran's top nuclear scientist, Mohsen Fakhrizadeh, died in a carefully planned ambush. According to one recent account, he was shot with a 1-ton Israeli machine gun smuggled into the country.[1]

No one has officially claimed responsibility for the assassination—but Iranians and many intelligence analysts blame Israel and believe the Trump administration knew about the operation in advance.[2]

Although many details about Fakhrizadeh's death remain unclear, assassinations have come to play a larger role in Israeli and U.S. attempts to counter Iran and its nuclear weapons development program. Debate continues over the killings' effectiveness, legality and political repercussions, especially as President Biden seeks talks with Iran to limit its nuclear capabilities, its activities in Iraq and its human rights abuses.

Since 2007, Israel's Mossad intelligence organization has killed at least five Iranian nuclear scientists, media reports say.[3] According to a 2018 book by Israeli journalist Ronen Bergman, Meir Dagan, the former Mossad director who initiated the plans to kill Iranian scientists, said bluntly in an interview that one killing is insufficient, as the threat of death must be constant to have an effect on the nuclear program.

"Sporadic eliminations are worth nothing," Dagan said.[4]

In his book, Bergman argued that killing the scientists has set the Iran's nuclear program back years. Human knowledge and leadership were lost, he said, and the Iranians were forced to invest an immense effort in inspecting equipment for possible sabotage. "These efforts greatly slowed down other aspects of the nuclear project, even bringing some to a standstill," Bergman wrote.[5]

But others say the killings have had little effect, and that actions such as the 2015 international agreement known as the Joint Comprehensive Plan of Action, in which Iran agreed to limit uranium enrichment in return for softening economic sanctions, have done more to curb Iran's capabilities.

"The Iranian project was too extensive and mature for a few killings to substantively affect it," wrote Shlomo Brom and Shimon Stein, senior researchers at Tel Aviv University's Institute for National Security Studies. "In the case of the Fakhrizadeh assassination, it is doubtful . . . the killing will significantly serve the objective of damaging and delaying the Iranian nuclear project."[6]

The United States first used the tactic against Iran in January 2020, when it assassinated Iranian Gen. Qassim Soleimani near Baghdad, striking his convoy with a drone. The attack also killed several of his allies in Iraq-based militias.[7]

"Because there have been many other targeted killings, in a way it made it easier to apply this to Soleimani, or the U.S. became more willing to apply it," says David Sterman, senior policy analyst at New America, a Washington think tank. "The war on terror and all the drone killings opened the space for the United States to target an Iranian government official. So they approached him more as a terrorist rather than a government official. But the primary story here is the Iranian-U.S. conflict, not terrorism."

While Soleimani's killing did not trigger a widely expected major backlash, some analysts say it, along with

By this time, human rights groups concerned about the growing number of civilian casualties—as well as international legal experts and members of Congress who said they had been kept in the dark over the program—began criticizing targeted killings and demanding more information.[56]

The United Nations also criticized U.S. drone use, and in 2010 it started calling for international agreements to limit armed drones and targeted killings, many of which violate international law.[57]

In a 2013 report, Christof Heyns, then the U.N.'s special rapporteur on extrajudicial, summary or arbitrary executions, warned that armed drones' relative ease of use would lead states to carry out longer and more numerous conflicts, risking an end to the notion that war should be something temporary or limited.

the more recent killing of Fakhrizadeh, has led Iran to increase its enrichment of uranium and refuse to renew talks with the United States about limiting its nuclear program. The Trump administration pulled out of the Joint Comprehensive Plan of Action in 2018.[8]

And some warn that the killings could lead to a dangerous escalation of violence and jeopardize long-accepted rules of engagement.

Assassinating scientists differs from the thousands of targeted killings of suspected terrorists and militants Israel has carried out over the years, says Daniel Statman, a professor of political philosophy and ethics at the University of Haifa in Israel. Scientists, he says, do not likely present an immediate threat to life, and international rules of conventional warfare forbid the killing of researchers and scientists working for sovereign states.

"These are not exactly fighters, they are civilians. [Assassinations] might lead to undermining conventions that have been around for years," Statman says. "The international community has a strong interest in making sure people take these limitations on fighting very seriously, and this could lead to the other side doing the same thing to our scientists."

For the United States, targeting Soleimani, a government official, marked a turn away from targeted killings that focused mainly on nonstate actors, such as members of terrorist or militant organizations, says Claire Finkelstein, director of the Center for Ethics and the Rule of Law at the University of Pennsylvania's law school.

"We are at an inflection point," she says.

In 2019, the United States designated as a terrorist organization the Quds Force, the Islamic Revolutionary Guards' military unit that Soleimani oversaw. But despite this designation, Soleimani also remained an official of the sovereign Iranian government. "Being a state actor should take precedence over being a non-state actor," Finkelstein says.[9]

Meanwhile, Iran's current top nuclear scientist, Ali Akbar Salehi, recently told the *PBS News Hour* that Iran plans to continue enriching uranium—unless the United States returns to the original deal brokered in 2015, whose terms Biden has indicated he wants to renegotiate. Salehi also said he did not fear for his life.

"I don't worry about it, because we believe in destiny. Destiny is in the hand of God," he said. "Eventually, we have to die, sooner or later. OK. You die as a martyr, so much the better."[10]

—*Sara Toth Stub*

[1] Stephen Farrell, "Iranian nuclear scientist killed by one-ton automated gun in Israeli hit: Jewish Chronicle," *Reuters*, Feb. 10, 2021, https://tinyurl.com/25fdx5pd.

[2] Chas Danner, "What We Know About the Assassination of Iran's Top Nuclear Scientist," *New York Magazine*, Nov. 27, 2020, https://tinyurl.com/2e8vzptn.

[3] Oliver Holmes, "Iranian scientist's death only the latest in long line of attacks blamed on Israel," *The Guardian*, Nov. 27, 2020, https://tinyurl.com/8zd77kv6.

[4] Ronen Bergman, *Rise and Kill First: The Secret History of Israel's Targeted Assassinations* (2018), p. 581.

[5] *Ibid.*, p. 609.

[6] Shlomo Brom and Shimon Stein, "Does the Cost of the Fakhrizadeh Assassination Outweigh the Benefits?" Institute for National Security Studies, Tel Aviv University, Dec. 2, 2020, https://tinyurl.com/4k78vf79.

[7] Karen Zraick, "What to Know About the Death of Iranian General Suleimani," *The New York Times*, Jan. 3, 2020, https://tinyurl.com/u4xs9pe9.

[8] Sune Engel Rasmussen and Laurence Norman, "Iran's Nuclear Scientist: How Will the Killing of Mohsen Fakhrizadeh Affect Tehran's Nuclear Program?" *The Wall Street Journal*, Dec. 1, 2020, https://tinyurl.com/bxmv4jr5.

[9] Miriam Berger, "What is Iran's Revolutionary Guards Corps that Soleimani Helped to Lead?" *The Washington Post*, Jan. 4, 2020, https://tinyurl.com/ff8vjhdr.

[10] Nick Schifrin, "Iran's top nuclear scientist discusses the potential for a nuclear deal with the U.S.," *PBS News Hour*, March 9, 2021, https://tinyurl.com/33mnx8ds.

"The expansive use of armed drones by the first States to acquire them, if not challenged, can do structural damage to the cornerstones of international security and set precedents that undermine the protection of life across the globe in the longer term," Heyns wrote.[58]

During his second term, Obama began to speak more openly about the program, defending its precise nature and releasing figures on civilians killed, although those White House figures fell far below those compiled by human rights groups.[59]

Further public scrutiny of targeted killings came after a 2011 American drone strike in Yemen killed Anwar al-Awlaki, who was a U.S. citizen, a Yemeni national and a suspected Qaeda operative. In 2014, in response to a lawsuit brought by *The New York Times* and the American Civil Liberties Union against the U.S.

government, a federal appeals court in New York released a partially redacted government memo justifying the targeting of Awlaki, and exposing more details of the targeted killing program, including the CIA's official role.[60]

The memo said that although targeting the New Mexico-born Awlaki carried a risk of depriving him of his liberties, "the continued and imminent threat of violence or death" that he presented to Americans outweighed his rights and justified his killing, although the memo did not detail what sort of threat he posed.[61]

Ultimately, the court dismissed a lawsuit brought by Awlaki's family against the Obama administration, saying it could not rule on matters of "military planning."[62]

The Trump Era

When Trump entered the White House in 2017, he expanded the targeted killing program, especially in Somalia, where he ordered 40 airstrikes in 2020 alone, up from 41 carried out by Bush and Obama combined from 2007 to 2016. He also walked back transparency measures that Obama had introduced, stopping for example the release of the number of civilians killed in strikes each year. This change was mainly possible because Obama's measures were executive actions rather than legislated rules that would have continued to apply beyond his presidency.[63]

Eventually, the United States came to use targeted killings to counter Iran. This was especially the case after 2018, when the Trump administration withdrew the United States from the 2015 Joint Comprehensive Plan of Action, in which several countries had lifted some economic sanctions on Iran in exchange for that regime's agreement to limit its nuclear program. Under Trump, the United States killed leaders of Iranian-backed militias that had targeted American troops and civilian contractors in Iraq.[64]

And, in a move that drew sharp domestic and international criticism, as well as raising fears of retaliation, the Trump administration in January 2020 used a drone to kill Iranian Gen. Soleimani while he was in Iraq, marking the first time that the authorization of military force following the Sept. 11 attacks was applied against a state official. Unlike most other U.S. targeted killings, this one was not secret.[65]

CURRENT SITUATION
Policy Review

Since President Biden entered the White House in January, administration officials and members of Congress have been taking steps to review and possibly change or limit the targeted killings program and the ongoing military force authorizations that support it.

The administration, which apparently has not carried out any targeted killings since one was reported in Iraq in January, now requires that the military and CIA seek White House permission before carrying out drone strikes outside the war zones of Syria and Afghanistan, officials have told *The New York Times*. This is a possible departure from the Trump-era policy that allowed military and intelligence officials to decide on their own whether to target individuals.[66]

The change has halted drone strikes but is only temporary, as Biden reviews policy.

"This review includes an examination of previous approaches in the context of evolving counterterrorism threats in order to refine our approach going forward," said Emily Horne, a spokeswoman for the White House's National Security Council. "In addition, the review will seek to ensure appropriate transparency measures."[67]

Avril Haines, Biden's director of national intelligence, who served in the Obama administration and was one of the architects of the drone program, supports returning to Obama-era rules that required the government to report the number of civilian casualties in drone strikes.[68]

The Biden administration is also considering tightening the requirements for ensuring that women and children are not in strike areas and requiring more surveillance before and during strikes. And it is weighing whether the United States should follow general rules for strikes, giving the operators freedom to make decisions, which was Trump's approach, or whether each strike should be approved in a more centralized manner, as was the policy under Obama since 2013.[69]

But until the administration releases an official statement or announces a change in policy, legal and human rights experts are expressing concern.

"The U.S. still claims the authority and power to kill terrorism suspects in violation of international human rights law," the ACLU's Shamsi says. "Until this changes,

AT ISSUE

Are targeted killings legal?

YES — **Abraham Bell**
Professor of Law, University of San Diego

Written for *CQ Researcher*, April 2021

Targeted killings have always been lawful under international law.

Modern international law emerged in Renaissance Europe, and its earliest versions assumed that states could legitimately kill.

The laws of war that emerged then (and persist until today) approve the killing of enemy combatants—not only of soldiers, but of everyone who participates in combat on behalf of the enemy. Under modern laws of war, states may kill innocent people as well, so long as the innocents are "collateral damage" to enemy combatants in an amount that is not "excessive." Within the bounds of these rules, states can and do target specific enemy targets for killing. For instance, during World War II, Allied forces famously targeted and killed Reinhard Heydrich, the acting Reich-protector of Bohemia and Moravia for Nazi Germany, and Marshal Adm. Isoroku Yamamoto of the Imperial Japanese Navy.

Some have objected to targeted killings in open-ended conflicts against nonstate armed forces, such as the United States' targeted killings of Qaeda terrorists. Such objections rest on a misunderstanding of the relationship between the law governing the conduct of combat and the rules that tell states when they are permitted to initiate military action. The same targeting rules apply to all combat, no matter whether the armed conflict was lawfully initiated. Even if it initially had no right to engage in armed conflict against al Qaeda or the Taliban, the United States still has a right to target specific Qaeda or Taliban combatants today.

A more difficult question arises where the targeted killing takes place outside armed conflict. Here, too, it has been clear for centuries that states may employ their militaries to kill combatants outside formal war. International law uses a variety of terms to describe occasions where military force is legitimately used outside armed conflict, such as "frontier incidents," armed reprisals and self-defense. In such cases, targeted killings are as legal as in armed conflict.

Perhaps the most frequent controversy over targeted killings is over identifying targets. Critics argue that persons such as Brig. Gen. Mohsen Fakhrizadeh of the Islamic Revolutionary Guard Corps should not have been considered legitimate targets because they had prominent civilian roles; in addition to his rank in Iran's military nuclear program, Fakhrizadeh was a physics professor at Imam Hossein University.

But this too misapprehends relevant international law. International law classifies civilians with combat roles or actively involved in combat as legitimate targets.

NO — **Algernon Biddle**
Professor of Law and Professor of Philosophy, University of Pennsylvania

Written for *CQ Researcher*, April 2021

Extrajudicial killings outside of active military hostilities have grown exponentially since the 9/11 attacks, particularly using drones. Drone technology has provided many advantages in the fight against violent nonstate actors. Compared with in-person "kill or capture" missions, drones have reduced the risk to our military in the fight against terrorists, minimized the collateral damage our strikes inflict, and reduced invasiveness to sovereign nations with whom we were not at war.

Despite these benefits, the legal framework for targeted killings remains nebulous, and it is still unclear what conditions must be satisfied before lethal force can be used outside the context of armed conflict. International law requires that we attempt to capture rather than kill nonstate actors who pose an imminent risk of harm, unless capture is "infeasible." But defining terms like "imminence" or "infeasibility" remains an elusive task, one largely left to the subjective judgment of presidents who have enjoyed discretion over such operations without much congressional or judicial oversight.

The recent killing of Iranian Gen. Qassim Soleimani made matters murkier still. This was the first time the United States had openly killed a state actor outside the context of armed conflict. In the absence of a clear justification grounded in the law of national self-defense, there is no basis for thinking such strikes legal under international law. Lack of clarity surrounding the use of targeted killing of nonstate actors is arguably responsible for this expansion, since it allowed previously clear rules to be manipulated for the sake of short-term gain.

An additional worry is that these practices have effaced the distinction between war and crime, given that we have weakened the line between combatants and civilians and thus eroded the protected status of civilians under the laws of war. If we continue down this path, we will begin to weaken the constitutional guarantees protecting domestic criminal suspects as well.

The results could be disastrous. We currently imagine, for example, that targeted killing would never be deployed on U.S. soil. Radicalization of the U.S. population, however, creates a grave risk that previously clear distinctions will no longer hold. We might thus find drones with lethal capacity deployed in domestic law enforcement, just as we have already seen with regard to surveillance. For this and many other reasons, we need legal clarity in the domain of targeted killing, and we should dial back our use of this technique except in cases where that clarity has been achieved.

Discussion Questions

Here are some questions to think about regarding targeted killings:

- Why are targeted killings on the rise? Who pioneered these operations and why?
- What is a targeted killing? Do you believe they are legal under international law?
- What do critics say about targeted killings? And what do its defenders argue in response?
- Are targeted killings the best way to stop Iran from developing nuclear weapons? If not, what would be more effective?
- Do you support using armed drones to carry out targeted killings, rather than human-piloted aircraft? Why or why not?
- How are drones changing the nature of war? What do ethicists argue about the costs of this type of warfare?

A young woman runs off as a fighter approaches a man outside a tent at a refugee camp near the Yemeni city of Marib on March 28, 2021. President Biden announced the United States will end support for Saudi Arabia's military campaign against Iranbacked Houthi rebels in Yemen.

our reputation for adherence to law and the norms that safeguard this are in tatters."

At the same time, some congressional Republicans oppose the suspension of drone strikes and the policy review.

"This action is yet another bureaucratic impediment created by the Biden administration that will give our enemies an advantage over the United States and our allies," Rep. Mike Rogers of Alabama, the senior Republican on the House Armed Services Committee, said in March.[70]

The United States also continues to expand the infrastructure needed to continue the drone program, including developing a CIA base in Niger dedicated to drones. Although no drone strikes from the base have been reported, the military is using it to surveil suspected terrorist groups in places such as Mali and Libya, and it appears prepared to expand drone strikes in Africa's Sahel region if policy permits.[71]

On a related note, some also worry that even though Biden has announced the United States will end support for Saudi Arabia's military campaign against Iran-backed Houthi rebels in Yemen—support that started under Obama when Biden was vice president—drone strikes and other targeting of suspected terrorists could continue or even increase, because Biden stipulated that the United States could still defend American and Saudi interests and continue fighting al Qaeda and linked groups there.[72]

"I'm cautiously optimistic," says Gibson of Reprieve. "But I am also disappointed that Biden did not address this issue of targeted killings and implied that anti-terrorism operations would continue."

Congressional Debates

In Congress, some lawmakers are renewing efforts to repeal two laws the United States relies on to justify targeted killings: the 2001 authorization to fight terrorism globally and the 2002 authorization for military force in Iraq. They say these declarations are outdated and should not be used to allow targeted killings in multiple countries.

Administrations have cited the 2001 authorization, written with the main goal of fighting bin Laden and al Qaeda, 41 times for attacks in 19 countries.[73] These authorizations of force allow the president to order killings without having to consult Congress, as long as officials cite some link to anti-terrorism.

"This approach has essentially written Congress out of its role of deciding war powers," the ACLU's Shamsi says.

The effort is somewhat bipartisan. While Democrats such as Rep. Barbara Lee of California want to cancel the authorizations to end the conflicts, Republican support for the issue stems from a desire to limit the White House's power and put the authorization for military action more firmly in Congress. Both sides of the aisle hope that the Biden administration will examine the issue.

"I think there is a bigger window of opportunity right now," said Rep. Don Bacon, a Nebraska Republican and retired Air Force brigadier general who served as a commander in Iraq. Bacon said the authorizations are out of date and cannot be used to justify current military operations. "I can't say I have math behind it," he said. "It's just my gut."[74]

Human rights organizations are lobbying lawmakers on the issue, with 25 prominent organizations sending a letter to Biden in February, urging him to end the authorizations, which they say have been stretched beyond their limits to create "endless war."[75]

"We want a revocation of that and a move back from the idea that we can carry out attacks anywhere we want in the name of a global war on terror," says Merryman-Lotze of the American Friends Service Committee.

The fallout from the Trump administration's killing of Soleimani, along with the alleged Israeli killing of nuclear scientist Fakhrizadeh, also continues and is among the contributing factors to Iran's refusal to return to negotiations limiting its nuclear capacity. The killing of Soleimani—using a tool reserved for suspected terrorists on a state official—also shows how enemies can blur, New America's Sterman says.

"It shows that the conflict with Iran is not entirely separate from the war on terror," he says. "It's a concerning sign that the conflicts can expand and enemies can blur together."

Although Biden said during his campaign that he would re-enter the 2015 nuclear agreement with Iran, Tehran is stepping up its uranium enrichment and says it will not return to negotiations until the United States lifts debilitating economic sanctions.[76]

Many former top U.S. officials have condemned those targeted killings and say Biden must do everything possible to return to the table with Iran—or face the prospect of war with the Islamic Republic.

"War with Iran would be an unmitigated disaster," a group of more than 40 former national security, military and diplomatic officials wrote to Biden. "While there is no question that the U.S. would prevail, military conflict with Iran would incur unacceptable costs to the United States and ultimately fail to advance U.S. national security. We must urgently reverse course, beginning by rejoining" the 2015 nuclear pact.[77]

OUTLOOK
An End to "Forever Wars"?

Many experts expect Biden to continue targeted killings to some extent, but say the policy governing them will likely more closely resemble Obama's than Trump's. For example, they expect more transparency, and for the White House and military to have authority over the majority of such operations instead of the CIA.

"Generally, the personality of the president doesn't change these things," says New America's Sterman. "But I think we may see more transparency requirements and more requirements to report on civilian deaths."

But some analysts see the chance for a larger change, especially because Biden has pledged to end the "forever wars" in places such as Afghanistan and Iraq, where drone killings have played a large role.[78]

Even though many of the same people from Obama's administration, which expanded drone strikes, are serving in the Biden administration, "we are waiting to see whether and how they learned a lesson about their approach, and how that approach perpetuates forever wars," the ACLU's Shamsi says. "It remains to be seen."

Analysts and legal rights advocates also worry about the use of drones on the domestic front, as more law enforcement agencies adopt them, mainly for surveillance assistance.[79] Finkelstein of the University of Pennsylvania worries that armed drones could be deployed to track or target people inside the United States, especially as the label of "domestic terrorism" is used more often to describe extremist movements across the political spectrum, including in events such as the Jan. 6 storming of the U.S. Capitol by Trump supporters.

"I'm concerned about the future," Finkelstein says. "When this way of dealing with security threats becomes a common practice, it's hard for it not to leak into other areas."

Analysts predict the gap between militaries will continue, especially as new technology emerges.

"Drones are part of that larger trend of military disparity, which will continue," Georgetown's Byman says.

Drones and technology used for surveillance are also becoming more advanced, incorporating elements of artificial technology and machine learning.[80] But the University of Haifa's Statman says that new technology, such as artificial intelligence (AI) or smarter drones will not necessarily mean more civilian casualties, as many fear.

"These AI-based robots might make mistakes, but humans are even more prone to error," Statman says. "We will be relying more on AI and robots for everything in our lives, so I see no reason to be more worried about them in war."

The United Nations has called for limits on the development and use of drones, and more oversight and international standards for when targeted killings are appropriate.[81] But some say this is unlikely to happen.

"There is a huge difference in opinion between various experts on what is considered a proportional attack," Statman says. "When people will assess as proportional or disproportional is often tied to their opinion on whether the conflict itself is justified."

New methods will likely emerge for targeted killings, however, says Hebrew University's Shereshevsky, especially with the growth of cyberwarfare.

"Maybe there will be targeted cyberattacks, targeting people by turning off their electricity, or causing their self-driving car to crash," Shereshevsky says. "You can imagine many things. But the new era of fully autonomous technology raises the ability to find and target people. The question will be how much humans will control the decision-making."

NOTES

1. Missy Ryan and Souad Mekhennet, "In a first, Yemenis seek redress for U.S. drone strikes at Inter-American Rights Body," *The Washington Post*, Jan. 27, 2021, https://tinyurl.com/3hjy9wxk.

2. "Who Has What: Countries that have Conducted Drone Strikes," New America, March 23, 2021, https://tinyurl.com/8cweyjcw.

3. "Drone Warfare," Bureau of Investigative Journalism, accessed March 8, 2021, https://tinyurl.com/5cvph66r.

4. Nick Cumming-Bruce, "The Killing of Qassim Suleimani Was Unlawful, Says U.N. Expert," *The New York Times*, July 9, 2020, https://tinyurl.com/3p4bxkae.

5. "Targeted Killings," International Committee of the Red Cross, https://tinyurl.com/netpab24; Kelsey D. Atherton, "Trump Inherited the Drone War but Ditched Accountability," *Foreign Policy*, May 22, 2020, https://tinyurl.com/r7f4bpw4; Peter Bergen, David Sterman and Melissa Salyk-Virk, "America's Counterterrorism Wars," New America, March 30, 2020, https://tinyurl.com/58k344mr.

6. Jane Arraf and Falih Hassan, "U.S. Airstrike Kills Top ISIS Leader in Iraq," *The New York Times*, Jan. 29, 2021, https://tinyurl.com/u63tattx; Charlie Savage and Eric Schmitt, "Biden Secretly Limits Counterterrorism Drones Strikes Away From War Zones," *The New York Times*, March 3, 2021, https://tinyurl.com/pbs63ms.

7. Jessica Purkiss and Jack Serle, "Obama's Covert Drone War in Numbers: Ten Times More Strikes Than Bush," Bureau of Investigative Journalism, Jan. 17, 2017, https://tinyurl.com/uned55rr; Atherton, *op. cit.*; "Strikes in Pakistan," Bureau of Investigative Journalism, accessed March 8, 2021, https://tinyurl.com/23f86bw3; "Strikes in Yemen," Bureau of Investigative Journalism, accessed March 8, 2021, https://tinyurl.com/4dybbn3u; and "Strikes in Somalia," Bureau of Investigative Journalism," accessed March 8, 2021, https://tinyurl.com/ekyjt4s2.

8. "Strikes in Afghanistan," Bureau of Investigative Journalism, accessed March 8, 2021, https://tinyurl.com/4aczfkhh.

9. Michael Eisenstadt, Kori Schake and David Deptula, "U.S. Strategy Toward Iran: Restoring Deterrence, Enabling Diplomacy," The Washington Institute for Near East Policy, Feb. 14, 2020, https://tinyurl.com/3ca4fcpc.

10. "United States, Use of Armed Drones for Extraterritorial Killings," International Committee of the Red Cross, https://tinyurl.com/senx7res.

11. Dina Smeltz *et al.*, "Rejecting Retreat: Americans Support US Engagement in Global Affairs," Chicago Council on Global Affairs, 2019, p. 16, https://tinyurl.com/3f7umpt5.

12. Dan Sabbagh, "Targeted killings via drone becoming normalised—report," *The Guardian*, Jan. 19, 2020, https://tinyurl.com/us3tzcj8; Angela Charlton and

Krista Larson, "France says it carried out first armed drone strike in Mali," *The Associated Press*, Dec. 23, 2019, https://tinyurl.com/827nx8v9; Peter Burt, "Joint Enterprise: An overview of US-UK co-operation on armed drone operations," The European Forum on Armed Drones, June 2020, https://tinyurl.com/2bfe7kht; and Marcus Müller, "The Fog of Drone War: Lessons from the U.S. and European Armed Drone Policy," American Institute for Contemporary German Studies at Johns Hopkins University, April 10, 2019, https://tinyurl.com/d7kpx4w.

13. Müller, *ibid.*

14. David M. Halbfinger, Ben Hubbard and Ronen Bergman, "The Israel-Iran Shadow War Escalates and Breaks Into the Open," *The New York Times*, Aug. 28, 2019, https://tinyurl.com/mph2mnb6; David E. Sanger, "Assassination in Iran Could Limit Biden's Options. Was that the Goal?" *The New York Times*, Nov. 28, 2020, https://tinyurl.com/uft4x39x; and Ronen Bergman, *Rise and Kill First: The Secret History of Israel's Targeted Assassinations* (2018), p. xxii.

15. Laurenz Gehrke, "German SPD under attack after shooting down armed drones," *Politico*, Dec. 18, 2020, https://tinyurl.com/yv9tsa2a.

16. Sophy Antrobus, "How Are Drones Changing Warfare?" Gresham College, Nov. 11, 2020, 7:24, https://tinyurl.com/3smyv2w5.

17. *Ibid.*, 12:09-12:24.

18. David Hambling, "U.S. Army's New Drone Swarm May Be a Weapon of Mass Destruction," *Forbes*, June 1, 2020, https://tinyurl.com/sad9fs.

19. *Ibid.*

20. "Remarks by the President at the National Defense University," The White House, May 23, 2013, https://tinyurl.com/mwn5cznb.

21. Shahaf Rabi and Avery E. Plaw, "Do Israeli Targeted Killings Comply with High Court of Justice's Guidelines?" *Israel Law Review*, June 2020, p. 56, https://tinyurl.com/drhmtw97.

22. "UN Rights Rapporteur Calls U.S. Killing of Top Iranian General 'Unlawful,'" RadioFree Europe Radio Liberty, July 7, 2020, https://tinyurl.com/jx65dmr7.

23. Rabi and Plaw, *op. cit.*

24. Cumming-Bruce, *op. cit.*

25. Ryan and Mekhennet, *op. cit.*

26. Cumming-Bruce, *op. cit.*

27. "The Secret Death Toll of America's Drones," *The New York Times*, March 30, 2019, https://tinyurl.com/2w8hxt98; Atherton, *op. cit.*

28. Robin Wright, "Why the Assassination of a Scientist Will Have No Impact on Iran's Nuclear Program," *The New Yorker*, Nov. 30, 2020, https://tinyurl.com/6ywm8s.

29. Amos Yadlin and Assaf Orion, "The Assassination of Fakhrizadeh: Considerations and Consequences," *INSS Insight*, Dec. 2, 2020, https://tinyurl.com/5fnhfae2.

30. Jennifer Varriale Carson, "Assessing the Effectiveness of High-Profile Targeted Killings in the 'War on Terror': A Quasi-Experiment," *Criminology and Public Policy*, February 2017, https://tinyurl.com/42e9z3jj.

31. Peter Kenyon and Greg Myre, "A Look Back at What Happened After the Killing of Iranian Gen. Qassim Soleimani," *NPR*, Jan. 1, 2021, https://tinyurl.com/y2tyfxzs.

32. Wright, *op. cit.*

33. "Treaties, State Parties and Commentaries," International Committee of the Red Cross, https://tinyurl.com/4394fp5r.

34. Nobuo Hayashi, "The Role and Importance of the Hague Conferences: A Historical Perspective," United Nations Institute for Disarmament Research, 2017, p. 4, https://tinyurl.com/3dvv6n6x.

35. Bergman, *op. cit.*, pp. 8-10.

36. *Ibid.*, pp. 16-17.

37. Frans Viljoen, "International Human Rights Law: A Short History," *UN Chronicle*, https://tinyurl.com/rkzavjws; Agnes Callamard, "The Targeted Killing of General Soleimani: Its Lawfulness and Why it Matters," *Just Security*, Jan. 8, 2020, https://tinyurl.com/7mxxv9pf.

38. John Daniszewski, "Was the drone attack on Iranian general an assassination?" *The Associated Press*, Jan. 4, 2020, https://tinyurl.com/4cz8jcx4.

39. Bergman, *op. cit.*, pp. 63-71.
40. *Ibid.*, pp. 31, 35.
41. Stephan Weissman, "The Lumumba Assassination and CIA Accountability," Wilson Center, April 9, 2012, https://tinyurl.com/adzryh5t; Luca Trenta, "The U.S. has blurred the lines on assassinations for decades," *The Conversation*, Aug. 26, 2016, https://tinyurl.com/8uynu7ud.
42. Trenta, *ibid.*
43. Andris Banka and Adam Quinn, "Killing Norms Softly: U.S. Targeted Killing, Quasi-secrecy and the Assassination Ban," Security Studies, 2018, https://tinyurl.com/e5522m; Tim Weiner, "George P. Shultz, Top Cabinet Official Under Nixon and Reagan, Dies at 100," *The New York Times*, https://tinyurl.com/8fymhwxc; and Bernard Weinraub, "U.S. Calls Libya Raid a Success; 'Choice is Theirs,' Reagan Says; Moscow Cancels Shultz Talks," *The New York Times*, April 16, 1986, https://tinyurl.com/3a5bvkj4.
44. Walter J. Boyne, "El Dorado Canyon," *Air Force Magazine*, March 1, 1999, https://tinyurl.com/5h2xc294.
45. Seymour Hersh, "Target Qaddafi," *The New York Times*, Feb. 22, 1987, https://tinyurl.com/4n4mnpak; "Memorandum of Law," Department of the Army, Nov. 2, 1989, https://tinyurl.com/2p7unehb.
46. Trenta, *op. cit.*
47. *Ibid.*
48. Daniel L. Byman, "Targeting Killing, American-style," Brookings, Jan. 20, 2006, https://tinyurl.com/45x2n6j9; Banka and Quinn, *op. cit.*
49. Jane Mayer, "The Predator War," *The New Yorker*, Oct. 19, 2009, https://tinyurl.com/jrzxzuy.
50. Charlie Savage, "Secret U.S. Memo Made Legal Case to Kill a Citizen," *The New York Times*, Oct. 8, 2011, https://tinyurl.com/rvdha3pf; Atherton, *op. cit.*
51. Cora Currier, "Everything you need to know about drone strikes," *ProPublica, PBS*, Jan. 11, 2013, https://tinyurl.com/vn8kh9a8; "Yemeni, Reported U.S. Covert Actions 2001-2011," Bureau of Investigative Journalism, accessed Jan. 23, 2021, https://tinyurl.com/2ps4npzw.
52. Chris Woods, "The Story of America's Very First Drone Strike," *The Atlantic*, May 30, 2015, https://tinyurl.com/dbnnd8v7.
53. Mayer, *op. cit.*
54. Banka and Quinn, *op. cit.*; Mayer, *ibid.*
55. Charlie Savage, "How 4 Federal Lawyers Paved the Way to Kill Osama bin Laden," *The New York Times*, Oct. 28, 2015, https://tinyurl.com/efxm464.
56. Mayer, *op. cit.*
57. Charlie Savage, "U.N. Report Highly Critical of U.S. Drone Attacks," *The New York Times*, June 2, 2010, https://tinyurl.com/6c7za8yh.
58. "Extrajudicial, Summary or Arbitrary Executions," United Nations General Assembly, Sept. 13, 2013, https://tinyurl.com/h9676kxc.
59. Purkiss and Serle, *op. cit.*
60. Greg Miller, "Legal memo backing drone strike that killed American Anwar al-Awlaki is released," *The Washington Post*, June 23, 2014, https://tinyurl.com/y32825sb; Charlie Savage, "Court Releases Large Parts of Memo Approving Killing of American in Yemen," *The New York Times*, June 23, 2014, https://tinyurl.com/8bbftujf.
61. Miller, *op. cit.*
62. Pete Yost, "Judge dismisses lawsuit over drone strikes in Yemen that killed American Anwar al-Awlaki," *The Washington Post*, April 4, 2014, https://tinyurl.com/yhk849d4.
63. Atherton, *op. cit.*
64. Dan Lamothe and Mustafa Salim, "U.S. Strikes in Iraq and Syria target Iranian-backed militia, Pentagon says," *The Washington Post*, Dec. 29, 2019, https://tinyurl.com/4m4kx696; David Brennan, "Joe Biden Must Rejoin Iran Nuclear Deal To Avoid 'Unacceptable' War, Former Officials Say," *Newsweek*, Feb. 5, 2021, https://tinyurl.com/aksjvauv.
65. Atherton, *op. cit.*
66. Charlie Savage and Eric Schmitt, "Biden Secretly Limits Counterterrorism Drone Strikes Away From War Zones," *The New York Times*, March 3, 2021, https://tinyurl.com/pbs63ms.
67. *Ibid.*

68. Brianna Rosen, "To End the Forever Wars, Rein in the Drones," *Just Security*, Feb. 16, 2021, https://tinyurl.com/sjms6jvd.
69. Savage and Schmitt, *op. cit.*
70. Eric Schmitt and Christoph Koettl, "Remote CIA Base in the Sahara Steadily Grows," *The New York Times*, March 8, 2021, https://tinyurl.com/y87na5an.
71. *Ibid.*
72. Rebecca Kheel, "Biden's Move on Yemen Sparks New Questions," *The Hill*, Feb. 13, 2021, https://tinyurl.com/47pe5fj3; Joseph Hincks, "Leading Aid Official David Miliband on What Joe Biden's Pivot Means to Yemen," *Time*, Feb. 5, 2021, https://tinyurl.com/5y5p47vv.
73. Andrew Bacevich, "Has Biden forgotten he's commander in chief? Here's America's national security to-do list," *Los Angeles Times*, Feb. 3, 2021, https://tinyurl.com/2y8jkaca.
74. Jennifer Scholtes and Connor O'Brien, "Adios AUMF? Democrats press Biden for help in revoking old war powers," *Politico*, Jan. 21, 2021, https://tinyurl.com/3dfz8xpt.
75. Ellen Mitchell, "Group of 25 prominent nonprofits urge Congress to pull war powers," *The Hill*, Feb. 17, 2021, https://tinyurl.com/4sa46tfb.
76. David E. Sanger, "Assassination in Iran Could Limit Biden's Options. Was That the Goal?" *The New York Times*, Nov. 28, 2020, https://tinyurl.com/uft4x39x; Kali Robinson, "What Is the Iran Nuclear Deal?" Council on Foreign Relations, Feb 25, 2021, https://tinyurl.com/y2ub8srs; and David Brennan, "Joe Biden Must Rejoin Iran Nuclear Deal to Avoid 'Unacceptable' War, Former Officials Say," *Newsweek*, Feb. 5, 2021, https://tinyurl.com/aksjvauv.
77. Brennan, *ibid.*
78. Gerald F. Seib, "Biden's Opposition to 'Forever Wars' Being Tested in Afghanistan," *The Wall Street Journal*, March 1, 2021, https://tinyurl.com/8xfervj8.
79. "Domestic Drones," American Civil Liberties Union, https://tinyurl.com/yh23nfu3.
80. Will Knight, "Anduril's New Drone Offers to Inject More AI into Warfare," *Wired*, Sept. 10, 2020, https://tinyurl.com/wyfjww94.
81. "All drone strikes 'in self-defence' should go before Security Council, argues independent rights expert," United Nations, July 9, 2020, https://tinyurl.com/t3k2yjzt.

BIBLIOGRAPHY

Books

Bergman, Ronen, *Rise and Kill First: The Secret History of Israel's Targeted Assassinations*, Random House, 2018.
An investigative journalist outlines the history of Israel's targeted killing program, from pre-1948 militias to the modern day.

Frantzman, Seth J., *Drone Wars: Pioneers, Killing Machines, Artificial Intelligence, and the Battle for the Future*, Bombardier Books, June 2021.
A journalist explores the development, current uses and the future role of unmanned drones in warfare.

Meisels, Tamar, and Jeremy Waldron, *Debating Targeted Killing: Counter-Terrorism or Extrajudicial Execution?* Oxford University Press, 2020.
Two academics examine the legal and ethical debates around targeted killings.

Senn, Martin, and Jodok Troy, eds., *The Transformation of Targeted Killing and International Order*, Routledge, 2019.
Two scholars present a collection of essays on the political, ethical and legal issues involved in modern targeted killings.

Articles

Atherton, Kelsey D., "Trump Inherited the Drone War but Ditched Accountability," *Foreign Policy*, May 22, 2020, https://tinyurl.com/vas552uk.
A journalist argues that President Donald Trump expanded the use of drones and made the program more secretive.

Banka, Andris, and Adam Quinn, "Killing Norms Softly: U.S. Targeted Killing, Quasi-secrecy and the Assassination Ban," *Security Studies*, 2018, https://tinyurl.com/xw78yub.
Two academics explore how leaks to the press lend legitimacy to secret military programs, including targeted killings.

Callamard, Agnes, "The Targeted Killing of General Soleimani: Its Lawfulness and Why It Matters," *Just Security*, Jan. 8, 2020, https://tinyurl.com/7mxxv9pf.
The U.N. special rapporteur on extrajudicial, summary or arbitrary executions analyzes the legal issues surrounding the U.S. killing of an Iranian general and the precedent it sets.

Carson, Jennifer Varriale, "Assessing the Effectiveness of High-Profile Targeted Killings in the 'War on Terror': A Quasi-Experiment," *Criminology and Public Policy*, February 2017, https://tinyurl.com/42e9z3jj.
In a comprehensive study, an associate professor of criminal justice at the University of Central Missouri argues that the United States' targeted killings since Sept. 11, 2001, have yielded "negligible" results.

Ryan, Missy, and Souad Mekhennet, "In a first, Yemenis seek redress for U.S. drone strikes at Inter-American rights body," *The Washington Post*, Jan. 26, 2021, https://tinyurl.com/f9s4bcvb.
A news article details how Yemeni families are challenging U.S. drone strikes in an international human rights court.

Sabbagh, Dan, "Targeted killings via drone becoming 'normalised'—report," *The Guardian*, Jan. 19, 2020, https://tinyurl.com/2rvk6fmh.
The public is increasingly accepting of targeted killings as they become more common, argues the group Drone Wars, which opposes the use of drones.

Savage, Charlie, and Eric Schmitt, "Biden Secretly Limits Counterterrorism Drone Strikes Away from War Zones," *The New York Times*, March 3, 2021, https://tinyurl.com/aunrfx46.
The Biden administration is considering tightening Trump-era rules for targeted drone strikes.

Wright, Robin, "Why the Assassination of a Scientist Will Have No Impact on Iran's Nuclear Program," *The New Yorker*, Nov. 30, 2020, https://tinyurl.com/t8u57pc.
A foreign-affairs journalist argues that the recent killing of a top Iranian nuclear scientist will not limit that nation's arms program.

Yadlin, Amos, and Assaf Orion, "The Assassination of Fakhrizadeh: Considerations and Consequences," *INSS Insight*, Dec. 2, 2020, https://tinyurl.com/vt63bjkj.
Two researchers at the Institute for National Security Studies, an Israeli think tank, write that the killing of the nuclear scientist could slow the progression of Iran's nuclear program.

Reports and Studies

Bergen, Peter, David Sterman and Melissa Salyk-Virk, "America's Counterterrorism Wars," New America, March 30, 2020, https://tinyurl.com/2pnreye3.
A comprehensive report by a Washington think tank tracks U.S. drone strikes in Pakistan, Yemen, Somalia and Libya, including the number of civilian casualties.

Burt, Peter, "Joint Enterprise: An overview of US-UK co-operation on armed drone operations," *Drone Wars UK*, June 2020, https://tinyurl.com/d2773jda.
A report by an anti-drone group details how the British military has joined U.S. drone missions and adopted American tactics.

"Use of armed drones for targeted killings," U.N. Special Rapporteur on Extrajudicial, Summary or Arbitrary Executions, United Nations Digital Library, 2020, https://tinyurl.com/2mtfxfz8.
The U.N.'s special rapporteur on arbitrary executions looks at the increase in targeted killings and the proliferation of armed drones, and recommends the United Nations adopt international regulations.

THE NEXT STEP

Biden Administration

Schmitt, Eric, and Christoph Koettl, "Remote C.I.A. Base in the Sahara Steadily Grows," *The New York Times*, March 8, 2021, https://tinyurl.com/y87na5an.
A CIA base in Niger is expanding its ability to launch armed drone strikes, but there is no public evidence it has conducted a strike against terrorism suspects yet.

Sen, Sudhi Ranjan, "India to Buy First U.S. Armed Drones to Counter China, Pakistan," *Bloomberg*, March 9, 2021, https://tinyurl.com/79c94wck.

India plans to buy 30 armed drones from the United States as the Biden administration seeks closer military ties with the Asian nation.

Stone, Mike, "Exclusive: Biden wants to keep Trump policy that boosted armed drone exports," *Reuters*, March 25, 2021, https://tinyurl.com/3h8epyff.
The administration will continue to sell drones abroad, even to countries whose human rights records are under scrutiny, according to sources.

Israel

Khoury, Jack, "Hamas Says Gaza Fishermen's Deaths Caused by Explosive-laden Israeli Drone," *Haaretz*, March 11, 2011, https://tinyurl.com/7ctnej9c.
Three fishermen in Gaza died in an explosion after snaring an armed Israeli drone in their nets.

Kirkpatrick, David D., Farnaz Fassihi and Ronen Bergman, "Killer Robot? Assassination of Iranian Scientist Feeds Conflicting Accounts," *The New York Times*, Dec. 9, 2020, https://tinyurl.com/ymvk5yrd.
Political factions in Iran disagree about the details surrounding the killing of one of the country's top scientists, believed to be the work of Israel, as each wants to avoid responsibility for the security lapse.

"Lebanon's Hezbollah group says it shot down Israeli drone," *The Associated Press*, Feb. 1, 2021, https://tinyurl.com/4p5pf272.
The militant group Hezbollah shot down an Israeli drone after vowing to avenge the killing of one of its fighters in an Israeli strike in Syria.

Terrorists

Barakat, Matthew, "Former Air Force analyst pleads to leaking secrets about drone program," *The Associated Press*, WTSP, April 1, 2021, https://tinyurl.com/scztbnpj.
A former Air Force intelligence analyst pleaded guilty to leaking classified documents about drone strikes conducted against al Qaeda and other terrorist targets.

Cooper, Helene, and Eric Schmitt, "U.S. Airstrikes in Syria Target Iran-Backed Militias That Rocketed American Troops in Iraq," *The New York Times*, Feb. 25, 2021, https://tinyurl.com/49see9z4.
The Biden administration authorized airstrikes against a militia in Syria that had recently attacked American and allied personnel in Iraq.

"Saudi energy ministry condemns terrorist drone attack on Riyadh oil refinery," *Arab News*, March 26, 2021, https://tinyurl.com/4sn3n3fn.
The perpetrators of a drone strike on an oil refinery in Riyadh have yet to be officially confirmed, but Jordan believes a Houthi terrorist group was responsible.

Yemen

Al-Batati, Saeed, "Senior Houthi leader killed in Arab coalition airstrike on Marib," *Arab News*, March 21, 2021, https://tinyurl.com/5c7y3hum.
Major Gen. Zakaria Yahiya Al-Shami, at the top of the Arab coalition's most wanted list, was killed while leading rebel Houthis in an offensive.

Frantzman, Seth J., "Reports say Iran has expanded 'kamikaze drone' base in Yemen," *The Jerusalem Post*, Jan. 14, 2021, https://tinyurl.com/b8cbtxcs.
Iran has reportedly sent to Houthi rebels "suicide drones" that operate like cruise missiles.

"Yemen's Houthis say they launched drone attacks on Saudi capital," *Al Jazeera*, April 1, 2021, https://tinyurl.com/vmjsmba2.
A Houthi spokesman says the group sent four drones to attack Riyadh, but Saudi officials have not confirmed the story.

For More Information

American Civil Liberties Union, 125 Broad St., 18th Floor, New York, NY 10004; 212-549-2500; aclu.org. Group whose work includes advocating for Americans hurt or killed in targeted killing overseas.

Bureau of Investigative Journalism, PO Box 76421, London EC2P 2SH, United Kingdom; +44 203 892 7490; thebureauinvestigates.com. Independent reporting organization that tracks drone strikes and deaths.

Drone Wars UK, Peace House, 19 Paradise St., Oxford, OX1 1LD, United Kingdom; +44 1865 243688; dronewars.net. Nongovernmental organization that maintains a database of countries with armed drones.

European Forum on Armed Drones, Sint Jacobsstraat 12, 3551 BS Utrecht, The Netherlands; +31 30 233 33 46; efad.org. European group focused on research about armed drones and advocating limits on their use in an effort to end armed conflicts.

Human Rights Watch, 350 Fifth Ave., 34th Floor, New York, NY 10118-3299; hrw.org. International nonprofit whose work includes tracking civilian deaths in drone strikes.

Institute for National Security Studies, 40 Haim Levanon St., Tel Aviv, Israel; +972 3 640 0400; inss.org.il. Think tank at Tel Aviv University that focuses on Israeli security, including the role of targeted killings.

New America, 740 15th St., N.W., Suite 900, Washington, DC 20005; 202-986-2700; newamerica.org. Think tank that tracks U.S. drone strikes.

U.S. Department of Defense, 1400 Defense Pentagon, Washington, DC 20301-1400; 703-697-5131; defense.gov. Federal department that oversees the armed forces and weapons research.

Child Trafficking

Can the world reduce a growing scourge?

By Jonathan Broder

Ethnic minority Rohingya children play at a temporary shelter in Indonesia in October 2020. Rohingya refugees fleeing persecution in nearby Myanmar are easy prey for traffickers, who exploit their desperate situation.

THE ISSUES

Sasha was just 14 when she turned her first trick as a victim of child sex trafficking.

The teenager had grown up in a poor, dysfunctional home in Florida, then endured soul-crushing bullying in high school after her family moved to Atlanta. Lonely and suffering from low self-esteem, Sasha said, she leapt at a chance for social acceptance when a classmate befriended her.

The friend then introduced her to an older man, who listened to Sasha sympathetically as she poured her heart out. He soon became, in her mind, her boyfriend and surrogate father. For the first time, "He made me feel like I was special," Sasha recalled tearfully in a CNN documentary on child trafficking.[1]

Soon, however, the man began exploiting Sasha's trust by pressuring her to have sex with other men for money in the back of a friend's Atlanta barber shop. Fearing the loss of his love and attention, Sasha agreed. But, finally, after being forced to sexually service nearly 40 men in one day, Sasha told the boyfriend she was fed up and wanted out.

"You ain't going nowhere," he said, pulling out a gun and daring her to walk away. Trapped between fear and dependence, Sasha continued to meet the man's demands until she finally found the courage to seek help from a safe house for victims of sex trafficking.[2]

From *CQ Researcher*,
April 16, 2021

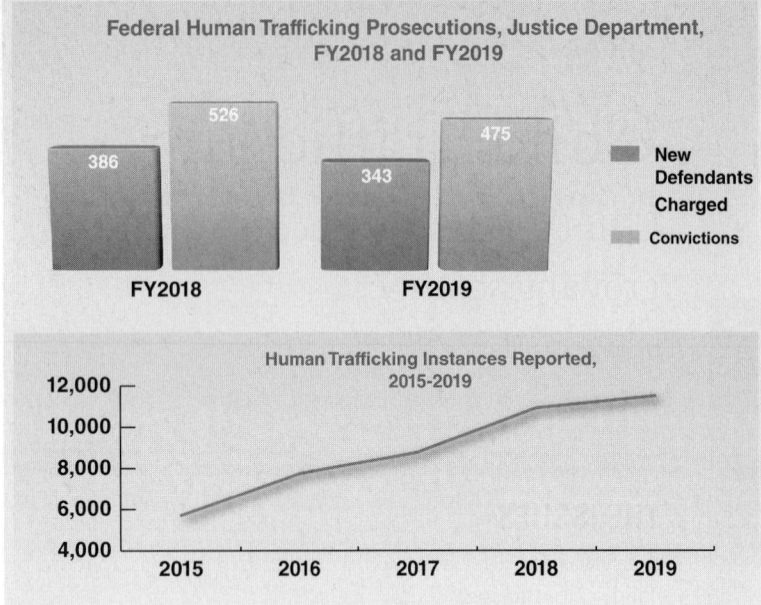

U.S. Trafficking Prosecutions Fall as Reported Cases Rise

Prosecutions and convictions of human traffickers by the U.S. Justice Department declined from fiscal 2018 to fiscal 2019. Yet reported instances of trafficking have risen steadily since 2015, according to the Polaris Project, a nonprofit that runs a national trafficking hotline.

Sources: "Trafficking in Persons Report, 20th Edition," U.S. Department of State, June 2020, pp. 515-516, https://tinyurl.com/kdm3enkh; "2019 Data Report: The U.S. National Human Trafficking Hotline," Polaris Project, https://tinyurl.com/3w5du39c

in the Department of State's 2020 annual report on global human trafficking.[4]

And, despite the more than a dozen U.S. and international laws and treaties enacted over the past century banning child trafficking and forced labor, the problem continues to grow. Experts say today's traffickers are tech-savvy and highly skilled at using technology to cover their tracks and stay ahead of law enforcement. While many U.S. tech companies voluntarily police their platforms for child sexual abuse materials, other companies are far less attentive and fail to cooperate fully with law enforcement when they do find such materials, experts say.

Even the Department of Justice, which Congress made the tip of the U.S. spear in the fight against human trafficking, has encountered difficulties fulfilling this mission in recent years. Prosecutions and convictions of traffickers fell nearly 10 percent in 2019 compared to the previous year, despite an 11 percent spike in online child sex trafficking reports.[5]

"Last year, we got 18 million reports of child sex abuse materials being posted online," an FBI agent told a Carnegie Mellon University information technology class earlier this year. "That's a 10,000 percent increase over the last six years."

A Justice Department spokesman said U.S. prosecutions had declined in recent years even as reports of child trafficking rose because it is "a hidden crime. Minors are almost never advertised as minors, and the victims are often trained to hide their age from those who might help them," he says. In addition, victims—who often come from abusive homes or foster care—"typically harbor conflicted emotions about their trafficker," ranging from trauma-bonding to fear of retaliation if they cooperate with law enforcement.

Sasha's story is not unique—in the United States or elsewhere. Between 25 million and 40 million people worldwide are victims of human trafficking and modern slavery, 10 million of them under age 18, according to various sources. The vast majority are girls forced by threat, deception or economic desperation into the underground sex trade. Even United Nations peacekeepers have been accused of sexually trafficking women, girls and boys in countries where the soldiers are stationed. Exploitation includes online imagery of rape and abuse of toddlers, shared and sold to pedophiles around the world. Cyber-facilitated exploitation has grown exponentially in recent years, FBI officials say, overwhelming federal, state and local law enforcement.[3]

"We and our allies and partners find ourselves confronting a crisis that has reached previously unimagined proportions," then-Secretary of State Mike Pompeo wrote

But Luis C. deBaca, former head of the Justice Department's human trafficking section and of the

Office to Monitor and Combat Trafficking in Persons during the Obama administration, also blames Republican deficit hawks in Congress for reducing by half the $60 million annual anti-trafficking budget. And the Trump administration shifted nearly $6 million from the Department of Homeland Security's cybercrimes unit in 2019—40 percent of the department's discretionary budget—to immigration enforcement, he says.

A new U.S. law designed to curb online child sex trafficking faces legal challenges from free-speech advocates, and critics say it inadvertently endangers minors by forcing them to take their business dealings offline and into the street. For U.S. anti-trafficking efforts to be more effective, critics say, Congress should require law enforcement and tech companies to work together to stop online trafficking, instead of relying on the voluntary arrangement that currently governs their relationship. Others say the United States should embrace a sweeping U.N. agenda for sustainable development that would enlist labor, health and financial institutions—in addition to law enforcement—in the fight.

Child trafficking, which takes several forms in addition to sexual exploitation, is the world's second most lucrative crime after the drug trade, earning traffickers some $150 billion a year. In what the U.N.'s International Labour Organization (ILO) calls the modern equivalent of slavery, millions of the world's children are trafficked and forced to work for little or no pay in farming, mining, fishing and in garment factories and restaurant kitchens. Or they are forced to work off a family debt. Traffickers also use children to run drugs, beg for money on the street or serve as soldiers in rebel armies. Others are trafficked for the forced removal and sale of their organs. Some infants are kidnapped and sold for adoption.[6]

A common misconception about child trafficking is that a minor must be transported across state lines or an international border to legally qualify as a trafficking

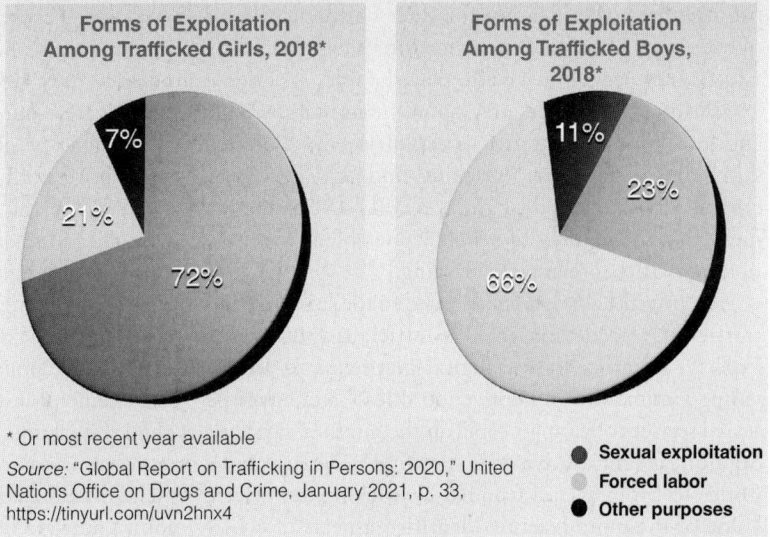

Girls Usually Trafficked for Sexual Exploitation, Boys for Labor

Most girls trafficked in 2018 were victims of sexual exploitation, while most boys were trafficked for forced labor, according to United Nations estimates of detected victims provided by 115 countries.

Forms of Exploitation Among Trafficked Girls, 2018*

Forms of Exploitation Among Trafficked Boys, 2018*

* Or most recent year available

Source: "Global Report on Trafficking in Persons: 2020," United Nations Office on Drugs and Crime, January 2021, p. 33, https://tinyurl.com/uvn2hnx4

- Sexual exploitation
- Forced labor
- Other purposes

victim. But a U.S. law enacted in 2000, commonly called the Trafficking Victims Protection Act, and several U.N. human rights conventions state that anyone under 18 recruited for sex work, labor or organ removal is a trafficking victim—regardless of whether they are transported across a border.[7]

However, the United States, the U.N. and many anti-trafficking groups differ on the definition of child trafficking. The ILO's estimates that 40 million people worldwide are trafficked each year includes 15 million women and girls who have been coerced into marriage. The organization argues that child brides qualify as trafficking victims because they routinely are coerced to become sexual and domestic slaves for their spouses.[8]

The U.S. government, which estimates that 25 million people are trafficked each year, does not specify how many are children. U.S. officials also say forced marriage is a complicated issue, often involving cultural traditions and norms. Other experts say research has not definitively identified forced marriage as a form of human trafficking.[9]

However, there is widespread agreement that child trafficking is on the rise. The U.N.'s Vienna-based Office on Drugs and Crime says children now make up a third of the world's trafficking victims, with girls comprising 19 percent, and boys, 15 percent.[10]

The spike is caused by poverty as well as natural disasters, such as typhoons, earthquakes or tsunamis, that leave struggling families vulnerable to traffickers who promise jobs or education for their children in safer places, say U.S. and international experts. The COVID-19 pandemic has also played a role.

"[H]uman traffickers prey upon the most vulnerable and look for opportunities to exploit them," Pompeo said in the 2020 report. "Instability and lack of access to critical services caused by the [COVID-19] pandemic mean that the number of people vulnerable to exploitation by traffickers is rapidly growing."[11]

The internet also has contributed to the spike in child trafficking, according to U.S. officials and outside experts. "Traffickers use digital platforms to recruit young victims with deceptive job offers" and advertise sexual services of young people on the internet, says Jane Sigmon, a senior adviser in the State Department's Office to Monitor and Combat Trafficking in Persons. "One of the more recently identified aspects of cyber-facilitated trafficking is [the use of] phones and webcams to live-stream acts of sexual abuse of children for profit."

Such live streams and photos appear on popular porn sites, where customers use search terms such as "young tiny teen," "extra small petite teen" or simply "young girl," according to *New York Times* columnist Nicholas Kristof, who has written extensively on child trafficking.[12] The most depraved live streams, showing rapes of children as young as 2 and 3 years old, appear on so-called dark web sites frequented by hardcore pedophiles, according to researchers and law enforcement.

But arresting the creators of such sites is "very, very difficult," Sigmon says. "Most law enforcement don't have the technical capacity or the resources to investigate and prosecute these crimes." And traffickers "move quickly [and] morph their techniques. They can just take down a site and move to a different site."

Several technical experts and Silicon Valley companies voluntarily help law enforcement identify such sites. Some have created algorithms that detect images of child sexual abuse.

Still, law enforcement officials are overwhelmed and underfunded, according to Michael D. Smith, a professor of information technology at Carnegie Mellon University and an expert on the role that technology plays in human trafficking. An FBI agent told one of Smith's classes this year that despite the huge increase in online child exploitation, "we had no increase in funding [so] we only investigate when we believe the victim is under the age of 6."

"Federal prosecutors are swamped," says Smith. "So, if there's a picture of a sexually abused 7-year-old posted online, they don't have the time or resources to investigate—not because they don't care but because they're already too busy with younger victims."

Followers of QAnon conspiracy theories have drawn attention to the child trafficking problem with their widespread use of seemingly altruistic hashtags, such as #SavetheChildren. However, QAnon falsely claims that Satan-worshiping pedophile elites are operating a global child sex-trafficking ring. Experts say QAnon followers divert scarce police manpower when they inundate law enforcement and rescue hotlines with false reports of child trafficking. (*See Short Feature.*)

Meanwhile, some countries have done little to prosecute offenders. A 2017 Associated Press investigation found nearly 2,000 allegations that U.N. peacekeepers had sexually trafficked, abused and exploited women, girls and boys in the Democratic Republic of Congo, the Central African Republic, Liberia and Haiti. And, although the U.N. has adopted numerous international treaties and conventions aimed at eradicating child trafficking, only a handful of the alleged offenders among its peacekeepers went to prison. Most were merely returned to their home countries, according to the AP.[13]

Sigmon says the lack of programs to mitigate poverty and family dysfunction contributes to the problem. "It's a real challenge to get enough resources for prevention, which is really critical to increasing child protection," she says. While the United States provides aid to several countries to help fight child trafficking, governments must "invest more in addressing these root causes of child trafficking, particularly by providing for the needs of marginalized communities."

Amid such challenges, here are some key questions being asked by officials, activists and experts:

Should the United States define forced marriage as a form of child trafficking?

Speaking to journalists in the Malaysian capital of Kuala Lumpur, the 13-year-old Rohingya girl tearfully recounted her ordeal in 2017, when her family fled government persecution of their ethnic group in their home country of Myanmar. She was caught by traffickers in Thailand, who sold her as a bride to a Rohingya man in Malaysia who was nearly twice her age.

He was cruel and controlling, she said, and confiscated her cell phone and left her alone in their home for days on end. After eight months, she managed to contact her father, who traveled to Malaysia to rescue her. She now lives with her family near Kuala Lumpur. But the husband refuses to grant her a divorce, and she fears he will force her to return to him.[14]

According to the ILO, the girl is one of some 40 million trafficking victims worldwide, with more than a third of the 15 million females coerced into marriage in 2016 under the age of 18 when they wed. And 44 per cent of those were under 15, while some were as young as 9, the organization said. While boys also can be victims of forced marriage, girls make up 96 percent of all victims of such coerced arrangements, the ILO says.[15]

Although the United States officially disagrees with calling such women and girls trafficking victims, experts on forced marriages have been urging the State Department to reconsider that position. If the United States were to classify forced marriage as human trafficking, it would affect country assessments in the department's annual report on human trafficking, which tracks worldwide compliance with the 2000 Trafficking Victims Protection Act and determines U.S. aid to countries accordingly.

A U.S. official points out that not all forced or arranged marriages constitute trafficking and must be assessed on a case-by-case basis.

The ILO's 2017 report on global slavery contends those millions of girls locked into marriages without their consent qualify as trafficking victims because "they were enduring a situation that involved having lost their sexual autonomy and often involved providing labour under the guise of 'marriage.'" Such circumstances fit the criteria for trafficking and involuntary servitude in international anti-slavery conventions, to which the United States is a signatory, the report said.[16]

In addition, say some U.S. anti-trafficking groups, forced marriage fits the Trafficking Victims Protection Act's description of involuntary servitude. The law defines involuntary servitude as being "induced by means of any scheme, plan or pattern intended to cause a person to believe that, if the person did not enter into or continue in such condition, that person or another person would suffer serious harm or physical restraint; or the abuse or threatened abuse of the legal process."[17]

"Because forced marriage happens as a result of various threats, pressure or coercion, where one or both participants do not or cannot consent, forced marriage is human trafficking," wrote Anita Teekah, an attorney who heads the anti-trafficking program at the New York-based Safe Horizon organization.[18]

But former U.S. officials question how the ILO derived its 15 million figure for forced marriage victims. Sarah Mendelson, a former U.S. ambassador to the U.N. for human rights, says representatives of Australia's anti-trafficking Walk Free Foundation briefed her in 2016 on how the ILO, working with the foundation, came up with its figures. "And I must say, the methodology didn't really hold up," she says.

DeBaca, the former head of the FBI's human trafficking section, also questions whether forced marriage should qualify as human trafficking. Like others, he stresses the complexity of the issue, noting that in many countries, 16- and 17-year-olds can marry with a parent's consent or a judicial ruling. And in some societies, he notes, a forced marriage occurs when a rapist is permitted to escape criminal prosecution by marrying the victim, usually with the consent of her family.

"If you are a person in a particular legal tradition where your father still has ownership over you in the way that most people in the West no longer assume for women, to what extent is that person a forced marriage victim?" he asks. "And how do cultural practices play into that determination?"

"It's horrifying," Martina E. Vandenberg, president of the Human Trafficking Legal Center, says of societies that permit rapists to escape prosecution by marrying their victims. Her Washington, D.C.-based organization provides pro bono legal assistance to trafficking victims.

But Vandenberg, like previous U.S. administrations and others in the anti-trafficking community, questions the practice of defining all forced child marriages as trafficking.

DeBaca, now a lecturer at Yale Law School, also questions whether a single ILO report provides sufficient grounds to warrant a change in how the United States counts trafficking victims. "To have the ILO frame applied to child marriage has to presuppose that this is a form of labor," he says. "And there are a lot of people that have a real hard time with that idea."

More research is needed to resolve the issue, he says. "In the last 10 years," he notes, "we have not had the academic work ... that it takes in international law and national law here in the United States to be able to say, as a matter of public policy, that child marriage is a form of slavery."

Should the U.S. incorporate the U.N.'s Sustainable Development Goals into its anti-trafficking efforts?

Until now, the United States has focused on using law enforcement as its primary tool to fight child trafficking. But a shortage of resources among federal and state police has limited their ability to respond to the growing number of reported cases.

As the Biden administration prepares to confront human trafficking, some activists say it should view the problem not only as a criminal justice issue but also as a global development challenge. That would enable the United States to enlist a broader range of institutions, organizations and businesses in the anti-trafficking fight, they argue.

To do that, they say, the United States would have to officially embrace the U.N.'s Sustainable Development Goals (SDGs), a collection of 17 broad objectives—such as ending poverty and hunger, promoting economic growth and fostering gender equity—along with 179 specific targets to achieve them.

"Child trafficking is a profound development problem," says Mendelson, the former U.N. ambassador for human rights. "In development, if you have a collection of countries, cities, the private sector, that feel there's value in this common framework, then you can make a change."

She and other former senior U.S. officials say implementing the 17 U.N. development goals would spread the word about the evils of child trafficking beyond the law enforcement community and build greater support for the cause.

A recent report by the United Nations University's Centre for Policy Research found that anti-trafficking and anti-slavery efforts can help achieve up to 113 of the 179 U.N. development targets, particularly those addressing poverty, gender equality, quality education, justice and strong institutions.[19]

For instance, Mendelson cites the goal of preventing the use of child labor in global supply chains. Besides the Justice Department, she says, under the SDG framework such efforts would involve other government agencies, including the departments of Labor, Health and Human Services and Commerce, as well as U.S. corporations and nongovernmental anti-trafficking organizations.

"Sometimes people will come up to me and they'll say, 'This issue of child labor in supply chains seems so abstract,'" she continues. "Well, do you drink coffee? Do you eat chocolate? Do you wear cotton? Do you have an iPhone? It's not abstract at all. It's part of the economy, and we need to address it. And SDGs are a way to do it."

"I'm not saying that the prosecution of human traffickers isn't important," Mendelson says, but "it hasn't got us to where we want to go. We need to broaden constituencies that know about this issue and are demanding changes in behavior by companies."

Mendelson and other anti-trafficking advocates concede that sustainable development goals such as ending poverty are long-term aspirations. But those in the thick of the battle against child trafficking need more money and manpower right now for federal and state law enforcement, more training for investigators and more prosecutors fluent in human rights law. "It's not just one or the other," Mendelson says. "Both are needed."

Experts say other countries and their companies have taken the U.N. development goals far more seriously than U.S. agencies and businesses. Former President Donald Trump's "America First" foreign policies often distanced Washington from the U.N. and multilateralism, leading his administration to ignore the SDGs. For example, during the four years Trump was in office, the United States did not produce a single Voluntary National Review, the periodic reviews used by the U.N. to track how member countries are complying with the development goals. As of 2019, 142 countries had filed such reviews at least once, according to Cooperation Canada, an independent Ottawa-based think tank that tracks global compliance with the goals.[20]

Children Make Up a Growing Share of Trafficking Victims

Minors made up 34 percent of the world's trafficking victims in 2018, up from 13 percent in 2004.
The share of victims who were girls nearly doubled, and the share who were boys increased fivefold.

Age and Gender of Trafficking Victims, 2004 and 2018

2004: Women 74%, Men 13%, Girls 10%, Boys 3%
2018: Women 46%, Men 20%, Girls 19%, Boys 15%

Source: "Global Report on Trafficking in Persons: 2020," United Nations Office on Drugs and Crime, January 2021, p. 32, https://tinyurl.com/uvn2hnx4

Several former Trump officials declined to comment on his administration's record of compliance with the U.N. development goal agenda. But a former member of the Trump administration's interagency committee tasked by Congress with collecting data on the administration's progress in implementing the goals, who asked not to be identified, says the administration deliberately refused to implement them for trade, climate change and, particularly, gender equity.

"Those two words—gender equity—was language that the U.S. would try to strike in every U.N. resolution that came up, which of course meant they would never go anywhere," the former official says, alluding to the veto the United States wields as a permanent member of the U.N. Security Council. "Really, what it came down to was the issue of sovereignty. Anything that called for the U.S. or other countries to contribute to gender equity or climate change or what have you, that was stuff that the administration would oppose."

Nevertheless, the former official says, "A lot of this is stuff that the U.S. government already does," such as alleviating poverty and hunger, fighting international crime and encouraging supply chains that are free of forced labor and trafficking.

So far, the Biden White House has given no guidance on whether it will incorporate the U.N. goals into its anti-trafficking efforts. But if it does, the administration's first challenge will be educating skeptics and those unfamiliar with the goals on how helpful they can be in broadening the fight against child trafficking beyond law enforcement, experts say.

"There's a whole bunch of folks out there for whom trafficking is purely a criminal issue, that it's about interdicting girls at the border who have duct tape on their mouths," deBaca says. "But child trafficking also touches upon things like poverty and hunger, health and education and the institutions that deal with those issues. So many of the SDGs can be brought to bear on the issue of child trafficking."

Has a U.S. law blocking websites that facilitate child sex trafficking inadvertently endangered its victims?

In 2018, President Trump signed into law the Fight Online Sex Trafficking Act (FOSTA), which authorized federal and state prosecution of internet platforms that knowingly facilitate child sex trafficking.[21] Lawmakers and child advocates have repeatedly hailed the law, saying it protects underage victims and gives them legal recourse in state courts against internet providers who fail to remove child sex trafficking websites from their platforms. Several other laws also give victims recourse in federal courts.

The law amended Section 230 of the Communications Decency Act, which had defined internet service providers, such as Google, Facebook and Twitter, not as publishers but as mere distributers of content, such as a phone company or a utility. Thus, under that provision, internet companies had been immune from liability for content provided by entities using their platforms.

Before FOSTA was enacted, platforms such as Backpage, a major online marketplace for ads selling sex, had successfully used Section 230 to argue that they were not responsible for third-party ads on their platforms that offered sex with minors. But after lawmakers heard emotional testimony from child sex trafficking victims,

FOSTA sailed through Congress with overwhelming majorities.[22]

A week before FOSTA was enacted, federal agents had shut down Backpage and charged its executives with child sex trafficking, including facilitating the sale of minors for sex and publishing abusive pictures of young girls. Before its demise, Backpage was earning more than $100 million annually, lawmakers say.[23]

After FOSTA's enactment, internet service providers became liable for knowingly allowing sex trafficking ads and child sexual abuse materials to appear on their platforms, so they either closed or scrubbed their sites of all sex ads. Craigslist eliminated its "Personals" section, including nonsexual subcategories such as "Missed Connections" and "Strictly Platonic," along with its "Therapeutic Services" section.

"We are finally decimating the online sex trafficking industry," Republican Rep. Ann Wagner of Missouri, the chief sponsor of the bill, said in a statement. "FOSTA gives federal, state and local prosecutors the tools they need to take down the websites selling our children with impunity."[24]

But critics say the law has had some unintended consequences that hurt both voluntary adult sex workers and adult and child trafficking victims being exploited by pimps who routinely use threats and violence to prevent them from quitting.

Kristen DiAngelo, a former sex trafficking victim who now heads the Sex Workers Outreach Project, a Sacramento, Calif.,-based organization that advocates for sex trafficking victims, said FOSTA endangered them by shutting down websites that allowed them to conduct their business safely online. Both sex trafficking victims and voluntary adult sex workers have been forced to return to the streets, where they are vulnerable to rape and robbery, she told lawmakers in a letter.[25]

Both supporters and opponents of FOSTA agree that Backpage deserved to be shut down because it catered largely to pedophiles, posting ads for sex with children as young as 2 years old and photos and videos of young children being raped, according to law enforcement officials.

But FOSTA critics say Craigslist and now-shuttered specialized websites such as Eros, a site advertising escorts, and sex worker directories such as CityVibe and NightShift helped both voluntary adult sex workers and trafficking victims vet potential clients by offering so-called bad date lists, which flagged clients with histories of violence, nonpayment or being police informants.[26]

In a recent study on the fallout from FOSTA, Danielle Blunt, a Brooklyn sex worker who holds a masters' degree in public health, noted that the law also forced the closure of VerifyHim, an encrypted website that required potential clients to get previous sex workers to vouch for them.[27]

DeBaca, the former head of the FBI's human trafficking section, says such arguments do not sway FOSTA'S supporters in the anti-trafficking community.

"Some FOSTA supporters are basically saying, 'We don't really care if the law has shut down the websites you used to screen your dates, because you aren't the children that we were concerned about. And if protecting the children means shutting down the entire sex market, then we don't mind that either, because there shouldn't be a sex market in the first place,'" deBaca says.

DeBaca concedes that the new law has made it harder for law enforcement to catch child predators. Before FOSTA, he explains, "one cop could make 40 arrests in a day by crafting an online sex ad that said the person is a child and then just scoop up all of the Johns when they showed up at the hotel room that the police rented for the sting.

"Before, it was like shooting fish in a barrel," he says. "After FOSTA was enacted, it was more like finding fish in an ocean."

Meanwhile, the Electronic Frontier Foundation, an organization that advocates for free speech, privacy and innovation on the internet, has filed a lawsuit against FOSTA, claiming it is an unconstitutional restriction on free speech. And in January, more than 70 civil rights groups and social justice organizations wrote to Congress and the Biden administration, urging them to investigate FOSTA's impact on human rights because it led to the removal of important online resources for vulnerable and marginalized people.[28]

Yiota Souras, senior vice president and general counsel of the National Center for Missing & Exploited Children, the national clearinghouse for reports of child trafficking and online child sexual abuse, says she understands the plight of adult sex workers, but for her there is no contest when it comes to which sex workers are being hurt the most.

"It's always been very interesting to me that when the sex workers and their proponents make their safety argument, they never acknowledge the value of not having children sold to somebody against their will and raped a dozen times a night while someone else pockets the money," she says. "Let's not forget these children suffer incredible and really long-lasting damage as a result of that experience."

BACKGROUND
Banning Trafficking

The sexual and commercial exploitation of children is as old as human civilization. But it was not until the early 1900s that serious efforts to halt such practices emerged—and those contained a strong element of racism in an era when legal and social discrimination against people of color was widespread.

The international movement against "white slavery," as it was then called, defined as the forceful procurement of a white woman or girl for prostitution, grew out of concerns about increased migration of European women seeking work in other European countries and the United States. Police investigations in early 1900s showed that many were being trafficked for prostitution.

Following conferences in Paris, London and Budapest in 1902, officials of several European countries crafted the 1904 International Agreement for the Suppression of the White Slave Traffic, which focused largely on the repatriation of trafficked women and girls. A second agreement signed by 13 countries—the 1910 International Convention for the Suppression of the White Slave Trade—criminalized trafficking in white females.[29]

Concerns also spread to the United States, prompting Congress in 1910 to pass the Mann Act, which made it a felony to transport any woman, regardless of her race, across state lines for "prostitution or debauchery, or for any other immoral purpose." The law was used primarily to criminalize interracial marriage and restrict immigration. Once restrictions were relaxed on marriage and immigration in the 1950s and '60s, human trafficking was not considered a major issue in the United States until several decades later.[30]

In 1921, the recently formed League of Nations held an international conference in Geneva, where delegates from 34 countries agreed to replace the term "white slave traffic" with "trafficking in women and children," a change that added nonwhite women and children, including boys, to the definition of trafficking victims.

The conference also produced the International Convention for the Suppression of the Traffic in Women and Children, which required its 33 signatory countries to prosecute traffickers and protect potential victims, thereby placing the 1910 convention under the league's authority. The League of Nations also published reports in 1927 and 1932 that examined the trafficking of European and Asian victims to destination countries, as well as traffickers' financial incentives and the methods they used to entice and retain women and girls in the illicit sex trade.

The reports described the "heartless fraud and cruelty of a different character" used by traffickers, similar to the methods of control and exploitation used today, according to Kristiina Kangaspunta, the head of applied research at the U.N. Interregional Crime and Justice Research Institute.[31]

Banning Child Labor

Meanwhile, social reformers were pushing to ban child labor in Europe and the United States, where the Industrial Revolution was in full swing. Children were considered ideal workers because they could be paid less, were small enough to perform tasks that adults could not and were less likely to strike. By 1900, 18 percent of all American workers were under the age of 16.

In 1904 reformers established the National Child Labor Committee, which aimed to regulate and

> "Federal prosecutors are swamped. So, if there's a picture of a sexually abused 7-year-old posted online, they don't have the time or resources to investigate – not because they don't care but because they're already too busy with younger victims."
>
> — Michael D. Smith
> Professor of Information Tecnology
> Carnegie Mellon University

CHRONOLOGY

1900s-1950s *International organizations and treaties outlaw slavery and trafficking.*

1904 The leaders of several European countries sign the International Agreement for the Suppression of White Slave Traffic, aimed at preventing white women and girls from being forced into prostitution.

1910 The U.S. Congress passes the Mann Act, making it a felony to transport a woman across state lines for the purpose of prostitution, debauchery or any other immoral purposes.

1926 The League of Nations adopts the Slavery Convention, requiring signatory countries to suppress all forms of slavery.

1948 The United Nations' Universal Declaration of Human Rights prohibits all forms of slavery and servitude, including forced and bonded labor.

1949 The U.N. adopts the Convention for the Suppression of the Traffic in Persons and of the Exploitation of the Prostitution of Others, which takes effect in 1951. The treaty focuses on repatriating sex workers and requires signatory countries to pass and enforce similar repatriation laws.

1990s-2000s *The Soviet collapse spurs an increase in human trafficking, leading to a global response.*

1991 The breakup of the Soviet Union prompts migration to Western Europe from former Soviet republics and Eastern Europe in search of jobs, accompanied by a surge in human trafficking, often organized by Russian crime syndicates.

2000 Convention 182 to eliminate the worst forms of child labor, sponsored by the International Labour Organization (ILO), goes into force after ratification by more than 100 countries. . . . President Bill Clinton signs the Trafficking Victims Protection Act, which establishes methods to prevent human trafficking, prosecute traffickers and protect victims. . . . U.N. adopts Protocol to Prevent, Suppress and Punish Trafficking in Persons, especially Women and Children, the first international instrument to criminalize human trafficking.

2002-04 The U.S. Department of State issues its first report on human trafficking, which grades nations on their efficacy in combating trafficking. . . . Major chocolate companies and anti-slavery groups adopt the International Cocoa Initiative, the first time an entire industry tries to eliminate child slavery in its supply chain.

2005 The ILO estimates the number of enslaved people worldwide at 12 million. A 2012 update puts the number at nearly 21 million.

2008 Council of Europe's Convention on Action Against Trafficking in Human Beings takes effect, providing greater protections for trafficking victims than U.N. treaties and establishing a monitoring system to oversee compliance by its 47 signatories.

2010-Present *Despite multiple efforts to curb human trafficking and sexual exploitation of children, the number of victims keeps rising, aided by the internet.*

2011 The ILO adopts a convention establishing basic rights for domestic workers. . . . The state of California requires companies to ensure their products are not made with trafficked or slave labor.

2013-16 The Walk Free Foundation's first Global Slavery Index estimates nearly 30 million people worldwide are enslaved as of 2013. By 2016, the figure is nearly 46 million. The United States, which does not include the victims of forced marriages in its compilation, says there are 25 million enslaved people worldwide.

2015 Under intense pressure from anti-trafficking activists, the British Parliament passes the Modern Slavery Act, which stiffens penalties for human traffickers, increases protections for victims and requires businesses to disclose their efforts to ensure their supply chains are free of slave labor. . . . U.N. adopts 17 Sustainable Development Goals, including the targets of ending slavery, forced labor and human trafficking.

2016 To strengthen its 1930 Forced Labour Convention, which criminalized forced labor, the ILO adds provisions to prevent forced labor and protect victims and provide access to legal remedies, including compensation.

2018-20 President Donald Trump signs the Fight Online Sex Trafficking Act, which authorizes federal and state prosecutors to go after internet platforms that knowingly facilitate child sex-trafficking and allow third parties to post images of child rape. . . . Several child trafficking scandals emerge involving high-profile figures, including financier Jeffrey Epstein. . . . Acting to disrupt what they mistakenly believe to be a secret ring by Satan-worshiping, child-trafficking pedophiles, QAnon followers threaten the lives of U.S. politicians, stage an armed standoff near the Hoover Dam, derail a train in Los Angeles, kidnap children in Colorado, Kentucky, Massachusetts and Utah, and allegedly kill a man in New York City.

2021 QAnon followers are among those who attack the U.S. Capitol (January). . . . *The New York Times* reports that the Justice Department is investigating whether U.S. Rep. Matt Gaetz, R-Fla., violated child trafficking laws by having sex with a 17-year-old. Gaetz denies any wrongdoing.

---

ultimately eliminate child labor in the United States. Along with state child labor committees, the reformers lobbied lawmakers and the public, using pamphlets and photographs of the deplorable working conditions for children in factories and mines. Studies also described how such conditions were harming children's health and educational development.[32]

While many state legislatures regulated the use of child labor, Congress did not immediately enact national legislation, largely because Southern states, where plantation owners relied heavily on Black child labor, resisted such laws. In 1916, Congress passed the country's first national child labor law, which banned interstate commerce involving certain products made with child labor.

But in 1918, the Supreme Court ruled the law unconstitutional on the grounds it exceeded the government's authority to regulate interstate commerce. In 1924, Congress passed a constitutional amendment that authorized federal child labor laws, but both the Southern states and several New England manufacturing states that used child labor combined to block its ratification.[33]

Child labor was not regulated on a national scale in the United States until the Great Depression and the sweeping measures enacted under President Franklin D. Roosevelt's New Deal. The National Industrial Recovery Act of 1933 reduced child labor for two years, but in 1935, the Supreme Court ruled it was also unconstitutional because it violated the constitutional separation of powers by delegating legislative powers to the executive branch.

In 1938 Congress passed the Fair Labor Standards Act, which prohibited employers from using children under 18 for certain hazardous jobs and banned children under 16 from working in factories and mines during school hours.[34] The law also limited the number of hours a child could work in nonagricultural jobs.

Unlike previous child labor laws, the Fair Labor Standards Act was firmly rooted in the Constitution's clause allowing federal regulation of interstate commerce. Thus, it excluded from coverage children not involved in activities affecting such commerce or children employed by a parent or guardian on a family farm or in a small business, such as a "mom and pop" grocery store.

During the 1930s, the ILO, an independent body created by the Allied powers after World War I, worked to prevent all forms of forced labor worldwide, including the exploitation of child labor. In 1946, the ILO became a specialized agency within the newly formed United Nations. However, the ILO did not take its first meaningful steps against child labor until 1973, when it created the Minimum Age Convention, which prohibited employment of children under 15 and banned children under 18 from certain hazardous jobs.[35]

In 1989 the United Nations Convention on the Rights of the Child, a legally binding international agreement, established the civil, political, economic, social and cultural rights of every child, regardless of their race, religion or abilities, supposedly protecting them against abuse, neglect and exploitation. To date, 196 countries have ratified the convention. Although the United States helped draft the convention and signed it, the treaty was never submitted to the Senate for ratification because conservatives, citing concerns it would undermine U.S. sovereignty, opposed it.[36]

QAnon Steals Charity's Hashtag

Misinformation "has nothing to do with keeping children safe."

The latest conspiracy theories about child trafficking began cropping up on social media last July. One insisted that texts purportedly from the U.S. Postal Service were connected to child trafficking. Another alleged that some unusually high-priced furniture with girls' names that online retailer Wayfair was advertising were actually ads for the sale of missing children.[1]

"#HumanTrafficking #wayfair ugh reading all of this is making my heart sank (sic)," tweeted a woman who called herself Black Cherie. "These poor kids.... Jesus Christ.... I believe it... there's too many 'coincidences' for it to be fake. $10,000+ for furniture with a missing child's name attached."[2]

Even though Wayfair explained that the items' prices were mismarked, and the postal service flagged the texts as a phishing scam, both posts went viral. Within a month, alarmed citizens, responding to calls on Facebook, held anti-trafficking rallies in some 200 cities and towns across the country, where many held up placards that read "Save the Children." By the first week of August, the hashtag #SavetheChildren was used more than 800,000 times on Twitter, according to an analysis by the media intelligence firm Zignal.[3]

Most of the demonstrators did not know at the time that followers of QAnon had organized the rallies. QAnon is a movement of internet conspiracy theorists who believe a secret group of Satan-worshiping pedophiles in government, Hollywood and the media—primarily Democrats—operate an international child trafficking ring. The theory has spread to millions of people on Facebook and has been linked to several violent crimes, including threats against politicians, an armed standoff near the Hoover Dam in Nevada, two kidnappings and a 2019 murder in Staten Island, N.Y.[4]

QAnon had resurrected a discredited allegation spread online during the 2016 presidential election by far-right figures, the Turkish press and Russian intelligence agencies. They claimed that Democratic nominee Hillary Clinton and other high-ranking government officials were trafficking children for sex, operating from the basement of a neighborhood pizzeria in Washington, D.C. The conspiracies led a North Carolina man to drive to Washington, enter the restaurant armed with an assault rifle and fire several shots, claiming he was there to rescue the children. Although no one was injured, the man was sentenced to four years in prison on weapons charges.[5]

Last year, the FBI branded QAnon a potential domestic terrorism threat—a warning that proved prescient when the group's supporters were among the most visible participants in the storming of the U.S. Capitol in January.[6]

In 2019, however, many had written off QAnon after the internet message board 8chan—where the group's mysterious pseudonymous seer, Q, had posted his theories—was shut down. But at the height of last summer's presidential campaign, QAnon came roaring back, this time both online and in town squares, using the "Save the Children" slogan.

QAnon followers had hijacked the trademarked name of Save the Children, the respected Connecticut-based humanitarian organization that provides medical, food and emergency aid to millions of children worldwide. The real charity has repeatedly said it has no connection to the #SavetheChildren hashtag used to spread QAnon's conspiracy theories.[7]

"In the United States, Save the Children is the sole owner of the registered trademark 'Save the Children,'" the charity said in a statement. "While people may choose to use our organization's name as a hashtag to make their point on different issues, we are not affiliated or associated with any of these campaigns."[8]

Then, during last year's presidential campaign, President Donald Trump helped move QAnon into the mainstream, when at a nationally televised town hall he answered a question about the group by saying: "I do know they are very much against pedophilia. They fight it very hard."[9]

There is no evidence that QAnon followers have ever saved a child from traffickers, a Justice Department spokesman says.

In 2020, Facebook removed QAnon content from its platforms to limit the risk to public safety, and Twitter followed suit in January. But the movement's followers managed to get around the companies' content moderators by creating "Save the Children" Facebook groups that serve as "soft fronts" for the movement, said Marc-André Argentino, a doctoral student at Concordia University who studies QAnon. He called such groups "pastel QAnon."[10]

Argentino said last year he had found 114 Facebook groups identifying themselves as anti-trafficking forums that were crammed with QAnon conspiracy theories. Between July and the end of September last year—in the run-up to the 2020 elections—membership in these groups and activity within them surged by 3,000 percent, he said. "Save the Children really revitalized the community after Twitter and Facebook took action against QAnon," Argentino said. "It's introduced an entire new population to QAnon."[11]

Researchers say QAnon's rebrand has attracted parents and grandparents, evangelicals, and online communities focused on health, wellness and yoga. "The way in which people encounter QAnon now is through relatively mainstream, non-absurd topics," Melanie Smith, the head of analysis for the social media research firm Graphika, told the House Intelligence Committee last October. "We're seeing a huge explosion in content around child sex trafficking and child exploitation through the Save the Children movement."[12]

Meanwhile, QAnon followers have inundated law enforcement and legitimate anti-trafficking organizations with false tips of child trafficking, diverting scarce resources from real cases. Polaris, an anti-trafficking organization that operates the U.S. National Human Trafficking Hotline, added a page to its website last year in an effort to dispel the misinformation spread by QAnon's Save the Children movement.

"QAnon and similar groups have an agenda that has little or nothing to do with reducing human trafficking and whose real aim is creating an atmosphere of fear and division. All evidence shows that QAnon is behind the #SaveTheChildren hashtag and various rallies, events and misinformation spread under that umbrella. Research into the way such groups operate shows very clearly that the best way to spread fear and division online is to focus on issues and topics—such as child exploitation—that spark strong emotions and inspire people to act on those emotions—whether they are based on real, factual information or not," Polaris cautioned.[13]

QAnon supporters recently added a new conspiracy theory to their canon of beliefs. When a large container ship became stuck in the Suez Canal and blocked shipping for a week, QAnon supporters claimed that Hillary Clinton was at the helm of the ship and that its 20,000 containers were packed with child sex slaves.

Their reasoning: The Taiwanese company that operates the ship is called Evergreen—which was Clinton's Secret Service code name when she was first lady.[14]

—*Jonathan Broder*

---

[1] Rachel E. Greenspan, "Trump's description of QAnon as being 'against pedophilia' follows its insidious takeover of the 'Save the Children' movement," *Business Insider*, Oct. 16, 2020, https://tinyurl.com/fzu8h8h9.

[2] Mami Fat Staxx, Twitter post, July 11, 2020, https://tinyurl.com/ujujx766.

[3] Amanda Seitz, "QAnon's 'Save the Children' morphs into popular slogan," *The Associated Press*, Oct. 28, 2020, https://tinyurl.com/r2usnju5.

[4] Lois Beckett, "QAnon: a timeline of violence linked to the conspiracy theory," *The Guardian*, Oct.16, 2020, https://tinyurl.com/a56nszy8.

[5] Michael E. Miller, "Pizzagate's violent legacy," *The Washington Post*, Feb. 16, 2021, https://tinyurl.com/365aymeh.

[6] Becket, *op. cit.*; Ryan J. Foley, "QAnon backer from Iowa was among first to breach Capitol," *The Associated Press*, Jan. 12, 2021, https://tinyurl.com/sp33w8xm; and Richard Ruelas and Craig Harris, "Jake Angeli, who wore fur hat and horns as mob raided U.S. Capitol, arrested and charged," *Arizona Republic*, Jan. 9, 2021, https://tinyurl.com/5yv5yabb.

[7] Kevin Roose, "How 'Save the Children' Is Keeping QAnon Alive," *The New York Times*, Sept. 28, 2020, https://tinyurl.com/4su8a3zc.

[8] "Save the Children Statement on use of its name in Unaffiliated Campaigns," Save the Children, Aug. 7, 2020, https://tinyurl.com/xj9rfwpy.

[9] "Donald Trump Town Hall With Voters," *NBC News*, Oct. 15, 2020, https://tinyurl.com/mxkxpa6r.

[10] Roose, *op. cit.*

[11] *Ibid.*

[12] Seitz, *op. cit.*

[13] "#SavetheChildren Questions and Answers," Polaris Project, https://tinyurl.com/8akaax88.

[14] Daniel Funke, "The Evergreen ship blocking the Suez Canal is not linked to Hillary Clinton," *Politifact*, March 25, 2021, https://tinyurl.com/sz4v3k2v.

Tours Educate Visitors about Child Trafficking

The hope is "everybody will walk away with a deeper understanding of the issues."

As travelers begin slowly returning to the skies, a unique tourism company is again offering groups with a social conscience trips to Colombia and Thailand, where they can get an unvarnished look at child trafficking and the modern slave trade.

The Hawaii-based company, AltruVistas, has specialized since 2013 in what some call "advocacy journeys." Their tours combine sightseeing, shopping and relaxation with educational programs aimed at raising awareness of the social, political, economic and environmental challenges in more than two dozen countries.

"The intention is that everybody will walk away with a deeper understanding of the issues and the work done on the ground," said AltruVistas' founder, Malia Everette.[1]

After a 2017 trip to study the child trafficking that underpins Thailand's infamous sex tourism, participant Karen Weiss was asked if the trip was depressing.

"I assure you that it was not," said Weiss, a board member of the U.S. branch of the anti-trafficking group End Child Prostitution and Trafficking (ECPAT), which helped organize the trip in partnership with AltruVistas. "It combines the excitement of visiting a fascinating country with a rare opportunity to broaden your understanding of the problem of human trafficking."[2]

The company hopes to resume some tours this fall and is accepting reservations now for Colombia and Thailand trips tentatively set for the fall of 2022, according to Everette.

The pandemic forced Everette to cancel nearly a dozen tours in March 2020, including a trip to the Balkans to learn about conflict resolution, to the Middle East for lessons on the region's chronic tensions and to New Zealand, Romania and Peru to study various environmental challenges. Before the pandemic struck, AltruVistas had led groups to Cuba for lectures on the communist country's history, health care system and agricultural ecology.

In previous years, the company ferried tour groups to Ghana to learn about slavery from the spot where millions of Africans were led in chains through the "door of no return" to lives of bondage in Brazil, the Caribbean and North America. Other groups traveled to India for lessons about sustainable agriculture and to Iran to learn about Persian culture.

Advocates for human rights, cultural diversity, political freedom or the environment accompany the groups, depending on their focus, Everette says. Once in-country, the groups meet local activists, who in turn introduce participants to people deeply affected by the problems they are studying. Local guides handle the sightseeing and shopping days.

Everette says some of the revenue earned from the tours is earmarked for philanthropy. Of the $3,500 fee for the 2017 Thailand trip, for example, $500 went to a tax-deductible donation to ECPAT-USA. Another 10 percent was donated to local anti-trafficking organizations that the

---

In 1999, the ILO wrote the Worst Forms of Child Labor Convention, which required all U.N. member states to eliminate child slavery, forced prostitution and the use of children for abusive sexual materials, criminal or hazardous activities and soldiering in armed conflict. The convention has been ratified by all 187 ILO members, including the United States. Each member state is responsible for enforcing it, with the ILO monitoring compliance.[37]

Sex Trafficking

Meanwhile, the fight against international sex trafficking shifted from the League of Nations, to the U.N., which replaced the league as the world's premier international body. In 1949, the Convention for the Suppression of the Traffic in Persons and of the Exploitation of the Prostitution of Others, which entered into force in 1951, became the international body's first legally binding instrument to address human trafficking.[38]

The United Nations defines a convention as legally binding when a member state ratifies it. But such conventions have no international enforcement mechanism, leaving implementation and enforcement to each ratifying member state.

group visited, while 25 percent of the fee paid for hotels, transportation and guides. "Around half of the tour fee stays in the country," she says.

Another participant on the Thailand trip, freelance writer Daniela Petrova, recounted the experience in *The New York Times*. "Instead of spending our days lounging by the pool between visits to tourist sights and attractions—although we did find time for some of that—we attended meetings with government representatives and local organizations involved in the fight against trafficking," such as the headquarters of ECPAT International and the local offices of the International Labour Organization, she wrote.[3]

The group also visited Thailand's Ministry of Social Development and Human Security, where officials had struggled to curtail the growing trafficking industry before the pandemic shut down sex tourism, leaving up to 300,000 sex workers with no clientele or livelihoods.[4]

Sex tourism, which is openly practiced in Bangkok's red-light districts and in the nation's beach resort cities, generated as much as 7 percent of Thailand's prepandemic GDP, the Netherlands Embassy in Bangkok said in a briefing paper.[5]

Although technically illegal in Thailand, prostitution remains a thriving business, regularly greased by bribes to police and drawing tourists from around the world looking for cheap sex with women, girls and boys. In Thailand, a 30-minute trick with a sex worker can cost as little as the equivalent of $16, according to End Slavery Now, a Cincinnati-based organization that educates the public on modern slavery around the world.

Trafficked children typically work in Bangkok in seedy basement brothels, garishly lit sex clubs, remote massage parlors and on the streets, as well as in the beach cities of Phuket and Pattaya.

Many of the exploited children are Thai, but some come from neighboring Myanmar, Laos and Cambodia, where traffickers have capitalized on wars, political upheaval and poor economic conditions to lure children with false promises of a better life in Thailand. There they are sold to brothel owners or pimps for the equivalent of $200 to $875 and then must work off their purchase price. Lately, Russian and Japanese criminal gangs have trafficked Russian and Eastern European children to Thailand, according to End Slavery Now.[6]

"We learned that behind the ornate temples, polite smiles and colorful baskets of fruits and vegetables, there was a grim reality," Petrova said.

—*Jonathan Broder*

---

[1] Daniela Petrova, "A Vacation With a Purpose: Fighting Trafficking in Thailand," *The New York Times*, May 11, 2017, https://tinyurl.com/kteyv4am.

[2] Ed Upright, "Fight trafficking on the beaches: 'advocacy tourism' is here," Thomson Reuters Foundation, June 1, 2017, https://tinyurl.com/vawtectp.

[3] Petrova, *op. cit.*

[4] *Ibid.*, Zsombor Peter, "COVID Lockdown Pumps Brakes on Thailand's Billion-dollar Sex Trade," VOA, May 29, 2020, https://tinyurl.com/39p4s2x3.

[5] "Tourism Industry in Thailand," Kingdom of the Netherlands, March 2017, https://tinyurl.com/4fpxkpyv.

[6] Cazzie Reyes, "History of Prostitution and Sex Trafficking in Thailand," End Slavery Now, Oct. 8, 2015, https://tinyurl.com/3u27kwyn.

With the collapse of the Soviet Union in 1991, human trafficking became a subject of growing concern in the United States, as people from the former Soviet republics and Eastern Europe migrated to the West seeking jobs. Transnational criminal gangs began making huge profits from sex trafficking and the forced labor of women from those countries, according to U.S. intelligence agencies.

The Trafficking Victims Protection Act provided the legal tools necessary to protect victims of sex and labor trafficking, prosecute traffickers and prevent trafficking in the United States and abroad. It also allowed the government to withhold certain kinds of U.S. aid from countries that did not comply with the law's standards—but also permitted waivers for national security reasons. For example, President Trump granted waivers to Iraq, Afghanistan, the Democratic Republic of Congo, Mali, South Sudan and Yemen.[39]

Also in 2000, the U.N. adopted the first legally binding instrument focusing on human trafficking since the 1949 Convention. The Protocol to Prevent, Suppress and Punish Trafficking in Persons defined trafficking in persons for the first time and reaffirmed its criminalization,

Empty desks commemorate the schoolgirls still missing in 2019 after the Islamist group Boko Haram abducted 276 girls to use as sex slaves in Nigeria's Borno state in 2014. Although many of the girls either escaped or were released after negotiations, more than 100 are still missing.

along with all forms of exploitation.⁴⁰ To date, 117 countries have signed onto the protocols, including the United States.

In 2001, the 15 member countries of the Economic Community of Western African States agreed on a plan to tackle slavery and human trafficking in that region, which supplies much of the world's cocoa. The following year, anti-slavery groups joined the world's major chocolate makers to create the International Cocoa Initiative, a Swiss-based nonprofit that advocates eliminating child labor by working with cocoa farmers, governments, international organizations and donors. The International Cocoa Initiative represented the first time members of an entire industry joined forces to tackle child slavery in its supply chains.

Brazil followed suit in 2004, launching its National Pact for the Eradication of Slave Labour. The move brought together government, businesses and civil organizations to pressure companies to eradicate forced labor in their supply chains, primarily in the country's coffee industry. Using the so-called "name-and-shame" approach, participants created the "Dirty List" of companies found selling products produced by child slaves and cut commercial ties with them.⁴¹

Trafficking Peacekeepers

In 2005, after reports emerged that U.N. peacekeepers in the Democratic Republic of Congo were involved in child trafficking, the world body established a new Conduct and Discipline Unit, responsible for preventing sexual exploitation and abuse by U.N. peacekeepers and enforcing a new zero-tolerance policy toward such crimes, as well as assistance for victims. From 2007 to the end of this January, the United Nations says it received 1,102 allegations that U.N. peacekeepers had sexually exploited or abused women and girls, not only in the Democratic Republic of Congo but also in the Central African Republic, Colombia, Guinea-Bissau, Jerusalem, Lebanon Liberia, Mali, Sudan, South Sudan and Haiti.⁴²

The 2017 Associated Press investigation reportedly found 2,000 allegations of abuse by U.N. peacekeepers over the course of 12 years. The reports from Haiti were particularly disturbing: Some Sri Lankan peacekeepers in Haiti allegedly would coerce children as young as 12 to provide sex by denying them food and other necessities and then paying them with cookies and small change.

"I did not even have breasts," one girl told U.N. investigators, adding that for three years, from age 12 to 15, she had sex with nearly 50 peacekeepers, including a "commandant" who paid her 75 cents per encounter.⁴³

Despite the U.N.'s disciplinary procedures, it has struggled to hold perpetrators accountable, in part because victims often are reluctant to testify under oath to investigators, fearing retribution. With their allegations left unsubstantiated, their cases often were dropped. From 2010 to 2020, a decade in which the United Nations received 777 allegations of sexual exploitation and abuse by peacekeepers, U.N. investigators substantiated only 255 accusations.⁴⁴

And while the United Nations repatriated nearly all of the alleged perpetrators and withheld their pay in those cases, criminal punishment fell to the home countries of the perpetrators. Of the 255 substantiated cases of sexual exploitation and abuse, only 57 soldiers were jailed, according to U.N. figures.⁴⁵

"The U.N. does not have its own courts," says a spokesperson for the U.N. Department of Peace Operations. Thus, it is up to member states to ensure appropriate follow-up on investigations, as well as accountability and disciplinary procedures, says the spokesperson, who requested anonymity. "They must ensure that the uniformed personnel they contribute are selected and trained in a way that entrenches zero-tolerance for sexual exploitation and abuse. They must act quickly on credible allegations, have the required legislation and processes in place so perpetrators can be held to account and victims receive effective remedies."

The U.N. and member states also are working to facilitate "claims of paternity and child support," the spokesperson says.

Jenna Stern, a former member of the U.N.'s Conduct and Discipline Unit, said many countries that contribute troops "are reluctant to admit the misconduct of their peacekeepers, especially where such misconduct can be traced back to inadequate training, and would rather sweep allegations under the rug."[46]

Stopping Cybertrafficking

Meanwhile, in 2008, as use of the internet exploded, President George W. Bush signed the PROTECT Our Children Act, landmark legislation that ordered the Justice Department to develop and implement a national strategy to protect children from the growing problem of online sexual exploitation and prosecute violators.[47] But since then, experts say, many of the law's key provisions—such as full funding for investigations, broad authority for the strategy's coordinator and regular progress reports to Congress—have remained unfulfilled.

The Justice Department did not respond to a request for comment, but in the past it has blamed insufficient congressional funding for its failure to fulfill the law's provisions.

Meanwhile, the Council of Europe's 47 members ratified the Convention on the Protection of Children against Sexual Exploitation and Sexual Abuse. The treaty, which entered into force in 2010, required members to fight child trafficking, prosecute traffickers and protect their victims. The treaty differed from previous international conventions because it empowered a group of experts to monitor member countries' anti-trafficking measures and publish public reports evaluating their progress.[48]

Besides governments, some corporations joined in the fight against child trafficking. In 2010, the Body Shop, an U.S. company that sells beauty products, launched a campaign against child sex trafficking, displaying eye-catching posters with headlines that read "Slavery Wasn't Abolished in 1865," referring to the end of the Civil War, and "Drugs Guns Kids—Sold on a Street Corner Near You." The posters urged people to

Jeffrey Epstein, a New York financier and registered sex offender, is pictured in 2005 with his companion Ghislaine Maxwell. Both were accused of trafficking and facilitating the abuse of underage children. Epstein died in jail in 2019 while awaiting trial, in a death that was ruled a suicide; Maxwell is in jail awaiting trial in New York City.

donate money to ECPAT International, a global network of anti-trafficking organizations.[49]

In 2014, child trafficking made international headlines when the extremist Islamist group Boko Haram kidnapped 276 girls from a school in northern Nigeria and sold them as sex slaves to fellow fighters for the equivalent of $12 each. Many of the girls eventually were rescued or escaped, but six died in captivity; more than 100 never returned.[50]

Meanwhile, some U.S. states and the federal government focused on ridding manufacturers' supply chains of human trafficking. In 2011, California enacted the Transparency in Supply Chains Act, which required major manufacturers and retailers to disclose their efforts to eliminate forced labor and human trafficking from their supply chains.[51]

In 2013, Australia's Walk Free foundation released its first Global Slavery Index, which estimated there were 29.8 million slaves globally, including children. A year later, the estimate had grown to 35.8 million. That same year, Najat Maala M'jid, the U.N. special rapporteur on the sale of children, child prostitution and child pornography, said children were more at risk than ever of being sexually exploited or sold.[52]

"Millions of girls and boys worldwide are victims of sexual exploitation, even though this issue in recent years has gained increased visibility," she said.[53]

In 2015, Britain's Modern Slavery Act required businesses to disclose how they ensured that their supply chains were free of slave labor. The law also mandated maximum life-in-prison sentences for convicted traffickers and compelled them to compensate their victims. In the same year, the United Nations adopted the 17 Sustainable Development Goals, which included ending slavery and eradicating forced labor and human trafficking.[54]

In the fall of 2016, at the height of a U.S. presidential election, phony allegations of child sex trafficking that spread online figured prominently in a conspiracy theory that was debunked but later became the basis for the QAnon movement. It claims that a cabal of Satan-worshipping, cannibalistic pedophiles—including 2016 Democratic presidential nominee Hillary Clinton—is running a global child sex-trafficking ring.[55] (*See Short Feature.*)

By 2017, the ILO estimated that 40.3 million people worldwide were victims of trafficking—one-quarter of them under the age of 18.[56]

After several child trafficking scandals in 2019 involving figures such as financier Jeffrey Epstein, a friend of U.S. politicians and Prince Andrew of the British royal family, and Robert K. Kraft, owner of the New England Patriots pro football team, Trump held a White House summit on human trafficking. He issued an executive order establishing a new White House position focused on trafficking, created a new government website devoted to the issue and directed his administration to develop better methods in quantifying the problem.[57]

But critics said the administration's past performance belied Trump's professed concern for trafficking victims. Some cited the State Department's 2020 human trafficking report, which noted that the Homeland Security Department ignored several cases of forced labor trafficking inside private detention facilities holding, among others, women and children trafficked into the United States from Mexico.[58]

"The administration has been especially dismissive of claims by women and children who have been trafficked over the U.S. southern border," said Eric Schwartz, president of Refugees International, a humanitarian organization that advocates for displaced people. He called the summit little more than a "photo op."[59]

CURRENT SITUATION

High-Profile Cases

Despite the nearly two dozen laws and treaties designed to halt child trafficking and forced labor, minors are being coerced, intimidated and duped into forced labor and the sex trade in growing numbers, with some of the most disturbing instances emerging in the past three months.

One of the most high-profile cases involved John Geddert, the former coach of the U.S. women's Olympic gymnastics team. Shortly after being charged in February with human trafficking and sexually assaulting children between the ages of 13 and 16, Geddert killed himself.

The charges stemmed from the 2018 investigation and conviction of Larry Nasser, the team's doctor, who was sentenced to life in prison after being convicted of sexually abusing more than 150 female gymnasts during their training. During Nasser's trial, team members recounted how Geddert had physically and mentally injured them as part of his harsh coaching practices, and then insisted that they train while injured.

Gymnast Makayla Thrush described Geddert's constant intimidation and mental abuse, which included urging her to kill herself when she failed to meet his

Law enforcement officers investigate the scene where two FBI agents were killed and others shot on Feb. 2, 2021, as they served a warrant on David Huber in Sunrise, Fla. Huber, who was suspected of involvement in violent child pornography, reportedly killed himself as agents closed in. The thriving market for child pornography is a major driver of child trafficking.

training demands. She said Geddert had thrown her onto the uneven bars, tearing her stomach muscles, rupturing lymph nodes in her neck and giving her a black eye.[60]

In bringing human trafficking charges against Geddert, Michigan Attorney General Dana Nessel used the language of the 2000 Trafficking Victims Protection Act, which defines human trafficking as any kind of labor that is forced, coerced through threats or intimidation or attained by fraud. In her indictment, Nessel said Geddert "subjected his athletes to forced labor or services under extreme conditions that contributed to them suffering injuries and harm."

"It checks all the boxes," said Ouleye Ndoye, a member of the board of directors of Wellspring Living, an Atlanta shelter for trafficking victims, referring to the "force, fraud and coercion" that defines human trafficking. "They don't have to be kidnapped."[61]

Also this year, an FBI investigation into child sex abuse turned into one of the deadliest shootings in the bureau's history, and a Canadian fashion mogul was indicted for sex trafficking.

In February, FBI agents investigating David Huber, 55, suspected of being involved in violent online child pornography, approached his apartment in Sunrise, Fla., to execute a search warrant. Huber allegedly opened fire on the team, killing two agents and wounding three others. Huber's body was later found inside the apartment, an apparent suicide.[62]

The shooting has focused attention on the soaring numbers of online child sexual abuse cases that have overwhelmed federal and state law enforcement.

The National Center for Missing & Exploited Children often gets tips about child trafficking from social media companies such as Facebook, which are required to report child sex abuse imagery or other materials on their platforms. Last year, the center turned over 21.7 million such reports to the FBI and local law enforcement, says the center's Souras.

FBI officials say the bureau's investigations into child trafficking reports are among the most difficult assignments, because agents must watch deeply disturbing online images and videos of very young children being sexually abused. "There's even a category called pre-verbal, which is kids who are abused before they can talk," says Hany Farid, a computer science professor at the University of California, Berkeley, who created an algorithm that helps social media platforms spot child sexual abuse imagery. "I saw an ad where a predator posted an ultrasound image of a fetus in the womb of his girlfriend or wife, saying, 'I have new material coming soon.' That's the world we're dealing with."

The bureau also monitors pedophile forums on the dark web, where members are anonymous and trade graphic images of child sexual abuse. Some such websites have "private rooms," which only admit members willing to share imagery of themselves sexually abusing children, according to FBI officials.

Suspicions that Huber engaged in such abuse triggered the search warrant in the Sunrise case, FBI officials say. The shooting occurred amid a spate of high-profile arrests involving online child exploitation, including three others in Florida involving a pediatrician in Broward County, a fourth-grade teacher in Boca Raton and a pastor in Central Florida.

Meanwhile, FBI agents in Los Angeles recovered 33 missing children in an operation against child traffickers in January. Eight of the children were being sexually exploited at the time of their rescue, the FBI said.[63]

In December, sex trafficking charges were handed down against the 79-year-old Canadian fashion magnate Peter Nygard, who built a multinational women's fashion empire. With his flowing mane of silver hair,

Rep. Matt Gaetz, R-Fla., addresses the Conservative Political Action Conference in Orlando, Fla., on Feb. 26, 2021. As part of a sex trafficking probe, federal authorities are investigating whether Gaetz had sex with a 17-year-old girl and paid for her to travel with him, a charge he denies.

AT ISSUE

Does the U.S. law against child sex trafficking online endanger its victims?

YES **Robert Winterton**
Director of Public Affairs, NetChoice

Written for *CQ Researcher*, April 2021

Despite the best intentions of the Fight Online Sex Trafficking Act (FOSTA), statistics show the law has not achieved its goal and has proven to be harmful since its passage in 2018. The most recent Department of State statistics show the fight against sex trafficking has stalled—convictions fell almost 10 percent from 2018 to 2019, even though potential cases identified through the National Human Trafficking Hotline rose more than 11 percent during that period. The State Department also admits the numbers of prosecutions and victims served have decreased since FOSTA was implemented.

FOSTA also has harmed vulnerable communities. Just this January, 70 civil rights and social justice groups pleaded with Congress to examine FOSTA's impact on human rights. These groups hoped to highlight how amending Section 230 of the Communications Decency Act to make online intermediaries legally responsible for vaguely "facilitating" someone else's creation of illegal content led to the mass removal of important online resources for vulnerable and marginalized people.

If we make websites legally responsible for the content of their users, we should not be surprised when they end up removing legitimate and important content to ensure they do not run into trouble with the law. FOSTA led to the removal of content related to sex trafficking from legitimate forum sites and social media, even as it failed to save victims from sex traffickers and did little to remove sex trafficking from the web. A study from 2018 showed that after FOSTA was signed, there was no long-term reduction in the number of sex ads displayed online.

Recent progress in the fight against sex trafficking has not relied on FOSTA. Before FOSTA was enacted, the FBI was able to take down Backpage.com, a website that a Senate report identified as knowingly facilitating sex trafficking. The law also was not used in more recent online sex trafficking suits filed by New York and Texas.

Given these important concerns, Congress should investigate whether FOSTA has failed. That is why NetChoice supported legislation introduced by Sens. Elizabeth Warren, D-Mass., Bernie Sanders, I-Vt., and Ron Wyden, D-Ore., to review the impact of FOSTA on vulnerable communities. Unfortunately, FOSTA's congressional supporters have not yet backed such a review.

NO **Yiota Souras**
Senior Vice President, General Counsel, National Center for Missing & Exploited Children

Written for *CQ Researcher*, April 2021

Between 2011 and 2017, courts across the country struggled to provide legal relief to children sold for rape and sexual abuse on websites that facilitated such trafficking. One appellate court dismissed a case involving 15-year-olds raped more than 900 times after being sold for sex online. Section 230 of the Communications Decency Act, the court said, required it to "deny relief to plaintiffs whose circumstances evoke outrage." Another court dismissed trafficking charges, saying Section 230 provides immunity even to internet platforms "alleged to support the exploitation of others by human trafficking."

Faced with such judicial outcomes, Congress narrowly revised Section 230 to remove blanket immunity when website operators knowingly facilitate sex trafficking. Since the law was enacted, victims can now get their day in court against everyone, including a website operator, who knowingly facilitates their trafficking, and website operators have legal incentives to ensure they do not facilitate online sex trafficking.

The new law, the Fight Online Sex Trafficking Act (FOSTA), threw open the courthouse doors for sex trafficking victims. Since then, it has been used in at least 10 cases against website operators that allegedly facilitated trafficking. These narrowly drafted cases are far from the flood of frivolous suits FOSTA opponents predicted. Courts are no longer compelled to dismiss such cases as soon as Section 230 is invoked, but they have dismissed some cases after initial review, while others have been allowed to move forward. Far from endangering victims, the law empowers them by giving them access to justice against everyone—including website operators that facilitate trafficking and abuse.

After enactment of FOSTA, certain websites where our organization knew children were regularly trafficked for sex shut down. While content can move to other websites, the shutdown of such sites causes disruption and makes it more difficult for a trafficker to market and sell children for sex online and for buyers to purchase them. FOSTA also forces website operators to consider potential liability and ensure that they are not knowingly facilitating online trafficking.

FOSTA's encouragement of self-regulation is a tremendous benefit for victims and potential victims. While we must do much

> Holding legitimate, well-intentioned websites liable for their users' posts is evidently not the quick fix FOSTA's proponents claimed. If we want to make genuine progress in the fight against sex trafficking, we should enable law enforcement and tech to work together, rather than against each other.
>
> more to keep children safer online, FOSTA is an essential step forward and an important model to give victims their day in court and apply market pressure to create incentives for websites to ensure bad actors are not using their sites to profit from the rape of children.

Nygard was often photographed with an entourage of attractive young women and teenage girls.

After federal agents raided his Nygard International corporate headquarters in New York and his Los Angeles home, Nygard stepped down as head of the company, which then filed for bankruptcy protection. He is in jail in Winnipeg, Canada, and U.S. authorities are seeking to extradite him to face charges of child sex trafficking, racketeering and other crimes. The U.S. attorney's office in Manhattan claims that over a 25-year period Nygard used his wealth and influence to recruit women and underage girls in Canada, the United States and the Bahamas to have sex with him and his associates. Some in the media now refer to him as "the Jeffrey Epstein of Canada."[64]

In March, *The New York Times* reported that the Justice Department is investigating Rep. Matt Gaetz, R-Fla., an outspoken supporter of former President Trump, as part of a federal sex trafficking probe. The investigation, which began in the final months of the Trump administration, grew out of a sex trafficking indictment of a former Florida state tax official and friend of Gaetz, who allegedly used a website that connected men with women and girls for sex in exchange for gifts and travel.[65]

According to the indictment, one of the girls is 17. Federal authorities are investigating whether Gaetz had sex with her and paid for her to travel with him, *The Times* reported. Gaetz denies he has been romantically involved with minors and says the investigation is part of a $25 million extortion plot against him and his family.[66]

Congressional Action

Some U.S. lawmakers, looking for new ways to crack down on cybertrafficking, are expected to reintroduce a bipartisan bill to remove some of the exemptions that protect internet platforms from liability. The Eliminating Abusive and Rampant Neglect of Interactive Technologies bill, or the EARN IT Act, died at the end of the 116th Congress on Jan. 3.

Its co-sponsors, Republican Sen. Lindsey Graham of South Carolina and Democratic Sen. Richard Blumenthal of Connecticut, say they will reintroduce the measure, which would allow states to sue service providers who allow end-to-end encryption on their platforms without enabling law enforcement to decrypt the material, according to a spokesperson for Blumenthal.

The measure would be the latest attempt to roll back civil immunity provided to internet service providers in Section 230 of the Communications Decency Act. However, Section 230 does require service providers to remove criminal content from their platforms, such as child sexual abuse imagery and materials that facilitate child sex trafficking.

Meanwhile, many are watching the Electronic Frontier Foundation's lawsuit challenging the constitutionality of FOSTA on grounds that it limits free speech. The law makes internet companies liable for knowingly failing to remove content that facilitates child sex trafficking.

The law's "broad language makes criminals of those who advocate for and provide resources to adult, consensual sex workers and actually hinders efforts to prosecute sex traffickers and aid victims," said David Greene, the foundation's senior staff attorney.[67]

Souras, of the National Center for Missing & Exploited Children, dismisses the free speech argument. "Speech is speech, and criminal conduct is criminal conduct," she says. "You can promote prostitution. You can talk about it. That's free speech. But you can't facilitate the prostitution of another person, which is another way of saying trafficking. There's just nothing speech-like about it."

Meanwhile, Sen. Mark Warner, D-Va., has introduced a bill that would allow Web users to sue Facebook, Google and other tech giants if a company's refusal to

Discussion Questions

Here are some issues to discuss regarding child trafficking:

- Why do you think child trafficking is still proliferating, despite a century of efforts to ban it through laws and treaties?

- What do you think would best solve the problem of child trafficking?

- Do you think internet service providers are doing enough to keep child traffickers from using their platforms? If not, what regulations or penalties should be enacted to spur greater efforts?

- Some civil libertarians argue that laws permitting the prosecution of websites that facilitate child trafficking violate free speech. What is your view of this debate?

- Why do some people argue that a broad United Nations agenda of programs for sustainable development would aid the fight against child trafficking?

- If you were a parent, what steps would you take to protect your children against child trafficking? How would you sort out genuine threats from imagined, conspiratorial ones?

---

police the photos, videos and posts on its platform results in real-world harm, such as child sex exploitation, child rape, fraud, cyber-stalking or the spread of child sexual abuse materials. Free-speech and internet privacy advocates oppose the measure.[68]

In other legislative moves, Sens. Elizabeth Warren, D-Mass., Ron Wyden, D-Ore., and Bernie Sanders, I-Vt., have introduced bills that would require Congress to investigate the impact FOSTA is having on marginalized populations. In the House, a bipartisan group has reintroduced a measure to require tech companies that report child sexual abuse materials on their platforms to preserve those materials for 180 days—double the current 90-day requirement—to give law enforcement more time get to those cases.[69]

State Efforts

Advocates for sex trafficking victims are pushing states to expand laws that seal or expunge criminal convictions connected to the trafficking.

Most states have criminal record relief laws that expunge a trafficked person's criminal convictions for prostitution. But many victims have convictions—and sometimes prison records—for additional crimes their pimps forced them to commit, such as drug possession and theft.

Without expanded record-relief laws, advocates say, sex trafficking victims cannot get legitimate jobs to rebuild their lives once they have broken free from their traffickers. Connecticut, Kansas, Michigan, New York and Virginia are among the states considering new criminal record relief legislation for trafficking victims.

Erin Marsh, a research and policy analyst at Polaris, an anti-trafficking nonprofit that operates the National Human Trafficking Hotline, said some state laws are so restrictive that trafficking victims cannot get their records expunged. And in many states where some relief is available, Marsh said the application process is so cumbersome and expensive victims cannot seek relief.

Marsh said lawmakers often say they are afraid of expanding the offenses for which records can be expunged because "they don't want to open the floodgate. They are afraid that they are going to have people convicted of murder who are trying to clear their record." But, she added, "that is not what we see."[70]

Marsh recommends that lawmakers authorize judges to decide on a case-by-case basis whether criminal record relief should be granted to a trafficking victim.

OUTLOOK
"Storm Clouds" Ahead

Most experts expect child trafficking to continue to rise in the coming years. Most such trafficking occurs behind closed doors and in the recesses of the dark web. And, as with illicit drug trafficking, the exploitation of children for sex and slavery is simply so lucrative it is difficult to eliminate, the experts say.

In addition, researchers say, the world's widening economic and demographic inequalities, armed conflicts and climate change will leave more children in desperate straits and thus more vulnerable to traffickers, further fueling the rise in trafficking.

Meanwhile, it is unclear how the Biden administration will handle the issue. Whatever its priorities, former officials say, the administration will need to do some significant catching up, since the United States failed to meet some of its own minimum global standards for combating human trafficking during the Trump administration.

According to the State Department's 2020 human trafficking report, the Trump administration failed to inform Congress of its anti-trafficking actions for the past two years. In addition, the report says, the United States must increase investigations and prosecutions of labor trafficking cases; restore the full range of congressionally mandated legal services for trafficking victims; and strengthen, rather than erode, protections for immigrant survivors of human trafficking.

DeBaca, the former head of the FBI's human trafficking section, was unsparing in his concerns over Washington's future rankings on its anti-trafficking efforts.

"This year's report, though it commemorates the 20th Anniversary of the modern anti-trafficking movement, should be read not as a triumphalist document but as a warning of storm clouds on the horizon," he said.[71]

Souras says, "You can't look at laws alone to solve a problem like trafficking, which is so broad in scope, multifaceted and complicated by a lot of societal factors. We need strong laws, absolutely, but that alone won't solve the tragedy of trafficking, especially in many international settings."

Also needed, and working in concert, she says, are "enforcement, prosecution, judicial and societal acceptance of child trafficking as a crime, laws to protect and provide recovery services for child victims, prevention and education." In some international settings, she says, "the array of needed solutions is even broader, especially when you factor in a weak or nonexistent rule of law in many geographic regions."

Carnegie Mellon's Smith says child trafficking will probably continue to rise because of a combination of lax law enforcement, increased demand and the ease—and profitability—of creating markets on the dark web to connect perpetrators with victims.

"The reality is so depressing and so emotionally draining that it's hard to get any sort of sustained attention among voters, who would rather think about less draining subjects that are easier to solve," he says.

In addition, he says, "crime generally outpaces the law, especially when there is a technological component, as with child sex trafficking." For example, he says, FOSTA updated the 1910 Mann Act to criminalize managing or operating a website with the intent to facilitate prostitution.

"That was just in 2018—many years after websites were being used to facilitate prostitution," he says, but more than a century later, "the law was just catching up to where the crime had gone. This is a constant part of the work advocates have to do: continue to push for the laws to modernize and become more robust and to follow the crime trends, while also pushing for better enforcement, prosecution, resources, education and awareness around the problem."

NOTES

1. "Children For Sale," The CNN Freedom Project, July 21, 2014, https://tinyurl.com/5etyt87w.

2. *Ibid.*

3. "Trafficking in Persons Report, 20th Edition," Office to Monitor and Combat Trafficking in Persons, U.S. Department of State, June 2020, https://tinyurl.com/kdm3enkh; "Global Estimates of Modern Slavery," International Labour Organization and Walk Free, Sept. 19, 2017, https://tinyurl.com/5x2upbke.

4. *Ibid.*

5. "Trafficking in Persons Report," *op. cit.*; "2019 Data Report," U.N. National Human Trafficking Hotline, Polaris Project, Dec. 31, 2019, https://tinyurl.com/3w5du39c.

6. "Global Estimates of Modern Slavery," *op. cit.*; "ILO says forced labour generates annual profits of US$150 billion," International Labour Organization, May 20, 2014, https://tinyurl.com/uzm4jt7k.

7. "Summary of the Trafficking Victims Protection Act (TVPA) and Reauthorizations FY 2017," Alliance to End Slavery & Trafficking, Jan. 11, 2017, https://tinyurl.com/58u67cxs.

8. "Global Estimates of Modern Slavery," *op. cit.*

9. "Trafficking in Persons Report," *op. cit.*

10. Kristiina Kangaspunta *et al.*, "2020 Global Report on Trafficking in Persons," United Nations Office on Drugs and Crime, January 2021, https://tinyurl.com/2xnpw8hf.

11. "Trafficking in Persons Report," *op. cit.*

12. Nicholas Kristof, "The Children of Pornhub," *The New York Times*, Dec. 4, 2020, https://tinyurl.com/zvkajfbf.

13. Paisley Dodds, "AP Exclusive: UN Child Sex Ring Left Victims But No Arrests," *The Associated Press*, April 12, 2017, https://tinyurl.com/yjcyc74k; Azad Essa, "Why do some peacekeepers rape? The full report," *Al Jazeera*, Aug. 10, 2017, https://tinyurl.com/29ww843k.

14. Rozanna Latiff and Ebrahim Harris, "Sold into marriage—how Rohingya girls become child brides in Malaysia," *Reuters*, Feb. 15, 2017, https://tinyurl.com/53498dzb.

15. "Global Estimates of Modern Slavery," *op. cit.*; for background, see Amy Yee, "Girls' Rights," *CQ Researcher*, April 17, 2015, pp. 337-360.

16. "Global Estimates of Modern Slavery," *ibid.*

17. "H.R. 3244-Victims of Trafficking and Violence Protection Act of 2000, Section 103 Definitions (5)," Congress.gov, Oct. 28, 2000, https://tinyurl.com/2b59jz9d.

18. Anita Teekah and William Sheehan, "Forced Marriage is Human Trafficking: We Explain How and Why," SafeHorizon, Dec. 11, 2019, https://tinyurl.com/2kzesx6k.

19. James Cockayne, "Developing Freedom: The Sustainable Development Case for Ending Modern Slavery, Forced Labour and Human Trafficking," United Nations University Centre for Policy Research, Jan. 25, 2021, https://tinyurl.com/yfyvn9b8.

20. Shannon Kindornay and Renee Gendron, *Progressing National SDGs Implementation: An independent Assessment of the Voluntary National Review Reports Submitted to the United Nations High-Level Political Forum on Sustainable Development in 2019* (2020). For earlier reports, see https://tinyurl.com/53sz9fk5.

21. Tom Jackman, "Trump signs 'FOSTA' bill targeting online sex trafficking, enables states and victims to pursue websites," *The Washington Post*, April 11, 2018, https://tinyurl.com/4jhe3psp.

22. "Yvonne Ambrose Testimony to Call on Congress to End Child Sex Trafficking," YouTube.com, March 13, 2018, https://tinyurl.com/nmmpnx8.

23. "Justice Department Leads Effort to Seize Backpage.Com, the Internet's Leading Forum for Prostitution Ads, and Obtains 93-Count Federal Indictment," Department of Justice, April 9, 2018, https://tinyurl.com/du68wc42.

24. "Wagner Statement on President Signing FOSTA Into Law," press release, Office of U.S. Rep. Ann Wagner, April 16, 2018, https://tinyurl.com/ynj5dc29.

25. "Kristen DiAngelo Letter to Senate Commerce Committee," Electronic Frontier Foundation, undated, https://tinyurl.com/32jxfwft.

26. Liz Tung, "FOSTA-SESTA was supposed to thwart sex trafficking. Instead, it's sparked a movement," *WHYY*, July 10, 2020, https://tinyurl.com/yybpd2cj; Danielle Blunt and Ariel Wolf, "Erased: The Impact of FOSTA-SESTA," *Hacking/Hustling*, https://tinyurl.com/4yfsveh9.

27. *Ibid.*

28. David Greene, "EFF Sues to Invalidate FOSTA, an Unconstitutional Internet Censorship Law," Electronic Frontier Foundation, June 28, 2018, https://tinyurl.com/ktuhnjx3; "Groups call on Congress to investigate the harm done by SESTA/FOSTA and hold hearings on the human rights impacts of altering Section 230," *Fight for the Future*, Jan. 27, 2021, https://tinyurl.com/xn7x7pyn.

29. Kristiina Kangaspunta, "A Short History of Trafficking in Persons," *Freedom From Fear Magazine*, October 2008, https://tinyurl.com/y9vy-5wmm.
30. Eric Weiner, "The Long, Colorful History of the Mann Act," *NPR*, March 11, 2008, https://tinyurl.com/5p2aybf8.
31. Kangaspunta, *op. cit.*
32. "Child Labor," History.com, April 17, 2020, https://tinyurl.com/4nb6zyjp; Grant Oster, "The History of Human Trafficking," Hankering for History, 2015, https://tinyurl.com/dts6d4w.
33. "Child Labor," *op. cit.*
34. "Oppressive Child Labor," Fair Labor Standards Act, Title 29, Section 203, Definitions, Cornell Law School, Legal Information Institute, https://tinyurl.com/tvbupr7v.
35. ILO Activities in the post-war world 1946 (Part 1 1946-1959), last updated Feb. 23, 2015, https://tinyurl.com/pcs3e5dv.
36. Karen Attiah, "Why won't the U.S. ratify the U.N.'s child rights treaty?" *The Washington Post*, Nov. 21, 2014, https://tinyurl.com/3dk9uvyd.
37. "History of the ILO," International Labour Organization, undated, https://tinyurl.com/476fp956; ILO and today's global challenges 1999 (Part 2 1999-), International Labor Organization, last update: Feb. 23, 2015, https://tinyurl.com/y34erc5m; and "Convention on worst forms of child labour receives universal ratification," *UN News*, Aug. 4, 2020, https://tinyurl.com/ud6c-wdsh.
38. Kangaspunta, *op. cit.*
39. "Victims of Trafficking and Violence Protection Act of 2000," govinfo.gov, Oct. 28, 2000, https://tinyurl.com/y4zkv63e; "Trafficking in Persons Report," *op. cit.*
40. Kangaspunta, *op. cit.*
41. Astrid Zweynert and Alex Whiting, "TIMELINE-Milestones in the fight against modern slavery," Thomson Reuters Foundation, May 30, 2016, https://tinyurl.com/54fhc45r.
42. "Conduct in U.N. Field Missions, Sexual Exploitation and Abuse, Table of Allegations," unmissions.org, 2021, https://tinyurl.com/4fxj5zbh.
43. Dodds, *op. cit.*
44. "Conduct in U.N. Field Missions," *op. cit.*
45. *Ibid.*
46. Jenna Stern, "Reducing Sexual Exploitation and Abuse in U.N. Peacekeeping," The Stimson Center, Feb. 12, 2015, https://tinyurl.com/zm28dcrp.
47. "PROTECT Our Children Act of 2008," Congress.gov, Oct. 13, 2008, https://tinyurl.com/9kx8f2zm.
48. Zweynert and Whiting, *op. cit.*
49. Stuart Elliott, "Body Shop Begins a Campaign Against Sex Trafficking," *The New York Times*, March 17, 2010, https://tinyurl.com/9sazc47.
50. Boko Haram: "Nigerian Terror Group Sells Girls Into Slavery," *NBC News*, May 1, 2014, https://tinyurl.com/yphyb3m8.
51. Kamala D. Harris, "The California Transparency in Supply Chains Act: A Resource Guide," California Department of Justice, 2015, https://tinyurl.com/bcksa9vw.
52. Global Slavery Index, Walk Free, 2018, https://tinyurl.com/3a4y7wyc; "Child Trafficking, exploitation on the rise, warns U.N. expert," *U.N. News*, March 13, 2014, https://tinyurl.com/ypb5aj6y.
53. *Ibid.*
54. Zweynert and Whiting, *op. cit.*
55. Brandy Zadrozny and Ben Collins, "How three conspiracy theorists took 'Q' and sparked Qanon," *NBC News*, Aug. 14, 2018, https://tinyurl.com/a3z3366x.
56. "Global Estimates of Modern Slavery," *op. cit.*
57. Katie Rogers, "White House Holds Trafficking 'Summit,' but Critics Dismiss Lack of Dialogue," *The New York Times*, Jan. 31, 2020, https://tinyurl.com/2ern988k.
58. "Trafficking in Persons Report," *op. cit.*
59. Rogers, *op. cit.*

60. Allyson Waller and Juliet Macur, "Human Trafficking Charges and Coach's Death Reopens Gymnastics' Deep Wounds," *The New York Times*, Feb. 25, 2021, https://tinyurl.com/3xfd652v.
61. Ibid.
62. Patricia Mazzei et al., "2 F.B.I. Agents Killed in Shooting in Florida," *The New York Times*, Feb. 2, 2021, https://tinyurl.com/tp6zmjed; Johnny Diaz et al., "Killing of F.B.I. Agents Comes Amid Explosion of Child Sex Abuse Reports," *The New York Times*, Feb. 3, 2021, https://tinyurl.com/ssrc74rt.
63. Minyvonne Burke, "33 missing children rescued in Los Angeles Trafficking Operation," *NBC News*, Jan. 23, 2021, https://tinyurl.com/mdja4v6b.
64. Benjamin Weiser et al., "Fashion Mogul Peter Nygard Indicted on Sex-Trafficking Charges," *The New York Times*, Dec. 15, 2020, https://tinyurl.com/4rbvpvr4; Marcy Nicholson, "Peter Nygard Denied Bail in U.S.-Canada Extradition Case," *Bloomberg*, Feb. 5, 2021, https://tinyurl.com/53benn7d.
65. Michael S. Schmidt et al., "Matt Gaetz Is Said to Face Justice Dept. Inquiry Over Sex With an Underage Girl," *The New York Times*, March 30, 2021, https://tinyurl.com/5xd4eprs.
66. Ibid.
67. Greene, op. cit.
68. Oscar Gonzalez, "Bill unveiled to reduce Section 230 protections for social media companies," *CNET*, Feb. 5, 2021, https://tinyurl.com/a6drp3fc.
69. Dean DeChiaro, "Sex workers, sidelined in last Section 230 debate, seek a seat at the table," *Roll Call*, Feb. 23, 2021, https://tinyurl.com/8hhrdsv5.
70. Sarah Martinson, "Erasing Criminal Records Lets Trafficking Victims Rebuild," Law360.com, Feb. 7, 2021, https://tinyurl.com/92j8mwy8.
71. Luis C. deBaca, "OPINION: Storm clouds on the horizon for U.S. human trafficking rankings," Thomson Reuters Foundation, June 29, 2020, https://tinyurl.com/yf3xuctr.

BIBLIOGRAPHY

Books

Belles, Nita, *In Our Backyard: Human Trafficking in America and What We Can Do to Stop It*, Baker Books, 2015.
A nationally recognized expert on human trafficking describes all forms of the practice in the United States, identifies risk factors and proposes steps to prevent its spread.

Clark, Jennifer Bryson, and Sasha Poucki, eds., *The SAGE Handbook of Human Trafficking and Modern Day Slavery*, SAGE Publications, 2018.
The co-founders of Azimuth180°—a nonprofit organization that aims to prevent labor exploitation and trafficking—provide a comprehensive collection of essays exploring the history, politics, economics and geography of human trafficking and slavery since 1945.

Flores, Theresa, *The Slave Across the Street*, Ampelon Publishing, 2019.
A moving memoir describes how a 15-year-old suburban Detroit girl became a victim of sex trafficking, her arduous road to recovery and the emotional scars that remain.

Shelley, Louise, *Human Trafficking: A Global Perspective*, Cambridge University Press, 2010.
An expert on transnational crime explains human trafficking's various business models around the world and forecasts its continued growth because of economic and demographic inequalities, armed conflict and global climate change.

Articles

Dodds, Paisley, "AP Exclusive: UN child sex ring left victims, but no arrests," *The Associated Press*, April 11, 2017, https://tinyurl.com/yjcyc74k.
An investigative reporter breaks the story of rampant child sex trafficking by U.N. peacekeepers in Haiti and several African countries and the failure of either the United Nations or the peacekeepers' home countries to punish the perpetrators.

Jackman, Tom, "Trump signs 'FOSTA' bill targeting online sex trafficking, enables states and victims to pursue websites," *The Washington Post*, April 11, 2018, https://tinyurl.com/4jhe3psp.

The Fight Online Sex Trafficking Act targets online sex trafficking, triggering free-speech and privacy controversies.

Kristof, Nicholas, "The Children of Pornhub," *The New York Times,* **Dec. 4, 2020, https://tinyurl.com/zvkajfbf.**
A columnist explores the dark world of pornographic images of child sexual abuse on the internet and its lasting damage to the victims.

Latiff, Rozanna, and Ebrahim Harris, "Sold into marriage—how Rohingya girls become child brides in Malaysia," *Reuters,* **Feb. 15, 2017, https://tinyurl.com/53498dzb.**
Young Rohingya girls fleeing violence in Myanmar are often abducted by traffickers and sold to male Rohingya refugees in Malaysia.

Mendelson, Sarah E., "Combating Human Trafficking and the Biden Administration," Council on Foreign Relations, Jan. 28, 2021, https://tinyurl.com/5svkr3tv.
A former U.S. ambassador to the United Nations for human rights argues that the U.S. government should align its policies against human trafficking with the U.N.'s Sustainable Development Goals to broaden the number of agencies that can be enlisted for the fight.

Teekah, Anita, and William Sheehan, "Forced Marriage is Human Trafficking: We Explain How and Why," SafeHorizon, Dec. 11, 2019, https://tinyurl.com/2kzesx6k.
A lawyer with an anti-trafficking organization argues that forced marriage qualifies as a form of human trafficking.

Reports and Studies

Cockayne, James, "Developing Freedom: The Sustainable Development Case for Ending Modern Slavery, Forced Labour and Human Trafficking," United Nations University Centre for Policy Research, Jan. 25, 2021, https://tinyurl.com/yfyvn9b8.
A report argues that the global development community should prioritize anti-slavery and anti-trafficking as part of its commitment to the U.N.'s Sustainable Development Goals.

"Global Estimates of Modern Slavery," International Labour Organization and Walk Free Foundation, Sept. 19, 2017, https://tinyurl.com/5x2upbke.
A study estimates that 40.3 million people worldwide are enslaved, including those forced into labor for private companies, adults and children who are sexually exploited for commercial purposes and victims of forced marriage.

Kangaspunta, Kristiina, *et al.,* **"2020 Global Report on Trafficking in Persons," Office on Drugs and Crime, United Nations, January 2021, https://tinyurl.com/2xnpw8hf.**
This report provides an overview on human trafficking worldwide during 2020, with chapters on socioeconomic factors, the impact of the COVID-19 pandemic, cybertrafficking and regional assessments.

"Trafficking in Persons Report, 20th Edition," Office to Monitor and Combat Trafficking in Persons, U.S. Department of State, June 2020, https://tinyurl.com/kdm3enkh.
The Trump administration's final report on global human trafficking notes major lapses in the U.S. government's performance.

THE NEXT STEP
Cybertrafficking

Bell, Christel, "Cyber crime experts warn of Omegle chat site, growing in popularity with kids—and predators," *Fox 4,* **Nov. 10, 2020, https://tinyurl.com/uvcpcaue.**
A video and text chat site that encourages users to "meet strangers" is becoming increasingly popular with teens and has been used by predators, police in Missouri warn.

Brown, Desmond, "Human trafficking survivor teaches kids, adults how to be safer online during COVID-19," *CBC,* **Oct. 22, 2020, https://tinyurl.com/rem9kjs.**
A Canadian victim of trafficking offered a free streamed event on online safety, as the Ontario government begins distributing educational materials for children on the issue.

Shelton, Caitlyn, "450 cyber crimes against children tips; TBI uncertain if correlation to online schooling," *Fox 17,* **Aug. 20, 2020, https://tinyurl.com/ew76nvjz.**

Cybercrimes against children, often by sexual predators, are rising in Nashville, Tenn., as kids spend more time on the computer for virtual learning.

Forced Marriage

Bloomberg, Matt, "Cambodia adds human trafficking lessons to schools," *Reuters*, Dec. 24, 2020, https://tinyurl.com/3jdyjx8w.
Primary and high school students in Cambodia will learn about the dangers of trafficking, after thousands of Cambodian women and girls have been trafficked internationally, often for forced marriages in China.

Currie, Kelley E., John Cotton Richmond and Samuel D. Brownback, "How China's 'missing women' problem has fueled trafficking and forced marriage," *South China Morning Post*, Jan. 13, 2021, https://tinyurl.com/h4k3a5m.
In an opinion column, U.S. officials urged China—where a decades-long, one-child policy and a preference for boys left the country with 30 million more men than women—to punish perpetrators of forced marriages and sex trafficking in the country's rural regions.

Sullivan, Helen, "Pandemic forcing girls in south-east Asia and Pacific out of school and into marriage—study," *The Guardian*, March 15, 2021, https://tinyurl.com/478nwnku.
With the pandemic raging, girls are increasingly seen as an economic burden, and forced marriages are sharply increasing as a result.

QAnon and Misinformation

Davis, Kristina, and Joshua Emerson Davis, "Experts worry QAnon conspiracies are overshadowing fight against child trafficking," *San Diego Union Tribune*, Sept. 30, 2020, https://tinyurl.com/yt47jp27.
Debunked conspiracies perpetrated by the QAnon movement, which uses misleading statistics, inspired several protests last fall.

Landers, Jamie, and Richard Ruelas, "These Arizona anti-trafficking groups say QAnon misinformation is derailing their efforts," *Arizona Republic*, Oct. 20, 2020, https://tinyurl.com/h9wjmbcv.
Anti-trafficking organizations worry that false conspiracies promoted by QAnon reduce the battle against child trafficking to a partisan political issue.

Rogers, Kaleigh, "Trump Said QAnon 'Fights' Pedophilia. But The Group Has Made It Harder To Protect Kids," *FiveThirtyEight*, Oct. 15, 2020, https://tinyurl.com/25u7fb8t.
Experts say child trafficking victims are more likely to have been part of the foster care system or immigrants than random children abducted on a playground.

Recent Scandals

Garrett, Major, et al., "Matt Gaetz trip to Bahamas is part of federal probe into sex trafficking, sources say," *CBS News*, April 8, 2021, https://tinyurl.com/2na2vzk7.
Justice Department investigators are examining whether Rep. Matt Gaetz, R-Fla., violated sex trafficking laws while on a recent trip to the Bahamas.

Gentile, Dan, "Bay Area EDM DJ Bassnectar accused of sex trafficking and child pornography," *SFGate*, April 7, 2021, https://tinyurl.com/3sp4wu8z.
Two women are suing a Bay Area DJ, accusing him of befriending them online to have sex with him when they were underage. He has denied the allegations.

Schneier, Matthew, "Ghislaine Maxwell Now Faces Two Sex-Trafficking Charges," *The Cut*, March 29, 2021, https://tinyurl.com/jyy3wcu7.
An amended indictment against Ghislaine Maxwell, the confidante of deceased accused sex trafficker Jeffrey Epstein, charges her with conspiring to conduct sex trafficking, and includes four victims, one of whom says they were asked to recruit other underaged girls.

For More Information

Alliance to End Slavery and Trafficking, 1320 19th St., N.W., Suite 600, Washington, DC 20036; 202-370-3625; endslaveryandtrafficking.org. A coalition of 15 U.S. and international organizations that works to address the political, legal and humanitarian challenges posed by slavery and human trafficking.

American Civil Liberties Union, 125 Broad St., 18th Floor, New York, NY 10004; 212-549-2500; aclu.org. A leading constitutional rights advocacy organization that lobbies for free speech and privacy on the internet, among other things, and challenges legislation that it alleges curtails those rights.

ECPAT International, 328/1 Phayathai Road, Khwaeng Thanon Phetchaburi, Ratchathewi, Bangkok 10400, Thailand; +66-2-215-3388; ecpat.org. An international organization that fights the sexual exploitation of children by supporting shelters for survivors, training law enforcement, lobbying governments and conducting research.

Electronic Frontier Foundation, 815 Eddy St., San Francisco, CA 94109; 415-436-9333; eff.org. An advocacy organization that fights for free speech, privacy and innovation on the internet.

International Labour Organization, 4 Route des Morillons, CH-1211, Geneva 22, Switzerland; +41-0-22-799-6111; ilo.org. A U.N. agency that brings together governments, employers and workers of 187 member states to establish labor standards, promote workers' rights and protect children against forced labor.

National Center for Missing and Exploited Children, 333 John Carlyle St., Suite 125, Alexandria, VA 22314; 703-224-2150; missingkids.org. National clearinghouse that works with law enforcement to rescue sexually exploited and missing children and provides legal resources to families, legislators and internet service providers.

Office to Monitor and Combat Trafficking in Persons, 2201 C St., N.W., Washington, DC 20520; 202-647-4000; state.gov/bureaus-offices/under-secretary-for-civilian-security-democracy-and-human-rights/office-to-monitor-and-combat-trafficking-in-persons/. U.S. State Department agency that produces an annual report on human trafficking, which determines U.S. foreign aid for anti-trafficking efforts.

Polaris, PO Box 65323, Washington, DC 20035; 202-790-6300; polarisproject.org. Advocacy organization that operates the U.S. National Human Trafficking Hotline and shares its data with law enforcement, researchers and the anti-trafficking movement.

Walk Free Foundation, PO Box 3155, Broadway, Nedlands, Western Australia 6009; +61-8-6460-4949; walkfree.org. Human rights organization that produces the Global Slavery Index, reports and policy papers and lobbies governments, international organizations and businesses to help eradicate modern slavery.

14

Fuel Efficiency Standards

Will Trump's rollbacks increase greenhouse gas emissions?

By Reed Karaim

A polar bear and her cubs walk on an Arctic ice floe. Polar bears use offshore floes for hunting platforms, but as a warming climate depletes Arctic ice, they can be forced to swim longer distances to reach floes.

THE ISSUES

On March 31, 2020, President Trump turned to his favorite means of communication, Twitter, to laud his administration's just-announced decision to roll back automobile fuel efficiency standards implemented under his predecessor, Barack Obama.

"Great news!" Trump tweeted. "American families will now be able to buy safer, more affordable, and environmentally friendly cars with our new SAFE VEHICLES RULE."[1]

But Trump's Safer Affordable Fuel-Efficient (SAFE) Vehicles rule quickly generated opposition from critics, including some within his own Environmental Protection Agency—and in May 2020, 23 states, led by California, filed suit to block the order. They were joined by a dozen environmental and consumer groups suing separately to block the SAFE rule.[2]

"Because of this change, we will breathe more polluted air, suffer more premature deaths and see a net loss of jobs in the automobile industry," said Mary Nichols, chair of the California Air Resources Board, a state entity charged with fighting air pollution and climate change, in a statement announcing the lawsuit.[3]

The court cases are the latest round in a heated battle between the Trump administration and both states and environmental groups over a key question: How efficient and clean-running should U.S. vehicles be to limit their impact on climate change and protect the public from pollution? The battle is being waged not only over the automobile regulations known as Corporate Average Fuel Economy (CAFE) standards, but also California's long-standing authority to set emission rules stricter than those of the federal government.[4]

Trump's SAFE standard replaces rules the Obama administration negotiated with automakers in 2012 that required a 5 percent annual increase in vehicle fuel efficiency. The Trump standards mandate only a 1.5 percent annual increase. Under the Obama plan, an automaker's vehicle fleet would have averaged about 54 mpg by 2025. Under the SAFE rule, the standard will be 40 mpg by 2026.[5]

The clash over the greenhouse gases and pollutants that come out of vehicles' tailpipes has consequences for automobile manufacturers, car buyers, public health and the global climate. It has divided the major automakers, with some supporting Trump's new rule and others agreeing to the stricter CAFE standards set by California, which several other states also follow.[6]

It also presents a stark contrast between the environmental positions of Trump and presumptive Democratic presidential nominee Joe Biden as they head into the November 2020 election. Trump has hailed the new car standards as part of his administration's broader reversal of Obama-era environmental regulations he says stifled American business.[7] Biden has promised to impose standards even stricter than those under Obama to tackle climate change and accelerate the country's move to clean, renewable energy.[8]

The Trump administration and its supporters say the SAFE rule still provides adequate environmental protection, while lowering the cost of cars for consumers because manufacturers will no longer have to spend as much on technology to boost mileage. The administration maintains the new rule will save automakers up to $100 billion in compliance costs and will reduce the average price of a new vehicle by $1,000.

That price cut, they say, will spur Americans to buy new, safer and cleaner-running cars, which will not only improve air quality but save thousands of lives. "This rule reflects the Department's No. 1 priority—safety—by making newer, safer, cleaner vehicles more accessible for Americans who are, on average, driving 12-year-old cars," said U.S. Transportation Secretary Elaine Chao. "By making newer, safer, and cleaner vehicles more accessible for American families, more lives will be saved and more jobs will be created."[9]

Opponents of weakening the standards say the administration's claims are built on a series of flawed estimations. "The federal agencies used questionable science, faulty logic and ludicrous assumptions to justify what they wanted from the start: to gut and rewrite the single most important air regulation of the past decade," said Nichols, the California Air Resources Board chair.[10]

Federal CAFE standards are developed through a collaboration between the National Highway Traffic Safety Administration (NHTSA) and the Environmental Protection Agency (EPA). Opponents note the EPA's internal review of the SAFE rule disputed several of the administration's public arguments, including the central assertion that it would reduce tailpipe pollutants and emissions that cause climate change compared to "the absence of regulation." According to documents obtained by Sen. Tom Carper, D-Del., the EPA review stated, "This is not correct. 'The absence of regulation' . . . would be the existing EPA standards, which are more stringent than those finalized in this action."[11]

The EPA assessment dismissed another key contention: that weaker standards would lead automakers to build cheaper cars and thus spur consumers to buy newer vehicles with better safety features. The EPA said this argument was built on the unfounded assumption "that it's necessary to give up fuel savings to get other attributes" in vehicle design. Anticipating the possibility of court challenges, an EPA staffer wrote in an internal email that the rule had "numerous factual inaccuracies which litigants can easily disprove."[12]

An EPA spokesperson described the documents as part of the internal deliberative process between the federal agencies. EPA Administrator Andrew Wheeler has publicly supported the SAFE rule, saying it "strikes the right regulatory balance that protects our environment, and sets reasonable targets for the auto industry. The rule supports our economy, and the safety of American families."[13]

Analysts on both sides of the debate say the severe economic downturn tied to the COVID-19 pandemic has upended certainty about the impact that the revised standards could have on the industry and the car-buying public. Some believe car shoppers are likely to be even more price-sensitive, while others say Americans are unlikely to be buying new cars under any circumstances.

The shutdown imposed due to the coronavirus pandemic produced a dramatic improvement in Los Angeles' air quality, as this view of MacArthur Park and downtown in April 2020 showed. Advocates of tougher auto emissions standards say this indicates what can be accomplished through regulatory action.

it had to apply for a waiver in each case.[16] That authority remained in effect for nearly half a century. The Trump administration revoked it last year, claiming it gave California de facto power to set national standards because several states followed its lead, forcing automakers to build more-expensive vehicles overall.[17]

California officials say courts have upheld their state's right to set emissions standards and contend the Trump administration is acting illegally in revoking the authority.[18] Analysts say the different lawsuits involving emissions policies could end up before the U.S. Supreme Court.

The key underlying issue is climate change. Transportation of all kinds, from automobiles to trucks to airplanes, is the United States' single largest source of the greenhouse gases—predominantly carbon dioxide (CO_2)—that almost all scientists accept are warming the planet. Transportation accounted for 29 percent of such

Ironically, the pandemic-triggered quarantines and business shutdowns have led to the cleanest air in decades, just as the issue of vehicle efficiency and emissions is being hotly debated. In late March and early April of 2020, Los Angeles, which historically has had some of the worst air pollution in the country, recorded its longest stretch of clean air since the EPA began recording data in the early 1970s.[14]

Los Angeles and California have long been at the center of America's battle to reduce the pollution coming out of tailpipes. California was the first state to regulate vehicle emissions in the 1960s.[15]

The 1970 federal Clean Air Act recognized California's unique challenge by giving the state authority to set stricter standards than the federal government, although

Transportation Is Most Common Emissions Source

The transportation sector accounted for 29 percent of U.S. greenhouse gas emissions in 2017, according to the Environmental Protection Agency. Light-duty vehicles were the biggest source of transportation emissions, generating 59 percent of emissions in that sector.

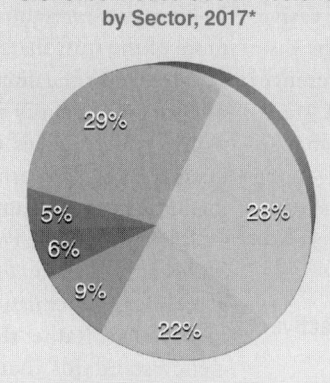

U.S. Greenhouse Gas Emissions by Sector, 2017*

- Transportation
- Electricity
- Industry
- Agriculture
- Commercial
- Residential

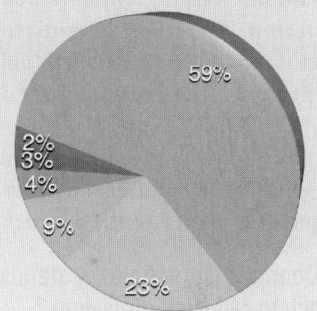

U.S. Transportation Greenhouse Gas Emissions by Source, 2017

- Light-duty vehicles
- Medium and heavy-duty trucks
- Aircraft
- Other
- Ships and boats
- Rail

* Totals may not add to 100 percent due to rounding.
Source: "Fast Facts on Transportation Greenhouse Gas Emissions," Environmental Protection Agency, July 16, 2019, https://tinyurl.com/y2vqneto

emissions in 2017. The power industry was second at 28 percent.[19]

Within the transportation sector, so-called light-duty vehicles—essentially the cars, sport utility vehicles and pickup trucks Americans love to drive—produce the biggest share, 59 percent, of those emissions.[20] More than 284 million cars and trucks are registered in the United States.[21] A typical gasoline-powered passenger vehicle emits 4.6 metric tons of carbon dioxide per year.[22] Improving the fuel efficiency to reduce greenhouse gas emissions is key to limiting climate change, according to environmentalists and others concerned by how the planet is warming.

"Based on what the science is telling us, we have a limited amount of time to act," says Andrew Linhardt, former deputy director of advocacy for the clean transportation program at the Sierra Club, an environmental group. "Getting vehicles to be as efficient as possible [and] moving into a market where vehicles are electrified is the only way we're going to be able to tackle the climate crisis."

But the administration and many supporters of rolling back CAFE standards say the issue of climate change is less pressing—or dismiss it outright.

Nicolas Loris, an energy and environmental policy fellow at the Heritage Foundation, a conservative think tank in Washington, does not fall into the dismissal camp. But when considering the difference between Obama's and Trump's fuel efficiency standards, he says, "The overall impact on climate change would be trivial."

As the Trump administration and its opponents battle over fuel efficiency and emissions standards, here are some questions central to the debate:

Were Obama's fuel efficiency standards an effective approach to reducing emissions?

When the Obama White House announced that the administration's clean car fuel efficiency standards had been finalized in 2012, the official statement emphasized the difference the new rule would make in the battle against climate change.

The standards would cut greenhouse gases coming from U.S. cars and light trucks—trucks weighing 8,500 pounds or less—in half by 2025, the administration said, reducing emissions by 6 billion metric tons, more than the total amount of carbon dioxide emitted by the United States in 2010.[23] The White House also said the rules would save a total of 12 billion barrels of oil, reducing consumption by more than 2 million barrels a day by 2025.[24]

By 2030, the standards would have produced a reduction in greenhouse gases equivalent to shutting down 140 coal-fired power plants for an entire year, according to the Union of Concerned Scientists, a science advocacy group based in Cambridge, Mass.[25]

Environmental activists say discarding the Obama fuel efficiency requirements will have a significant impact on climate change. "The standards President Trump is rolling back represent the single biggest step any nation has ever taken against global warming," says Dan Becker, director of the Safe Climate Transport Campaign at the Center for Biological Diversity. The campaign is an advocacy group working to reduce greenhouse gases.

Trump's SAFE rule, Becker says, makes American air quality worse. Even though tailpipe exhaust is far cleaner than it was decades ago, it still contains nitrogen oxides, particulate matter and other compounds that can hurt human health. Lower fuel efficiency standards mean more exhaust as Americans burn more gasoline, he says.[26]

"It makes everything worse," Becker says. "It means more of the stuff that you breathe that makes you sick. And that's just the direct health effects. In addition, in a way we can't quantify as easily, it makes global warming worse, which makes the likelihood of all the consequences of global warming worse—sea level rise, flooding, droughts, you name it."

But the Heritage Foundation's Loris says the United States accounts for only about 14 percent of global greenhouse gas emissions, and the transportation sector even less. Rather than mandate changes in fuel efficiency standards that raise the price of vehicles, he says, a more effective approach to tackling climate change would be to focus on bringing down the costs of technologies that can reduce emissions, which could speed their adoption both in the United States and abroad.

"If you're increasing the cost, whether it's new vehicles or . . . other energy technology, you're only going to disincentivize the investment in those projects," Loris says. "The best way to be a leader is to lower the cost so that

[U.S.] consumers and consumers in other countries can more readily adopt them."

The Trump administration's analysis of the SAFE rule acknowledges it will lead to an increase of 2 to 3 percent in U.S. oil consumption, which would amount to half a million more barrels a day. However, it says that will amount to an increase in global temperatures of only three-thousandths of a degree Celsius by 2100.[27]

"The opponents of the rule try to portray it as if terrible things are going to happen imminently . . . and the numbers certainly do not support that kind of assessment, to put it charitably," says Marlo Lewis Jr., a senior fellow at the Competitive Enterprise Institute, a public policy group based in Washington dedicated to promoting free markets. Lewis' group says it will sue to weaken the fuel efficiency standards even further.

But a research paper published in *Science*, the peer-reviewed journal of the American Association for the Advancement of Science, concluded the Trump administration's projections about the rule's impact are based on faulty underlying assumptions.

Antonio Bento, a professor of public policy and economics at the University of Southern California and a lead author of the paper, told a U.S. House committee that one significant error is a large undercount in the number of vehicles the administration projects to be on the road by 2029. This means there will be more miles driven than the administration forecasts, he said, and "increased driving translates into increases in gasoline consumption and the external effects" of greenhouse gas emissions and local air pollution.[28]

Other analysis indicates that even the Trump forecast for the increase in greenhouse gas emissions with the new rule is equivalent to about four years' worth of those emissions from the entire U.S. transportation sector, not just vehicles.[29]

The Sierra Club's Linhardt says the effect of greenhouse gases is cumulative, with a growing impact that becomes harder to mitigate over time. "Billions of tons of CO_2 is nothing to dismiss as small," he says. "Transportation emissions are not small and tackling them now is essential."

Other advocates of the Obama rules say focusing on greenhouse gases neglects the fact that reducing emissions also cuts other pollutants coming out of tailpipes, and even small changes make a difference. "California has 26 million passenger vehicles, and we drive about 350 billion miles a year in those 26 million vehicles," says Steven Cliff, deputy executive officer of the California Air Resources Board. "So the incremental pollution from each vehicle is extremely important."

Did Obama's stricter standards impose an undue financial burden on automakers?

The fuel efficiency standards set out in Obama's 2012 clean car rule were the result of lengthy negotiations with 13 major foreign and U.S. automakers, including General Motors, Ford and Chrysler, which all agreed to the annual increases in efficiency outlined in the rule.

But Lewis, of the Competitive Enterprise Institute, says the Obama rule was partly based on a faulty forecast. "The fuel economy standards and even the CO_2 standards are based on expectations of what fuel prices will be over the next 13 years," he says, with those estimates determining "how much fuel savings are worth to consumers and, thus, how much it is reasonable for consumers to invest in fuel-saving technology."

Fuel Efficiency Rises in U.S.

Fuel efficiency for light vehicles—which include cars, sport utility vehicles and light trucks—has increased by 10 mpg to 34.6 mpg over the past two decades, according to an analysis by the Rhodium Group, a New York City research institute.

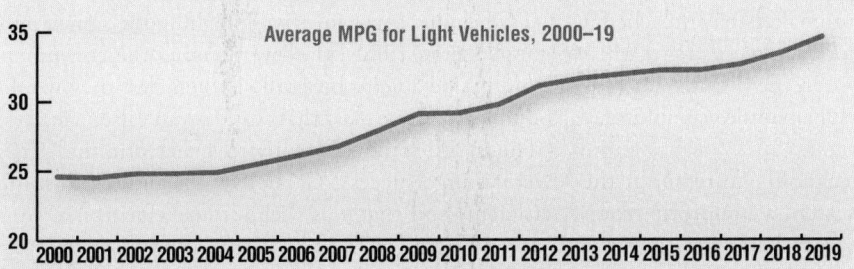

Source: Zeke Hausfather, "Analysis: How Trump's rollback of vehicle fuel standards would increase US emissions," Carbon Brief, July 10, 2019, https://tinyurl.com/y8y2lzvf

The forecasts saw gasoline prices reaching $4.50 a gallon by 2025, he says. However, the growth of U.S. production from shale oil fields has helped keep fuel prices below predicted levels, he says, which has changed the equation and made it more difficult for auto manufacturers to meet the standard.

"They forecast that one way people would deal with rising fuel costs, which they expected, was to buy compact cars, coupes and sedans," Lewis says. "Because consumers decided they wanted more heavier, taller vehicles than the agencies forecast, it meant that it was more difficult for the automakers to comply with the 2012 standards."

But Ann Carlson, a professor of environmental law at UCLA, says the technological capability to meet the Obama standards exists and the case for the effort still holds. "Both California and the EPA took a really careful look at the question and concluded that automakers could meet those standards, and that seemed quite justifiable to me," she says.

Carlson says that when car manufacturers first approached the Trump administration, they were not asking for a big rollback of standards. "The automakers didn't ask for a freeze, and they didn't ask for the cuts the Trump administrations has agreed to," she says. "What they were arguing for was little tweaks around the edges."

That was essentially the message Bob Holycross, then global director for sustainability and vehicle environmental matters at Ford, delivered at a hearing held by federal regulators in 2018. "Let me be clear: We do not support standing still," Holycross said. "Clean-car standards should increase year over year, with the inclusion of provisions that promote ongoing investment in technology that will further drive greenhouse gas reductions."[30]

Carlson adds that five automakers have reached a separate agreement with California to meet stricter emissions requirements than those in the SAFE rule. This undermines the case that the Obama rule was an undue burden, she says.

However, Brett Smith, technology director at the Center for Automotive Research, a nonprofit group based in Ann Arbor, Mich., says there were signs the Obama standards were going to be harder for automakers to meet going forward.

Under the complicated system that exists for meeting efficiency rules, car companies can bank credits for overperforming in early years and can also trade credits—so Ford, for example, could buy credits from Hyundai to meet the standards in a given year if Hyundai had credits to spare. Car companies are using up their credits, Smith says, and could have trouble meeting the standards in the next few years while still providing the vehicles consumers want.

"If you look at the data, if you look at the credits available, and if you look at how severe [the Obama rule] gets for pickup trucks in next few years, the car companies were probably going to be in trouble," Smith says.

Thomas Pyle, president of the American Energy Alliance, a Washington-based public interest group that promotes market-oriented energy and environmental policies, says the efficiency requirements backed by Obama and California distort the car market and hurt sales. "By making the mpg mandate so high, they're forcing the auto industry to make cars that currently consumers don't want or can't afford," says Pyle. "Consumers are buying crossovers and SUVs and pickup trucks. That's what their preferences are. That's what they want."

Advocates of stricter fuel efficiency standards sharply dispute the idea they are restricting either carmakers or consumer choice. "Nobody is being forced into any kind of car. Look—on the market, there's a wide range of vehicles available," says Bill Magavern, policy director of the Coalition for Clean Air, a California organization that works to promote air quality.

"The auto companies were making the same arguments in the 1970s; they were saying the consumers wouldn't be able to buy full-size vehicles, they would be too expensive—all that was proven false," he says. "The CAFE standards that were enacted in the 1970s were a huge success. Cars got safer and much more efficient, and that was without any sacrifice in consumer choice."

More recently, Magavern says, automakers have been prospering under the Obama rules while selling plenty of bigger vehicles. "They recovered from the [2007-09] recession, and they were having their best years, even as the fuel efficiency standards were going up under that agreement."

Will Trump's rollback on standards spur a move to newer, cleaner cars?

The biggest single influence on car sales this spring had nothing to do with fuel efficiency or pollution control costs. Sales tumbled an estimated 53 percent in April for major automakers, in a collapse that analysts say was the result of the severe economic downturn resulting from the pandemic.[31]

Given the economy's uncertain future, analysts say, it is hard to determine what impact other factors, including sticker price and fuel efficiency ratings, might have on car sales. "It's all going to depend on what the recovery looks like and what consumer confidence looks like," says the Heritage Foundation's Loris.

But even before the pandemic, analysts were casting doubt on the Trump administration's claim that the reduction in fuel efficiency requirements would lead to lower vehicle prices that would spur a car-buying spree. "The cost per vehicle to meet the fuel efficiency requirements is relatively small in the overall cost of a new car," says the Sierra Club's Linhardt. "Depending on the model, it's somewhat like $800 to $1,200 per vehicle, and [when] you compared those numbers to [the cost of] all the new bells and whistles, it's not that much."

The average cost of a new car in the United States in January was $37,851, according to analysts at Kelley Blue Book, the car pricing firm.[32]

Pyle, of the American Energy Alliance, says the cost of meeting fuel efficiency standards built into that price does inhibit buyers. "What this is doing is making it harder to buy a new car. It's pricing people

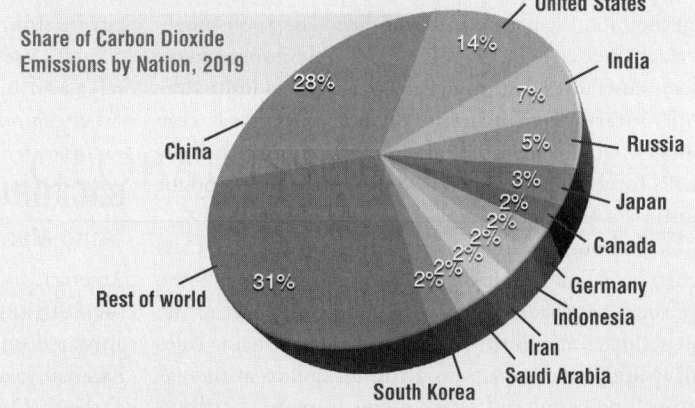

China, U.S. Are World's Top Carbon Emitters

China was responsible for 28 percent of all the carbon dioxide emitted globally in 2019, according to the Union of Concerned Scientists. The United States was second at 14 percent, and India was third at 7 percent.

Share of Carbon Dioxide Emissions by Nation, 2019

Source: "Each Country's Share of CO_2 Emissions," Union of Concerned Scientists, May 11, 2020, https://tinyurl.com/yyxgukld

out of the purchasing deal, and who gets hit the hardest? It's the poor," says Pyle. "It's preventing poor people from having the freedom and mobility of a new, safer car."

The money automakers will save by meeting the SAFE rule instead of the more stringent Obama standards will bring new vehicles within range of more Americans, Pyle says. "If you don't have [a lot] of disposable income and you need a car, if a new car is more affordable, then at least it's an option for you," he says.

Linhardt, however, doubts consumers will see savings from the SAFE rule. "If anyone thinks that automakers are going to lower the cost of their vehicles because they're not doing fuel efficiency, they haven't been paying attention to the auto industry for the last 30 years," he says.

Loris says the issue is how much prices will increase. "One of the benefits of the SAFE rule compared to the Obama era standards is that it's less aggressive. The 1.5 percent increase is pretty modest comparatively, so it shouldn't result in as much investment in changing vehicle technology and design," he says. "In that regard, I think automakers will be better off in terms of how they can meet the standard in a way that doesn't significantly raise prices."

Supporters of the stricter Obama standards counter that they actually provided greater benefits to consumers through fuel savings, making automobiles more attractive financially. They point to the Trump administration's internal analysis that showed the SAFE rule rollback would lower the price of new cars and light trucks by about $1,000, but would increase the amount consumers would pay for gasoline by $1,400.[33]

Even though gasoline prices fell to an average of less than $2 a gallon this spring and have not increased at the rate the Obama administration predicted, Becker of the Safe Climate Transport Campaign says the Obama rules still would "save consumers a trillion dollars at the gas pump long-term, and that's down from $1.7 trillion before gas prices fell."

The $1.7 trillion figure was the savings the Obama administration projected from their 2012 efficiency standards.[34] Critics of those standards say the projection was always unrealistic because it included accumulated savings over an excessively long period of time and assumed ever higher gasoline prices.

The critics also question how much consumers actually value the savings they get from higher fuel efficiency when shopping for a new vehicle. The Center for Automotive Research's Smith says it only has a limited impact. "Consumers are interested in saving money at the pump, but it's not a high priority," he says. "It's just not that big a deal for most people. With gas relatively inexpensive, [car shoppers feel] 'I'd rather have that sunroof' or the newest tech or something else."

Researchers have reached contradictory conclusions on the effect of fuel savings on sales. The National Bureau of Economic Research, a nonpartisan group that distributes economic research to policymakers and others, found buyers steeply discount fuel efficiency when making price considerations and are willing to pay only $380 extra for $1,000 savings in fuel costs.[35] However, a study by Consumers Union, a public interest advocacy group, found car buyers were willing to pay $1,000 more for a vehicle to save $100 per year in fuel costs.[36]

The National Automobile Dealers Association, which supports Trump's SAFE rules, feels the rollback has more value than the fuel savings from Obama's standards and will boost car sales. "Regulatory standards that embrace marketplace realities will accelerate, not inhibit, fleet turnover," said Peter Welch, the association's president and CEO, "and ensure that newer, safer and more fuel-efficient cars and trucks get on America's roads."[37]

BACKGROUND
"Auto Mania"

America's love affair with the automobile began early in the 20th century, when the first "horseless carriages" appeared on the nation's roads. But it exploded into a national passion with the arrival of Henry Ford's Model T, the first relatively affordable, mass-produced car.

Before the Model T, automobiles came with a variety of power sources, including steam engines, alcohol-fueled motors and even battery-powered electric vehicles. Tom McCarthy, author of *Auto Mania: Cars, Consumers, and the Environment*, a history of the car in American society, says that some of today's concerns about the gasoline engine were present in the earliest days of the automobile.

Model Ts fresh off the assembly line are parked outside the Ford plant in Highland Park, Mich., in 1913. Ford built 15 million Model Ts between 1908 and 1927, helping to make automobiles ubiquitous.

"I was amazed . . . to find people who, from the very beginning, were picking up on these problems," says McCarthy, a historian at the U.S. Naval Academy in Annapolis, Md. "There was a whole big debate on electric versus gasoline versus alcohol: 'Shouldn't we burn alcohol? It's so much cleaner.'"

In 1900, most of the roughly 8,000 automobiles on U.S. roads were steam-powered. About a quarter of the vehicles built in America were electric powered. But the power and range advantage gasoline-fueled engines enjoyed gave them the edge over other power sources. By the time Henry Ford designed the Model T, they had already come to dominate automobile design.[38]

The initial Model T rolled off the assembly line on Oct. 1, 1908. Between that year and 1927, Ford built about 15 million of them.[39] Their sales, along with those of models from General Motors, formed in 1908, and other companies, would transform the nation.

In 1908, the United States had fewer than 200,000 motor vehicles. Twenty years later, more than 24 million cars and trucks were on the nation's roadways. By 1948, that number had grown to more than 41 million, and more rapid growth was ahead in the prosperous decades of the 1950s and 1960s.[40]

The original Model T got up to 21 mpg, but as cars grew heavier and more powerful, fuel efficiency shrank.[41] By 1950, average mileage was down to slightly under 13 mpg.[42] More cars burning more gasoline meant much more automobile exhaust. But as millions of vehicles crowded roadways, officials were slow to connect the growth in traffic with the increasingly dirty air in major metropolitan areas.

Reckoning in California

In the summer of 1943, a thick blanket of smog—a combination of fog and atmospheric pollutants—descended on Los Angeles, limiting visibility to only three blocks and leaving people with burning eyes and lungs and nausea. Officials at first thought a local chemical plant was to blame. But when the plant was shut down, the smog continued.[43]

In 1947, Los Angeles County formed a special board to control air pollution, the first such body in the United States. But the city's smog continued despite the board's effort to regulate power plants, oil refineries and other industrial sites it thought might be to blame.[44]

In the 1950s, Arie Haagen-Smit, a bio-organic chemistry professor working for the Los Angeles air district, finally connected the smog to automobile exhaust. He determined that airborne hydrocarbons and nitrogen oxides released when gasoline was burned in car engines were responsible for the polluted air.[45]

His conclusions were disputed by oil companies, which hired their own experts to challenge his findings.[46] But by the 1960s, the connection had been established and California began to build a regulatory framework to control auto exhaust. In 1966, the state created the first tailpipe emissions standards in the United States and, a year later, launched the California Air Resources Board to work for clean air.[47]

On the national level, growing environmental awareness and rising concern about air pollution led to the 1970 Clean Air Act. The law authorized the development of regulations to limit vehicle emissions. The EPA was created the same year to implement the law.[48] Recognizing California's earlier efforts and pollution challenges, the Clean Air Act also authorized the state to set emissions regulations that were stricter than federal standards by applying for a waiver from the EPA.[49]

Shift to Fuel Efficiency

From 1950 to 1975, American cars grew bigger, more powerful and more luxurious—but slightly less fuel efficient. In 1950, U.S. vehicles averaged 12.8 mpg, according to the U.S. Energy Information Administration. By 1975, that had fallen to 12.2 mpg, with mild ups and downs along the way.[50]

The inattention to fuel efficiency was made possible by a sustained era of relatively cheap fuel. From 1950 to 1975, the average gasoline price in the United States climbed from 27 cents a gallon to 57 cents a gallon. Yet when adjusted for inflation, gasoline was cheaper in 1975 that it had been 25 years earlier.[51]

But by then, the price was already climbing as a result of events in the Middle East. For decades, the United States had been growing increasingly

CHRONOLOGY

1943-1967 *California leads the way in regulating tailpipe emissions.*

1943 Severe smog in Los Angeles reduces visibility and causes burning eyes and lungs, but scientists do not consider automobiles to be the cause.

1950 California Institute of Technology chemistry professor Arie Haagen-Smit identifies automobile tailpipe emissions as the cause of Los Angeles' smog.

1966 With air pollution worsening, California establishes the first tailpipe emissions standards in the nation.

1967 Gov. Ronald Reagan creates California's Air Resources Board to address pollution.

1970-1975 *Concerns about the environment, auto safety and dependence on foreign oil spur regulation.*

1970 Congress passes the Clean Air Act, requiring a 90 percent reduction in harmful emissions from new automobiles by 1975. The law gives California the authority to set its own standards.

1973 The Environmental Protection Agency (EPA) releases a study confirming that lead from automobile exhaust threatens public health and issues regulations to reduce the metal in gasoline. . . . An oil embargo by Arab nations sends U.S. gasoline prices soaring, spurring interest in more-efficient vehicles, which boosts sales of smaller four-cylinder Japanese models.

1975 The Energy Policy and Conservation Act sets the first fuel economy goals through the Corporate Average Fuel Economy (CAFE) program.

1981-1996 *Growing focus on tailpipe emissions' health hazards sparks further action.*

1981 A new generation of catalytic converters with sensors and onboard computers appears in new cars, reducing pollutants from tailpipes.

1985 EPA issues regulations to cut the amount of lead in gasoline by 90 percent starting Jan. 1, 1986.

1992 Senate approves and President George H.W. Bush signs the United Nations Framework Convention on Climate Change, committing countries to fight global warming.

1996 EPA completes its 25-year mission to completely remove lead from gasoline, banning it from gasoline as of Jan. 1.

2003-2012 *Rising fuel prices and global warming concerns lead to renewed focus on fuel efficiency.*

2003 A spike in gasoline prices that would last until 2008 spurs interest in hybrid and electric vehicles.

2007 The U.S. Supreme Court rules that the EPA has authority to regulate carbon dioxide and other greenhouse gas vehicle emissions as pollutants under the Clean Air Act.

2008 Federal government offers a tax credit of up to $7,500 to purchasers of qualified plug-in electric vehicles.

2012 The Obama administration finalizes standards to increase fuel economy standards to roughly 54 mpg for cars and light-duty trucks by 2025.

2017-Present *President Trump vows to reduce government regulation and boost the U.S. oil industry.*

2017 President Trump tells autoworkers he will review fuel efficiency standards that automakers had agreed to during the Obama administration.

2018 California Gov. Jerry Brown commits the state to getting nearly 5 million electric vehicles on the road by 2030 to reduce greenhouse gas emissions.

2019 The Trump administration revokes the waiver giving California the authority to set its own, stricter vehicle emission standards, which are also followed by several other states. . . . California sues the Trump administration in federal court over the revocation of its emissions waiver.

2020 The Trump administration finalizes rules rolling back fuel efficiency standards to 40 miles mpg by 2026, saying the change will lower car costs (March). . . . Twenty-three states, the District of Columbia and a dozen environmental and consumer groups file suit to block the administration's decision to weaken fuel efficiency standards (May).

dependent on oil from that region to feed its gasoline habit. By the mid-1970s, about one-third of the oil refined into gasoline was coming from outside the United States.[52]

When Israel faced off against Egypt and Syria in a 1973 war, Arab oil-producing nations imposed an embargo on sales to the United States in retaliation for U.S. support of Israel. The embargo would lead to a quadrupling of oil prices, gasoline shortages, long lines at filling stations and the nation's first fuel efficiency standards.[53]

In 1975, President Gerald Ford signed the Energy Policy and Conservation Act, which included a provision establishing mandatory fuel efficiency standards for automakers that would gradually rise to 27.5 mpg for 1985-model cars.[54]

The requirement spurred a revolution in U.S. automobile design, says Smith, of the Center for Automotive Research. Manufacturers switched from heavier body-on-frame construction, in which the car's body is mounted on a rigid frame, to lighter unibody construction, in which the vehicle's body and chassis are integrated into a single structure. They also shifted more production to smaller cars.

In both cases, Japanese and European automakers had an edge, because they were already making smaller, more fuel-efficient unibody cars. "It took [U.S. automakers] a long time to get really good at unibody cars," Smith says, "and over that time, they lost a lot of market share to international companies."

At the time, U.S. automakers complained the fuel efficiency mandate would mean the end of full-sized cars and would destroy their business. A Ford executive testified before Congress in 1974 that the standards "would result in a Ford product line consisting . . . of all sub-Pinto-sized vehicles." (The Pinto was a small Ford hatchback.)[55]

Larger vehicles did not disappear, and the 1975 mandate succeeded in raising fuel efficiency. By 1985, average mileage for cars had reached 27.5 mpg. But the rule had a separate, lower standard of 19.5 mpg for light trucks, which included minivans and sport utility vehicles as well as pickup trucks. In 1986 automakers successfully lobbied President Ronald Reagan's administration to lower the standard to 26 mpg for cars. At the same time, two of the vehicles designated as light trucks were taking off in popularity: The first minivan was introduced by Chrysler in 1983 and become an immediate hit, while SUVs grew in popularity in the 1990s.[56]

The consumer shift toward these less efficient vehicles, along with a lack of interest on Capitol Hill in increasing standards, stalled fuel efficiency for two decades. In 1995, Democratic President Bill Clinton tried to raise light truck efficiency standards, but a Republican-controlled Congress responded by stripping the administration's authority to increase vehicle efficiency. The withdrawal of authority remained in place until 2000.[57]

Removing Lead

The Clinton administration was more successful in continuing the effort to make vehicle exhaust cleaner. In 1996, the EPA completed a 25-year effort to remove lead, a human health hazard, from gasoline. Two years later, the administration, automakers and Northeastern states agreed to put cleaner cars on the roads before it was mandated under the Clean Air Act. The cars produced under this National Low Emission Vehicle program first became available in New England in 1999.[58]

California continued on its own aggressive path, starting a "zero emissions" vehicle program in 1990 requiring automakers to offer a specific number of the very cleanest vehicles available, including electric vehicles and some hybrids—vehicles powered by both gasoline and batteries.[59]

In 2000, oil prices again soared, renewing interest in stricter federal fuel efficiency standards. The Clinton administration modestly raised the light truck requirements that year, but oil prices continued to be high, and in 2007 Congress passed the Energy Independence and Security Act, raising CAFE standards for cars and light trucks by 40 percent.

When Obama took office in 2009, he accelerated those improvements, requiring automakers to reach a fleetwide average of 35.5 mpg by 2016. He also took steps to bring federal standards in lines with California's, a move referred to as "harmonization," which ended an ongoing concern of automakers that they would be required to meet two separate standards.[60]

U.S. Lags in Fuel Economy

China, EU are moving aggressively to cut tailpipe emissions.

President Trump's rollback of U.S. fuel efficiency standards will leave the United States far behind most of the developed world in reducing tailpipe emissions over the next decade.

The European Union (EU) has forged ahead with an ambitious—critics say unrealistic—schedule to cut the vehicle greenhouse gases responsible for climate change, requiring cars to average the equivalent of 57 mpg by 2021 and 92 mpg by 2030.[1] Trump's fuel efficiency rule requires that automakers' U.S. vehicle fleets reach 40 mpg by 2026.[2] (Trump rolled back a more ambitious standard set by the Obama administration, calling it overly burdensome; critics say the rollback is unneeded and will result in greater pollution.)

China has made a major commitment to developing, building and promoting the use of electric vehicles, setting a goal that 25 percent of automobiles and trucks sold in the country will be zero-emission, meaning primarily electric, by 2025. That goal increases to 50 percent by 2030.[3]

In addition, China has adopted stricter fuel efficiency requirements than the United States. The average for new vehicles sold in China in 2018 was already 41 mpg, exceeding the U.S. 2026 requirement.[4] Japanese standards also exceed U.S. requirements.[5]

Europe, the United States and China use different methods to track the progress limiting greenhouse gases from vehicles. The Europeans record and publish grams per kilometer of carbon dioxide (CO_2), the principal greenhouse gas. China also focuses on the volume of certain tailpipe gases. The United States uses miles per gallon as a way to determine the amount of emissions.

"But the bottom line is, our [standards] are worse. They're worse than the 'godless communists' in China. They're worse than Europe," says Dan Becker, director of the Safe Climate Transport Campaign at the Center for Biological Diversity. The campaign is an advocacy group that works to reduce greenhouse gases.

China, the United States and the EU are the world's three largest automobile markets, in that order, with Japan a distant fourth. Climate change activists consider drastically reducing the CO_2 that comes from vehicles a key part of limiting climate change.

The global commitment to cutting emissions is strong enough that a study by the International Council on Clean Transportation (ICCT), a global environmental think tank, concluded, "An increasing number of local and national governments are signaling their intention to phase out combustion-engine-powered vehicles altogether."[6]

China invested nearly $60 billion between 2009 and 2017 in electric vehicles. About 450 manufacturers working on electric vehicles are registered with the Chinese government, including domestic and foreign companies. Tesla, the leading U.S. electric car manufacturer, recently announced plans to increase production of its Model 3 electric cars to 4,000 vehicles a week at a plant in Shanghai.[7]

China's electric vehicles industry has been hurt by the global recession tied to the coronavirus pandemic, as well as a decision by the Chinese government to trim subsidies.[8]

In 2011, after lengthy negotiations with automakers, the Obama administration announced even stricter CAFE requirements, which reflected growing concern about the role that the greenhouse gases in auto exhaust, particularly CO_2, were playing in climate change.

When Obama's clean car standards were announced in 2011, 13 auto executives joined Obama on stage for the announcement. Margo Oge, director of the EPA's office of transportation and air quality and a lead EPA negotiator of the agreement, remembered the scene:

"A fleet of shiny new cars, SUVs, and pickup trucks serves as a gleaming backdrop for President Obama as he strides across a brightly lit convention center stage. He quickly shakes the hands of thirteen smiling auto CEOs and senior executives before stepping to the lectern and announcing some of the stiffest new regulations on automobiles in decades. The executives sit listening agreeably,

But analysts believe the country's leaders remain committed to the industry long-term.

The EU's clean-vehicle goals include stiff fines for automakers that fail to meet the emissions requirements. The European Automobile Manufacturers Association has called the standards unrealistic, saying they "are driven purely by political motives, without taking technological and socioeconomic realities into account."[9]

Those realities, said Erik Jonnaert, the association's secretary general in 2019, are the still higher-than-average cost of electric vehicles (EVs) and the shortage of charging stations to make EVs widely acceptable to consumers.[10]

But some European countries already are transitioning to electric vehicles. In March, nearly 60 percent of all cars purchased in Norway were fully electric, continuing a trend that has the country on course to meet its goal of phasing out gasoline- and diesel-powered vehicles by 2025.[11]

Aggressive government policies have helped make EVs popular in Norway. Norwegians who go electric get an exemption from the country's steep vehicle purchase tax, as well as a 50 percent discount on tolls, ferries and parking rates (originally 100 percent). They also can use the traffic lanes reserved for buses if they have one passenger.[12]

Nic Lutsey, who directs the ICCT's electric vehicle program, says setting emissions requirements for manufacturers that lead them to invest in clean-car technology and offer more zero-emission models, combined with purchasing incentives for consumers, are the keys to getting the public to try EVs. He adds that electric vehicles are cheaper to operate than gasoline-powered cars. "Every market has found the same thing: Consumers don't naturally take up that offering, but it overwhelmingly offers a cost benefit for consumers when they do," Lutsey says.

In Norway, the combination appears to be working. "It's actually quite amazing how fast the mindset's changed," said Christina Bu, secretary general of the Norwegian Electric Vehicle Association. "Even in 2013 or 2014, people were skeptical. Now, a majority of Norwegians will say: 'My next car will be electric.'"[13]

—*Reed Karaim*

---

[1] Ethan N. Elkind, "Trump's Flawed Rollback of Fuel Economy Rules," *Regulatory Review*, May 18, 2020, https://tinyurl.com/y77f2bqs.

[2] Coral Davenport, "Trump Calls New Fuel Economy Rule a Boon. Some Experts See Steep Costs," *The New York Times*, March 31, 2020, https://tinyurl.com/rvjbasw; David Shepardson, "U.S. to finalize fuel efficiency rewrite through 2026: sources," *Reuters*, March 30, 2020, https://tinyurl.com/y857alev.

[3] Elkind, *op. cit.*

[4] *Ibid.*

[5] Zifei Yang and Dan Rutherford, "Japan 2030 fuel economy standards," International Council on Clean Transportation, Sept. 27, 2019, https://tinyurl.com/y32v93zj.

[6] "The end of the road? An overview of combustion-engine car phaseout announcements across Europe," International Council on Clean Transportation, May 2020, https://tinyurl.com/ybu864do.

[7] Eleanor Albert, "Can China's Electric Car Industry Weather the COVID-19 Storm?" *The Diplomat*, May 8, 2020, https://tinyurl.com/y8vwjc2o.

[8] *Ibid.*

[9] "Auto industry reacts to deal on CO_2 targets for cars and vans," European Automobile Manufacturers Association, Dec. 17, 2018, https://tinyurl.com/y9zuo5bw.

[10] *Ibid.*

[11] Jon Henley and Elisabeth Ulven, "Norway and the A-ha moment that made electric cars the answer," *The Guardian*, April 19, 2020, https://tinyurl.com/yblyo6t4.

[12] *Ibid.*

[13] *Ibid.*

---

even proudly, to the plan that would compel their companies—representing 90 percent of the American market—to double the fuel efficiency of their products and cut greenhouse gas emissions in half by 2025."[61]

The Center for Automotive Research's Smith, however, says the automakers agreed to the new rules only reluctantly. "They knew going in, it was going to be really, really hard, especially if fuel prices didn't drastically increase because most people don't value fuel efficiency, and certainly at that time very few people understood or valued" lowering greenhouse gas emissions, he says.

But an EPA report found that through 2018 automakers scored record-breaking gains in fuel efficiency and in limiting greenhouse gas emissions under the Obama rules. In 2018, average fuel economy reached a record 25.1 mpg and CO_2 emissions from new U.S. vehicles fell to the lowest level ever recorded. The EPA projected further gains for 2019.[62]

Electric Vehicle Boosters Eye Greater Growth

California leads with an ambitious goal for 2030.

When climate change activists envision a future where greenhouse gas emissions have been brought under control, electric vehicles play a critical part.

"Between 2040 and 2050, getting to all zero-emission vehicles is basically what the science would say is needed for climate change mitigation," says Nic Lutsey, who directs the electric vehicle program for the International Council on Clean Transportation, a global think tank that provides research to fight climate change.

Electric vehicle advocates believe a significant transition to electric vehicles (EVs) in the United States is possible within the next few decades. "I like to think in 10 years we'll be closing in on all new sales of vehicles being electric or highly efficient," says Andrew Linhardt, former deputy director of advocacy for the clean transportation program at the Sierra Club, an environmental group.

But electric vehicle skeptics doubt EVs can gain sufficient traction to seriously dent the market for gasoline-powered vehicles. "There is a market for EVs. It's a niche market, and it should not be forced on people," says Thomas Pyle, president of the American Energy Alliance, a Washington-based group that works to promote market-oriented energy policies.

California has led the charge in the United States for electric vehicles, setting an ambitious goal to have 5 million zero-emission vehicles on the road by 2030, up from about 700,000 this year.[1] Those vehicles would almost all be purely electric vehicles or plug-in hybrids, in which a battery-powered electric motor drives the wheels but a gasoline-fueled engine can charge the battery when it starts to run down. Cars or trucks powered by hydrogen fuel cells could account for a small portion of zero-emission vehicles.

In early 2020, California had roughly half of all zero-emission vehicles in the United States.[2] A more than sevenfold increase would be required to meet the state's 2030 goal.

California is committing significant resources to making that happen. By the end of 2019, the state had about 21,000 electric vehicle charging stations. The California Air Resources Board, whose mission includes fighting climate change, has committed nearly $1.1 billion to EV projects, the bulk of it going to charging stations.[3] By 2025, the state hopes to have 250,000 such stations in place.[4]

California's zero-emissions vehicle program, largely adopted by 10 other states, requires that a certain number of the vehicles sold in the state by any manufacturer be zero-emission vehicles, with the number linked to their total California sales.[5]

Last year, President Trump revoked California's authority to set its own emission standards, including its zero-emissions vehicle program. The state is challenging Trump's move in court.

The program does seem to have spurred EV sales. The number of zero-emission vehicles in California has grown by 30 percent annually in the last two years.[6]

The agency also found that automakers were developing a range of approaches to meet the standards. "Technological innovation in the auto industry has led to a wide array of technology available to manufacturers to achieve CO_2 emissions, fuel economy and performance goals," the report stated.[63]

All the major automobile manufacturers were in compliance with the Obama clean car standards at the end of 2018, the EPA said. The wider use and refinement of established technologies such as turbocharged engines and gasoline direct injection—in which fuel is injected directly into the combustion chamber, improving efficiency—contributed. So did newer approaches such as cylinder deactivation that uses only part of an engine when less power is necessary and stop/start systems that shut down the engine entirely at idle, the EPA

The rest of the country, however, lags far behind. Electric vehicle sales have been less than 3 percent of U.S. sales overall, even with federal tax credits and additional incentives offered by some states.[7]

EV skeptics say consumers simply prefer the gasoline-powered vehicles they are familiar with, and which are still cheaper to buy on average. They say consumers are unfamiliar with EV technology, and worry about how far electric vehicles can go on a charge and whether they will be able to find a charging station when needed.

Lutsey, of the International Council on Clean Transportation, acknowledges significant barriers remain to widespread adoption of EVs. The foremost remains cost, he says, with EVs selling at a price premium compared with gasoline-powered vehicles, but he says that could change soon: "Our analysis indicates that cost parity will happen before 2030."

The two largest U.S. automakers say they remain committed to producing electric vehicles. Ford is reportedly investing $11 billion to produce 20 new EV models by 2023, including the Mustang Mach-E, which brings the company's most venerated model name to an electric compact sport utility vehicle. General Motors says it will spend $20 billion in the next three years on EVs, with 60 percent of its research and development going to developing new EV technology and vehicles.[8]

Currently, one company, Tesla, sells 80 percent of all the EVs bought in the United States. The relative paucity of available electric vehicle models compared to gasoline models is one of the barriers to wider adoption, Lutsey says, which the investments by GM, Ford and other large automakers could address.

Vehicle range, once a limiting factor, is becoming less important as battery power and range increase, he says. Several models from different manufacturers can now go more than 200 miles on a single charge.[9]

But a lack of consumer knowledge about electric vehicles remains a problem, Lutsey says. "Some people don't know that EVs exist. People confuse EVs and hybrids," he says. "There are all these barriers in just understanding what the technology is."

Still, studies forecast U.S. EV sales will grow significantly in the coming decades, despite a temporary downturn associated with the coronavirus, and will account for as much as one-third of sales in the 2030s.[10] EVs already have taken off in parts of Europe, largely as a result of government policies encouraging adoption, says Lutsey. (*See Short Feature.*)

In the United States, he says, maintaining the zero-emission standards established by California is key to the future. "Taking that away," Lutsey says, "would be a massive deterrent to electric vehicles."

—*Reed Karaim*

---

[1] David Shepardson, "California looks to ramp up electric vehicle sales," *Reuters*, Jan. 26, 2018, https://tinyurl.com/yd375vpc; Skip Descant, "Reaching California's EV Goals Will Take Policy, Partnerships," *Government Technology*, March 6, 2020, https://tinyurl.com/y7pye5wc.

[2] *Ibid.*

[3] Rob Nikolewski, "California electric vehicle sales are up. But will we reach the 5 million goal by 2030?" *Los Angeles Times*, Dec. 1, 2019, https://tinyurl.com/ycfb5spx.

[4] Shepardson, *op. cit.*

[5] "What is ZEV?" Union of Concerned Scientists, Sept. 12, 2019, https://tinyurl.com/ybf9a9uc.

[6] Nikolewski, *op. cit.*

[7] "Electric Vehicle Sales: Facts and Figures," Edison Electric Institute, October 2019, https://tinyurl.com/y8ve634u.

[8] Henry Payne, "As GM and Ford ramp up for EVs for U.S., Europeans retreat," *The Detroit News*, March 11, 2020, https://tinyurl.com/yaceuqy3.

[9] Kelly Lin, "Longest-Range Electric Cars of 2020: 19 EVs That Can Go the Distance," *Motor Trend*, Dec. 23, 2019, https://tinyurl.com/y9hymuhw.

[10] "Electric Vehicle Outlook 2020, Executive Summary," *BloombergNEF*, May 19, 2020, https://tinyurl.com/ybzo4wmh.

---

said. In addition, the growth of hybrid and all-electric vehicles contributed to the gains.[64]

To allay concerns about the new standards, however, the administration had agreed to a midterm review. In the review, the Obama administration concluded the standards were still reasonable—but at the request of some automakers, the Trump administration reopened the review shortly after taking office.[65]

The reassessment was part of a larger review of environmental regulation, which Trump had criticized during the 2016 campaign as stifling business. The Trump administration initially floated the idea of freezing fuel efficiency standards, but some automakers opposed the proposal, causing a split within the industry.[66]

The administration then began considering the 1.5 percent annual increase they finalized this March, which provides automakers regulatory relief while still allowing the car companies to say they are steadily improving fuel efficiency and fighting climate change.[67]

CURRENT SITUATION
Final Rule

Trump's SAFE rule is scheduled to go into effect on June 29. The impact will not be felt immediately as automakers work on car designs years ahead. Court challenges could also derail the regulation.

But the final order, posted April 30 in the *Federal Register*, outlines the requirements automakers will be expected to meet if the rule stays in force. As was the case with the earlier CAFE and greenhouse gas emission standards established by the Obama administration, the requirements are partly "vehicle-footprint-based," which means they take the number of larger, less efficient vehicles automakers produce into account when calculating the requirements for each manufacturer's vehicle fleet. As the standards become more stringent each year, they move the entire vehicle fleet toward the required average.[68]

In concluding the new rule will save automakers money and lower new-car costs, NHTSA and EPA said they "believe their analysis of the final rule represents the best available science, evidence and methodologies for assessing the impacts of changes in CAFE and CO_2 emission standards."[69]

Even before the rule was formally announced, however, Carper, the senior Democrat on the Senate Environment and Public Works Committee, had asked the EPA's inspector general to open an investigation into how the rule was put together. Carper said he had received reports that EPA political appointees may have violated the law by avoiding the required steps associated with finalizing the rule, "including potential efforts to conceal documents that should eventually be made public."[70]

Carper is now asking the inspector general to expand its investigation based on new evidence he said shows his concerns were justified. "My previous request to you observed that an effort to conceal further interagency disagreement could result in the concealment of embarrassing and legally risky information related to flaws in the final rule," the senator wrote to the inspector general. "I have learned that this is exactly what has occurred."[71]

Court Action

At least four different lawsuits are pending concerning fuel efficiency standards and the Trump administration's decision to revoke California's authority to set stiffer rules.

The most recent is the suit filed by 23 states, four cities and the District of Columbia on May 27, 2020, challenging the Trump administration's plan to relax the fuel efficiency requirements established by the Obama administration through Trump's SAFE rule.[72]

The suit, filed in the U.S. Court of Appeals for the District of Columbia Circuit, contends the Trump rule violates the Clean Air Act as well as procedures for rulemaking established in the Administrative Procedure Act.[73] "The EPA and NHTSA improperly and unlawfully relied on an analysis riddled with errors, omissions and unfounded assumptions in an attempt to justify their desired result," said California Attorney General Xavier Becerra when announcing the lawsuit.[74]

NHTSA did not comment on the lawsuit, while the EPA restated earlier comments that its rule "provides a sensible, single national program that strikes the right regulatory balance, protects our environment and sets reasonable targets for the auto industry, while supporting our economy and the safety of American families."[75]

The suit will not be heard until 2021, says Craig Segall, assistant chief counsel at the California Air Resources Board. The case is expected to end up before the U.S. Supreme Court. "There's no world in which this is resolved before the election," says Segall.

Twelve environmental and consumer groups are also suing the administration over the SAFE rules based on largely the same contentions. They include the Sierra Club, the Natural Resources Defense Council, the Union of Concerned Scientists and the Consumer Federation of America.[76]

In a separate action filed last year, California, 23 other states and the cities of Los Angeles and New York are suing to overturn the administration's decision to revoke California's authority to set its own emission standards. The suit contends NHTSA's decision exceeds the authority granted the agency by Congress and is based on arguments rejected by the courts in the past.[77]

Segall says final arguments are expected before the Court of Appeals for the District of Columbia Circuit sometime after October.

Finally, the Competitive Enterprise Institute, the libertarian think tank, announced in May it is suing the administration because it did not roll back the fuel efficiency standards far enough. The institute contends the government's analysis indicates the public would benefit if the standards were weakened further or frozen entirely.[78]

The Alliance for Automotive Innovation, a newly formed group that represents all the major automobile manufacturers, has announced it will oppose the Competitive Enterprise Institute lawsuit, saying automakers support continued improvements in the standards.[79] However, several members of the alliance are supporting the Trump administration in the lawsuit over whether California has the right to set stricter emission and fuel efficiency standards.[80]

California's Separate Deal

Volvo is joining four other major automakers who have struck a separate deal with California to follow stricter fuel efficiency and emission standards than those in the Trump SAFE rule.[81]

Volkswagen, Ford, BMW and Honda earlier agreed to meet higher standards negotiated with the state. The deal negotiated between the state and the companies stretches out the original schedule in the Obama rules by one year to 2026 and lowers the required annual reduction in greenhouse gas emissions from 4.7 percent to 3.7 percent, says Cliff, the deputy executive officer of the California Air Resources Board. The agreement "basically does what the Obama standards would have done in four years in five," he says.

The agreement could boost the average fuel efficiency of an automaker's fleet to about 50 mpg by 2026, below the Obama standard's goal of 54.5 mpg but significantly higher than the 40 mph in Trump's SAFE rule.[82]

Cliff says the state plans to go ahead with its new standards even if it loses the suit to overturn the SAFE rule in court. "The outcome of any of this litigation is really not important for the purpose of this agreement," he says. "The automakers are agreeing to this outcome no matter what happens."

The same is true if California loses its other lawsuit against the Trump administration in which it seeks to regain authority to set its own emission standards. "These are fairly robust agreements," which would still be in force, says Segall.

Trump lashed out at the original four automakers who reached an agreement with California, dismissing them as "politically correct" and calling their leaders "Foolish executives!" He reiterated administration claims that the SAFE rule would lead to safer, cheaper cars with very little impact on the environment.[83]

In a joint statement, the four automakers said the deal was driven by a need for the predictability and reduced costs that come with embracing one standard and a wish to be good environmental stewards.[84]

Legislative and Administrative Policy

The Clean and Efficient Cars Act of 2019, a bill sponsored by 75 House Democrats that would restore the Obama fuel efficiency rules, is one of several pieces of legislation introduced in Congress that would require the government to support cleaner, more efficient vehicles.[85]

They include bipartisan legislation in the House and Senate called the Driving America Forward Act. The measure would extend and restore tax credits for electric vehicle purchases and encourage vehicles fueled by hydrogen fuel cells, a technology that releases only water vapor into the air.[86] The electric vehicle credit, which can reach $7,500 for some vehicles, currently phases out as a manufacturer sells 200,000 electric vehicles.[87] For example, the federal tax credit for Tesla, manufacturer of the most popular U.S. electric vehicle models, expired at the start of this year.[88]

Rep. Alexandria Ocasio-Cortez, D-N.Y., announces the introduction of the Green New Deal legislation to address climate change in 2019, joined by co-sponsor Sen. Ed Markey, D-Mass. (right) and other lawmakers.

AT ISSUE:

Will Trump's fuel efficiency standards harm efforts to contain climate change?

YES **Dan Becker**
Director, Safe Climate Transport Campaign, Center for Biological Diversity

James Gerstenzang
Editorial Director, Safe Climate Transport Campaign, Center for Biological Diversity

Written for *CQ Researcher*, June 2020

NO **Marlo Lewis**
Senior Fellow in Energy and Environmental Policy, Competitive Enterprise Institute

Written for *CQ Researcher*, June 2020

President Trump's rollback of clean-car rules halts the biggest single step any nation has taken to cut global warming pollution. The rules took effect in 2012 and would deliver a new-car fleet in 2025 that averages 37 mpg, while cutting auto emissions in half. By trashing the rules, the president is leaving the world at far greater risk of the climate catastrophes we are already witnessing.

Before Trump gutted them, the rules not only reduced pollution—they were saving Americans hundreds of billions of dollars at the pump. Even after paying for the gasoline-saving improvements—more-efficient transmissions and safe, lightweight materials—consumers would come out $4,000 to $6,000 ahead because their cars would need less fuel.

Each gallon of gasoline we burn pumps 25 pounds of carbon dioxide (CO_2), the primary global warming pollutant, into the atmosphere. The stringent standards were designed to prevent release of 6 billion tons of CO_2 by eliminating our need for 12 billion barrels of oil.

CO_2 creates an invisible heat-trapping blanket close to Earth. The energy from that heat is making tropical storms and wildfires more frequent and fierce. The heat is helping spread tropical diseases to once-temperate climates and is making increasing swaths of the globe unfit for human habitation.

Ignoring science, Trump is ending widely popular rules that would improve the cars we drive for years to come and keep as much CO_2 out of the atmosphere as shutting all U.S. coal-fired power plants for more than a year.

By adopting these responsible rules, the United States had signaled it was committed to tackling the planet's biggest environmental threat—rather than burying its head in the warming sand.

Trying to justify the rollback, the Trump administration falsely claimed that stronger rules would make us less safe on the road. As we wrote in *The New York Times*:

"This is auto mechanics, not rocket science. Ford proved that efficiency and safety go hand in hand when it converted the steel bodies of its F-150 pickups to aluminum. It lopped 700 pounds from America's best-selling model and helped lift mileage by 4 mpg. The [government] upgraded the truck to a five star safety rating."

The Trump administration's Safer Affordable Fuel-Efficient (SAFE) Vehicles rule is deregulatory compared to the 2012 Obama administration rule it replaces. The SAFE rule increases the stringency of corporate average fuel economy (CAFE) standards by 1.5 percent annually. If still in effect today, the 2012 rule would increase regulatory stringency by 5 percent annually.

California and its allies tout the 2012 rule as a "climate solution" and slam the SAFE rule as a planet wrecker. In fact, both rules are irrelevant to the climate.

Under the SAFE rule, national gasoline consumption and the associated carbon dioxide (CO_2) emissions will decline by 32 percent during 2020-50, whereas consumption and emissions would decline by 43 percent under the 2012 rule. Will the SAFE rule's slower rate of decline doom humanity to planetary ruin? Will future generations pay a terrible price for the Trump agencies' deregulatory ambitions? No.

Compared to the 2012 rule, the SAFE rule will, in 2100, increase CO_2 concentrations by 0.66 parts per million, global average temperatures by 0.003 of a degree Celsius, and sea levels by 0.06 centimeters—about two-hundredths of an inch. Those numbers come from the Environmental Protection Agency's standard climate policy calculator, a model called MAGICC.

Climate sensitivity—the long-term change in global average surface temperature after a doubling of atmospheric CO_2 concentration—is a key variable in climate assessments. The Intergovernmental Panel on Climate Change estimates that climate sensitivity is "likely in the range of 1.5 degrees-4.5 degrees Celsius."

Accordingly, the Trump agencies used sensitivities of 1.5 to 4.5 degrees Celsius and 6.0 degrees Celsius to estimate the SAFE rule's potential climate effects. Even under the least stringent regulatory option considered (freezing CAFE standards at model year 2020 levels) and assuming the highest sensitivity (6.0 degrees Celsius), the global mean surface temperature in 2100 is only 0.006 of a degree Celsius higher than under the 2012 rule.

Six-thousandths of a degree Celsius is 13 times smaller than the margin of error for measuring changes in annual average global temperatures. That tiny temperature increase 80 years from now would have no discernible impact on weather patterns, crop yields, species habitat or any other environmental condition people care about.

> Yet while touting "safety," the administration ignored deadly air pollution from refineries needed to keep more gas guzzlers on the road. This will kill an estimated 18,000 people.
> To justify its attack, the Trump administration has fabricated a false conflict between safe cars and a safe climate. Americans can and must have both.

> The SAFE rule's alleged evisceration of "critical climate protections" is political theater. In contrast, the rule's reduction in vehicle ownership costs is real. By helping middle-income families afford new, safer, more fuel-efficient vehicles, the SAFE rule will benefit people more than the rule it replaces.

The most high-profile piece of environmental legislation that concerns vehicle emissions is the Green New Deal, which lays out a multiyear roadmap for tackling the causes of climate change and includes investing in electric vehicles. The Green New Deal is often mischaracterized as mandating changes, but the bill that was introduced last year by Rep. Alexandria Ocasio-Cortez, D-N.Y., and Sen. Ed Markey, D-Mass., is a nonbinding resolution, so its provisions would not become law without further legislative action.[89]

Congressional observers say none of this legislation is likely to become law in this congressional session given the bitter divisions between the two political parties over the need to address climate change, a phenomenon about which many Republicans are skeptical. Instead, the direction of fuel efficiency and emissions policy is likely to continue to be set by regulatory action by the executive branch, which will be determined by the upcoming presidential election.

The Trump campaign website, as of early June, did not include a section outlining plans to address vehicle emissions or climate change. But in an "Energy and Environment" section listing Trump's achievements, it notes that the administration has "rescinded many costly Obama-era regulations."[90]

Biden, the presumptive Democratic nominee, has called the Green New Deal "a crucial framework for meeting the climate challenges we face."[91] His environmental plan, which his campaign site calls "a Clean Energy Revolution," includes several proposals to dramatically reduce vehicle emissions, with the goal of getting to a 100 percent clean energy economy by 2050.[92]

Those plans include developing new fuel economy standards that not only reverse the Trump SAFE plan but go "beyond what the Obama-Biden administration put in place" and are aimed at ensuring 100 percent of new sales for light- and medium-duty vehicles will be electrified.

Biden also promises to "work with our nation's governors and mayors to support the deployment of more than 500,000 new public charging outlets by the end of 2030." In addition, his administration would restore the "full electric vehicle tax credit to incentivize the purchase of these vehicles."[93]

OUTLOOK
An Inevitable Change?

With stark differences between Biden and Trump toward climate change and federal regulation, analysts say the 2020 election obviously will play a huge role in determining the direction of fuel emissions and efficiency policy over the next four years.

Still, several advocates of stronger policies believe a longer-term shift to cleaner, even zero-emission vehicles is inevitable. The Safe Climate Transport Campaign's Becker says the need for U.S. automakers to compete globally—particularly in China, which is making a commitment to shift to electric vehicles—along with gasoline prices he expects to rise again, mean that vehicles will be much cleaner and burn much less—or no—gasoline in the next decade. "I think we're on a one-way street toward cleaner, more efficient vehicles after the detour and stall of the Trump administration is behind us," he says.

But Smith, at the Center for Automotive Research, says there is a good chance the U.S. market goes its own way and, when it comes to electric vehicles and fuel efficiency, the United States could become "a technology backwater. We already are in some ways."

That would simply reflect the desire of American consumers for larger, less fuel-efficient vehicles, says Smith. "The reality is the markets are different and they're going to be different for a long time.... The U.S. consumer, at least until there's a real change in beliefs on greenhouse gases, which is slowly happening, we're not going to value [greenhouse gases] as much as Europe does," he says. "We're not going to value [a government-established] industrial policy as much as China does. They're going to be different models."

UCLA's Carlson sees policy at the state level, supported by several automakers, continuing to move the United States toward a zero-emissions future. "I do think the push to electrify the transportation sector is going to continue," she says. "We're seeing investments in infrastructure, and I don't think California will back away."

Electric vehicles, whether purely electric or plug-in hybrids that also burn gasoline, accounted for less than 3 percent of automobile sales last year, but surveys show that nearly a third of Americans now say they would consider an electric vehicle for their next purchase.[94]

The Coalition for Clean Air's Magavern believes that sentiment means the transportation industry could be on the verge of a dramatic shift. "In 10 years we'll have seen the transition really pick up steam and, at that point, it will appear inevitable that we'll be going to fully electric vehicles," he says.

Cliff, at the California Air Resources Board, says the investments automakers are making in the next generation of zero-emission vehicles to respond to global concerns about climate change have created a momentum within the industry that shifts in U.S. federal regulations cannot derail. "There's really no going back at this point," he says.

But other experts say the American public, which has valued style, convenience and price more than environmental considerations, does not share the same urgency. McCarthy, the author and historian, believes concern about climate change has become more dominant in recent years, but the attitudes that govern vehicle purchases are likely to remain largely the same, with fuel efficiency or emissions not the primary concern for many buyers.

"Consumers quite understandably have other priorities than solving world problems when buying automobiles," McCarthy says. "You're really talking about having to transform an entire culture, how you think about the world, what we value in the world and how we should value it. That's a pretty big step."

NOTES

1. Coral Davenport, "Trump Calls New Fuel Economy Rule a Boon. Some Experts See Steep Costs," *The New York Times*, March 31, 2020, https://tinyurl.com/rvjbasw.

2. Rebecca Beitsch, "States, green groups sue Trump over rollback of Obama fuel efficiency regulations," *The Hill*, May 27, 2020, https://tinyurl.com/yd2k5w8g.

3. "California and 22 other states take Trump Administration to court over vehicle emissions rollback," California Air Resources Board, May 27, 2020, https://tinyurl.com/ydbuswdy.

4. "Attorney General Becerra Files Lawsuit Against EPA for Attacking California's Advanced Clean Air Standards," State of California Department of Justice, Nov. 15, 2019, https://tinyurl.com/y7p7g7q8.

5. Davenport, *op. cit.*; David Shepardson, "U.S. to finalize fuel efficiency rewrite through 2026: sources," *Reuters*, March 30, 2020, https://tinyurl.com/y857alev.

6. David Shepardson and Ben Klayman, "California, four automakers defy Trump, agree to tighten emission rules," *Reuters*, July 25, 2019, https://tinyurl.com/y5v8u2ol.

7. "Energy and Environment, President Donald J. Trump achievements," Donald Trump for President, accessed June 11, 2020, https://tinyurl.com/uzjtkmk.

8. "Climate: Joe's Plan for a Clean Energy Revolution and Environmental Justice," Joebiden.com, accessed June 11, 2020, https://tinyurl.com/y65rc9fr.

9. "U.S. DOT and EPA Put Safety and American Families First with Final Rule on Fuel Economy Standards," National Highway Traffic Safety Administration, March 31, 2020, https://tinyurl.com/yas28cx4.

10. "California and 22 other states take Trump Administration to court over vehicle emissions rollback," op. cit.

11. Rebecca Beitsch, "New documents show EPA rolled back mileage standards despite staff, WH concerns," The Hill, May 20, 2020, https://tinyurl.com/yauwkpte.

12. Ibid.

13. "U.S. DOT and EPA Put Safety and American Families First with Final Rule on Fuel Economy Standards," op. cit.

14. Ann Carlson, "Los Angeles Air Quality in the Time of Covid-19," LegalPlanet, April 21, 2020, https://tinyurl.com/ybvfsgha.

15. "History," California Air Resources Board, 2020, https://tinyurl.com/ycs3awya.

16. Ibid.; "Vehicle Emissions California Waivers and Authorizations," U.S. Environmental Protection Agency, Feb. 20, 2020, https://tinyurl.com/ycgt4ntm.

17. Kevin Liptak and Gregory Wallace, "Trump revokes waiver for California to set higher auto emission standards," CNN, Sept. 18, 2019, https://tinyurl.com/yyxm2yxb.

18. Dino Grandoni and Juliet Eilperin, "California sues Trump administration over revoking authority to limit car pollution," The Washington Post, Sept. 20, 2019, https://tinyurl.com/y3ozv9zu.

19. "Fast Facts on Transportation Greenhouse Gas Emissions," U.S. Environmental Protection Agency, July 16, 2019, https://tinyurl.com/y2vqneto.

20. Ibid.

21. "U.S. Vehicle Registration Statistics," Hedges & Company, 2020, https://tinyurl.com/ycnkclv4.

22. "Greenhouse Gas Emissions from a Typical Passenger Vehicle," U.S. Environmental Protection Agency, May 10, 2018, https://tinyurl.com/yad7qmts.

23. "Obama Administration Finalizes Historic 54.5 MPG Fuel Efficiency Standards," The White House, Aug. 28, 2012, https://tinyurl.com/r5jej4u.

24. Ibid.

25. "A Brief History of U.S. Fuel Efficiency Standards," Union of Concerned Scientists, Dec. 6, 2017, https://tinyurl.com/y89wtz6q.

26. "Smog, Soot and Other Air Pollution from Transportation," U.S. Environmental Protection Agency, March 18, 2019, https://tinyurl.com/y7zhkty4.

27. "The Safer Affordable Fuel-Efficient (SAFE) Vehicles Rule Model Year 2021-2026 Passenger Cars and Light Trucks, Final Environmental Impact Statement," National Highway Traffic Safety Administration, March 2020, https://tinyurl.com/ydaaooql.

28. Antonio M. Bento, "Written Testimony," U.S. House Committee on Oversight and Reform, Subcommittee on Environment, Oct. 29, 2019, https://tinyurl.com/ych8xhy9.

29. Jessica McDonald, "The Facts on Fuel Economy Standards," Factcheck.org, May 3, 2019, https://tinyurl.com/yxrzjvb7.

30. Michael Wayland, "Ford, UAW voice opposition to freezing fuel economy standards," Automotive News, Sept. 25, 2018, https://tinyurl.com/y9u3q97c.

31. Michael Wayland, "Coronavirus pandemic tanks U.S. auto sales in April," CNBC, May 1, 2020, https://tinyurl.com/y8xnqa8l.

32. "Average New-Vehicle Prices Up 3.5% Year-Over-Year in January 2020 on Sales Mix, According to Kelley Blue Book," PR Newswire, Feb. 18, 2020, https://tinyurl.com/y7rspfk6.

33. Coral Davenport, "U.S. to Announce Rollback of Auto Pollution Rules, a Key Effort to Fight Climate Change," The New York Times, March 30, 2020, https://tinyurl.com/yx5j28bg.

34. "Obama Administration Finalizes Historic 54.5 MPG Fuel Efficiency Standards," op. cit.

35. Simon Constable, "Detroit's Headache: Car Buyers Don't Seem to Care About Fuel Efficiency," Forbes, June 10, 2019, https://tinyurl.com/ydbqo6tj.

36. "New Study Finds Consumers Are Willing to Pay More for Fuel Economy as Auto Regulators Look to Roll Back Efficiency Standards," Consumer Reports, June 12, 2018, https://tinyurl.com/y7cnlzpm.

37. "NADA Supports Right-Sizing Fuel Economy Standards for Current Market Realities," National Automobile Dealers Association, March 31, 2020, https://tinyurl.com/yd44s89u.

38. Martin Melosi, "The Automobile and the Environment in American History," Automobile in American Life and Society, 2010, https://tinyurl.com/ycjmc2o5.

39. "Ford Motor Company unveils the Model T," History, 2020, https://tinyurl.com/qquqmjy.

40. "State Motor Vehicle Registrations by Years, 1900-1995," U.S. Department of Transportation Federal Highway Administration, https://tinyurl.com/ycxl9xz3.

41. Meredith Bennett-Smith, "From Model T to Prius: 13 big moments in fuel efficiency history," The Christian Science Monitor, March 7, 2012, https://tinyurl.com/y9c7yk78.

42. "Table 2.8—Motor Vehicle Mileage, Fuel Consumption, and Fuel Economy, 1949-2010," U.S. Energy Information Administration, Sept. 27, 2012, https://tinyurl.com/ya3pzyr7.

43. "History," California Air Resources Board, op. cit.

44. Ibid.

45. Ibid.

46. "Fifty Years of Clearing the Skies," CalTech, April 25, 2013, https://tinyurl.com/ybjgvqcd.

47. "History," California Air Resources Board, op. cit.

48. "Evolution of the Clean Air Act," U.S. Environmental Protection Agency, Jan. 3, 2017, https://tinyurl.com/ydhc27nt.

49. "History," California Air Resources Board, op. cit.

50. "Table 2.8—Motor Vehicle Mileage, Fuel Consumption, and Fuel Economy, 1949-2010," op. cit.

51. "Fact #915: March 7, 2016 Average Historical Annual Gasoline Pump Price, 1929-2015," Office of Energy Efficiency and Renewable Energy, Energy.gov., March 7, 2016, https://tinyurl.com/y6gdo8zk.

52. "Table 5.1a—Petroleum and Other Liquids Overview, Selected Years, 1949-2011," U.S. Energy Information Administration, Annual Energy Review, 2011, https://tinyurl.com/yd2brk2l.

53. "Energy Crisis (1970s)," History, Aug. 21, 2018, https://tinyurl.com/y7ekxmyx.

54. Philip Shabecoff, "Ford Signs Bill on Energy that Ends Policy Impasse and Cuts Crude Oil Prices," The New York Times, Dec. 23, 1975, https://tinyurl.com/ycjxybxl.

55. "History of Fuel Economy—One Decade of Innovation, Two Decades of Inaction," The Pew Environment Group, April 2011, https://tinyurl.com/y7eokqu7.

56. Bob Sorokanich, "30 Years Ago Today, Chrysler Invented the Minivan, And Changed History," Gizmodo, Nov. 2, 2013, https://tinyurl.com/y88ow4um.

57. "History of Fuel Economy—One Decade of Innovation, Two Decades of Inaction," op. cit.

58. "Timeline of Major Accomplishments in Transportation, Air Pollution and Climate Change," U.S. Environmental Protection Agency, Jan. 10, 2017, https://tinyurl.com/ybv4ocht.

59. "Zero-Emission Vehicle Program," California Air Resources Board, 2020, https://tinyurl.com/ycxyhyxy.

60. John M. Broder, "Obama to Toughen Rules on Emissions and Mileage," The New York Times, May 18, 2009, https://tinyurl.com/yam3er9b.

61. Margo T. Oge, "Driving the Future: Combating Climate Change with Cleaner, Smarter Cars," Arcade, 2015, Kindle edition, location 2613.

62. "The 2019 EPA Automotive Trends Report, Executive Summary," U.S. Environmental Protection Agency, March 2020, https://tinyurl.com/y9fpf8ss.

63. Ibid.

64. Ibid.

65. Steven Overly and Juliet Eilperin, "President Trump to reopen review of Obama-era fuel economy standards," The Washington Post, March 13, 2017, https://tinyurl.com/zazs4fz.

66. Rebecca Beitsch, "Trump administration backing off plans to freeze fuel economy: WSJ," The Hill,

Oct. 31, 2019, https://tinyurl.com/yc4gvg6b; Wayland, "Ford, UAW voice opposition to freezing fuel economy standards," *op. cit.*

67. *Ibid.*

68. "A Rule by the Environmental Protection Agency and the National Highway Traffic Safety Administration on 04/30/2020," *Federal Register*, April 30, 2020, https://tinyurl.com/ya3tsz8x.

69. *Ibid.*

70. "After Reviewing New Documents, Carper Urges Expansion of EPA Inspector General Investigation into the SAFE Vehicles Rule," U.S. Senate Committee on Environment and Public Works, May 19, 2020, https://tinyurl.com/yd3tutow.

71. *Ibid.*

72. Jace Lington, "Group of states and cities sue Trump administration over rollback of Obama administration fuel efficiency standards," Ballotpedia News, June 2, 2020, https://tinyurl.com/ycjx9t3o.

73. *Ibid.*

74. "Attorney General Becerra Files Lawsuit Challenging Trump Administration's Reckless Rollback of America's Clean Car Standards," State of California Department of Justice, May 27, 2020, https://tinyurl.com/y9ybz3sq.

75. Beitsch, "States, green groups sue Trump over rollback of Obama fuel efficiency regulations," *op. cit.*

76. "Trump Administration Sued for Gutting Clean Car Standards," Natural Resources Defense Council, May 27, 2020, https://tinyurl.com/y93nbq9f.

77. "Attorney General Becerra Files Lawsuit Challenging Trump Administration's Attempt to Trample California's Authority to Maintain Longstanding Clean Car Standards," State of California Department of Justice, Sept. 20, 2019, https://tinyurl.com/y9hh9bv2.

78. Rebeca Beitsch, "Conservative group sues administration, arguing rollback of Obama mileage rule wasn't aggressive enough," *The Hill*, May 1, 2020, https://tinyurl.com/y82lt98j.

79. "Auto Innovators Intervenes in Fuel Economy Litigation," Alliance for Automotive Innovation, May 22, 2020, https://tinyurl.com/ybwu6pvp.

80. Tom Krisher and Ellen Knickmeyer, "Automakers side with Trump in legal fight with California," *The Associated Press*, Oct. 29, 2019, https://tinyurl.com/y843ktp7.

81. Bradley Berman, "Volvo joins automakers siding with California on emissions, opposing Trump administration," electrek, April 7, 2020, https://tinyurl.com/vko97bo.

82. Brakkton Booker and Jennifer Ludden, "Trump Administration Challenges California And Automakers On Fuel Economy," *NPR*, Sept. 6, 2019, https://tinyurl.com/y662orgk.

83. "Trump Lashes Out After Automakers Agree to California's Standards," *Bloomberg/IndustryWeek*, Aug. 21, 2019, https://tinyurl.com/yc7ge6ub.

84. Juliet Eilperin and Brady Dennis, "Major automakers strike climate deal with California, rebuffing Trump on proposed mileage freeze," *The Washington Post*, July 25, 2019, https://tinyurl.com/yyho54u8.

85. "Matsui Introduces Legislation that Pushes Back on the Trump Administration Attempts to Roll Back the Fuel Economy and Vehicle Emissions Standards," press release, Office of Rep. Doris Matsui, Feb. 5, 2019, https://tinyurl.com/yajb8rab.

86. "Stabenow, Alexander, Peters, Collins, Kildee Introduce Bipartisan Bill to Expand Electric Vehicle and Hydrogen Fuel Cell Tax Credits," press release, Office of Sen. Debbie Stabenow, April 10, 2019, https://tinyurl.com/yaha29fy.

87. "Federal Tax Credits for New All-Electric and Plug-in Hybrid Vehicles," U.S. Department of Energy, Office of Energy Efficiency and Renewable Energy, May 14, 2020, https://tinyurl.com/nba8gs2.

88. Eric Walz, "Tesla is Without the Federal EV Tax Credit for the First Time Since the Introduction of the Model S in 2012," *FutureCar*, Jan. 2, 2020, https://tinyurl.com/yafzjn92.

89. Lisa Friedman, "What Is the Green New Deal? A Climate Proposal, Explained," *The New York Times*, Feb. 21, 2019, https://tinyurl.com/y4kw8pmz.

90. "Energy and Environment, President Donald J. Trump Achievements," Donald Trump for President, *op. cit.*
91. "Climate: Joe's Plan for a Clean Energy Revolution and Environmental Justice," Joebiden.com, *op. cit.*
92. *Ibid.*
93. *Ibid.*
94. "Electric Vehicle Sales: Facts and Figures," Edison Electric Institute, October 2019, https://tinyurl.com/y8ve634u; "New Survey Shows Strong Support for Electric Vehicles Across Economic Spectrum," Union of Concerned Scientists, July 18, 2019, https://tinyurl.com/ya5vkatn.

BIBLIOGRAPHY
Books

Doyle, Jack, *Taken for a Ride: Detroit's Big Three and the Politics of Pollution,* **Four Walls Eight Windows, 2000.**
A former analyst with the Environmental Policy Institute, a Washington think tank, documents a 50-year history of General Motors, Ford and Chrysler resisting anti-pollution technology.

Gardiner, Beth, *Choked: Life and Breath in the Age of Air Pollution,* **University of Chicago Press, 2019.**
A journalist examines air pollution and the toll it takes on human health around the world, including pollution from automobiles, and the efforts underway to get to a future of zero-emission vehicles.

McCarthy, Tom, *Auto Mania: Cars, Consumers, and the Environment,* **Yale University Press, 2007.**
A historian looks at America's love affair with the car, particularly large, less fuel-efficient vehicles, and how that and the efforts of automakers have made effective environmental regulation of automobiles difficult.

Oge, Margo T., *Driving the Future: Combating Climate Change with Cleaner, Smarter Cars,* **Arcade, 2015.**
A former director of the federal Office of Transportation and Air Quality recounts the story behind the Obama administration's 2012 deal with automakers to double vehicle fuel efficiency.

Articles

Dennis, Brady, and Juliet Eilperin, "GM, Toyota and Chrysler side with White House in fight over California fuel standards, exposing auto industry split," *The Washington Post,* **Oct. 28, 2019, https://tinyurl.com/y4hv3cku.**
A group of automobile manufacturers, including General Motors and Toyota, backed the Trump administration's effort to restrict California's authority to set stricter vehicle emission standards, while other carmakers, including Ford and Volkswagen, agreed to follow California's standards.

Meyer, Robinson, "Trump's New Auto Rollback Is an Economic Disaster," *The Atlantic,* **April 13, 2020, https://tinyurl.com/ybtyfgqu.**
According to the government's own analysis, the Trump administration's fuel efficiency rollback will not create auto industry jobs as the president has stated, but instead will eliminate nearly 13,500 jobs.

Shepardson, David, "Trump finalizes rollback of Obama-era vehicle fuel efficiency standards," *Reuters,* **March 31, 2020, https://tinyurl.com/yak2rg6f.**
The Trump administration reduced the annual requirement for automakers to improve the fuel efficiency of their vehicle fleets from 5 percent to 1.5 percent through 2026, a move it said will cut the cost of a car; critics said the change will lead to more harmful vehicle emissions.

Tabuchi, Hiroko, "States Sue to Block Trump From Weakening Fuel Economy Rules," *The New York Times,* **May 27, 2020, https://tinyurl.com/ybyvwvsq.**
Twenty-three states, led by California, are suing the Trump administration over its new vehicle fuel efficiency standards, arguing the move is based on bad science.

Reports and Studies

"Final Regulatory Impact Analysis, The Safer Affordable Fuel-Efficient (SAFE) Vehicles Rule for Model Year 2021-2026 Passenger Cars and Light Trucks," National Highway Traffic Safety Administration and the Environmental Protection Agency, March 2020, https://tinyurl.com/yb4cjxyh.
Two federal agencies' analysis of the Trump administration's rollback of vehicle fuel efficiency standards

concludes that the benefits to consumers and the auto industry in reduced costs outweigh the increased emissions of greenhouse gases and pollutants.

Harto, Chris, Shannon Baker-Branstetter and Jamie Hall, "The Un-SAFE Rule: How a Fuel-Economy Rollback Costs Americans Billions in Fuel Savings and Does Not Improve Safety," *Consumer Reports*, **August 2019, https://tinyurl.com/yb54awmc.**
A study by a consumer advocacy organization finds that the administration's pullback on fuel efficiency standards will not improve vehicle safety and will cost consumers billions in extra costs at the gas pump through increased consumption.

Reidmiller, David, *et al.*, **"Fourth National Climate Assessment Volume II: Impacts, Risks, and Adaptation in the United States," U.S. Global Change Research Program, 2018, https://tinyurl.com/y93ha5f5.**
The latest U.S. government assessment of climate change predicts increasingly severe consequences for the nation, including heat waves, reduced crop yields, flooding, severe storms and hundreds of billions of dollars in economic damage.

Smith, Brett, "Fuel Economy and Greenhouse Gas Regulation in the United States: Change is Coming," Center for Automotive Research, March 19, 2019, https://tinyurl.com/ydxkajt5.
The director of propulsion technologies and energy infrastructure at the Center for Automotive Research examines Trump's fuel efficiency rule and the possible outcomes from the new standard.

THE NEXT STEP
Electric Vehicles

Geman, Ben, "Tesla says air quality jumps from coronavirus lockdowns make case for electric vehicles," *Axios*, **June 9, 2020, https://tinyurl.com/y8lko4e5.**
The coronavirus shutdowns show how much air quality would improve if electric cars replaced gasoline-powered vehicles, Tesla argues.

"A Million-Mile Battery From China Could Power Your Electric Car," *Bloomberg*, **June 7, 2020, https://tinyurl.com/y7v4pnoe.**
A Chinese company that produces batteries for Tesla and Volkswagen electric cars has developed a battery that lasts for 16 years and 1.24 million miles.

Stevens, Pippa, "Meet Nikola, the speculative electric vehicle stock that traders believe is as valuable as Ford," *CNBC*, **June 9, 2020, https://tinyurl.com/yadbvogn.**
An electric vehicle company that has not generated any revenue currently has about the same market capitalization as Ford.

Emissions During the Pandemic

Cohan, Daniel, "The COVID-19 shutdown leaves the air cleaner, but it isn't getting cooler," *MarketWatch*, **May 11, 2020, https://tinyurl.com/ybe89ks6.**
Air quality is improving during the COVID-19 shutdowns because of falling carbon emissions, but temperatures will continue to rise until the planet reaches net-zero emissions, according to an atmospheric scientist.

Fox, Alex, "Carbon Emissions Are Decreasing During the Pandemic but Could Bounce Back Fast," *Smithsonian Magazine*, **May 22, 2020, https://tinyurl.com/ybh57f9w.**
At the height of the coronavirus shutdowns in April, global carbon emissions dropped 17 percent year-over-year, but quickly began to rebound.

Plumer, Brad, and Nadja Popovich, "Traffic and Pollution Plummet as U.S. Cities Shut Down for Coronavirus," *The New York Times*, **March 22, 2020, https://tinyurl.com/tebno2n.**
Satellites detected significant declines in emissions in metropolitan areas during the shutdowns.

Environmental Protection Agency

Beitsch, Rebecca, "House Oversight seeks docs from oil giant Marathon after Trump mileage rollback," *The Hill*, **May 28, 2020, https://tinyurl.com/y7hyaw6n.**
The Democratic-led House Oversight and Reform Committee asked Marathon Petroleum for documents regarding meetings with Environmental Protection Agency (EPA) officials and the U.S. Department of Transportation after the Trump administration revised Obama-era fuel efficiency regulations.

Daly, Matthew, "Democrats decry 'pandemic of pollution' under Trump's EPA," *The Associated Press*, May 20, 2020, https://tinyurl.com/y95rlqog.
Sen. Ed Markey, D-Mass., said the Trump administration has turned the EPA into "Every Polluter's Ally"—a charge agency Administrator Andrew Wheeler denied.

Eilperin, Juliet, and Brady Dennis, "EPA staff warned that mileage rollbacks had flaws. Trump officials ignored them," *The Washington Post*, May 19, 2020, https://tinyurl.com/ybm45tts.
Government documents show that political appointees sidelined EPA officials when the EPA officials questioned revised mileage standards.

New Rules

Beitsch, Rebecca, "Automakers fight effort to freeze fuel efficiency standards," *The Hill*, May 22, 2020, https://tinyurl.com/y8t9ddwo.
A conservative organization has filed suit arguing that the Trump administration's fuel efficiency standards are actually too ambitious—but a group of automakers is opposing the lawsuit.

Chuang, Tamara, "Colorado, Denver join 25 other cities and states in suing EPA for relaxing clean-car rule," *The Colorado Sun*, May 27, 2020, https://tinyurl.com/yb6fm9na.
Concerned that lower clean-car standards could undercut the state's zero-emissions policy, Colorado joined a lawsuit against the Environmental Protection Agency.

Shaw, Adam, "Trump administration eases Obama-era regs on vehicle fuel economy," *Fox News*, March 31, 2020, https://tinyurl.com/ybvpequn.
Trump administration officials argue the new fuel efficiency rules will save hundreds of lives and balance environmental concerns with affordability, but Democrats disagree.

For More Information

Alliance for Automotive Innovation, 1050 K St., N.W., Suite 650, Washington, DC 20001; 202-326-5500; autosinnovate.org. Advocacy group that represents the auto industry, including its suppliers.

American Energy Alliance, 1155 15th St., N.W., Suite 900, Washington, DC 20005; 202-621-2940; americanenergyalliance.org. Alliance that works to enlist consumers to support anti-regulatory, free market policies regarding U.S. energy and fuels.

California Air Resources Board, 1001 I St., Sacramento, CA 95814; 800-242-4450; https://ww2.arb.ca.gov. State agency charged with protecting Californians from the harmful effects of air pollution and developing programs to fight climate change.

Competitive Enterprise Institute, 1310 L St., N.W., 7th Floor, Washington, DC 20005; 202-331-1010; cei.org. Libertarian think tank that opposes government actions to limit climate change, including regulation of greenhouse gas emissions.

Environmental Protection Agency, 1200 Pennsylvania Ave., N.W., Washington, DC 20460; 202-564-4700; epa.gov. Federal agency whose mission is to ensure that Americans have access to clean air, water and land.

International Council on Clean Transportation, 1500 K St., N.W., Suite 650, Washington, DC 20005; 202-798-3986; theicct.org. Research organization that seeks to improve the environmental performance of all modes of transportation.

National Highway Traffic Safety Administration, 1200 New Jersey Ave., S.E., Washington, DC 20590; 888-327-4236; nhtsa.gov. Federal agency charged with enforcing vehicle safety and performance standards.

Safe Climate Transport Campaign, Center for Biological Diversity, 1411 K St., N.W., Suite 1300, Washington, DC 20005, 202-494-5577, safeclimatecampaign.org. Advocacy group that fights global warming by lobbying for measures to reduce greenhouse gas emissions, including slashing auto emissions and cutting U.S. oil use in half.

Sierra Club, 2101 Webster St., Suite 1300, Oakland, CA 94612; 415-977-5500; sierraclub.org. Leading environmental organization that seeks to mitigate climate change.

Union of Concerned Scientists, 2 Brattle Square, Cambridge, MA 02138; 800-666-8276; ucsusa.org. Science advocacy group that favors more stringent fuel efficiency standards.

15

Zoonotic Diseases

Can future pandemics be prevented?

By Sarah Glazer

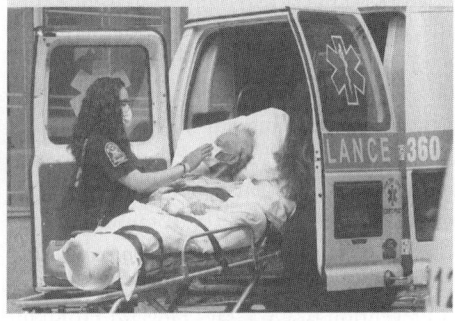

A COVID-19 patient is transported by ambulance to Mt. Sinai Morningside hospital in New York City on May 18, 2020. The virus is only the most recent example of a disease that originated in animals and then spread widely and lethally among humans.

From *CQ Researcher,*
June 26, 2020

THE ISSUES

In the second week of January 2020, a 61-year-old man died from a mysterious pneumonia that was causing a spate of illnesses from an unknown virus in Wuhan, China. The man was a regular customer at Wuhan's giant seafood market, which also sold exotic animals, some live, for meat. Of the first 41 cases of pneumonia tied to the viral infection that first arose in December 2019, two-thirds had either been workers or customers at the market.[1]

According to a widely circulated menu and to reports from vendors and observers, offerings at the market included snakes, dogs, baby crocodiles, arctic foxes, raccoon dogs, bamboo rats and civet cats, sometimes butchered on site.[2]

At such Asian markets, exotic animals are often stacked in cages on top of animals they would never encounter in nature. Exchanging excretion and saliva under stressful conditions makes animals prone to contagion and creates a petri dish for viruses to jump from one species to another, scientists say.

Speculation was rampant that the Wuhan market was the source of the virus that causes COVID-19, which erupted into a pandemic that has killed hundreds of thousands of people across the globe. But in recent months, scientists have cast doubt on the theory. They instead fear that the virus jumped earlier from an animal to a human, perhaps in the wild, and that the market's crowded conditions simply helped to spread the virus from one infected human to many others.[3]

Regardless of what exactly happened, COVID-19 is just the most recent example of a growing threat to human health—zoonotic diseases, which leap from animals to humans and which, if the virus mutates successfully in humans, can also be transmitted from human to human. Researchers believe COVID-19 spilled over from a horseshoe bat in China, possibly to another intermediate animal, such as an endangered pangolin, considered a culinary luxury in China, and then to humans.[4]

Scientists have long warned of a new epidemic of zoonotic diseases, but it is only recently that the environmental roots, such as human encroachment on wild habitats, are gaining the kind of public and media attention given to climate change.

Some of the most well-known epidemics originated with animals, including HIV (from chimpanzees), severe acute respiratory syndrome or SARS (from bats) and Middle East respiratory syndrome or MERS (from camels). An epidemic is a disease that affects a large number of people within a community or region, as opposed to a pandemic, which affects most of the globe.

Scientists say the frequency of such outbreaks has been increasing in recent years. According to estimates, 60 to 75 percent of newly emerging infectious diseases can be traced to animals and more than 70 percent of those come from wildlife.[5]

In fact, scientists have been predicting a zoonotic epidemic similar to COVID-19 for more than a decade, and some even targeted coronaviruses from bats, which likely produced both SARS and COVID-19. For example, in 2007, a Hong Kong scientists' study of SARS said the presence of SARS-like coronaviruses in horseshoe bats, "together with the culture of eating exotic mammals in southern China, is a time bomb."[6]

Andrew Cunningham, a professor of wildlife epidemiology at the Institute of Zoology, London, said in March, "The emergence and spread of COVID-19 was not only predictable, it was predicted [in the sense that] there would be another viral emergence from wildlife that would be a public health threat."[7]

Some scientists and advocacy groups say the spread of both new and existing zoonotic diseases can be attributed to declining biodiversity in natural animal habitats, as humans slash forests for agriculture, mining, roads or housing. Other studies pinpoint increasing human contact with wild animals as the root of growing risks.

With the human population growing and global trade and travel expanding, the human activities that trigger outbreaks "are accelerating and magnifying globally, which is why we're seeing more and more outbreaks happening and will continue to," says Jonathan Epstein, one of the researchers who discovered that horseshoe bats were the likely origin of the SARS virus, and who is vice president for science and outreach at EcoHealth Alliance, an environmental health research group in New York. "The single biggest cause of these epidemics is people. . . . We're encroaching on natural systems and disrupting them, and it's leading to epidemics and pandemics."

Yet traditional public health approaches to disease outbreaks have ignored the role played by environmental destruction, says Samuel S. Myers, an environmental health scientist at Harvard University's School of Public Health, who is promoting a new discipline, planetary health, to unite environmental health and medicine.[8]

"The way we're transforming our natural systems is a dominant driver of the global burden of disease," he says, but "we're completely unequipped to confront these [environmental] problems as a public health community."

That problem extends to the approach to pandemics such as COVID-19 by the U.S. Centers for Disease Control and Prevention (CDC), says Howard Frumkin, a former director of the CDC's National Center for Environmental Health and professor emeritus at the University of Washington School of Public Health. "If you focus on vaccines and public health strategies like contact tracing and isolation, you may overlook some of the root causes of diseases that lie outside the biomedical world," he says.

Along similar lines, several bills in Congress aim to promote greater collaboration among environmental experts, veterinarians and human health experts to anticipate and tackle future pandemic threats in an approach known as One Health.[9]

Some scientists are trying to raise money to create a comprehensive library of zoonotic viruses, saying such a repository could predict and prevent pandemics. But critics point out that similar efforts along those lines, including one funded by the U.S. Agency for International Development (USAID), failed to find COVID-19.[10]

"It's hard to claim success in searching the world over for the virus that will cause the next pandemic when this virus eluded all that tremendous effort," says Richard S. Ostfeld,

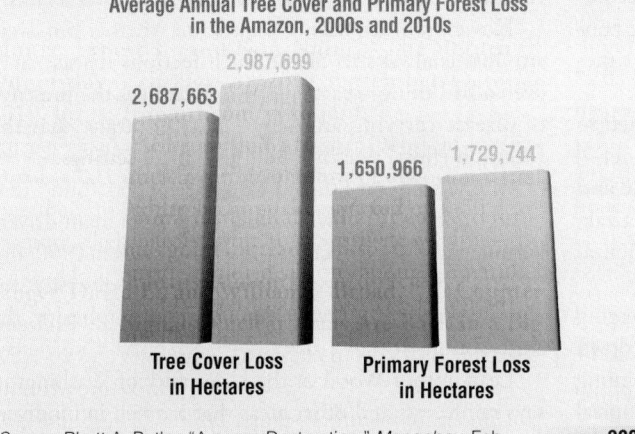

Amazon Deforestation Accelerated in Past Decade

The Amazon rainforest continues to lose tree cover in general and primary forest—forest that has existed undisturbed for a long period of time—in particular. During 2010–19, the average annual number of hectares of forest lost increased from the previous decade. (One hectare equals 2.47 acres.)

Average Annual Tree Cover and Primary Forest Loss in the Amazon, 2000s and 2010s

Tree Cover Loss in Hectares: 2,687,663 (2002-09), 2,987,699 (2010-19)
Primary Forest Loss in Hectares: 1,650,966 (2002-09), 1,729,744 (2010-19)

Source: Rhett A. Butler, "Amazon Destruction," *Mongabay*, Feb. 26, 2020, https://tinyurl.com/ydxcx7kr

a disease ecologist at the Cary Institute of Ecosystem Studies, a private research center in Millbrook, N.Y.

Many scientists agree that the dramatic changes humans have imposed on the planet as a result of world population growth is one major reason for the increase in new zoonotic diseases. "The 21st century is paying the price for what happened in the 20th century," when the world population grew from 1.6 billion to more than 6 billion and humans pushed deeper into virgin forests, says Dennis Carroll a former USAID official who oversaw efforts to forecast zoonotic disease outbreaks.[11] "As we're accommodating this increasing population, we're seeing the increasing frequency and intensity of these spillover events" when diseases leap from animals to humans, he says.

As the world's population heads toward a projected 11 billion people in 2100, developing countries are increasing their wealth and their appetite for meat, with an accompanying demand for more agricultural land in the vast tropical rain forests of the Amazon and Congo River basins.[12]

The loss of biodiversity that results is a major cause of zoonotic disease, according to Ostfeld. As humans cut down and transform virgin forests, coming into extended contact with displaced wild animals and their viruses for the first time, "we've made [these regions] increasingly dangerous by disturbing them and fragmenting the natural habitats," he says. But other scientists question Ostfeld's biodiversity theory, arguing that urbanization and growing wealth helped reduce infectious disease rates between 1990 and 2010.[13]

"Cities bring people into close contact with doctors, make it efficient for public health to do mosquito spraying, vaccinations, offer drugs to infected people. Cities are good for people's health," says Chelsea L. Wood, assistant professor at the University of Washington School of Aquatic and Fishery Sciences. "When you stack up biodiversity against all these other drivers, biodiversity is totally inconsequential."

Experts also disagree on whether governments should ban the trade in exotic animals for human consumption.

"We're creating the perfect storm. If you're a virus whose goal is to spread, you couldn't design a better system to aid and abet a pandemic than these wildlife markets" in Wuhan and across Asia, said Steven Osofsky, professor of wildlife health and health policy at the Cornell University College of Veterinary Medicine. "A lot of these pathogens are meeting species they've never met before, and that's when we have these viral jumps—and create the situation we're in now."[14]

Some researchers and environmentalists argue that certain kinds of well-regulated legal wildlife trade pose little danger of transmitting disease, but other environmental groups dispute that.

As scientists, conservationists and members of government in the United States and around the world debate the threat of zoonotic disease, here are some of the issues they are considering:

Is loss of biodiversity increasing the spread of diseases from animals to humans?

Environmental advocacy groups and some scientists say human incursion into natural habitats is causing viruses that circulate harmlessly in animals to jump increasingly to humans, with sometimes fatal consequences. Other scientists, however, argue that the loss of biodiversity is not necessarily a bad thing because it can reduce the populations of disease-carrying animals.

A widely cited study by British and American ecologists estimated that outbreaks of newly emerging zoonotic diseases are occurring about two to three times more frequently per decade than in the 1940s.[15]

That increasing frequency is "pretty clearly linked to our human footprint and what we do on the planet—building roads, cutting down forests, global trade and travel—all increasing exponentially," says Peter Daszak, president of EcoHealth Alliance, a nongovernmental research organization, and a co-author of the study.

"In some areas where there is a high risk of emerging zoonotic disease, maybe we shouldn't cut the forest down and have people move in and eat wildlife," he says, pointing to his group's research finding that cutting down tropical forests in Asia for palm oil is leading to workers contracting malaria and occasionally a new zoonotic disease.

Two New York-based researchers argue that the reduced diversity of animals that results from such human activity is leading to an increase in zoonotic disease and that conserving biodiversity can protect against such new diseases emerging and spreading.

The researchers, Ostfeld of the Cary Institute and Felicia Keesing, professor of science, mathematics and computing at Bard College in Annandale-on-Hudson, N.Y., say they have demonstrated this theory in their study of Lyme disease in the U.S. Northeast. (See Short Feature.)

The number of ticks carrying the disease is lower in undisturbed forests—areas with more animal diversity—than in the fragmented forests typical of suburban sprawl, their research finds. They theorize that is because expansive forests can support more large predators of the mice that are the hosts of Lyme disease, and can also support opossums, which typically remove the ticks through grooming and also transmit Lyme to far fewer ticks than mice do.[16]

"The species we lose in the Northeast when we lose biodiversity are foxes and bobcats, and those species actually protect us because they keep mouse numbers low," says Keesing. "We should be protecting biodiversity far more than we're doing now; because the best way to keep [the animals that host] these pathogens in check is to let biodiversity do it."

Keesing and Ostfeld say this conclusion—that more diversity equals less disease, which they call the "dilution" theory—is applicable globally, and they argue for resisting land development that cuts up natural forests.

However, other scientists question whether biodiversity loss is always to blame for infectious disease or is even a bad thing—particularly if it reduces the presence of disease-carrying animals. They also argue that the "dilution effect" does not hold true in all settings.

In one study of 60 countries, researchers found that urbanization and growing wealth were the main drivers behind reducing infectious diseases between 1990 and 2010. Contrary to the dilution theory, biodiversity was not correlated with improvements in human health, the study found.[17]

Lead author Wood of the University of Washington says rainforests and other areas that are rich in biodiversity also tend to be rich in viruses and parasites that circulate in animals, so in some cases, when humans preserve those areas or reforest them, "we're also potentially facilitating other diseases."

Both sides in the debate agree that the more contact people have with wild animals, the greater the possibility of animal diseases jumping to people, especially as humans enter natural habitats. But the solution proposed by some environmentalists—to turn those habitats into national parks—"doesn't necessarily recognize the reality of people's lives; lots of people who live near biodiverse forests depend on those forests for their livelihoods, so saying they can't live there is akin to taking away their livelihoods," Wood says.

Some researchers have found that it is often degraded areas on the edge of pristine habitats, rather than the undisturbed core, where humans are most likely to come in contact with animals in ways that could lead to a spillover—when a virus or other disease pathogen jumps from an animal to a human.

In a recent study of farmers living next to Kibale National Park in Uganda, Stanford University researchers found that fragments of residual forest, not larger expanses of habitat, were most likely to be the site of human contacts with primates because they shared borders with farms. For example, a monkey bit a boy digging in his garden, according to lead author Laura Bloomfield.[18]

"We humans go to these animals," said study co-author Eric Lambin, professor of earth system science at Stanford. "We are forcing the interaction through transformation of the land."[19]

In such situations, where humans are chopping up a natural habitat into a mosaic of forest and human dwellings, the loss of diversity may be the "visible result," but the real driver of zoonotic disease is the man-made environment, says Roger Frutos, an infectious disease specialist at CIRAD, a French government research center working in developing countries.

A study from the University of California, Davis, finds the more abundant a species, the more likely it is to carry a disease that jumps to humans. Domestic animals such as cattle have been the most frequent carriers of a zoonotic disease. But among wild mammals, most zoonotic diseases can be found in three groups—rodents, bats and primates.[20]

"They're super-adaptable" animals, explains Christine Johnson, lead author of the study, and professor of epidemiology and wildlife health at the University of California, Davis, School of Veterinary Medicine. She points to rats and mice that feed on human garbage and white-faced monkeys that steal tourists' food in Costa Rica. Once people clear land for farming and housing, she says, these animals "move right in, they shelter with us, they depend on our food."

Ostfeld says Johnson's research is consistent with his findings about Lyme disease—that such diseases thrive best in ecosystems that have been highly disturbed by humans. "It's the little weedy species [like mice] that are often the best reservoirs for zoonotic pathogens; they're the ones that benefit when we muck things up," he says.

Since 1940, agricultural drivers such as clearing land for farms have been linked to about half of emerging zoonotic diseases, according to a study co-authored by Jason R. Rohr, a professor of biological sciences at Notre Dame University.[21]

Growing demand for meat among developing nations means agricultural production will need to double or triple to feed the planet's population by 2100, Rohr projects, posing the threat of more land clearance and more zoonotic disease. At the same time, he says, more food and meat protein equate to better health. "We shouldn't be thinking of biodiversity and disease in a bubble. We have to think about the cost and benefits," he says. "In some cases, the land may be better used for agriculture."

Should selling wildlife for human consumption be banned?

Many critics point to markets in China and other parts of Asia where wild animals in cages are often stacked on top of chickens and in close proximity with humans, making it more likely that they will get sick and transmit viruses to other animals and people.

Species that are endangered because of hunting, wildlife trade and habitat loss have twice the number of zoonotic diseases as other threatened species, according to a recent study by University of California, Davis, researchers.[22]

The stress that wild animals experience in being transported to markets is akin to the "shipping fever" contracted by cows that get sick after being crowded into a trailer for the slaughterhouse, says Johnson, the study's lead author. "Basically, we've given these viruses a unique evolutionary pathway," she says.

The Wildlife Conservation Society, together with other environmental groups, has formed an "End the Trade" coalition, urging governments around the world to enact legislation to "permanently end commercial trade and sale of terrestrial wild animals" for human consumption.[23]

Susan Lieberman, vice president for international policy at the Wildlife Conservation Society, says there is clear evidence that wildlife markets have contributed to zoonotic disease epidemics such as SARS. "Do we spend years investigating which might be the next one? Or do we say we can't accept any risk of this happening again? . . . If we stop the commercial markets where people eat wildlife, the chances of this happening again are infinitesimal."

But some experts say some kinds of legal wildlife trade pose little danger of transmitting disease. For example, kudu and springbok, two species of antelope, are raised in South Africa in settings "almost like farmed systems, controlled and traceable—that's a really important food source there," says Catherine Machalaba, policy adviser at the EcoHealth Alliance. She argues that any ban should be limited to the species experts know are most likely to put humans at risk of disease, such as rodents, bats and primates.

EcoHealth is supporting a more restrictive proposal to ban high-risk wildlife, an approach taken in a

Nurse's aide Benetha Coleman, herself an Ebola survivor, comforts an infant girl with symptoms of the disease in Paynesville, Liberia, in 2015. Following the Ebola outbreak in West Africa in 2014-16, governments imposed a ban on hunting wild animals and eating their meat in an effort to halt the spread of zoonotic diseases.

bipartisan bill introduced by Sens. Lindsey Graham, R-S.C., and Chris Coons, D-Del., and supported by the World Wildlife Fund.[24]

In that proposed ban, "we're not including farmed wildlife, livestock that has appropriate veterinary management and that is well regulated," says Jan Vertefeuille, senior adviser for wildlife conservation advocacy at the World Wildlife Fund.

In a recent opinion piece, economists at the University of Oxford in England wrote that "banning all wildlife trade is a knee-jerk and potentially self-defeating measure." Bans, especially those that remove currently legal supplies of farmed wildlife, could "drive up black market prices and increase incentives for poaching," they wrote.[25]

In China, the wildlife breeding farms and the associated trade are estimated to involve 14 million people and be worth $74 billion, so the impact of a ban on that economy would be "uncertain," the economists said. In January, China imposed a temporary ban on the wildlife trade in the wake of the Wuhan outbreak, and in May 2020, China's legislature began consideration of a permanent ban.[26]

A previous Chinese effort to ban wildlife trade in southern China in the wake of the SARS outbreak in 2002-03, which was traced to a market, was a failure, critics say. Wildlife markets in Guangdong closed down, but reopened a few months later. Black market activity ramped up, and after the outbreak ended the ban was abandoned under a combination of cultural and economic pressures.[27]

Following the 2013-16 Ebola outbreak in West Africa, governments across the region imposed a ban on hunting and eating meat from wild animals.[28]

But those bans led to illegal markets and sometimes a boomerang effect, where consumption of bush meat actually increased, perhaps because the meat became more desirable after the ban took effect, says Diogo Verissimo, an economist and research fellow at Oxford. "We also saw unequal impacts," he says, where communities dependent on bush meat suffered nutritionally.

Harvard's Myers points to research he has overseen in Madagascar villages where people eat wild lemurs and tenrecs (a mammal resembling a hedgehog). "If people in those villages stopped giving bush meat to their children, you would see a 30 percent increase in anemia rates in those kids," he says. "It means a blanket policy [banning wildlife] could cause a lot of hardship and suffering."

Verissimo says that although cattle have often been the source of outbreaks of illnesses such as mad cow disease, "our response to those pandemics was not to ban that industry, because we understand that millions of people rely on that for nutrition, and lots of livelihoods depend on it. What we did was to say, we need to improve regulation."

Many experts say a ban alone will not change traditional food habits. Verissimo has been studying a different strategy—using advertisements with celebrities to shift consumer preferences away from eating pangolin, an anteater-like animal that is the most highly trafficked mammal in the world, prized for the supposed medicinal properties of its scales and its meat. Some scientists think the pangolin may have been the intermediate animal that passed the COVID-19 virus from bats to people.[29]

In one such ad, Miss Universe Vietnam looks horrified and stalks away when her host ceremoniously presents her with a pangolin dish at a restaurant.[30]

Finally, wildlife markets are not the biggest cause of zoonotic epidemics. Research shows that land use changes, such as farmers cutting into forests and moving closer to bat habitats, are a much bigger factor—and the leading cause of new diseases.[31]

"If you blocked the wildlife trade completely in China you would still get lots of people infected every year by bat coronaviruses," says Daszak of EcoHealth Alliance.

Is it possible to predict the next pandemic?

In the wake of the 2003-06 H5N1 bird flu that provoked fears of a global pandemic, USAID in 2009 created a program called PREDICT, charged with strengthening "global capacity for detection and discovery of zoonotic viruses with pandemic potential."

From 2009 to 2019, PREDICT funded research to find viruses among animals in the wild, trained about 5,000 people around the world to identify new diseases and helped develop 60 research labs.[32]

The program found about 1,000 viruses, including bat coronaviruses similar to the ones that caused SARS and COVID-19, but it did not discover the virus causing the current pandemic. Critics say hunting for the next pandemic virus in nature is like looking for a needle in a haystack, because thousands of zoonotic viruses are present and are frequently mutating in ways that could change their potential to infect and thrive in humans.

"The difficulty with that approach is that there are so many viruses, and the vast majority of them are undescribed and harmless," says Barbara Han, disease ecologist at the Cary Institute of Ecosystem Studies. She uses a different strategy, one of constructing computer models based on the distinctive traits of animals that have given humans viruses in the past to forecast which animals are most likely to host new zoonotic diseases.

Some prominent scientists have called for reorienting the government's approach.

"Although PREDICT almost certainly discovered hundreds of potential zoonoses [zoonotic diseases], their true zoonotic potential is almost impossible to assess," wrote Colin J. Carlson, a biologist at Georgetown University who studies newly emerging infectious diseases. "For now, the only real way" to distinguish potentially zoonotic viruses from their low-risk counterparts is to observe a human infection caused by a virus that has spilled over from animals, he said. The government's approach "oversells basic science" and detracts from funding for primary health care, diagnosis and other efforts to catch clusters of human infection early, according to critiques cited by Carlson.[33]

Daszak's group EcoHealth Alliance is one of the most prominent funded by PREDICT to perform virus-hunting research in the wild. After the SARS outbreak, the group's hunting led it to a group of bat coronaviruses that it concluded were the likely source.[34] After 20 years of studying animals that cause zoonotic outbreaks, Daszak says, "it's clear to me there are patterns to disease emergence that are predictable. It doesn't mean that we can predict the next one." But much like an earthquake forecaster, he says, his research can point to the hotspots where clusters of animal viruses are likely to jump to humans, then take steps to limit people's contact with the host animals.

In 2015, Daszak's group, together with Chinese researchers, found 3 percent of people living near bat caves in Yunnan province, China, where hunting and eating bats is common, had antibodies to a SARS-like coronavirus found in bats. That finding suggested bats could directly infect people, the researchers said.[35] (See Short Feature.)

As for the argument that it would be better to focus on early clusters of people infected with a new disease, Daszak says that is essentially what countries are doing now with their public health approach: "We wait for pandemics to emerge and hope we'll get a vaccine. It's not a strategy at all."

Daszak wants to raise private and public funds for a $1.2 billion project to discover and catalog the majority of the 1.5 million zoonotic viruses—mostly unknown—in mammals, humans and waterfowl. "To prevent the few that could cause a pandemic, we have to discover all of the potential ones," Daszak says. This proposed atlas of viruses, dubbed the Global Virome Project, would be a logical successor to PREDICT, supporters say.

"The Global Virome Project will begin lowering risk of spillover because we'll have greater granularity about where and what needs to be done," says Dennis Carroll, the project's chair, who founded PREDICT when he led USAID's emerging pandemic threats program. The new project would expand the kind of research done in Yunnan province that discovered antibodies in people to animal viruses, Carroll says, then use that knowledge as an early-alarm system to work closely with communities and national governments to prevent an epidemic.

But some scientists say the government should shift away from this biomedical approach. "Rather than emphasizing virological research in places where people

CHRONOLOGY

1300s-1800s *Bubonic plague and influenza cause worldwide pandemics.*

1346 Bubonic plague arrives in Europe from China, killing 30 to 60 percent of Europeans.

1688 Influenza strikes England, Ireland and Virginia.

1889 Influenza pandemic spreads from Britain to continental Europe and the U.S., infecting 40 percent of Boston.

1900s-1960s *The world suffers three flu pandemics, and scientists isolate the flu virus.*

1918-19 The Spanish flu kills 40 million to 100 million, including an estimated 675,000 Americans.

1939 Invention of the electron microscope permits scientists to see a virus for the first time.

1942 Studies begin on first flu vaccine after scientists isolate two strains of influenza.

1953 DNA is discovered, permitting scientists to identify the building blocks of a virus.

1957 Hong Kong flu (H2N2) becomes a worldwide pandemic but kills relatively few compared to 1918—116,000 in the U.S.

1968 Asian flu (H3N2) pandemic causes 100,000 U.S. deaths.

1970s-1990s *Animal-origin viruses spur outbreaks of AIDS, Ebola and Nipah viruses.*

1976 Ebola cases erupt in South Sudan and the Democratic Republic of Congo with fatality rates of more than 80 percent. The likely origin was fruit bats, with primates as intermediate animals.

1981 AIDS epidemic is first recognized in the United States. Similar viruses long existed in primates.

1995 Gabon and Zaire (now Democratic Republic of the Congo) report clusters of Ebola virus, linked to gorilla and chimpanzee carcasses in nearby forests.

1999 Nipah breaks out among pig farmers in Malaysia; researchers later trace the virus to bats. Fatality rate is 40 to 75 percent.

2000s-Present *Three major coronavirus outbreaks erupt, and COVID-19 pandemic shuts down the globe.*

2001 Nipah breaks out in Bangladesh, linked to sap from date palms contaminated by bats, that is then consumed by people.

2002 First death from severe acute respiratory syndrome (SARS) is recorded in China's southern Guangdong province. More than 8,000 people are infected, with a fatality rate of about 10 percent.

2003 After a tourist returns to Toronto from Hong Kong in February, SARS spreads from Asia to North and South America and Europe. The World Health Organization (WHO) declares the pandemic contained in July.

2004 WHO reports first case of human-to-human transmission, in Thailand, of bird flu (H5N1). Fears of a worldwide pandemic fail to be realized.

2005 In response to the bird flu threat, President George W. Bush requests and Congress approves $3.8 billion to develop vaccines and stockpile anti-flu medications.

2007 Ebola outbreak in Gabon is linked to hunters eating bats during massive bat migration.

2009 WHO declares the swine flu (H1N1), which scientists trace to pig and poultry farming and to human contact with waterfowl, a pandemic; the flu eventually infects millions and kills thousands.

2010 WHO declares an end to the swine flu pandemic.

2012 In Saudi Arabia, the first death from Middle East respiratory syndrome (MERS) is recorded. The fatality rate is about 35 percent, and the disease kills 866 people.

2014-16 Largest outbreak of Ebola occurs in West Africa since the virus was discovered, with more cases and deaths in this outbreak than all others combined.

2019 In December, WHO receives first report of COVID-19 cases in Wuhan, China; most are linked to a live-animal market.

2020 China closes the Wuhan market and announces temporary ban on wildlife trade (January). . . . Chinese government proposes limiting types of wildlife sold for meat (April). . . . Chinese legislature begins drafting permanent ban on wildlife sale and consumption (May). . . . U.S. House passes recovery act, which includes a ban on imports of high-risk wildlife (May). . . . A bipartisan bill authorizing presidential sanctions against nations that sell high-risk wildlife, supported by environmental groups, is introduced in the Senate (May).

and wildlife come into dangerously close contact, investments should be dramatically shifted to focus on making such human-wildlife contact much less likely in the first place," wrote Cornell's Osofsky. The focus, he said, should be on preventing the risky behaviors likely to cause future outbreaks—eating and trading the body parts of wild animals, mixing species in markets and human incursions into wild areas that increase contact with wildlife.[36]

Governments should focus on catching the disease in animals before it even gets to humans and then act quickly, according to Larry Brilliant, a leading epidemiologist who helped the World Health Organization (WHO) eradicate smallpox and is now board chair of Ending Pandemics, a group that advises governments on the early discovery and containment of pandemics.

He pointed to a Cambodian program where a farmer "can call the government and say, 'I have 20 dead chickens,' and they'll come and bring you 30 live ones and clean up your place. That's a phenomenal bi-direction system that cleans up the virus for you, puts you back into business, and the epidemic is aborted. Being able to survey bats, pigs, birds . . . that's what we're going to have to do in the age of pandemics."[37]

The main reason a zoonotic disease emerges "is not biology, it's sociology; it's human," says Frutos, a molecular microbiologist at CIRAD. "It's not possible," he says, to predict which virus will cause the next pandemic because that requires a chain of largely accidental events triggered by humans, from destroying wild places to successful spillover to the mutation into a human disease. "We should put the filter at the bottleneck" of human activity, he says. "Whatever the virus, it has to go through the bottleneck."

An artist depicted an outbreak of plague in Florence in the 14th century based on the description of writer Giovanni Boccaccio. A bubonic plague pandemic in that century, which killed between 30 percent and 60 percent of Europe's population, originated from fleas on black rats.

BACKGROUND
Rodents and Plagues

One of the most notorious early zoonotic diseases was the Black Death, the name given to bubonic plague carried by rodents that devastated Europe in successive waves starting in the 14th century. The plague first reached Europe in 1346, most likely carried by fleas on black rats that inhabited merchant ships. The disease wiped out as much as 30 to 60 percent of Europe's population.[38]

Recent genomic research has revealed that the plague originated in China, then traveled through Asia, Europe and Africa from 1346 to 1351.[39]

Bats Can Harbor and Transmit Many Viruses

"It's just a matter of probability for disease to happen."

In 1998, people started getting sick in northern Malaysia with fever, headache, drowsiness and convulsions. All of them were pig farmers or involved in the pork industry. By the end of the outbreak, at least 283 people had been infected and almost 40 percent had died.

Scientists would later trace the illness—Nipah virus—to bats that had roosted in fruit trees above the pig sties, dropping chewed mango and water apple into the sties. The pigs ate the droppings, contracted the virus and passed it on to the rest of the herd, infecting their human handlers.[1]

Bats have also been linked to coronaviruses, including severe acute respiratory syndrome (SARS), Middle East respiratory syndrome (MERS), two coronaviruses that cause the common cold and the virus behind COVID-19. In a new study, researchers from the EcoHealth Alliance, a New York City-based environmental research group, and China's Wuhan Institute of Virology identified more than 780 new coronaviruses in bats and traced the likely origin of the viruses behind both SARS and COVID-19 to horseshoe bats.[2]

Why have bats been linked to so many outbreaks of human disease? They are highly social animals, roosting in packed groups as large as millions. The authors of the new study point out that horseshoe bats in southern China often share their roost with other bat species, which may make it easier for coronaviruses to leap to different species.[3]

The lineage of bats can be traced back about 50 million years, and scientists believe they may have co-evolved with viruses in a way that permits them to carry viruses without being affected by them—a trait that is perhaps related to their ability to fly.[4]

"They have an interesting immune system," says Peter Daszak, EcoHealth Alliance president and a co-author of the recent paper. "There's pretty good evidence that bats reduce their natural immune response to viruses. Maybe it's part of the [evolutionary] cost of flight, which is energetic; they have to reduce stress."

Bats "seem to be able to recover from infection from a pathogen but not completely clear it from their system, which they do by suppressing their immune system," said Kate Jones, professor of ecology and biodiversity at University College London. "[An] over-responsive immune system is sometimes what actually kills you—from organ failure."[5]

Bats are attracted to human habitation and farms, especially if the bats have been disturbed from their natural habitat. That is one reason they showed up in such large numbers on pig farms in Malaysia. Booming pork demand contributed to slash-and-burn deforestation as farmers cut into the forests where bats lived to create industrialized pig operations, while vast tracts were logged.[6]

Light from houses attracts insects, which in turn attract the bats that eat them, says Roger Frutos, a microbiologist with the French government research agency CIRAD, who focuses on infectious diseases. EcoHealth researchers expect as many as 10,000 to 15,000 bat coronaviruses have yet to be discovered in addition to the 781 they recently discovered and the 509 previously known bat coronaviruses.[7]

"Since we attract bats to human environments, we therefore attract a very large reservoir of viruses," Frutos says. "After that, it's just a matter of probability for disease to happen: The more contact you have, the higher the presence of bats, the higher the probability to get emergence [of disease]—and contamination of humans."

The first step to prevention, he says, is to fortify barns and pig sheds against bats—the United Nations recommends applying wire screens to open-sided pig sheds, installing roofing and placing netting over ventilation openings.[8] Such

The bacterium that causes the plague, *Yersinia pestis*, still resides in rodents indigenous to North and South America, Africa and Central Asia.[40] Plague is now treatable with antibiotics. Human plague infections continue to occur in rural areas in the western United States, but significantly more cases occur in Africa and Asia, according to the CDC.[41]

Zoonotic diseases predated the plague. Today, they account for more than 60 percent of human infectious diseases.[42] Zoonoses include diseases that cross routinely from animals to humans, such as rabies, or have recently crossed and now pass from human to human, such as HIV, which originated in a chimpanzee.[43]

Many diseases that people now consider human-to-human—including smallpox and measles—are believed to have originated with animals in the distant past.[44] For example, researchers believe influenza jumped from

steps, along with the Malaysian government's ban on pig farming in high-risk areas following the Nipah outbreak, helped to eradicate the disease from Malaysia, according to Dennis Carroll, who oversaw the pandemics prevention program at the U.S. Agency for International Development.[9]

The area where southern China converges with Laos, Myanmar and Vietnam is likely to be a future hot spot for emerging disease, EcoHealth researchers predict, because a growing human population, urbanization and intense poultry and livestock farming all provide opportunities for a virus to jump from animals to people.[10]

One study by Daszak's group found about 3 percent of a human community in southern China living near bat caves had antibodies to SARS-like bat coronaviruses, despite recalling no SARS symptoms.[11] He says his organization wants to conduct more such studies to anticipate viruses likely to cause epidemics.

However, EcoHealth's funding for this work was abruptly terminated in April by the U.S. National Institutes of Health (NIH) after EcoHealth's grant got caught up in a political controversy over the Wuhan lab. The $3.7 million grant was canceled a few days after President Trump responded to a question at a press conference from a reporter who erroneously claimed that millions of dollars in grants were going to the Wuhan Institute. Trump told the reporter the grant would be ended immediately, amid mounting but unproven theories targeting the Wuhan lab as the source of the coronavirus.[12]

In fact, only about 10 percent of that grant was slated for the Wuhan Institute for collecting and analyzing samples, according to EcoHealth's Daszak.[13]

Thirty-one U.S. scientific societies and 77 Nobel laureates wrote to the NIH calling for an investigation into the grant's cancellation. The Nobel laureates said the termination of the grant "sets a dangerous precedent by interfering in the conduct of science."[14]

"Our future plans were to sequence whole genomes" of viruses, EcoHealth said in a statement accompanying the recent study, "particularly . . . to see if any of these viruses are likely able to infect humans. That work will not happen without the funding from NIH."[15]

— *Sarah Glazer*

---

[1] David Quammen, *Spillover: Animal Infections and the Next Human Pandemic* (2012), pp. 314-328.

[2] Alice Latinne *et al.*, "Origin and cross-species transmission of bat coronaviruses in China," bioRxiv, posted June 1, 2020, https://tinyurl.com/y85f63fc.

[3] *Ibid.*

[4] Quammen, *op. cit.*

[5] Kate Jones *et al.*, "FAQs—Relationship between habitat loss, biodiversity, bats and live wildlife markets," 2020, https://tinyurl.com/yaz2csh9.

[6] Tom Evans *et al.*, "Links between ecological integrity, emerging infectious diseases originating from wildlife, and other aspects of human health—an overview of the literature," Wildlife Conservation Society, April 2020, https://tinyurl.com/y8dd4ac4.

[7] "Talking points from Latinne *et al.*, Origin and cross transmission of bat CoVs in China," EcoHealth Alliance, June 1, 2020.

[8] "Nipah Virus Frequently Asked Questions," Food and Agriculture Organization of the United Nations, https://tinyurl.com/ybhp37p8.

[9] Ferris Jabr, "How Humanity Unleashed a Flood of New Diseases," *The New York Times Magazine*, June 17, 2020, https://tinyurl.com/yc26pngc.

[10] Latinne *et al.*, *op. cit.*

[11] Nin Wang *et al.*, "Serological Evidence of Bat SARS-Related Coronavirus Infections in Humans, China," Virologica Sinica, March 2, 2018, https://tinyurl.com/ycqze63h.

[12] James Gorman, "Prominent Scientists Denounce End to Coronavirus Grant," *The New York Times*, May 21, 2020, https://tinyurl.com/y9vl62de.

[13] Nurith Aizenman, "Why The U.S. Government Stopped Funding A Research Project On Bats And Coronaviruses," *NPR*, April 29, 2020, https://tinyurl.com/yc47l3po.

[14] Gorman, *op. cit.*

[15] "Talking points from Latinne *et al.*, Origin and cross transmission of bat CoVs in China," *op. cit.*

---

horses to humans soon after horses were domesticated and then made additional jumps to humans from other domesticated animals, such as poultry and swine.[45]

The moment when a pathogen leaps from a member of one species into members of another is known as a spillover. Spillover leads to the emergence of a new disease only when the alien pathogen thrives in a new species and spreads among its members.[46]

Spillovers are actually "fairly common events," says the Global Virome Project's Carroll: In studies, 10 to 15 percent of communities that have routine exposure to wildlife test positive for antibodies to wildlife viruses. But many animal pathogens that make the jump to humans "fizzle out," says the Cary Institute's Han, either failing to transmit to another human or infecting only a limited number of people.

As Deer Population Explodes, Lyme Disease Spreads

"We're placing homes, dogs and kids right in the hot zone we've created."

The first thing many summer visitors see on the ferry to Martha's Vineyard is the pamphlet warning them to beware of Lyme disease.

Martha's Vineyard, an island off Cape Cod in Massachusetts that is famed for its beaches, has consistently ranked among the top 10 counties in the country for Lyme disease rates.[1]

But old-timers who grew up on the island in the 1950s or earlier "say they never saw a tick here" of the Lyme variety, the blacklegged or deer tick, says Richard Johnson, director of the Martha's Vineyard Tick Program, a county effort that educates the public about Lyme.[2]

Many people think of Lyme as a recent invader, because it was first identified in Lyme, Conn., in 1976. Cases have risen steadily from just under 10,000 in 1991 to more than 300,000 a year, according to the U.S. Centers for Disease Control and Prevention (CDC). Initial symptoms include skin rash, headache, fever and fatigue. Lyme can be treated with antibiotics, but if not caught early, the infection can spread to joints, the heart and the nervous system.[3]

It turns out the Lyme bacterium has been in North America for at least 60,000 years, circulating unnoticed in forests, according to recent genomic analysis by Yale University researchers. The researchers concluded that the suburban explosion of the deer population—without predators—allowed the tick population to soar in New England and the Midwest.[4]

Like many parts of the Northeast, the Vineyard was originally covered by virgin forest, then turned into treeless pastureland for sheep by European colonists starting in the 18th century. With the collapse of the sheep industry in the early 1900s, the trees started growing back.

They provided cover for deer, which carry the adult ticks, and for white-footed mice, which carry the poppy seed-sized tick nymphs, the stage when ticks bite people. Deer ticks reappeared in the 1960s or '70s, Johnson estimates, when second-growth forest blanketed the island's pastures.

While it is true that some forest seems to be a prerequisite for ticks and their hosts, humans have made it worse by cutting up the forest into small fragments, where large predators of mice and deer can no longer survive, says Richard S. Ostfeld, a disease ecologist at the Cary Institute of Ecosystem Studies, a research center in Millbrook, N.Y.

Ostfeld's research finds more infected ticks in small patches of woods than in undisturbed forest, where predators of mice such as foxes live, as do opossums, which eat most of the ticks on them.[5]

In suburban developments, "we're placing homes, dogs and kids right in the hot zone we've created," Ostfeld says. "If you're right next to a bit of forest, that's more dangerous than living next to a big continuous forest." One solution he proposes is building houses together in clusters.

Yet on the Vineyard, as in much of the Northeast, it would be hard to change the longstanding suburban and

Carroll says, "What is less common is a virus that is able to spread human to human after the initial spillover."

One characteristic that makes zoonotic pathogens so problematic is that they can hide in "reservoir hosts," animals that carry the pathogen while suffering little or no illness, such as the white-footed mice that carry Lyme disease.[47]

By contrast, eradicating smallpox worldwide, as the WHO announced had been accomplished in 1980, was feasible because it lacked the ability to live anywhere but in the human body, according to science writer David Quammen in his 2013 book, *Spillover*. The virus could not hide in animals.

It would be far more difficult to eradicate yellow fever, a zoonotic disease that is infectious to both monkeys and people and is passed by mosquitoes. It will continue to occur in humans unless the WHO "kills every mosquito vector or every susceptible

rural patterns, where houses abut small patches of woods, observes Johnson.

Traditional approaches to controlling Lyme disease have been to clear vegetation and cull the animals hosting the ticks, says Chelsea L. Wood, an assistant professor at the University of Washington's School of Aquatic and Fishery Sciences in Seattle. "The unfortunate reality is that is the only strategy that's ever worked for us in the past," she says.

For example, Monhegan Island off Maine employed sharpshooters to kill the entire herd of 100 deer on its four-and-a-half square miles between 1996 and 1999.[6] By 2004, no ticks could be found on the island.[7]

If an adult tick can no longer feed on a deer, she can no longer reproduce, so killing one fed adult female tick is the equivalent of killing 2,000 larvae or several hundred nymphs.[8]

Looking to Monhegan, Martha's Vineyard has been encouraging more deer hunting, offering bow hunters a bounty of $100 for taking their third doe. It also has been encouraging homeowners to allow hunting on their property.[9] Last year, hunters took almost twice as many deer as in 2015, according to Johnson.

But simply reducing the deer population will not necessarily eliminate ticks, cautions Ostfeld. Ticks are constantly seeking a host, he says, noting one case where halving the deer population led to twice as many ticks living on each deer. However, other studies find that reducing the deer population dramatically resulted in a significant reduction in Lyme cases.[10]

"I don't think there's any doubt that reducing deer will eventually reduce ticks," says Johnson, explaining his strategy for the Vineyard. "The question is how low do you have to get the numbers."

Reducing density to eight or fewer deer per square mile might break the cycle of ubiquitous Lyme disease, according to one estimate Johnson cites. That would be an ambitious goal for the Vineyard, which averages 30 to 50 deer per square mile on its approximately 100 square miles.

"No one has tried it on the scale we're doing it on the Vineyard," Johnson says. As an island, the Vineyard has an advantage: Deer cannot walk over a land border from a neighboring county to replace those that have been killed.

Success, for Johnson, would be to return the island to "the way it used to be 60 years ago"—before the ticks arrived.

— *Sarah Glazer*

---

[1] Noah Asimow, "Funding for Tick Program Runs Out; Tick Spread Marches On," *Vineyard Gazette*, June 27, 2019, https://tinyurl.com/y6w5hace; Matt Rocheleau, "Mass. counties have some of the highest rates of Lyme disease in the U.S.," *The Boston Globe*, May 10, 2018, https://tinyurl.com/y9l8o4s2.

[2] "MV Tick Program," Dukes County, https://tinyurl.com/ycfk7tol.

[3] "Lyme Disease," U.S. Centers for Disease Control and Prevention, https://tinyurl.com/yx9fq6n2.

[4] "Ancient History of Lyme Disease in North America Revealed with Bacterial Genomes," Yale School of Medicine, Aug. 28, 2017, https://tinyurl.com/yakh9mxz.

[5] Felicia Keesing *et al.*, "Hosts as ecological traps for the vector of Lyme disease," *Proceedings, Biological Sciences*, Aug. 19, 2009, https://tinyurl.com/ycqkl4a3.

[6] George Smith, "Monhegan killed all its deer and eliminated Lyme disease," *George's Outdoor News*, Oct. 28, 2016, https://tinyurl.com/yb5r6bs8.

[7] Joseph Piesman, "Strategies for Reducing the Risk of Lyme Borreliosis in North America," *International Journal of Medical Microbiology*, May 2006, https://tinyurl.com/y6vsqbn3.

[8] "Could Reducing Deer Populations Reduce Lyme Disease?" *Entomology Today*, Sept. 28, 2017, https://tinyurl.com/ycl7y4jw.

[9] Julia Wells, "Bow Hunters Offered Financial Incentive to Take More Deer," *Vineyard Gazette*, Sept. 30, 2019, https://tinyurl.com/yakwamw2.

[10] Howard J. Kilpatrick *et al.*, "The Relationship between Deer Density, Tick Abundance, and Human Cases of Lyme in a Residential Community," *Journal of Medical Entomology*, July 1, 2014, https://tinyurl.com/y9ym5k25.

---

monkey in tropical Africa and South America," Quammen wrote.[48]

Zoonotic diseases include several diseases better known in the United States, including Lyme disease (from mice), West Nile virus (mosquitoes), hantavirus pulmonary syndrome (rodents) and monkeypox (monkeys).[49]

COVID-19 is the third coronavirus (so-called because of its crown-like structure) to cause an outbreak of serious illness in the past 20 years. All three—SARS, MERS and COVID-19—have been linked to animal origins. Many of the most serious recent zoonotic outbreaks can be traced to environmental causes, often to human contact with animals disturbed from their natural habitats, according to the Wildlife Conservation Society.[50]

Influenza Outbreaks

Influenza pandemics were first documented about 300 years ago. The 20th century alone saw three such

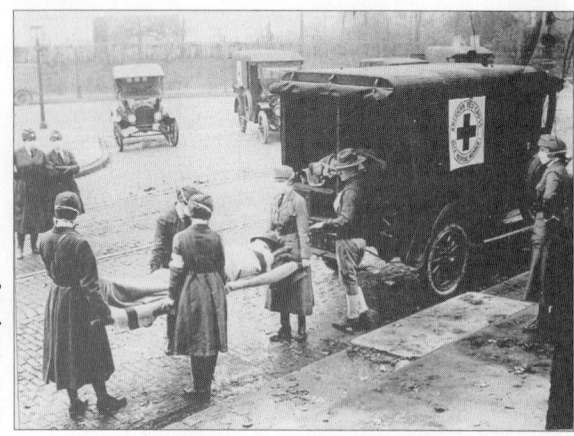

Red Cross medical personnel transport a victim of the 1918 influenza pandemic in St. Louis. The disease killed 675,000 Americans and at least 40 million people worldwide.

pandemics: Two were comparatively mild, but the 1918-19 "Spanish flu" pandemic infected an estimated 25 to 30 percent of the world's population. About 675,000 Americans died from the flu in 1918—nearly half of all U.S. deaths that year. Worldwide, 40 million to 100 million people died.[51]

The two milder 20th-century pandemics, in 1957 and 1968, were probably caused by the exchange of genes between human and avian flu viruses. The 1957 and 1968 outbreaks caused about 116,000 and 100,000 U.S. deaths, respectively.[52]

The 1918 flu was a novel, or new, virus that originated in birds and then spent some time in another host, perhaps pigs or horses, before it emerged as a human disease. Striking during World War I, it was able to spread quickly among soldiers in cramped army barracks and steerage-like transports. The majority of deaths probably resulted from secondary infections, such as bacterial pneumonia, which were deadly before the discovery of antibiotics. The death rate in the 1918 flu was 20 times greater than that for today's influenza, which kills fewer than 0.1 percent of those who catch it.[53]

In 1939, the newly invented electron microscope took a picture of a virus—the first time in history it could be seen. By the 1940s, scientists had isolated two strains of influenza and had begun to test vaccines. After the discovery of DNA in 1953, scientists were able to identify the building blocks of a virus.[54]

Ebola, Nipah and AIDS

The Ebola virus causes a hemorrhagic fever that is among the most virulent known diseases.[55]

It first appeared in two separate outbreaks in 1976 in the African countries of South Sudan and the Democratic Republic of the Congo (formerly Zaire) near the Ebola River with fatality rates of more than 80 percent. Researchers suspect fruit bats are the natural hosts of Ebola virus.[56]

Although the exact origin of Ebola is unknown, the virus is introduced to humans through contact with the blood, organ or secretions of bats or from chimpanzees, gorillas, monkeys, antelopes or porcupines found ill in the forest.[57]

Beginning around 1995, Gabon and the Democratic Republic of the Congo reported clusters of the disease—in each case linked to gorilla and chimpanzee carcasses in nearby forests that were sometimes eaten by villagers. As researchers searched for the cause between 2001 and 2005, they discovered that bats, which carried the virus, came into contact with apes during the dry season when fruits become less plentiful and they compete for the same food. A 2007 outbreak in Gabon was linked to hunters eating bats during a massive migration when fruits were plentiful.[58]

Although the AIDS epidemic was first recognized in 1981 in the United States, researchers say it originated far earlier, as similar immunodeficiency viruses long existed in primates. The first spillover to humans likely occurred in the course of hunting, butchering and eating primates carrying viruses. One of these events likely occurred in Africa between 1910 and 1930, some researchers believe, giving rise to the HIV strain behind AIDS.[59]

Nipah virus, which can cause severe respiratory infection and encephalitis, broke out among pig farmers in Malaysia in 1999, followed by Bangladesh in 2001. Nipah virus has a fatality rate of 40 to 75 percent, and it has no cure or vaccine.[60]

Since 2001, Bangladesh has had nearly yearly outbreaks and India has had several. In Malaysia, the virus has been traced to fruit bats that roost above pig sties, with pigs passing the disease via direct contact with people who work in the pork industry.[61]

Slash-and-burn deforestation, together with drought, initially drove bats into fruit orchards adjoining pig farms that had recently expanded into forests.[62]

The 2014-16 Ebola outbreak in West Africa was the largest since the virus was discovered in 1976, with more cases and deaths in this outbreak than all others combined. A total of 11,310 deaths were reported in Guinea, Liberia and Sierra Leone.[63] Vaccines are under development and have been used to control outbreaks in Guinea and the Democratic Republic of the Congo, according to the WHO.[64]

Ebola reappeared in the Democratic Republic of the Congo in August 2018, causing more than 2,000 deaths by November 2019 at a 67 percent mortality rate, the second-largest Ebola outbreak in history.[65]

21st-Century Outbreaks

The first pandemic of the 21st century started in China's southern Guangdong province in 2002 after a patient died from an unusual pneumonia, later identified as SARS.[66]

SARS has infected at least 8,000 people and killed about 10 percent of them.[67]

Early cases were linked to wildlife markets and restaurants in Guangdong, where coronaviruses were found in masked palm civets, a cat-like mammal considered a culinary delicacy in China. Chinese authorities responded by imposing a temporary ban on the hunting, sale, transportation and export of all wild animals in southern Chinese provinces. They also culled and quarantined civets in the region's many civet farms.[68]

Horseshoe bats have been identified as the likely origin of the virus, while farmed civets probably served as an intermediary, passing the disease to humans. The disease spread to four continents (Asia, North and South America and Europe) after a tourist returned to Toronto in February 2003 from a Hong Kong hotel, spurring a planetary public health panic. The WHO declared the outbreak contained on July 5, 2003.[69]

Bird flu, a highly contagious disease among chickens in Asia, Africa and Europe, raised fears of a worldwide pandemic after the WHO reported the first case of human-to-human transmission in Thailand on Sept. 28, 2004, from the H5N1 flu strain.

In December 2005, in response to an emergency request from President George W. Bush, Congress approved $3.8 billion to develop vaccines and stockpile anti-flu medications.[70]

Dozens of human cases and some deaths were reported in Turkey in January 2006.[71] But the outbreak failed to turn into a transmissible disease between humans. Most of the 648 cases since 2003 have occurred in people who had close contact with poultry.

Currently, human infection is rare, and there is no ongoing transmission in humans, according to the CDC, but the bird flu can be fatal, with a 60 percent mortality rate. The first case in North America occurred almost a decade after the first outbreak, in Canada in 2014, when a person who had recently returned from China died.[72]

Swine flu (H1N1), meanwhile, killed thousands and infected millions in 2009, when it was declared a pandemic by the WHO in June of that year, the last declared pandemic before COVID. The WHO declared an end to the pandemic on Aug. 10, 2010. The WHO said H1N1 had become much like any other flu strain, no longer causing the majority of flu outbreaks or triggering outbreaks during the summer.[73] Globally, an estimated 151,700 to 575,400 people died from swine flu in the first year of the pandemic.[74] It has been traced to pig and poultry farming and contact with wild waterfowl.[75]

MERS, a severe respiratory disease caused by a coronavirus, was first reported after a 60-year-old man died of a novel virus in Saudi Arabia in 2012. Across the globe, 27 countries have reported cases of MERS, but about 80 percent occurred in Saudi Arabia. The disease, which has a fatality rate of about 35 percent, has killed 866 people. There is no specific treatment and no vaccine.[76]

Although the disease emerged from dromedary camels in Saudi Arabia, some researchers view them as an intermediary, since the virus is found in bats and African dromedaries.[77]

COVID-19's Emergence

On Dec. 31, 2019, the WHO received a report from China of a cluster of cases in Wuhan with a pneumonia of unknown cause, later identified as COVID-19.[78] Of the first 44 patients hospitalized, 27 had been exposed to the local seafood market in December 2019, where live wildlife was also sold.[79]

Authorities closed the Wuhan market in January 2020. They also reported finding environmental samples of COVID-19 virus (on sewage and surfaces) in the area where wild game was sold.[80]

Since then, however, cases of COVID-19 have been traced back to November 2019, and some scientists began questioning in early 2020 if the market was the source.[81]

In late May 2020, George Gao Fu, the director of the Chinese Center for Disease Control and Prevention, said the center had been unable to trace the virus to an animal in the market. "At first, we assumed the seafood market might have the virus, but now the market is more like a victim," Gao Fu told the state-owned *Global Times*.[82]

It remains unclear how the virus was transmitted to humans. Many scientists believe the virus probably came from a horseshoe bat, where a virus whose genome is 96 percent similar to COVID-19's has been identified. One scientist at the Sorbonne University in Paris has suggested that the virus may be the result of a recombination of two different viruses—one closer to the horseshoe bat's and the other closer to a pangolin virus.[83]

A pangolin, an endangered species that is the most highly trafficked mammal in the world, was rescued from poachers in Uganda in April 2020. Pangolins are prized in China as a culinary delicacy and for alleged medicinal purposes, and may have been part of the transmission chain of the COVID-19 virus.

CURRENT SITUATION
International Developments

Moving toward its first permanent national ban on the trade in wildlife food, China's legislature is considering changes to the nation's wildlife law that would outlaw the sale and human consumption of some wild animals; the drafting of new legislation is likely to take at least until the end of the year.[84] That change would replace the temporary wildlife ban issued in January 2020 in the wake of the coronavirus outbreak in Wuhan, which was to stay in effect until the pandemic ended.[85]

In April 2020, the Chinese government issued a proposed list of animals that could be sold for meat, drastically curtailed from the species that are currently legal. Notably, the approved list left out some of the animals of most concern for zoonotic disease, such as pangolins, civet cats and bamboo rats—a large rodent that lives in bamboo thickets—as well as dogs, which Chinese markets have long sold for food.[86]

Some provinces have begun to offer farmers cash to end the practice of rearing civets and other wild animals.[87]

In May 2020, Guangdong province, a prime center for wildlife gastronomy where SARS originated, started imposing tough fines for ordering restaurant dishes, such as bat soup, a positive sign that the provinces are prepared to enforce a stronger national law, according to Aili Kang, executive director of the Wildlife Conservation Society's Asia program. But she says some of the biggest industries, such as breeders of bamboo rats, are seeking exemptions from the ban.

Wildlife advocates say the proposed law still has big loopholes—permitting wildlife trade for traditional Chinese medicine, for fur and for exotic pets. Pets such as "rare reptiles or turtles may not be as risky as primates or rodents, but they still have risky pathogens," says Kang.

China's wildlife ban will have limited effect if nearby countries continue the exotic animal trade, experts say. In March, Vietnamese Prime Minister Nguyen Xuân Phúc requested draft legislation by April 1, 2020, to restrict the trade and consumption of wildlife, but no information about a ban has been made public, raising concerns among conservation groups as to the government's seriousness.[88]

In May 2020, the WHO said it was not recommending a ban on live animal markets globally, despite urging from some environmental groups and members of the U.S. Congress.[89] WHO food safety and animal diseases expert Peter Ben Embarek said live animal markets—which exist in many countries, including in Africa—are essential to providing food and livelihoods to millions around the world and that governments should focus on improving the markets' hygiene and food safety standards.[90]

The Wildlife Conservation Society and other conservation groups are calling on national governments to issue bans on all wildlife for human consumption, with narrow exceptions for indigenous communities that rely on wildlife for subsistence.[91]

AT ISSUE:

Should the trade in wildlife for human consumption be banned?

YES
Susan Lieberman
Vice President, International Policy, Wildlife Conservation Society

Written for *CQ Researcher*, June 2020

In only four months, people everywhere have awakened to the massive global tragedy that can result from zoonotic pandemics, when animals pass on pathogens to humans. If we want to avoid the next COVID, we need to accept that tweaks to current policies or targeted closures of some risky wildlife markets will be irresponsibly insufficient. Business as usual and mere improvements to existing policies will not prevent the next zoonotic pandemic.

Global public opinion is moving rapidly to a place where decision-makers can adopt policies that once would have been considered radical but seem sensible now as people experience the impact of this pandemic on their economies, well-being and lives. If governments view the challenges of avoiding a future pandemic through this newly shifted Overton Window, they will see how bold policies that reorder our relationship with wildlife will allow for solutions that reflect local realities. Nuanced changes to current policies or targeted closures of only today's problem markets will not prevent future zoonotic pandemics.

This shift in public opinion means we need lawmakers and decision-makers to know that now is the time to make wholesale changes to our fractured relationship with wildlife. For example, we need to stop relentlessly destroying wildlife habitat for logging, mining and agriculture, which increases the possibility of spillover of deadly pathogens from wildlife to humans. Protecting ecological integrity should be a priority within any comprehensive plan to avoid future zoonotic outbreaks.

With large-scale reform of the global wildlife trade, we can then support local solutions that will preserve wildlife for those who depend on it for food security or sustainable income-generating enterprises such as wildlife-based tourism. Indeed, under this new framework, locally and socially accepted solutions will be stronger and more sustainable. Globally, the commercial trade in wildlife for human consumption, particularly birds and mammals, poses an enormous risk to humans. This trade for urban consumers is especially unnecessary, because they do not need to eat wildlife; it is neither a dietary nor a cultural necessity for them, as it still is for some rural communities.

With bold action for an overarching change in our relationship to wildlife, we can significantly reduce the risk of zoonotic pandemics; help address the world's biodiversity crisis; support local economies through nonconsumptive industries such as ecotourism; and preserve wildlife for those who depend on it for their well-being and cultural identity. It is only through recognizing that we are at a global inflection point with our relationship with wildlife that we will make progress.

NO
Amy Hinsley
Senior Research Fellow, Wildlife Conservation Research Unit, Department of Zoology, University of Oxford

Stephanie Brittain
Postdoctoral Researcher, Interdisciplinary Centre for Conservation Science, Department of Zoology, University of Oxford

Written for *CQ Researcher*, June 2020

With the highly publicized links between the coronavirus that caused COVID-19 and wild animal meat, banning wildlife trade and consumption has been widely suggested as the only way to stop future pandemics. This is a simple and powerful message, but this very simplicity means this approach is unlikely to work.

Proposed bans ignore the complexity of the wildlife trade and the diversity of both its consumers and of the plant, animal and fungal species being consumed. Wild meat is not just threatened high-disease-risk animal species being traded illegally in the tropics, but also pigs, deer, birds, antelope and rodents hunted globally. Further, while wild meat may be consumed as a luxury in high-income areas, it contributes to the food security and livelihoods of millions of people globally, especially those in rural communities.

Banning wildlife consumption presents the real risk of unintended consequences and perverse outcomes. Markets can be driven underground where monitoring and regulation are impossible, potentially increasing zoonotic disease transmission by reducing the potential and incentives for applying food hygiene standards. Where bans are successful, wild-meat traders, who are often women, lose valuable employment. Further, viable alternative sources of food and income are rarely available or provided, which could result in increased malnutrition and poverty.

Alternatives such as livestock or poultry are often named but, in the Congo Basin, an estimated additional 4.5 million tons of pigs or chickens would be needed to replace wild meat, requiring millions of hectares of forest clearance. Deforestation would destroy globally important habitats. Further, disease emergence from domestic animals is also a real risk, and agricultural intensification and land use change, particularly in tropical regions where wildlife biodiversity is high, are root causes of disease emergence. It is time to learn from past mistakes, not repeat them.

This is not to say that nothing should change following the COVID-19 pandemic. We must dramatically re-evaluate our relationship with animals and with nature more broadly. A priority should be better regulation rather than outright bans, focused on addressing illegal, unsustainable and high-disease-risk trade, whether this involves wild or domestic animals. We should also carefully consider the impact of regulation on food security, and focus efforts on areas where wild meat is a luxury. While a blanket ban may sound good on paper, in reality, long-term policy changes need to be designed with enough nuance to be feasible, to be effective, and to not cause further harm.

Some environmentalists are seeking an international ban on all live wildlife trade, including pets, working through existing treaties. The Convention on International Trade in Endangered Species of Wild Fauna and Flora (CITES), a legally binding accord agreed to by 183 countries, is one possible avenue, according to Elly Pepper, deputy director of the International Wildlife Conservation Initiative at the Natural Resources Defense Council, a New York-based environmental group.[92]

The treaty prohibits international commercial trade in about 670 animal species threatened with extinction and regulates trade in more than 5,000 species that could become threatened. But most wildlife species traded for food are not covered.[93]

"The purpose of CITES is to address unsustainable trade, and this pandemic has made us realize that the wildlife trade has a component we haven't thought about—human health," says Pepper. She wrote in a blog that the leadership of CITES should be "scouring" the treaty's text to bring changes in that direction and not "shrugging its shoulders."[94]

However, the CITES secretariat said recently that "matters regarding zoonotic diseases are outside of CITES's mandate," and other experts agree that the treaty would have to be amended to make public health a reason for prohibiting trade in a designated species.[95]

"Amending treaties is really complicated—it would not happen quickly," says Lieberman of the Wildlife Conservation Society, noting that the last time the treaty was amended it took 30 years, requiring a two-thirds majority.[96]

Pepper says another possible international forum is the United Nations Convention on Biological Diversity, signed by 150 government leaders at the 1992 Rio Earth Summit, which calls for commitments by nations to prevent the long-term decline of biodiversity. The United States is not a party to that treaty.

The next meeting of the diversity convention in 2021 should pledge to meet the Natural Resources Defense Council's goal of protecting 30 percent of the Earth's land and water by 2030, according to Pepper. "When thousands of acres of the Amazon are destroyed for agriculture, for example, the risk to humans from contact with wildlife increases," she said.[97]

But the convention, while filled with commendable recommendations, has "no teeth" to enforce any actions by governments, according to Machalaba, the policy adviser at the EcoHealth Alliance. Machalaba says she wants zoonotic risk made part of risk assessments for new development projects, much like environmental impact statements used by governments, corporations and international agencies such as the World Bank.

U.S. Efforts

To prevent another zoonotic epidemic, leading members of Congress are pushing for more funding to enforce laws against illegal wildlife trafficking and legislation to encourage a ban on overseas markets that sell live and exotic animals.

Sen. Tom Udall, D-N.M., said in April that congressional members were pushing for a "substantial increase" in funding for the U.S. Fish and Wildlife Service to stop illegal wildlife from other countries. Udall is the ranking Democrat on the Senate Appropriations subcommittee that oversees the Fish and Wildlife Service. Subcommittee Chairman Lisa Murkowski, R-Alaska, said she was also concerned about the link between the illegal wildlife trade and public health.[98]

In early February 2020, in its fiscal 2021 budget request, the Trump administration proposed a 16 percent cut in the Fish and Wildlife Service, the agency charged with enforcing wildlife anti-trafficking laws.[99] However, Congress rejected many of Trump's proposed cuts in environmental agencies when it passed the 2020 appropriations package, so it is questionable whether Trump's cuts will make it into the final bill for 2021 intact.[100]

Several bills seek to prohibit zoonotically dangerous imports from wildlife markets overseas and offer incentives to other countries to ban these markets. Buried in the $3 trillion act passed by the House to deal with the pandemic-caused economic downturn is a section making it illegal to import species designated by Fish and Wildlife as a "biohazard to human health." It authorizes $111 million to help foreign countries end the trade in animals that pose a disease risk to human health and to strengthen early detection of zoonotic diseases.[101]

However, the Democratic-controlled House passed the bill in a party line vote, and Senate Majority Leader Mitch McConnell, R-Ky., has said it has "no chance of becoming law" and will not pass in the Republican-controlled Senate.[102] Some environmental groups think a bipartisan measure dealing with wildlife may have more chance of success than the Democrats' bill—perhaps as part of a future economic stimulus measure.

In one such effort in the Senate, Republican Graham and Democrat Coons have introduced a measure aimed at banning the sale of "high-risk" wildlife in live animal markets for human consumption. The more than $1 billion bill requires federal agencies to identify which species have a high risk of spreading a zoonotic disease and authorizes the president to use sanctions against nations that continue to permit markets selling those animals, along with aid to help communities that depend on wildlife for subsistence.[103]

"How can we prevent this from happening again?" Graham asked in a statement referring to the COVID-19 pandemic. "Governments in Asia and elsewhere should immediately shut down markets that sell high-risk wildlife for human consumption and fully enforce laws already on the books to end the global illegal trade in wildlife."[104]

Several mainstream conservation groups, including the World Wildlife Fund and the Nature Conservancy, have endorsed the bill.

However, two environmental groups say it does not go far enough. The trade in all live wildlife should be banned, not just those designated "high-risk," say the Natural Resources Defense Council and the Center for Biological Diversity, based in Tucson, Ariz.

The bill's approach—directing federal agencies to predict a species' risk before banning its import—is "like playing Russian roulette," considering some 5,000 species are traded internationally, says Brett Hartl, the Center for Biological Diversity's government affairs director: "Every single species on the planet has viruses and bacteria. So the notion that somehow we could ever determine what species and combination of events are likely to cause a disease is extremely low."

Moreover, he says, the bill ignores the United States' own role in the trade; it is the No. 1 importer of exotic animals for pets and the site of markets selling live reptiles and amphibians for food in large American cities.

The bill also encourages the federal government to use a so-called One Health approach to detection and response to pandemic threats, uniting expertise from animal health, human health and environmental health experts.[105]

Earlier this year, the Trump administration had planned to shut down USAID's 10-year PREDICT program, which trains science and lab workers in developing countries to identify potential zoonotic diseases. Sens. Elizabeth Warren, D-Mass., and Angus King, I-Maine, protested the shutdown in late January, saying COVID-19 "heightens the need for a robust, coordinated, and proactive response to emerging pandemics—one of the roles that PREDICT played."[106]

In an about-face effective April 1, the administration extended the program's funding for six months. With the $2.26 million extension, PREDICT will continue to provide technical expertise to support detection of cases of COVID-19 in Africa, Asia and the Middle East to support the public health response.[107]

OUTLOOK
Growing Pressures

Pressure to clear land for agriculture and hunt bush meat for food is expected to increase with an expanding world population, raising worries about increasing spillovers of zoonotic diseases in degraded landscapes.

"The intensity and frequency of outbreaks will continue in China, but we will see parallel events beginning with much greater intensity in areas that were remote and isolated," predicts the Global Virome Project's Carroll, pointing to Africa, where the population is expected to boom along with a growing middle class. "If they assume the dietary patterns that are prevalent in the U.S., then we will have a huge problem in land use, because they will demand cattle protein."

Sharing similar concerns, Harvard's Myers says habitat destruction in Africa and the Amazon basin for agriculture could be stemmed by innovations in food production, including artificial milk and eggs, plant-based meat substitutes along the lines of the Impossible Burger, insect-based foods and new crop varieties. "It's not too late, but we absolutely can't continue on our current trajectory without paying enormous human health costs," he says.

Some scientists hope that advances in interpreting the genome of viruses will help predict and prevent zoonotic pandemics.

"Ultimately, one of our big goals—the holy grail—is to look at the genome of a virus before it's caused even a single human infection and understand whether it will cause disease," says EcoHealth scientist Epstein, who sees the Global Virome Project's proposed virus library as one step in that direction. Each experience of studying these viruses in animals and people "brings us closer" to that goal, he says.

For bat coronaviruses, which EcoHealth has studied extensively, "we're five to 10 years from being able to break down the risk of them emerging and disrupt them from emerging," says EcoHealth President Daszak. "In a few decades, we'll be able to prevent many pandemics."

Daszak adds, "Fifty years from now, people will look back on this time and say, 'That was the pandemic era and thank goodness they got to grips with that.'"

In the meantime, COVID-19 has been a reminder of how much faster a disease can spread in the modern world via planes and global trade than in earlier centuries. "The rate of spread of the [bubonic] plague from Central Europe took years; now it's hours," says Stanford's Lambin, who calls COVID-19's "double whammy" of zoonotic disease plus globalization "a very dangerous cocktail."

One of the biggest obstacles to attacking the environmental roots of zoonotic epidemics, scientists and advocates agree, is getting the world to listen. Many of them hope that will change because of the current pandemic.

"The issue of high-risk wildlife trade has been around forever," says the World Wildlife Fund's Vertefeuille. "What's new and different right now is the entire world and the global economy is bearing the costs of that risky wildlife trade. So we really have a moment in time to address this issue—that if we act quickly and aggressively we can try to stop the next pandemic."

The current pandemic is just one of many signals, along with a changing climate, that our planet is in trouble, says Myers.

"I'm hoping COVID-19 will be the loudest and most immediate of these warning bells that we've been hearing, that it will be a wake-up call," he says. "We need to pause and address this relationship we have with our natural systems."

NOTES

1. Andrew Joseph, "First death from Wuhan pneumonia outbreak reported as scientists release DNA sequence of virus," *STAT*, Jan. 11, 2020, https://tinyurl.com/s4wx3nk; Derrick Bryson Taylor, "How the Coronavirus Pandemic Unfolded: a Timeline," *The New York Times*, June 9, 2020, https://tinyurl.com/wb48cut; and Chaolin Huang *et al.*, "Clinical features of patients infected with 2019 novel coronavirus in Wuhan, China," *The Lancet*, Jan. 24, 2020, https://tinyurl.com/w5qfs4w.
2. Jeremy Page and Natasha Khan, "On the ground in Wuhan, Signs of China Stalling Probe of Coronavirus Origins," *The Wall Street Journal*, May 12, 2020, https://tinyurl.com/ycqtmqkp.
3. James T. Areddy, "China Rules out Animal Market and Lab as Coronavirus Origin," *The Wall Street Journal*, May 26, 2020, https://tinyurl.com/yb7jyb78.
4. David Cyranoski, "The biggest mystery: what it will take to trace the coronavirus source," *Nature*, June 5, 2020, https://tinyurl.com/yd7ooc6a; Alexandre Hassanin, "Coronavirus origins," *The Conversation*, March 24, 2020, https://tinyurl.com/rynx542.
5. Kate E. Jones, "Global trends in emerging infectious diseases," *Nature*, Feb. 21, 2008, https://tinyurl.com/y8676bqx; "One Health, Zoonotic Diseases," Centers for Disease Control and Prevention, last reviewed July 14, 2017, https://tinyurl.com/yaxup36m.
6. Vincent C.C. Cheng *et al.*, "Severe Acute Respiratory Syndrome Coronavirus in an Agent of Emerging and Reemerging Infection," *Clinical Microbiology Review*, October 2007, https://tinyurl.com/w2yjfj6.
7. Damian Carrington, "Coronavirus: 'Nature is sending us a message,' says UN environment chief," *The Guardian*, March 25, 2020, https://tinyurl.com/ycvgc7lt.
8. "Our health depends on our environment," Planetary Health Alliance, https://tinyurl.com/yaospq78.
9. "Global Wildlife Health and Pandemic Prevention Act," Sen. Chris Coons and Sen. Lindsey Graham, https://tinyurl.com/ya72mg34; "Bi-Partisan One Health Congressional Bills introduced in U.S. Senate and House," One Health Commission, 2020, https://tinyurl.com/yyn8b8vj.
10. "Reducing Pandemic Risk, Promoting Global Health," USAID, accessed June 17, 2020, https://tinyurl.com/yad4gotw.

11. "World Population by Year," worldometer, https://tinyurl.com/y2nw28sa.
12. Anthony Cilluffo and Neil G. Ruiz, "World's population is projected to nearly stop growing by end of the century," Pew Research Center, June 17, 2019, https://tinyurl.com/yd2kw8j2.
13. Chelsea L. Wood et al., "Human infectious disease burdens decrease with urbanization but not with biodiversity," *Philosophical Transactions of the Royal Society B*, April 24, 2017, https://tinyurl.com/ya89fgmg.
14. "The Wildlife Origins of SARS-COV2 and Employing a One Health Approach," podcast interview with Dr. Steve Osofsky, Excellsior, April 3, 2020, https://tinyurl.com/yacvagop.
15. Kate E. Jones et al., op. cit.
16. "Forest ecology shapes Lyme disease risk in the eastern US," *Science Daily*, July 9, 2018, https://tinyurl.com/y7h82kja; Richard S. Ostfeld et al., "Tickborne disease risk in a forest web," *Ecology*, May 8, 2018, https://tinyurl.com/ybskbxce.
17. Wood et al., op. cit.
18. Laura S.P. Bloomfield et al., "Habitat fragmentation, livelihood behaviors, and contact between people and nonhuman primates in Africa," *Landscape Ecology*, April 1, 2020, https://tinyurl.com/y8uxnems.
19. "How forest loss leads to spread of disease," Stanford University, April 8, 2020, https://tinyurl.com/yahrzsuu.
20. Christine K. Johnson et al., "Global shifts in mammalian population trends reveal key predictors of virus spillover risk," *Proceedings of the Royal Society B*, April 8, 2020, https://tinyurl.com/rcjgms2.
21. Jason R. Rohr et al., "Emerging human infectious diseases and the links to global food production," *Nature Sustainability*, June 11, 2019, https://tinyurl.com/y9uuc5y9.
22. Johnson, op. cit.
23. "End the Trade: Coalition Invites Global Community to Take a Stand Against Future Pandemics," WildAid, April 20, 2020, https://tinyurl.com/y7amshwc.
24. "A Global Call to Action on Covid-19 and Wildlife Trade," preventpandemics.org, https://tinyurl.com/ybhcdpb7.
25. Dan Challender et al., "Coronavirus: Why a blanket ban on wildlife trade would not be the right response," *The Conversation*, April 8, 2020, https://tinyurl.com/y8exr4sf.
26. "China Suspends Wildlife Trade to Curb Novel Coronavirus," Xinhuanet, Jan. 26, 2020, https://tinyurl.com/yag4e22g.
27. George Wittemyer, "The new coronavirus emerged from the global wildlife trade and may be devastating enough to end it," *The Conversation*, March 31, 2020, https://tinyurl.com/spztlfm.
28. Jesse Bonwitt et al., "Unintended Consequences of the 'Bushmeat Ban' in West Africa during 2013-2016 Ebola Virus Disease Epidemic," *Social Science & Medicine*, March 2018, https://tinyurl.com/yc4p9bq9.
29. "Wildlife Crime: Pangolin Scales," United Nations Office on Drugs and Crime, 2020, https://tinyurl.com/yablpa5e.
30. Candace Famiglietti and Maria Ivanova, "We must address exotic wildlife consumption to avoid the Next Global Pandemic," *New Security Beat*, April 20, 2020, https://tinyurl.com/ybgucocn.
31. "One Health," World Bank Group, 2018, p. 15, https://tinyurl.com/t6gbr7e.
32. "Shutdown of PREDICT Infectious Disease Program Challenged by Senators Warren and King," *Global Biodefense*, Feb. 4, 2020, https://tinyurl.com/y8pzml9p.
33. Colin J. Carlson, "From PREDICT to prevention, one pandemic later," *The Lancet Microbe*, March 21, 2020, https://tinyurl.com/yaw424hr.
34. Cyranoski, op. cit.
35. Nina Wang et al., "Serological Evidence of Bat SARS-related Coronavirus Infection in Humans, China," *Virological Sinica*, March 2, 2018, https://tinyurl.com/y8e4j53b.
36. Steve Osofsky, "Emerging 'dis-ease': US foreign assistance needs to focus on the root causes of pandemics," *The Hill*, May 24, 2020, https://tinyurl.com/ycds8yoa.

37. Steven Johnson, "How Data Became One of the Most Powerful Tools to Fight an Epidemic," *The New York Times Magazine*, June 10, 2020, https://tinyurl.com/y9mk9vt8.
38. Christian Nordqvist, "Origins of the Black Death Traced Back to China, Gene Sequencing Has Revealed," *Medical News Today*, Nov. 1, 2010, https://tinyurl.com/yd27waez.
39. Ibid.
40. "The History of Plague—Part 1. The Three Great Pandemics," *Journal of Military and Veterans Health*, https://tinyurl.com/yckb75kl.
41. "Plague," Centers for Disease Control and Prevention, https://tinyurl.com/saz8w86.
42. "One Health, Zoonotic Diseases," *op. cit.*
43. David Quammen, *Spillover* (2013), p. 427.
44. *Ibid.*, p. 137.
45. Jason R. Rohr, *op. cit.*
46. Quammen, *op. cit.*, p. 43.
47. *Ibid.*
48. *Ibid.*, pp. 22-23.
49. *Ibid.*, p. 31; "Monkeypox," Centers for Disease Control and Prevention, https://tinyurl.com/y726qbrh.
50. Tom Evans et al., "Links between ecological integrity, emerging infectious disease originating from wildlife, and other aspects of human health," Wildlife Conservation Society, April 2020, https://tinyurl.com/y8dd4ac4.
51. Sarah Glazer, "Avian Flu Threat," *CQ Researcher*, Jan. 13, 2006, https://tinyurl.com/ycb53he2.
52. "Influenza; 1957-1958 Pandemic (H2N2 Virus)," Centers for Disease Control and Prevention, Jan. 2, 2019, https://tinyurl.com/ycqqgbqb; "Influenza; 1968 Pandemic (H3N2 virus)," Jan. 2, 2019, https://tinyurl.com/ybxo853d.
53. Jeremy Brown, *Influenza: The Hundred-Year Hunt to Cure the Deadliest Disease in History* (2018), p. 60.
54. *Ibid.*, p. 65.
55. "Hot Spots for Emerging Diseases," *The New York Times*, July 15, 2012, https://tinyurl.com/y5kl5vhu.
56. Warren Andiman, *Animal Viruses and Humans, a Narrow Divide* (2018), p. 165, p. 167.
57. "Ebola Virus Disease," World Health Organization, Feb. 10, 2020, https://tinyurl.com/y24gcxvg.
58. Andiman, *op. cit.*, pp. 170-173.
59. Evans et al., *op. cit.*
60. "Nipah virus," World Health Organization, May 30, 2018, https://tinyurl.com/y8hudome; Paul M. Sharp and Beatrice H. Hahn, "Origins of HIV and the AIDS Pandemic," *Cold Spring Harbor Perspectives in Medicine*, September 2011, https://tinyurl.com/y5pftt2w.
61. "Hot Spots for Emerging Diseases," *op. cit.*
62. Evans et al., *op. cit.*
63. "2014-2016 Ebola Outbreak in West Africa," Centers for Disease Control and Prevention, March 8, 2019, https://tinyurl.com/y7aqqxp2.
64. "Ebola virus disease," *op. cit.*
65. "Top 9 Infectious Disease Outbreaks of 2018," Contagion Live, Dec. 31, 2018, https://tinyurl.com/y8los7fp; Grant M. Gallagher, "The Ebola Outbreak Response So Far," Contagion Live, Jan. 2, 2020, https://tinyurl.com/y8ryuglp; and "Ebola Virus Disease," *op. cit.*
66. "CDC SARS Response Timeline," Centers for Disease Control and Prevention, April 26, 2013, https://tinyurl.com/vsp9qng.
67. Brown, *op. cit.*, p. 6.
68. Diana Bell, "Coronavirus: We still haven't learned the lessons from Sars," *The Conversation*, Jan. 24, 2020, https://tinyurl.com/yc5u86el.
69. "SARS (Severe Acute Respiratory Syndrome)," World Health Organization, 2020, https://tinyurl.com/vnwflw4; "Update 95—SARS: Chronology of a Serial Killer," World Health Organization, Nov. 16, 2002, https://tinyurl.com/y8p2uuxy.
70. Glazer, *op. cit.*
71. *Ibid.*
72. "Influenza (Flu)," Centers for Disease Control and Prevention, Jan. 8, 2014, https://tinyurl.com/u4jjgh5.

73. Martin Enserink, "WHO Declares Official End to H1N1 'Swine Flu' Epidemic," *Science*, Aug. 10, 2010, https://tinyurl.com/ybxkojbb.
74. Mackenzie Bean, "A look back at swine flu," *Becker's Hospital Review*, March 12, 2020, https://tinyurl.com/t5n5jpk.
75. "Hot Spots for Emerging Diseases," *op. cit.*; Jim Robbins, "The Ecology of Disease," *The New York Times*, July 14, 2012, https://tinyurl.com/qpmwpry.
76. Yella Hewings-Martin, "How do SARS and MERS Compare with COVID-19?" *Medical News Today*, April 10, 2020, https://tinyurl.com/y77vpj7t.
77. Roger Frutos *et al.*, "COVID-19, The Conjunction of Events Leading to the Coronavirus Pandemic and Lessons to Learn for Future Threats," *Frontiers in Medicine*, May 12, 2020, https://tinyurl.com/yd388hkr.
78. "Pneumonia of Unknown Cause-China," World Health Organization, Jan. 5, 2020, https://tinyurl.com/qwxenbk.
79. Chaolin Huang *et al.*, "Clinical features of patients infected with 2019 novel coronavirus in Wuhan, China," *The Lancet*, Jan. 24, 2020, https://tinyurl.com/w5qfs4w.
80. Hassanin, *op. cit.*
81. Daniel Lucey, "Recent Data and Maps to help find origin of COVID-19," *Science Speaks: Global ID News*, March 15, 2020, https://tinyurl.com/szykfa2; Frutos, *op. cit.*; Josephine Ma, "Coronavirus: China's first confirmed COVID-19 case traced back to November 17," *South China Morning Post*, March 13, 2020, https://tinyurl.com/sdajymy; and Page and Khan, *op. cit.*
82. Jackie Salo, "Wuhan market is the 'victim' of coronavirus outbreak," *New York Post*, May 27, 2020, https://tinyurl.com/y89u8g3m.
83. Hassanin, *op. cit.*
84. Steven Lee Meyers, "China Vowed to Keep Wildlife off the Menu, a Tough Promise to Keep," *The New York Times*, June 7, 2020, https://tinyurl.com/y9havdyf.
85. David Stanway, "China legislators take on wildlife trade, but traditional medicine likely to be exempt," *Reuters*, May 20, 2020, https://tinyurl.com/y8pmgfnj.
86. Ben Westcott, "Chinese government reveals draft list of animals which can be farmed for meat," *CNN*, April 10, 2020, https://tinyurl.com/s9fpupq.
87. "China offers farmers cash to give up wildlife trade," *AFP, Bangkok Post*, May 19, 2020, https://tinyurl.com/ydcwt343.
88. Michael Tatarski, "Vietnam wildlife trade ban appears to flounder amid coronavirus success," *Mongabay*, May 25, 2020, https://tinyurl.com/ya7k2uqy.
89. Jackie Northam, "Calls to Ban Wildlife Markets Worldwide Gain Steam Amid Pandemic," *NPR*, April 19, 2020, https://tinyurl.com/yceea6rd; Helen Briggs, "Coronavirus: WHO developing guidance on wet markets," *BBC News*, April 21, 2020, https://tinyurl.com/y7rx5j6x.
90. "UN: Live Animal Markets Shouldn't Be Closed Despite Virus," *The Associated Press/U.S. News & World Report*, May 8, 2020, https://tinyurl.com/y9sjswby.
91. "End the Trade: New Coalition Invites Global Community to Take a Stand Against Future Pandemics," WSCNewsroom, April 21, 2020, https://tinyurl.com/yajo6ys8.
92. "What is CITES?" CITES, https://tinyurl.com/zrccyqb.
93. Susan Lieberman, "CITES, the Treaty that Regulates Trade in International Wildlife, Is Not the Answer to Preventing Another Zoonotic Pandemic," *National Geographic*, May 22, 2020, https://tinyurl.com/y8d5qzk6.
94. Elly Pepper, "We must prevent future viruses by ending the wildlife trade," NRDC, April 14, 2020, https://tinyurl.com/ya6gdy99.
95. "CITES Secretariat's statement in relation to COVID-19," CITES, https://tinyurl.com/ydgudnxy.
96. Lieberman, *op. cit.*
97. Pepper, *op. cit.*
98. Stephen Lee and Dean Scott, "As Lawmakers Push Global Wildlife Market Ban, U.S. Issues Remain,"

Bloomberg Law, April 28, 2020, https://tinyurl.com/ybjungch.

99. "U.S. Fish and Wildlife Service: FY2021 Appropriations," Congressional Research Service, March 20, 2020, https://tinyurl.com/yclp53wu.

100. John R. Platt, "Trump's Budget Plan: A Push for Even Greater Environmental Regression," *EcoWatch*, Feb. 12, 2020, https://tinyurl.com/y79sor5s.

101. Rebecca Beitsch, "Two green groups call for end to wildlife trade to prevent next pandemic," *The Hill*, May 18, 2020, https://tinyurl.com/yasezlar.

102. Lauren Frias, "House passes $3 trillion coronavirus relief bill dubbed HEROES Act," *Business Insider*, May 15, 2020, https://tinyurl.com/yaccyogl.

103. "Discussion Draft," coons.senate.gov, accessed June 17, 2020, https://tinyurl.com/y7wxw5mu.

104. "Sens. Coons, Graham introduce legislation to shut down high-risk wildlife markets that could ignite another global disease outbreak," press release, Sen. Chris Coons, May 19, 2020, https://tinyurl.com/y77otomf.

105. "Global Wildlife Health and Pandemic Prevention Act," *op. cit.*

106. "Senators Warren, King Question USAID on Decision to Shutter Global Infectious Disease Prevention Program," press release, Elizabeth Warren, Jan. 31, 2020, https://tinyurl.com/y8u6nw7m.

107. Kristin Burns, "PREDICT Receives Extension for COVID-19 Pandemic Emergency Response," UCDavis, March 31, 2020, https://tinyurl.com/ybcw8p35.

BIBLIOGRAPHY
Books
Andiman, Warren A., *Animal Viruses and Humans, A Narrow Divide: How Lethal Zoonotic Viruses Spill Over and Threaten Us,* **Paul Dry Books, 2018.**
A professor emeritus of pediatrics and epidemiology at the Yale University Schools of Medicine and Public Health explains the science behind some of the biggest zoonotic outbreaks in recent years, including MERS, SARS and Ebola.

Brown, Jeremy, *Influenza: The Hundred-Year Hunt to Cure the Deadliest Disease in History,* **Touchstone, 2018.**
The director of the Office of Emergency Care Research at the National Institutes of Health provides a readable history of flu epidemics, including the 1918 Spanish flu, and traces scientific and governmental efforts to cure the disease.

Quammen, David, *Spillover: Animal Infections and the Next Human Pandemic,* **W.W. Norton, 2012.**
A science writer accompanies prominent virus hunters into the wild to illustrate how scientists have tried to trace zoonotic diseases such as SARS, Ebola and AIDS back to their animal origins and how animal diseases spill over to humans.

Articles
Areddy, James T., "China Rules Out Animal Market and Lab as Coronavirus Origin," *The Wall Street Journal*, **May 26, 2020, https://tinyurl.com/yb7jyb78.**
In an interview with Chinese state media, the head of China's Center for Disease Control and Prevention said his scientists were unable to trace the virus that caused COVID-19 to an animal at the Wuhan seafood market, originally suspected as a source.

Beitsch, Rebecca, "Two green groups call for end to wildlife trade to prevent next pandemic," *The Hill*, **May 18, 2020, https://tinyurl.com/yasezlar.**
Two environmental groups urged Congress to ban the trade in all live wildlife, saying the recent House-passed Heroes Act does not go far enough.

Bell, Diana, "Coronavirus: We still haven't learned the lessons from Sars," *The Conversation*, **Jan. 24, 2020, https://tinyurl.com/yc5u86el.**
A professor of conservation biology at the University of East Anglia in England argues that the world should learn the lesson from the 2002-03 SARS outbreak—that the wildlife trade is a "threat to human health."

Meyers, Steven Lee, "China Vowed to Keep Wildlife Off the Menu, a Tough Promise to Keep," *The New York Times*, **June 7, 2020, https://tinyurl.com/y9havdyf.**
A journalist discusses the economic pressures to narrow China's wildlife ban as the government considers permanent legal changes.

Osofsky, Steve, "Emerging 'dis-ease': US foreign assistance needs to focus on the root causes of pandemics," *The Hill*, May 24, 2020, https://tinyurl.com/ycds8yoa.
A wildlife veterinarian at Cornell University argues that the government should reorient its efforts away from hunting for the viruses that could cause the next pandemic and toward stopping root causes such as wildlife trade and deforestation.

Watts, Jonathan, "'Promiscuous treatment of nature' will lead to more pandemics—scientists," *The Guardian*, May 7, 2020, https://tinyurl.com/yaf3l4gr.
A journalist quotes scientists who say human beings' destruction of nature, such as habitat occupied by bats in Asia, will lead to more pandemics of diseases jumping from animals.

Reports and Studies

Evans, Tom, *et al.*, "Links between ecological integrity, emerging infectious diseases originating from wildlife, and other aspects of human health—an overview of the literature," Wildlife Conservation Society, April 2020, https://tinyurl.com/y8dd4ac4.
A global conservation group that also runs the Bronx Zoo summarizes research showing links between human incursions into the environment and outbreaks of infectious diseases.

Keesing, Felicia, *et al.*, "Impacts of biodiversity on the emergence and transmission of infectious diseases," *Nature*, Dec. 2, 2010, https://tinyurl.com/yaja4q8j.
A Bard College professor and other environmental health researchers conclude that preserving ecosystems "should generally reduce the prevalence of infectious diseases."

Magnusson, Magnus, *et al.*, "Effect of spatial scale and latitude on diversity-disease relationships," *Ecology*, December 2019, https://tinyurl.com/yab8tbbg.
This meta-analysis by Swedish and American ecology experts found that high biodiversity was linked to reduced risk of infectious disease in large regions in the temperate zone.

Wood, Chelsea L., *et al.*, "Human infectious disease burdens decrease with urbanization but not with biodiversity," *Philosophical Transactions of the Royal Society B*, April 24, 2017, https://tinyurl.com/ya89fgmg.
In this study of 60 countries, researchers from universities in Washington, California and Maryland find that urbanization and growing wealth have been the main drivers in reducing infectious diseases, while biodiversity has had a minimal to negative effect.

THE NEXT STEP

Biodiversity

Hall, Louise, "World Bee Day: Are we ignoring biodiversity risks in the same way we ignored the pandemic?" *The Independent*, May 20, 2020, https://tinyurl.com/y85s2j6s.
Experts warn that losses of biodiversity, especially bees, constitute a crisis that people are unprepared for, much the way many were caught off guard by the coronavirus pandemic.

Rankin, Jennifer, "EU plan for 3bn trees in 10 years to tackle biodiversity crisis," *The Guardian*, May 19, 2020, https://tinyurl.com/ybku3t9q.
A European Union initiative calls for one-third of the continent to become protected zones, but some scientists say the strategy is not specific enough.

Win, Thin Lei, "Will pandemic push humans into a healthier relationship with nature?" *Reuters*, May 21, 2020, https://tinyurl.com/yagvjtf8.
The coronavirus pandemic has hampered ongoing efforts to preserve biodiversity, according to environmentalists.

Coronavirus and the Environment

Beitsch, Rebecca, "Efforts to rescue recycling complicated by coronavirus," *The Hill*, June 17, 2020, https://tinyurl.com/ybnznbzo.
Municipalities facing budget shortfalls due to the coronavirus pandemic might be forced to recycle less material, and the recycling industry has turned to Congress for help.

Harvey, Fiona, "Covid-19 pandemic is 'fire drill' for effects of climate crisis, says UN official," *The Guardian*, June 15, 2020, https://tinyurl.com/ycu6ww4c.
A United Nations business chief warns that crises like the coronavirus pandemic will multiply until humans adopt more environmentally sustainable practices.

Miller, Ryan W., "'More masks than jellyfish': Environmental groups worry about coronavirus waste in oceans," *USA Today*, June 9, 2020, https://tinyurl.com/ydfe6rlw.
Environmentalists warn that masks, gloves and other pandemic-related waste are polluting the ocean.

Regulations

Challender, Dan, et al., "Coronavirus: why a blanket ban on wildlife trade would not be the right response," *The Conversation*, April 8, 2020, https://tinyurl.com/y8exr4sf.
Environmental researchers argue blanket bans on wildlife consumption would encourage illegal sales, but that targeted regulations would make wildlife trade safer.

Khadka, Navin Singh, "Coronavirus: China wildlife trade ban 'should be permanent,'" *BBC*, Feb. 4, 2020, https://tinyurl.com/ybve9hom.
Conservationists called on China to make its temporary wildlife trade ban permanent, and state-run media in the country denounced the lack of regulations in the wildlife market.

Londoño, Ernesto, Manuela Andreoni and Letícia Casado, "Amazon Deforestation Soars as Pandemic Hobbles Enforcement," *The New York Times*, June 6, 2020, https://tinyurl.com/y9tqce7v.
Illegal loggers and miners in the Amazon see little chance of punishment because deforestation regulations are going unenforced during the pandemic.

Wildlife Consumption

Alden, Chris, and Ross Harvey, "A South African proposal to allow the breeding of wildlife for slaughter could end in disaster," *Quartz Africa*, June 15, 2020, https://tinyurl.com/y9rbc2q9.
South Africa is considering expanding the number of species that can be bred for slaughter, raising the risk of humans contracting zoonotic diseases, according to the authors.

Kays, Roland, "Can Asia end its uncontrolled consumption of wildlife? Here's how North America did it a century ago," *The Conversation*, June 17, 2020, https://tinyurl.com/yazbkl3d.
North America limited wildlife consumption in the early 1900s, after many species were driven nearly extinct, and China could pursue a similar conservation plan, according to a scientist.

Stanway, David, "China legislators take on wildlife trade, but traditional medicine likely to be exempt," *Reuters*, May 20, 2020, https://tinyurl.com/y9h6skc4.
Wildlife continues to be used in medicine and in the fur trade in China, because those practices are exempt from the country's ban on consumption.

For More Information

Center for Biological Diversity, PO Box 710, Tucson, AZ 85702-0710; 520-623-5252; biologicaldiversity.org. Advocacy group working to protect endangered species.

Centers for Disease Control and Prevention, 1600 Clifton Road, Atlanta, GA 30329; 800-232-4636; cdc.gov. Federal government's lead public health agency.

EcoHealth Alliance, 520 Eighth Ave., Suite 1200, New York, NY 10018; 212-380-4460; ecohealthalliance.org. Research group developing science-based solutions to prevent pandemics and promote conservation.

One Health Commission, PO Box 972, Apex, NC 27502; 984-500-8093; onehealthcommission.org. Nonprofit advocating "One Health" approaches, which join experts in animal, plant and human health with ecosystem professionals.

Wildlife Conservation Society, 2300 Southern Blvd., Bronx, NY 10460; 718-220-5100; wcs.org. Global advocacy and research group dedicated to protecting wildlife and wild places.

World Health Organization, 1 Dag Hammarskjöld Plaza, 885 Second Ave., 26th floor, New York, NY 10017; 646-626-6060; who.int. United Nations agency that is responsible for international public health.

World Wildlife Fund, 1250 24th St., N.W., Washington, DC 20037; 202-293-4800; worldwildlife.org. Global conservation group dedicated to protecting wildlife and natural habitats.

16

The Future of Meat

Can the industry navigate health and environmental concerns?

By Sara Toth Stub

Ryan MacKay checks on his cows at Lilac Hedge Farm, where cattle, sheep, pigs and chickens are raised using sustainable methods in Hudson, Mass. Since the coronavirus pandemic began, the small farm's home deliveries have increased, as customers turned to locally raised meats.

From *CQ Researcher*, September 25, 2020

THE ISSUES

Ranchers Mac and Celsie Sussex are trying to figure out how to set up their own meat-processing facility in Goshen, Wyo., to slaughter and pack cuts of their grass-fed cattle, after Wyoming in July became the first state to allow farmers to sell portions of their cows directly to Wyoming consumers.

Selling directly to consumers cuts out the intermediaries, such as meat processing companies and retailers, making locally raised meat more affordable and helping small ranchers stay in business, say the Sussexes and other ranchers.[1]

"We put a bunch of feed in our cattle and then grocery stores and the packers are making the extra money off it," Celsie Sussex said.[2]

Whether Wyoming's new policy will aid small ranchers or help diversify the increasingly consolidated U.S. meat industry remains to be seen, but it is one of a growing number of issues facing an industry dominated by big players. As beef, poultry and pork producers try to determine how to keep up with the growing global demand for meat, policymakers and consumers are raising concerns about industry consolidation and its effect on the environment and human health. Responses to those concerns could have a lasting impact on the industry and the planet.

"All the pressures on the industry are adding up," says Joshua Specht, assistant professor of history at Notre Dame and author of

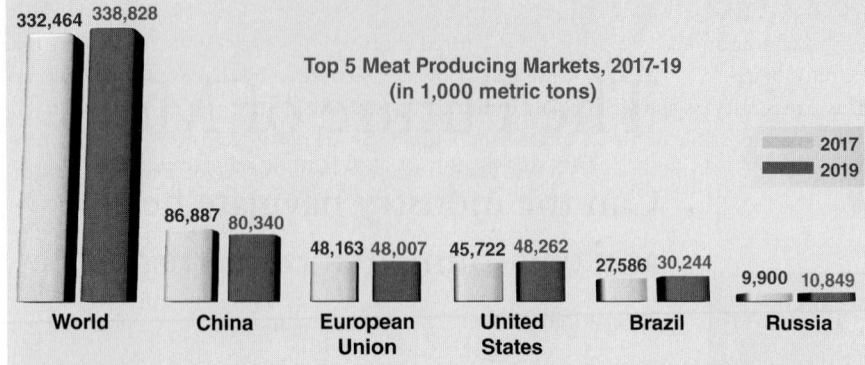

Global Meat Production on the Rise

Total world production of meat rose by 6 million tons between 2017 and 2019, but fell in China, the world's largest producer, and in the European Union after outbreaks of African swine fever in 2018 required large numbers of hogs to be destroyed. Production rose in the United States, Brazil and Russia.

Top 5 Meat Producing Markets, 2017-19 (in 1,000 metric tons)

Region	2017	2019
World	332,464	338,828
China	86,887	80,340
European Union	48,163	48,007
United States	45,722	48,262
Brazil	27,586	30,244
Russia	9,900	10,849

Sources: "China: pork production drops by 5.5%," Pig333, July 22, 2019, https://tinyurl.com/yyrwxqsm; "Meat Market Review," U.N. Food and Agriculture Organization, March 2019, https://tinyurl.com/yybvv4vr; and "Meat Market Review," U.N. Food and Agriculture Organization, April 2020, https://tinyurl.com/y5hr2syo

Red Meat Republic: A Hoof-to-Table History of How Beef Changed America. "It's not exactly a moment of revolutionary change, but all the issues about meat are now in the public conversation." Nearly one in four Americans say they are eating less meat, with most citing health reasons.[3]

Nevertheless, overall meat consumption in the United States has grown steadily in recent years, and global consumption has increased even faster, as incomes rise across the world. The U.S. meat industry, which produces beef, pork, lamb and poultry, recorded sales of $218 billion in 2019 and produced about 100 billion pounds of products. Globally, the industry is valued at $945.7 billion, and produced more than 725 billion pounds in 2018.[4]

This has also led to increased trade in meat, international consolidation of producers and U.S. producers' growing reliance on selling to foreign markets such as Japan, South Korea and Mexico.[5]

Exports "deliver value for cuts and variety meat items that command a better price internationally," says Joe Schuele, vice president of communications at the U.S. Meat Export Federation, a trade association representing American exporters of beef, pork, lamb and veal. He says that animal parts not widely consumed in the United States, such as organ meats, can be sold abroad: "International demand maximizes carcass value and helps fuel expansion in the U.S. meat and livestock industries."

But the hegemony of U.S. beef exports has been challenged lately, with countries such as Australia and Brazil emerging as competitors. Other countries are partly closing their doors to American meat in response to increased U.S. tariffs and concerns about the use of hormones, antibiotics and genetically modified feeds in American products.[6]

Four companies control 85 percent of U.S. beef and pork production, and three companies control 90 percent of the chickens raised for meat. The pork and poultry sectors are also vertically integrated, with a small number of companies owning multiple parts of the production chain, from animals to feedlots to slaughterhouses. This, along with a reliance on a cheap labor force for slaughtering and processing meat, means Americans pay less for their meat than people in most other developed countries. For example, one kilogram—2.2 pounds—of beef round costs, on average, $12.45 in the United States, compared to $19.01 in France and $20.96 in Hong Kong.[7]

Critics of the U.S. meat industry say it puts profit above health, safety and the environment, creates a vulnerable workforce and makes it very difficult for smaller players to compete with large companies that have strong political lobbying power.

"Meat companies make profits by pushing workers to their limits," says Specht, adding that meat plant workers often are immigrants, refugees or people of color. The average U.S. hourly wage for meat processing in 2018 was $13.68, compared with an average of $16.58 overall in the manufacturing sector.[8]

In addition, the per capita rate of workplace illnesses and injuries in U.S. meat processing is nearly 40 percent higher than the average rate for all industries, with a slaughterhouse worker losing a body part or sustaining another serious injury every 48 hours in the United States.[9]

In addition, as the coronavirus pandemic has shown, the U.S. meat industry supply chain is susceptible to disruptions, potentially putting the nation's food supply at risk. Last spring, meat shortages developed across the country after thousands of meat plant workers contracted COVID-19 and processing plants had to close. Some ranchers had to cull thousands of animals because there was nowhere to slaughter them.[10]

Since March, more than 42,500 meatpacking workers have tested positive for the virus in nearly 500 meat plants, and at least 203 meatpacking workers have died. Medical experts say the close quarters, low temperatures and poor ventilation in plants create ideal conditions for the virus to spread.[11]

The industry's concentration and vertical integration, along with the fact that most meat processing is regulated at the federal level, instead of by the states or local health departments, have contributed to the decline in independent farms and meat processors, according to experts, historians and industry analysts. Experts say federal inspection standards, introduced in the 1960s, were designed for large facilities and are too expensive for smaller processors to meet. Many remaining small farms have become part of the consolidated industry and now raise hogs, chickens or cattle under contracts with large companies.[12]

Big companies such as Tyson Foods and Perdue say this system reduces farmers' risks and provides them with a guaranteed buyer and professional support. But small producers who contract to raise animals for the large companies complain that they often have to borrow money to meet the companies' specifications for growing conditions and end up in debt and trapped in an industry in which they have no control.[13]

"Small farms are in crisis mode," says Joe Maxwell, co-founder of Family Farm Action Alliance, a nonprofit group involved in research, policy development and advocacy for independent farmers. "There is almost no market for independent livestock producers because a few big companies have a lock on the market."

While the industry has a long history of consolidation and poor working conditions, changing consumer preferences and increased scrutiny of the industry's impact on human health and the environment present new challenges.

The United Nations' Intergovernmental Panel on Climate Change recently declared that eating less meat is a key to mitigating climate change and ensuring an adequate food supply for the world's growing population. Globally, 14.5 percent of emissions of planet-warming greenhouse gases come from livestock, and the sector requires other resources, such as water and land for grazing and growing feed crops.[14]

But industry proponents argue that other sectors, such as transportation, produce more greenhouse gas pollution, and that emerging technologies could make livestock farming more environmentally efficient. In addition, the industry has reduced its carbon footprint over the last four decades in the United States, even as it has increased production, they say.[15]

"The beef industry has a great sustainability story to tell," says Ethan Lane, vice president of government affairs at the National Cattlemen's Beef Association, the beef producers' trade association and lobbying group. "The cattle we raise turn nutrient-poor grass that is inedible to humans into high-quality, protein-dense beef."

Debate is also growing over the negative health and environmental effects created by factory farms, called concentrated animal feeding operations, or CAFOs. The share of U.S. beef raised in these massive facilities, which house thousands of animals under one roof, grew 7.6 percent between 2011 and 2017. Most of the world's poultry and pork is also produced in such facilities.[16]

Critics say CAFOs create large amounts of manure, more than 13 times the amount of waste created by people each year, which often is stored, untreated, in sheds, open

> **"All the pressures on the industry are adding up."**
>
> — *Josh Specht*
> *Assistant Professor of History*
> *Notre Dame*

pits, lagoons and barn basements. This manure can contaminate water and air and contribute to antibiotic resistance and the spread of zoonotic diseases, infections that spread from animals to humans. One proposed congressional bill would phase out CAFOs in the United States.[17]

Industry supporters say such threats can be mitigated and that CAFOs are needed to ensure a robust and affordable food supply.

In the last two years, the popularity of plant-based meat alternatives has grown, and scientists have made progress developing lab-grown meat, although it is not yet on the market. Some analysts expect these products to take significant market share away from meat producers, and the meat industry has begun investing in these alternatives.

Other food analysts say such alternatives will remain niche products due to their high prices, uncertainty over processed or unfamiliar ingredients and the difficulty of changing consumer habits.

The industry also faces shifting global trade policies, struggles to automate meatpacking, federal investigations of industry consolidation and proposed legislation to limit the power of large companies.

As environmentalists, lawmakers, industry leaders and small ranchers contemplate the future of the global meat industry, here are some of the questions they are asking:

Does meat production accelerate climate change and put food supplies at risk?

Many scientists and policymakers say meat production, especially of beef, contributes to climate change and uses large amounts of land, threatening global food security for a growing human population. Eating less meat, they say, is key to stopping this cycle and producing enough calories for everyone.[18]

"Increasing the production of animal-based protein isn't a viable solution, as it would irreparably deplete natural resources," say Jessica Fanzo and Claire Davis, researchers at Johns Hopkins University. The "livestock sector contributes significantly to climate change," according to the U.N.'s Food and Agriculture Organization. Cows account for 65 percent of the global greenhouse gas emissions emitted by all livestock, primarily methane emitted from manure and from cows' digestive process.[19]

To prevent the spread of the coronavirus, workers at a JBS meat plant in Greeley, Colo., get their temperatures checked before entering the facility in April 2020. The company was fined $15,000 for failing to protect its workforce during the pandemic, an amount critics charge is inconsequential for the billion-dollar company.

Methane only remains in the atmosphere for 12 years, unlike carbon dioxide (CO_2), which remains for hundreds of years. But methane is 28 times more powerful in warming Earth's atmosphere during a 20-year period than CO_2. Yet scientists attribute about 20 percent of the planet's warming since the Industrial Revolution to methane.[20]

Beef production also contributes to climate change by encouraging deforestation to make way for grazing cows and feed crop production. For example, during the last 50 years, 17 percent of the Amazon rainforest, which cleans huge amounts of the planet's CO_2 emissions from the atmosphere, has been cleared for such uses. With up to 10,000 square miles of the Amazon being cleared annually during the past two decades and wildfires destroying more, the world's rainforests could disappear in 40 years, experts say.[21]

While chickens and pigs do not emit as much methane as cattle, their manure emits greenhouse gases, and large swaths of land must be cleared to raise feed crops for poultry and pork.[22]

The use of land to graze animals or grow feed for them also means less space to raise crops for the world's burgeoning population, which by 2050 will require about 70 percent more calories than today, according to Fanzo and Davis. Grazing and growing crops for animal feed take up 77 percent of total global farmland, but livestock produces only about 18 percent of the world's calories and 37 percent of its protein, according to experts.[23]

Signs that climate change threatens global food supplies are already emerging, with increased flooding, rising seas and longer-lasting and more intense heat waves triggering record-breaking wildfires that can decimate forests, towns and farms.[24]

"You're sort of reaching a breaking point with land itself and its ability to grow food and sustain us," said Aditi Sen, a senior policy adviser on climate change at Oxfam America, an antipoverty advocacy organization.[25]

But other researchers, including many in the meat industry, say animal grazing and feed crop production contribute a relatively small amount of greenhouse gases, especially in developed countries. In addition, they say, as technology and efficiency progress, meat production will help ensure the global food supply.

"These models about climate change and food security don't account for innovation, or shifting agriculture to other places," says Ted Nordhaus, founder and executive director of the Breakthrough Institute, a research group in Oakland, Calif., that promotes technological solutions to energy, conservation and farming challenges. "We are tying all these complex issues of meat production and climate change and food output together, with long chains filled with assumptions."

A 2019 study, partly funded by the National Cattlemen's Beef Association, published by the U.S. Agriculture Department's Agricultural Research Service, found that beef production in seven U.S. cattle-producing regions accounted for just 3.3 percent of the nation's greenhouse gas emissions in 2016, compared to 56 percent produced by transportation and electricity generation. In the United States and Europe, the agriculture industry, including livestock, accounts for only about 10 percent of greenhouse gas emissions.[26]

"The truth is, we can't stop temperature rises with our diets," said Bjorn Lomborg, a former director of Denmark's Environmental Assessment Institute, a government agency. He is now president of the Copenhagen Consensus Center, a think tank focusing on solutions for global problems.[27]

Sarah Little, vice president for communications at the North American Meat Institute, a Washington-based trade association, says increased productivity and improved use of manure can make meat production key to boosting global food supply.

"U.S. meat production is becoming more and more efficient," she says. "There is great promise for research about livestock helping to cool the planet, from improved animal husbandry and improved genetics—producing cattle that use less feed—to better understanding methane's role in global emissions."

Frank Mitloehner, a professor of animal science and director of atmospheric science at the Air Quality Research Center at the University of California, Davis, points out that farmers increasingly are using biodigesters, devices that use bacteria to digest organic matter. For instance, methane gas from cattle and hog manure can be used to make electricity or power cars. In California alone, this has resulted in an annual methane reduction equivalent to removing 460,000 cars from the roads.[28]

Greenhouse gas emissions, both overall and from the livestock sector, are growing faster in developing countries, but those nations could reduce them by implementing stricter standards and adopting U.S. and European animal feeding and breeding practices, Mitloehner says.

Moreover, deforestation is mainly a problem in South America, Africa and Asia, so cutting back on meat consumption in the United States would have little impact, according to Mitloehner and Nordhaus.

In addition, says Lane at the National Cattlemen's Beef Association, cattle turn otherwise unproductive land into a source of food. "Cattle are able to be raised on lands that are not suitable for other crops raised for human consumption," he says.

Does industrial meat production threaten human health?

Public health experts say concentrated populations of animals in CAFOs contaminate air and water supplies and contribute to antibiotic-resistant infections and increased outbreaks of zoonotic diseases.

"CAFOs are directly associated with occupational and community health risks," said a statement from the American Public Health Association, which backed a bill introduced in December by U.S. Sen. Cory Booker, a Democrat from New Jersey. The measure would ban the construction of new factory farms and phase out existing ones by 2040, while providing aid to farmers

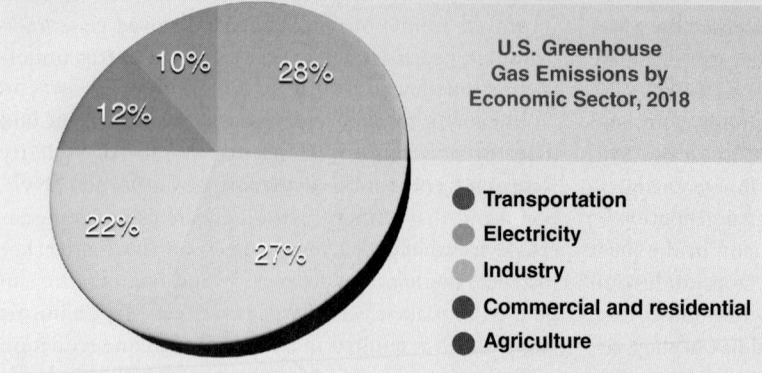

Agriculture Accounts for 10 Percent of U.S. Greenhouse Gases

Farming, including livestock production, emitted 10 percent of all greenhouse gases in the United States in 2018, well below other sectors of the economy, according to the Environmental Protection Agency.

U.S. Greenhouse Gas Emissions by Economic Sector, 2018

- Transportation
- Electricity
- Industry
- Commercial and residential
- Agriculture

Source: "Sources of Greenhouse Gas Emissions," U.S. Environmental Protection Agency, undated, https://tinyurl.com/y5jtrep2

who want to switch from running CAFOs to running smaller operations. Although the legislation has gained several co-sponsors, it remains in discussion in the Senate Agriculture Committee, with no date scheduled for a vote.[29]

One large CAFO can produce as much manure as the amount of sewage produced by the city of Philadelphia, says Valerie Baron, a senior attorney and director of the animal agriculture, health and food division at the Natural Resources Defense Council, an environmental advocacy group in Washington. "But unlike cities, CAFOs don't treat waste," Baron says.

Large concentrations of untreated manure, stored in unlined ponds or lagoons or spread on open fields, can leak nitrates into groundwater, polluting drinking water, says Baron. Nitrates are linked to numerous health problems, including cancer, thyroid dysfunction and infant mortality.[30]

Current state regulations rely on CAFO operators to self-report leaks into groundwater, rather than requiring mandatory testing of such water. Thus, it is difficult to track instances of pollution from factory farms, according to Baron's group. "But water pollution from CAFOs is widespread and ubiquitous," she says. In California alone, for instance, about 1 million people living in the farming areas of the state's Central Valley have high levels of potentially cancer-causing chemicals in their drinking water.[31]

Farm runoff from manure pits also can trigger harmful algal blooms that kill fish and other wildlife, which happened recently in the Chesapeake Bay and occurs every summer in the Gulf of Mexico.[32]

In recent years, Baron says, some farms have begun irrigating their fields with liquified manure, and the spray sometimes blows onto neighboring properties, creating a stench and air pollution that can damage mental and physical health. People living near such farms are more likely to report asthma symptoms, and CAFO workers often suffer from respiratory illnesses and allergies, according to researchers at the University of Wyoming.[33]

Animals raised in CAFOs also routinely receive antibiotics to help protect them from infection, contributing to the rise of drug-resistant bacteria. Incidents of bacteria found in farm animals that did not respond to antibiotics tripled between 2000 and 2018, according to an analysis by scientists of 900 studies. These bacteria can infect humans who eat undercooked meat or come into contact with animal waste.[34]

"These operations are creating superbugs that are extremely hard or impossible to treat," Baron says.

Eating animals treated with antibiotics can also damage the so-called good bacteria that live in the human digestive tract and help break down food.[35]

The federal government's Centers for Disease Control and Prevention (CDC) says factory farms also can introduce new diseases to humans, making them a potential source of pandemics. Factory farms use breeding techniques that make animals less able to resist disease, critics say. Previous outbreaks of novel diseases linked to domesticated animals include the H7N9 virus, or bird flu, that jumped from chickens and other fowl to humans in China beginning in 2013.[36]

"Put all these factors together and you have a perfect-storm environment for the emergence and spread of disease," said Michael Greger, a public health physician and the author of *Bird Flu: A Virus of Our Own Hatching*. "If you actually want to create global pandemics, then build factory farms."[37]

Other researchers and industry leaders say the health risks from industrial farms can be managed without making meat unaffordable. "It's very unlikely that operation size has any impact on emissions or human health," says Mitloehner, the University of California professor, pointing out that all farms, regardless of size, must manage manure. The livestock industry says government efforts to monitor water sources near factory farms for pollution are too burdensome. Leaks and other issues are rare, the industry says.[38]

"CAFOs are not dumping manure and water waste indiscriminately all over the country," said Steve Dittmer, executive vice president of the Agribusiness Freedom Foundation, an anti-regulation organization that, along with several industry groups, opposes Booker's proposed farm reform bill.[39]

"Banning efficient and responsible feeding methods means it will take longer to grow cattle to full size, thereby actually *increasing* impacts on the environment," said Lane of the National Cattlemen's Beef Association.[40]

The use of antibiotics in farm animals is crucial to maintaining animal health and an adequate food supply and is not a major contributor to antibiotic resistance in humans, says Ron Phillips, vice president for government and public relations at the Animal Health Institute, an industry lobbying group for companies that produce veterinary medications. Only three of the 21 pathogens the CDC says cause the most antibiotic resistance are passed to people through undercooked meat, he says.

"Additional regulations are being tightened, including ensuring all uses of medically important antibiotics require veterinary supervision," Phillips says. He also says the U.S. Food and Drug Administration (FDA) monitors antibiotic residues in meat, and that such residues usually are detected in less than 1 percent of products sampled for routine testing.

Alex Smith, a food and agriculture analyst at the Breakthrough Institute, said large livestock operations do not pose a greater risk for spreading zoonotic diseases than smaller farms. In fact, he said, expanding industrial facilities in the developing world would make meat more affordable there, reducing reliance on wild animals—a source of zoonotic diseases. Well-run industrial operations also are better able than scattered, small-scale agriculture to take sanitary, veterinary and other steps necessary for guarding against zoonotic diseases, he said, especially in places where wild animals may come into contact with farm animals.[41]

"To combat the main drivers of zoonotic diseases, we must sustainably intensify our food system, not pine for a romanticized and inefficient production system that brings people and wild animals in closer contact," Smith wrote.[42]

Could alternative products jeopardize the meat industry?

Lab-grown and plant-based meat alternatives are poised to capture greater market share as consumers worry more about the toll that meat production takes on the climate and human and animal health, some industry observers say. In 2019, sales of plant-based meat alternatives grew 18 percent in the United States.[43]

"This is not a fad," says Caroline Bushnell, associate director of corporate engagement at the Good Food Institute, a nonprofit that promotes plant-based and other meat alternatives. "The industry is poised to further accelerate."

Lab-grown meat, also known as clean or cultured meat and produced by growing muscle, fat and flesh from

Climate change activists outside the Brazilian Embassy in London protest the deforestation of the Amazon rainforest in 2019. Some environmentally conscious consumers favor plant-based foods—or possibly lab-grown meat in the future—to reduce the negative environmental impact of meat production.

animal cell cultures, remains in the developmental stages. But the sector is growing, with about 30 companies operating around the world, says Chase Purdy, a food journalist and author of *Billion Dollar Burger*, a book that chronicles the development of lab-grown meat.[44]

"You can't just bury your head in the sand and say cultured meat isn't coming," says Purdy, who expects lab-grown meat to be available to consumers by 2021. "There's too much investment and too much science."

In fact, plant-based meat alternatives and lab-grown meat, which currently account for about 1 percent of sales in the sector, could make up to 10 percent of the market by 2029, according to Barclays Investment Bank.[45]

Many plant-based meat substitutes are aimed at meat-eaters and have gained increased attention after showing up on menus at fast-food restaurants such as White Castle, Burger King and McDonald's.[46]

"The whole point of our product is not to be successful as a new product, but to be successful at the expense of the incumbent industry," said Pat Brown, chief executive and founder of Impossible Foods, an Oakland, Calif.-based company that makes plant-based burgers and other products.[47]

Surveys also indicate that younger consumers are more interested in these products, another sign of growth potential.[48]

Meat companies have begun reacting to this emerging competition, with big players such as Tyson and Cargill investing in plant-based meat alternative startups or launching their own plant-based products.[49]

"We're creating new products for the growing number of people open to flexible diets that include both meat and plant-based protein," Noel White, president and CEO of Tyson Foods, said in 2019, when the company announced its new Raised & Rooted line of plant-based products and meat-and-plant protein blends.[50]

Meanwhile, livestock ranchers are worried about losing market share to plant-based proteins after watching cow milk consumption decline as soy, oat, almond and other alternative products have grabbed about 10 percent of total milk sales in recent years.[51]

Livestock producers have ramped up campaigns emphasizing what they claim are the benefits of animal meat, and successfully lobbied for state label laws requiring plant-based products to be labeled "imitation" meat. They also support a pending federal bill that would require similar labels.[52]

Some food analysts remain skeptical of predictions that lab-grown meat and plant-based meat alternatives will disrupt the meat sector anytime soon, due to the difficulty in changing consumer habits, uncertainty about the products and their higher cost.

"I do believe we will continue to see growth in these plant-based and lab products, but it doesn't present an immediate threat to the meat industry," says Nick Masters, an analyst at IBIS World, a U.S. market research firm, citing the relatively small market share of the new products.

About 70 percent of Americans are not interested in cutting back on meat consumption, says Mark Lang, associate professor of marketing at the University of Tampa and an expert in the food sector. He says many people will try new products, but few buy them again.

"We have to realize that the percent of the population demanding these products is really small," he says.

The fact that plant-based alternatives contain multiple unfamiliar and highly processed ingredients, like soy leghemoglobin and expeller-pressed canola oil, will also hold them back, he says, because polls show consumers want fewer—and recognizable—ingredients.[53] "Really it's a highly processed food, and people will come to realize this," Lang says.

Kate Kavanaugh, co-owner of Western Daughters Butcher Shoppe in Denver, which sells locally raised and slaughtered meat, also points out that plant-based products do not solve many environmental-impact concerns. For example, Impossible Burger relies on genetically modified ingredients and soy, often the sole crop grown in fields, a practice that depletes the soil and encourages deforestation, she says.[54]

"I do not see them as a competitive threat," Kavanaugh says. "We work with meat where farmers and ranchers are using regenerative practices that help restore soil and grassland health, building topsoil and sequestering carbon, all while raising a product that is biologically near ideal for us to consume. . . . Impossible Burgers contribute massively to deforestation, monocropping [and] carbon release—all while offering something that is nutritionally a packaged food packed full of . . . ingredients that take away from health. Our customer base understands the difference."

Christine McCracken, executive director of the animal protein division at Rabobank's RaboResearch Food & Agribusiness, headquartered in the Netherlands, says the higher prices of plant-based products means they likely will "remain a relatively niche product," and not offer significant competition to meat.

Lab-grown meat also faces hurdles, including designing economical and efficient bioreactor machines that grow the meat and the nutrient-dense liquid mediums to grow it in, Purdy says. And although the energy and resources needed to grow it are certainly less than those required to raise, feed and slaughter livestock, "we don't know exactly how much energy is needed," Purdy says.

BACKGROUND
From Local to National

Until the mid-19th century, most farm animals were slaughtered and eaten or sold locally. This began to change after 1850, when the advent of industrialized slaughter in the United States began consolidating meat production, increasing the availability of meat and lowering its cost.[55]

The advent of railroads enabled ranchers and farmers to raise their animals on cheap, abundant land in the American West and ship them to markets in the Midwest and East. By the 1860s, the beef industry became the first to use modern production lines, as assembly-line facilities for slaughtering and packing meat emerged in cities such as Cincinnati and Chicago. Such a system, in which each worker repeatedly performed one task, eliminated downtime and made it easier to train employees.[56]

With the invention of refrigerated rail cars, Chicago's packing companies began distributing fresh meat and pork nationwide; by 1890, four companies controlled the majority of U.S. beef and pork and other companies connected to the meat sector.[57]

The industry relied heavily on European immigrant workers, who were desperate for jobs. The work was brutal and dangerous. *The Jungle*, a 1905 novel by investigative journalist Upton Sinclair about a Chicago immigrant family working in the industry, showcased the filth and lack of sanitation standards in meatpacking facilities.[58]

Upton Sinclair's novel *The Jungle* focused attention on the unsafe working conditions in U.S. meatpacking plants at the turn of the 20th century. Public outcry about the revelations led to passage of the 1906 Pure Food and Drug Act and the Federal Meat Inspection Act, which aimed to improve the safety of the nation's meat, food and drugs.

The book triggered a public outcry that spurred government officials to take action on food safety. In 1906, Congress passed the Pure Food and Drug Act, mandating ingredient labeling, and the Federal Meat Inspection Act, which required the inspection of live animals and slaughtering facilities. The inspection law did not apply to poultry, which still consisted mainly of backyard hens raised for eggs and, occasionally, for meat.[59]

In 1917, a Federal Trade Commission investigation documented long-suspected price-fixing and collusion among the five largest beef processing companies, nicknamed the Beef Trust. As a result, the companies had to sell their nonslaughter operations, which led to more competitive conditions for ranchers wanting to sell their meat.[60]

As unions gained strength in the 1930s, conditions and salaries for meatpacking workers improved.[61]

Meanwhile, the poultry industry evolved as the government encouraged development of new breeds

CHRONOLOGY

1860s-1940s *Meatpacking industry emerges in the United States and the federal government introduces regulation.*

1867 Mining entrepreneur Philip Danforth Armour opens Armour & Co. in Chicago to process cattle arriving on trains from the American West.

1878 Chicago meatpacking giant Swift & Co. commissions the Peninsula Car Co. to build a refrigerated freight train car for fresh meat, which proves more economical to transport than live animals.

1905 Publication of *The Jungle*, Upton Sinclair's book describing unsafe and unsanitary working conditions in the meatpacking industry, leads to enactment of the Pure Food and Drug Act and the Federal Meat Inspection Act to ensure consumer safety.

1917 Federal Trade Commission investigation uncovers anti-competitive practices by the five largest U.S. beef processing companies.

1940 Early antibiotic gramicidin is used to treat an outbreak of cow udder infections at the New York World's Fair.

1943 United Packinghouse Workers of America union is founded in Chicago.

1948 U.S. officials approve Merck's antibiotic sulfaquinoxaline as a routine additive to chicken feed to prevent disease. . . . Brothers Dick and Mac McDonald open a quick-service hamburger restaurant in California, soon turning the business into a franchise-based company.

1950s-1960s *Fast-food industry and factory farms expand.*

1951 Agricultural irrigation expert Earl Brookover opens Feedyards Inc. in Kansas, one of the earliest industrial feedlots for livestock. . . . Food and Drug Administration (FDA) approves first animal feeds containing antibiotic growth promoters for use in the United States.

1954 FDA approves the hormone diethylstilbestrol, a synthetic growth stimulant, for use in cattle feed.

1956 Kentucky businessman Col. Harland Sanders franchises his famous fried chicken, laying the foundation for the Kentucky Fried Chicken fast-food chain.

1959 FDA bans diethylstilbestrol for use in chickens after it is found to cause male breast growth in humans.

1967 The Wholesome Meat Act imposes federal meat processing standards, in addition to state standards, even if the meat will only be sold in-state, leading many smaller plants to close.

1970s-1990s *Demand for chicken rises as health and ethical concerns grow about eating red meat.*

1975 The publication of two books, *Eat Your Heart Out: Food Profiteering in America* and *Animal Liberation*, reflect emerging concerns about the ethics of eating meat.

1977 U.S. Senate Committee publishes "Dietary Goals for the United States," recommending reduced meat consumption; a revised version walks back on the original and recommends reducing "animal fat" and choosing leaner meats.

1979 FDA bans the use of diethylstilbestrol in cattle due to concerns that it causes cancer.

1983 McDonald's introduces the Chicken McNugget, fueling the growth of the processed poultry market.

1985 U.S. chicken consumption surpasses pork, but beef remains ahead of both.

1992 U.S. chicken consumption surpasses beef.

1997 After outbreaks of mad cow disease in Europe, United States bans feeding protein from cows, sheep and other animals to cattle.

2000-Present *Health and environmental concerns related to meat consumption intensify.*

2004 U.S. per capita consumption of red meat and poultry reaches a record 220.2 pounds.

2006 U.N. Food and Agriculture Organization report attributes 18 percent of greenhouse gases worldwide to livestock production.

2009 The so-called swine flu pandemic begins in Mexico, eventually killing more than 12,000 Americans. . . . Ethan Brown, former CEO of a hydrogen fuel cell company, founds Beyond Meat in El Segundo, Calif., to make plant-based meat substitutes.

2010 New FDA guidelines link eating processed meat to higher risk of cancer.

2013 A group of Dutch scientists create the first lab-grown hamburger.

2013 Shuanghui International, China's largest pork producer, buys Virginia-based meat processor Smithfield Foods.

2018 African swine fever spreads among pigs in China, disrupting global pork supply.

2019 U.N. Intergovernmental Panel on Climate Change urges people to cut meat consumption to stop climate change and ensure food security. . . . Beyond Meat earns $298 million in net revenue, a 239 percent increase over 2018. . . . U.S. per capita meat consumption sets new record of 224.3 pounds.

2020 Nearly one in four Americans say they are eating less meat, mainly citing health reasons. . . . COVID-19 sickens thousands of meat workers, causing processing plants to close and leading to product shortages.

---

especially suited for their meat. The first factory that plucked feathers by machine and sold packaged, ready-to-cook chickens opened in Chicago in the 1940s. In addition, fast-food outlets, including hotdog stands and drive-ins, began to proliferate in the 1940s and '50s, with the rise of Carl's Jr, McDonald's and Kentucky Fried Chicken. Meat consumption became tied to American leisure culture.[62]

By the 1950s, a hamburger and french fries had become the quintessential American meal.[63]

Rise of Factory Farms

Due to government policies, technological developments, the growth of the fast-food sector and rising global demand, the second half of the 20th century saw further industrialization and consolidation of animal agriculture and meat production.

Beginning in the 1950s, cows were taken off ranches after a couple of years and moved to feedlots, penned areas for raising animals, where they ate cheap government-subsidized corn, rather than grass, to speed up their growth. Corn also produced fat in the muscle tissue, giving the meat a marbled texture, which American consumers came to love.[64]

The use of hormones, first approved by the FDA in the 1950s, further shortened the time it took to grow animals to slaughter weight. And farmers began to routinely put antibiotics in the feed for chicken, cattle and pigs to prevent infections and, in some cases, to promote faster growth.[65]

In the late 1960s, the Wholesome Meat Act and Wholesome Poultry Products Act required that state inspectors use federal inspection standards. As a result, 17 states ended their inspection programs and allowed federal ones to take over. The laws burdened smaller processors with more expenses, causing many to close. The rise of fast-food chains also contributed to consolidation among processors, as companies such as McDonald's sought uniformity. By the mid-1970s, McDonald's was buying all its beef from just five suppliers.[66]

Consolidation continued to increase during the 1980s and later. And by 2000, four companies controlled 84 percent of beef production, similar to a century earlier. Many mergers also occurred in the chicken-processing sector in the 1980s, as consumption grew rapidly. By 1992, chicken would surpass beef as the most popular animal protein in the United States. By 2000, eight chicken processors controlled two-thirds of the market.[67]

Meanwhile, as farms got bigger, their numbers dwindled, falling from about 3 million in 1960 to just 2 million in 2000.[68]

The consolidation created industry characteristics resembling those of the early 20th century, with the workforce again dominated by poor immigrants and people of color. Union membership began declining after the mid-1960s, leaving workers with little power. By 1990, only about 60 percent of meatpackers were unionized.[69]

But the industry differed from earlier in the century in one respect: By the end of the 20th century, meat

Rise of Industrial Farms in China Raises Health, Environmental Concerns

Small farmers also fear losing livelihoods.

By the end of 2020, the outskirts of Beijing will be home to 11 new farms raising hundreds of thousands of hogs, as China races to keep up with growing demand for meat.[1]

"We're one of the key projects aimed at stabilizing Beijing's meat supplies and protecting livelihoods," said Zu Sheng, owner of Sifanghong Agriculture and Animal Husbandry, which is building one of the farms, a multi-story facility that will raise 60,000 pigs for slaughter each year.[2]

Desperate to produce more meat, China is allowing livestock operations to locate in and near cities, reversing previous efforts to keep agricultural facilities out of urban areas because of health and environmental risks.

China's rapidly industrializing meat sector also includes larger processing and distribution facilities and a shift toward modern retailers rather than traditional animal markets, where wild and farmed animals are slaughtered on site and where scientists say some animal-borne diseases have jumped to humans.

Many consumers welcome the changes, saying they make food safer. But the rapid shift has raised concerns about the impact such large livestock operations will have on the environment and health of those living nearby, as well as on the livelihoods of small farmers.[3]

Meat consumption in China has more than doubled since the 1990s, as its citizens' earning power has grown.[4] While imported meats have satisfied some of this demand, "China has an oft-repeated goal of self-sufficiency," says Christine McCracken, executive director of the animal protein division at RaboResearch Food & Agribusiness, the research arm of Rabobank, a Dutch company that is a global leader in food and agriculture financing.

To move toward that goal—and to feed one-fifth of the world's population on about one-tenth of its arable land—the Chinese government has encouraged the growth of large, concentrated animal feeding operations (CAFOs), where thousands of animals are raised inside massive buildings rather than on traditional pasture lands.[5]

The share of China's pork coming from small and backyard farms has dropped to about half, down from 80 percent in the 1990s. And by 2012, 80 percent of the country's chickens were being raised in large industrial operations.[6]

Manure from such facilities has been shown to contribute significantly to the production of carbon dioxide, a major cause of climate change, as well as nitrogen and phosphorus runoff that can pollute nearby waterways. "It is obvious that livestock and poultry farming has become a key source of environmental pollution in China," wrote a group of Chinese scientists.[7]

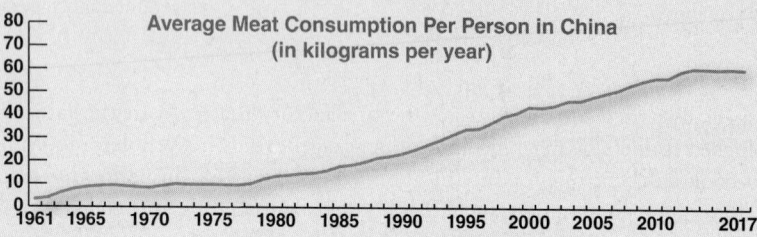

China's Meat Consumption Has Risen Sharply

Average meat consumption in China more than doubled between 1993 and 2017, according to data from the U.N. Food and Agriculture Organization. Meat supply per capita rose consistently from 1980 until 2013 but has plateaued in recent years.

Source: Hannah Ritchie and Max Roser, "Meat and Dairy Production," Our World in Data, November 2019, https://tinyurl.com/y5c2tloj

The rapid expansion of industrial animal agriculture also requires harmful land-use changes. As China imports vast amounts of feed for its growing livestock population, large swaths of the Amazon rainforest, key to absorbing atmosphere-warming carbon, have been cut down to grow soybeans to feed Chinese farm animals.[8]

"Given the sheer population size, even small increases in individual meat intake will lead to outsized climate and environmental consequences worldwide," said Pan Genxing, director of the Institute of Resources, Environment and Ecosystem of Agriculture at Nanjing Agricultural University.[9]

Government regulations aim to prevent leakage of contaminants from livestock operations, and farms near cities are subject to stricter standards. But many farms do not meet those standards. For example, fewer than half of the livestock facilities in Heilongjiang province in northeast China were properly collecting manure and other waste in 2018, according to the national Ministry of Ecology and Environment.[10]

Factory farms also are breeding grounds for diseases, including African swine fever, which spread through Chinese pig farms in 2018 and resulted in 40 percent of the nation's pigs being euthanized. While small farms also suffered, some scientists said the growth of CAFOs allowed the disease to spread more rapidly.[11]

Scientists say confining large groups of animals in close quarters near rapidly expanding cities risks exposing people to zoonotic diseases, infections that jump from animals to humans. This year, for example, a new variety of flu related to the H1N1 strain that caused a pandemic in 2009 was detected in hogs and hog farmers in China. Some scientists say Chinese farms do not properly prevent and contain disease outbreaks among animals. China has also seen increased domestication of wild animals, including snakes and civet cats for food, another source of zoonotic diseases.[12]

Meanwhile, many of the country's remaining small farmers say they may not survive financially, due to increased competition from industrial farms and the government's failure to provide promised compensation for pigs euthanized during the African swine fever outbreak. Rabobank has projected that half of China's small hog farmers would leave the sector.[13]

African swine fever "continues to spread in China, but at a slower pace," a Rabobank report said, citing better prevention measures. "Despite this, small to medium farms are cautious to restock or expand production."[14]

—Sara Toth Stub

---

[1] "Cheek by jowl: China pork crisis spurs pig farms' return to cities," *Reuters*, June 10, 2020, https://tinyurl.com/yxn9nots.

[2] *Ibid.*

[3] Tracie McMillan, "How China Plans to Feed 1.4 Billion Growing Appetites," *National Geographic*, February 2018, https://tinyurl.com/y7q5xewn.

[4] *Ibid.*

[5] *Ibid.*; Yuanan Hu, Shu Tao and Hefa Cheng, "Environmental and Human Health Challenges of Industrial Livestock and Poultry Farming in China and their Mitigation," *Environment International*, October 2017, p. 112, https://tinyurl.com/yxuvx8s7.

[6] Michael Standaert, "African swine fever destroying small pig farms, as factory farming booms: Report," *The Guardian*, March 11, 2020, https://tinyurl.com/yaoyzhpu; Dominique Patton, "China supersizes pig farms to cut costs in world's top pork market," *Reuters*, Feb. 7, 2018, https://tinyurl.com/yxbm95be; and Yuanan, Shu, and Hefa, *op. cit.*, p. 112.

[7] *Ibid.*, Yuanan, Shu, and Hefa.

[8] Melissa Chan and Heriberto Araújo, "China Wants Food. Brazil Pays the Price," *The Atlantic*, Feb. 15, 2020, https://tinyurl.com/yyo7nwuj.

[9] Marcello Rossi and Undark, "China's Love for Meat is Threatening its Green Movement," *The Atlantic*, July 31, 2018, https://tinyurl.com/y8epxz8a.

[10] "Cheek by jowl," *op. cit.*

[11] "China tries to lure small farmers back to pigs amid pork shortage," *Reuters*, Dec. 17, 2019, https://tinyurl.com/y5el4fsh; "Building a factory farmed future, one pandemic at a time," *Grain*, March 3, 2020, https://tinyurl.com/y5b8oyxn.

[12] Betsy McKay and Phred Dvorak, "A Deadly Coronavirus was Inevitable. 'Why Was No One Ready?' " *The Wall Street Journal*, Aug. 13, 2020, https://tinyurl.com/y4rfbaen; Tom Philpott, "Industrial Hog Farms are Breeding the Next Pandemic," *Mother Jones*, Aug. 11, 2020, https://tinyurl.com/yyd8ahp6; Simone McCarthy, "Industrial farming of livestock a ticking pathogen bomb, scientists say," *South China Morning Post*, June 2, 2020, https://tinyurl.com/y5c2y2ms; and Ben Westcott and Shawn Deng, "China has made eating wild animals illegal after the coronavirus outbreak. But ending the trade won't be easy," *CNN*, March 6, 2020, https://tinyurl.com/waoq2ww.

[13] McMillan, *op. cit.*; Michael Schuman, "China's Small Farms Are Fading. The World May Benefit," *The New York Times*, Oct. 5, 2018, https://tinyurl.com/y3wlb2jg; and "China tries to lure small farmers back to pigs amid pork shortage," *op. cit.*

[14] "African Swine Fever: A Global Update," Rabobank, Feb. 27, 2020, p. 4, https://tinyurl.com/y6b7gfpo.

Small Meat Processors Enjoy Surging Demand Amid Pandemic

"This has marked the first time we have been profitable."

Since 2013, Kate Kavanaugh and Josh Curtiss have been selling locally sourced beef, pork and other products at their Western Daughters Butcher Shoppe in Denver. The two took special pride in looking out for the health of their customers and the animals, even if that made it difficult to compete with mass-produced meat selling for a fraction of the price at nearby grocery stores.

Since the coronavirus pandemic began, however, business is booming. Kavanaugh and Curtiss are working around the clock to keep up with burgeoning demand and have begun offering daily home delivery.

"This, in fact, has marked the first time we have been profitable," Kavanaugh says. "The volume we are experiencing is what the shop needs to be sustainable."

Western Daughters is one example of the many small butchers and meat producers whose sales are soaring as the pandemic disrupts industrial meat production and spotlights the dangers to employees' health posed by crowded working conditions at large-scale meat processing plants.[1] Makers of plant-based meat substitutes also are seeing a surge in business.

The U.S. Department of Agriculture defines a small processor as one with fewer than 500 workers; very small processors employ fewer than 10 people.[2]

By September, about 42,500 meat-processing plant workers at nearly 500 plants had been diagnosed with COVID-19, the disease caused by the coronavirus, and more than 200 had died. Investigations by media and workers' rights organizations have described the lack of antivirus precautions at some large meat plants, especially in the early days of the pandemic. Two meat processing companies have been fined for safety violations by the U.S. Occupational Safety and Health Administration.[3]

In addition, the pandemic caused meat shortages at grocery stores after many large plants had to close temporarily due to virus outbreaks in their plants. Smaller meat producers, by contrast, have largely avoided coronavirus outbreaks and closures as they do not have as many employees to potentially spread the virus, are often located in isolated rural communities and can allow more distance between workers.[4]

And the meat-buying habits of some U.S. consumers appear to be shifting, according to both anecdotal evidence and data. "Demand is off the charts," said Donna Kilpatrick, co-founder of Grass Roots Farmers' Cooperative, which sells meat online from more than 30 Arkansas farms, including her own 1,200-acre ranch for grass-fed beef and pastured chicken and pork. "That's what I hear from everybody."[5]

Unlike large meat producers, smaller operations say they are keeping up with demand and even increasing supply. "We have been able to double, even triple, the volume of meat coming through our shop," Kavanaugh says.

Smaller meat processors say they are often more adaptable than large operations, allowing them to quickly pivot to meet changing market trends. For example, with most restaurants closed and people cooking at home during the COVID-19 lockdown, smaller operations could quickly cut back on processing meat for restaurants and begin focusing on packaging meat for individual sales in grocery stores.

"We were able to do that quick, where a lot of these big companies, they can't do that," said Chris Kurzweil of Kurzweil's Country Meats, a butcher shop in Garden City, Mo. His company is receiving more orders from grocery stores trying to keep up with consumer demand, so they began creating smaller packages for retail rather than focusing on large orders for restaurants and food service companies.[6]

Meanwhile, retail sales of plant-based meat substitutes jumped 35 percent during the height of the coronavirus-related lockdown—from April 12 to May 9—compared to the previous four weeks. Meat sales during the same period increased about 28 percent. Companies making plant-based substitutes such as Impossible Foods, Beyond Meat and Tofurky Co. said they have increased production, lowered some prices and begun marketing to more retailers.[7]

"With disruption in the animal-based meat supply, they're more motivated than ever," Impossible Foods CEO Pat Brown said of retailers interested in his company's products.[8]

Small meat producers said they are using their expanding market share to push for changing federal regulations that they say disadvantage small players. Backers of three congressional bills—the bipartisan Prime and Expanding Markets for State-Inspected Meat Processors acts, along with the Democratic-backed Local Food Assistance and Resilient Markets Act—cite COVID-19 meat industry disruptions as a reason to increase competition in the sector.

Among other things, small producers say, the bills would allow small farmers to charge more competitive prices for their animals by reducing industry consolidation and easing slaughtering regulations so they are less cumbersome for small players.[9] For example, the Prime Act would give states total control over the safety of meat processed and sold within their borders, while the Expanding Markets bill would allow some state-inspected meat to be sold across state lines.

Some experts say the bills have little chance of passage, noting that the original Prime Act, introduced in 2015, was never called up for a vote.[10] The measure was re-introduced after the COVID-19 pandemic, but no hearings have been held on it in the pertinent House or Senate committees.[11]

Groups representing large meat companies and consumer groups oppose the Prime and the Expanding Markets measures, citing health concerns and the fact that they would produce different safety standards and levels of enforcement among the states.[12]

The Prime Act "would allow for the commercial sale of non-inspected meat products," the National Pork Producers Council said. The current federally regulated inspection systems "are essential partners, along with producers, packers and processors, in delivering safe meat products."[13]

However, Joe Maxwell, co-founder of the Family Farm Action Alliance, an advocacy group for small farmers, says the pandemic may force long-term changes regarding industry consolidation and the prices small farmers get from large processors for their animals. "The decisions made in Washington, D.C., in the near future are vital to determining if we even have any small or independent farmers left in America," he says.

Kavanaugh says for her business to survive long-term, policy changes are needed to encourage smaller local and regional players. "Things really need to change on a legislative level," she says. "Legislation that opens up state processing can radically change the food system."

—*Sara Toth Stub*

---

[1] Stephen Miller, "As COVID-19 hobbles industrial meat, small producers are having a moment," The Food and Environment Reporting Network, May 6, 2020, https://tinyurl.com/y6jpa4dr.

[2] Ximena Bustillo, "Small meat processors get little aid as demand grows," *Politico*, June 15, 2020, https://tinyurl.com/ybqhu88s.

[3] Kimberly Kindy, "More than 200 meat plant workers in the U.S. have died of covid-19. Federal regulators just issued two modest fines," *The Washington Post*, Sept. 13, 2020, https://tinyurl.com/y5dyt8sk.

[4] Leah Douglas, "COVID-19 shows no sign of slowing among food-system workers," Food and Environment Reporting Network, June 22, 2020, https://tinyurl.com/y447glos; Michael Grabell, Claire Perlman and Bernice Yeung, "Emails Reveal Chaos as Meatpacking Companies Fought Health Agencies Over COVID-19 Outbreaks in Their Plants," *ProPublica*, June 12, 2020, https://tinyurl.com/yyn92wne; and Baylen Linnekin, "As major meat processors buckle under COVID-19 crisis, busy smaller competitors fight red tape," *The Counter*, May 7, 2020, https://tinyurl.com/y4c8p3lv.

[5] Lisa Held, "As COVID-19 Disrupts the Industrial Meat System, Independent Processors Have a Moment to Shine," *Civil Eats*, May 19, 2020, https://tinyurl.com/y5n5yvkj.

[6] Frank Morris, "Small Meatpacking Plants Thrive as COVID-19 Forced Bigger Ones to Close," *NPR*, April 30, 2020, https://tinyurl.com/y4f7xne9.

[7] Amelia Nierenberg, "Plant-Based 'Meats' Catch on in the Pandemic," *The New York Times*, May 22, 2020, https://tinyurl.com/y66p8eyc; Jacob Bunge and Heather Haddon, "Coronavirus Meat Shortages Have Plant-Based Foods Makers' Mouths Watering," *The Wall Street Journal*, May 13, 2020, https://tinyurl.com/yb8uoy6g.

[8] Bunge and Haddon, *ibid*.

[9] "Sen. Booker Introduces Legislation to Strengthen Food System in Response to COVID-19 Disruptions," press release, Office of Sen. Cory Booker, July 2, 2020, https://tinyurl.com/y49urk4a; "Cheney Introduces Bill to Open New Markets for State-inspected meat," press release, Office of Rep. Liz Cheney, June 12, 2020, https://tinyurl.com/y66fhfcy; Stephen R. Miller, "Amid COVID-19 bottleneck in meat industry, PRIME Act gains support," *Fern's AG Insider*, June 3, 2020, https://tinyurl.com/yyr3hfgp; "Bill would OK interstate sales of state-inspected meat, poultry," *Food Safety News*, May 14, 2018, https://tinyurl.com/y3wgx4yg; and Ezra Klein, "Farmers and animal rights activists are coming together to fight big factory farms," *Vox*, July 8, 2020, https://tinyurl.com/ybhwxwdn.

[10] Hollie McKay, "Revived legislation seeks to end monopoly of meat industry, open markets to small farmers amid coronavirus pandemic," *Fox News*, May 12, 2020, https://tinyurl.com/ybzdjqct; Jesse Rifkin, "As Trump Executive Order Forces Meat Plants Open, PRIME Act Would Permit the Industry More Potential Sales," *Govtrack Insider*, June 1, 2020, https://tinyurl.com/y4xv6awl.

[11] "H.R. 2859—PRIME Act," U.S. Congress, https://tinyurl.com/y6oauevl; "S-1620 PRIME Act," U.S. Congress, https://tinyurl.com/yyawmqcy.

[12] McKay, *op. cit.*

[13] "PRIME Act," National Pork Producers Council, https://tinyurl.com/y4d9t6qh.

processors were located mainly in rural areas instead of cities, partly to take advantage of the new cheap labor force and to be closer to large feedlots.[70]

Amid these developments, some critics raised concerns about the economics, ethics and health of the industry. In the 1970s, as expanding food chains threatened to take business away from independent restaurants and smaller meat suppliers, Texas activist and writer Jim Hightower, author of *Eat Your Heart Out: Food Profiteering in America*, warned of what he called the "McDonaldization of America." A nascent vegetarian movement, including the establishment of the Farm Animal Rights Movement organization in 1976 to promote a vegetarian lifestyle, also highlighted what its supporters called cruel practices on farms, including cutting off chickens' beaks to prevent pecking and destroying male chicks because they do not produce eggs.[71]

In 1977, the government published federal dietary goals linking heart health risks to meat consumption. At the same time, medical professionals and consumers began to raise questions about the routine use of hormones and antibiotics in farm animals. Worried that residues of such products would end up in milk and meat, federal regulators began banning them or regulating their use.[72]

By the 1990s, overuse of antibiotics was causing drug-resistant infections, and many European countries limited their use in agriculture. However, powerful drug company lobbies in Washington fought similar actions by U.S. government officials.[73]

Red meat consumption in the United States began to decline in the 1980s amid growing concerns about levels of fat and cholesterol, and people began to eat more chicken. Beef suffered yet another blow in the late 1980s when mad cow disease, a neurological condition affecting cattle that are fed the processed remains of other infected bovine animals, emerged in England and spread across Europe. A few outbreaks of the disease, which can cause a fatal brain disorder in humans who eat meat from infected cows, also occurred in the United States.[74]

Partly in response to such health concerns, organic meat, raised without growth hormones or antibiotics, became more widespread in the 1990s, even though it was more expensive.[75]

A Global Industry

Since the beginning of the 21st century, the meat industry has grown increasingly global and interconnected, with world consumption rising rapidly. The last two decades have also seen intensified concerns about the health and environmental impact of meat, evidenced in part by rising demand for organic, local and free-range products and plant-based meat substitutes.[76]

Between 2000 and 2014, global meat production rose 28 percent—and totaled nearly 330 million metric tons in 2017—fueled mainly by growing demand in developing countries, where populations were becoming wealthier and more urbanized. Expanded use of feed grains, driven by government subsidies and increased use of genetically engineered crops, played a key role in this growth. Between 1990 and 2015, corn production doubled, and soybean production tripled globally.[77]

A trend toward lower tariffs and more free trade agreements encouraged increased trade in feed grains and meat. Global meat exports doubled between 1998 and 2015, with a few big producers such as the United States and Brazil dominating production of beef, poultry and pork, as well as corn for animal feed.[78]

Large meat companies also became more international. Brazil's JBS, for example, opened processing plants in the United States in 2007 and bought U.S. processing companies, growing into one of the biggest players in the American market. In 2013, a Chinese-controlled company bought U.S. meat producer Smithfield Farms and began importing meat slaughtered in the United States. As this global consolidation increased, consumer prices fell and choices available on grocery store shelves increased.[79]

Meanwhile, more small players—especially those raising animals—went out of business. The number of farms in the United States dropped from 2.2 million in 2007 to 2 million in 2019.[80]

The income farmers receive per animal also declined, with a pound of beef bringing a rancher 93 cents in 2009, down from $1.97 in 1980. Consolidation-related health concerns also began to grow as hormones and antibiotics were used more widely. In addition, the government increasingly recalled meat products contaminated with bacteria such as salmonella and E. coli, a situation that has been exacerbated by the growth of CAFOs.[81]

In developing countries, where live animals are often sold in largely unregulated markets, fears increased about zoonotic diseases spreading from both wild and domesticated animals. Raising wild animals for meat exposes humans to diseases for which they do not have immunity, such as when civet cats in China likely passed the virus that causes severe acute respiratory syndrome to humans, killing more than 700 people in 2002-03. But farm animals also can be a source of zoonotic diseases, either harboring viruses themselves or acting as a vehicle to pass viruses from wild animals to humans, especially as farms, wild animals and humans live in closer proximity as urban expansion causes deforestation. For instance, the 2009 swine flu outbreak, which began in Mexico, was tied to the livestock trade. In addition, there were worries that farm animals could be another source of zoonotic diseases.[82]

In 2018, outbreaks of African swine fever, a virus deadly to pigs but that does not infect humans, in China and Europe caused those regions to seek more imports—pushing up global food prices—and highlighted how local events can reverberate in an interconnected global meat market. China's increased demand for meat for its growing middle class also caused it to relax import and trade restrictions, despite simmering political and trade tensions with the Trump administration. China increased its meat imports by 63 percent in 2019.[83]

Meanwhile, organic, grass-fed and other specialty meat markets continued to grow, as concerns increased about animal welfare and health. Large meat companies such as Perdue and Conagra Foods launched lines of organic, grass-fed and pastured products.[84] Meat companies also have begun to invest in plant-based alternatives and lab-grown meat, hinting that they realize such options could reshape the market.

Meanwhile, closures of meat-processing plants due to COVID-19 have focused increased public attention on issues that had been building in the meat industry, including consolidation, globalization and poor working conditions.

CURRENT SITUATION
New Challenges

Today, the global meat industry is dealing with increased automation and reliance on overseas trade and proposed legislative changes in the United States.

The U.S. beef industry promotes its products at a press conference in Tokyo in 2015. Japan recently agreed to lower tariffs on American beef, opening up a new market for U.S. producers.

Growing overseas demand for meat, especially in Asia, is opening new markets for U.S. producers. Japan, for example, recently struck a trade deal with the United States in which it agreed to lower tariffs on imported American beef. And Chinese imports of U.S. pork and chicken increased sharply after Chinese production declined in 2019 due to outbreaks of African swine fever.[85]

Heavier reliance on overseas markets also means increased vulnerability to protectionist policies and other trade barriers, says Masters, at IBIS World. Both Trump and Chinese officials have threatened to back out of a new trade deal involving exports of U.S. pork and other agricultural products, causing meat producers to worry about future growth.[86]

"The U.S.-China Phase One Trade Agreement is critical to both the near- and longer-term success and growth of American agriculture—and the millions of American jobs the agricultural sector sustains," said nearly 200 U.S. agricultural associations and companies in a June letter to Trump. Producers in the United States and elsewhere also worry about a fall in demand and price when China's pork industry recovers.[87]

As foreign meat industries become more global, U.S. producers face increased competition, especially from Brazil, the world's leading producer and exporter of beef. The number of beef cattle in Brazil grew 56 percent between 1990 and 2018. U.S. agriculture officials

AT ISSUE

Are meat processing workers adequately protected against COVID-19?

YES — Julie Anna Potts
President and CEO, North American Meat Institute

Written for *CQ Researcher*, September 2020

Every day, the meat and poultry industry works hard to produce safe food and ensure the well-being of the men and women who work in its facilities. Meatpackers learned early in the COVID-19 pandemic what a terrible toll it would take on their employees, and companies mourn the teammates who lost their lives.

Contrary to sensational news reports, the industry invested hundreds of millions of dollars to protect employees—and continues to invest. From partitions to face masks to staggered shifts and much more, the meat and poultry industry overhauled its facilities and procedures and was able to significantly reduce COVID-19 cases among meatpacking employees during the summer.

Companies acted early to protect employees. By the time the Centers for Disease Control and Prevention (CDC) issued guidance for meat and poultry plants, the industry was educating employees about stopping the virus in their communities. If companies could find tests, they tested. If they could find face masks and shields, they gave them to employees and federal inspectors, who are required to be present whenever a facility is open. Companies installed additional sanitization, conducted contact tracing and communicated with local, state and federal authorities. Perhaps most importantly, they provided paid leave for sick workers, quarantined employees and expanded health care benefits.

When facilities were initially shut down, beef and pork production dropped 40-50 percent. But after extensive safety measures were put in place, the dedicated men and women working in processing facilities returned operations to normal faster than anticipated. Despite reduced choices in some areas, stores have had enough meat and poultry to help consumers keep food on the table.

Protecting workers is equally important to livestock producers. As plants shut down, producers had to house more and more cattle and pigs, driving prices down. Again, thanks to the efforts of packing-plant workers, widespread euthanasia of pigs was unnecessary, and prices for cattle are rebounding.

But the industry's successful efforts to reduce COVID-19 cases and make up for lost production have gone largely unrecognized. This pandemic should show the industry's critics how much companies rely on and value the men and women working in their facilities—and how important these team members are in providing safe, affordable food.

As infectious disease experts predict a possible second COVID-19 wave in the fall, the meat and poultry industry will remain vigilant and innovative in protecting and supporting its workers.

NO — Melissa J. Perry
Chair, Department of Environmental and Occupational Health, Milken Institute School of Public Health, George Washington University

Written for *CQ Researcher*, September 2020

Since March, more than 42,500 meatpacking workers have tested positive for the virus in nearly 500 meat plants, and at least 203 workers have died. Public health experts say the close quarters, extreme temperatures and poor ventilation in plants create ideal conditions for the virus to spread.

The coronavirus spreads via viral particles—respiratory droplets and aerosols emitted when an infected person speaks, coughs, sneezes, laughs or sings. Keeping a distance of six feet or more is necessary to prevent droplet transmission from person to person. Workers on meatpacking lines are always standing elbow to elbow and shoulder to shoulder. Unless they are spaced 6 feet or more apart, workers are not maintaining a safe distance.

To avoid the spread of viruses and bacteria, every person needs to be vigilant about personal hygiene. However, our research in meatpacking plants has demonstrated that workers have, on average, 4.5 seconds to perform their task before the next piece of meat comes along. This means workers have no time to step off the line to cough or sneeze into a tissue, wipe their mouths or noses, or wash their hands. The fast pace of the work prevents meatpacking workers from practicing personal sanitation and hygiene, putting the workers (and their family members) at greater risk of coronavirus infection.

During the pandemic, all citizens have been instructed to stay at home when they are feeling sick so that they will not spread illnesses to others. Meatpacking companies are creating an incentive for workers to ignore symptoms of illness because workers can get bonus pay when they do not take sick days. This practice is counterproductive to sound public health measures.

The notion that the United States must choose between safe conditions for meatpacking workers or a dependable supply of meat is a false dichotomy. Companies can slow line speeds to enforce 6-foot distancing between workers and allow workers to step off the line to attend to basic hygiene needs. They can also provide pandemic sick leave so workers are not encouraged to come to work sick. Instead of hampering production, these practices will prevent shutdowns, preserve a healthy workforce and ensure a safe, reliable national meat supply.

decided early this year to lift import bans on some Brazilian beef products—in place since 2017 due to health concerns. That has raised fears among U.S. ranchers about losing market share to Brazilian beef, which is usually about 30 percent less expensive.[88]

"To me, it's almost like a slap in the face," said Michael Lee, a cattle rancher in Faulkner County in Arkansas.[89]

Russia, which has banned many U.S. agriculture imports since 2014 in response to economic sanctions imposed on Moscow after its invasion of Ukraine, has increased its production and exports of poultry and beef, presenting yet another source of competition.[90]

Meanwhile, the meat processing industry continues to lag behind other sectors in automating, largely because of the difficulty of designing machines that can deal with the many sizes and shapes of animals and animal parts.[91]

"Protein producers have long looked at these technologies but struggled to implement them at scale," says Jordan Bar Am, an industry consultant and associate partner at McKinsey & Co., a U.S.-based global management consulting firm. Despite the dangers involved, including injuries to limbs, humans are better at meat processing and do it more cheaply than machines, according to Masters at IBIS. But low unemployment levels in the last decade—before the emergence of COVID-19—made it difficult to retain workers, causing frequent turnover and labor shortages.[92]

Now, the risks of relying on cheap labor are even clearer and more controversial amid the coronavirus pandemic, which has infected thousands of workers in meatpacking plants in the United States, South America and Europe, temporarily closing some plants.[93]

In the United States, for example, even though more than 42,500 meatpacking workers have tested positive for the virus and 203 have died, the U.S. Occupational Safety and Health Administration (OSHA) has issued only two fines, totaling $29,000, on companies for failing to protect workers. Critics blasted the fines as being ridiculously low, given that the two companies—Smithfield Foods and JBS—had combined revenues last year of $65 billion.[94]

"This 'teeny' citation . . . is less than a slap on the wrist. It's a 'get out of jail free' card and a signal to the industry that there are no consequences for failing to protect these vital and essential workers who process the meat and poultry that we eat," said Debbie Berkowitz, a former OSHA chief of staff and now program director for worker safety and health at the National Employment Law Project. "This industry decided to thumb its nose at the basic CDC guidance on social distancing and wearing masks. In these two plants, more meatpacking workers died in last couple of months than in the entire industry last year."[95]

But the companies said they will challenge the citations, which are "without merit," and that they instituted safety improvements long before OSHA issued guidelines, which both the companies and worker advocates have said were not adequate or timely. OSHA said the penalties are the maximum allowed by law.[96]

Masters, of IBIS World, says the virus has made it "even more clear that labor is a weak point in this industry," and said that "COVID could be a catalyst" for increased automation to reduce the number of people handling meat and the instances of food-borne illness. About 70 percent of pathogens enter food through human contact. Robotics could also cut down on the high injury rates among meatpackers, industry experts say.[97]

But the industry has been slow to adopt new technologies, experts say, and it often does so in a piecemeal way, without effective strategies or reliable data collection to assess the results. Meat processing also requires gentle handling, an area in which robots still trail humans.[98]

New Legislation

Pending state and federal legislation is challenging U.S. meat industry consolidation.

In the wake of meat shortages caused by the pandemic, lawmakers, small farmers and ranchers say support is growing for a bipartisan congressional proposal that, like Wyoming's new law, would lift a ban on the intrastate sale of beef and pork slaughtered at plants not inspected by federal or state authorities meeting federal standards. Some say the ban is costly and has contributed to the decline in the number of slaughterhouses in the United States.

First proposed in 2015, the measure—called the Processing Revival and Intrastate Meat Exemption or Prime Act—is one of three pieces of federal legislation related to the meat industry pending in Congress.[99]

"There is a lack of smaller processors across the country—it is a pinch point for local food systems," says

Kavanaugh of Western Daughters Butcher Shoppe in Denver.

Currently, about 50 plants process 98 percent of the nation's beef, pork and chicken. Many farmers struggle to find facilities that will take their business and often must drive hours with their livestock to get to a processing facility. Supporters of the Prime Act say it would enable more small and medium-sized slaughterhouses to open, making processing more affordable and convenient for smaller farmers and ranchers, and lowering the cost of local meat for consumers.[100]

Although the bill has been awaiting a vote for a few years, some supporters say they feel there is now a better chance of it passing due to the meat shortages caused by the COVID-19 pandemic.[101] States would regulate the facilities.

Large meat producers and industry groups oppose the Prime Act.[102]

"A robust and consistent U.S. meat inspection system is critical to ensuring food safety, maintaining consumer confidence and safeguarding animal health," the National Pork Producers Council said in a statement.[103]

In another attempt to spur competition in meat processing, U.S. Rep. Liz Cheney, a Republican from Wyoming, in June introduced the national Expanding Markets for State-Inspected Meat Processors Act of 2020, which would allow meat and poultry that is inspected by states using U.S. Department of Agriculture standards to be sold across state lines. Currently, 27 states allow such products to be sold only within their own states.[104]

Meanwhile, Booker's proposed Farm Reform Act aims to disrupt vertical integration in the chicken and poultry sectors by, among other things, providing aid for farmers who want to become independent and stop raising animals on contract for big meat companies.[105]

Federal officials also are increasing scrutiny of meat industry consolidation, with the four largest meatpackers currently under investigation by the Justice Department for possible collusion on prices. A separate investigation of price-fixing in the poultry industry resulted in charges against four industry executives.[106]

While the companies have declined to comment, farmers say such steps are in the right direction of enforcing laws about industry concentration.

"Price fixing in the agricultural industry is extremely harmful to everyone besides the companies who engage in this unethical practice," stated the National Farmers Union. "Ultimately, it means those companies pay farmers even less for their hard work while charging restaurants, grocery stores and American consumers more for food. But price fixing is only a symptom of the much bigger problem of corporate consolidation."[107]

OUTLOOK
Changes on the Horizon

Economic uncertainty, supply and demand changes and a growing role for technology are among the factors determining the near future of the meat industry.

Global meat consumption is expected to drop 4 percent in 2020, largely due to growing poverty in the developing world—which is increasing for the first time in more than two decades—linked to the COVID-19 pandemic.[108]

"Robust meat trade depends on global economic growth and a reasonable level of economic prosperity," says Schuele at the U.S. Meat Export Federation. "It is important to put the COVID-19 crisis behind us so that economic activity can achieve a sustained recovery." This is particularly important for the U.S. market, says McCracken of RaboResearch Food & Agribusiness.

"With growth in U.S. per capita meat and poultry consumption slowing, much of the future growth for U.S. protein processors will come from export markets," says McCracken.

In addition to falling demand in some places, meat producers say supply issues are likely to linger at least as long as the pandemic lasts, and prices likely will rise.[109] McCracken says this could force meat processors to add more automation to their supply lines and switch more quickly between retail and wholesale products.

"Companies will need to be more flexible going forward and be able to adjust to temporary disruption more easily," she says. "This may force big changes."

To maintain long-term growth, the industry will have to further address its environmental impact, which will likely include developing new technologies to improve efficiency and reduce emissions and wasted meat, analysts say.

"The global industry will need to continue to focus on neutralizing the impact of production on the environment if it wants to compete in the long term," McCracken says. Analysts say consumers will increasingly demand fresh products with less environmental impact, fewer antibiotics and good animal welfare—all for low prices.[110]

"We'll see a combination of the [established meat companies] making moves to address those demands like we have seen some experiment with the elimination of antibiotics from poultry and lower-methane beef, as well as innovative startups creating solutions where they see unmet consumer needs," says McKinsey's Bar Am. "It will be interesting to see if the carbon [impact] labeling of food products takes off, as some predict, and whether that drives consumers to adopt lower carbon diets that reduce or shift the mix of animal proteins."

The meat industry says technology, including artificial intelligence, is key to meeting demand and satisfying future environmental regulations. The North American Meat Institute says one of its main goals is to find new ways to reduce environmental impact.

"Companies will share best practices with each other to the benefit of the industry as a whole," says the institute's Little.

NOTES

1. Baylen Linnekin, "New Wyoming Law Lets Local Ranchers Sell Cuts of Meat Directly to Consumers," *Reason*, April 4, 2020, https://tinyurl.com/vrerzx9.
2. Denise Heilbrun-Ellis, "Local ranchers work toward offering locally fed, processed beef," (Scottsbluff) *Star Herald*, May 5, 2020, https://tinyurl.com/y6p9d2qn.
3. Justin McCarthy and Scott Dekoster, "Nearly One in Four in U.S. Have Cut Back on Eating Meat," Gallup, Jan. 27, 2020, https://tinyurl.com/y6a3a6fm.
4. "The Meat and Poultry Industry: Basic Statistics," *The Market Works*, https://tinyurl.com/yxdatue8; "Meat Sector Value Worldwide in 2018 and 2023," Statista, Sept. 30, 2019, https://tinyurl.com/y3z7psup; and Hannah Ritchie and Max Roser, "Meat and Dairy Production," Our World In Data, November 2019, https://tinyurl.com/y5xbpst6.
5. John Miller, "Is global meat trade overdone?" *IHS Markit*, May 29, 2018, https://tinyurl.com/yyhjjfcl.
6. *Ibid.*; Aerin Einstein-Curtis, "U.S. meat industry set to expand, may face stiffer competition in export markets," *FeedNavigator*, Feb. 15, 2018, https://tinyurl.com/y68exnot.
7. Jane Mayer, "How Trump is Helping Tycoons Exploit the Pandemic," *The New Yorker*, July 20, 2020, https://tinyurl.com/y4d27n7g; Ally Marotti, "Second lawsuit against poultry giants alleges chicken price-fixing conspiracy," *Chicago Tribune*, Jan. 15, 2018, https://tinyurl.com/y6rwfpvx; Deena Shanker, "There Aren't Enough Slaughterhouses to Support the Farm-to-Table Economy," *Bloomberg*, May 23, 2017, https://tinyurl.com/y8nx53uq; Phillip Clauer, "A Small Overview of the Modern Commercial Poultry Industry," *Penn State Extension*, Dec. 16, 2011, https://tinyurl.com/y3n5cg67; "Facts and Myths of Vertical Integration," *Farm Journal's Pork*, Jan. 17, 2011, https://tinyurl.com/yxwm28sc; "The Meat and Poultry Industry: Basic Statistics," *op. cit.*; and "Price Rankings by Country of Beef Round (1kg) (or Equivalent Back Leg Red Meat) (Markets)," *Numbeo*, https://tinyurl.com/ycdmtdac.
8. "Occupational Employment Statistics," U.S. Bureau of Labor Statistics, May 2018, https://tinyurl.com/y2qrgs7u.
9. Jacob Bunge and Jesse Newman, "Tyson Turns to Robot Butchers, Spurred by Corona Outbreaks," *The Wall Street Journal*, July 9, 2020, https://tinyurl.com/ybsww4to; Mayer, *op. cit.*
10. Mitchell Hartman, "COVID-19 exposes U.S. meat supply's dependence on a few large plants," *Marketplace*, May 6, 2020, https://tinyurl.com/y2n8xwbs; Ted Genoways, "Beyond Big Meat," *The New Republic*, Aug. 4, 2020, https://tinyurl.com/yymjg6eq.
11. Kimberly Kindy, "More than 200 meat plant workers in the U.S. have died of covid-19. Federal regulators just issued two modest fines," *The Washington Post*, Sept. 13, 2020, https://tinyurl.com/y5dyt8sk; Megan Molteni, "Why Meatpacking Plants Have Become COVID-19 Hot Spots," *Wired*, May 7, 2020, https://tinyurl.com/y8kvh27b.
12. Shanker, *op. cit.*; Genoways, *op. cit.*
13. "Become a Perdue Poultry Farmer," Perdue Foods, https://tinyurl.com/y39zmu5h; "Contract Poultry

Farming," Tyson Foods, https://tinyurl.com/y6ruea98; and Annie Lowrey, "The Human Cost of Chicken Farming," *The Atlantic*, Nov. 11, 2019, https://tinyurl.com/y48zdlhn.

14. Abigail Abrams, "How Eating Less Meat Could Help Protect the Planet From Climate Change," *Time*, Aug. 8, 2019, https://tinyurl.com/yyeqvgwy; "Key Facts and Findings," U.N. Food and Agriculture Organization, https://tinyurl.com/zonnqet.

15. "New Analysis Shows U.S. Agriculture Reducing Per-Unit GHG Emissions," American Farm Bureau Federation, April 14, 2020, https://tinyurl.com/yxbbykl8.

16. Marian Swain, "The Future of Meat," Breakthrough Institute, May 18, 2017, https://tinyurl.com/y3gwk8ru; H. Claire Brown, "Two new bills would blunt the impact of factory farms on public health and the environment," *The Counter*, Dec. 16, 2019, https://tinyurl.com/y428kpqj.

17. "What Happens to Animal Waste?" FoodPrint, https://tinyurl.com/yxzr5uh7; "Animal Feeding Operations," U.S. Department of Agriculture, https://tinyurl.com/z8b3tzw.

18. Justin Worland, "If We Want to Stop Climate Change, Now is a Moment of Reckoning for How We Use the Planet, Warns U.N. Report," *Time*, Aug. 8, 2019, https://tinyurl.com/yy6xpvtc; Abrams, *op. cit.*

19. "Livestock and Climate Change," U.N. Food and Agriculture Organization, 2016, https://tinyurl.com/y5x8bh2t; "Key Facts and Findings," *op. cit.*

20. "Key Facts and Findings," *ibid.*; Thin Lei Win, "Fighting Global Warming, One Cow Belch at a Time," *Reuters*, July 19, 2018, https://tinyurl.com/y56bpfg3; and Alejandra Borunda, "Methane, Explained," *National Geographic*, Jan. 23, 2019, https://tinyurl.com/y3s7zwa6.

21. "Deforestation and Forest Degradation," World Wildlife Fund, https://tinyurl.com/y2bqou3h; "Rainforest Facts: The Disappearing Rainforests," Rain-Tree Publishers, https://tinyurl.com/y2m9qkm3; and Alejandra Borunda, "See how much of the Amazon is burning, how it compares to other years," *National Geographic*, Aug. 29, 2019, https://tinyurl.com/y2nr54og.

22. Leah Garces, "Replacing beef with chicken isn't as good for the planet as you think," *Vox*, Dec. 4, 2019, https://tinyurl.com/y45uajt7; Aaron E. Carroll, "The Real Problem With Beef," *The New York Times*, Oct. 1, 2019, https://tinyurl.com/y3lyakmo.

23. "World must sustainably produce 70% more food by mid-century: UN report," *UN News*, Dec. 3, 2013, https://tinyurl.com/y5vktvf5; Hannah Ritchie, "Half of the world's habitable land is used for agriculture," Our World In Data, Nov. 11, 2019, https://tinyurl.com/y3p5yqc8.

24. Christopher Flavelle, "Climate Change Threatens the World's Food Supply, United Nations Warns," *The New York Times*, Aug. 8, 2019, https://tinyurl.com/y627ppqu.

25. *Ibid.*

26. Jan Suszkiw, "Study Clarifies U.S. Beef's Resource Use and Greenhouse Gas Emissions," Agricultural Research Service, U.S. Department of Agriculture, March 11, 2019, https://tinyurl.com/y5pjdjmy; "Sources of Greenhouse Gas Emissions," Environmental Protection Agency, https://tinyurl.com/y5jtrep2; Dennis Silverman, "New Summary of California Greenhouse Gas Emissions in 2016," *Energy Blog*, July 16, 2018, https://tinyurl.com/yykm74c6; and "Agri-environmental indicator—Greenhouse gas emissions Statistics Explained," undated, https://tinyurl.com/y345r3zc.

27. Bjorn Lomborg, "Don't let vegetarian environmentalists shame you for eating meat. Science is on your side," *USA Today*, July 31, 2019, https://tinyurl.com/y55zjzep.

28. Gregory Meyer, "Methane from manure offers green fuel revenue for US farmers," *Financial Times*, June 25, 2020, https://tinyurl.com/y3pc8crh; Jim Morrison, "Turning Manure into Money," *The Washington Post*, June 16, 2020, https://tinyurl.com/y4ffdw4l; and "What is a dairy digester, and how does it affect methane emissions?" CLEAR Center at the University of California, Davis, April 23, 2020, https://tinyurl.com/yxzqqjjs.

29. "Booker Unveils Bill to Reform Farm System," press release, Office of Sen. Cory Booker, Dec. 16, 2019,

https://tinyurl.com/y3j43xns; Robert P. Martin, "Public Health Experts Support a Ban on CAFOs. New Polling Suggests the Public Does, Too," *Civil Eats*, Dec. 17, 2019, https://tinyurl.com/y3apkg6o; Ezra Klein, "Farmers and animal rights activists are coming together to fight big factory farms," *Vox*, July 8, 2020, https://tinyurl.com/ybhwxwdn; and "Farm System Reform Act of 2019," U.S. Congress, https://tinyurl.com/y5yvfngd.

30. Prafulla Kumar Sahoo, Kangjoo Kim and M.A. Powell, "Managing Groundwater Nitrate Contamination from Livestock Farms: Implication for Nitrate Management Guidelines," *Current Pollution Reports*, 2016, https://tinyurl.com/y52yt-bae; "Animal Feeding Operations," *op. cit.*

31. "How Industrial Agriculture Affects Our Water," FoodPrint, undated, https://tinyurl.com/yyeqvgwy.

32. "Industrial Agricultural Pollution 101," Natural Resources Defense Council, undated, https://tinyurl.com/y4ws27eh.

33. John Flesher, "Factory Farms Provide Abundant Food but Environment Suffers," *PBS NewsHour*, Feb. 6, 2020, https://tinyurl.com/r2h8cko; Amy A. Schultz *et al.*, "Residential proximity to concentrated animal feeding operations and allergic and respiratory disease," *Environment International*, September 2019, https://tinyurl.com/y3vdg539.

34. Maryn McKenna, "Farm Animals Are the Next Big Antibiotic Resistance Threat," *Wired*, Sept. 19, 2019, https://tinyurl.com/y24lx6uh; "Antibiotic Resistance, Food, and Food Animals," Centers for Disease Control and Prevention, undated, https://tinyurl.com/y63ven3o.

35. William D. Cohan, "Antibiotics in Meat Could be Damaging Our Guts," *The New York Times*, May 25, 2018, https://tinyurl.com/y8hdrn92.

36. Lisa Held, "Industrial Meat 101: Could Large Livestock Operations Cause the Next Pandemic?" *Civil Eats*, May 29, 2020, https://tinyurl.com/yxl4mrcq.

37. Sigal Samuel, "The meat we eat is a pandemic risk, too," *Vox*, Aug. 20, 2020, https://tinyurl.com/yb2mfpqo.

38. "Comments in response to the U.S. Environmental Protection Agency's 2020 National Pollutant Discharge Elimination System (NPDES) general permit for stormwater discharges associated with industrial activity, Docket ID# EPA-HQ-OW-2019-0372," U.S. Poultry & Egg Association, June 1, 2020, https://tinyurl.com/y6jsm77f; "CSB Accidental Release Reporting," U.S. Poultry & Egg Association, Jan. 13, 2020, https://tinyurl.com/yxuacx9b; "Concentrated Animal Feeding Operation," National Pork Producers Council, https://tinyurl.com/y5qh9pou; and John George, "Defending Agriculture: What Environmental Activists Don't Want the Public to Know about CAFOs," *Feedlot*, https://tinyurl.com/y53uyd9b.

39. Steve Dittmer, "Legislation introduced to eliminate modern animal agriculture," *Beef Magazine*, Dec. 19, 2019, https://tinyurl.com/y5zsdr58.

40. Steve Davies, "Booker bill would place moratorium on large CAFOs," *Agri-Pulse*, Dec. 16, 2019, https://tinyurl.com/yy4f79em.

41. Alex Smith, "To Combat Pandemics, Intensify Agriculture," Breakthrough Institute, April 13, 2020, https://tinyurl.com/y4gqtpgk; "Wildlife Trade, COVID-19, and Other Zoonotic Diseases," Congressional Research Service, April 6, 2020, https://tinyurl.com/yy82jb6p.

42. Smith, *ibid.*

43. "Plant-Based Market Overview," Good Food Institute, 2020, https://tinyurl.com/yya2xhax.

44. Chase Purdy, *Billion Dollar Burger* (2020), https://tinyurl.com/y2l755yv.

45. "Carving up the alternative meat market," Barclays Investment Bank, Aug. 19, 2019, https://tinyurl.com/yxuj4rp7.

46. Jacob Bunge and Heather Haddon, "America's Cattle Ranchers Are Fighting Back Against Fake Meat," *The Wall Street Journal*, Nov. 27, 2019, https://tinyurl.com/w9w38oa.

47. *Ibid.*

48. Sheril Kirshenbaum and Douglas Buhler, "Americans, especially millennials, are embracing

plant-based meat products," *The Conversation*, Oct. 21, 2019, https://tinyurl.com/y2lmkpew.

49. "Plant-based Meat Market," MarketsandMarkets, 2019, https://tinyurl.com/y3y96gu7.

50. "Tyson Foods Unveils Alternative Protein Products and New Raised & Rooted® Brand," news release, Tyson, June 13, 2019, https://tinyurl.com/y5llqv2u.

51. Heather Haddon and Jacob Bunge, "Meat, Milk Groups Seek to Defend Supermarket Turf," *The Wall Street Journal*, Oct. 7, 2019, https://tinyurl.com/y4tfmf5e.

52. Bunge and Haddon, *op. cit.*

53. Jade Scipioni, "Whole Foods CEO on plant-based meat boom: Good for the environment but not for your health," *CNBC*, Aug. 21, 2019, https://tinyurl.com/y4maurbw.

54. Alina Tugend, "Is the New Meat Any Better Than the Old Meat?" *The New York Times*, Sept. 21, 2019, https://tinyurl.com/y3xnruoq; Nicole Rasul, "Impossible Foods and Regenerative Grazers Face Off in a Carbon Farming Dust-Up," *Civil Eats*, June 19, 2019, https://tinyurl.com/y5d9d3r2.

55. Amy J. Fitzgerald, "A Social History of the Slaughterhouse: From Inception to Contemporary Implications," *Human Ecology Review*, Vol. 17, 2010, p. 60, https://tinyurl.com/yy9ufwhw.

56. *Ibid.*; Joshua Specht, "The price of plenty, how beef changed America," *The Guardian*, May 7, 2019, https://tinyurl.com/yxm4zoa3.

57. Specht, *ibid.*

58. *Ibid.*; Upton Sinclair, *The Jungle* (1905).

59. "Upton Sinclair, Whose Muckraking Changed the Meat Industry," *The New York Times*, June 30, 2016, https://tinyurl.com/y7coyqy4; "Celebrating 100 years of FMIA: Overview," U.S. Department of Agriculture, https://tinyurl.com/ybdb5ekh; and "U.S. Chicken Industry History," The National Chicken Council, https://tinyurl.com/y6xyye5d.

60. Eric Schlosser, *Fast Food Nation* (2001), p. 137.

61. Fitzgerald, *op. cit.*

62. Maryn McKenna, "The Surprising Origin of Chicken as a Dietary Staple," *National Geographic*, May 1, 2018, https://tinyurl.com/y3fw232f; Schlosser, *op. cit.*, pp. 21-22.

63. Schlosser, *ibid.*, p. 5.

64. Michael Pollan, "Power Steer," *The New York Times Magazine*, March 31, 2002, https://tinyurl.com/y6bukhos.

65. "Steroid-Hormone Implants Used for Growth in Food-Producing Animals," U.S. Food and Drug Administration, https://tinyurl.com/y6yhmzwp; Claas Kirchhelle, "Pharming animals: a global history of antibiotics in food production," Palgrave Communications, Aug. 7, 2018, https://tinyurl.com/ybubtnob.

66. Michelle R. Worosz *et al.*, "Barriers to Entry into the Specialty Red Meat Sector: The Role of Food Safety Regulation," *Journal of Rural Social Sciences*, June 30, 2008, https://tinyurl.com/y3pp7nky; Schlosser, *op. cit.*, p. 136; and "Poultry Inspection: The Basis for a Risk-Assessment Approach," National Academies Press, 1987, chapter 2, https://tinyurl.com/yxvh5dqc.

67. Schlosser, *ibid.*, pp. 136-140.

68. "United States Farm Numbers, 2000-2011," U.S. Department of Agriculture, Aug. 30, 2012, https://tinyurl.com/y5tcbk2p; "Farming and Farm Income," U.S. Department of Agriculture, https://tinyurl.com/yazhmopv.

69. Fitzgerald, *op. cit.*, p. 61.

70. *Ibid.*

71. "Who We Are," Farm Animal Rights Movement, https://tinyurl.com/y4hezqqv.

72. Gerald M. Oppenheimer and I. Daniel Benrubi, "McGovern's Senate Select Committee on Nutrition and Human Needs Versus the Meat Industry on the Diet-Heart Question," *American Journal of Public Health*, January 2014, https://tinyurl.com/yx8wlrd3; Kirchhelle, *op. cit.*

73. Kirchhelle, *ibid.*

74. "Mad Cow Disease Fast Facts," *CNN*, July 1, 2020, https://tinyurl.com/y6cc6w8s.

75. Fitzgerald, *op. cit.*; "Going Mainstream: Meat and Poultry Raised Without Routine Antibiotics Use,"

National Resources Defense Council, December 2015, https://tinyurl.com/y3h28vte.

76. "Going Mainstream," *ibid.*; Jonathan Shieber, "Lab-grown meat could be on store shelves by 2022, thanks to Future Meat Technologies," *TechCrunch*, Oct. 10, 2019, https://tinyurl.com/y5ng7d23.

77. "Meat Consumption," Organisation for Economic Co-operation and Development, accessed Aug. 10, 2020, https://tinyurl.com/yxfajf2s; Bill Winders and Elizabeth Ransom, *Global Meat* (2019), p. 13; "Harnessing the power of livestock to drive sustainable development," U.N. Food and Agriculture Organization, Oct. 17, 2018, https://tinyurl.com/y3fsc9v6; and Hannah Ritchie, "Which Countries Eat the Most Meat?" *BBC*, Feb. 4, 2019, https://tinyurl.com/y7lyh5xe.

78. Winders and Ransom, *ibid.*, p. 10.

79. Kimberly Kindy, "This foreign meat company got U.S. tax money. Now it wants to conquer America," *The Washington Post*, Nov. 7, 2019, https://tinyurl.com/yyndk98b; Tom Polansek, "At Smithfield Foods' slaughterhouse, China brings home U.S. bacon," *Reuters*, Nov. 5, 2019, https://tinyurl.com/u5ytqul.

80. "Total number of farms in the U.S. from 2000 to 2019," Statista, April 21, 2020, https://tinyurl.com/y2q6nvyf.

81. Stephanie Ogburn, "Ranchers struggle against giant meatpackers and economic troubles," *Grist*, April 15, 2011, https://tinyurl.com/y2h4snn7; Kindy, "This foreign meat company got U.S. tax money," *op. cit.*; and "Proposed bill would allow FDA access to CAFOs to investigate foodborne outbreaks," *FoodSafety Magazine*, Feb. 12, 2020, https://tinyurl.com/y47vbemf.

82. Tom Levitt, "Farm animals and pandemics: nine diseases that changed the world," *The Guardian*, Sept. 15, 2020, https://tinyurl.com/y2v7e3no; Ignacio Mena *et al.*, "Origins of the 2009 H1N1 influenza pandemic in swine in Mexico," *eLife*, June 28, 2016, https://tinyurl.com/r5n9zvt.

83. Adam Vaughan, "African Swine Fever Helps Drive World Food Prices to Two-Year High," *NewScientist*, Dec. 5, 2019, https://tinyurl.com/y5pbsej2; Emiko Terazono, Andres Schipani and Jamie Smyth, "How swine fever is reshaping the global meat trade," *Financial Times*, Jan. 9, 2020, https://tinyurl.com/tngscr7.

84. Keith Loria, "Organic Meat Demand Continues to Grow," *Meat + Poultry*, April 20, 2020, https://tinyurl.com/yyep76pq; "Grass-fed Beef Market Size, Share 2020 Regional Trend, Future Growth, Leading Players Updates, Industry Demand, Current and Future Plans by Forecast to 2023," *MarketWatch*, July 6, 2020, https://tinyurl.com/y3xohsdj.

85. Yohei Matsuo, "Japan is hungry for meat but domestic producers aren't feasting," *Nikkei Asian Review*, March 27, 2019, https://tinyurl.com/y58xq5df; Burt Rutherford, "Japan puts final stamp of approval on U.S.-Japan trade agreement for beef," *Beef Magazine*, Dec. 4, 2019, https://tinyurl.com/y67xrrs9; "EU Agricultural Outlook 2019-2030 Meat and Dairy," European Commission, Dec. 10, 2019, https://tinyurl.com/y4krep68; and Karen Braun, "U.S. Faces Meat Shortage While its Pork Exports to China Soar," *Reuters*, May 5, 2020, https://tinyurl.com/y43rsqfy.

86. P. Scott Shearer, "Keep China Phase One trade agreement," *National Hog Farmer*, June 19, 2020, https://tinyurl.com/y3tb9u4z; Keith Johnson, "China Puts the Final Kibosh on Trump's Trade Deal," *Foreign Policy*, June 1, 2020, https://tinyurl.com/y2seqha7.

87. Shearer, *ibid.*; "EU Agricultural Outlook 2019-30: African swine fever continues to affect global meat market," European Commission, Dec. 10, 2019, https://tinyurl.com/y4krep68.

88. Mustafa Zia *et al.*, "Brazil Once Again Becomes the World's Largest Beef Exporter," Economic Research Service, U.S. Department of Agriculture, July 1, 2019, https://tinyurl.com/yy3mgclt; Nathan Owens, "Brazil's beef gets cool U.S. reaction," *Arkansas Democrat Gazette*, Feb. 29, 2020, https://tinyurl.com/y284jfg8.

89. Owens, *ibid.*

90. "Russian Federation," Foreign Agricultural Service, U.S. Department of Agriculture, July 1, 2019, https://tinyurl.com/y5dvhftq; Vladislav Vorotnikov, "Russian poultry exports booming thanks to China," *Poultry World*, Feb. 19, 2020, https://tinyurl.com/y32mhkrd.
91. Bunge and Newman, *op. cit.*
92. *Ibid.*; Megan Pellegrini, "State of Meat & Poultry Industry Workforce 2019," *The National Provisioner*, Oct. 25, 2019, https://tinyurl.com/yxjjcndz.
93. Megan Durisin, "Virus Can Travel 26 Feet at Cold Meat Plants with Stale Air," *Bloomberg*, July 23, 2020, https://tinyurl.com/y44yzkt4.
94. Kindy, "More than 200 meat plant workers in the U.S. have died of covid-19," *op. cit.*
95. "Slap-on-the-wrist fine for multi-billion-dollar meat corporations," "Rachel Maddow Show," *MSNBC*, Sept. 16, 2020, https://tinyurl.com/y3ulj6wp.
96. Kindy, "More than 200 meat plant workers in the U.S. have died of covid-19," *op. cit.*; "U.S. Department of Labor Cites Smithfield Packaged Meats Corp. for Failing to Protect Employees from Coronavirus," Occupational Safety and Health Administration, Sept. 10, 2020, https://tinyurl.com/y4x9gd5p.
97. Milane Haboon, "How Meat Producers Can Improve Food Safety with Robotic Automation," *Robotics Business Review*, June 9, 2020, https://tinyurl.com/y2cse4yb; Pan Demetrakakes, "Automation Makes Meat Cutting Faster, Safer," *Food Processing*, April 18, 2019, https://tinyurl.com/y2ggmbmf.
98. Pan Demetrakakes, "Food Industry Struggles with Barriers to Automation," *Food Processing*, May 1, 2020, https://tinyurl.com/y2w8j3v9.
99. Stephen R. Miller, "Amid COVID-19 bottleneck in meat industry, PRIME Act gains support," *Fern's AG Insider*, June 3, 2020, https://tinyurl.com/yyr3hfgp.
100. *Ibid.*; Kevin Killough, "The meat producer's bottleneck," *Powell Tribune*, July 23, 2020, https://tinyurl.com/y38stkyn; and Michael Corkery and David Yaffe-Bellany, "The Food Chain's Weakest Link: Slaughterhouses," *The New York Times*, April 18, 2020, https://tinyurl.com/y8pwmqtf.
101. "Meat processor shutdowns = prime time for PRIME Act," Farm & Ranch Freedom Alliance, April 25, 2020, https://tinyurl.com/yxm395cl.
102. Miller, *op. cit.*
103. "PRIME ACT," National Pork Producers Council, https://tinyurl.com/y4d9t6qh.
104. "Cheney Introduces Bill to Open New Markets for State-inspected meat," press release, Office of Rep. Liz Cheney, June 12, 2020, https://tinyurl.com/y4hfn6gn.
105. Dan Nosowitz, "Cory Booker Announces Legislation to Scale Back Factory Farms," *Modern Farmer*, Dec. 16, 2019, https://tinyurl.com/y2ym97p6; "Sen. Booker Introduces Legislation to Strengthen Food System in Response to COVID-19 Disruptions," press release, Office of Sen. Cory Booker, July 2, 2020, https://tinyurl.com/y49urk4a.
106. Jacob Bunge and Brent Kendall, "Justice Department Issues Subpoenas to Beef-Processing Giants," *The Wall Street Journal*, June 5, 2020, https://tinyurl.com/y3xgmts6; Cade Metz, "Pilgrim's Pride Chief Executive Is Accused of Price Fixing," *The New York Times*, June 3, 2020, https://tinyurl.com/y7qyt7fb.
107. "Price-fixing indictment highlights need for stronger antitrust enforcement, protections for farmers," National Farmers Union, June 2, 2020, https://tinyurl.com/ycfa6rce.
108. "Livestock and Poultry: World Markets and Trade," U.S. Department of Agriculture, July 10, 2020, https://tinyurl.com/n2wdnuk; "Novel Coronavirus," Food and Agriculture Organization of the United Nations, undated, https://tinyurl.com/yy3mezfv; and "Poverty," The World Bank, undated, https://tinyurl.com/y2n8dm5c.
109. Tatiana Freitas, "Beef prices will remain high for months as producers work to rebuild capacity, executive warns," *Time*, May 19, 2020, https://tinyurl.com/y23kwnh7.
110. "Smart Livestock Farming," Deloitte, November 2017, https://tinyurl.com/y4vrq5zp.

BIBLIOGRAPHY

Books

Purdy, Chase, *Billion Dollar Burger: Inside Big Tech's Race for the Future of Food,* **Portfolio/Penguin, 2020.**
A journalist writes about the doctors, scientists and others working to develop meat from microscopic animal cells, a technology that aims to virtually end animal slaughter and the environmental damage linked to traditional meat production.

Schlosser, Eric, *Fast Food Nation: The Dark Side of the All-American Meal,* **Houghton Mifflin Company, 2001.**
In this landmark exposé, an investigative journalist chronicles the rise of fast food and how it shaped the development of the modern industrialized meat industry.

Specht, Joshua, *Red Meat Republic: A Hoof-to-Table History of How Beef Changed America,* **Princeton University Press, 2019.**
A University of Notre Dame history professor traces the sometimes-violent evolution of the U.S. beef industry.

Winders, Bill, and Elizabeth Ransom, eds., *Global Meat: Social and Environmental Consequences of the Expanding Meat Industry,* **MIT Press, 2019.**
An associate sociology professor at Georgia Tech (Winders) and an associate professor of international affairs at Penn State (Ransom) examine the environmental, social and economic issues linked to the rise of the global meat industry.

Articles

Bunge, Jacob, and Heather Haddon, "America's Cattle Ranchers are Fighting Back Against Fake Meat," *The Wall Street Journal,* **Nov. 27, 2019, https://tinyurl.com/w9w38oa.**
Beef producers are responding to the growing popularity of plant-based protein products by trying to convince consumers that alternatives are not healthier than meat.

Bunge, Jacob, and Jesse Newman, "Tyson Turns to Robot Butchers, Spurred by Coronavirus Outbreaks," *The Wall Street Journal,* **July 9, 2020, https://tinyurl.com/ybsww4to.**
Meat processors are beginning to adopt automation in response to the pandemic.

Contrera, Jessica, "The lives upended around a $20 cheeseburger," *The Washington Post,* **July 7, 2020, https://tinyurl.com/ycao72zn.**
A journalist traces the story of a single hamburger from the cow to the table, focusing on the challenges faced by people at all stages of production.

Friend, Tad, "Can a Burger Help Solve Climate Change?" *The New Yorker,* **Sept. 23, 2019, https://tinyurl.com/y23hsdas.**
A magazine writer profiles Impossible Foods, which makes a variety of plant-based meat substitutes and whose CEO wants to eliminate animal agriculture.

Held, Lisa, "Industrial Meat 101: Could Large Livestock Operations Cause the Next Pandemic?" *Civil Eats,* **May 29, 2020, https://tinyurl.com/yxl4mrcq.**
A food journalist discusses whether crowded conditions inside large-scale animal feeding operations could lead to future pandemics of viruses that jump from livestock to humans.

Klein, Ezra, "Farmers and animal rights activists are coming together to fight big factory farms," *Vox,* **July 8, 2020, https://tinyurl.com/ybhwxwdn.**
A journalist chronicles how people on opposite sides of the political spectrum have found common ground in a fight to revamp some agricultural policies, including changes that would create more competition in the livestock sector and better protect the environment.

McKenna, Maryn, "Farm Animals Are the Next Big Antibiotic Resistance Threat," *Wired,* **Sept. 19, 2009, https://tinyurl.com/y24lx6uh.**
A magazine writer and book author outlines how antibiotic-resistant infections are rising among livestock.

Reports and Studies

"Climate Change and Land," Intergovernmental Panel on Climate Change, August 2019, https://tinyurl.com/y4tp6u2g.
The United Nations agency explains how the production of meat and other foods contributes to climate change and puts future global food supplies at risk.

"The future of food and agriculture: Alternative pathways to 2050," U.N. Food and Agriculture Organization, 2018, https://tinyurl.com/uyrezsx.
In this data-heavy policy paper, the U.N.'s anti-hunger agency recommends changes in meat and other food production to create a more environmentally sustainable food supply.

Schultz, Amy A., *et al.*, "Residential proximity to concentrated animal feeding operations and allergic and respiratory disease," *Environment International*, September 2019, https://tinyurl.com/y3vdg539.
Researchers at the University of Wisconsin document increased health problems affecting people living near large factory farms.

Theurer, Benjamin M., and Antonio Hernandez, "Carving up the Alternative Meat Market," Barclays, Aug. 19, 2019, https://tinyurl.com/yxuj4rp7.
Two researchers at an international investment bank examine challenges facing the industries that make plant-based meat substitutes and develop meat from cultures grown in labs.

THE NEXT STEP

China

"China Importing Record Pork Volumes," *Hoosier Ag Today*, Aug. 2, 2020, https://tinyurl.com/y697zthz.
China's pork imports continue to soar, even as the country has slowed the import process by implementing coronavirus checks on frozen food containers.

Hong, Jinshan, "Impossible Foods Awaits Nod as Beyond Meat Muscles In," *Yahoo Finance*, Sept. 9, 2020, https://tinyurl.com/y28f6osl.
Alternative meat company Impossible Foods fears missing out as it awaits regulatory approval to sell products in China, where competitor Beyond Meat has already entered the market.

Stickler, Jordan, "China Continues to Scale Back Meat Imports Amid Pandemic," *Forbes*, July 9, 2020, https://tinyurl.com/y6co9jdl.
China added two Brazilian pork companies to its list of restricted imports, following similar bans on meat imports from Europe, Canada and the United States, citing coronavirus outbreaks as a concern.

Health and Environment

Colley, Claire, "European meat plants posing 'avoidable risk' of disease, inspectors say," *The Guardian*, Sept. 14, 2020, https://tinyurl.com/yxqeh5nj.
European meat inspectors say simplifying inspections throughout the continent since 2014 has led to greater health risks for meat consumers.

Dunne, Daisy, "Interactive: What is the climate impact of eating meat and dairy?" *Carbon Brief*, Sept. 14, 2020, https://tinyurl.com/y4xb8enc.
Fifteen times more animals are raised to be eaten than the number of wild animals on the planet, according to a study published in the *Proceedings of the National Academy of Sciences*, an academic journal, with beef leaving the largest carbon footprint.

Dutkiewicz, Jan, "The Climate Activists Who Dismiss Meat Consumption Are Wrong," *The New Republic*, Aug. 31, 2020, https://tinyurl.com/yxfj8toh.
A meat expert argues that the climate movement focuses too much on big oil companies, while ignoring how much greenhouse gas the meat industry generates.

Meat Alternatives

Hager, Emily, and Mark Abadi, "Alternative-meat startup is hoping a 3D-printed steak can upend the meat industry," *Business Insider*, Aug. 31, 2020, https://tinyurl.com/yy47nsre.
An Israeli startup is developing meat alternatives produced on a 3D printer using soy and pea proteins, coconut fat and sunflower oil.

Jibilian, Isabella, "Beyond Meat just announced meatless 'meatballs' will soon be sold at grocery stores, expanding its plant-based portfolio beyond burgers," *Business Insider*, Sept. 14, 2020, https://tinyurl.com/y6lalh4p.
Beyond Meat recently introduced pre-shaped "meatballs," made of pea protein and brown rice, in grocery stores.

Money, Jack, "Alternative meat maker fights back against Oklahoma labeling requirement," *The Oklahoman*, Sept. 17, 2020, https://tinyurl.com/y2b7tzw5.
A Chicago producer of meat alternatives is challenging an Oklahoma law that requires its packaging to include a large label saying the product is plant-based.

Worker Safety

Chadde, Sky, Kyle Bagentose and Rachel Axon, "A week before Trump's order protecting meat plants, industry sent draft language to feds," *USA Today*, Sept. 14, 2020, https://tinyurl.com/y3h44vpk.
A meatpacking trade group sent the U.S. Department of Agriculture a draft of an executive order that would allow plants to remain open during the coronavirus pandemic—a week before President Trump signed a similar order.

Kindy, Kimberly, "More than 200 meat plant workers in the U.S. have died of Covid-19. Federal regulators just issued two modest fines," *The Washington Post*, Sept. 13, 2020, https://tinyurl.com/y5dyt8sk.
Six months after several meat plants became coronavirus hotspots, companies, worker safety groups and meat plant workers are criticizing how long it took the Occupational Safety and Health Administration to issue fines against companies that allegedly failed to protect workers.

Nieberg, Patty, "Workers protest $15,000 COVID-19 fine issued to JBS meat plant in Greeley," *The Denver Post*, Sept. 16, 2020, https://tinyurl.com/y6tua7wm.
A union representing meatpackers at a Colorado plant staged a protest calling for federal officials to levy a larger fine against the company after several workers died of COVID-19.

For More Information

Food and Agriculture Organization of the United Nations, Viale delle Terme di Caracalla, 00153 Rome, Italy; +39-06-57051; fao.org. U.N. agency that leads international efforts to improve global agriculture and food security.

Good Food Institute, 1380 Monroe St., N.W. #229, Washington, D.C. 20010; 866-849-4457; gfi.org. Organization that promotes plant-based eating and lab-grown meats.

National Cattlemen's Beef Association, 9110 East Nichols Ave., Suite 300, Centennial, CO 80112; 303-694-0305; ncba.org. Marketing and trade organization for U.S. ranchers.

National Chicken Council, 1152 15th Street, N.W., Suite 430, Washington D.C. 20005; 202-296-2622; nationalchickencouncil.org. Trade association and lobbying group for broiler chicken producers.

National Pork Producers Council, 122 C St., N.W., Suite 875, Washington, D.C. 20001; 202-347-3600; nppc.org. Lobbying and industry association for hog farmers.

Natural Resources Defense Council, 40 West 20th St., 11th Floor, New York, N.Y. 10011; 212-727-2700; nrdc.org. Environmental advocacy group that works to improve animal farming practices.

North American Meat Institute, 1150 Connecticut Ave., N.W., Washington, D.C. 20036; 202-587-4200; meatinstitute.org. Meat and poultry industry trade association.

U.S. Department of Agriculture, 1400 Independence Ave. S.W., Washington, D.C. 20250; 202-720-2791; usda.gov. Federal department that oversees inspection of farm animals, slaughtering practices and meatpacking operations.